STANFORD'S
WALLACE
STERLING

STANFORD'S
WALLACE
STERLING

PORTRAIT OF A PRESIDENCY

1949–1968

ROXANNE L. NILAN AND CASSIUS L. KIRK JR.

Karen E. Bartholomew, Contributing Editor

STANFORD HISTORICAL SOCIETY

SOCIETY FOR THE PROMOTION OF SCIENCE AND SCHOLARSHIP

*Production of this book was underwritten
by the Stanford Historical Society
from generous donations provided by*

Claude S. Brinegar Fund

*Robert and Charlotte Beyers Fund
(endowed by Lorry Lokey)*

Boyce and Peggy Nute

Larry Horton

Sunny Scott

*and with special assistance of
Richard Eberli to Cassius L. Kirk Jr.*

STANFORD HISTORICAL SOCIETY
P.O. Box 20028, Stanford, CA 94309
historicalsociety@stanford.edu

Distributed by and available through
STANFORD UNIVERSITY PRESS (sup.org)

ISBN: 978-0-9847958-8-8   LCCN: 2023939018

Printed in Canada

ENDPAPERS: Front of the Quad as Wallace Sterling would have known it during his 1930s
graduate-student days.   BERTON CRANDALL / STANFORD UNIVERSITY ARCHIVES

FRONTISPIECE: John Ewart Wallace Sterling (1906–1985), in 1960.   JACK FIELDS / STANFORD UNIVERSITY ARCHIVES

PAGE VI: President J. E. Wallace Sterling walks along the allée of London plane trees on the west side
of Memorial Auditorium in 1960. Serra Street (today, Jane Stanford Way) is in the background.
JACK FIELDS / STANFORD UNIVERSITY ARCHIVES

IN MEMORY OF
CASSIUS L. KIRK JR.
1929–2014

One thing is certain about the verdict that historians will pass on Wallace Sterling's administration as President of Stanford University: It will be said that during his time the University flourished. They will say that for Stanford it was a time of extraordinary gains in every dimension. The faculty was enormously strengthened, the intellectual life of the University was never more lively, new construction was at a peak and the University's reputation reached new heights. . . . Somehow [Wallace Sterling] created a climate in which good and constructive things happened, a climate in which growth and dynamic movement seemed natural and easy. . . . To us he is first of all a kindly, warm, wholehearted man with a sparkling sense of humor, a way with words, and a gift for friendship. Thanks to those qualities, he accomplished something that is almost impossible in a great university today. He created a sense of community that held together the varied parts of the University family and enabled it to remain a coherent and self-confident institution.

JOHN W. GARDNER, '35
CHAIRMAN, THE URBAN COALITION
PER/SE MAGAZINE, FALL 1968

CONTENTS

Stanford's Wallace Sterling: Portrait of a Presidency—the title defines both this book's subject and the perspective from which it traces J. E. Wallace Sterling's 19 years as Stanford's fifth president. This is a biography of a man and an institution, both seen from Building Ten, the President's Office on the Inner Quad. Because Sterling's own nearly complete draft account of his presidency was destroyed when an arsonist set fire to his office in 1968, our view of the president is mostly from the outside, based on the memories and written records of those who worked closely with him. Inevitably, the book focuses on the problems that ended up on the president's desk, those crises and opportunities that remorselessly confront a university president every day.

Historians and social scientists have written a great deal about the qualities that make an effective leader. As the authors make clear, Wallace Sterling had many of these qualities: a commanding presence tempered by natural charm and ready wit, the courage to make decisions, the ability to select and attract talented associates, and, perhaps most important of all, the capacity to recognize and take advantage of opportunities.

< Determined to brighten up commencement, President Sterling turned to English-born Professor Eric Hutchinson, an accomplished calligrapher and manuscript illuminator. Combining heraldry and Stanford's emblematic redwood tree, Hutchinson designed shields, banners, and flags for Stanford's seven schools, the graduate division, the university, and the president. The flags were first unfurled (opposite) at the 1967 commencement. STANFORD NEWS SERVICE

Together these qualities are what Machiavelli would have called *virtu*, those elements of mind and character that are essential for the success of presidents as well as princes. But Machiavelli also knew that no less essential was what he called *fortuna*, the outside forces and existing conditions over which even the most effective leader has little or no control. Successful leaders are people lucky enough to live at a time and place in which their qualities mesh with these external circumstances, when their distinctive *virtu* matches *fortuna*'s ebb and flow. For most of his presidency, this was Sterling's situation: by 1949, when he took office, the restraints of economic depression and the world war were gone, replaced by the onset of that great postwar economic boom that was nowhere more apparent than in California. At the same time, new generations of students and professors were reshaping higher education, new disciplines (computer science, for instance) were emerging, and many established disciplines (linguistics, psychology, biology) were being transformed. These developments created possibilities for growth and innovation that had not existed ten, even five years earlier. Sterling did not create these developments, but he knew how to use them for Stanford's benefit.

Merely to list the major events of the Sterling years is enough to demonstrate his importance for Stanford's future: moving the medical school from San Francisco to the main campus; developing Stanford's land for faculty housing, the industrial park, and the shopping center; establishing the Stanford Linear Accelerator; opening campuses overseas; and many more. Like most decisions that turn out well, deciding to do these things may seem obvious enough in retrospect, but at the time many of these actions—especially the decision to move the medical school—were hotly contested. We should not overlook the courage and foresight required to choose what often seemed like a very risky alternative.

Although we can see the contours of the future taking shape, Sterling's Stanford reflected a world that has, in many ways, disappeared. In the first place, Stanford in 1949 was, and largely remained, a predominantly local institution, run by men with deep local roots. Of the 15 members of the Board of Trustees who selected Sterling in 1948, 12 were from the Bay Area, most of them lawyers and business leaders from San Francisco. They were all men except for the daughter of the publisher of *L.A. Times*, who was the first woman on the board since Jane Stanford. No more than 6 of the 54 trustees who served while Sterling was president were women. Both physically and culturally, the campus in the fifties and early sixties was very different from what it would become just a few years later. When I used to tell a later generation of students that when I was an undergraduate, coed dorms were unimaginable, and then went on to point out that women were allowed to stay out after 10:30 only a limited number of times each quarter, they would look at me with amazement, perhaps touched by a certain amount of pity.

By March 1967, when Sterling informed the trustees that he intended to leave the presidency by September of the following year, the Stanford he had known, both as a graduate student in the 1930s and as president since 1949, had been

transformed. By the late sixties, the foundations he had established for the university's future were in place, but his accomplishments were obscured by a wave of protests and conflicts among both students and faculty. The final chapters in *Stanford's Wallace Sterling* provide a moving account of the last two years of his presidency, which were shadowed by his own failing health and the demands of an increasingly turbulent and occasionally violent campus community. This was not a world that Sterling could have mastered nor even fully understand, but the dignity and fortitude with which he confronted its challenges were, I believe, among his most impressive achievements. *Fortuna* had turned against him; his *virtu* remained.

I experienced the Sterling years as an undergraduate from 1954 to 1958, and then as Western Civilization instructor from 1962 to 1964 (when I had the rare and unforgettable opportunity to teach at the Florence campus). The Stanford to which I returned as a faculty member in 1979 was a dramatically different place than the one I had entered as a rather bewildered freshman a quarter century earlier. Many of these differences were the result of the innovations that are described in the pages that follow. Yet institutions, like individuals, have characters that persist even as they evolve. It is that complex interplay of change and continuity that makes history such a fascinating subject. Seeing the changes and continuities at work in the university that Wallace Sterling did so much to create is one of the enduring pleasures of this richly informative book.

James J. Sheehan, '58
Professor of History and
Dickason Professor in the
Humanities, Emeritus

J. E. Wallace Sterling was a master of polished prose as well as an engaging raconteur, with a fund of stories he could put to use on formal and informal occasions alike. He was the only academic leader, wrote a *San Jose News* reporter, who could put the fate of man and "I Love Lucy" into the same speech.[1]

Sterling took great care in writing, adeptly using press releases, speeches, and the Alumni Association magazine to talk about his university. He was a careful and meticulous wordsmith, preferring ample time to compose his text, editing "even as he walked to the rostrum," said presidential assistant Fred Glover. "And that's why we couldn't get a text in advance."[2]

On accepting Stanford's presidency, in late 1948, Sterling persuaded the trustees to allow him to forgo the *Annual Report of the President,* a Stanford tradition dating back to 1904. Instead, he suggested, at the end of his tenure he would write a review of the major national issues in American higher education and use this as a backdrop to evaluate developments at Stanford during his presidency. The materials he had gathered for this review, along with a nearly complete first draft of the analysis he had been working on since 1966, were in his office when, in July 1968, an arsonist set it ablaze. A subsequent busy schedule as chancellor and ongoing ill health prevented his piecing these materials together again.[3] Unfortunately, today's historian is left without either his review of his 19-year presidency, 1949–68, or the sort of valuable year-by-year documentation that had been recorded by his predecessors.

While renowned for his congeniality, Sterling nevertheless cherished his privacy and that of his family. Although he loved to read biographies of historical figures, he seemed reluctant to engage in producing a formal autobiography. "As to my own presidency, any comment thereon risks being autobiographical," he told a campus audience in 1960, "and this risk I am unwilling to take except with strict reserve and without any relish whatsoever." He preferred, as he said later in an informal memoir, to let his record at Stanford speak for itself.[4]

Although a recipient of many honors and accolades, Sterling, along with his era, has receded in Stanford's rear-view mirror as the university accelerates along the steep trajectory his administration had set. Now the stuff of Stanford legend, his aura of success nevertheless underpins the story of Stanford's rise to become one of the world's most respected universities.

It is not easy to portray a complex man and his evolving presidency. We are fortunate to have invaluable glimpses into this transformational era, however, from scholars who chose to investigate Stanford in studies of its time and place within American academia. Historian of science Stuart W. Leslie first brought attention to the impact of Cold War federal funding with his studies of MIT and Stanford, culminating in *The Cold War and American Science: The Military-Industrial-Academic Complex at MIT and Stanford* (1994). As a counterpoint, historian Rebecca S. Lowen provides a critique of Stanford's growth in engineering and the sciences during the Sterling era in her *Creating the Cold War University: The Transformation of Stanford* (1997), examining the implications of Stanford's increasingly close relations with federal and corporate research agendas. Urban historian Margaret Pugh O'Mara subsequently featured Stanford in her *Cities of Knowledge: Cold War Science and the Search for the Next Silicon Valley* (2005), placing its development at this time within the larger framework of postwar urbanization and the geopolitics of its region.

Frank A. Medeiros' 1979 dissertation, "The Sterling Years at Stanford: A Study in the Dynamics of Institutional Change," remains the only analysis of the intersection of academic change with aggressive and wide-ranging fundraising at Stanford during this time. Historian of science C. Stewart Gillmor, in *Fred Terman at Stanford: Building a Discipline, a University, and Silicon Valley* (2004), included a scholarly exploration of Sterling's relationship with his provost of 10 years, Frederick Terman, and especially the influence of this partnership on faculty recruiting and department building. Stanford President Emeritus Richard W. Lyman began his 2009 memoir of the turbulent 1960s and '70s, *Stanford in Turmoil: Campus Unrest, 1966–1972*, with an examination of events and policies of Sterling's last two years in office while Lyman was an associate dean and then provost.

Sterling's Stanford, however, is too often absent from broader studies of this dynamic period, such as those investigating the impact of McCarthyism on academia or the growth of professionalism and economic influence in collegiate

athletics. Even more surprising is the absence of any general, much less scholarly, biography of the man described in 1967 by renowned social reformer John W. Gardner, '35, as having "contributed more than any other human being to the remarkable advancement Stanford has made."[5]

In 1992, the Stanford Historical Society partially filled this void when it published a biography of Sterling's predecessor, Donald B. Tresidder, to counterbalance a pervasive but superficial storyline of faculty unhappiness during his tenure. With his *Don Tresidder: Stanford's Forgotten Treasure*, journalist Edwin Kiester Jr. provided a long-overdue examination of this difficult wartime presidency and the beginnings of significant postwar changes and experiments later fully credited to the Sterling administration, notably land development, faculty recruiting, and reconsideration of the Medical School program.

It was the need for a similar overview of Sterling's era that Cassius (Cash) Kirk Jr. '51, JD Cal '54, hoped to fill. During his retirement, in the early 1990s, Cash Kirk had begun exploring the J. E. Wallace Sterling papers in the Stanford University Archives to compile an account about a man he greatly admired. Cash previously had served as staff counsel to Vice President Alf Brandin in Stanford's Business Office (1960–78), where he was involved in university land development and intellectual property issues. He readily admitted that he was not in President Sterling's inner circle, but he was clearly impressed with the man as well as the administrator and came to know many who served in the Sterling administration. Cash went on to become business manager of Menlo College, as well as a successful real estate investor.

Cash did not intend to write a definitive or scholarly biography but rather to offer a portrait, admittedly selective and impressionistic. He sought to provide something for the general reader, at the very least, and even better, to generate interest in further study of the Sterling era. It is this intention that Karen Bartholomew, as contributing editor, and I, as co-author, committed to completing.

Little did we know that, when Cash asked us to help with his growing manuscript in 2010, it would become more than a decade-long project. He was unflagging in his support and enthusiasm for our work, patient with suggestions, edits, additions, and substantive rewriting. He was intrigued by new sources and enjoyed discussing, and at times debating, the additional viewpoints and stories we brought to the work. It was a truly collaborative project, periodically highlighted by delightful lunches that he graciously hosted at his favorite restaurants.

While we have rewritten the text and have added extensive footnotes, illustrations, appendices, and a bibliography, this biography has remained something of a travelogue, covering highlights of an important era in Stanford history and touching on areas Cash thought most interesting as he explored Sterling's presidential records. His selection of initial chapter topics reflected his own personal interests and his modesty. We have expanded on these topics but have refrained, as he did, from analyzing the full nature of the evolution of academic fields, departments, and programs. Fortunately, scholars have as stepping-stones the works previously mentioned and many other primary and secondary sources named in the endnotes and bibliography.

Cash died in 2014, reading revised chapters and enjoying the biographer's journey to the end. He was especially interested in the ballooning chapter (now two chapters) on land development. With this volume, we honor his memory as a devoted and generous Stanford alumnus and benefactor, and a wonderful colleague and friend. We hope we have interpreted his intentions accurately and that our work will encour-

age readers to delve more deeply into, and explore in their own way, Stanford's rich archival collections of this period.

Finally, a word on our own perspectives. In the 1970s, we were among the next generation of young staff members who had been undergraduates—albeit at rival campuses—during the turbulent late 1960s and early '70s and who would be part of the Stanford administrations that succeeded Sterling's. We were welcomed wholeheartedly by the "older generation" of Fred Glover, Pete Allen, Don Carlson, Bob Beyers, Lyle Nelson, Ralph Hansen, and many others who had worked together as part of Sterling's (and, later, President Richard Lyman's) extended team. We benefited from their enthusiasm and deep affection for Stanford, but also from their willingness to think beyond the triumphal language of Stanford's success. They helped us—me as Ralph Hansen's successor as Stanford's second university archivist, and Karen, '71, as reporter and editor in Bob Beyers' Stanford News Service—to better understand the campus community and how to document it for future scholars. We often thought of our mentors as we worked on this book and have tried to incorporate their voices and stories where we could.

Don Carlson, then director of university relations, once said that none of them had had the courage to attempt a biography of Wally Sterling, knowing from the inside the complexities of the time and of the man. Yet Carlson, Glover, and Allen made an invaluable contribution to the University Archives by gathering nine colleagues together shortly after Chancellor Sterling's death, in 1985. The result, transcribed as "A Session on Wally" (1985), provides crucial insights into the workings of the Sterling administration. This book benefited enormously from that effort, along with Fred Glover's own lengthy 1993 oral history and the many interviews conducted in the late 1970s, 1980s, and early 1990s with faculty and administrators as Fred and I set in motion the Stanford Oral History Project. Our special thanks to Susan Schofield, '66, who, as chair of the Historical Society's Oral History Committee, revitalized the program at the turn of the millennium and especially for her leadership of the program's "Diversity Project" interview series that proved to be a vital source for later chapters.

Our work has also benefited in many ways from Bob Beyers' long-standing interest in documenting post-1945 Stanford. Following on the efforts of Glover (1946–52) and Allen (1952–61) as News Service directors, Bob and his staff built a remarkable collection of reference files. Far more than the usual newspaper morgue, the files cover a vast array of campus topics, people, events, issues, and developments that allowed us to fill out the story of this era. Bob often set aside other things for me, as university archivist, pulling a tape recording or document out of his desk drawer and taking the time to explain its particular significance. Later, as chair of the SHS Publications Committee, Bob encouraged Karen and me, then editors of the society's journal, *Sandstone & Tile*, to include post–World War II stories. How fitting that Bob should be remembered, through the generosity of his friend and news colleague Lorry Lokey, '49, with an endowed fund for society publications targeting this period. We know Bob would be pleased that the Beyers Fund is a major supporter of this biography.

Claude S. Brinegar, '50, Ph.D. '54, Karen's late husband and a friend I admired greatly, would have thoroughly enjoyed working on this project with us, as he did on many other SHS ventures, including his co-authorship of *A Chronology of Stanford University and Its Founders, 1824–2000* (2001). He and Karen created the Claude Brinegar Fund for just such a project as this one, and we are thrilled to honor his memory using the Brinegar Fund to support the book's publication.

We would like to thank those unsung donors who facilitated and funded digitization of the *Stanford Daily* archives. Partway through our project, the *Daily*'s back issues became available online, making this important window on campus viewpoints far more accessible, particularly during the pandemic campus shutdown. Many, though by no means all, of Stanford's student, alumni, and administrative publications also are now available online through the auspices of the Stanford University Archives. We hope this volume will help expand support, moral and financial, for their efforts.

There were many others who have helped bring this long project to fruition. Cash Kirk's close friend and business partner in later years, Richard Eberli, helped him put his research notes into an initial body of text. Margaret Kimball, '80, Stanford's third university archivist, helped Cash in his journey through the Sterling archives and has been unfailing in her encouragement of our work. Maggie, and her successors, Daniel Hartwig and Josh Schneider, and the staff of Stanford's Special Collections and University Archives, especially Tim Noakes, MLA '13, and Aimee Morgan, were unstintingly patient. Stanford's News Service, especially Pamela Moreland, Linda Cicero, and Michelle Futornick, allowed us to spend many hours perusing old News Service photos and reference files. Similarly, at Stanford's Maps and Records Office, Suman Prasad was unflappable in guiding Karen through original building records of the era, and Dobie Howard and others capably provided statistical details.

Sunny Scott not only helped with historical photographs but also wandered Stanford hills and Stanford Research Park helping us pin down particular vantage points. Margaret McKinnon, Jean Deken, and Carol Blitzer spent many hours carefully reading and copyediting every sentence with gratifying enthusiasm. Miriam Palm and

Don Price, '53, MBA '58, who both spent their careers at Stanford, helped confirm obscure campus historical details.

Many colleagues read individual chapters and gave sage advice: Bob Hamrdla, '59, MA, '64, secretary of the university emeritus and former SHS president; Jean Marie Deken, SLAC senior archivist; Elena Danielson, Ph.D. '75, Hoover archivist emerita; Larry Cuban, educational historian and Graduate School of Education professor emeritus; Peter Stansky, Frances and Charles Field professor of history emeritus; Gene Kershner, retired associate director of Facilities Project Management; and Jim Madison, '53, LL.B. '59, former *Daily* sportswriter and *Daily* editor.

We also received unflagging support from Larry Horton, '62, director of government relations emeritus and SHS colleague, who took on marketing tasks with aplomb; Charlie Junkerman, dean of continuing studies emeritus and SHS colleague; David Kennedy, '63, Donald J. McLachlan professor of history emeritus; Boyce Nute, '57, former head of the SHS Publications Committee; Norris Pope, director emeritus, Stanford University Press; Steve Staiger, Palo Alto historian, and his colleagues; and the late Bill Wyman, former associate dean of students.

We have been beneficiaries of the work of staff in the Stanford University Archives and the Stanford News Service who, over many decades, developed magnificent historical photograph collections. Among these is the work of several notable photographers employed by the university on special assignments. We are especially indebted to Bay Area photographer Leo Holub, who covered many bases and passed on many prints and negatives to the university, and to Jack Fields, who took hundreds of photographs of Sterling and Stanford for a December 1960 *Saturday Evening Post* feature article. Luckily, many of Field's negatives and prints not used for the article were turned over to the University Archives.

Christine Taylor and her staff at Wilsted & Taylor Publishing Services of Oakland, California, have been a joy to work with. We are grateful for their professionalism, excellent judgment, and patience during the lengthy, complicated production of this book.

Perhaps no one except us has read and reread as many draft chapters as my husband, James Axline. With the cold eye of a Cal alumnus confronted with Stanford stories, he has provided us not only with excellent editing suggestions but unconditional moral support and a heavy dose of Sterling-style pragmatic advice. (For him—and throughout his favorite chapter of this biography—it shall always be "Cal," not "UC Berkeley.")

Roxanne L. Nilan, Ph.D. '99
(Cal '73, MLS '74)
Los Gatos, 2023

FOLLOWING >
Sailors enjoy a full Lagunita in 1965, with the boathouse beyond and Hoover Tower in the distance.
STANFORD NEWS SERVICE

STANFORD'S
WALLACE
STERLING

STANFORD AT A CROSSROADS

THE PRESIDENCY OF J. E. WALLACE STERLING

by Roxanne L. Nilan

The campus, conditioned by one of the most beautiful spring-times of many a year, has experienced a great lift with the arrival of Dr. Sterling," announced the *Stanford Alumni Review* in May 1949. "It has been fifteen months since Don Tresidder died so unexpectedly. The University has moved ahead in that time, but the arrival of Dr. Sterling has imparted the vigor and security of permanent leadership."

Forty-two-year-old John Ewart Wallace Sterling had seemed a dark-horse candidate from Southern California for Stanford's fifth presidency. The Canadian-born historian with a Stanford Ph.D. (1938) had been a history professor for 10 years at a noted engineering institute with no history department and had recently become director of the Huntington Library and Art Gallery. He had few scholarly publications to his name. Yet Sterling had earned a reputation among trustees, donors, alumni, and faculty at the California Institute of Technology (Caltech) for his qualities as a charismatic teacher and an

effective faculty leader. He was well known in Southern California philanthropic circles for articulating a vision for well-supported private higher education. His deep, resonant voice could be heard on the CBS radio network, where, since 1942, he had been a popular news analyst covering wartime events, political conventions, and the creation of the United Nations. And he had maintained close ties with Stanford faculty.

Sterling had turned away other college presidency offers (among them, he had withdrawn, in 1946, from consideration while a final candidate for the top job at the University of Southern California). He had hoped that, after years of a heavy teaching and administrative load, his new position at the Huntington would offer a scholarly haven. But when opportunity for a return to his Northern California alma mater presented itself, it proved irresistible. He knew he was at a crossroads, he later recalled.[1] So, too, was Stanford.

Wallace Sterling's presidency is now considered the springboard to modern Stanford, a university at the front ranks of American higher education and academic research. Sterling was not the first Stanford president to dream of the

< President J. E. Wallace Sterling, at his desk in 1960. That year he told students: "I can tell you without equivocation that I found my job puzzling and exhausting, but always stimulating and rewarding." JACK FIELDS / STANFORD UNIVERSITY ARCHIVES

After several years of drought, students enjoyed boating and swimming again after the largest rainfall on record filled Lagunita to capacity in March 1951. Photographer Bob Bishop, a former Navy aeronautical engineer, was among the many World War II veterans studying at Stanford. Scenes of the lake and rolling hills beyond gave Stanford, still called "The Farm," a special bucolic aura.   BOB BISHOP / STANFORD NEWS SERVICE

university's potential as a premier academic program, nor was he its first president to try new fundraising strategies or explore new academic opportunities. As a historian, Sterling appreciated the work of the presidents he succeeded, and he looked back fondly on his graduate-student years in Stanford's close-knit community of the 1930s.

Sterling was keenly aware that President David Starr Jordan (1891–1913) and his pioneer faculty had catapulted a small, remote school into national academic recognition with a firm grounding in research as well as teaching; Stanford had been, after all, one of the 14 founding members, in 1900, of the prestigious Association of American Universities (AAU). Ray Lyman Wilbur (1916–43), adept at attracting private foundation support, had encouraged development of graduate and professional schools and had fortified undergraduate student services despite the economic trials of the Depression. Sterling already had seen, from his Caltech vantage point, the many changes World War II brought to academe. The pace of change at postwar Stanford had only escalated as Donald Tresidder (1943–48) sought to improve the university's medical school, student scholarship, and faculty recruiting, and as he began to explore opportunities for land development.

Before Sterling, Stanford's was not a mediocre academic program, nor was it any more or less regional than the vast majority of America's private universities, but it certainly was "a limping college," as one of Sterling's assistants later wrote, and not as well known as it deserved to be. Stanford had survived the Depression and World War II better than many other campuses, avoiding faculty layoffs and dwindling enrollments. The trade-off was delayed maintenance: "The university had virtually eaten the roofs off its buildings."[2] The Depression had also stunted growth in Stanford's research program, which had yet to live up to expectations for a top AAU campus. An observation made about his alma mater during the busy wartime years by talented physicist William W. Hansen is instructive: He considered Stanford to be a sunny place with a good golf course and a football team.[3]

Sterling recognized, on taking the job, that the university needed more than a quick fix-up. Aside from maintenance issues, faculty salaries were notoriously low, scholarship support was inadequate, and labs and libraries needed expansion as well as modernizing. It would have required a crystal ball, Stanford's seventh president, Richard W. Lyman, mused years later, "to have predicted with confidence in 1949 that

the Sterling Era would see so remarkable and sustained a rise in the University's fortunes."[4]

Ten years into his presidential term, Wallace Sterling had become an intrinsic part of the postwar Stanford success story. In December 1960, a national magazine dubbed him "Stanford's Man with the Midas Touch," the personification of the university's rise to national prominence through an ambitious faculty recruiting campaign and construction of major research facilities. Four months after the article appeared, Stanford would begin a pathbreaking fundraising campaign, building on earlier significant injections of foundation and federal funding, and on an innovative, and increasingly controversial, program to develop thousands of acres of non-academic campus land.[5]

By 1968, at the end of his 19-year presidency, the numbers were even more compelling. The university's operating budget was nearly nine times the size it had been when he took office, growing from $13 million to more than $115 million. The endowment had jumped from $41.2 million in 1949 to $268.2 million in 1968. Fundraising during the Sterling era had brought in more than 10 times what the university had raised between 1905 and 1949. Despite implementation of Stanford's increasingly selective admissions policy, the size of the student body grew by 40 percent, with graduate students accounting for much of the increase, while undergraduates from across the country broadened its geographical diversity. The professorial ranks had nearly tripled in size, while per capita faculty salaries had more than doubled.[6]

The Sterling era is known for the university's new major teaching and research facilities, among them the Stanford Medical Center and the Stanford Linear Accelerator Center. Sterling also launched the university's first broad curriculum review, the development of an overseas studies program, a review of education at Stanford in all

Changes underway can be seen from Hoover Tower in 1956: The Florence Moore complex, opening later that year, was slated to house 350 undergraduate women. Dinkelspiel Auditorium, also under construction, dwarfs the 1901 Stanford Post Office, at its side. The little brick and stucco building would be replaced in 1960 by the new Post Office, across the street. The Knoll, formerly President Wilbur's residence, sits on the hill above "Flo Mo." STANFORD NEWS SERVICE

its aspects, and initial reforms of student regulations and judicial procedures. While the administration grew in size and complexity, so, too, did faculty participation in governance through university committees and advisory groups.

By any conventional measure, concluded John Walsh in a 1973 Carnegie Commission study, "Stanford rose to a place among the best half-dozen American universities and is still on top of it, a marvelously pleasant place."[7]

THE RIGHT MAN AT THE RIGHT TIME

Many scholars have explored Stanford's near-perfect storm of advantages: a postwar boom in the economy, a willingness to engage in Cold War military-industrial research, the GI Bill, and the university's remarkable inheritance of more than 8,000 acres of prime real estate in a thriving location; in short, being in the right

place at the right time. Sterling himself acknowledged that his administration had "blue skies and a fair wind to sail by":

> During the 1950s and early '60s, the general climate for educational advancement was propitious; there was economic prosperity; there was public interest in higher education; a court decision opened the way for corporate philanthropy; there was the new and wealthy Ford Foundation; the Cold War, despite its tensions and tragedies, turned on the federal spigot in support of research; the first Eisenhower administration made available millions for health research facilities. And while all this was going on, an ever-swelling number of Stanford Associates and friends served faithfully and well to enhance the University's financial well-being.[8]

Even so, trustees, faculty, staff, and alumni alike would credit Sterling with being the right man at the right time, bringing something special

A *Daily* editor called him a manager of complexity, an alumnus described him as the ringmaster of a three-ring circus, but Sterling likened his work to that of an orchestra conductor. Here, in July 1962, Sterling works at his two desks in Building 10. (His windows face north, with a view across the courtyard to Building 170.) STANFORD NEWS SERVICE

to Stanford in both his administrative style and his personality. For Eastern collegiate rivals, Sterling personified Stanford's exuberant pride and youthful (in their eyes, adolescent) competitiveness. After all, his "Midas touch" and his faculty raiding ventures were often at their expense. Closer to home, and especially among those who knew and worked with him, he was the quintessential coach: a superb recruiter who searched for talent and then gave his team his full confidence; a charismatic leader who promoted dreams and winning ways while urging careful planning and pragmatic problem solving. And at the heart of it all, he built a small and intensely loyal administrative staff who worked closely with a growing cadre of faculty leaders.[9]

From the beginning, Sterling carefully built his good credit among trustees and alumni, keeping them well informed while challenging them to think boldly and to take a more active role in attracting new sources of financial support. He drew faculty members into university planning based on rigorous academic self-study and financial analysis, and pushed department heads and deans to always aim higher. He urged students to take risks and explore their opportunities, but also to remember the values of diligence, responsibility, and accountability. "It is hard to think of a university president in the years immediately past who was so firm an administrator and phenomenal a fundraiser, and at the same time, maintained such esteem among alumni and students," noted the 1973 Carnegie Report. "He personified the university in a way that Jordan had in an age vastly less skeptical of authority figures, and preserved into an era of the impersonal university what is, in the literal sense, a personal style."

Sterling always seemed comfortable among strangers, the center of any crowd, whether it was at a student dining hall, a faculty get-together, a Bohemian Club gathering with corporate leaders, or a visiting entourage of foreign dignitaries. His memory for names was legendary, as were his efforts to put others at ease. He was skillful and generous in thanking others for their work, and was a master of the personal note to staff, faculty, alumni, and students, as well as donors, large and small, statesmen, and generals. Students as well as faculty utilized his open-door policy.

Yet while Sterling avoided the humorless pomposity and pretense he found annoying in some authority figures (young as well as old), he maintained a strong sense of propriety, of his own responsibilities, and of the dignity of his office. He could be coolly correct or warmly enthusiastic, as one *San Jose News* reporter commented, but despite his reputation as Stanford's best salesman, he was never unctuous. No one ever doubted that the buck stopped with him. Chet Huntley, Sterling's CBS radio colleague, described his friend succinctly: "Intelligence and ability and good humor, suspended on the chassis of an All-America tackle, carry a considerable degree of authority."[10]

Bruce Bliven, '11, retired editor of the *New Republic*, had known Stanford's first five presidents. At Sterling's retirement in 1968, Bliven wrote admiringly that he "knows the greatest of all tactics—defeating an opponent without letting him lose too much face." Equally important, he added, was Sterling's principle of gradualism, which the president himself described as "the art of doing easily tomorrow what could be done today only over a dead body."[11]

Sterling believed that faculty members and students were the measure of a university. "It is they who determine its life, its variety, its drive, its innovation, and its experiment," Sterling told

President Sterling with class of 1953 officers, ceremonially placing their class plate in the Inner Quad arcade. From left: Joseph W. St. Geme, Charlotte E. Mesick, Sterling, Ann C. Alabaster, and John F. Shea. The changing relationship between students and administration would be a major theme of his later years in office.
STANFORD NEWS SERVICE

a journalism student in 1964. But the university's president, he added, was there to give them a push in "the way he uses his opportunities, authority, and judgment, the way he persuades others."[12] In his autobiography, Ray Lyman Wilbur, Stanford's third president, had described the essential characteristic for presidential success as durability of mind and body. Such durability was required, Wilbur said, "not only to carry out long-term programs but to last out and get the final word in discussions and debates on subjects in which the trustees, faculty, and the public are all involved."[13] Getting the last word was something Sterling did exceptionally well.

While Sterling welcomed discussion and believed strongly in the collegiality of academic life, his final decisions were rarely open to debate. In tough times, his nerves didn't fray, commented prominent trustee and international law expert Herbert Phleger, who admired the president's even temper and sense of humor, but, Phleger added, "no one ever made the mistake twice of thinking he would yield to pressure, or ever give up on a point of principle on which he thought he was right." A Sterling aide once quipped to a local reporter that "Wally…will listen to all the advice without committing himself, then do it his own unorthodox way. And he is usually right."[14]

THE MAN IN THE MIDDLE

Bliven used the imagery of the three-ring circus to describe Wally Sterling's job as that of a ringmaster. *Stanford Daily* associate editor Nancy Steffen, '65, saw Sterling as an adept manager of complexity. Sterling likened it to being an orchestra conductor. It was certainly a balancing act.[15]

Sterling was a buffer between ambitious academic officers and faculty colleagues on the one hand, and trustees focused on fiduciary responsibility on the other; between alumni (and often

parents) who worried that change might not be for the better, and students, who felt change was not happening fast enough; between the university and the general public, be it neighbors who had their own agenda for Stanford's land or letter writers on the hunt for Communists among the professoriate.

Sterling was also a man in the middle of changing times. Steffen credited Sterling with moving Stanford "from the brink of certain fiscal disaster to the precarious edge of academic greatness on which she seems to be tottering today," but Steffen's praise was tempered with a student's healthy skepticism of the later years of his administration. She would not quarrel with Stanford's success, which had "garnered a fair share of unmitigated praise and/or grudging admiration," but she worried that this success was "clearly measured in dollars and cents."[16]

During the last two years of his presidency, 1966–68, Sterling's personal style and the strength of his office made him both campus hero and villain. Seven years after the reorganization and streamlining of Sterling's administration, newer faculty and students perceived the university as authoritarian and bureaucratic. While the *Daily* now criticized its centralization, the 1959 reorganization in fact had significantly decentralized decision making by shifting authority from the president's desk to the provost and new vice presidents of business and of finance and development, while deans became significantly more independent than under previous administrations. Despite the criticisms, however, few faculty or students wanted to go back to a smaller, quieter, less prosperous Stanford.[17]

Reflecting the tenor of the times on campuses across the nation in 1967 and 1968, Stanford's arguably more sophisticated young faculty and student body seemed leery of President Sterling's accessibility. Some young critics were suspicious, even contemptuous, of Sterling's attempts to maintain a congenial, or at least civil, relationship with the student body. In 1968, leaders of the Old Union sit-in made headlines by refusing his invitation to talk. At the ensuing faculty meeting, a young professor even attempted, unsuccessfully, to physically push the 6-foot-2 former football player away from the microphone.[18]

Sterling, as an administrator and a historian of modern political institutions, admittedly had little patience with those who sought quick, easy answers to complex social questions, or those who wanted to immediately change institutions without delving deeply into either the problems they hoped to solve or the implications of their proposed solutions. He continued to hold students in high esteem, praising their intellectual ability and moral fiber, and thought Stanford students were now better prepared to take advantage of opportunities. But he worried that they also were increasingly arrogant and humorless. As always, he counseled pragmatism, civility, and thorough study before leaping to either conclusions or solutions.[19]

In summer 1968, as his administration drew to a close after nearly two decades in office, and suffering from recurring health problems, Sterling got the last word, in his own way. Only weeks before he turned over his work to a new administration, an arsonist set fire to his office. He refused to take the attack personally and turned his attention to those who prevented the fire from spreading and to others who helped him with the ensuing public attention. "You once told a reporter the university president's job was to take all the blame and share all the credit," News Director Bob Beyers wrote Sterling after receiving a personal note of appreciation from the busy president. "To me and many others, students as well as staffers, you have provided a splendid example of what a major university president can and should be." Despite the fire and the campus disruptions of previous months, Beyers wrote, "where other men, with justice, were reduced to tears and rage, your concern for the university remained steadfast and central."[20]

Memorial Court hosts a class on a sunny California day, around 1960. The Inner Quad Courtyard can be seen through the arcade. STANFORD NEWS SERVICE

View across White Plaza and the "Claw" fountain toward Engineering Corner in 1968. The recently remodeled Career Planning and Placement Center is on the right (formerly Stanford's Bookstore, 1913–60), backed by the Education Building. The relative calm of the Plaza on this afternoon contrasts with other afternoons of speech making and protests during the previous two years.   STANFORD NEWS SERVICE

"I know of no university which is all things to all people," Sterling had told an alumni audience earlier that year. He remained convinced that universities were "essential to a humane, enlightened, and improving society" just as the American public was wavering in its support of higher education. Once again in the middle of student and alumni quarrels, and faculty and public differences, Sterling remained as steady in his conviction in 1968 as he had in 1949: Stanford belonged in the front rank of universities, "a Stanford proud of its past, relevant to the present, and open to the future."[21]

It is not easy to encapsulate the uncommon man who was Stanford's fifth president, a university figure whose image today is inseparable from what Stanford University has become. We can, however, provide a glimpse of some of the experiences and perspectives J. E. Wallace Sterling brought to his presidency, and of some of the events that shaped Sterling's Stanford University.

Today, J. E. Wallace Sterling is memorialized at the university he loved by a dormitory complex, two endowed humanities professorships, awards of excellence to 25 graduating seniors, an alumni association award, and a medical alumni award. While this may seem a modest tribute, President Richard Lyman offered a different perspective. "For Wally Sterling at Stanford," he wrote following Sterling's death, in 1985, "it is impossible not to think of Sir Christopher Wren's epitaph in the great Cathedral of St. Paul's: *Si monumentum requiris, circumspice*—If you seek his monument, look about you! He will need no other, he deserves no less."[22]

1

FINDING STANFORD'S
FIFTH PRESIDENT

On November 19, 1948, Stanford University's Board of Trustees announced its unanimous decision: J. E. Wallace Sterling, the 42-year-old director of the Huntington Library and Art Gallery and former Caltech professor, would become Stanford's fifth president. The Canadian-born Sterling was, seemingly, something of a dark horse in this nationwide search, but his selection reflected the hopes and expectations of a university community eager to take the next step in its development. His acceptance would propel his career as dramatically as it would enrich Stanford.

Ten months earlier, the Stanford community had been shocked by the loss of its 53-year-old president, Donald B. Tresidder, who died January 28 of a heart attack while on university business in New York City. Under Tresidder, Stanford had emerged from wartime uncertainties of unpredictable enrollments, deferred maintenance, and diverted faculty, to embrace postwar opportunities. By 1947, Tresidder could share his dream for a

revitalized institution with the faculty's Academic Council: Underway were efforts to build a stronger faculty, foster a higher level of student scholarship, renovate and expand campus facilities, and experiment with creative fundraising. The loss of this vigorous outdoorsman, and of the momentum Tresidder had initiated during his five years at the helm, were much on trustees' minds.[1]

SELECTING A PRESIDENT

Board of Trustee President W. Parmer Fuller Jr., a close friend of Tresidder, set the search process in motion before stepping aside in grief. Ira Lillick, '97, one of the board's longest serving and most tactful members, chaired a search committee that included some of the board's most esteemed and opinionated trustees: from New York, former U.S. President Herbert Hoover, '95; from San Francisco, *San Francisco News* Editor Paul C. Edwards, '06, international law expert Herman Phleger, Cal '12, and banker and philanthropist Lloyd Dinkelspiel, '20; Stockton lawyer George Ditz, '11; and from Los Angeles, cardiologist and cancer researcher Seely G. Mudd, Columbia '17, Harvard '24. Each had

< J. E. Wallace Sterling poses outside his office on the Quad a week after taking over as Stanford's fifth president in April 1949. He would go on to serve 19 years, playing a major role in catapulting the university to national distinction.
MOULIN STUDIOS / STANFORD NEWS SERVICE

Stanford trustee Ira S. Lillick (left) chaired the presidential search committee and served as an important intermediary between alumni and the President's Office. As a maritime law expert, he had a strong interest in legal ethics and served on many trustee and university committees. Dean of Engineering Frederick E. Terman (right) led the faculty's presidential search advisory committee but stepped down when his name came up as a strong candidate for the post.
STANFORD UNIVERSITY ARCHIVES / STANFORD NEWS SERVICE

Frank Fish Walker, who resigned as a trustee to become university financial vice president, 1940–46, took charge of the alumni presidential search advisory committee. STANFORD NEWS SERVICE

worked closely with Tresidder, some becoming his good friends, and all would have to work well with his successor.[2]

Paul Edwards, a veteran Scripps-Howard editor, took over the board presidency from Fuller on short notice. Edwards had been active in alumni affairs, and particularly fundraising, for more than a decade. He remained a key member of the search committee while overseeing the university's progress and administrative transition.[3]

While looking for Tresidder's successor, Edwards maintained a good working relationship with Alvin C. Eurich, Tresidder's vice president and now acting president. Edwards knew that Eurich was a polarizing figure, as popular with the board as he was unpopular among faculty department heads. (Eurich would eventually withdraw his name from consideration.)[4]

Two advisory committees assisted the trustees' search committee. The faculty advisory committee, initially chaired by Frederick E. Terman, '20, had its own set of criteria, strong on scholarship and academic leadership that many faculty felt had been missing in the Tresidder-Eurich administration. The faculty search committee considered itself more than an advisory body, calling itself the Academic Council Committee on Selection of the University President. Terman stepped down when his own name was presented as a candidate; he was replaced by Edgar E. Robinson, chair of the History Department. Another strong internal candidate was English professor and former Dean of Humanities John W. Dodds, a gifted teacher, eloquent speaker, and respected administrator.[5]

John W. Dodds, English professor and former dean of humanities, was another strong internal candidate for the Stanford presidency.   STANFORD NEWS SERVICE

An alumni committee was led by Frank Fish Walker, '18, a former trustee active in the Alumni Association. The group endorsed the faculty's hope of finding someone with solid scholarly credentials, but with the personality to bring unity to Stanford, engage faculty, alumni, and students alike, and interest the public in Stanford affairs. While not insisting on a Stanford alumnus, they urged the trustees to develop leadership from within.[6]

The trustee search committee fielded 117 serious recommendations during its nine-month nationwide search, but their work was hampered by stiff competition. Many other major colleges and universities were looking for presidents during this postwar period of renewed interest in American higher education. Many of the suggestions echoed strategies of other universities similarly faced with expanding public and alumni expectations but limited resources. Some looked beyond accomplished scholars to select

senior statesmen, as had Columbia University (General Dwight Eisenhower) and the University of Pennsylvania (former Minnesota governor and perennial Republican presidential candidate Harold Stassen). Nominations included California Governor Earl Warren, U.S. Secretary of State Dean Acheson, and U.S. Senator J. William Fulbright, along with two generals and an outspoken Nobel Prize–winning scientist.[7]

Sterling's record seemed slim by comparison: With a 1938 Stanford Ph.D., he had only 10 years of academic experience and a meager record of published research. He had neither national political status nor military leadership experience. Yet Sterling's name appeared on each of the initial lists compiled by the trustee, alumni, and faculty committees. Months later, he was still among the half-dozen names seriously considered. By the time trustees decided to aggressively recruit him, it was clear that his background, interests, breadth of experience, and charisma fit well with each committee's distinct expectations.

In late 1937, just before his dissertation was accepted, Wallace Sterling had joined the Caltech faculty as an assistant professor. He rose quickly through the faculty ranks, winning a full professorship by 1942. Three years later he was named to the endowed Edward S. Harkness Professorship of History and Government. Sterling had carried a heavy teaching load during and after the war, while rising as an effective faculty diplomat and administrator. Named to Caltech's Executive Committee in 1940, he was elected secretary of the faculty by his colleagues (1941–44) and subsequently chairman of the faculty (1944–46). His contacts had expanded rapidly as he came to know influential college trustees, philanthropists, and business and academic leaders throughout Southern California. By 1946, he had rebuffed attempts to recruit him for the presidencies of the University of Southern California and of Scripps College.[8]

Notable, too, was his parallel career as a popular CBS radio news analyst; his sonorous voice had been heard up and down the West Coast since 1942, as he brought historical context and insight to the events unfolding around the world during and after the war.

Sterling's responsibilities on and off campus, however, had taken a toll on his research and publishing. In July 1948, he changed direction to become director of the Henry E. Huntington Library and Art Gallery, with a continuing connection to Caltech's Humanities Department. Sterling followed in the footsteps of two distinguished scholar-directors, Max Farrand and Louis B. Wright, and looked forward to years of study and scholarship in beautiful surroundings, while applying his experience with library problems to advancing the Huntington's collections, financial support, and scholarly reputation.[9] As a graduate student and research assistant, he had seen the inner workings of Stanford's Hoover War Library, and maintained a close relationship with its directors, Professor Ralph Lutz, also Sterling's dissertation advisor, and Lutz's successor, Professor Harold Fisher. (In 1946, Sterling had turned down the opportunity to follow Lutz as Hoover Institution director.)[10]

The Huntington appointment also reflected Sterling's ever-widening associations. Its Board of Trustees included many he had come to know during his Caltech years. Robert Millikan, retired head of Caltech, now presided over the Huntington's Board of Trustees.

Barely a month into his new work, Sterling was visited by Huntington trustee Dr. Seeley Mudd, a fellow Caltech faculty member.[11] Sterling was unaware, he later claimed, that Mudd was also a trustee of Stanford University and a member of its presidential search committee. Given Sterling's expertise in modern history, their increasingly personal discussion of Sterling's views of the New Deal and Franklin D.

Roosevelt raised no flags with him about Stanford's interest. Nor was Sterling aware that he was being looked over when Mudd introduced him to Herman Phleger over lunch at the Century Club of Los Angeles (both Sterling and Mudd were members). Phleger had served as legal counsel to the U.S. Military Government in postwar Germany and—unbeknownst to Sterling—was a Stanford trustee.[12]

Mudd's mission, at the request of fellow Stanford and Huntington trustee Herbert Hoover, had been to ascertain Sterling's political views. Mudd had been pleased to hear that Sterling thought Roosevelt egotistical and intellectually dishonest. While he admired some New Deal social objectives, Sterling told Mudd, he felt its programs were not well implemented. Washington, D.C., he believed, needed a thorough housecleaning. Without knowing it, Sterling had passed the Mudd-Hoover political litmus test. Armed with Mudd's reassurance, Herbert Hoover now enthusiastically supported Sterling's candidacy. Hoover may not have played as decisive a role in finding Sterling as he later claimed, but his disapproval would have put an end to Sterling's candidacy.[13]

Phleger, too, was impressed. Alerted to Sterling's potential by Union Oil President Reese Taylor, a Caltech trustee, Phleger was among the Northern California trustees who knew little about Sterling. After their Century Club meeting, Phleger, too, became a firm advocate for Sterling's candidacy.[14]

Sterling's good friend and colleague Harold Fisher followed the recruiting process with some amusement. Before the San Francisco dinner, the trustees studied Sterling's listing in *Who's Who in America*. Edwards asked Fisher for clarification. Hoover staff member X. J. Eudin had been listed with Sterling and Fisher as co-editor of the memoirs of V. I. Gurko, published in 1939 as part of the Hoover Institution's *Features and Figures of the Past* series. Was Eudin a Russian, Edwards asked, and, if so, what *kind* of a Russian? Fisher assured Edwards that Eudin, a Russian-born American citizen, was "not under the pay of Uncle Joe [Stalin]."[15]

Edwards also asked about Sterling's citizenship status and activities during World War II. Sterling, in Canada in 1938 as war broke out in Europe, had asked the Canadian Government for a service assignment but had been told his Caltech responsibilities were more valuable to the war effort. Sterling's back injuries, suffered during his college football years and still painful in 1938, also rendered him ineligible for active duty. He subsequently took on administrative duties that aided Caltech's contribution to the war effort. Sterling had delayed completing his U.S. citizenship application until 1940 to remain eligible for Canadian war service, if needed. (Canada, as part of the Commonwealth, was at war, but the United States was not.) Sterling was granted U.S. citizenship in 1947.[16]

By the time Sterling visited Fisher, during an October weekend at Stanford, the intentions of the trustee search committee were obvious. That weekend, Sterling was among the dinner guests of trustee Lloyd Dinkelspiel, where he met board President Paul Edwards and other members of the search committee. "He made a most engaging impression," recorded Edwards. In addition to his accomplishments as a faculty leader and CBS news broadcaster, Sterling impressed the trustees with his strong attachment to Stanford and his connections with many faculty members following his years as a graduate student. Both were essential factors in accommodating the requirements of the faculty and alumni advisory committees.[17]

By late October, the trustee search committee, with endorsements from the faculty and alumni committees, settled firmly on Sterling. Then began what Edwards called "delicate diplomatic moves" to determine if he genuinely was interested in the position. If so, would the Huntington Library board release him so soon after his taking their directorship?[18]

ACCEPTING THE PRESIDENCY

Sterling followed his discussions with Edwards, Phleger, Mudd, and Lillick with a November 17 memorandum confirming his interest and outlining his thoughts about the presidency.[19]

In it, he reiterated his belief that despite financial challenges, the university must attract both the best faculty possible and a student body capable of high academic performance. Stanford, he said, "has ground to gain in both these endeavors." Sterling had high expectations of the role of faculty in the formulation of the university's educational policy. This could be done through formal faculty interchanges as well as through faculty-administration cooperation and faculty interactions with trustees. Both of these goals—improving faculty and student quality and faculty involvement—would become hallmarks of the Sterling administration.

As an experienced faculty leader, he believed in accountability as well as the sharing of opinion, noting that "large faculties are frequently too readily given to cliquishness and to sniping at trustees and administrative officers. In some universities indeed the president, second only to the football coach, is the one university game that enjoys a completely open season." This could be avoided, he said, if faculty representatives participated "strongly and deliberately in the formulation of university policy and, through participation, to accept responsibility."

Sterling echoed Donald Tresidder in insisting that the president be the only administrative officer directly responsible to the board for university operations. (Tresidder, on agreeing to move from board president to university president in 1943, had demanded that the university's treasurer report to the president, not the board, as had been the case.) Sterling, too, would pay close attention to finances, and would build a staff adept at financial analysis and budget forecasting.

Foreshadowing future land development projects that would mark his administration, Sterling also noted Tresidder's precedent and its potential: "The board has already under consideration methods by which the potentially great assets in land which the university possesses may be translated into university income." This was a direction he had every intention of pursuing.

Sterling still hoped he would make headway with his three writing commitments. He proposed July 1, 1949, the end of the Huntington's fiscal year, as a starting date. "Acceptance of the Presidency of Stanford University would, of course, preclude the undertaking of any more scholarly works of this sort," Sterling told the board. "Thereafter academic exercises of this nature would have to be confined to projects susceptible of briefer treatment," he optimistically concluded.

Paul Edwards offered the presidency to Sterling and after Sterling's conditional acceptance was reviewed, a final special November 19 meeting of the Board of Trustees confirmed the appointment.

At that meeting's conclusion, M. C. Sloss, vice president of the Stanford board, signaled to Frederic O. Glover, Stanford's director of information, to publicly announce the appointment to a waiting room filled with newspaper reporters. Edwards, alert to the need to mend fences within the Stanford community, personally made a simultaneous announcement on campus to the faculty's representative body, the Academic Council. The *Stanford Daily* set in motion its special "extra" edition, ready to roll off the press.

Glover carefully timed the announcement to coincide with that of acting President Alvin

Eurich as president of the newly created State University of New York.[20]

The nine-month-long search for a new president had ended, and a dynamic new era for Stanford University was about to unfold.

The decision to accept the Stanford presidency was, of course, one of the most important decisions that Sterling would ever make. "This was a decision which could not be made by formula," he told Peter C. Allen, editor of the Alumni Association magazine, the *Stanford Alumni Review*. "I realized that I stood at a fork in the road." Had he continued as head of Huntington, he could have conducted research that might bring him national recognition as a historian. He was determined to complete his three book manuscripts. The family would have a beautiful home at the Huntington Library, surrounded by more than 200 acres of famously landscaped grounds. They had privacy and time to pursue personal goals. In addition, their three children did not want to leave friends. Despite this, the Sterlings embraced the opportunity.[21]

QUICK VISIT FOR BIG GAME

Sterling's appointment had been announced on Big Game Friday, the day before the annual gridiron clash between Stanford and Cal. At a football luncheon in San Francisco that day, some alumni suggested to Edwards that Sterling, then in Pasadena, should be present for Saturday's 51st Big Game in Berkeley. A doubtful Edwards agreed to phone Sterling, whose immediate response was "That might be helpful, mightn't it."[22]

Sterling and his wife, Ann, took the Lark passenger train that night and arrived in Palo Alto early the next morning. After breakfast with General Secretary Tom Carpenter, the university's chief fundraiser, Sterling went to Edwards' Los Altos home, where he also conferred, for more than two hours, with Fred Glover and

At the time Wallace Sterling became president, the Stanford Union complex was the heart of undergraduate socializing on campus. The Cellar (entrance beneath the awning) was its popular eatery and soda fountain (left). STANFORD NEWS SERVICE

A 1950s view from Men's Clubhouse (now Building 590) across Panama Street at Lasuen Street. Beyond are the 1913 Stanford Bookstore (right), the Education Building (center), and the Engineering Building (left) that later would be named for Fred Terman. Hoover Tower looms over the School of Education. STANFORD NEWS SERVICE

Students in the mid-1950s often relaxed outside The Cellar. The Post Office, on Lasuen Street, is in the background. Within a few years, a new Bookstore and Post Office would be built off to the left, and the street and old Post Office area would become White Plaza. An arcade along the front of the Stanford Union complex connects its three buildings, replicating the arcade theme of the Main Quad. STANFORD NEWS SERVICE

CHAPTER 1: FINDING STANFORD'S FIFTH PRESIDENT | 19

The Post Office, around 1950, looking north on Lasuen. The building was torn down after the 1959–60 Post Office was built across the street. The Stanford Union complex is in the distance.
STANFORD NEWS SERVICE

Looking up Lasuen Street at History Corner, site of Sterling's graduate studies and early teaching, and the east side of the Quad. After decades of being able to drive from the Oval to the Post Office and beyond, in fall 1938 cars finally were blocked 24 hours a day due to frequent traffic accidents.
KEN REICHARD / STANFORD NEWS SERVICE

Pete Allen. Sterling already seemed to embrace his presidential role, Allen remembered. "As I walk around the campus," Sterling told Allen, "it seems to me that the housekeeping could be just a little bit better," and he suggested setting up a $10,000 fund to improve maintenance. "He was very forthcoming," Allen recalled. "He knew, with his radio background and journalistic slant, almost before we asked a question what we wanted."[23]

The problem of acquiring scarce Big Game tickets emerged. Al Masters, Stanford's director of athletics, rose to the occasion, saying, "I always hold a couple of tickets for the Second Coming." At halftime, with Cal ahead 7–0, Masters took Sterling to the dressing room to meet the team. Stanford, widely viewed as a 20-point underdog, faced a powerful Cal team. As a former collegiate football player and coach, Sterling spoke encouragingly: "You fellows are putting up a magnificent fight. All through the first half as I sat in the stands, my feet were

On the day following his appointment as Stanford's fifth president, J. E. Wallace Sterling attended the 51st Big Game. Although Berkeley was greatly favored, after the former collegiate athlete gave a rousing half-time pep talk to his team, Stanford kept the game close, losing 6–7. SAN FRANCISCO EXAMINER / STANFORD NEWS SERVICE

itching to be down there in uniform on the field with you. But I had to remind myself that I was about twenty-five years too late for that." While Stanford ultimately lost the game, they surprised onlookers with an unexpectedly close score of 6–7. This was to be Sterling's introduction as president-elect to Stanford intercollegiate football, a sport he enjoyed, but that would sorely try his patience in future years *(see Chapter 16)*.[24]

After the game, there was a problem of protocol—how to present the Sterlings to important alumni and faculty before his return to San Marino? An impromptu invitation to a party at the campus home of Jack W. Shoup, director of the Alumni Association, and his wife, Peg, turned out to be just the thing—a crowd of 200, everyone happy, and no problems of academic formality. Thus ended Sterling's first foray on the campus in his role as president-elect.[25]

DELUGE OF CONGRATULATIONS

Immediately following the announcement, Sterling and the university received hundreds of congratulatory letters and telegrams. Many of them were addressed to "Dear Wally," revealing the breadth of his personal friendships even at this relatively early stage in his career, and many came from Stanford faculty members who had been colleagues during the years he was working for his doctorate.

Professor John Dodds wrote Sterling presciently: "You'll have a great opportunity here, for you'll find many people who will share with you a deep belief in the potentially brilliant future which lies ahead for the University."[26]

In her matter-of-fact letter of congratulations, former campus first lady Mary Tresidder said: "Dr. Hutchins wrote an article about the University Administrators which Dr. Tresidder enjoyed and which might interest you if you haven't seen it. . . . It is a very graphic description of the pitfalls and contradictions of that elusive position." She later wrote from Yosemite, "I hope that your years at Stanford will be fruitful both for you and the University and that your days may be long in the land."[27]

Southern California developer and businessman Preston Hotchkis was one of several who claimed he had suggested Sterling's name as a candidate. In his congratulatory letter, he cautioned Sterling about taking on too much of a burden, recalling a recent conversation with General Dwight D. Eisenhower, now president of Columbia University. Hotchkis thought Eisenhower found the unavoidable demands for luncheons, dinners, and speaking engagements left him no time for himself and his wife.[28] Having been in academia all his adult life, Sterling very likely understood the enormous demands the presidency would entail, although he was overly optimistic about completing his pending writing commitments once he assumed Stanford's presidency.

Caltech president and eminent physicist Lee A. DuBridge wrote, "Stanford University's recent raid on Pasadena kidnapping Wallace Sterling was really no surprise to his friends who long had anticipated that he would be a logical choice for this important post. We are delighted for his sake and for the sake of Stanford though losing him from the Pasadena area is a serious personal blow to us."[29]

"I think the possibilities for Stanford's development are unlimited," wrote Stanford history Professor William Bark prophetically. (Bark had first met Sterling during their days as instructors in the Western Civilization program in the 1930s.) "But it will be a hard piece of work and it needs someone like you to do it. I know the temptation to stay at the Huntington must have been very great. You chose the right way and I'm sure you will not regret it."[30]

Grayson Kirk, then with the School of International Studies at Columbia University and later president of Columbia, wrote Sterling, "With your background of experience at Stanford and your wide contacts among the Stanford faculty, you should be able to avoid a great many of the headaches which any outsider encounters when he comes into a responsible position in a university community."[31]

Complimenting Sterling, if somewhat backhandedly, Thomas A. Bailey, professor of history, wrote: "The general [faculty] feeling is one of immense relief, in view of the many horrible alternatives that had been rumored about, and great satisfaction that Stanford has at long last broken away from the medical tradition and turned to a scholar in the Social Studies." (Sterling's two immediate predecessors were physicians, although Tresidder had not practiced medicine but instead had spent most of his adult life prior to Stanford as president of the Yosemite Park and Curry Company.)[32]

On learning of his son's appointment, the Rev. William Sterling telegraphed Sterling from Ontario: "Congratulations. More than proud of you. Dad."[33]

Newspaper coverage was equally laudatory. On November 23, the *Cleveland Plain Dealer* noted that other colleges and universities had appointed presidents from other professions than education. It was refreshing to see, it editorialized, "an outstanding American university choose as its chief executive officer [one] who has devoted his entire adult life to educational and cultural pursuits. Such a choice has been made by Stanford University." Two days later, the *San Francisco Chronicle* commented: "As head of the distinguished Huntington Library in Pasadena [*sic*], Dr. Sterling found it not inconsistent to be a first-rate historian and to share his knowledge with the public by going on the radio as a news analyst. This willingness to transcend from the ivory tower is essential in a modern university and is one among many reasons why Stanford is to be congratulated on its choice."

The November 29 issue of *Time* magazine reporting the appointment described Sterling as "cob-nosed" and stated that he described himself as "a regular guy." This created quite a local stir. One angered friend of Sterling's wrote *Time*, saying that those with prominent noses "were behind our proboscis for keeps, and not for comment."[34] *Time*'s December 17 reply:

Time didn't mean to be unkind to Wallace Sterling in the November story about his appointment as Stanford's new president. Nor did we intend any lack of dignity in describing his nose. We wanted to give readers who had never seen President-elect Sterling some idea of his appearance. You will agree that his nose is prominent, and we mentioned it simply because it is the most striking of his features. Our story told about his talents both as an administrator and a scholar, so our readers should have good reason to share your admiration for Wallace Sterling.

Trustee President Paul C. Edwards smoothed Sterling's move into the presidency. The two quickly developed a productive working relationship and close friendship. This is one of a series of photos taken by San Francisco's Gabriel Moulin Studio in April 1949, commissioned by the university.   MOULIN STUDIOS / STANFORD NEWS SERVICE

"Running a university is a difficult task," the *Stanford Daily*'s November 23 editorial commented about Sterling's appointment. "Keeping harmony among the faculty, students, and alumni, and keeping the university solvent and attractive to the public requires the greatest tact, judgment, and ability. Wasn't it Woodrow Wilson who said that running the nation was a cinch compared to running a university?"[35]

PLANNING THE MOVE TO HOOVER HOUSE

Wally Sterling made several visits to campus over the next five months, as did Ann Sterling. She was enthusiastic about the move north and socialized easily with trustees and faculty as she planned for the relocation of her family. "Ann's competence, her keen insight, and clear judgement excite my constant admiration," Paul Edwards wrote Wally Sterling after Ann's January 1949 visit. "I'd like to have listened in on the conversation between her and Parmer Fuller at dinner Friday night. I'll bet it sparkled."[36]

Sterling had made clear in his November memorandum of conditions that he was not convinced that the Lou Henry Hoover House, the university's official presidential residence since 1945, could be "adapted in the first instance to a happy family life and in the second instance to the responsibility of entertaining faculty, students and friends of the University." Even Herbert Hoover, meeting with Sterling in New York in January 1949, expressed some concern about the Hoover House not being suited to a family with small children. "Maybe," Hoover suggested to Sterling, "you could cut it up." Sterling replied, "Oh, no one would want to do much cutting up to THAT house."[37]

Don and Mary Tresidder, who had no children, had changed the ambiance of the Hoover House, exchanging the Hoovers' antiques for some of their own Craftsman-style furnishings from their Ahwahnee Hotel suite, their Yosemite home. They opened the house to students at small, casual dinners and large, monthly open houses.[38] Ann Sterling, who favored 18th-century English antiques, was now eager to plan for her own change of style.

Mary Tresidder, who had succeeded her husband as president of Yosemite Park and Curry Company, was in the process of moving back to Yosemite following her husband's death. The transition from one lady of the house to another, during a time of grieving, was difficult.

The ever-diplomatic Paul Edwards helped smooth the way. While helping Ann with her plans to update the house before the Sterling family moved from Pasadena, he expedited renovation of the house at 415 Gerona that the Tresidders had bought in 1939, when Don

Tresidder joined the Board of Trustees, and where Mary could look out at the rolling hills behind the campus.[39]

THE FINAL ARRANGEMENTS

During the presidential search, Eurich, as acting president, had maintained excellent relations with the board and oversaw a stable transition. The Board of Trustees had not expected him to leave the university, much less so promptly, after their announcement. To fill in between Eurich's departure for New York in early January and Sterling's presumed July 1949 arrival, the board named Clarence H. Faust as acting president. In 1947, Eurich, as vice president for academic affairs, had appointed Faust, an English professor and dean from the University of Chicago, to the faculty without conferring with the English Department. Faculty resistance was significant enough for Faust to be appointed instead as director of libraries. With a reorganization of university departments and schools in 1948, Eurich then named Faust dean of the newly formed School of Humanities and Sciences.

Faust's appointment as acting president was no more popular with the Faculty Advisory Board than his earlier appointments. Noting this opposition, Eurich asked the other deans who among them would be willing to serve as acting president instead of Faust. Each demurred. Only Engineering Dean Fred Terman refused to endorse Faust's selection. Without faculty support, Faust's brief tenure as acting president was not a happy one.[40]

By mid-December, Edwards already had resolved to move up Sterling's starting date. With the backing of the Huntington board, Sterling agreed to shift from July 1 to April 1, 1949.[41]

EARLY LIFE

CANADA AND CALIFORNIA

The man who would become an influential commentator on international affairs and an esteemed president of Stanford University was shaped by the influence of a modest, hardworking boyhood spent in rural Canada. Wallace Sterling's future success was nurtured during his years as a university student and in his early years as a student athlete, when his social skills, leadership abilities, athletic prowess, and academic interests were first recognized and rewarded.

GROWING UP IN RURAL CANADA

John Ewart Wallace Sterling was born in the Ontario farming village of Linwood on August 6, 1906, the second child of the Rev. William Sterling and Annie Wallace Sterling. The Sterlings had lived in Canada for little more than a year, having arrived from England, in 1905,

with their 7-year-old daughter, Elizabeth. (Their third child, Eileen, was born in 1915.)[1]

Annie Wallace and William Sterling had grown up among the collieries of County Durham, in North East England. She was descended from generations of coal miners; William's father, John Ewart Sterling, an engine fitter, was Durham-born but of Scottish descent. William listed his occupation as miner as late as the 1901 census, but his calling was that of preacher. For William and Annie Sterling, family life and work were framed by strongly held values of hard work, sociability, personal accountability, and compassion.[2]

Both Annie and William were lay preachers in County Durham, with Annie's contribution enlivened by her musical ability, an important element in Methodist chapel worship. The Durham chapels promoted lively congregational singing, as well as musical performances at outdoor church gatherings and miners' meetings.

William Sterling, formally ordained in 1907, served as a minister in farming communities along Lake Erie in Southwest Ontario. Like many of his colleagues, he served congregations too small to afford a full-time pastor. His home

< While studying for his master's degree in history at the University of Alberta, Sterling coached Alberta's formidable football team for two years. His Alberta Golden Bears won the prestigious Hardy Cup in 1929, setting up Sterling for the head coaching job with Calgary's professional football team. UNIVERSITY OF ALBERTA ARCHIVES

As president of the Athletic Union of Victoria College at the University of Toronto, 20-year-old Wallace Sterling was in charge of all sports during the 1926–27 school year.
TORONTOENSIS, UNIVERSITY OF TORONTO, 1926–27

parish changed often; the Sterlings lived in at least eight small country towns until his retirement, in 1945.[3]

Wallace Sterling grew up amid rich, hilly farmland, once heavily wooded but still known for its excellent hunting and fishing. In a 1956 address he titled "Fathers and Sons," Wallace Sterling reflected on his boyhood in Southwest Ontario:[4]

> I was always close to the land. I knew what it was to see seed sown and harvests reaped. I felt the excitement of barn-raisings when neighbors for miles around gathered to do a good turn for one who was getting a stake in life or who had been visited by misfortune. I had the adventure of tracking rabbits over the snow in winter and the thrill of making maple syrup in the spring. I knew the exhilaration of the early frost and the late October moon that set the stage for Halloween. And what pranks Halloween brought to the rural countryside forty years ago!

Sterling also valued the self-reliance of the people of these communities:

> I think of their readiness to make their own way in the world by hard work; of the fact they did much to create their own fun and entertainment, of the interest of parents in advancing the education of their children. . . . And I find myself hoping that the virtues of self-reliance, of hard work, of genuine good neighborliness will remain strong within us even in this fast-moving atomic and Phenobarbital age.

The Rev. William Sterling and Annie Wallace Sterling (right), parents of Wallace Sterling. At left is Annie's brother Thomas Wallace and his wife, Annie Jones Wallace. The Sterlings had encouraged the Wallaces to join them in Canada, where Thomas followed William into the ministry.   STARK FAMILY

Later known and respected for his empathy and ability to communicate with people of all social levels, Sterling drew from both family values and his own work experience in Western Ontario's farm country. He worked at a wide array of jobs: pitching hay, stringing telephone lines, working on a construction gang, selling furniture polish, serving as an advance man for a Chautauqua show, and playing professional baseball. For a short time, to please his father, he rode circuit as a pinch-hitting lay preacher, an experience that convinced him he was not cut out to be a minister.[5]

His father was a particularly strong influence. William Sterling, 6-foot tall and 235 pounds, was powerfully built and, as his son recalled, was "as strict as he was strong. . . . And my early impression of his strength and strictness will be with me forever." William had an enduring influence on all of his children, who in turn grew into tall, imposing figures.

Some of his father's spirit of independence rubbed off on him, Sterling later remembered.

Their relationship was one of ongoing, if often frustrated, attempts at mutual reform. As a boy, young Wallace tried at least twice to bring his father "to his senses" by running away from home. Each time, the boy returned on his own, about nightfall, walking back after some 5 or 6 miles.[6]

Several things about his father had given him hope, Sterling said. "When it dawned on me that he planned to have the fastest horse on the road, I thought my father might be well worth saving." On one occasion when his father took him to a local rugby football game, the home team recruited the Rev. Sterling, known as an exceptional player back in County Durham, as a substitute fullback. "I figured that any man who liked fast horses and could, at short notice, star in a [rugby] soccer game, would one day overcome his shortcomings and learn more about bringing up children."

Coming home from college on vacations, fortified with new learning, young Sterling continued his self-imposed and fruitless task of saving his father from ignorance and mysticism. On one summer visit, his father took him to a nearby lake for a bonfire and picnic supper. "The sunset on the lake was magnificent," Wallace Sterling recalled. "The heavens were lit up with an entire spectrum of glorious color. We watched the changing splendor in silence. Then he said to me: 'Do you enjoy the sunset?' I said 'Yes, sir, I do.' He went on: 'Explain it to me in terms of reason, will you please.' I didn't even try!"

Sterling also fondly recalled those visits home: snowshoe hikes with his father in winter, their occasional visits to big-league baseball games in the summer, "the wonderful stories he told on all occasions, and his tremendous kindliness." His father's politics were simply put: "Son, if a man is not something of a radical at twenty, there is something wrong with his heart; and if he is not something of a conservative at forty, there is something wrong with his head."

As this was a speech to graduating seniors, Wallace Sterling ended with observations on the ultimate agreement between father and son on

During inaugural events as Stanford's fifth president in October 1949, Wallace Sterling visited with his father. The Rev. William Sterling had served small farming communities of Canada's Southwest Ontario for nearly 40 years before retiring in 1945. He died in February 1950, four months after attending his son's inauguration.
STANFORD NEWS SERVICE

the virtues of self-reliance and of hard work as the honest application of one's talents, whatever those may be. His relationship with his father "is the story of the kindliness that is apt to permeate each of us when, around a campfire, we feel the beauty of a sunset or the soaring magnificence of mountain peaks, for in such circumstances we are in the presence of something that is beyond the power of man to create, and we are humbled."

Although there are few references to Sterling's mother, Annie Wallace Sterling, in his archives, she, too, was a strong influence. An accomplished musician, she taught him to play the piano, with a repertoire ranging from English music hall ditties to contemporary songs, and to use it to bring together people from all walks of life. Sterling deftly used the piano, as a student, faculty member, and university administrator, to liven up social gatherings.[7]

Annie Sterling died in 1931, when Sterling was 25. As a friend of his mother's wrote him, in 1948, on his appointment as Stanford's president:

"Never, Wallace, have I found anyone so true, so good, so unselfish, so utterly satisfying to my soul as was your Mother. You have a wonderful heritage in your parentage." She would have rejoiced at his success, but "she expected it of you."[8]

COLLEGE AND UNIVERSITY YEARS IN CANADA

William and Annie Sterling made sure their three children attended school in whichever small, rural village they resided at the time; each of them moved on to college. Wallace would later recall with amusement that at least one of his high school teachers, Hazel Hay, was not particularly impressed with his scholarship. She told him he would make "a good ditch-digger." Miss Hay, he added, "was something of a disciplinarian but one of the best high school teachers I ever had."[9]

In fall 1923, Wally Sterling entered Victoria College of the University of Toronto, where his sister Elizabeth had studied. This esteemed

In fall 1923, Wallace Sterling entered Victoria College, the esteemed coeducational, liberal arts college of the University of Toronto. His sister Elizabeth had graduated from Victoria College in 1920.
UNIVERSITY OF TORONTO ARCHIVES

Wallace Sterling (at center), representing the Athletics Union, was an influential member of the Victoria College Students' Parliament, the college's student executive committee. *TORONTOENSIS*, UNIVERSITY OF TORONTO, 1926–27

coeducational liberal arts college, founded by the Wesleyan Methodist Church of Canada and in 1890 federated with the University of Toronto, maintained a strong reputation for academics and public service. Elizabeth had studied history and English, graduating in 1920, but was best known as a "theatre star" and as the dynamic president of the Women's Drama Club.[10]

Victoria College challenged Sterling's mind and body, and he quickly became engaged in college life there. In addition to his studies in history, philosophy, and economics, he became active in student affairs and joined the Victoria College Glee and Choral Club. Sterling served as secretary and later president of the Victoria College Athletic Union, which managed both men's and women's sports for the college. As Union president, he also served on the Victoria College Students' Parliament. In addition, he participated in the Victoria Students' Christian movement. Under Sterling's senior photograph was the traditional pithy quote, in his case: "Why should such things be mixed: muscle and music, sense and nonsense."[11]

Sterling also served on his Victoria College senior class executive committee. Ann Marie Shaver, of Ancaster, Ontario, was the committee's vice president. Their relationship would

Student athlete, legislator, and comic-opera star? Wally Sterling, with fellow student Page Tor in a Gilbert and Sullivan production while at the University of Toronto. STANFORD UNIVERSITY ARCHIVES

last the rest of their lives. She, too, was busy at Victoria College, participating in *Acta Victoriana*, the well-respected undergraduate magazine, and the Annesley Student Government Association, the women's self-governance committee. (In Canadian census and birth records, as well as the Toronto yearbook, her name is variously spelled Anne and Anna, but she preferred "Ann.")[12]

Ineligible to serve on the all-male Victoria College executive committee, in 1906 the women of Victoria College's Annesley Hall created a women's self-governance committee. Ann Shaver (first row, third from left) was elected a member of its governing committee, 1926–27.   *TORONTOENSIS*, UNIVERSITY OF TORONTO, 1926–27

At 6-foot-2 inches, and 215 pounds, Sterling had a tall, athletic body and long, strong hands. While at the University of Toronto, a university with a notable sports tradition, he could indulge in his love of athletics, particularly basketball and football. Basketball, invented by Ontario native James Naismith in 1891, had become a highly popular indoor sport for cold-weather Canada, and Sterling played guard on Victoria College's team.

It was Canadian football, however, and the success of Toronto's "Varsity Blues," that held popular imagination. Toronto had a distinguished football tradition, dating to the first documented gridiron match in Canada, in 1861. Canadian and American football were diverging in rules, but both versions required versatility as well as stamina. Sterling played at center, quarterback, end, and guard on a team that was just 3 points short of winning its fifth Grey Cup his senior year.[13] He later said of his football career, "I was definitely not a star; I was probably least ineffective at end." Despite his modesty, Sterling had made a name for himself at Toronto as a multi-sport athlete. A football career, as player or coach, was a serious possibility.[14]

After Sterling graduated from the University of Toronto, with honors in history and philosophy, he accepted a position as lecturer in Canadian, British, and European history for the 1927–28 academic year at Regina College, a small Methodist private school that had recently become a branch of the University of Saskatchewan. While in Regina, he took a job coaching basketball and continued his football career playing on the Regina town team.

In fall 1928, Sterling headed west again, to Edmonton and graduate study at the University of Alberta. His sister Elizabeth, shortly after her 1922 marriage, had moved to Edmonton, where she inspired development of a strong local and regional theater scene. At least equally important, Ann Shaver had already moved to the University of Alberta, where she taught marketing and household management in the university's Home Economics Department.[15]

Sterling studied for his master's degree with the head of Alberta's History Department, Professor A. L. Burt, soon to become one of Canada's most influential historians. Burt was, like Sterling, an Ontario-born alumnus of the University of

Toronto, and he was highly respected as a stimulating teacher, a tireless researcher, and a graceful writer. Sterling happily delved deeply into England's revolution of the 1640s, and then into the French Revolution, as Burt encouraged him to consider becoming an academic historian. He was appointed a sessional assistant (lecturer) in history and taught a course in modern European history as he worked to complete his degree by 1930.[16]

With his playing time limited by a back injury, Sterling was hired to replace retiring football coach Jimmy Bill, as well as to coach basketball. Coach Bill, who had taken the Alberta Golden Bears to their first conference title, the Hardy Cup, in 1922, and second in 1926, was a tough act to follow. Sterling was fortunate to have Fred Hess, destined to be ranked one of Alberta's best players, as his football captain. During Sterling's two years as coach, the Golden Bears consistently defeated teams throughout the province. At the end of his first season, they won Alberta's third Hardy Cup, but the following year lost the cup to the University of British Columbia.[17]

Following graduation from the University of Alberta, Sterling spent the summer of 1930 arranging the papers of W. S. Pearce, a surveyor for the Canadian Pacific Railway interested in Alberta's natural resources and irrigation problems. While considering his next step— an advanced degree at Harvard, Stanford, or the University of London—Sterling was offered the position of coach of Calgary's professional

Football practice during 1924's first snow attracted a good audience to the commons in front of University College at the University of Toronto. The university had a long football history, dating back to 1861, before Canadian and American rules diverged. Sterling made a name for himself as both a football player and a coach. UNIVERSITY OF TORONTO ARCHIVES

football team, the Tigers, precursor of today's Calgary Stampeders. "Sterling was about to spurn the lucrative offer for the monastic life of a scholar," Frank Taylor later recorded, when Ann Shaver "undertook to straighten him out on the economic facts of life." She convinced him that if he coached at Calgary during the fall, he could study at Stanford University during the other three academic quarters, then return to Calgary the following fall, thereby providing sufficient income to allow them to get married. Sterling took the Calgary coaching job, and he and Ann were married on August 7.[18]

JOINING THE STANFORD COMMUNITY

After a challenging 1930 fall season, the newlyweds left for Stanford University, arriving shortly before Christmas. Stanford, some 35 miles southeast of San Francisco, sprawled over more than 8,000 acres, much of it rolling coastal foothills to the west, down across a broad fertile plain to the college town of Palo Alto. Opened in 1891, the campus still had a rural feeling when Sterling joined some 890 graduate students and 2,700 undergraduates on campus. A herd of 300 sheep was used to mow athletic fields and to keep outlying fields of wild oats and hay surrounding the main campus buildings under control (motorized farm equipment would be introduced the next year). Peacocks roamed the arboretum.[19]

No doubt a Canadian, reading the university's *Bulletin* in winter, would take note of the following: "The Santa Clara Valley is one of the most attractive portions of the state in fertility, in natural beauty, and in the excellence of its climate. In winter the mercury rarely falls below 30 degrees, with an average midday temperature of about 55 degrees. In summer, the midday temperature ranges between 60 and 80 degrees. . . ."

Hay mowing and baling operations, seen here in the mid-1930s behind Stanford's Main Library, carried on farming functions close to campus buildings. For Sterling and his classmates, Stanford was still truly The Farm.   STANFORD UNIVERSITY ARCHIVES

A 1930s view of Toyon Hall (center), with Encina Commons to the left. The path led across a hayfield toward the Stanford Union, behind (out of sight in this photo). A portion of Encina Hall can be seen at far left. Cars in transit are on Galvez Street. STANFORD UNIVERSITY ARCHIVES

As they had traveled across the Canadian and American west at the end of 1930, however, economic collapse was written across the landscape. Stanford University itself presented a confident and prosperous public image. Its most distinguished alumnus, Herbert Hoover, was president of the United States, and another, Dr. Ray Lyman Wilbur, served as Hoover's secretary of the interior while continuing to hold the title of Stanford president. Yet there were homeless camps growing on the edges of Palo Alto, and breadlines in San Jose and San Francisco. A 15-year-long building boom, with new dormitories, gymnasiums, sporting facilities, and an attractive new golf course, had come to an end, while the extensive orchards and fertile farms of Santa Clara County's "Valley of Heart's Delight" were visibly suffering from unpaid debt. Coach Glenn S. (Pop) Warner's football teams were making headlines, but jobs were scarce and wages quickly declining, which made it especially difficult for students to pay the rising costs of tuition (recently raised 25 percent to $300 a year), not to mention costs of room and board, books, and lab fees.

The young couple soon learned that Calgary's

football team had been hard hit as well, and Sterling's coaching position was cut. As Sterling enrolled in winter quarter 1931, they both set out to find jobs that would make ends meet.[20]

Stanford's History Department, one of the university's oldest, had not flourished as much as some others, but the number of graduate students was increasing, in part due to an array of available library research resources. Financial support was undependable, however, with the department offering very few stipends in 1930. Scholarships were rare. Ann, a trained dietitian, landed a position as a biochemistry assistant in the Chemistry Department, then became assistant director of dining at the women's dormitory, Roble Hall. Sterling's first jobs were humble, including a stint behind a cafeteria counter, until, in 1932, his History Department connections paid off.[21]

Typical of graduate student life, the young couple lived in a succession of apartments and cottages in Palo Alto and College Terrace: a duplex at 519 Addison Street (1931); a cottage at 534 Guinda (1931–32); 173 Madroño (1932–34), where their landlord was Coach Pop Warner (who lived at 175 Madroño until his departure

An aerial view of campus after 1938 construction of the School of Education Building, next to the Main Library (the two light-colored buildings at lower right). Faculty housing from the 1890s on Alvarado Row (bottom middle) still reached nearly to the Quad. Beyond the Quad are the Chemistry Building and the Stanford Museum, and a vast expanse of Stanford land separating the campus from Menlo Park. ROGER WHITE / STANFORD UNIVERSITY ARCHIVES

at the end of 1933); and, finally, a cottage at 570 Amherst Street (1934–37) in College Terrace.[22]

Although his earlier work might have led him to study English and Canadian history with Professor Carl Brand, it was Ralph Lutz who became Sterling's dissertation advisor and mentor. In his studies and student teaching, Sterling had become particularly interested in British and European foreign policy following the Great War, including diplomatic relations between Great Britain, France, Japan, and the United States. Sterling gravitated to Lutz, an expert on postwar

Germany and a key player in the early development of the Hoover War Library, who served as the library's director from 1924 to 1943. Both the War Library's collections and the History Department faculty associated with it had a defining influence on Sterling's academic friendships and his academic and administrative careers.[23]

Harold Fisher, professor of Russian history and Lutz's assistant chairman at the Hoover War Library, found Sterling part-time work there. Beginning in fall 1932, Sterling was appointed as a full-time research assistant. By 1934, Sterling

The Main Library (today's Green Library Bing Wing), around 1925. In the 1930s, Sterling spent much of his time as a graduate student and research associate in the Hoover War Library, then located on the first floor. The arcade at right extended beyond the building, in expectation of connecting to a library quadrangle.   STANFORD UNIVERSITY ARCHIVES

Hoover War Library reading room, seen here around 1930. The War Library and Archives attracted scholars from around the world, including Sterling, who completed his dissertation in modern European history in 1937.   HOOVER INSTITUTION ARCHIVES

History Professor Ralph H. Lutz was an expert on post–World War I Germany and a key player in the early development of the Hoover War Library. STANFORD UNIVERSITY ARCHIVES

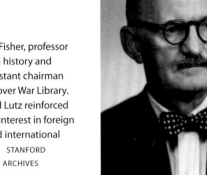

Harold K. Fisher, professor of Russian history and Lutz's assistant chairman at the Hoover War Library. Fisher and Lutz reinforced Sterling's interest in foreign policy and international relations. STANFORD UNIVERSITY ARCHIVES

Japan, and the United States, particularly the influence of economic considerations on Britain's diplomatic policy toward France. Included is an analysis of the impact of religious disputes in Northern Ireland, and an overview of Middle Eastern politics of the period, including competing claims for oil concessions in Arab countries. With Lutz as his mentor, Sterling used the extensive collections of the Hoover Library to study the role of the European press on diplomatic relations during the midsummer crisis of 1914. His dissertation, a study of Austro-Hungarian diplomacy and the Austro-Hungarian press in 1914, would be submitted to his committee in fall 1937 and accepted January 1938.[25]

Sterling augmented his meager Hoover Library salary in 1935 with an appointment as an instructor in history, teaching sophomore courses in English and European history and substituting for Fisher and Lutz to lecture to advanced classes on modern Europe. Soon after, he joined the staff of the History of Western Civilization Program, Stanford's year-long, required freshman introductory course. "Western Civ" had replaced a similar required series, Problems of Citizenship, devised in 1923 by historian Edgar Eugene Robinson. The influential Robinson, at Stanford since 1911, was a gifted speaker and an energetic and exacting professor and department head (1930–53), who fostered many innovative courses and programs. His goals for both programs were ambitious: to offer "a deeper sense of the long view of history, and a zest for relating the various parts of the university's program of study."[26]

Robinson also had intended the course series to be a way to recruit recent Ph.D.s from other campuses to Stanford as instructors, expanding its teaching staff. Despite this goal, Stanford's low salaries, uncertain appointments, and lack of guaranteed faculty status turned this opportunity into an important apprenticeship and means of financial support for the department's

was listed as working in the War Library's Russian Revolution Institute, where he collaborated with Fisher on two memoirs of the Czarist regime.[24]

Sterling's relationships with Lutz and Fisher reinforced his interest in foreign policy and international relations, past and present, as well as his career as both an academic and an interpreter of current events for general audiences. Sterling's files for the period include a broad-ranging 54-page essay on British foreign policy between the end of World War I and the beginning of World War II. In it, he explores the complex diplomatic relations between Great Britain, France,

American historian Edgar Eugene Robinson, an energetic and exacting professor seen here in 1943, was the long-serving head of Stanford's History Department, spanning Sterling's graduate student days into his presidency. STANFORD NEWS SERVICE

more promising graduate students. Some of Sterling's Western Civ colleagues—among them George H. Knoles (who would succeed Robinson as Byrne Professor of American History), Rixford K. Snyder (later professor of history, then Stanford's head of admissions), and Easton Rothwell (future director of the Hoover Institution and later president of Mills College)—became his lifelong friends.

Robinson kept close watch on young instructors and the department's graduate students, no matter their field. Although Sterling's knowledge of American history "left a great deal to be desired," as he later admitted, his 1933 orals committee included the irascible Robinson, an expert on 19th-century American political history. Sterling's interaction with the legendary Robinson would later become a popular anecdote. During his exam, Robinson asked the budding Europeanist to name one president of the United States. Sterling did so. Robinson asked him to

Faculty of the History Department, one of Stanford's original departments, in front of the Stanford (Old) Union, ca. 1935. In the back row are several department instructors, including Wallace Sterling, standing tall at the center. STANFORD UNIVERSITY ARCHIVES

name two more. After Sterling had named at
least eight presidents, Robinson said, "Now, Wallace, name one more and let's talk about him."
Years later, with Robinson still a forceful campus
presence, President Sterling joked that "I never
quite forgave Edgar for that."[27]

Wally and Ann Sterling could not help but
enjoy Stanford as a lively and sociable community. His earlier football back injury had ended
his playing career, but he played on the faculty
softball team and easily made friends among
Stanford coaches, particularly John Bunn, the
university's very successful basketball coach.[28]

During these years, Sterling observed the benefits and costs of Pop Warner's win-at-all-costs
approach compared to the approach of his successor, Claude (Tiny) Thornhill, in 1933. Thornhill,
a former college and professional player, was
heavily criticized for his insistence that collegiate
football belonged to the athletes, not to well-paid
coaches, fans, and sports reporters. Athletes were
at Stanford, Thornhill said, primarily to get an
education. His team, initially heckled for not taking the game seriously enough, proved they could
be both students and athletes. Thornhill's "Vow
Boys" turned Stanford's losing trend upside
down, going 25–4–2 in three seasons, including
annual wins against arch rivals Cal and USC,
and three trips to the Rose Bowl (1934–36).

THE CALTECH YEARS

In May 1937, before submitting his dissertation,
Sterling received a consequential letter from
Professor William Bennett Munro, an authority
on American government and highly regarded
professor and administrator at the California
Institute of Technology (Caltech) in Pasadena.
Sterling had become acquainted with Munro,
a fellow Canadian, at academic conferences, then
as now a principal networking source for graduate
students. The esteemed Munro, who had served

on the Harvard faculty before joining Caltech
in 1924, also was highly influential in Southern
California educational and philanthropic circles.
Munro suggested a position at Caltech: "From
my very agreeable acquaintance with you I am
inclined to think that you would greatly enjoy college teaching and that you would do very well."[29]

Sterling enthusiastically responded, giving
a detailed account of his scholarly work at
Toronto, Regina, and Alberta, and particularly
his research interests and teaching at Stanford.
Munro then offered a post in modern history that
would involve holding sophomore sections, six or
seven a week, in connection with the course on
modern European history and giving occasional
lectures to the sophomore class. "Our proximity
to the Huntington Library is, of course, a certain allurement," he added, "because it affords
unusual facilities for continuing research work."

Sterling was frank with Munro about his
current Stanford salary: $1,800 per annum
from the History Department, and an expected
$600 from the Hoover Library, where he was
due for promotion to research associate. In late
June, Munro offered Sterling a one-year post as
assistant professor, at $3,000, with the expectation
that it would continue. The rank and title were
"quite acceptable," Sterling responded, and he
looked forward to expanding his dissertation for
publication and completing editorial work on a
manuscript for the Hoover Library.

Sterling had hoped that Caltech would pay
his way back to Stanford whenever necessary to
conduct research at the Hoover Library, on the
grounds that the Caltech library was inadequate.
Munro finessed this by agreeing to the more
pragmatic, and less costly, alternative of purchasing the books Sterling felt he needed. Sterling
subsequently became chair of the Library Committee, the first of many committee assignments.

As a new assistant professor at Caltech in fall
1937, Sterling became popular among students,

parents, and alumni. He kept a letter written several years later, in January 1945, by the parents of one of his students: "We have received several enthusiastic letters from our son regarding your particular course of study. Current issues are presented in an interesting way—it has made quite an impression—favorable too. . . . The boy is beginning to think and I want to thank you for a very wholesome stimulation to the process."[30]

At Caltech, Sterling and other humanities professors took on increasingly time-consuming duties and speaking engagements as the institute's scientists and engineers became deeply engaged in the emerging war effort. Recognizing an able administrator, his colleagues elected him as secretary, 1941–44, and then chairman of the faculty, 1944–46. A tenured associate professor by 1940, Sterling was promoted to full professor in 1942, with the substantive salary of $3,600. Salary increases were severely limited in those financially straitened times. On Munro's retirement, in 1945, as Edward S. Harkness Professor of History and Government, Sterling was named to the endowed chair.[31]

Throughout the 1930s and '40s, Sterling took advantage of research opportunities supported by the Social Science Research Council, an organization sponsored by the Rockefeller Foundation. The council was determined to keep interest in social sciences alive during World War II so that it would have bargaining power for postwar research projects. Less than two years after his arrival at Caltech, Sterling won a sabbatical when he was awarded a Research Council fellowship (with a stipend of $2,500, plus a travel allowance of $1,000) for the 1939–40 academic year. His plan was to study British imperialism in the Western Pacific, particularly the Fiji Islands. Professor Munro's desire to continue active involvement with the sophomore class gave Sterling the opportunity to spend a year away at this early stage of his career without jeopardizing his academic future.[32]

He hoped to leave in early September, sailing to England with Ann and his baby son, William, born the previous July, for a long research trip. Three or four months in Fiji were to follow. The outbreak of war in Europe that fall, and ensuing air battle over southern England, ended

In 1937, Sterling was hired as an assistant professor at Caltech, where he became a popular professor of modern (20th-century) European history. He quickly rose within the faculty ranks, becoming a full professor in 1942. He served as chairman of the Caltech faculty from 1944 to 1946 and was named Harkness Professor of History and Government in 1945.

COURTESY OF THE ARCHIVES, CALIFORNIA INSTITUTE OF TECHNOLOGY the Sterlings' planned trip to London. Rather than postpone the project, the council accepted an alternative, a study of Canadian immigration and assimilation. After six months in Ontario, chiefly in Toronto, then Kingston, Montreal, and Ottawa, Sterling traveled west to Saskatoon, Edmonton, Vancouver, and Victoria, then returned eastward through Calgary, Moose Jaw, Regina, and Fort William to Toronto. After visits to Quebec and the Maritime Provinces, he visited Ontario before heading back to California. He completed a lengthy bibliography and compiled extensive materials on both pre-Dominion immigration from Europe to Canada, as well as current Canadian public opinion on European immigration and refugee issues.

Canada was at war, if not under direct attack. As a Canadian citizen, Sterling volunteered for military service while in his native Ontario but was turned down due to his football-related back injuries. When he returned to Pasadena later in 1940, he applied for U.S. citizenship, beginning the seven-year process leading to his naturalization in 1947.

Although he did not apply for any additional Social Science Research Council fellowships, Sterling actively participated in Research Council activities, including chairing a roundtable at the council's Asilomar Conference in Pacific Grove, California, in 1941, and chairing a subcommittee on public opinion.

HISTORIAN AS CBS NEWS ANALYST

In spring 1942, at Caltech's annual alumni weekend conference, Sterling gave a public lecture titled "The War in Review and in Prospect." Three weeks later, Hal Hudson, a Columbia Broadcasting System (CBS) executive, asked Sterling if he'd like to go on the air. Someone in the audience had reported very favorably on the lecture. (This was not Sterling's first time on

radio. About a year earlier, he had appeared on a well-received CBS forum moderated by political scientist and journalist Leo Rosten.) After negotiating and signing a contract at the CBS Hollywood office, Sterling found himself in an elevator with three men, whom he later learned were radio time salesmen assigned to find a sponsor for Sterling, but who had not been introduced to him. "Do you think we can sell him?" asked one. "We sure as hell won't," said another, "if we say the son of a bitch is a college professor."[33]

Sterling became a news analyst for CBS in September 1942 and took part in a variety of CBS news programs until July 1948. CBS World News Roundup first went on the air in 1938 from various locations around the world, focusing on the growing international crisis. Edward R. Murrow, Harry W. Flannery, and William L. Shirer broadcast on-the-scene reports from London, Berlin, and Vienna. Murrow's 1939 report during the London Blitz firmly established CBS as the place for wartime coverage.

For much of the war, Sterling, as expert commentator, was on the air live for 15 minutes, three to five times a week, broadcasting from the KNX station at Columbia Square, Hollywood, a convenient drive from Pasadena. KNX, "The Voice of Hollywood," was among the handful of original West Coast CBS-owned-and-operated stations and featured some of Hollywood's most popular musical and comedy stars.

He was a dedicated analyst, typing his own scripts and spending 2 to 20 hours on each 15-minute broadcast. He regularly read *Foreign Affairs*, *The Atlantic*, *Harper's*, *The Economist*, *Pacific Relations*, the *Bulletin of International News*, and *The New York Times*. "He feels it's wholesome for him to get away from the strictly academic atmosphere of the campus into the less formal air of the broadcasting studio," reported Radio News in 1943. "Straightforward! That's what we liked about Dr. Sterling, the man behind the quietly authoritative voice." The article also noted that this quietly authoritative voice also managed to grow "the best delphiniums in Pasadena."[34]

Sterling's first broadcasts were so successful that CBS decided to sponsor a 12-week series. He earned $25 for each sustaining program, $50 for each local sponsored broadcast, and $60 for each sponsored program on the CBS Pacific Network. These payments were gradually increased over the years but remained at modest levels. However, they were a welcome supplement to his Caltech salary, also modest in those early postwar years. He was meticulous about payments, once complaining about an underpayment of $25.50 because his 15 minutes on Saturday were paid at the same rate as his 5-minute broadcasts during the week.[35]

Sterling's first commercial sponsor was Adohr Milk Farms. Gayb Little, whose advertising firm represented Adohr, felt free to advise Sterling, and they exchanged views congenially and often. Little wanted Sterling's broadcasts to be "the most widely, most eagerly listened to broadcasts on the air." As the professor's "original booster and first sponsor," he had a suggestion. "Your material is always factual and analytical. I believe, however, that you would increase your audience if you could inject a little more personality and feeling into your material. . . . Yours is such an interesting personality that I am sure our audience would appreciate knowing you better."[36]

Two years later, representing a different advertiser (Kenu, a cleaning product presumably used "almost exclusively" by women), Little wrote Sterling that "we should soft-pedal the more technical aspects of the war and put into our program as much color, glamour and romance as possible." Sterling replied, "I just can't see myself as a dispenser of color, glamour, and romance—at least in the Hollywood connotation of those terms but am terribly

As an expert in international affairs, Sterling served as a news analyst for CBS radio's World News during World War II and its aftermath. His deep and resonant voice, and his ability to explain complex wartime and early cold war events, brought him together with many of the leading radio journalists of the era.   CBS / STANFORD UNIVERSITY ARCHIVES

encouraged by your reaction to my ventures into tying up the historical past with the palpitating present."

Sterling's broadcasts differed in format over his six years with CBS. He quickly learned the uncertainties of radio talent contracts. In June 1943, he accepted a role as one of a board of experts on a program known as the Signal Round Table, or The War Question Board, scheduled from 4:30 to 5 p.m. each Sunday. Questions were posed to a panel of experts: former Berlin correspondent and "brilliant radio commentator" Harry Flannery; John B. Hughes, "ace news analyst" and an expert on Japan and the Pacific; and "Caltech's esteemed professor of modern European history," Dr. Wallace Sterling, the "possessor of a fascinating radio delivery," as a CBS flyer about the program declared. "Dr. Sterling throws a powerful spotlight on fundamental history, which is the necessary third side of today's news drama."[37] The term was for 52 weeks, at $100 a program, but these broadcasts did not last the full year.

During January 1944, he substituted for analyst Harry Flannery, but by March, Sterling wrote to Little: "Radio plans are a bit vague for the immediate future. I am enjoying the vacation from the air because it affords opportunity to catch up on other commitments. But I feel that radio is now in my blood, so I shall probably go rushing for any new prospect that looms on the horizon."[38]

Sterling's broadcasts soon resumed. CBS selected him to join a distinguished team to cover the June 1944 Republican convention in Chicago. At the 1945 conference in San Francisco at which the United Nations charter was signed, he joined not only his colleague Chet Huntley from Los Angeles but also William Shirer and Robert Trout, in from New York, Eric Sevareid from Europe, and San Francisco newsman Don Mozley.

In April 1945, Sterling won his own billing: "Wallace Sterling, News Analysis." By late September, he joined his old friend and mentor Harold Fisher, director of the Hoover Library, doing alternating 10:15 p.m. broadcasts. Sterling took

Sunday, Tuesday, and Thursday; Fisher took Monday, Wednesday, and Friday. These broadcasts followed Chet Huntley's popular newscast at 10 p.m. Huntley had been playing a key role in molding news policy at KNX. Sterling was perceptive in recognizing the abilities that would lead Huntley to great success not only in radio but as a television news anchor in the 1960s with colleague David Brinkley. Responding to Huntley's request for suggestions of background reading in foreign affairs, Sterling wrote him:

> I cannot conclude without saying once more how fortunate KNX is to have you take over at this juncture a large share of the responsibility for shaping the news policy and output for at least the immediate future and for what I hope will be an extended period. I shall say again, although I don't think I need to do so, that I am solidly behind the things you want to do and hope that I may have some small share in achieving their realization.[39]

In fall 1945, Sterling was the moderator of a program called "Citizens Forum" from 9:30 to 10 on Thursday evenings, sponsored by Citizens National Trust and Savings Bank of Los Angeles. These were thoughtful and lucid broadcasts,

Sterling's work as a CBS radio news commentator led to many friendships in journalism, including with Chet Huntley (looking over Sterling's shoulder), who would become a top television news anchor with David Brinkley during the 1960s.
STANFORD UNIVERSITY ARCHIVES

often laying out the factual and legal background of a current major item of news, such as the U.S. coal strike of November 1946. In May 1947, Sterling analyzed the Truman Doctrine, initiated with a $400 million Greece-Turkey aid bill, and objections voiced by former Vice President Henry Wallace. Sterling's concluding comment: "Mr. Wallace's eyes are fixed on the horizon. In consequence, it is possible to claim him a man of vision. But if a people is to reach the horizon of the future, it cannot be ignorant of the past, or blind to the obstacles of the present. Cooperation is a two-way street."[40]

In November 1946, Sterling concluded a broadcast with a reference to the recent election, when Republicans won a majority in both houses of Congress for the first time since 1928:

> The Republicans may be able to provide more efficient federal administration, it is hoped that they will, but whether they will be able to . . . nourish prosperity by taking the government out of business . . . when the trend has been for nearly a century all in the opposite direction; whether they will be able to make headway in decentralizing government as society adds to its own complexities, all this remains to be seen. They, like their predecessors, will have the task of harmonizing liberty and order for it is a perennial one. There are two strong bulwarks of continuing liberty; one is a government strong enough to protect the interests of all the people, the other is a people strong enough and well enough informed to maintain its sovereign control over its government.[41]

Sterling whimsically prefaced a broadcast he had been asked to give on the subject of "Winning the Peace":

> As I understand my assignment, I am to shed light on the role which the writer shall have to play in winning the peace. It is always flattering to be asked to shed light—it suggests that one has some sort of cosmic relationship with the sun, or some hidden power stored up in a kind of private [Tennessee Valley Authority]. Sometimes,

> I confess, wild flights of fancy carry me beyond the bounds of rational thought, but never to a point where I aspire to be the center either of the solar system or, and for a different reason, the [TVA]. I hope to be forgiven, therefore, if whatsoever light I may shed is rather diffuse.[42]

In a broadcast in July 1947, at the beginning of the Cold War, Sterling said of postwar relations between the U.S. and the Soviet Union:

> These two powers are at the moment engaged in a serious, perhaps ominous, contest of strength and influence. The contest is reflected in the opposing views held concerning the making of peace with Austria and with Germany; in the fact that Russian efforts to strengthen Soviet political and economic domination of eastern Europe is in conflict with the Truman Doctrine and the Marshall Plan. It is noteworthy that Washington has just protested to Moscow against Russian seizure of Italian and German assets in the Balkans in violation of the peace treaties with the satellites. It is difficult to see how improved relations within the U.N. can be achieved until there has been prior improvement in relations between Moscow and Washington. This will take some doing, given the present state of affairs.[43]

Sterling took time to respond to many listeners' letters. He rarely settled for the superficial quick response, and did not avoid controversial subjects, from the atomic bomb to the political influence of the Catholic Church. Occasionally he received hate mail: "Listening to you this evening, news or no news, I came to the conclusion that you are either a Jew or a stooge for the Jews. . . . Personally, I believe there will be no enduring peace in the world until the Jews are put in ghettos or reservations and kept there—and the Indians are freed." At least one letter was passed on to the FBI.[44]

Sterling enjoyed his success as a radio news commentator and had made a great many valuable contacts outside the Caltech academic community, and reluctantly gave up his broadcasts

With the Cold War underway, Sterling spent his 1947–48 sabbatical year teaching European and British history and Soviet international affairs at the National War College, Fort McNair, Washington, D.C.

when offered the presidency of Stanford. The broadcasts gave him a name throughout Southern California and along the Pacific Coast. Ernest Arbuckle, a Stanford friend who would later serve as a trustee and dean of the Business School, was reminded of Eric Sevareid. Sterling "was lucid, he was always thoughtful, and he really had the news," remembered Arbuckle.[45]

NATIONAL WAR COLLEGE

In 1946, Sterling hoped to step away from Caltech administrative duties and planned a sabbatical leave to continue his study of British colonial policy. He hoped to complete two projects: his earlier study, titled "Canada and the Refugee Problem," and an ambitious undertaking with English historian Godfrey Davies on British foreign policy since 1783. Living conditions and limited housing options in war-damaged London, however, meant he could not take his growing family along. Research trips on his own to Washington, D.C., Toronto, and Ottawa were substituted, followed by a new opportunity, a round of teaching at the recently established National War College (NWC) in Washington, D.C., where he was appointed to teach a course on European history.

The NWC recently had been created to unify in one institute the study of war, national power, and foreign policy and was considered the highest educational institution of the armed forces and the State Department. Vice Admiral Harry W. Hill and his principal deputy, Major General Alfred M. Gruenther, depended on attracting distinguished visiting lecturers to the program. Sterling's invitation to teach was a prestigious one. Hill and Gruenther had also signed up Leslie R. Groves, military director of the Manhattan Project; Columbia political scientist Grayson Kirk, who had played a role in creation of the United Nations Security Council and later was president of Columbia University; British Labour Party leader and economics scholar Harold L. Laski; China scholar Owen Lattimore; former ambassador to the Soviet Union and Britain W. Averell Harriman, now Truman's secretary of commerce; and historian and political scientist George F. Kennan, who would play a key role in American Cold War strategy. This considerable honor led to important contacts for Sterling, and lasting friendships.[46]

Sterling based his 1947–48 lectures on topics assigned to him by the NWC or suggested by his students. With the Cold War now underway, most of them dealt with the Soviet Union: the role of Manchuria in Soviet foreign policy, the power of the Soviet Union, the Soviet answer to the Marshall Plan, Soviet interests and policies in the Arctic, Soviet intentions in Austria, the strength and weakness of Russia's geographic position, the Iberian Peninsula in Soviet foreign policy, the significance of the eastward shift of Soviet industry, Soviet intentions in Germany, and the growth of communism in Latin America.

Other topics drew on Sterling's expertise in modern British history. He used one lecture, "The Patterns of British Foreign Policy," covering foreign policy in sweeping terms from the Tudor period to 1947, as a chance to outline the substance of his intended book on British foreign policy. Sterling's lectures were more than a scholarly review. He was now highly experienced at analyzing and explaining complex issues for a listening audience, placing current events clearly and compellingly in historical context.

His success led to a request from Admiral Raymond A. Spruance, president of the Naval War College in Newport, Rhode Island, to lecture on U.S. foreign policy and its influence on American naval strategy. Sterling felt his "knowledge of naval strategy is seriously deficient," but Spruance, who was noted for his role in winning the battle of Midway, ignored Sterling's caveat, and Sterling's lecture was well received.

CIVIC AND EDUCATIONAL SERVICE

While at Caltech, Sterling also served on 16 governmental, educational, and civic boards.[47] Long interested in the formation of public opinion on American foreign policy issues, he joined the Los Angeles Committee of the Council on Foreign Relations, which published the influential quarterly *Foreign Affairs*. Fellow members included Karl Brandt, professor of agricultural economy at Stanford's Food Research Institute, and Harold Fisher, director of the Hoover Library.[48]

Sterling's many outside activities while at Caltech also included committee work for the Western College Association and for the Advisory Board of the Institute of World Affairs. He became a member of the Board of Visitors of the U.S. Naval Academy and of the Board of Trustees of the Thacher School in Ojai, California. He returned to Stanford as a member of a committee to foster an annual conference, hosted by the History Department, for college and university teachers of American history.

He also served with or spoke to business-related groups throughout Southern California, often the result of his CBS news analyst broadcasts.

During the early years of the war, Sterling briefly served as secretary-treasurer of the Caltech Defense Group, in cooperation with the Coordinator of Information in Washington, D.C. (later renamed the Office of Strategic Services and, after the war, the Central Intelligence Agency). The group explored attitudes in the foreign language press on the Pacific Coast regarding the Soviet Union and communism. It discontinued operation in 1943.

The year after his National War College experience, Sterling visited General Lyman Lemnitzer, a respected diplomat and negotiator, before touring Canada for the Council on Foreign Relations. Lemnitzer, deputy commandant of the War College, also was the Army representative on the Strategic Survey Committee of the Joint Chiefs of Staff. Learning that Sterling was going to Ottawa, Lemnitzer insisted that Sterling call on "Alex," that is, Harold R. L. G. Alexander, the popular governor general of Canada.

Sterling demurred, concerned about intruding on such an august person. Alexander had had a distinguished military career in both world wars and had been made 1st Viscount of Tunis in 1944 for his leadership in North Africa and Italy. (In 1952, he would become 1st Earl of Tunis.) Lemnitzer, who had served on General Dwight Eisenhower's staff and as commanding general of the 34th Anti-Aircraft Brigade in North Africa in 1944, had served as Alexander's chief of staff when he was Supreme Allied Commander of the Mediterranean Theater, 1944–45.[49]

Before he left Washington, D.C., however, a courier brought a letter of introduction from Lemnitzer to Alexander and a copy of Lemnitzer's letter to the governor general, telling him to expect a call from the young professor. "So, I was stuck!" Sterling later recalled. His appointment was arranged for a lunch in February 1948. He rode to the end of the streetcar line and then plodded through the snow to his destination, apprehensive about the reception he might receive. At Government House, a servant helped him off with his overcoat and galoshes and then turned him over to a colonel, who showed him to a drawing room and offered him a martini. When Sterling heard children romping upstairs, he relaxed. Later, as Stanford president, Sterling mingled with many famous and not-so-famous people, and, like Alexander, deftly put people at ease.[50]

Sterling encountered Alexander for a second time when the governor general visited the Huntington Library and Art Gallery in summer 1948, while Sterling was the Huntington's director. Alexander had come to California to give the Charter Day address at UCLA and was staying with a Stanford alumnus, Thomas E. Gore, '12, a prominent Southern California citrus grower and an old hunting companion. Gore had asked Sterling to show Alexander the Art Gallery in the morning when it was normally closed to the public. Viewing the Huntington's famous collection of English 18th-century portraiture, he asked if many Englishmen visited the gallery. The curator, Maurice Block, replied that many did so. Alexander then asked if these visitors complained that the portraiture was in Southern California rather than England. Block could recall only one complaint, then suggested that when the British government returned the Elgin Marbles to Greece, the Huntington trustees might return the portraits to Britain. "Jolly good," said Alexander.[51]

TARGET FOR RECRUITMENT

Stanford was not the first educational institution to try to entice Sterling for a senior administrative post during his tenure at Caltech. In early January 1943, Sterling was taken to lunch by Irving M. Walker, chairman of the board of Scripps College and a socially prominent Los Angeles attorney, and William B. Stevens, bishop of the Episcopal diocese of Los Angeles. Walker and Stevens were members of a committee searching for a new president for Scripps College. Scripps, a women's liberal arts college known for rigorous academics, had been founded in 1926. (It later became a member of the Claremont Colleges in Southern California.) They offered Sterling the position.

Concerned about the toll his wartime activities were taking on his research and writing, Sterling declined the offer. "My main interest in life is to do a good job of teaching on the university level," he told them, "to do some popular writing on contemporary events, and over a period of years to make some contribution to knowledge as a result of scholarly research."[52]

University administration, however, was on his mind. He went on to tell Walker that if he were president, he would have three goals: to strengthen the college's financial position; to restore balance among the various departments and improve teaching personnel; and to raise student scholarship, through both entrance requirements and undergraduate accomplishments.

In 1946, Sterling was approached by Harry J. Bauer, president of Southern California Edison, who, in addition to serving on Caltech's Board of Trustees and Executive Committee, was a University of Southern California trustee. Bauer told Sterling that he was seriously considered as a final candidate for USC's presidency. Sterling, however, still hoped to find a means of returning to the role of scholar, and asked that his name be withdrawn:

> My preference is to make a career for myself, if I can, in the fields of teaching, research, and writing. To accomplish that will require heavy expenditures in time and energy. These I am prepared to make, but I did not see how I could possibly make them and at the same time meet the challenge and discharge the responsibilities that the presidency of the university would entail. I hope you will not regard the basis of my decision as rooted in selfishness . . . I repeat that this decision has been a hard one to make, but believing as I do that a man does best what he enjoys most, I am satisfied that my decision is the right one.[53]

Sterling was not opposed to an administrative post more closely related to his research interests, however, particularly one at Stanford. In October 1944, Harold Fisher, then temporarily Hoover Institution chairman in the absence of the ill Ralph Lutz, wrote to Sterling proposing him as Lutz's successor. Fisher favored a fundamental reorganization and a considerable increase in its financial resources. His wish list included separation of the Hoover Library and research institute from the Stanford Libraries, and the appointment of a full-time head of Hoover Library who would have no teaching obligations in the History Department, as he and Lutz had carried. Fisher already had suggested to President Donald Tresidder, then visiting Herbert Hoover in New York, that he propose Wallace Sterling for the position. "Of course I'm interested. And you may tell Dr. Tresidder as much," Sterling replied. "I am interested in the thing itself and not as any [leverage] to use here. . . . I shall keep the whole matter a deep, dark secret and shall not allow it to disturb my digestion until the time has come for definite action one way or the other."

Fisher's efforts to find a successor at that point collapsed, but two years later Sterling again was recruited, this time by Stanford Vice Presi-

dent Alvin Eurich. In 1946, the job description was not Fisher's, but an earlier, lesser concept. Sterling's status in Southern California, however, and his contributions to Caltech and to CBS had become more noteworthy. Eurich thought the position should continue its combination of teaching and administration, and only as a 9-month appointment rather than 12. Sterling declined Eurich's offer.[54]

Sterling explained his decision to his mentor Ralph Lutz: "Turning the offer down was the hardest thing I have ever done and it practically broke my heart to do so." He still had three major writing commitments to complete by spring 1946, and he was not interested in a significant pay cut. The vice president expected Sterling to find summer teaching work elsewhere, and he was similarly eager for Sterling to continue his radio work, another source of non-Stanford income. To do so out of San Francisco was far more inconvenient than his CBS work in Southern California, Sterling concluded, and "another straw for the camel to carry." Sterling had countered with a four-fifths salaried position, but "Eurich could not see it this way. My responsibilities to my family, including my Father, are so heavy at this time I could not afford to give up the extra radio income."[55]

HUNTINGTON LIBRARY AND ART GALLERY

Back at Caltech in spring 1948, Sterling tried to work on the Canada volume while he and Ann speculated on a family trip to Europe. The family now numbered five, with the addition of daughters Susan Hardy Sterling in 1941 and Judith Robinson Sterling in 1944. An ideal opportunity intervened, however, with both publishing and travel plans.

The Henry E. Huntington Library and Art Gallery, next door to Caltech in neighboring San Marino, was located on 200 acres of the former

Caltech faculty had long taken a keen interest in development of the Huntington Library and Art Gallery. As the Huntington's new director in 1948, Sterling had a Board of Trustees that included (from this 1939 photo, left to right) astronomer Edwin P. Hubble; historian and mentor William Munro; physicist Robert A. Millikan; former U.S. President Herbert Hoover; and Los Angeles art patron, gas and electric entrepreneur, and Caltech trustee Allan C. Balch.
COURTESY OF THE ARCHIVES, CALIFORNIA INSTITUTE OF TECHNOLOGY

estate of railroad magnate and land developer Henry E. Huntington. By 1914, Huntington had become an avid and notable collector of British and American literary works and art. His library, art gallery, and 60 acres of botanical gardens had been established as a trust in 1919 and were opened to the public in 1928. The esteemed library of rare books, manuscripts, and ephemera attracted scholars from around the world. On July 1, 1948, Sterling was appointed director, retaining a connection with Caltech as an associate in history.

Sterling's predecessors were Max Farrand and Louis B. Wright, both distinguished scholars and prolific authors. Farrand, formerly chair of Yale's History Department, was an authority on the American constitutional period when he was hired in 1927 to transform a collector's library to a research library. Wright, an authority on the English Renaissance and early American colonies, was teaching English history at the University of North Carolina when he succeeded Farrand on his retirement in 1941. Wright left in 1948 to head the Folger Shakespeare Library in Washington, D.C. Sterling, as Caltech's Harkness Professor of History and Government and heir presumptive to Humanities Chair Clinton K. Judy, was a natural choice to succeed Wright.[56]

The Huntington Library and Art Gallery

was dear to the hearts of many on Caltech's faculty. College co-founder George Ellery Hale had been instrumental in its founding, and a number of Caltech administrators, faculty, and trustees, including William B. Munro and Robert A. Millikan, also served on the library's Board of Trustees. It was Millikan, as chairman of the Huntington's Board of Trustees, who proudly announced the appointment of J. E. Wallace Sterling as Wright's successor, effective July 1, 1948.

Sterling had done extensive research at the Huntington Library during his Caltech years and, like other Caltech humanities professors, had arranged a research hideout there. Well versed with the inner workings of another major research library and archives, Stanford's Hoover War Library, he had retained close ties with colleagues who straddled the worlds of academia and research library and archival administration. The position afforded Sterling time for academic research as well as the opportunity to continue his CBS broadcasts. It also provided a lovely home on Huntington's extensive, beautifully manicured grounds, although the family continued living in their Pasadena home on tree-shaded Jackson Street. This enabled the children to remain at their schools—Bill, 9, and Susan, 7, at Polytechnic

Elementary School, and Judy, 4, at the nursery school at nearby Pasadena City College. Ann could continue her work on the board of the Pasadena Dispensary and as a director of the Pasadena Art Institute.[57]

Wallace and Ann Sterling pose at the Huntington Library and Art Gallery with their three children (Judith, William, and Susan), in 1948. In April 1949, they would leave San Marino for Stanford University.   STANFORD NEWS SERVICE

As director, Sterling dealt with the usual routine needs of a research library—permission requests to quote from Huntington Library manuscripts, staff budget requests, salary issues—all the while getting to know the staff, the board, and the 12 trustee committees that helped administer the institution. He studied the Huntington's articles of incorporation and bylaws and reconsidered the mission of the Friends and of the publications program. He worked with the directors to develop a tentative new research program, with money set aside for fellowships and two new appointments to the research staff built into the program.

Only four-and-a-half months later, on November 19, 1948, *The Pasadena Star-News* broke the story: "Dr. Sterling Named Head of Stanford: Widely Known as Huntington Library Director." The *Los Angeles Times* headline the following day announced simply: "Dr. Sterling Elected Head of Stanford." "The youthful, husky educator, a former football player, declined to make a formal statement immediately on his appointment," it went on to say, "but from his manner left no doubt that he is gratified and honored at having been chosen."

As his family prepared to leave Pasadena for Palo Alto the following spring, Sterling was hon-

ored by some 200 friends and Pasadena associates at a testimonial luncheon. The Elks Club event, sponsored by the Pasadena Junior Chamber of Commerce, paid tribute to his cultural, social, civic, and educational contributions to the community in his 11 years there. Toastmaster Lee DuBridge, Caltech's president, said his associates had anticipated that Stanford "would be looking Pasadena-way for a new president."[58]

Chet Huntley, Sterling's CBS radio news colleague for nine years, told the gathering: "Intelligence and ability and good humor, suspended on the chassis of an all-American tackle, carry a considerable degree of authority. Dr. Sterling, we are better people for having known and associated with you."[59]

LAUNCHING THE STERLING PRESIDENCY

Arriving at Stanford in April 1949, Wally and Ann Sterling were on the go constantly. "Everyone, it seems, wants to meet Dr. Sterling," noted Pete Allen, editor of Stanford's alumni magazine.[1]

On April 1, they settled in at the spacious Lou Henry Hoover House on San Juan Hill, with time set aside that weekend to watch Stanford's baseball team defeat Cal, 12–3. A press conference took up the morning of April 5, his first day in office, where he answered as many questions about his thoughts on Communists on American campuses as he did about himself, Stanford's future, and, inevitably, the state of Stanford football. On the morning of his second official day, he addressed the university's Academic Council in Memorial Auditorium, and on his third he spoke to the student body at a Traditions Week assembly in Frost Amphitheater.

< On arriving at Stanford in April 1949, Wallace and Ann Sterling moved into Lou Henry Hoover House, on Mirada Avenue, the university's official presidential residence since 1945. They initially were unsure the house would be suitable for a family with three young children, but it worked out. The house quickly became a center of university hospitality. MOULIN STUDIOS / STANFORD NEWS SERVICE

There, just days after assuming the presidency, Sterling described himself as "the most recently arrived freshman on the campus," before moving on to emphasize the importance of developing in students "the standards of honor and responsibility in which Stanford takes pride."[2]

Sterling returned to Frost a few days later to participate in the outdoor Easter Sunday service. During the next few weeks, he and Ann would be guests of honor at informal and formal receptions, from a student gathering at Lagunita Court to two elegant Stanford Associates dinners, the first at the Bohemian Club in San Francisco and a second in Los Angeles. Subsequent months would be equally busy, with a round of alumni conferences and a May speech on Canadian affairs at San Francisco's Commonwealth Club. Getting reacquainted in a variety of forums gave him the opportunity to articulate his vision of Stanford's place in the larger world of American higher education while he ruminated on the tools he had been given and those he would need to implement that vision. The new president's plans for a summer for research and reflection rapidly crumbled.

Faculty, alumni, and students alike seemed

This 1947 aerial photo, looking north, shows the campus that Wally Sterling would inherit. At the bottom is faculty housing. Palo Alto is at top right and Menlo Park at left, with the baylands in the distance. Much of Sterling's presidency would be consumed with building Stanford's academic program. Student housing eventually would fill the vast open area east of Hoover Tower, while science buildings, the medical school, and the shopping center would be sited west of the Quad and Oval. Prominent is a Palo Alto Farm leftover: the mile-long, double row of trees planted in the late 1870s by Leland Stanford on a true north axis. More than 700 Tasmanian blue gums connected the Stanford residence on San Francisquito Creek to the Farm's reservoir (Lagunita), where the carriage lane turned and continued to the Stock Farm's Red Barn (out of view). Also visible is Palm Drive, which runs magnetic north from the Oval to El Camino. BISHOP / STANFORD NEWS SERVICE

relieved by the easiness of Sterling's arrival. "He simply came home," reported the *Stanford Alumni Review*, "and the friendliness that has been a mark of Stanford since its opening has been greatly enhanced" by the university's fifth president. While few expected him to need time to get the feel of things, Sterling knew he was in the midst of a honeymoon period and "in due course I shall stub my toe," he wrote his publisher. "But I hope by that time I shall be able to weather the consequences."[3]

At the outset, Sterling was conscious of the need to quickly mend relations among administrators, faculty, and alumni, all of which had been strained during the previous administration as the university was emerging from the austerity and uncertainty of the immediate postwar years.[4]

BRINGING IN THE FACULTY

Stanford's new president had arrived at an especially opportune time. Federal and foundation support of university research was rising dramatically. Stanford was also in a highly advantageous geographical location for cultivating relationships with electronics and other technology-based industries developing along the San Francisco Peninsula and in Santa Clara Valley. The 1950s would provide an unprecedented opportunity for the development of American higher education.[5] At the outset of his administration, no one could have predicted this.

Everywhere Sterling went when he was first appointed, Pete Allen later recalled, "everyone wanted to know what his plans were, and he wasn't about to go on the record too soon. He was always careful and considered things very carefully before coming out with anything." In fact, as Sterling later admitted, when he arrived on campus in 1949, "I had very little experience and felt I had to know a lot more about the University than I did before I made any moves."

He set out, with an organizational plan and an even smaller staff than utilized by his predecessor, to maintain and build on Stanford's postwar momentum.[6]

The university community, if not its physical plant, had survived the turmoil of wartime pressures in relatively good condition. Amid dramatically falling enrollment, Stanford's administration and faculty had managed to carve out a role for the university within America's war effort. Postwar Stanford had to navigate an increasingly complex web of funding sources, find the means to make up deferred maintenance while supporting reinvigorated faculty research, deal with the sudden rise in enrollment due to the GI Bill, and nurture much-needed curriculum growth.

Sterling knew, from his ongoing contacts among the Stanford faculty over the years, that the Tresidder administration had faced a crisis of confidence between administrators and faculty. Donald Tresidder, in taking firm, business-like control, had held much close to his chest. While seeking to improve the faculty and curriculum, he had rarely engaged faculty members as individuals, relying instead on his confidante and executive officer, Alvin C. Eurich. Tresidder had met him while president of the Board of Trustees and felt Eurich "had the clearest pictures and had the most succinct answers" regarding campus issues, Fred Glover later recalled. "He just liked the way the man's mind worked."[7]

Even among his critics, Tresidder was recognized as having brought vigorous, if not always popular, leadership at a difficult time. He had attracted numerous outstanding academic figures, among them Law Dean Carl Spaeth, Creative Writing Program Director Wallace Stegner, and radiologist Henry Kaplan, initial steps that Sterling would vigorously follow and expand. Tresidder had made much-needed administrative changes by centralizing the president's authority over financial functions of the university and improving business and accounting procedures. He also set up a Planning Office, among the first established in a major university, and a news service that focused on faculty accomplishments and institutional news, not public relations. Other staff changes, many of them made by Al Eurich, as vice president and while acting president, were less successful, particularly appointments in fundraising and in the chaplaincy of Memorial Church.[8]

During Sterling's eight years on campus as a graduate student, instructor, and research assistant, he had become friends with many now on the faculty and administrative staff. During his Southern California years, he had kept in touch

with some of them, and was familiar with the wartime and postwar campus mood. Eurich later recalled that faculty morale and financial support were the biggest problems he and Tresidder had faced. Eurich's impersonal style and particularly his unwillingness to involve faculty in academic decisions made relations between the administration and faculty sour to a level that even alumni could taste. Despite record gifts and improved administrative processes and planning, said Eurich, 1948 had been a "tough year."[9]

Sterling would address the fundamental question—is a university a business enterprise?—in his discussions with Stanford's trustees in 1948. While Don Tresidder had accomplished many things for Stanford during the difficult years of World War II, Fred Glover later reflected, he seemed not to realize that the administration of

Stanford's fourth president, Donald B. Tresidder, who died of a heart attack in January 1948, shepherded the university through difficult war years. He initiated plans for faculty recruiting, land development and campus planning, and academic-industry ties that were accelerated by his successor, Wallace Sterling. STANFORD NEWS SERVICE

Vice President Alvin C. Eurich had a tough year as Stanford's interim president. He became president of the newly established State University of New York system in January 1949. STANFORD NEWS SERVICE

a university has "subtle but all-important differences" from that of a business corporation. Tresidder believed simply that it was his job to run the university and the faculty's job to teach. In his memorandum to the Board of Trustees in November, Sterling emphasized his intention to change this.[10]

In his November memorandum, Sterling observed that Tresidder had used military terminology to describe his preferred administrative structure, with a "chief of staff" (vice president) and other "staff officers" (business manager, etc.) running the university, but he appeared to have no formula for involving faculty. Sterling, who had chaired the Caltech faculty for two years, preferred to think of faculty deans as his general staff, with administrative posts as line officers whose work supported policy decisions made by the president, deans, and other faculty representatives. Deans and department heads, he believed, should have the training, knowledge, and ability necessary to formulate educational policy. One of the best ways to deal with faculty bickering and sniping at administrative officers and trustees, he added, was to encourage the faculty to participate actively and deliberately in policy formation, not only giving them a stake in the outcome but also giving them a sense of accountability and responsibility.

In his study of the Sterling administration, Frank Medeiros found that Sterling's relationship with the Academic Council and its Executive Committee was traditional. Unlike Tresidder, however, Sterling turned often to Stanford's Advisory Board, consisting of seven tenured full professors elected by the members of the Academic Council. The Advisory Board, unique to Stanford when created, in 1904, as part of the formal organization of the faculty, advised the president on issues he raised, but could also initiate recommendations. Special decisions regarding controversial appointments, dismissals,

Two months into what would become a 19-year presidency, the congenial Wally Sterling posed in front of Memorial Church, June 1949.   STANFORD NEWS SERVICE

promotions, or academic organizational changes required the Advisory Board's assent, and policy differences between the president and the Advisory Board were reported to the Board of Trustees. Matters of academic freedom would be just one notable area where Sterling consulted, and respected, the views of the Advisory Board. Writing to Herbert Hoover 10 years later, Sterling said that he turned often to the Advisory Board for assistance and appreciated its wise and constructive counsel. "If I were to lose its confidence, this fact would quickly be known to the faculty and my effectiveness would be diminished."[11]

Sterling's informal monthly meetings with deans were an especially distinctive means for the president and faculty leadership to exchange ideas. "Sterling consulted in this fashion extensively, revealing his ability to function equally well in both formal and informal settings," noted Medeiros.

"It was pretty much open door for any

member of the faculty," or Sterling would drop in on faculty in their offices, a roundtable of former presidential staff members recalled in 1985. "Even when he differed with individuals, they certainly had a hearing." Informality aside, "no one ever doubted that Wallace Sterling was the president."[12]

Sterling used his knowledge of the faculty to good advantage. With prewar faculty friends and acquaintances still on campus, he could recall with equal facility earlier curriculum reviews, budget problems, and department committee meetings, faculty softball teams, and billiards and poker games at the old faculty club. He could also speak with faculty from personal experience about wartime pressures on university budgets and administrative priorities, as well as changes in curriculum and student demographics.

Stanford faculty would soon be involved on advisory committees, temporary and standing, to consider expected academic topics, such as curriculum review and reconsideration of the Medical School program and location. They also became an important and ongoing counterpoint to the pro-development interests of Business Manager Alf Brandin and trustees on questions of land use through a new university committee on land and building development, established in 1950. The presidential advisory committee, chaired for many years by art Professor Ray Faulkner, pressed for redefinition of academic (campus) vs. non-academic land.

Under its influence, much more acreage was designated academic, and the committee played a key role in critiquing campus master plans and building programs (*see Chapters 5 and 6*).

BUILDING THE STERLING TEAM

While inserting faculty into the process, Sterling kept his own staff small, waiting for those he had inherited to prove themselves. His inclination was to keep it simple.

Keeping it simple had been a pre–World War II Stanford tradition. The university's early presidents had worked with small administrative structures. When the university opened in 1891, President David Starr Jordan (1891–1913) initially had only Registrar Orrin Leslie Elliott, who also served as *de facto* director of admissions and presidential assistant. Department heads reported directly to the president (no schools or deans yet existed) and, as the university's senior faculty, were especially influential. Faculty committees oversaw campus life, from student

Newly arrived President Sterling visited with Chancellor Ray Lyman Wilbur, Stanford's long-serving third president, at a Hoover Library event in April 1949. Wilbur, who had strongly supported Sterling's candidacy, died unexpectedly two months later.
STANFORD NEWS SERVICE

discipline and athletics to graduation requirements, curriculum, and public events.

Ray Lyman Wilbur (1916–43) replaced some of the administering faculty committees with university officers. The registrar continued to handle admissions with a faculty committee, but a dean of men and a dean of women looked after student behavior, and the Board of Athletic Control and a new athletics director took over Stanford's haphazard array of teams and athletic facilities. Wilbur also organized departments into several schools, but despite this new layer of deans, Wilbur's door was always open, and department heads remained powerful campus voices.

Stanford's use of vice presidents had been rare and idiosyncratic, largely an acting presidency during a president's absence from campus. Jordan's close friend John Casper Branner, head of the Geology Department, was unusually influential. Holding the title of vice president after 1899, Branner served as acting president during Jordan's many research and speaking trips. During Ray Lyman Wilbur's government service late in World War I, either professors John M. Stillman or Charles D. Marx served as acting president, while Robert E. Swain served a caretaker role as acting president during Wilbur's four-year absence, 1929–33, as Herbert Hoover's secretary of the interior. Wilbur, technically on leave, remained the final arbiter.

In 1944, President Tresidder was the first to grant the vice presidency full oversight of the academic program and to place the office between himself and the rest of the university when he hired Alvin Eurich. While Tresidder streamlined business functions, he also bulked up the President's Office staff with, in addition to his powerful vice president, a presidential assistant with a background in budgeting and federal interagency relations, a planning director, a news director, and a fortified staff for his business

manager. As acting president for the year following Tresidder's death, Eurich maintained the concept of an academic vice presidency (Douglas Whitaker, dean of Biological Sciences, shifted into the position). Eurich also created yet another vice presidency, for public affairs and development, and a new senior position at Memorial Church.

Within Sterling's first year, the vice presidents were the first to step aside. Whitaker became dean of graduate studies in 1949 (the former School of Biological Sciences had been absorbed into a new school, Humanities and Sciences), although he would be recalled to a similar position, as "provost," in 1952. By the end of 1949, Vice President for Development Louis Lundborg moved on to the Bank of America. He was not replaced. Nor was Chaplain Paul Covey Johnston. Johnston, unaccustomed to academic settings where he had no specific congregation to exhort, would be the first to challenge Sterling's authority, and would be gone by spring 1950 (see Chapter 15).

BUILDING 10: ASSISTING THE PRESIDENT

By 1952, the president's team was clearly Sterling's and, unlike Tresidder's, was definitely grounded in the Stanford experience. Some of Tresidder's appointments fit easily into the Sterling style, notably Alf Brandin, Fred Glover, and Lillian C. Owen, executive secretary. Sterling met others along the way, drawn from Stanford's faculty and alumni. With an aversion to organization charts and cramming people into established job descriptions, he built his team around people's strengths.

On arriving in his new office, Sterling was fortunate to have Lillian Owen to smooth the way. Owen, class of '20, and one of five Stanford alumni siblings, was active in alumni affairs (her brother-in-law was Alumni Association Director

Lillian Owen, who had been Tresidder's executive secretary, continued in that role and provided Sterling with invaluable institutional knowledge of university policies and practices. She had an unusually wide array of contacts throughout the faculty, alumni, and staff. Owen is seen here in 1964, two years before her retirement. STANFORD NEWS SERVICE

Jack Shoup) and had a wide array of faculty friends and extensive knowledge of university procedures and practices. She had served for 18 years in the Graduate School of Business as executive secretary and an instructor in business reports before beginning her work in the President's Office, in 1943, where she co-managed the budget of the Army Specialized Training Corps. She soon became Tresidder's executive secretary. Faculty and staff continued to consult her about university procedures and practices on everything from budgeting to faculty leave policy, until her retirement in 1966.[13]

Presidential assistant Thomas A. Spragens had first worked with Tresidder in Washington, D.C., where, in 1945–46, he helped manage Stanford's postwar relationship with the federal government. Spragens, a 1938 graduate of the University of Kentucky, had served as a senior analyst

at the Bureau of the Budget and as assistant chief of food allocations in the wartime Foreign Economic Administration (1940–45). On moving to campus, he spearheaded acquisition of the Dibble Army Hospital site in Menlo Park, which Stanford turned into married student housing as "Stanford Village." Spragens had two special responsibilities: trustee relations and building and land development. He worked well within Tresidder's expanding administrative structure but did not develop a similarly close relationship with Sterling. "It was a difficult thing to be assistant to one president and then to be accepted by the next president in the same role," noted Fred Glover (who would later find himself in a parallel situation). Nevertheless, Sterling appreciated Spragens' support during the transition (Spragens worked for two interim presidents as well as two presidents) and encouraged his later career as a college president.[14]

In July 1951, Spragens resigned to become executive assistant at the Ford Foundation's newly formed Fund for the Advancement of Education.[15] Sterling replaced him with a definitively Stanford man, Robert J. Wert, '43, who had returned to Stanford to earn his MBA, '50, and Ph.D., '52, in education. Although Wert stayed in this position only three years, he returned, in 1959, as a professor of education and vice provost, and as Stanford's first dean

Robert J. Wert, a Stanford alum and veteran then completing his Ph.D. in education, was Sterling's first major administrative hire. After serving as presidential assistant, and later professor, vice provost, and first dean of undergraduate education, he became president of Mills College. STANFORD NEWS SERVICE

of undergraduate education. (He was named president of Mills College in 1967.)[16]

In 1954, when Wert left Stanford for the Carnegie Corporation of New York, Sterling hired the legendary Kenneth M. Cuthbertson, '40. As presidential assistant (1954–59) and vice president of finance, with responsibility for development (1959–71), Cuthbertson played a pivotal role on the Sterling team *(see Chapter 7)*.

Few made the transition to Sterling's team more easily than Fred Glover, '33, Stanford's first news director (initially titled director of information). An accomplished journalist and former editor of the *Burlingame Advance*, Glover had been hired by Tresidder in 1946. That year, after service with U.S. Naval Intelligence in San Francisco, London, and Germany, the multilingual Glover had returned to his editorial job, but was considering an offer from the State Department when Stanford journalism professor and department head Chilton R. (Chick) Bush asked him to consider becoming the university's "director of information."

Stanford's unusual "news service" grew out of early fundraising attempts. Bush and Templeton Peck, '29, a professional journalist and journalism department lecturer, had provided well-written descriptive texts for fundraising campaigns sponsored by the independent Stanford Associates. The Alumni Association had kept Stanford alumni well informed of campus activities, beginning with its monthly *Alumnus* in 1899. Tresidder set up the Office of Information in fall 1945, hiring Oren M. Stephens, an Arkansas newsman who had worked for the U.S. War Information Office. Stephens had focused on publicity announcements. Bush recruited Glover when Stephens resigned to join *Newsweek* magazine.[17]

During his job interview, Glover told President Tresidder that his policy "would be to get things out, handle the bad news as well as the good." Tresidder was dubious, Glover later recalled, "but we finally decided, why don't we try it?" Returning to campus in August 1946, Glover spent the rest of his life at Stanford.[18]

That same year, the Alumni Association hired Peter C. Allen, '36, as editor of the monthly *Stanford Alumni Review*. Glover and Allen soon became an important team as well as good friends. Years later, when Allen took over Stanford's News Service from Glover, he continued its professional quality of news coverage and well-written and well-edited publications aimed at audiences on and off campus.[19]

As director of information, Glover had a small office on the Quad, a secretary, and, in 1951, an

As a former radio news analyst, Sterling was drawn to talented writers and editors like Peter C. Allen, seen here as editor of the alumni magazine in the early 1950s. For the next 25 years, the tall, soft-spoken, and modest Allen became the backbone of Stanford's publications, a key interpreter of its history, and an important member of Sterling's team. STANFORD NEWS SERVICE

THE INDISPENSABLE FRED GLOVER

"More than any other person in Stanford's post–World War II history," according to his Stanford obituary, "Glover was looked to by alumni and friends of the university as the embodiment of institutional memory and Stanford loyalty."[1]

Descended from Gold Rush San Franciscans, Frederic O. Glover (1912–93) was an unusually well-traveled young man when he enrolled at Stanford in 1929. He and his family had lived in Paris and later near Hamburg during the 1920s. Years earlier, Glover's father, a Coast Guard officer, had worried about his son's diminutive size, and had arranged for 9-year-old Fred to take boxing instruction from coaches at the University of California (where Fred's sister was an undergraduate). Later, while studying German in Hamburg, 17-year-old Glover joined a German boxing club and took lessons from the north German welterweight champion. He participated in some 20 fights under the name of "Fritz Glüber." His success in boxing strongly influenced his life, giving him exceptional courage and self-assurance despite being 5-foot-6.

The Glovers had returned to the United States during the Depression, settling in Palo Alto, where they would attract national attention for establishing and managing a successful homeless shelter built on the site of the present Sheraton Palo Alto Hotel on El Camino Real. Fred's mother, Mable Glover, "a consummate fund-raiser," talked the Palo Alto City Council into giving the Glovers a site for a shelter and a warehouse in which to collect food that was otherwise going to waste from restaurants and homes. For three years they ran that shelter and additional shelters in San Francisco as volunteers.[2]

At Stanford, young Glover joined Delta Tau Delta fraternity. He was captain of the boxing team in his junior and senior years and held the Pacific Coast Conference lightweight boxing title. President of his fraternity as a senior, he was appointed by President Ray Lyman Wilbur as one of three student representatives on the Board of Athletic Control. He graduated with distinction in economics in 1933 and was elected to Phi Beta Kappa. After graduating, Glover decided against Harvard Business School, returning instead to Europe for postgraduate work at the University of Hamburg.

He began his journalism career that year with a stirring account, published in *Esquire*, of a duel he witnessed in Hamburg. He reported his subsequent travels throughout Europe and Asia in a column, "A European Notebook," in the *San Francisco Argonaut*, which paid him $25 per piece.

On his return home, Glover, now an experienced journalist with more than 100 articles to his name, found a job with the *San Francisco Examiner*, then relocated to Redwood City, where he talked his way into a job at the *Redwood City Tribune* by telling the editor, who said there were no jobs available, that he would start Monday for free. After two weeks in sports, he was given a paycheck and permanent job. Within six weeks he was city editor. In 1936, he was appointed editor of the *Burlingame Advance*. In 1939, he offered his language skills to the U.S. Navy. He worked in San Francisco for Vice Admiral John W. Greenslade, commandant of the 12th Naval District, as an aide

Fred Glover capitalized on his wartime experience as an admiral's aide and military intelligence officer, along with years as an accomplished journalist and editor, to assist Sterling throughout his presidency.
STANFORD NEWS SERVICE

and interpreter, but was transferred to London when V-2 rockets were destroying the city. By the end of the war, Glover was head of U.S. Naval Intelligence for Germany.

While considering a post with the U.S. State Department, Glover was tapped by Don Tresidder, in 1946, to return to the university as director of information and founder of the future Stanford News Service. He moved to Sterling's office in 1952. Glover linked together the administrations of four presidents. After Sterling retired, Glover continued as executive assistant to Acting President Robert Glaser and then President Kenneth Pitzer (1968–70). In 1970, with the appointment of Richard Lyman as president, Glover was appointed a special liaison between the President's Office and the Board of Trustees, retiring in 1977 as secretary to the university.

Lyman called Glover "a one-man intelligence unit and sympathy squad—no one in the Stanford family suffered or gained glory without Fred's being among the first to know, and to spread the word, veteran newsy that he was, as widely as possible, and as sympathetically."[3]

Fluent in German, French, and Spanish, Glover served as interpreter and host for many important foreign visitors. He toured Europe with Professor Robert Walker, founding director of Overseas Campuses, in search of sites. Glover's language fluency, international travel experience, and knowledge of protocol proved essential in the program's early years.

Glover retained a strong connection to the Stanford chapter of Delta Tau Delta, serving as alumni advisor. In the 1960s, the Stanford chapter bucked the national fraternity's policy of racial discrimination to pledge its first Black member, resulting in suspension by the national organization. Glover wrote an eloquent defense that ultimately led the national organization to change its ban.

Glover never claimed to be a major decision-maker within the Sterling administration, but he played a key role in keeping communications open among Sterling and the growing layers of staff and between administrators and trustees. "Fred Glover was always there when we needed him," Sterling once commented. "He always seemed to know things that were happening before they did." At a Faculty Club reception honoring Sterling in 1974, he said, "The only quarrel I've ever had about Fred Glover is that his very energy made me feel tired. But I forgave him for that because in every way he was absolutely indispensable."[4]

The multilingual Fred Glover needed no interpreter when greeting Georges Pompidou (left) during the French president's February 1970 visit to the Stanford Linear Accelerator Center. Glover often translated for senior administrators and was an important resource regarding international etiquette.
STANFORD NEWS SERVICE

NOTES

1. "Aide to Four Presidents, Frederic O. Glover, Dies at 81," Stanford News Service press release, November 19, 1993 (reproduced as "Fred Glover: He Rejoiced in Stanford's Triumphs, Lamented Its Misfortunes," *Stanford Observer*, November-December 1993). Additional biographical information drawn from Glover's 1993 oral history; Karen Bartholomew, "Frederic O. Glover: Exceptional Stanford Man," *Sandstone & Tile* 18:1 (Winter 1994) 1–19; the Frederic O. Glover Papers, SC0468, and the Frederic O. Glover Papers, SC0234, SUA.
2. Glover (1993) session one.
3. "Fred Glover: 'He Rejoiced in Stanford's Triumphs, Lamented its Misfortunes,'" *Stanford Observer* (November-December 1993).
4. "Wally Recalls the Early Sterling Years as President, 25 Years Ago," *Campus Report*, April 24, 1974.

assistant. Former *Daily* reporter Donald T. Carlson, '47, had come to Stanford in the first wave of GI Bill students, and returned after working as a presidential assistant at Oregon State College. "We did whatever needed to be done, and that rather describes what I do now: write and rewrite copy, reports, memos; answer letters and phone inquiries; edit, plan publications; and greet, host, jolly, counsel, arrange and rearrange, follow up, listen, talk, worry, type, wrap, stamp, mail, hand deliver, sit in a lot of meetings, sweep up. . . ."[20]

Like Glover and Allen, Carlson became an integral part of Sterling's operation. After working with Glover, he became an assistant to the president, running Stanford's Southern California office of one (1954–59), then returning to campus to organize the Medical Center dedication and, more generally, to handle community relations. He set up the University Relations Office, in 1961, in time for the PACE (Plan of Action for a Challenging Era) fundraising campaign, and served as associate director of university relations until 1974, when he became university relations director.

Glover took a proactive approach to getting news out to the local and national press. As he searched for campus stories, he had a knack for getting faculty to explain their research. He pioneered medical coverage at a time when doctors were dismissive of reporters. He reported from the Chemistry Department that Stanford scientist Hubert Loring had isolated a strain of the polio virus and wrote about physicist William W. Hansen and his success accelerating electrons— work by Hansen that later led to the Stanford Linear Accelerator Center. "It was a wonderful time to be at Stanford. . . . I was free to roam the campus, and to get into the laboratories."[21]

Sterling had first met Glover while both were Stanford students in the early 1930s, and had long appreciated Glover's unusual abilities as an articulate and diplomatic problem-solver. "It did

me a lot of good to see you," he wrote Glover after his November 1948 visit to campus, "and I look forward with keen appreciation to the works we shall do together in the future."[22]

In spring 1952, Sterling chanced to meet Glover on the Quad. When the president asked his advice about a complicated issue, Glover responded that he would get back to him after he had done some research. Soon after, Glover provided Sterling with a one-page executive summary of pros and cons of the issue, appendices with additional information, and a letter for Sterling's signature. Sterling was delighted, and asked Glover to move to the President's Office. "That was the start," Glover later commented, "first his assistant and then his executive assis-

In 1952, Frederic O. Glover, Stanford's director of information since 1946, moved to the President's Office, giving him, as he said, "50-yard-line seats at university affairs." The editor of the *Palo Alto Times* commended the move, calling Glover "an unusual combination of brains, drive, and friction-eliminating personality." STANFORD NEWS SERVICE

History professor Rixford K. Snyder became admissions director (later dean) in 1950. Snyder and Sterling had been friends since their days as graduate students and instructors in Stanford's History Department. Early in his 20-year career in admissions, his office was on the second floor of a newly double-decked Inner Quad building.   STANFORD NEWS SERVICE

tant, a job which gave me 50-yard-line seats at university affairs." Elinor Cogswell of the neighboring *Palo Alto Times* applauded Sterling's decision, writing the president that Glover was "an unusual combination of brains, drive, and friction-eliminating personality."[23]

As presidential assistant, Glover kept Sterling up-to-date on campus and local events, and often filled in context through his notes on yellow paper. Some are masterpieces—succinct, informative, and often witty. He responded to many routine inquiries, and drafted many letters for Sterling's signature. In his oral history, Glover admitted that it was "tricky to write for Wally, because Wally's language was so selective. You were always pleased when a letter you had written for Wally came back with no changes."[24]

According to Glover, the distribution of staff work was simple: If academic, it went to the provost's office; if financial, it went to Wert; anything without dollar signs came to him. "Wally had an aversion to 'administration,'" said Don

Carlson. "He was a true man of the faculty. So we all had that same title [assistant to the president] and different jobs."[25]

By 1952, Sterling also had his "university officers" in place: his first provost, Doug Whitaker; Alf Brandin, business manager; Dave Jacobson, general secretary; Duncan McFadden, controller; Rix Snyder, admissions director; and Don Winbigler, dean of students. "At the time, Stanford operated like a large family trying to make do on a very modest income," noted Carlson, but it worked. Sterling "did it by leadership," recalled Ken Cuthbertson, "by encouraging people, by getting people he had confidence in, then encouraging them, and giving them his support."[26]

THE SHADOW OF COLD WAR

Sterling's seemingly easy transition was based as much on hope as fact. Beneath the sense of goodwill were potentially destabilizing controversies that could have set alumni against faculty and president, tried the patience of trustees, and deepened unease about the loss of prewar Stanford's smaller, close-knit, and neighborly self-image.

Sterling's first potential public controversy presented itself on his very first day in the office. Under the shadow of the Cold War, with its public scrutiny of potential Communist infiltration in academia, the new president faced questions, publicly and privately, about faculty political opinions.

The university enjoyed a good relationship with the news media, due in part to Tresidder's choice of journalism over public relations by hiring Fred Glover. The new president's press conference, organized by Glover, was intended to provide Sterling with his first opportunity to talk publicly about the university, on his own turf.

It was unusual for a university president to spend his first morning in office with news reporters rather than focusing his attention on campus issues, but no doubt Sterling and Glover agreed with the *San Francisco Chronicle*: "The taking over of the leadership of a university is a public event, not merely an academic event."[27]

Although Sterling was eager to place Stanford within a larger context of American higher education and democracy, he showed no surprise when reporters' first questions were about communism and Communist influence on American college campuses.

Three years earlier, Winston Churchill had warned an American audience of the "iron curtain" spreading over Eastern Europe. For the past two years, U.S. President Harry Truman had made opposition to communism the lynchpin of American foreign policy. That spring of 1949, newspaper headlines (including those of the *Stanford Daily*) reported the retreat of American-backed Nationalist Chinese forces, on the run from Mao Zedong's Chinese Communists. Congressional investigations of alleged Communists in the State Department had moved on to consider infiltration of Hollywood and academia. With national attention aimed at rumors of Communist recruiting on American college campuses, a congressional committee was investigating University of California physicists involved in the Manhattan Project, on the assumption that the Soviets could not have developed nuclear technology without help from American Communist sympathizers.

These were events that Caltech Professor Sterling had reported as a CBS news commentator. Sterling had raised the specter of communism himself during his November campus visit at a large, but informal, post–Big Game alumni gathering. Amid good-humored socializing, Sterling spoke in a more serious tone of his opportunity to perform "frontline duty" in the fight to preserve democracy, reported the *Alumni Review*. "You can't beat Communism by dynamite or mere

damnation. You can only beat it by proving that our system is best." Invigorated university education, Sterling said, would be a bulwark in the attack, and Stanford could take an important role in the fight.[28]

In early spring 1949, the California state legislature and the University of California became entangled in a caustic debate about the role of government in interpreting and monitoring faculty loyalty and regulating university curriculums. Only weeks before Sterling's press conference, state Senator Jack Tenney, chairman of California's Committee on Un-American Activities, had introduced 13 legislative bills aimed at hunting down suspected Communists in state government and, by extension, California's public schools. (One would amend the state constitution to give the legislature power to determine the loyalty of University of California employees; another made it a crime to teach anything but "Americanism" in public schools.) While none of these bills became law, their chances of passing looked good throughout the spring, and influenced decisions faced by UC administrators and regents.[29]

During Sterling's first month in office, the California loyalty-oath crisis became a public controversy. Fearing a loss of the University of California's traditional autonomy from political battles, UC President Robert Gordon Sproul had recently proposed a compromise: that UC employees take a newly worded loyalty oath that would replace the traditional affirmation of allegiance to the United States and state constitutions (as taken routinely by state employees since 1942) with one adding that the signatory was not a member of the Communist Party. The Board of Regents, in turn, would insist that the oath be taken yearly as a requirement for employment, disregarding university procedures on tenure, due process, and contractual obligations. In April 1949, few expected a complex debate that would

At his October 1949 inauguration, Sterling visited with (left to right) Caltech President Lee DuBridge, UCLA Provost Clarence Dykstra, and University of California President Robert Gordon Sproul. All were in the midst of the academic and public relations nightmare revolving around early state and federal anti-Communist investigations and the California loyalty oath. STANFORD NEWS SERVICE

last for years, spotlighting questions of the politically appointed Board of Regents' authority in individual faculty hiring, firing, and retention decisions.[30]

A proposed debate at UCLA on whether Communists could act as free and impartial scholars had caused a highly publicized uproar when it became known that one of the participants would be Herbert Phillips, an acknowledged Communist Party member recently fired by the University of Washington. Less well known was Stanford Dean of Students Lawrence Kimpton's denial of permission to a student organization hoping to host Phillips at a similar debate. Instead, Phillips spoke to a small public gathering in a Palo Alto park.[31]

Public interest was intense, if narrow: How would Sterling, an expert on international affairs, navigate the question: Were there Communists at Stanford? As a private university, Stanford could dodge the issue of loyalty oaths for public officials. Its faculty, administrators, and many trustees remained protective, however, of the role of

higher education in understanding controversial political views and world affairs. The limitation of discussion and debate touched on academic freedom, faculty integrity, trustee authority, contractual obligations and constitutional protections of personal freedom.

Stanford University was, by reputation and voting behavior, a significantly more conservative community than the UC campuses in Berkeley and Los Angeles. The influence of former U.S. President Herbert Hoover, as a prominent alumnus, trustee, and donor, was well known. The residential community of faculty and students had always leaned Republican in elections and political debates, consistently giving notable majorities to the opponents of Franklin D. Roosevelt, the man who beat Hoover. Stanford's Republicans, however, included many who still considered themselves Progressives from an earlier era, and the Board of Trustees, like the faculty, included many who considered themselves both Republican and liberal, or at least moderate—leaning more toward Governor Earl

Warren than rising California Republican star U.S. Senator Richard Nixon. Unlike the Board of Regents, Stanford trustees were self-selected and jealous of their independence from the political pressures of either voters or legislators. Over the ensuing decade, their trust in Sterling remained publicly steady despite increasingly vocal attacks on their president and faculty.

At Sterling's introductory press conference that April, reporters wasted little time in questioning the new president's stand on communism as a field of study: Did he think that basic facts about communism should be discussed in schools? "Certainly," replied the scholar of international relations. "How can you learn about Darwin if you don't read his books? Or understand Lenin if you don't read him? Wasn't it Job who said 'Oh, that mine enemy had written a book'?" Sterling also pointed out that Stanford had one of the finest Russian and Slavic collec-

tions in the world at the Hoover Library. "Mr. Hoover would not have brought the collection to its point of distinction if he had not intended it to be studied."[32]

Sterling stated that communism posed a real menace to the world, but added, "I hope the people who are responsible for combating it understand it. . . . I also hope that those who seem to be hysterical about it, understand it as well. Understanding tends to deflate hysteria." The Western world must "demonstrate that the Western system can do more for the individual. . . . It is obvious that education must share this responsibility."

Pressed further about Communists at American universities, Sterling stated firmly that an active Communist should not teach on campus. "I doubt very much if a member of the Communist Party is a free agent," Sterling said. "If he is not a free agent, then it would seem to follow

Sterling and Glover took the unusual step of calling a press conference for the president's first day in office, April 5, 1949. Reporters peppered him with questions on the two most important topics of the day: Stanford football and Communists on campus.   GABRIEL MOULIN / STANFORD NEWS SERVICE

that he cannot be objective. If he cannot be objective, he is precluded from teaching."

Sterling and Glover may have been amused at the variety of news headlines that ensued, ranging from the new "President's Assault on Reds" to "Teaching of Red Principles Urged." But despite Sterling's efforts to place education above fear, the "free agent" question alone would be at the heart of upcoming debates on the implications of state and federal investigations into alleged subversive behavior on college campuses and the authority of politicians, rather than academics, to determine the boundaries of academic freedom.[33]

In both public statements and private communications in the years that followed, Sterling reiterated his position: Universities were part of the solution, not the problem. A few weeks after the interview, Sterling delivered an Easter Sunday message, broadcast nationally by NBC, urging Americans "to take stock of what we ourselves are doing in our own local sphere and in our national community to advance the cause [of democracy] we proclaim and profess." Stanford students had recently collected some three tons of clothing and shoes to airlift to fellow students of the Free University of Berlin, in the U.S. Sector, now isolated by the Soviets.[34]

Unlike UC's regents, Stanford trustees did not pressure the university president to make a policy statement regarding the loyalty-oath controversy that unfolded during his first five years in office. Having passed the gauntlet of political tests by the trustee search committee, Sterling maintained broad trustee support and continued to develop congenial and constructive relationships with board members, with the help and ongoing support of trustee President Paul Edwards.

Influential alumni members of the Stanford Associates, however, were less trustful. Judge Louis Roseberry, '03, a highly influential South-

ern California alumnus and creator of the Associate's innovative "R" plan for fundraising, had not been alone in urging the 1948 presidential search committee to find a patriotic executive. Paul Edwards had reassured Roseberry that trustees intended to find "a man who believes thoroughly in and practices actively the principles of freedom underlying our American democratic system." But Edwards would not be prodded into allowing trustees to take a more invasive role in political tests of university staff and faculty. Edwards agreed that "our educational institutions have a great responsibility to teach the superior virtues of the free system of government and society we have developed in this country," but the trustees, he told Roseberry, would not move unilaterally in faculty selection or definition of curriculum. "How this teaching shall be accomplished is, of course, a matter for the administrations and faculties to determine. The roles of the trustees should be only to insist, as a broad general policy, that it be done."

Edwards further discouraged Roseberry's suggestions "that the board make a public declaration of policy in support of Americanism as it applies to Stanford University," doubting both the wisdom and the expediency of declarations like that implied by the loyalty oath. "It is obvious that a mere declaration would be meaningless unless followed by performance. And performance involves total cooperation of administration, faculty, students, and alumni."[35]

Roseberry was, in fact, delighted with Sterling's appointment, which he thought augured "a united Stanford family and an able, vigorous and constructive type of leadership which is bound to keep Stanford in the top notch of American universities." Others remained dubious, particularly when Sterling, less than a year in office, defended 245 Stanford faculty members who expressed sympathy for colleagues at the University of California who, having refused to abide by what they called the Regents' "sign or get out policy," were fired.

"In my mind and in the minds of a great many of my friends, a paramount issue today is whether or not a person is 100% loyal, not 99.9%," wrote L. R. Weinmann, '06 (LL.B. Cal '08), a prominent East Bay lawyer, when he learned that "employees of Stanford University had injected themselves into the controversy of the loyalty oath at Cal. If this is true, we would like to have a list of the names of these persons and their positions in the University."[36]

Edwards fielded numerous letters from Weinmann, and in response, enlisted the help of Leland Cutler, one of the board's oldest and most esteemed members, but Weinmann persisted. "I have a great respect for academic freedom," he wrote Edwards after he was visited by Cutler. "However, it should not be confused either with

In the midst of the University of California loyalty oath controversy, Governor Earl Warren (right) was an honored guest at Stanford's celebration of Herbert Hoover's 75th birthday, August 10, 1949. Warren, like Sterling, was leery of Communist witch-hunts in academia.
STANFORD NEWS SERVICE

a right to be disloyal to the United States Government or to needlessly meddle in the affairs of a sister institution," albeit a rival university that Weinmann thought "cannot be treated with confidence nor regarded as a friend of Stanford." He continued to insist that Stanford's trustees "should quietly go deeply into this situation with the idea of preventing any controversy at Stanford. This is the best way to keep Stanford strong and united." But Edwards refused to start a witch hunt. He had no list of Stanford's signers, he told Weinmann, and no copy of the letter of protest to share.[37]

Sterling's explicit defense of his faculty prompted personal attacks on his own background and character, and accusations of pro-communist sympathies. "The implication in your letter," Edwards wrote another alumnus, "that President Sterling is sympathetic with Communists and Communist teaching is somewhat of a surprise to me because he has made the contrary impression on everyone with whom I have had contact."[38]

Sterling's response to a request from the editor of the *San Francisco Chronicle* for an expression of opinion on "the oath question" was firmly in line with the moderate Republican views of Edwards, and of Governor Earl Warren, as well as the conclusions originally reached by UC's Academic Council. Insisting that his comments were unofficial and those of "a private citizen deeply interested in American higher education," Sterling reiterated that while he was on record believing that a Communist Party member was unfit to discharge a teacher's obligations, the newly worded loyalty oath was simply not an effective way to eliminate Communists from a campus setting. "Communist Party members will not shrink from perjury if they judge that such perjury will help to accomplish party ends." California's original oath, which had long been required of all public servants of the state, was sufficient. Any further change to the oath was not the responsibility of the Regents but required a constitutional amendment, according to Sterling.[39]

Sterling began his speech at the Spring 1950 Alumni Conference by quipping that he would "redirect the alarmists" by affirming that Stanford was not "afflicted" with a loyalty oath and moved on quickly to topics he believed to be more relevant—Stanford's academic strengths, concerns, and opportunities.[40]

CHALLENGES AHEAD

Sterling refused to let the issue of communist infiltration sidetrack his work. He was immersed in a re-evaluation of the Medical School's antiquated facilities and in exploration of non-academic landholdings as a resource to improve the university's financial base. He also faced financial problems at the Stanford Research Institute (established 1946) and at the near-bankrupt Stanford University Press, and personnel problems left by the previous administration.

As Sterling stood firm on the importance of building a more selective admissions policy, Stanford was faced with the implications of a significant drop in student enrollment (from 8,400 in 1949 to 7,700 in 1950) as the number of veterans on the GI Bill dropped, accompanied by the uncertainties of the Korean conflict, the draft, and uncertain and inconsistent college deferments.

Dean of Students Donald Winbigler found student morale hard hit by the international scene's uncertainties. Despite a 1948 law that allowed a college student to postpone induction until the end of the academic year, many local selective service boards were refusing to grant such postponements. Some states were granting deferments to students who maintained high academic records, but others were not. Win-

bigler's staff found themselves educating local boards around the country about the law and Selective Service regulations, help that was not always received "graciously." Some draft-eligible men decided to save tuition and drop out, finding jobs as they waited; others dropped out to enlist in the service of their choice, rather than wait for a regular Army assignment through the selective service board.[41]

Sterling worried about the heavy strain these students experienced. "Their morale is better than it has any right to be, given Congressional indecision on the manpower issue. Their performance, and stability, is a tremendous testimony to the moral asset that this country has in its youth," he told the *Alumni Review*.[42]

"Never has a national legislature played so fast and loose with the morale of the youth in the nation," Sterling told a large assembly of alumni in Salinas in April 1951. Neither college students nor prospective students could plan their future—remain in school, join up, or wait to be drafted, he said, and "we can't advise them what to do because no one now knows."[43]

As trustee President Paul Edwards reminded alumni, while the "winds of freedom" continued to blow at Stanford, the "economic storm" continued to swirl. The ambiguities of the draft situation had economic implications. After a wartime decrease followed by a peak of veterans on the GI Bill, student enrollment was expected to fall to 5,500 by the autumn 1951 quarter, due to the Korean conflict. This meant a significant drop in tuition income at a time of rising costs. Facing questions of tuition increases and size of the student body, Sterling refused to consider laying off faculty or dropping admissions standards to bring in more tuition income. Instead, he continued to urge public (non-government) support of Stanford and its fellow universities, as essential elements of a free American society.

"A LOFTY PURPOSE SHARED"
STERLING'S INAUGURATION

Sterling's formal inauguration as Stanford's fifth president on October 7, 1949, was the most elaborate in the university's 58-year history. Professor Marion Rice Kirkwood, former dean of the Law School, chaired the Inauguration Committee, with help from Lyle E. Cook, assistant general secretary.[1]

All offices and classes closed at 1:30 p.m. on Inauguration Day, a Friday. An academic procession of 575 included trustees, faculty members, student leaders, and invited delegates marched two abreast from Memorial Auditorium to a service at Memorial Church. The delegates included 235 representatives of 244 institutions and learned societies, and 32 presidents of other colleges and universities. The procession then walked to Frost Amphitheater, accompanied by 17th-century French and Italian music played by a brass ensemble from the top of Hoover Tower. Some 5,000 attendees were welcomed by a fanfare composed for the occasion by Professor Leonard Ratner and played by the University Band.

The ceremony was broadcast throughout the West, carried live by station KEEN, San Jose, as well as by CBS (over Station KNX in Hollywood), and NBC. Portions of trustee President Paul C. Edwards' introduction and all of Sterling's inaugural address were transcribed by NBC and KIBE, Palo Alto. As a gusty wind blew his voice around the amphitheater, Sterling, knowledgeable of the difficulties of outdoor broadcasting, doffed his mortarboard and "hunched over the microphone, looking much more like a football player . . . than a university president," reported the *San Francisco Examiner*.[2]

Sterling with trustee President Paul C. Edwards and Alumni Association President Frank Fish Walker at the pre-inauguration dinner hosted by the Stanford Associates and the Alumni Association at San Francisco's Palace Hotel, October 6, 1949. Walker, the evening's toastmaster, had also chaired the alumni presidential search committee.
STANFORD UNIVERSITY ARCHIVES

In his address, "A Lofty Purpose Shared," Sterling talked about the rapid changes occurring in higher education and the world for which universities prepare leadership. Higher education institutions were dazed, he said, by the exploding postwar demand for college. "If facilities can keep pace with enrollments, great gains would be brought in prospect for our democratic system by a raising of the general level of education."[3]

Sterling expressed strong support for taxpayer-supported public higher education but emphasized the special role to be played by private institutions, which "lend variety to our whole higher educational system. By their very nature they have greater opportunity and responsibility to experiment and thus to stimulate improvement, not only among themselves, but also among their larger, tax-supported sister institutions."

With World War II still fresh in the minds of his audience, Sterling added a warning.

Trustee President Paul Edwards and University President J. E. Wallace Sterling approached the podium at Sterling's October 7, 1949, inauguration ceremony at Frost Amphitheater.

Noting that the value of education and freedom of thought must be associated with democracy, Sterling said, "A state that fears to encourage independent thought does not trust itself."

"The age we live in has witnessed the aggrandizement of state power and the extension and ramification of its activities." The growing power of government, he believed, existed to "make men free to develop their faculties," but "its power is and should be limited," and government should be "made to accept the proper responsibility of explaining itself to its electorate."

In conclusion, Sterling said: "Education has enabled man to take the measure of many things. Its pre-eminent task today is to enable him to take his own measure—his own moral measure, and the moral measure of the society of which he is a part."

The night before the inauguration, the Stanford Alumni Association and the Stanford Associates jointly hosted an alumni banquet in the Gold Room of San Francisco's elegant, historic Palace Hotel. Six hundred alumni and friends dined, following a reception for a thousand guests.

Frank Fish Walker, president of the Alumni Association, read a telegram from Herbert Hoover, who was unable to make the trip to California: "In President Sterling there has been no risk and no error in choice. Character, understanding, scholarship, administrative ability, and love of youth are all combined in him. Stanford will march ahead to greater things under his leadership as it has done under every one of its presidents."

A month earlier, Sterling had received a personal letter from Hoover. "There is no one whose installation as President of Stanford I would rather attend than yours—because of Stanford and because of you," said Hoover. "I need not tell you of my faith and confidence in you. You are bringing to Stanford qualities of great understanding, statesmanship and leadership—and I only wish I could be there to say these things to you in person."[4]

In his speech at the dinner, Sterling asked for a tightening of educational practice and a toughening of educational standards. He said in part:

> In the past quarter century colleges and universities have been obliged to do work which was formerly and properly done in the grade schools. I see no reason for instance why colleges need to provide courses in "bonehead English." Nor do I see any reason why entering college students, as some I have taught, need to have the impression that George Washington was an approximate contemporary of Julius Caesar. . . . Even in exaggeration this experience bespeaks a lack of thoroughness in preparation, a lack which I personally deplore.
>
> My plea then is for a tightening of our educational practice and toughening of our educational standards all along the line. And I make this plea because I believe that education is a serious business; no business is so serious in a democratic society.[5]

Sterling's inaugural speech was widely covered by West Coast radio stations. His sonorous voice was already known to radio audience from his six years as a CBS wartime news analyst.
STANFORD NEWS SERVICE

For the Sterlings, a highlight of the inauguration celebrations was the presence of their fathers. The Rev. William Sterling, 73, traveled by train from Hamilton, Ontario, to the Bay Area. Ann's 75-year-old father, Albert M. Shaver, a rancher in Ancaster, Ontario, also attended the inauguration. He flew to California from Toronto, his first trip by air.

William Sterling had been in failing health for several years. Sterling had visited his father in Ontario whenever possible on his trips to the East Coast, but now the Rev. Sterling insisted on an October visit. "In the final preparation for the great event," he told his son, "I say to you both, go slow, as slow as possible."[6]

On the Saturday following the inauguration, the Sterlings hosted many friends at dinner in their campus home, with 40 students joining them for dessert. Sterling

Sterling's family had front-row seats. From left: his father, the Rev. William Sterling, Ann Sterling, daughters Judy and Susan Sterling, Ann's father Albert Shaver, unidentified woman, and son, Bill Sterling.
STANFORD NEWS SERVICE

also invited the King's Men, the popular radio quartet he had met during his first Bohemian Grove encampment the preceding July. The quartet sang before dinner and entertained again afterward. Sterling later recalled that a couple of the male students approached Ann at this point, and explained they had dates for the evening. Ann thought they wanted to leave, but no, they wanted to collect their dates and bring them back to the festivities as the King's Men sang on in the crowded living room. Sterling was amused when one of the students, thanking him for the wonderful time, admitted he had expected to be bored. He and the other students had thought that "The King's Men" was the president's nickname for the Board of Trustees. When Sterling suggested to his father it was his bedtime, the retired minister responded, "What! Go to bed and miss all this?"[7]

"I am no judge of inauguration parties, especially when I am the innocent victim, but it seemed to me that the one here on October 7 went off well enough," Sterling wrote his Caltech mentor William Munro. "My overriding reaction was one of thankfulness that it was all over."[8]

NOTES

1. Sterling Presidential Papers, SC0216 box 56 (contains Sterling inauguration files).
2. "Stanford Heritage is Entrusted to Dr. Sterling at Inauguration," *Stanford Alumni Review* (November 1949) 3–14. *San Francisco Examiner*, October 8, 1949.
3. "A Lofty Purpose Shared," *Stanford Alumni Review* (November 1949) 4, 9–11.
4. "To Greater Things," *Stanford Alumni Review* (November 1949) 13.
5. "Stanford Family Gathers for Inauguration Dinner," *Stanford Alumni Review* (November 1949) 13–14.
6. SC0216 box 56.
7. Sterling, "The Stanford Presidency: Part II, A Noble Purpose Shared," 7.
8. Sterling to Munro, November 2, 1949, in SC0216 box 23.

4

WALLY'S FOLLY
RELOCATING THE MED SCHOOL TO CAMPUS

One of Sterling's first major challenges as Stanford's new president was rehabilitation of the Stanford School of Medicine and Stanford Hospitals in San Francisco. "The facilities in San Francisco were in a deplorable state," he recalled later. "In the old buildings, rats ran in the basement. The newer hospital, built in 1917, was usable but it was clear to me that new facilities had to be built."[1]

At an estimated cost of no less than $15 million, the financial problem was daunting. But the situation was more complicated than a fundraising trial. Should the university renovate current facilities, at Sacramento and Webster streets, in San Francisco, or consolidate medical education on the main campus some 35 miles south? Or should it divest itself altogether of responsibility for medical education?

Amid sharply divided opinions, Sterling concluded that the university should remain committed to medicine and ultimately move the school to the main campus. There, he thought, it could thrive in new facilities with a renovated curriculum, expanded research resources, and a new hospital. The Stanford Medical School, dubbed "Wally's Folly" by its detractors, opened on campus in 1959. The decision to relocate it represented the sternest test of Sterling's mettle since assuming the presidency.[2]

Cooper Medical College, originally founded in San Francisco in 1858 by Dr. Elias Samuel Cooper, was the first medical school on the West Coast. Stanford University acquired it in 1908, when it became the Department of, and later the School of, Medicine. This was the university's first foray into postgraduate professional education and a major expansion of its academic program. At the time, it was a bold move, given the university's need to recover from both the 1906 earthquake's costly structural damage and from low faculty salaries. By 1949, the Stanford Medical School comprised several buildings, including two hospitals (the Lane Hospital, constructed in 1894, and Stanford Hospital, constructed in 1917).[3]

President David Starr Jordan had advocated

< A fall 1959 evening at the new Stanford Medical Center features the reflecting pool and fountains at its entrance. The center was designed around courtyards, patios, and urban landscaping. Concrete grillwork, with a motif inspired by Moorish Spain, embellishes the buildings and columns used to screen courtyards and walkways.
STANFORD MEDICAL HISTORY CENTER

Stanford's two San Francisco hospitals, seen in the mid-1950s: Lane Hospital (center) was constructed by Cooper Medical School in 1894 at the corner of Clay and Webster streets, San Francisco. In 1917, Stanford Hospital (far left) was built up the street on Clay. STANFORD MEDICAL HISTORY CENTER

and facilitated Stanford's entry into medical education. Jordan had hoped to create a more research-oriented medical program, but the school's funding continued to be a concern. His successor, John Casper Branner, facing significant budget problems and backed by Carnegie Foundation advisors, found the medical program absorbing far more than its share of the university's budget. To deal with trustee cuts to his budget, Branner proposed that the university terminate all financial support to the school as of July 31, 1914, and merge it with the University of California, which also had a medical school in San Francisco. Trustee Herbert Hoover opposed Branner's

efforts, however, and the Board of Trustees balked at giving up the school. Negotiations between officials of the two schools quickly broke down.[4]

At Branner's retirement, in 1915, the Board of Trustees selected Medical School Dean Ray Lyman Wilbur, who had received his M.D. degree from Cooper Medical College, as Stanford's third president, assuring continuance of the school. "President Branner saw the medical school as a menace to the future of Stanford University with its limited endowment," said Wilbur, "while I saw it as the first great gift to a Stanford that was to be one of the great universities of the world." Wilbur consistently promoted the relevance of medical education generally and advocated the effectiveness of linking a medical school to a university.

Wilbur had early fundraising success, leading to construction in 1917 of a new $500,000 Stanford Hospital for surgery and consultations adjacent to Lane Hospital (which became primarily a teaching hospital) and, in 1922, a $450,000 building devoted to training and housing for the School of Nursing. A 1923 fundraising drive, "Stanford's Medical Million," reached only $400,000. Nevertheless, in 1927, a Medical School committee worked with an architect to design a new facility in San Francisco; construction costs were estimated at $3.7 million. A donor offered $2.5 million on the condition that Stanford raise $1.25 million by 1932, but the effort failed as the Depression took hold. Plans for more than $3 million in improvements were cut short, sorely disappointing the school's faculty.

Although a three-story medical research building was added in 1939 as a gift from Lucie Stern, and the academic program continued to grow, the decline of the school's older facilities in San Francisco persisted.[5]

SAN FRANCISCO MEDICAL CAMPUS RECONSIDERED

The idea of moving the Medical School from San Francisco to the campus was not Sterling's. Wilbur, like Jordan and Sterling, considered research "one of the most important functions of the medical school," but Wilbur predicted that any move out of San Francisco hinged on available patients. The "deteriorating neighborhood" surrounding the San Francisco site was home to working-class patients who could not afford a doctor's private practice. Wilbur had expected that, one day, adequate population growth along the San Francisco Peninsula would justify making the move.[6]

In 1944, President Donald B. Tresidder considered the idea. As part of Tresidder's broad study of the state of the university, Professor Harold K. Faber chaired a three-man committee that recommended modernizing the medical buildings in San Francisco, backed by a targeted fundraising campaign, an approach strongly favored by the Medical School faculty. Tresidder, after visiting other university medical schools, reluctantly agreed. As yet there appeared to be too few clinical patients, and too much opposition by local physicians, to justify the expense of a move. In 1946, the Board of Trustees approved plans for a new medical building in San Francisco but did not allocate funds.[7]

By the time Dr. Henry S. Kaplan arrived in 1948, the conditions in which his Radiology Department worked in a corner of Lane Hospital were "god-awful. Our physical plant was indescribably bad." Cooper's original facilities, particularly the 1882 Medical School building and the 1894 Lane Hospital (formally opened January 1, 1895), were in urgent need of modernization.[8]

In the early years of his presidency, Sterling was pressured by Medical Dean Loren R. (Yank) Chandler and the medical faculty to move forward with expansion plans. Sterling initially endorsed a Board of Trustees 1951 reaffirmation of earlier plans to expand and modernize the school in San Francisco, but he soon concluded that this was a mistake and urged reconsideration. He appointed a Committee on Future Plans of the Medical School, made up of eight Medical School faculty members and chaired by Dean Chandler, to study a wide range of questions from curriculum to space, clinical material, public aspects of medicine, and prepaid medical care. Their voluminous 1952 report was a comprehensive study of past, present, and future. It concluded that a large capital outlay would be required either to refurbish the San Francisco facilities or to relocate to the campus, but it was inconclusive about relocation.[9]

Young surgery Professor Loren R. (Yank) Chandler was appointed dean, in 1933, to oversee President Wilbur's shake-up of the Medical School. Chandler, seen here in 1951, shepherded the school through the Depression, a world war, and three postwar Medical School evaluations. He had mixed feelings about the move from San Francisco and objected to the school's emerging focus on research over teaching. STANFORD UNIVERSITY ARCHIVES

In November 1952, Sterling surveyed 400 Medical School faculty and others related to the school, asking their preferences on location. He received only 30 responses, representing not only widely divided opinions about moving from San Francisco but also a lack of consensus on the school's mission.[10]

One respondent, an official of the San Francisco Department of Public Health, worried that the move would lead to an increased emphasis on research. He wrote that medical education should produce doctors who would care for the sick, not treat them as "a series of experiments." A Webster Street physician decried the lack of "challenge" available among suburban patients. "People on the Peninsula do not stab or shoot each other in sufficient numbers," he wrote. "They don't, by-and-large, contract syphilis or clap in suitable quantities; they don't suffer from the nutritional, metabolic or uncommon infectious diseases encountered in a brawling metropolitan area."

Proponents of the move, however, emphasized the valuable connections to be made among academic disciplines. Dr. Donald Stilwell, an assistant professor of anatomy, preferred moving the school to transferring such departments as bacteriology, chemistry, and anatomy, then on campus, up to San Francisco. "Moving would not only provide highly desirable liaison between all departments but would draw clinical researchers into the realm of work being carried on in such fundamental sciences as physics, biology, and engineering," he wrote.

"We would be in the strongest position scientifically" on the main campus, wrote Dr. Windsor Cutting, professor and chair of pharmacology. "I believe the practice of medicine is becoming increasingly dependent on fundamental science. . . . Our only rich potential is the strength of the campus. To me it seems foolish not to use it, and expeditiously." If the school did not move, he warned, within 10 years it would drift down to a second tier of medical schools.

Radiologist Kaplan noted that his house in Sausalito had a magnificent view of San Francisco and the Bay, but he was willing to move some 45 miles south to the main campus "and the opportunity to work hand-in-hand with members of the fundamental physical and biological science departments in pioneering new lines of medical research." Kaplan viewed medical research as "probably the major reason for the existence of the Medical School, although I would grant that teaching, with which it is inextricably interwoven,

Stanford engineer Edward Ginzton, director of the Microwave Laboratory (left), and Stanford radiologist Henry Kaplan adapted Stanford's Mark III linear accelerator to treat Hodgkin's disease, as well as retinoblastoma and other tumors. STANFORD NEWS SERVICE

In January 1956, Stanford's CLINAC (clinical linear accelerator) was used to begin six weeks of treatments on 7-month-old Gordan Isaacs for retinoblastoma. This photo was taken a year later to accompany Ellen Isaacs' news magazine account of her son's miraculous recovery.
MOULIN STUDIOS / STANFORD NEWS SERVICE

is virtually the same level of importance." Patient services and routine clinical activities, while necessary, "should never be the dominant factors in the program." (Kaplan would go on to build the Radiology Department from a two-man service unit, with bare wires dangling over the patients, into one of the most respected radiology departments in the world.)

Kaplan's work with Stanford physicist Edward Ginzton, director of the Microwave Laboratory, would adapt the Physics Department's Mark III linear accelerator for use in treatment of Hodgkin's disease, as well as retinoblastoma and other tumors. In January 1956, Stanford's CLINAC machine was used to begin six weeks of treatment on 7-month-old Gordon Isaacs for retinoblastoma.[11]

In addition to divided medical faculty opinion, many on campus felt that the Medical School was a significant financial drain on the university and should be abandoned. Sterling, however, remained convinced that professional training in health care was not only an important national asset but one to which Stanford should continue to make significant contributions.[12]

Sterling continued to seek advice, consulting with some 20 leaders in American medical education. Two fellow members of the Commission on Financing Higher Education, a nongovernmental organization funded by the Carnegie and Rockefeller foundations, were especially helpful: Dr. Lowell T. Coggeshall of the University of Chicago Medical School, highly regarded for his experience with national and international public health issues, and Dr. Alan Gregg of the Rockefeller Foundation, one of the most influential men of his generation in medical education and research.[13] Both men argued that medicine and medical science were dependent on the results of research in basic sciences, not only chemistry, biochemistry, and biology but also physics and engineering. Both predicted closer ties to social sciences, such as psychology, and added, presciently, that medicine eventually would also look to law and business.[14]

In June 1953, Sterling, backed by the trustees' Special Committee on the Medical School, recommended relocating the Medical School to the campus. He noted his earlier reluctant endorsement of the Medical School faculty (Faber) committee's recommendation, but now contended that the future of medical education depended on the course of medical science, which was itself increasingly dependent on the basic sciences. This key relationship could be strengthened by "bringing the Medical School into the closest possible physical and intellectual relationship to the whole University."[15]

Sterling created his own committee, which included himself and trustee President Lloyd Dinkelspiel, Henry Kaplan, and other younger Medical School faculty. "Our committee—which Sterling really ran because he knew where he was going—built a very strong case for the move," recalled Kaplan. Kaplan's assignment was to build the general argument "about the growing interdependence of the sciences, the increasing scientific basis of medicine and the fact that the medical school could not flourish unless it was located in proximity to the scientific departments of the main university."[16]

Unless there were a firm financial commitment to continue the Medical School, Sterling noted, its location was beside the point. Noting the board's fiduciary responsibility toward the school, he said, "I do not see how, in all conscience, the Medical School can be discontinued, at least until concerted efforts, which have not heretofore been made, have clearly demonstrated that continuance is financially impracticable."[17]

Population growth on the Peninsula since the end of World War II now assured a sufficient, if changing, clinical population. Formerly, clinical patients were largely drawn from the poor and indigent. Now, prepaid health-care plans were increasing the number of pay or part-pay patients. Sterling admitted that a move to the campus would impact the neighboring medical community, but local doctors had led him to believe "that the Medical School would be welcomed, not necessarily with nosegays and red carpets, but welcomed nonetheless."

Sterling concluded his report:

> I do not think my imagination is air-borne when it prompts me to urge due attention by the Board to the changes occurring on the Peninsula, to the changes that are on the march in the country in the whole area of medical care and education, and the opportunities which are to be plucked by courage and vision from these changing circumstances. Insofar as a president of Stanford University may be permitted to dream, I dream of a truly great center of medical teaching and research in the heart of a truly great university, and I know from reading the files in my office that, as a Stanford presidential dream, this one is not original with me. So, "Once more into the breach. . . ."

THE MOVE IS ON!

In July 1953, the full board approved Sterling's request to consolidate the School of Medicine on the main campus. The move was expected to take three to five years.[18]

Some changes at the school were immediate. Following the board's decision, Yank Chandler, who had been dean for 20 years, stepped down in August, saying his decision was necessary to keep "Stanford University vital and growing." Chandler had joined the staff in 1923, after he received his Stanford medical degree, and had been appointed dean in 1933 to oversee President Wilbur's shake-up of the Medical School faculty. A respected administrator as well as teacher and surgeon, Chandler shepherded the school through the Depression and World War II, and then through three postwar evaluations of the school's future.[19]

Chandler had long seen advantages to a move to campus but objected to the emerging focus on research, believing Stanford had failed in its commitment to improve the school's San Francisco facilities.[20] Sterling appointed Dr. Windsor C. Cutting, professor and chair of pharmacology, to succeed Chandler in 1953. Lacking confidence in Cutting, Sterling would replace him in March 1957 with Dr. Robert H. Alway, head of pediatrics, as acting dean *(see Chapter 11).*

In his oral history, presidential assistant Fred Glover later recalled how disturbing the decision to move the Medical School and hospital turned out to be. "The doctors in San Francisco would talk about those peasants down in Palo Alto, and the Palo Alto doctors would talk about those arrogant bastards in San Francisco. Any time you start disturbing a person's pocketbook, you invite all kinds of other reasons."[21]

"The situation was chaotic, because there were true believers on both sides," recalled Robert Alway. There were some "who knew it was an absolutely asinine idea to move, it would destroy all that was good about Stanford Medical School, and those who . . . were so sure they were right about what was going to be done that anybody of the old school was to be looked down upon." But

Robert H. Alway, head of pediatrics, served as acting dean from 1957 to 1958, when he reluctantly agreed to accept the Medical School deanship. Serving until 1965, Alway took the lead in reorganizing the Medical School's curriculum, recruiting new faculty, and guiding the 1959 move from San Francisco to the new campus medical center.
STANFORD NEWS SERVICE

only a small percentage allowed the fight to get nasty or vindictive, he said. "If I had been in the community for 5, 10, 15, 20 years and had a following, a practice, a clientele, I wouldn't want to leave it. It's just that simple. I would have to have a very good reason to leave. And most of them didn't."[22]

These differences could take a personal turn. "In those days neither Wally nor I dared to be ill," according to Glover. President Sterling was having problems with diverticulitis, which later became serious. "When Wally saw Dr. Russel Lee, he would get two minutes of medicine and an hour of medical politics. I was having a routine physical and had a cardiogram. The nurse started to heckle me about the move of the Medical School, and my rate picked up so much that they had to do the cardiogram over."[23]

Sterling, Cutting, and, later, Alway also faced antagonism from alumni. "There was vocal criticism of the change, as well as accusations that Stanford was heading toward socialized medicine," said Alway. Kaplan also recounted "howls of outrage" from some older faculty, who "kept after Wally, through the alumni, saying this was the worst decision imaginable—it would mean the death of the medical school, and so on. . . ."[24]

While opinion remained divided, Dr. William Lister (Lefty) Rogers, '23, a pioneering thoracic surgeon and chair of the Stanford Medical Alumni Fund, hosted a dinner at the Bohemian Club for some 100 influential Medical School faculty and alumni, with Sterling as a guest. Rogers, with both undergraduate (1923) and medical (1926) degrees from Stanford, had been a college athlete and member of the 1924 U.S. Olympic gold-medal rugby team. In his remarks, Rogers noted that the highly esteemed President Wilbur himself had foreseen a time when population growth on the Peninsula would make possible the move of the Medical School to the campus, an announcement that surprised many of his guests. Rogers then pointed out that President

A photo opportunity with a bulldozer at groundbreaking, September 11, 1956, for development of what President Sterling called "the most complete medical center we can achieve." From left, Dean of Medicine Windsor C. Cutting, Palo Alto Mayor Noel Porter, and Sterling. STANFORD NEWS SERVICE

W. Parmer Fuller III (left), chair of Stanford's $22 million Medical Center Fund campaign, and Dean Robert Alway (center) joined Medical Center architect Edward Durell Stone to look over a model of Stone's design. Photo taken 1957–58.
STANFORD MEDICAL HISTORY CENTER

Sterling thus could neither be blamed for the school's failure, nor claim all the credit if it succeeded. Sterling thought Rogers' generous gesture and inspired note of inevitability helped close ranks in support of the move.[25]

Former President Herbert Hoover, as honorary chairman, launched the Stanford Medical Center Fund campaign with a flourish on August 4, 1956, at a press conference. W. Parmer Fuller III served as campaign chair, with vice-chairs James B. Black and Charles R. Blyth, both trustees. They were aided by trustee Ernest Arbuckle and many Stanford Associates.

The immediate need for relocation, construction, and endowment was $22 million ($15.5 million for buildings and $6.5 million for endowment).[26]

Stanford also benefited from Sterling's 1956 appointment by the surgeon general to the U.S. Public Health Service's National Advisory Council on Health Research Facilities, whose purpose was to distribute federal funds as equitably as possible to hospitals and medical schools. During Eisenhower's first term, Congress had passed legislation

providing $30 million a year for three years to improve "health research facilities." Council members, in groups of three or four, visited facilities throughout the country, affording Sterling the opportunity to learn more about opportunities and problems experienced at other institutions as well as to make Stanford's case for assistance.[27]

Sterling and the trustees moved ahead quickly to select an architect. A Medical School faculty committee, headed by Dr. Henry Kaplan, interviewed candidates throughout 1953–54, and finally recommended Edward Durell Stone of New York in May 1954. Stone would submit designs a year later.[28]

Stone impressed Kaplan not only as innovative but also as a man of integrity and commitment. Stone also was the only major architect who offered to put other projects on hold and move to the Palo Alto area until construction was well underway. Known for a more romantic style, in contrast to contemporary glass and metal modernism, Stone had designed the American Embassy in New Delhi and the United States Pavilion at the Brussels World's Fair, and had just finished impressive buildings at Vanderbilt University and the University of Arkansas Hospital and Medical School. (Stone later designed major civic buildings for Palo Alto, including its 1959 main library and 1970 city hall.)[29]

Stone initially proposed a high-rise hospital intersecting a four-story clinic building, with the Medical School at the other end, but the Board of Trustees rejected the idea. Kaplan said that Stone predicted he, not the Board of Trustees, would eventually be blamed for the inefficiencies of the alternative horizontal layout.[30]

The renowned architect must have "wished he had never heard of Stanford," suggested the *Palo Alto Times* after the center's opening, in 1959:

As soon as the design was underway, a series of complicated feuds developed between Stanford and the city, Stanford and local doctors, "contract doctors" who supplied specialized service to the hospital and the city, and between individual Stanford doctors and individual Palo Alto doctors in the same specialties. All this ill feeling periodically erupted into the open, both at City Council meetings and at staff meetings of Stanford men. Stone was caught in the middle because the hospital's design depended in many ways upon the way in which the local and Stanford doctors were to share the joint hospital.[31]

As it turned out, Sterling's enthusiasm for Stone quickly faded. "We had some knotty problems with the architect during construction," Sterling told an interviewer years later. "Stone was great in his field. One of the difficulties was that Stone's staff did not include a good engineer."[32]

Equally important, said Sterling, "Stone seemed not to realize that if one added zero to a figure, he was actually multiplying by ten."[33] Costs for construction and for equipping the facility kept rising. "Even when we approximated what might be a good idea, it still wasn't enough," recalled Alway. While Sterling cajoled the trustees, Kenneth Cuthbertson was delegated to unravel financial problems arising from the construction. "Wally was always skeptical about architects after that," said Glover.[34]

Sterling's later views about Stone were summed up in a letter to the president of the University of Texas, who had solicited his opinion of Todd Wheeler, the architect brought in by Stanford to assist in the planning and construction of the Medical Center after problems arose with Stone's plans (Wheeler was seeking the commission to design the proposed medical school in Texas):

As you may or may not know, it was the architect Ed Stone who designed our new Medical Center. We are delighted with his design. But when we got down to the short strokes of the planning, we discovered that Stone's staff was not quite up to the detailed job. It was at this point that we asked Todd Wheeler to help us. His help was utterly invaluable. He is knowledgeable, hard-headed, and at the same time able to work effectively with others. Perhaps I can best put in my good word by telling you that it is my view we would have been in a bad way if we had not found Todd Wheeler to help us out.[35]

Groundbreaking took place on September 11, 1956, on the site reserved by the trustees "for ultimate development of the most complete medical center we can achieve." An earlier Stanford press release had described the Medical Center design as the first "garden hospital" ever built, with landscaping by the renowned San Francisco landscape architect Thomas Church. Stone turned for inspiration to Moorish Spain, in keeping with the tone and ambiance of the campus. To house some 525,000 square feet of hospital space, teaching facilities, clinics, and library, he designed a grouping of seven three-story buildings under one roof and connected by open walkways. Exterior walls of reinforced concrete, patterned to simulate the "rustic" cut sandstone of the Quad, were pigmented to harmonize with the university's older structures.[36]

Just three years later, the new 56-acre, $22 million Stanford Medical Center was dedicated. Medical departments had begun moving in to their new quarters on August 1, 1959, the day the first patients were admitted to the new joint Palo Alto–Stanford Hospital. Despite the differences over

Since the Stanford trustees did not want a high-rise building, Stone designed seven three-story buildings under one roof, joined by open walkways, to house 525,000 square feet of hospital space, teaching facilities, clinics, and a library. Noted San Francisco landscape architect Thomas Church designed the courtyard gardens. RAGNAR M. PETERSON / STANFORD UNIVERSITY ARCHIVES

For the September 18, 1959, evening outdoor dedication of the Medical Center, plans had been made to feature the building "in all its glory" by turning on lights in the open courtyard at a dramatic moment. An unexpected, heavy rainstorm just beforehand led pranksters on Sterling's staff to jokingly set out duck decoys. (An indoor ceremony was quickly improvised.)   STANFORD NEWS SERVICE

the design, *Architectural Forum* described the final result as "Medicine's Taj Mahal," while John Hill, manager of Stone's Palo Alto office, more modestly described it as "a little Versailles for the sick."[37]

On the evening of September 18, the stage was set in an open courtyard. "We had arranged that at the crucial moment of the evening ceremony, all the lights would be turned on, so that the building could be seen in all its glory," Sterling recalled. "Instead, torrential rains fell. We had to improvise and hold the ceremonies inside."[38]

Over the next two days, a symposium of distinguished guests spoke on "Medical Care, the University, and Society." The evening's principal speaker was Frank Stanton, president of Columbia Broadcasting System, then serving as chairman of the board of the Center for Advanced Study in the Behavioral Sciences at Stanford. "This new medical center here at Palo Alto will, I hope, begin a trend that will reintegrate medical schools with the universities," he stated, "and provide the opportunity for a close interrelationship with the college and other graduate schools, for the problems of health require this kind of educational integration."[39]

Reflecting on the challenge of relocating and rebuilding the Medical Center, Sterling added

a more personal observation. "On the basis of a quarter of a century in higher education," he said, "perhaps I am entitled to observe that no one knows how basically conservative faculties can be until he has experienced efforts to effect a change in educational procedures and programs."[40]

RETHINKING FACULTY AND CURRICULUM

The projected Medical School move also had set in motion a significant change in the composition of its faculty. To make up for their modest salaries, Stanford's pre–World War II physicians had been allowed to use Medical School facilities 25 percent of their time for their private practices.

The opportunity to develop private practices had been important in prewar recruiting, in some cases providing nearly all of the doctors' income. Some faculty members thus were virtually volunteers. Many had built considerable practices and were reluctant to give them up to come to the campus. This concept had also allowed many of the school's distinguished doctors to collaborate with University of California colleagues in joint undertakings at the San Francisco City and County Hospital and at other local hospitals.

Efforts by Provost Frederick Terman (seated, second from right) and Dean Robert Alway (right) to attract faculty to the new Medical School, beginning in 1957, were dubbed "The Big Raid" by Eastern rivals. Among the new faculty they successfully recruited were Joshua Lederberg (left) and Arthur Kornberg. JACK FIELDS / STANFORD UNIVERSITY ARCHIVES

Now, as part of the new program, physicians' salaries were raised, but they were required to work full-time. Many of the distinguished physicians at Stanford's San Francisco hospitals chose not to give up private practice to relocate down the peninsula.

The energetic Robert Alway, who agreed in May 1958 to remove "acting" and become dean, not only was an effective administrator and teacher but also had developed excellent relations with Palo Alto pediatricians, particularly the influential Dr. Esther Clark, a co-founder of the Palo Alto Medical Clinic. Sterling turned to Alway to move the faculty forward on relocation, curriculum reform, and faculty improvement.[41]

Beginning in 1957, Alway had worked closely with Sterling, Provost Frederick Terman, Humanities and Sciences Dean Philip Rhinelander, and the Rockefeller Foundation, to launch a large-scale recruiting effort dubbed "The Big Raid." These first efforts had been instigated when Harvard tried wooing Henry Kaplan away from Stanford. When Provost Fred Terman asked what would keep him at Stanford, Kaplan responded "playmates," colleagues he could work with who would share his insatiable curiosity.

Terman suggested Arthur Kornberg of Washington University in St. Louis, a good friend of Kaplan's. Kornberg was willing to come only if he could bring along his research staff. Stanford agreed to "lift" five staff members, leaving a large hole at Washington University. Among them was future Nobel laureate Paul Berg.[42]

Their hunt also landed Joshua Lederberg, a brilliant young bacteriologist from the University of Wisconsin to head a new Department of Genetics in 1958; J. Garrott Allen of the University of Chicago as head of surgery (and, later, hand surgeon Robert Chase from Yale, who succeeded Allen as head); pediatrician Norman Kretchmer from Cornell, who would take Alway's place as head of pediatrics; Halsted Holman, recruited from Rockefeller University to head the Department of Medicine; and David Hamburg from the National Institutes of Health, who would create a new Department of Psychiatry and Behavioral Sciences. Other significant appointments would follow as the buildings on campus inched toward completion.

The promise of new medical facilities also helped Stanford keep at least one key faculty member. "We are much heartened that our radiologist, Henry Kaplan, has turned down what is generally regarded as a fabulous position at Harvard," Provost Terman reported to a friend at UC Berkeley in 1957. "Kaplan's decision was based primarily on the challenging opportunity that is developing here from the association that the medical sciences will have with the corresponding science departments on campus when the medical school makes its move in 1959."[43]

Curriculum reform became an important element of the planning. The revisions and reorientation proved to be as controversial as the physical move and prompted yet more changes to the faculty ranks. In September 1953, backed by a $210,000 Commonwealth Fund grant, the Medical Council's Committee on Curriculum began a three-year review. By developing a distinctive new curriculum, Stanford captured the attention of educators, foundation officials, and others, which in turn helped the fundraising effort.

The new curriculum was described in a July 1956 publication by Sterling, "A Program of Education for Medicine at Stanford University":

> The eight years between graduation from secondary school and graduation from medical school are looked upon as a continuum. Students will be admitted to Medical School after three years of college work, as at present, but instead of devoting four years exclusively to the study of medicine, they will enter a five-year program of medical work, within the first three years of which each will complete the equivalent of an additional year of college work. Those with interests and talents in non-medical subjects will be encouraged to continue and broaden their interests and to develop their talents at the same time that they study medicine.[44]

Sterling used the 1956 press conference announcing the fundraising drive to point out that "at Stanford, emphasis remains on superior

professional training. The move to campus will bring medical education into a true University environment." A revised curriculum would broaden the education of medical students and afford better opportunities for student experience in research. "Students will receive the versatile education they need in a rapidly changing and expanding world of medicine, and for leadership roles in whatever area of medical activity they choose to enter," he said. The Medical School review paralleled a self-study (1954–56) on the main campus that Sterling considered "the most thorough review of undergraduate curriculum in 30 years."[45]

Recalled Robert Alway: "I don't believe that we would have gained the attention we did had we not pressed forward so vigorously in fighting through, getting acceptance of the markedly changed curriculum." Nevertheless, the novel approach was not entirely successful. The Medical School never succeeded in setting up blocks of time that matched the university calendar. The five-year program did not last through the 1960s but served to instill a concept of preparing physician-scientists and leaders. "I think the best thing," Alway concluded about the proposed five-year plan, "was that it enabled a great many students to become involved, one way or the other, in clinical and basic science investigation. . . . They got the taste of what it was really like and how god-damned-hard it was to do good research."[46]

Ernie Arbuckle later commented that the decision to move the Medical School "was one of the most courageous decisions that [Sterling] and the trustees made." Henry Kaplan felt that in the face of medical faculty and alumni opposition, "Wally deserves a medal for the courage he showed in sticking with [the] decision" to relocate.[47]

Even former Dean Loren Chandler was reconciled to the need to move on, becoming chief of surgery at the Palo Alto Veterans Administration Hospital, built on Stanford land in 1959, where he worked to develop its facilities as a teaching hospital.

While some Medical School faculty hoped that Stanford would continue to operate the San Francisco hospitals privately to train recently graduated physicians as residents and fellows, the Board of Trustees concluded the university had neither the financial nor staffing resources.

In 1958, the old Lane Hospital was condemned for further care of bed patients by the California State Bureau of Hospitals. The university transferred the old Medical School building and 1917 Stanford hospital to the Presbyterian Church, which operated it as Presbyterian Hospital. The facilities were later combined with Children's Hospital of San Francisco. As of 2020, the complex was part of the Pacific Heights campus of the California Pacific Medical Center.

Aerial photograph, 1966, of the Stanford Medical Center, featuring the fountains at its entrance and its extensive parking lots. Above, the back of the original 1891 Leland Stanford Junior Museum can be seen, with the long horizontal portion of its 1902–05 extension, all that survived the 1906 earthquake. In 1909, part of this extension had been fitted up for Anatomy and other science units, to ease space problems at the then-new Medical Department in San Francisco. AIR PHOTO COMPANY / STANFORD NEWS SERVICE

The Medical Center's large modernist reflecting pool and fountains, seen here in 1959, still decorate the entrance to the now-older portion of a much-enlarged complex.   STANFORD MEDICAL HISTORY CENTER

BUYING OUT PALO ALTO'S INTEREST IN THE MEDICAL CENTER

Years later, Fred Glover recalled Sterling's difficult decisions regarding the Medical School. The one error in judgment Sterling made at that time, Glover believed, was agreeing to joint management of the new hospital by Palo Alto and Stanford.

Local physicians had supported improving local hospital facilities, including enlarging the 200-bed Palo Alto Hospital, built in 1931 on Stanford land near El Camino (a large wing was added in 1942). Dr. Russel Lee had pressed for a postwar major addition, but President Tresidder had refused to consider Lee's plans. Years later, while Stanford mapped out its new medical center on campus, a survey suggested that one new hospital, operated jointly by Palo Alto and Stanford, could be built more inexpensively and operated more efficiently than two individual

hospitals. Palo Alto voters resoundingly passed a new bond to match Stanford funds to build a joint 440-bed "Palo Alto–Stanford Hospital" that could be designed as part of the new Medical Center. The trustees, in turn, also authorized Stanford's contribution to the shared facilities. In 1959, a new Palo Alto–Stanford Hospital opened as part of the new Stanford Medical Center.[48]

By the mid-1960s, however, the joint operation clearly was not working. The new hospital was virtually operated as two separate facilities, with the city controlling one wing known as the Palo Alto Pavilion and the university in charge of the Stanford Pavilion. Each group had its own staff and functioned under its own rules.

In 1965, Dr. Robert J. Glaser took over with the elevated title of vice president for medical affairs and dean of the medical school. Glaser, recruited from Harvard Medical School and the Affiliated Hospital Center in Boston, encouraged Sterling to attempt to acquire Palo Alto's share

Palo Alto Hospital, built on Stanford land near El Camino in 1931, served Peninsula communities for nearly 30 years. The building (seen here in the 1930s) and its extensions were closed in 1959, reopening six years later as medical office space (later as clinical space). Stanford purchased the building in 1968, renaming it Hoover Pavilion. An extensive renovation, completed in 2013, preserved its notable Art Deco features.
STANFORD NEWS SERVICE

of the joint hospital. Glaser's work in Boston had involved affiliating six Harvard teaching hospitals. Earlier, as vice president for medical affairs and dean of the University of Colorado Medical School, Glaser planned a $20-million hospital and research structure. Glaser quickly observed that the Palo Alto–Stanford Hospital did not function as a university hospital. "The present organizational and physical arrangements will neither support the University's long-term objectives in respect to medical education nor meet the community's pressing need," he said.[49]

A recent incident had proved especially provoking: In 1966, Stanford doctors recommended that the Palo Alto medical staff not appoint a man who had completed a Stanford internship in surgery "without distinction." The Palo Alto staff ignored the advice and admitted him to practice. Glaser wrote Sterling that while the quality of local medical practice was high, "it is nonetheless true that an open staff hospital, and that is what the Palo Alto side of the hospital is, is not compatible with quality medical education."[50]

That August, Stanford offered to purchase, for approximately $5 million, the city's share of the buildings and equipment. If the city accepted and would agree to terminate its lease of land under the new hospital, the university would make available additional land next to the original Palo Alto Hospital (renovated and reopened in 1964 as the Hoover Pavilion). At this point, the Palo Alto City Council was not interested in selling the municipally owned facilities, nor in spending its own funds to further expand the 1931 hospital. City officials proposed that Stanford construct a community hospital in exchange,

Robert J. Glaser, recruited from Harvard, became vice president for medical affairs and dean of medicine in 1965.
STANFORD NEWS SERVICE

In 1968, James Hildebrand (left, standing), Palo Alto city attorney, with Medical Vice President Robert Glaser, President Sterling, and Palo Alto Mayor Frances Dias signing off on the university's buyout of Palo Alto's interest in the Palo Alto–Stanford Hospital, which included Hoover Pavilion as well as Palo Alto's share of the 1959 Medical Center complex. STANFORD NEWS SERVICE

on a bed-for-bed basis. Stanford instead offered to sell the city its own interest in the joint Palo Alto–Stanford Hospital, and build its own new teaching hospital and ambulatory care center on lands adjoining the Medical Center.

In October 1967, city officials summarized Palo Alto's options: 1) Stay in place, and continue the costly operation of the Palo Alto Pavilion of the 1959 hospital for the benefit of Palo Alto residents and medical staff, not a terribly attractive alternative since it would compete with the proposed expansion of the Stanford facility; 2) sell the Palo Alto Pavilion to Stanford, as Stanford suggested, and use the proceeds to expand the Hoover Pavilion to a self-sufficient community hospital; or 3) sell both the Palo Alto Pavilion and the Hoover Pavilion to Stanford and use the proceeds to retire the city's bond debt and for other non-hospital purposes, or contribute all or part of the proceeds toward construction of a Palo Alto Clinic hospital then under consideration.[51]

In January 1968, the City Council decided to divest its hospital interests and leased lands to Stanford.[52] The details were worked out a few months later: Stanford would acquire Palo Alto's Medical Center buildings on campus. The university would grant staff privileges to those community physicians then on the hospital staff for the remainder of their professional careers, but the separate medical staffs would be unified. Stanford would pay the City of Palo Alto $1 million and assume the city's outstanding hospital bond payments, totaling $3.5 million in principal and interest, over a 20-year period. It also provided guarantees for specific community hospital services for the next 40 years.

Soon after, a Stanford press release announced, "After nearly three years of negotiations with the Palo Alto City Council, Stanford University finally assumed complete ownership of the jointly owned 580-bed Palo Alto–Stanford Hospital on July 1, 1968." At the time of the announcement, the Board of Trustees designated the entire complex—the School of Medicine and the newly designated Stanford University Hospital—as the Stanford University Medical Center.[53]

Agreement between Stanford and the city came on the eve of Wallace Sterling's retirement as president of the university and Dr. Robert Glaser's assumption of new responsibilities as acting president.[54]

AN EXERCISE IN SELF-HELP
ACCELERATING LAND DEVELOPMENT

Stanford's president oversees landholdings far larger and more complex than the usual suburban campus of academic buildings, student and faculty residences, and athletic fields. Wallace Sterling, an avid gardener as well as academic administrator, had 8,800 acres—two-thirds the size of Manhattan—of oak-studded foothills and open fields, much of it rural and undeveloped in 1949, to tend and nurture.

Senator Leland Stanford intended the university's land to be a major financial asset to the institution's original endowment, but the land also carried a growing financial burden not recognized by the public. Only a small portion of the land—roughly 100 acres comprising the central campus and immediate surroundings—was exempt from rapidly rising property taxation as San Francisco Peninsula land values skyrocketed after World War II. The university also faced pressure from local, state, and federal agencies that wanted to acquire, through condemnation, portions of its lands. Developers and neighboring city councils eyed "blue chip" pasture lands as potential suburbs and lucrative tax bases. With the university's academic ambitions gaining strength, Sterling's administration in the 1950s undertook a novel master planning effort for residential, commercial, and light industrial development amid postwar California's rapidly changing economy and demography.

Stanford's land development program offers the most visible change to the university during Sterling's 19 years as president. Its story is often told as one of certainty and success, centered on development of the Stanford Industrial (now Research) Park and Stanford Shopping Center. It was, however, more often the result of uncertainty, experimentation, learning, disagreement, accommodation, leaps of faith, and compromise among university officials, as well as between the institution and its neighbors.

Sterling, like predecessor Donald B. Tresider, believed that developing surplus lands was vital to improving the pool of unrestricted funds

< This early 20th-century view from Stanford's rolling hills looks northwest over Sand Hill Road to hills and mountains beyond. The photographer may have stood in the vicinity of today's Stanford Linear Accelerator Center. Stanford University, still nicknamed The Farm, had grown to 8,800 acres by the time Wally Sterling returned to campus in 1949.
BERTON CRANDALL / STANFORD UNIVERSITY ARCHIVES

for faculty salaries and student scholarships. It was no "get-rich-quick" scheme or magic bullet, as some may have hoped and the public at times assumed, but one element of a larger plan to bolster Stanford's income. Sterling had quickly found that the university had to prove it was making full use of its assets before it could attract major grants and donors. By way of explanation, Sterling enjoyed telling of a visit with the Rockefeller Foundation's new president, Dean Rusk, a UC Berkeley alumnus familiar with Stanford's land legacy. When Sterling inquired about a Rockefeller grant, Rusk asked what Stanford was doing by way of "self-help," not only with alumni support but also through development of its unusual land assets. Sterling pointed to planning efforts and projects already underway.[1]

AN UNFAILING SUPPORT, A HIDDEN PRICE

At the end of the 19th century, Senator and Mrs. Leland Stanford were among California's most prominent landowners, acquiring more than 200,000 acres in 17 counties from Shasta to Riverside. Three of their many properties, comprising some 78,000 acres of farmland, ranches, and vineyards in Northern California, provided the endowment for their 1885 Founding Grant for the Leland Stanford Junior University.[2] "The endowment of lands is made because they are, in themselves, of great value," Leland Stanford told the university's trustees, "and their proper management will ensure to the University an income much greater than would be realized were their value to be invested in any reliable interest-bearing security."[3]

In his November 1885 address to the newly assembled trustees, Senator Stanford stated that the lands were never to be "alienated" (sold or transferred), believing that the acreage would

"be an unfailing support to the institution which they are designed to benefit."[4] Ongoing financial troubles following the senator's 1893 death, however, led Jane Stanford to amend the Founding Grant in 1902 to allow the sale of two of the three properties: the Gridley Ranch, in Butte County, and Vina, in Tehama and Butte counties. As the site memorializing their son, the Palo Alto Farm remained sacrosanct and, in fact, kept growing. Composed of 6,996.75 acres, in Santa Clara and San Mateo counties in 1885, the Farm grew to 8,247.64 acres by 1908, according to official surveys.[5]

The Palo Alto Farm's extensive acreage carried a financial implication unforeseen in 1885: the gradual rise in property taxation. Although financial stability returned to the university in the late 1890s, Mrs. Stanford predicted that ever-increasing tax assessments on endowment lands could cripple the institution. Future trustee George Crothers, '95, and other young alumni spearheaded a successful referendum in 1900 amending the state constitution to exempt that segment of Stanford University's Palo Alto Farm property devoted to educational purposes. At the time, this was about 100 acres of the Quadrangle and surrounding buildings, but the new law provided significant tax relief as long as rural property values of the outlying acreage remained comparatively low. In 1934, the Board of Trustees officially increased the designated "campus" to 1,023 acres.[6]

The trustees were tempted from time to time to sell off outlying acreage during the economic woes of later decades—40 acres across El Camino Real, near Palo Alto High School, were sold to a residential developer in 1922—but they scrupulously maintained the Farm nearly intact, with only some minor boundary adjustments. Over the years, leases of small portions of surplus (non-"campus") acreage for agricultural purposes—

Archibald Treat captured this 1886 view of Leland and Jane Stanford's Palo Alto Farm from above the old county road (later Foothill Road/Junipero Serra Boulevard). In the distance are the well-kept paddocks of the trotting horse department. Between is the Farm's very full reservoir (Lagunita). In 1953, a controversial master plan recommended a vast residential community in these hillsides. ARCHIBALD TREAT / STANFORD UNIVERSITY ARCHIVES

a dairy, a flower and vegetable farm, a nursery, and cattle ranching generated enough income to pay property taxes. (The costly trotting horse stock farm and racing operations had been discontinued in 1903.)[7]

Trustees also experimented with leasing arrangements close to the Quadrangle. In the 1890s, they began leasing land to faculty, fraternities and sororities, and boarding-house landlords willing to build residences for students, faculty, and staff near the Quad, thus fostering a residential community. Eateries, a candy store, a gas station, and other small retail enterprises also were built on leased land, setting a precedent for later commercial leases, including a 1927 lease of 66 acres at El Camino and Stanford Avenue to the Palo Alto School of Aviation. Over time, leases were also made with outside research institutions, including the Carnegie Institution's Plant Biology Laboratory (1929), the U.S. Department of Agriculture (1922–44), the city of Palo Alto for the Palo Alto Hospital (1931) and, across El Camino Real, the school district for Palo Alto Union High School (1919). A 1927 proposal for a 1,500-acre botanical garden, to be located along a wide corridor adjacent to San Francisquito Creek, from El Camino Real into the foothills, fell short due to lack of outside funding. So, too, did 1925 plans by a Palo Alto consortium of businessmen for a luxury hotel, complete with 18-hole golf course, to be located to the southwest of the Lathrop residence on Alta Vista. (Four years later, the university built nearby the Stanford Golf Course and its clubhouse with its own funding.)[8]

After World War I, the university leased land for new government research ventures. In 1929, the Carnegie Institution built its Plant Biology Laboratory near the intersection of Governor's Avenue and Searsville Road. STANFORD UNIVERSITY ARCHIVES

In 1916, four acres at Lomita and Lagunita drives were leased to Sarah Gates Howard, widow of a Stanford professor. Her 1917 garden apartment complex of 26 units—the only apartments on campus—provided housing for professors and staff. After the 80-year lease expired, in 1997, Kingscote reverted to the university. It was remodeled in 2015–17 for student and employee services. STANFORD UNIVERSITY ARCHIVES

In 1927, the trustees leased 66 acres at the corner of El Camino and Stanford Avenue to the Palo Alto School of Aviation. The facility grew quickly to three runways and three hangars. The aviation school relocated, in 1935, as part of Palo Alto's new airport on the baylands. PALO ALTO HISTORICAL ASSOCIATION

POSTWAR PLANNING

As Stanford emerged from wartime conditions, President Don Tresidder's operating budget, heavily dependent on tuition and conservative investments, was inadequate to sustain postwar building renovations, much less growth. Income from agricultural leases no longer covered property taxes and minimal services for the tenants.[9] In addition, postwar Peninsula land values were skyrocketing with the suburban population boom. This subjected the university to significant property tax increases due to changing appraisal regulations. More than 7,500 acres of undeveloped land could now be assessed at "highest and best use" as represented by residential developments in neighboring Palo Alto and Menlo Park, regardless of whether Stanford leased to tenants or left the land undeveloped. Early in his brief tenure, Tresidder and the trustees had begun to study the implications of larger-scale commercial development.[10]

To set the stage for overall land use studies, as well as campus renovation, Tresidder turned to noted California architect Eldridge T. (Ted) Spencer, who had worked with Tresidder's Yosemite Park and Curry Company. (In 1927, he had founded Spencer Associates, a firm that would become noted for its mid-century contemporary designs for educational, civic, museum, and recreational projects.)[11] In November 1944, at Spencer's suggestion, Tresidder created a university planning office, the first academic architectural planning office in the United States. Spencer became its first director, reporting directly to Tresidder. Although the position was intended to be part-time, he spent considerable time at Stanford.[12]

Ted Spencer, a UC Berkeley- and Beaux Arts–trained architect, believed that "form follows function" through long-range pragmatic planning. Given changing postwar educational and residential demands, he questioned maintaining the style of Stanford's older, at times

Portrait of architect Eldridge T. Spencer, Stanford's first director of planning, by his friend Ansel Adams in 1953. Throughout his 15 years (1944–59) as part-time director, Spencer championed faculty concerns about the use of campus lands and warned against hasty residential planning.   ANSEL ADAMS / STANFORD NEWS SERVICE

idiosyncratic, buildings simply out of sentiment. He began the first of an eight-year series of surveys of campus needs, problems, and possibilities, aiming ultimately at an overall plan rooted in Frederic Law Olmsted's layout of the main campus but adapted to contemporary university needs.[13]

Initially, Spencer focused on the main campus, where the Quadrangle and science facilities needed significant upgrading and the expected influx of postwar students would need housing. But his charge was expansive. The Planning Office also studied broader issues of traffic and pedestrian flow, parking, utilities, green space, community amenities, and related needs. At the same time, he considered how the university might begin planning to develop small portions of unrestricted (non-academic) land.[14]

Spencer's approach to the whole campus was endorsed by Professor Lewis Mumford, the well-known architectural critic and planning advocate, who had taught at Stanford during the war. In a detailed 1947 memorandum to Tresidder, written at the president's request, Mumford reviewed Stanford's architectural legacy, prewar construction, and recent planning efforts.[15]

Mumford, like Spencer, was impressed with Olmsted's 1886–88 quadrangle conception of the university and its surroundings but despaired at its subsequent buildings, which, he said, had neither inner nor outer unity. "Almost every departure from [Olmsted's] conception has proved both an esthetic liability and an economic loss," Mumford wrote in his Tresidder memorandum. The original heavy masonry of the Quadrangle represented a high standard of the era but was now prohibitively costly and made further alternations to meet new needs expensive and unsatisfactory. "Later buildings like Encina [sic], the Library, and the Education Building completely lack the positive qualities of the Quad and repeat on a grand scale all the vices of an obsolete form of construction," he added.[16]

"A fresh, independent analysis of the problem brings one back to Olmsted's essential contribution: compactness, concentration, unity," Mumford told Tresidder, concluding that "the buildings of the University should, in future operations, be conceived as a concentrated urban group in a permanent rural setting." Mumford also recommended that "the tie-in between the new and the old should be, first, with respect to height and scale, and second in the use of the covered walk or arcade, the esthetic connecting thread between the individual buildings, and as a necessary functional adaptation to circulation on foot."

Mumford also suggested that the university architect should serve as a co-designer and oversee every phase of campus construction. "No single outside firm should be entrusted with future building; but one by one the best outside architects on the coast should be drawn into the design of successive buildings, to keep the design at the top levels of skill and imagination."[17]

Backed by Mumford, Spencer developed a series of planning documents from which Tresidder expected to revive the university's teaching, research, and residential facilities. Spencer also responded to the president's interest in commercial development, mapping out possible commercial and industrial sites along El Camino Real as early as 1946.[18]

It is not Spencer but Business Manager Alf E. Brandin who later would be credited with the initial steps toward the university's commercial and industrial zone land development. When appointed by Tresidder to head the reorganized Business Office in 1946, the 33-year-old Brandin, '36, became, in essence, Stanford's city manager, overseeing all business operations except finance and investments. One admirer noted, however, an obvious difference: "[C]ity managers are not responsible for housing and feeding their constituents. Very few have the responsibility of buying thousands of lab rats for medical school experiments or supervising the interior decoration of dormitories."[19]

By Wallace Sterling's arrival in 1949, Brandin was the most outspoken staff member advocating commercial, industrial, and residential development of Stanford land.

Unlike Spencer, Brandin quickly gathered important allies among Stanford trustees, including key members of their Land Development Committee: Charles R. Blyth, '08, John Cushing, '08, and George F. Morell, '09. They, in turn, introduced Brandin to Colbert Coldwell, California's "dean of real estate brokers."

Few outsiders would have as strong an

Alf Brandin, business manager and director of land development, in July 1957, with a Skidmore, Owings & Merrill land use plan. The plan recommended substantial housing construction for non-Stanford–affiliated residents in the lower foothills. Area 6, south of Sand Hill Road (noted by Brandin), instead was assigned to the Stanford Linear Accelerator Center. Near his thumb is a proposed route for Interstate 280.   STANFORD NEWS SERVICE

ALF E. BRANDIN, DEVELOPMENT ADVOCATE

When Sterling named Alf Brandin as Stanford's first director of land development, his responsibilities were already wide-ranging. As business manager, he oversaw the university's buildings and grounds, campus police and fire departments, purchasing and inventory, along with insurance, employee retirement, and medical coverage programs. He was responsible for housing and feeding thousands of students and watched over faculty-staff residential areas, as well as thousands of acres of farmland, hills, woodlands, water reserves, three lakes, and numerous isolated research areas.

He was also the master of negotiated contracts, be they research grants or utility services, land leases or construction contracts. This placed him in a pivotal role as the university's trustees stepped up commercial, industrial, and non-affiliated residential land development.

Brandin (1913–99) was already a popular campus figure when he returned to Stanford in 1946 to head its newly reorganized Business Office. The starting center for the legendary "Vow Boys" football teams, the 33-year-old Brandin, '36, also had been president of his Zeta Psi fraternity chapter, president of the senior honorary society Phi Phi, and a member of the Men's Council, a student judicial council. He had worked his way through Stanford "hashing" at Kappa Kappa Gamma and as campus representative for Phelps-Terkel, a Palo Alto men's clothing store.[1]

Brandin continued his campus presence after graduating, working with the Stanford Associates as a class of 1936 "agent" to foster fundraising among his former classmates and other alumni. After working for an insurance company, he joined the Navy, serving as an aviator during World War II. He had intended to go back to his insurance job after the war, but trustee President W. Parmer Fuller Jr. intervened. Fuller, '10, a former *Daily* editor with a long-standing interest in campus affairs, recommended him to President Don Tresidder, then rethinking how the university managed its business operations. Hitting it off with Tresidder, Brandin enthusiastically accepted the business manager position in 1946. Tresidder was "a do-er," an admiring Brandin later recounted, complaining that most faculty criticism of the businessman-president seemed to him unjustified "academic politics."[2]

Three years later, in 1949, Brandin fit in easily with incoming President Sterling (also a former collegiate football player) and his staff, some of whom had been fellow Stanford athletes and student leaders. Brandin also developed easy working relationships with influential trustees, particularly those with real estate experience, and notably with trustee advisor Colbert Coldwell, the prominent Bay Area executive of the Coldwell-Banker real estate firm. Brandin's ideas on land development matters, including an aggressive approach to town-gown relations, coincided with Coldwell's, and Coldwell, in turn, gave Brandin tremendous support.

During the Depression, Brandin, like many of his fellow class agents, had viewed development of university lands as a solution to Stanford's income problems. After becoming business manager, he later recalled, he better understood the limitations faced by university Comptroller Almon Roth, whose land development plans in the 1920s and '30s made little progress. Low land values and rents had yet to offset the high cost of providing utilities, and Roth had little success attracting outside investors. Brandin, however, had returned to campus just as the pressure of suburban growth in neighboring cities pressed against Stanford's open lands.[3]

Nearly every weekend Brandin, often on horseback, inspected portions of the university's broad acreage. It was a way to get to know agricultural tenants, but also afforded him firsthand knowledge of remote areas and a means to check for sagging fences, trees needing attention, or roads needing repair.

Although at times annoyed by faculty questions, and openly disagreeing with university planner Ted Spencer's caution, Brandin fully supported the university's singular obligation to develop its vast acreage to underwrite its academic program. Despite disagreements, he was praised by faculty for his "rigid commitment to flexibility" and his courtesy. He endorsed expansion of the academic reserve and shorter industrial leasing arrangements, and he questioned the trustees' unwillingness to reconsider the university's obligations toward fair housing in non-affiliated residential developments.[4]

For Stanford's suburban neighbors, few university officials—aside from Sterling—represented the university's physical presence and weighty local influence like Brandin. A man of great charisma and seemingly boundless energy, Brandin often had little patience with local real estate agents, large-scale real estate developers, and, especially, Palo Alto and Los Altos Hills officials.

In late 1959, Brandin's responsibilities were broadened yet again with his appointment as the university's first vice president for business affairs. His successor as land development officer, Tom Ford, reported to Brandin, as did a new, full-time university planner, Harry Sanders. (Ted Spencer, who stepped down in 1959, had been part-time, reporting to Sterling.)

After Sterling's retirement in 1968, Brandin's patience with student unrest and campus upheavals wore thin. He remained for two more years, sympathetic to then-President Kenneth Pitzer's difficulties, then stepped away from the administration in 1970. "The fun had gone out of working for Stanford," he concluded. He became senior vice president and a director of Utah Construction and Mining Company (later Utah International), presided over by trustee and friend Ed Littlefield. He retired in 1982.[5]

Brandin continued his long-standing interest in Stanford affairs, living at his home on Salvatierra Street until his death, in 1999. Deeply interested in Stanford history, he served as president of the Stanford Historical Society from 1991 to 1993, as well as on the Hoover Institution Board of Overseers and on the Stanford Athletic Board. He also was a Stanford Associate.

NOTES

1. "Alf E. Brandin: An Interview Conducted by Robert de Roos, Stanford Oral History Project" (1989); "Alf E. Brandin, Interview by Frederic O. Glover, Stanford Oral History Project" (1990); "Services Thursday for Alf Brandin, Former Vice President," *Stanford Report*, December 1, 1999; "Alf E. Brandin, '36: He Broke New Ground," *Stanford* [magazine] (March-April 2000); Rosemary McAndrews, "The Birthplace of Silicon Valley: A History of Land Development at Stanford University," *Sandstone & Tile* 19:1/2 (Spring 1995) 3–11; and "A Rich Harvest on His Farm," *Peninsula Living / Palo Alto Times*, September 24, 1955.
2. Brandin (1989) 23, Brandin (1990) 3–5, 10.
3. Brandin (1989) 33.
4. Brandin (1989) vi.
5. Brandin (1989) 31.

influence on the university's initial land planning of the late 1940s and 1950s as Colbert Coldwell. If Alf Brandin was the "ball carrier," one football-minded journalist noted in 1955, Coldwell was the coach. After Coldwell won an argument with a trustee in 1950, Brandin observed dryly to a colleague: "Mr. Coldwell had definite plans for the development of Stanford lands."[20]

Coldwell, a University of California alumnus and co-founder of the highly successful real estate firm Coldwell-Banker, had been the board's unofficial development advisor since 1941. (His relationship to Stanford was not made public until 1952, even though trustees had formalized it two years earlier.) He was behind early studies, like the 1941 soil survey, which, surprisingly, concluded that only small sections of The Farm's outlying acreage could be profitably farmed. In 1947, the Los Angeles firm of Cormac-McConnell conducted an economic feasibility survey of Stanford lands and the general area. This effort, funded by trustee George Morell, enthusiastically backed Coldwell's interest in commercial development, particularly a shopping center, an interest strongly shared by Alf Brandin.[21]

Asked to recommend a commercial site for perhaps a dozen stores, Cormac-McConnell recommended Stanford Lot 76, a small strip of about 11 acres of non-contiguous university land that lay between El Camino and the Southern Pacific railroad tracks just over the border in San Mateo County. (Some 109 lots, the vast majority assembled by Leland Stanford, made up the university's 8,800 acres.) Coldwell strongly disagreed, preferring a larger area adjoining the campus: Lot 1, 65 acres, sited between the Palo Alto Hospital and San Francisquito Creek, along El Camino (the present shopping center site). But this site presented a thorny public relations problem: In a controversial decision earlier in 1947, Tresidder had turned down Palo Alto's

request for major expansion of the Palo Alto Hospital into that area, claiming the university needed it for future academic growth. His refusal had caused tension in town-gown relations that would take years to repair. How could Stanford justify using this same area to create a shopping center, particularly one that would compete with Palo Alto's merchants?[22]

Acting President Alvin Eurich, in charge after Tresidder's sudden death in January 1948, made it clear that he, too, would not allow Lot 1 to be used for non-academic purposes, be it city hospital expansion or shopping center. Brandin stalled a trustee decision by recommending further study, and waited for a new president to settle in.

In March 1949, Spencer recommended a less controversial project: a light industrial development on campus land on Lot 41, lying along El Camino Real adjacent to Barron Park, in Stanford's easterly corner. El Camino Real, a major Peninsula thoroughfare, was lined on both sides with small-scale commercial development for much of its length from San Francisco nearly to San Jose. The flat, undeveloped fields along Stanford's border with Barron Park and Palo Alto offered an obvious spot to fill in, but Spencer had more in mind than a strip of commercial leases bordering a busy road.

His recommendations also included a more controversial suggestion. Behind the small commercial and industrial zones along El Camino, he proposed a residential development running alongside the College Terrace neighborhood, on both sides of Page Mill Road to Foothill Road. This planned neighborhood of multiple and single-family homes, schools, recreational areas, and a hotel in a "park like setting" was not a quick-built suburban development but was intended, he said, to "create a community based on the policies of the university."[23]

Acting President Clarence Faust (standing in

from January through March 1949) left Spencer's memorandum, along with the battle over Lot 1, for the arrival of Wallace Sterling.

AN EXERCISE IN SELF-HELP

As the new president evaluated the university's existing condition before leaping into its future, Sterling's approach to the land development questions before him had the hallmarks of his administrative style: he leaned toward cautious experimentation, backed by the full cooperation of the Board of Trustees and, unusually, a role for faculty.

Sterling's first concern was Stanford's continuing dependence on tuition. Throughout his presidential tenure, he would argue against increasing undergraduate enrollment to increase tuition income, insisting that the university's goal should be quality of scholarship, not quantity of students matriculated. While studying the university's budget, however, he saw a particular need to boost unrestricted funding. Gifts from alumni and friends, corporations, and foundations were vital to the institution's financial health, but these gifts were usually restricted to specific building projects, scholarships, programs, or improvements. Development of residual lands—part of the endowment—might provide a comparatively predicable source of unrestricted funds as well as tax relief. This, in turn, could provide flexibility to recruit top faculty in fields that did not easily attract corporate or government funding. Land development also was a means to attract reluctant foundation and other funding; Dean Rusk was not the only foundation officer to ask what Stanford was doing to utilize its remarkable land legacy. As Sterling told magazine writer Frank Taylor in 1960: "[W]hen I went around with my tin cup asking for funds, prospective donors were always asking me what we were doing to develop our unexploited assets."[24]

The new president had at hand conflicting site recommendations with an array of unresolved legal and town-gown issues. And each was based on differing assumptions of individual staff, trustees, and advisors. Over the next few years, Sterling experimented with new mechanisms to sort out the variables, and to plan, review, and oversee the developments.[25]

More than any other senior staff officer inherited from the previous administration, Alf Brandin provided a continuum from Don Tresidder's hopes to Wally Sterling's implementation. The president immediately warmed to his personable and energetic business manager who, like Sterling, was a former collegiate football player. Sterling tempered Brandin's urge to move ahead quickly, however. Spencer, with his architect's expertise and sympathy for faculty concerns, also often provided a counterpoint to Brandin's enthusiasms. Sterling had "a marvelous capacity for living with differences of opinion," recalled former presidential assistant Ken Cuthbertson. He picked strong people, added Howard Brooks, another former assistant, "and he was willing to let them argue."[26]

By the end of Sterling's first year, in April 1950, the Board of Trustees agreed to consider specific proposals from his administration for residential, light industry, and commercial leases. But the university had yet to deal with important policy questions regarding installation of utilities, annexation, incorporation, leasing, and land condemnation. Also unclear was Stanford's legal standing as a landlord, as well as its property and business taxation obligations, and the legal implications of financing such improvements as roads or commercial buildings.[27]

Brandin had potential tenants for Spencer's recommended Lot 41 (light industrial), but Sterling chose a small, non-controversial residential development along San Francisquito Creek as a first step in non-academic land development.

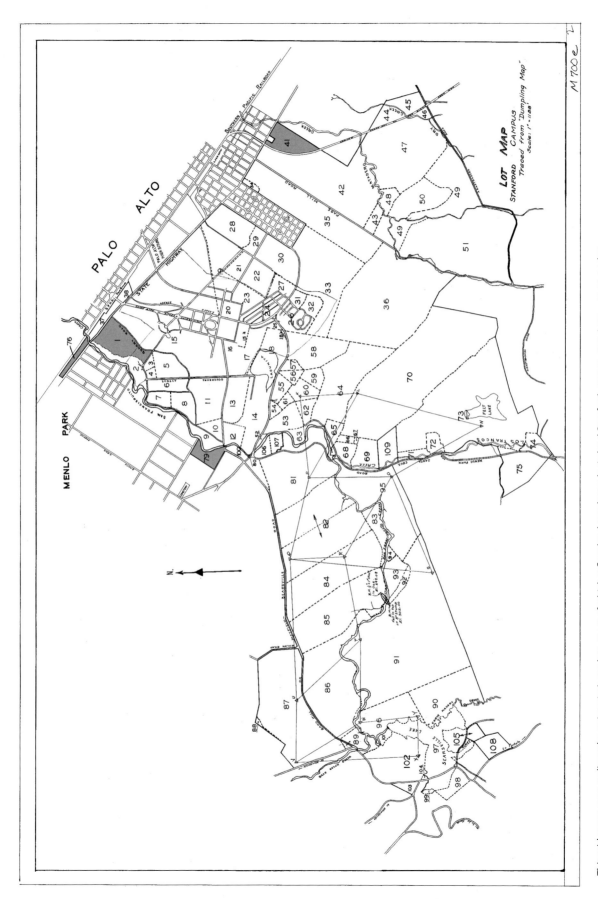

This mid-1920s map outlines the university's 109 lots, most of which reflect land purchases by Leland Stanford, 1876 to 1893. Lots 1, 41, 76, and 79 were earmarked for the Sterling administration's first non-academic land development projects. STANFORD UNIVERSITY ARCHIVES

THE TRIAL BALLOON
STANFORD OAKS

At least one senior Stanford official already had ruminated about large-scale non-university residential land development. In 1923, Comptroller Almon E. Roth proposed subdividing 7,000 acres of the Farm, most of it in the foothills, into exclusive suburban estates to create the finest residential enclave along the Peninsula. Only the difficulty of providing water, electricity, gas, and sewage utilities, particularly once the Depression struck, kept him from pursuing the idea. Ted Spencer's 1949 suggestion for a residential neighborhood on the other side of College Terrace, though far less sprawling than Roth's, was aimed at an academically oriented community, rather than a typical Peninsula suburb. Neither Sterling nor the trustees were, as yet, comfortable with either step.[28]

Sterling chose as his trial balloon a 24-acre parcel—Lot 79—on acreage located on the Menlo Park (San Mateo County) side of San Francisquito Creek, between Lemon and Vine streets, across from the fourth tee of the Stanford Golf Course. The land was the site of the original Cedro Cottage, built before 1877 and part of the Stanfords' Palo Alto Farm since 1882. It was later used by early faculty families. The lot, under review as early as spring 1949, could serve as an experiment in annexation, leasing, and working with real estate developers. If serious problems arose, it was expendable.[29]

In 1950, Brandin began negotiating with Harry L. Arnold, '27, and his Peninsula Pacific Construction Company of Menlo Park, to lease and build 45 three- to five-bedroom homes on nearly 16 acres of the site. Arnold agreed to rent the land as 99-year leaseholds, at a prepaid rental of $5,000 per acre, effective March 1, 1953. (When a home was sold, the remaining years of the lease would be passed on to the home buyer.) These three- to five-bedroom houses were on the higher end of local home sales, starting at $25,000, though Arnold agreed to build a few two-bedroom houses on request.[30]

Sterling asked that members of the "Stanford family" (faculty, staff, and alumni) be given preference, but residential leases on this portion of university land ultimately were not restricted to Stanford faculty and staff, the first time since 1921. Equally significant, the university had no role in monitoring sales to the public.[31]

During the process, university officials agreed to a friendly condemnation suit by San Mateo County, which legally allowed the sale of 8.9 acres to the county and school district for construction of Oak Knoll Elementary School. Cedro Cottage was torn down to make way for it. Menlo Park officials agreed to annex the remaining acreage and provide utilities to the new neighborhood dubbed "Stanford Oaks" (today's Stanford Creek).[32]

A second non-faculty neighborhood later would be part of Stanford's mid-century master plan. Stanford Hills, bounded by Sand Hill and

Harry L. Arnold of the Peninsula Pacific Construction Company, here in 1957 with Alf Brandin, won the contract to build Stanford Oaks, across San Francisquito Creek, as the university's first speculative, non-faculty housing neighborhood. His company later built 78 houses at Stanford Hills, off Sand Hill Road. Arnold was exasperated with university staff for exerting their role in overseeing his architectural and construction plans. STANFORD NEWS SERVICE

Alpine roads, just beyond the Meyer-Buck estate, was planned in 1957–59 for at least 700 homes. By the time the first 78 homes were built and annexed to Menlo Park, university officials had learned much about residential issues and had serious doubts about further unaffiliated residential development. By 1960, siting of the Stanford Linear Accelerator Center farther up Sand Hill Road officially ended further expansion of Stanford Hills (see Chapter 6).[33]

MORE STUDIES, MORE QUESTIONS

Stanford Oaks was not itself a troublesome site, but Arnold impatiently waited nearly two years before he could begin construction, in April 1952. Sterling and his staff, facing this precedent-setting arrangement, first had to work through important legal and pragmatic issues with trustees, faculty, local officials, and a new consultant.[34]

Soon after making their 1950 Stanford Oaks site decision, Sterling and the trustees hired an outside professional consultant to undertake a comprehensive use study of all university-owned land, excluding the main campus, with recommendations for a master plan. They chose, in July 1950, the San Francisco civil engineering firm of Punnett, Parez & Hutchison. Elmore E. Hutchison, a civil engineer who had done work for the Newhall Land Company in Southern California, was recommended by trustee Herman Phleger, who was also a member of the Newhall board. (The Newhall Company had a similar problem: When Los Angeles County decided, in 1950, to tax ranch lands for best potential use as reflected by its suburban neighbors, the company turned from agriculture to development, resulting in creation of the town of Valencia.)[35]

When prodded for news about future land developments, Sterling cautioned that Hutchison's was a long-range study only, and that no further construction, except for the two small sections

"on the edge of the campus" (Lots 41 and 79), was contemplated. Nevertheless, speculation ran wild as soon as Sterling, in October, announced the Hutchison hiring. The San Francisco Chronicle headline the following day was the most blatant: "New Stanford Housing: 7,000 acres of School's Farm Land to be Opened for Home Building!" (A representative of the New York firm of N. K. Wriston already had written Brandin of his company's interest in developing the university's 8,800 acres. The offer was politely declined.)[36]

Although seemingly sidelined, Ted Spencer fleshed out his earlier reports, focusing largely on academic land use in and around the main campus—not the purview of Hutchison. Spencer's September 1950 "Master Plan: Land Use, Showing Existing Leases and Proposed Zoning, Stanford University" also reiterated his earlier suggestions regarding commercial land along El Camino, with adjacent residential housing.

Spencer also analyzed the possibilities of a large-scale commercial area on Lot 1, Brandin and Coldwell's preferred shopping center site near San Francisquito Creek. Fueling Coldwell's push for Lot 1, Spencer suggested three different spatial arrangement possibilities: all commercial space under one roof, with surrounding parking; an arrangement of outlying, detached buildings around central parking; and the more traditional detached buildings with no internal parking.[37]

Elmore Hutchison's recommendations, issued in 1951, lacked Spencer's detail and were far more speculative and sweeping. Not surprisingly, Hutchison expanded on the 1947 Cormac-McConnell survey conclusions and endorsed both Sterling's recommendation for the Stanford Oaks (Lot 79) residential development and Spencer's original light industry zone (Lot 41).[38]

Hutchison's engineering studies, however, highlighted many still unresolved development issues: How would utilities be provided—through incorporation by a neighboring municipality, self-incorporation, or incorporation by specific power, sanitation, and water districts? What kind, and length, of leasing arrangements should be offered? How would arterial roads and traffic issues be worked out with neighboring munici- palities? And just what *were* the official bound- aries of Stanford's "campus," that is, land devoted to academic use as opposed to surplus lands?

Equally important, the Hutchison report underscored strong local interest in suburban residential development. The report did not ask *whether* extensive development of housing was appropriate, but rather "what type of town or city would be best for Stanford?" Hutchison answered this question by recommending a town of 44,000 people built on 5,600 acres in the foothills.

Ultimately, Hutchison's study raised more questions than it answered. Sterling's staff also raised legal and political questions, along with engineering and management concerns, prompt- ing the creation of new mechanisms for debate and resolution. In October 1950, the trustees created a new Special Committee on Land Development, chaired by board President Paul C. Edwards and made up of influential members of the board's Buildings and Grounds Commit- tee and its Investment Committee, along with Sterling and presidential assistant Tom Spragens. Although some trustees still leaned heavily on Colbert Coldwell for advice, not all were so eas- ily persuaded, particularly Herman Phleger and George Morell. Both had extensive land devel- opment experience, in the Central Valley and Southern California; both also owned significant undeveloped acreage in the Santa Cruz Mountains that would, years later, become public parkland.[39]

That same month, October 1950, Sterling set up a parallel faculty committee, the Advisory Committee on Plant Development, acting on a suggestion Spencer had made years before to Don Tresidder. Representatives were drawn from

across the faculty, along with Spencer, Brandin, Spragens, and trustee George Morell. Its portfolio initially focused on campus buildings but within its first month the committee began reviewing current and future campus academic land needs, along with Spencer's rudimentary master plan. Sterling soon charged the committee with advis- ing him on all proposals pertaining to land use and the structures built on them. (In 1951 it was renamed the Advisory Committee on Land and Building Development, later the University Com- mittee on Land and Building Development.)

Throughout Sterling's administration, the advisory Committee on Land and Build- ing Development played an important role in reviewing overall campus needs and develop- ment, particularly in articulating a more expan- sive concept of academic land reserve. In doing so, it served as a faculty mouthpiece, a setting in which faculty concerns were validated, if not always alleviated. "Sometimes [Sterling] took the faculty committee's advice and sometimes he didn't," recalled former presidential assistant Kenneth Cuthbertson. "He never made them feel that it was fruitless for them to argue." The faculty committee served as an effective watch- dog over land development initiatives by keeping attention on the university's ultimate goal: sup- port of the academic program. The committee gradually became an essential part of the review and approval process, from building designs and site selection to parking and traffic circulation.[40]

The committee broadened faculty thinking and problem solving, and balanced staff and faculty opinions. "The committee's early days were stormy ones," recalled longtime chair Ray Faulkner, professor of art and architecture, who also served four years as acting dean of Humanities & Sci- ences. In the beginning, "no[t] one of us under- stood the complexities of using Stanford's lands for the greatest long-term benefit to the University and the surrounding communities. It took a great

Art and architecture Professor Ray Faulkner (at right, with Ted Spencer) served as first chair of Sterling's faculty Advisory Committee on Land and Building Development. Faulkner worked closely with university planner Spencer to create an effective approval process, backing the architect's concern about incomplete plans and urban sprawl, and urging the trustees to consider future academic land needs.

STANFORD NEWS SERVICE

many meetings for us all truly to appreciate that the planning of 8,800 acres cannot please everyone, not even the ten members of a committee."[41]

The committee also served as a venue in which Alf Brandin and Ted Spencer were forced to work through their differences.

From the outset, the experimental residential development project had proved as unpredictable as Sterling suspected. Given Spencer's reservations about the Peninsula Pacific Construction Company, trustees raised questions about the financial stability of Arnold's company and the board considered at least two other developers. Brandin, however, was eager to move ahead

with Arnold and pressed for quick approval of Arnold's incomplete architectural plans by the Planning Office. Spencer, alert to the board's insistence that Arnold's houses be "in architectural harmony" with their residential neighbors, balked when he was given only vague architectural drawings, incomplete specifications, and what he considered a mediocre design.[42]

Arnold, thinking of Stanford Oaks as a typical local subdivision project, was surprised that the university planner was brought into the process. Nor did he agree with Spencer or Sterling that prospective buyers should be from "a restricted and selective group" connected to the university (ironically, he would later be accused of his own selectivity in excluding non-white home buyers). After a meeting between planner and builder, the increasingly unhappy Spencer documented his conclusion: "This project seems to have been developed [by the university] primarily on the basis of procurement of 'venture money.' I do not feel that such initial financing should play so dominant a part in the university's development."[43]

But Arnold seemed to have the upper hand. Separately, in mid-1951, Brandin started negotiations with Arnold to build 10 ranch-style faculty houses in a triangular tract between Foothill Road, Mayfield Drive, and Alturas Road, then an extension of Gerona Road. (Sterling had earlier asked the board to allow faculty to develop the last eight lots along Foothill Road, but provision of utilities remained a hurdle.) When Arnold offered to pay for installation of roads and utilities for this development to win the 10-house Alturas contract, the board acquiesced. This would "enable the area to be developed without cost to the university and on an economical basis," they concluded, "by production of 10 houses at once rather than one by one" (as was traditional with faculty homes).[44]

Arnold's building plans for the Alturas faculty housing project quickly became troublesome.

Spencer had carefully worked out an approval process that included timely consultation with the new faculty advisory committee. Brandin had touched base about site development with Spencer and the committee, but no actual architectural plans were available until contracts with Arnold were ready to be signed in July 1951. Again, Brandin pressured Spencer for quick approval, and again the planner protested. In a detailed letter to Sterling, Spencer complained of uninspired exterior designs that were "trivial and lack integrity. They would, I feel, bring considerable critics to the university, and in the end would be a bad investment."[45]

Spencer believed that if Stanford took on this type of speculative home development for faculty housing, it should not "submit to the hum-drum innocuous solutions offered by the commercial promoter. To this end," he said, "I hope that a competent architect can be appointed for the project so that the university can be assured of an outstanding, inspiring environment."[46] Spencer's view prevailed. Although faculty housing was a clear need, the Alturas subdivision went no further, and the lot remains undeveloped today. Additional faculty houses were built instead along Foothill Road (now Junipero Serra Boulevard), as well as off Santa Teresa Street (the "Searsville Block" on the other side of campus) in the traditional, individualistic fashion.[47]

Tension between Brandin and Spencer continued throughout the remainder of the decade. Spencer reported directly to Sterling until 1956, when Ken Cuthbertson took over as intermediary and facilitator.[48] Spencer was diverted from land development projects but continued to work closely with architects and contractors on campus buildings. After 1956 much of his time was spent on the new Medical School project and on planning for Stanford's academic acreage. He also remained an influential member of the advisory committee until he resigned from the

Planning Office in 1959. Throughout his 15 years working for Stanford, he advocated recognition of faculty concerns, and challenged development recommendations that he felt put contractors and developers before students and faculty.[49]

Brandin retained the trust of Coldwell, the trustees, and the president, as he adroitly dealt with the array of engineers, city and county planners, developers, and government officials required for large-scale planning. His knowledge of real estate, Fred Glover said, "often disconcerted the outside experts who were brought in to make recommendations." His firsthand understanding of the geography of Stanford lands was unparalleled.

In September 1952, Sterling appointed Brandin as executive officer for land development, in addition to his role as business manager. "[Sterling] gave me wide berth," Brandin later said confidently. "We never worked at cross purposes. The business operations had to be dealt with dispatch, no delays. We were action oriented. I knew what he wanted, and he trusted us to deliver the goods."[50]

WHERE TO BUILD A SHOPPING CENTER?

Before Elmore Hutchison's 1950–51 study was complete, the trustees moved ahead to select sites for commercial and light industrial development. The future of Lot 76, across El Camino Real, as a possible shopping center site was another matter.

Alf Brandin had been looking at the possibilities of a shopping center as early as 1946. Suburban customers still flocked to San Francisco's major stores, even though the trip often involved a long drive along two-lane highways and, perhaps, across one of the Bay's bridges. But with a rapidly growing suburban population, regional shopping centers were popping up around the Bay Area, with several new centers along the Peninsula already underway.[51]

The other clear enthusiast for a shopping center was Colbert Coldwell. In 1950, Coldwell-Banker was finding tenants for San Francisco's new Stonestown Shopping Center, off 19th Avenue near Lake Merced and San Francisco State College. With Stonestown in mind, Coldwell wanted the far more expansive Lot 1—not Lot 76, favored by the trustees—for Stanford's center. According to Bandin, Coldwell confronted individual trustees still favoring Lot 76, insisting that industrial development of Lot 41 must be postponed if Lot 1 were not chosen. Brandin, with two potential industrial tenants now in hand, had no intention of holding back on developing the industrial zone, and helped push Coldwell's recommendation.[52]

Coldwell then convinced the trustee Committee on Land Development, in 1951, to have architectural studies made of Lot 1, recommending the award-winning firm of Welton Becket

Real estate magnate Colbert Coldwell (seated), the trustees' influential real estate advisor for more than 20 years, reviews a model for the Stanford Shopping Center in 1955. Professors Robert Walker (left) and Ray Faulkner (right), members of the faculty land and buildings committee, were known for the challenging questions they posed to Coldwell and to Business Manager Alf Brandin (center).   STANFORD UNIVERSITY ARCHIVES

and Associates of Los Angeles, designers of Stonestown. Known for its Late Modern and International styles, the firm had just completed notable buildings for Bullocks of Pasadena, General Petroleum, and Prudential. Becket also had been named master planner for the UCLA campus in 1948 and was aware of campus-related pressures as well as the success of Westwood Village, which had opened with 34 stores in 1929 next to UCLA.[53]

In June 1952, Becket submitted a schematic plan, a site plan, and a color rendering of the entire project, as well as preliminary plans in sufficient detail both to obtain cost estimates and for Stanford to begin negotiations with prospective tenants. Becket offered to provide these services at no cost on the understanding that, if the project went forward, the firm would be retained as architect for the proposed anchor tenant, the Emporium, at the usual fee. (Coldwell had enticed the Emporium, one of San Francisco's premier department stores and a Stonestown anchor store, to take the lead at Stanford.) Becket gambled that Stanford would stick with his firm to supervise the entire project.[54]

On July 5, 1952, Sterling publicly disclosed that the university's trustees were "considering" plans to develop a 60-acre shopping center on the foothill side of El Camino. Becket's preliminary plans included a major department store and sites for additional food, drug, furniture, and apparel stores covering 780,000 square feet.[55] Despite the news, the board had, in fact, not yet decided to sign off with Becket, debating whether to use Stanford funds or seek outside financing. Brandin, wanting to move forward with prospective tenants, encouraged President Sterling to push the trustees on a positive decision. Competing shopping centers were popping up in San Mateo and Santa Clara counties. One would be a campus neighbor: R. H. Williams, a private developer, had just revealed his plan

The Stanford Shopping Center formally opened in 1956, with seven major buildings, 50 stores, and room for 4,000 cars. Fronting El Camino in this June 1959 aerial photo are (from left) the Emporium, Roos Brothers, Livingstons, Joseph Magnin, Blum's, and I. Magnin. The center also included a Woolworth's, a hardware store, a thrift store, a shoe repair shop, a bakery, and several other restaurants, including Woodlands and Sandy's Kitchen.   PALO ALTO AIR PHOTO CO. / STANFORD NEWS SERVICE

to build a competing center in Palo Alto, the $5 million Town and Country Shopping Center at El Camino Real and Embarcadero Road. In May, Morgan Stedman, a Palo Alto architect, had showed off his plans for Shopper's World (later Alma Plaza), a neighborhood 60-store center anchored by a grocery store, on Alma Street and Meadow Drive, southeast of California Avenue. (A year later, Hillsdale Shopping Center in San Mateo was started.)[56]

Stanford's announcement, like that of R. H. Williams, sparked both complaints and suggestions of alternate locations farther away from Palo Alto's University Avenue merchants. Brandin was unimpressed with such protests,

believing them driven simply by self-interest. "It is imperative that we develop our land according to the best planning techniques for maximum utility, life of development and greatest economic return," he wrote to Sterling. When he talked with realtors, businessmen, and residents at civic and business group meetings, he said, most of the criticism of the university's shopping center concept were "based on inadequate facts and local prejudices. The history of decentralized shopping centers has been to increase the business of the surrounding community rather than to run local merchants out of business." It was time for Stanford to take a firm stand, he urged. "We should be convinced that we are doing the right

Professor Ray Faulkner registered faculty concern about the loss of this section of the arboretum's natural vegetation to the expansive parking surrounding the shopping center (seen here in 1958). Colbert Coldwell, a vocal advocate for the development, responded bluntly: "Mr. Faulkner, we anticipate that those acres of concrete [asphalt] are going to be covered with automobiles." STANFORD NEWS SERVICE

thing; that we have the right people doing the job and push forward with our plans."[57]

Fred Glover, on the other hand, had warned Sterling earlier that timing was all-important. Palo Alto's cooperation was paramount, and the nearby Palo Alto Hospital and the Children's Convalescent Home had powerful backers with long memories of Tresidder's rejection. Brandin kept subsequent negotiations with the Emporium quiet, even denying an Emporium-Stanford arrangement early in 1953 when prodded by the *Palo Alto Times*. A public announcement would not, in fact, be made until Brandin's discussions with Palo Alto's city manager and city planner were further along.[58]

Knowing something was in the works, Palo Alto city officials denied sewer service to the area. A new city ordinance now prohibited furnishing municipal services outside city limits. Palo Alto's long-standing special utilities agreement with Stanford covered only property that housed the university and related activities (including campus faculty homes and medical facilities) and would not extend to non-university residential or commercial developments on Stanford land. While favoring the development in principle, Palo Alto's City Council wanted a bigger piece of the pie.[59]

It took another year of negotiation, nudging, and accommodation before details about utilities and annexation could be worked out, eased in part by Palo Alto City Manager Jerome Keithley's cooperation in providing utilities for the Varian Associates building in Lot 41.[60] Annexation discussions for Lot 1 began in fall 1953. Lot 76, tucked across El Camino Real, later would be leased to car dealerships, Christmas tree sellers, and other businesses, and annexed to Menlo Park.

Trustees approved the shopping center's first lease, in July 1954, with the Emporium, which agreed to construct its building at its own expense (as would I. Magnin and the Purity grocery store) and to pay the university a net annual rental of 0.9 percent of gross sales. Becket won the shopping center design contract. In March

1954, the trustees had authorized expenditure of $628,000 for on-site and off-site development of the shopping center, with an additional $435,025 allocated the following October. The university was now fully committed to building and financing a major regional shopping center with its own funds, an audacious move for an educational institution largely inexperienced in commercial development. With Wagner and Martinez as builders, construction began that summer in the oak-studded fields.[61]

The faculty advisory committee was watchful. When early excavation required extensive removal of trees, chair Ray Faulkner complained directly to President Sterling. Faulkner was subsequently introduced to Colbert Coldwell. When the professor shared the committee's concern that there would be acres of terrible-looking concrete around the center, Fred Glover recalled, Coldwell looked Faulkner in the eye and said, "Mr. Faulkner, we anticipate that those acres of concrete [asphalt] are going to be covered with automobiles."[62]

Neither Faulkner nor his committee were mollified. They raised more questions, prompting changes in seemingly mundane matters like parking lot design and landscaping to bring the shopping center's design up to a level comparable to the "imaginative architectural and landscape treatment" of the campus. They recommended hiring landscape architect Thomas Church, the university's longtime landscape advisor and a faculty favorite, but Coldwell suspected Church would be "too elaborate and costly." As a compromise, the university retained another influential California landscape architect, Lawrence Halprin. (Halprin, who had also worked with the University of California, was well known for his designs for noted California modernist architects but would come to national attention with his plans for the 1962 Seattle World's Fair, Mendocino's Sea Ranch, and renovation of Ghirardelli Square and other San Francisco settings.) Within a few years, the faculty advisory committee put limits on the extension of commercial and residential development between the shopping center and main campus, weighed in on countless other individual lot developments, and pressed for a more complex analysis of the merit of land development.[63]

The $15 million Stanford Shopping Center—a

A ca. 1958 view of the shopping center's mid-century modern architectural design, with Gallenkamp shoe store (left) and the iconic "five and dime" variety store F. W. Woolworth Co.
STANFORD NEWS SERVICE

name settled on by Sterling's staff after more than two dozen catchy names were rejected—formally opened for business in 1956 with seven major buildings, some 50 stores, and room for 4,000 cars. In addition to major department and clothing stores—Emporium, I. Magnin, J. Magnin, Roos Brothers, Livingstons, and Hastings—Stanford Shopping Center provided the basics: a Purity grocery store, Woolworth's, Donnelly's Hardware, a thrift store, a shoe repair shop, a bakery, and several restaurants, including Woodlands and Sandy's Kitchen, and, in a foreshadowing of a later California lifestyle, Eat-Rite and Slenderella. (Roos Brothers abandoned downtown Palo Alto to be the first store to open to the public, with J. Magnin soon after.) Major shopping centers farther south soon followed, including San Jose's Valley Fair (1956), Sunnyvale Plaza (1957), and San Antonio Shopping Center in Mountain View (1957).[64]

Signs here at the front of the "Mall Shops" (facing El Camino Real) point to the shopping center's two major restaurants, Woodlands and Blums. STANFORD NEWS SERVICE

Except for the ribbon cutting for Roos Brothers, the center's first completed building, in fall 1955, Sterling's staff insisted that Stanford in general, and Sterling in particular, remain in the background. Openings, news releases, and publicity were handled by the stores. (Pete Allen, who succeeded Fred Glover as director of the university's News Service, wanted to avoid news reports associating such commercial interests with news about academic plans and programs.)[65]

A MASTER PLAN FOR STANFORD
SKIDMORE, OWINGS & MERRILL

Hutchison's 1951 report, especially its recommendation of large residential communities in the foothills and its promotion of a shopping center, stirred public comment and newspaper headlines. Stanford's faculty, alumni, and neighbors pressed the Sterling administration for more details than could be gleaned from the university's brief press releases. Yet while Elmore Hutchison had fortified trustee interest in land development and had validated many of the legal and pragmatic questions raised by Sterling's staff, he was not up to creating a sweeping master plan. Hutchison was unable to provide further planning advice, being too absorbed with engineering and topographical studies for roads, utilities, drainage, and other services for projects already underway.[66]

"Time is in our favor, as more and more of the available [non-Stanford] property around us is used," Brandin told an Alumni Association interviewer early in 1953. "We must be sure that what we do is right from the University's standpoint."[67]

In March 1953, on Brandin's recommendation, the trustees appointed the architectural-engineering firm of Skidmore, Owings & Merrill (SOM) to provide a master plan for potential

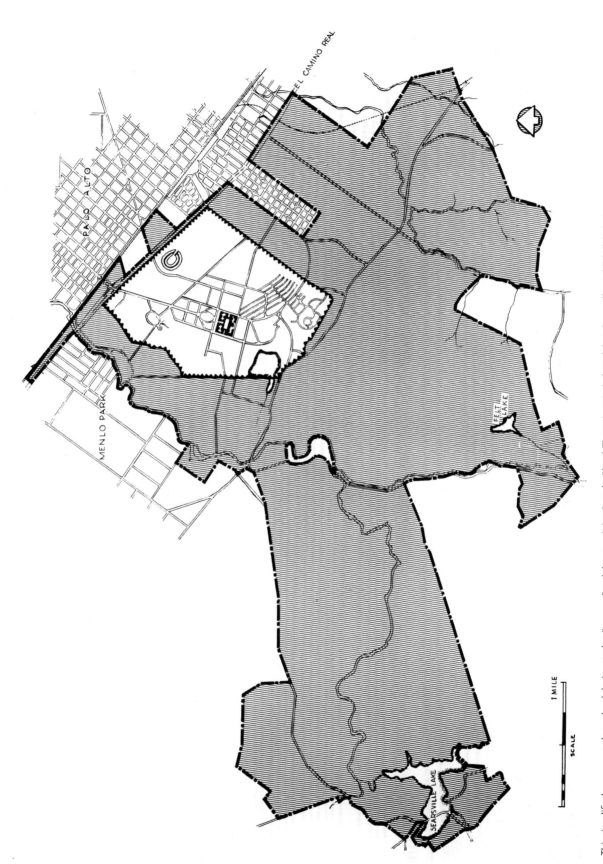

This simplified 1950s map shows land designated as "campus" and the remaining "surplus" land. The university's three lakes, Searsville and Felt (labeled) and Lagunita (on campus), can be seen, in white. The bulbous white "S" along Alpine Road is not a lake but Stanford Weekend Acres, a residential area developed in the 1920s on non-Stanford land in unincorporated San Mateo County.   STANFORD NEWS SERVICE

PALO ALTO

MENLO PARK

EL CAMINO REAL

FELT LAKE

SEARSVILLE LAKE

1 MILE

SCALE

development of all of Stanford's surplus lands. This nationally known firm was favored because of its capacity to carry out large projects, among them the 1939–40 New York World's Fair, the extensive facilities used by the wartime Manhattan Project in Oak Ridge, Tennessee, and a 4,000-acre site for Ford Motor Company in Detroit. Partners Louis Skidmore and Nathaniel Owings articulated four architectural design principles that appealed to university officials: group projects, innovative designs, social change, and "showmanship."[68]

The university's commission—to map out and plan development of nearly 6,000 bucolic acres—must have been mouthwatering. Skidmore, Owings & Merrill boasted that their plan would provide "the maximum flexibility in developing the University properties to attain the optimum balance between the sociological, aesthetic, and political considerations and with the maximum economic benefits to the University."[69]

The working draft of the master plan, overseen by engineer John Merrill, was completed in August 1953, with the final report submitted in September. Much of the 1953 study, in fact, focused on the shopping center, but SOM estimated that Stanford could build at least 9,000 houses on quarter- to four-acre lots (thus contributing dramatically to an estimated 80,000 new houses reportedly needed in the booming greater Bay Area). They recommended intensive development of 2,933 foothill acres into non-university residential communities and outlined which areas could be used for homes, stores, schools, shopping centers, recreation, churches, civic centers, and a new network of roads for a new residential population of around 40,000.[70]

In their interim report, SOM gave a green light to Brandin's Stanford Oaks project with Harry Arnold and endorsed immediate development of an additional 332-acre development proposed by Arnold's company in the southeast corner of Stanford lands, near Los Altos, straddling Foothill Road near its intersection with the railroad tracks. This area (site of current Gunn High School, the VA Hospital, and acreage devoted to the research park), they said, would fill the need for housing "employees of the industrial plants to be located on Stanford land, and to fill a long-felt need for housing University employees, both faculty and administrative." Assuming such employees to be less affluent than those interested in Stanford Oaks, these more modest homes were aimed at a lower price bracket ($12,000 to $15,000). (This was never built, but Arnold would be involved in the later Stanford Hills project, in 1957–59.)[71]

In addition to extensive residential zones and the shopping center, SOM also supported Brandin's concept of adjacent business and professional zones (the future Welch Road area of medical and professional offices). Interestingly, their recommendations limited the industrial park to its 1954 size of a few hundred acres.

Sterling, his staff, and his faculty advisory committee suspected that the report provided answers meant to please and support a trending trustee viewpoint. "My staff and I were somewhat under-whelmed by the consultants," Sterling later recalled. "When we plied them with questions, they sought to provide answers which would please us. It was experience such as this which persuaded me that there are few if any 'experts,' only 'professionals.'"[72]

Sterling's staff worried that they required a more precise definition of campus vs. surplus land needs and set to work to gather information to counterbalance SOM's residential recommendations. General Secretary David S. Jacobson, who oversaw university fundraising, had pressed Sterling to publicly clarify the amount of land reserved for educational purposes. The faculty advisory committee, mired in what they viewed as "misinterpretations of signals," had struggled

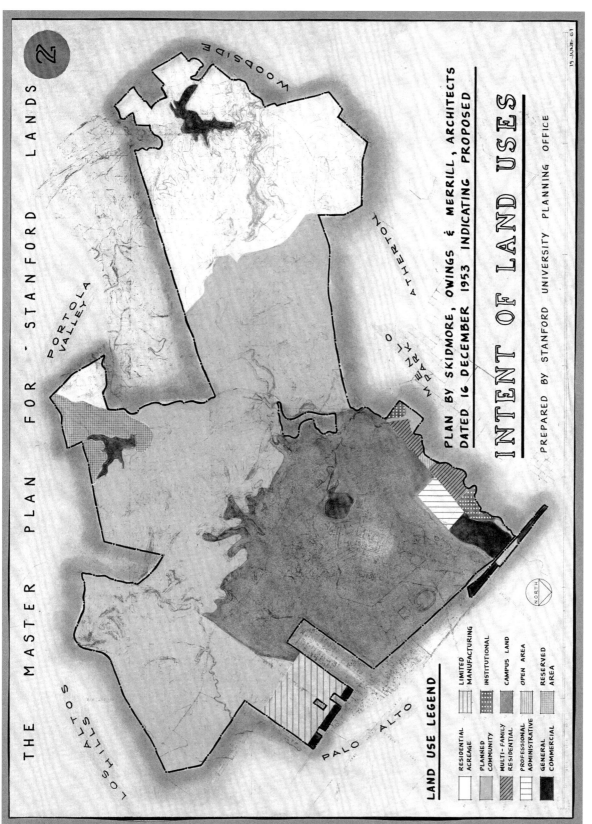

THE MASTER PLAN FOR STANFORD LANDS

2

PLAN BY SKIDMORE, OWINGS & MERRILL, ARCHITECTS
DATED 16 DECEMBER 1953 INDICATING PROPOSED

INTENT OF LAND USES

PREPARED BY STANFORD UNIVERSITY PLANNING OFFICE

19 JUNE 61

LAND USE LEGEND

RESIDENTIAL ACREAGE		LIMITED MANUFACTURING
PLANNED COMMUNITY		INSTITUTIONAL
MULTI-FAMILY RESIDENTIAL		CAMPUS LAND
PROFESSIONAL ADMINISTRATIVE		OPEN AREA
GENERAL COMMERCIAL		RESERVED AREA

WOODSIDE

PORTOLA VALLEY

ATHERTON

MENLO PARK

PALO ALTO

LOS ALTOS

NORTH

This 1953 "Intent of Land Uses" plan, *with north facing down*, illustrates Skidmore, Owings & Merrill's recommendations for developing nearly 6,000 Stanford acres. Campus lands had already expanded to include the planned medical school, some of the lower hills (where an early site for the linear accelerator was proposed), and eastward toward what became the industrial park. The outlying areas across much of the south were slated to be residential developments, including a massive "planned community" (in light gray) that would include services such as schools, churches, stores, and fire stations. (This version of the December 1953 SOM map was prepared, in color, in 1961 by the Planning Office.)   STANFORD UNIVERSITY ARCHIVES

thus far to convince the trustees and consultants that Stanford needed acreage for growth of academic programs. Sterling asked them to review the 1953 draft report, then gave them a boost by adding Dean of Engineering Fred Terman to the committee. Terman took charge of a new Campus Size and Boundaries subcommittee. The result was a vigorous discussion of how much land should be set aside as academic reserve versus how much should be developed and in what way.[73]

The subcommittee's report, written largely by Terman, was highly critical of the SOM master plan, which seemed little concerned with the educational mission of the university. "They [SOM] have shown an understandable tendency to think of the Stanford lands as a vast, potential subdivision which incidentally has a university occupying some of the area," the subcommittee's June 1954 review bluntly stated. "There seems to be an over-concern with planning Stanford lands to follow the trends indicated by other developers, rather than accepting the challenge to deal originally and imaginatively with the land that is at Stanford's disposal." (The industrial park, which Terman felt had stronger ties to the academic program than other land use recommendations, also was neglected by SOM.)[74]

Despite the subcommittee's advice, the trustees adopted the Skidmore, Owings & Merrill Master Plan in principle at their September 1954 meeting but concluded that the plan contained elements they would not pursue and assured the advisory committee that faculty concerns would be considered in subsequent land development decisions. Members of the trustees' Land Development Committee, however, remained interested in and alert to proposals, large and small, for residential developments.[75]

Despite—or perhaps due to—its limitations, the SOM planning process proved particularly

important in prompting trustees to rethink the concept of academic reserve and to consider the academic value of the industrial park. In 1955, the board reserved approximately 3,780 acres for educational use. By 1960, at the urging of the Faculty Advisory Committee and its Subcommittee on Campus Boundaries, among others, the acreage reserved for educational use was increased to 4,800.[76]

In June 1955, the board also adopted a policy that there would be no construction on hilltops and ridges that form skylines or on the slopes of the foothills that rise behind Foothill Road (Junipero Serra Boulevard) and furnish the "back drop" of the main campus.[77]

STANFORD UNINCORPORATED

As long-term leases were being negotiated in 1953, Sterling's staff and the Board of Trustees faced the need to quickly provide basic utilities, such as electricity, gas, sewer, and water, to the leased parcels. The mixed reactions of the Palo Alto City Council and city manager to Stanford's shopping center development and their possible rejection of annexation posed a considerable roadblock.

In July, a special meeting was held in the San Francisco office of Colbert Coldwell, who was joined by Alf Brandin, University General Counsel Robert Minge Brown, and John Rodgers and Lawrence Lackey of Skidmore, Owings & Merrill. The group evaluated three alternatives for Stanford lands: 1) remain as is, as unincorporated county land, and attempt to provide utilities as it did for other portions of the campus; 2) remain unincorporated, but encourage annexation of selected parcels by adjoining municipalities, particularly Palo Alto; or 3) incorporate on its own as a separate municipality or municipalities.[78]

Coldwell, hoping to find the alternative that

would result in the lowest taxes, thought Stanford already had a nucleus of municipal services and could therefore be expanded economically into an incorporated municipality—an unprecedented move for a university. Brandin disagreed, pointing out that while Stanford did have police and fire departments, they were so different from those of a city that he doubted they would be adequate. Brown noted the potential conflict of interest of having residential representatives, some university affiliated and some not, on different and perhaps opposing decision-making bodies—that is, as a municipal government, on the one hand, and university trustee, administrative, and faculty bodies on the other. Also, many older students would be able to vote and could be a significant element in the electorate. It also was noted that it would be too cumbersome for Stanford, straddling two counties, to obtain utility services through the formation of various separate utility districts.[79]

The Skidmore representatives were especially worried about timing. While obtaining gas and electrical access through Pacific Gas & Electric could be done relatively easily, getting water and sewer service to the shopping center quickly was vital to stay on schedule. Incorporation and special utility districts were time-consuming affairs at the very least.

Stanford remained unincorporated. The group recommended that the university move ahead with talks with Palo Alto officials, based on either annexation or contracting for specific services.

LIGHT INDUSTRY THAT WOULDN'T BE A "NUISANCE"

Some mark the beginning of Stanford Industrial Park (renamed Stanford Research Park in 1984) with the 1953 opening of the Varian Associates building, but this experimental industrial zone did not "open" so much as evolve, changing shape, size, and purpose during its first decade.[80]

Throughout much of the 1950s, no concerted effort was made to promote a uniquely high technology "research park" concept. Sterling's administration was fiercely proud of having no brochure, no salesmen, and no advertising program devoted to developing any of its properties.

University officials knew that the industrial area plan was unusual, Pete Allen wrote in 1954 to an inquiring editor of *Architectural Forum*. Unlike the typical developer, Stanford made no effort to lure in "a bell-wether plant," Allen wrote, and made no "ballyhoo of any kind" with offers of bargain land or special deals. Indeed,

In 1954, nearly a year after Varian Associates completed its first building, landscaping was still nonexistent. Soon after this photo, Varian enlarged the facility and added extensive landscaping. More Varian buildings were later added along Hansen Way. SHAPERO / STANFORD NEWS SERVICE

Bounded by Barron Park (left) and the curved railroad tracks, Stanford's Lot 41 was designated an "industrial zone" in 1951, and a small portion set aside for Varian Associates. Eastman Kodak followed (1953) on Lot 42. In this ca. 1955 photograph, Page Mill Road runs up the middle and out of the photo, while Junipero Serra Boulevard (Foothill Road) can be seen curving around at the top. The university's Ryan Lab, on Stanford Avenue, and a Palo Alto city reservoir's square cap can be seen near the top middle of the image. (Faculty housing had yet to expand into this area.) HATFIELD AERIAL SURVEYS / STANFORD UNIVERSITY ARCHIVES

Stanford not only did not cut deals—it drove a hard bargain. "We know of no other light industry area in the country with higher restrictions," yet prospective leaseholders continued to come in unasked. "We are not giving the area a high-powered promotional build up," concluded Allen. "It is selling itself." Although the original 40 acres had quickly expanded to nearly 225 acres, Allen admitted that the industrial park was "a stepchild" to the university's focus on opening the shopping center.[81]

Brandin later claimed that he had developed the idea of tucking the industrial area into the eastern corner of campus, but Eldridge Spencer, as early as 1946, had envisioned commercial-industrial use of this corner of land, framed by El Camino Real and the Southern Pacific Railroad spur to Los Gatos. In 1947, Spencer outlined park-like settings for a possible mixed-use area rising from El Camino to Foothill Road (later Junipero Serra Boulevard), along Page Mill Road, and advocated a 100- to 300-foot El Camino greenbelt, on Stanford's side, from Menlo Park to South Palo Alto. He also promoted the idea of a significant street realignment of Page Mill Road to connect it to Oregon Avenue.[82]

Brandin was masterful at attracting industrial leaseholders. In an unusual act of certitude, with two potential leaseholders but no paid lease in hand, the Board of Trustees in April 1950 had authorized Brandin to begin constructing streets and installing utilities for Lot 41. Hansen Way (named for recently deceased Stanford physics Professor William W. Hansen, a founding director of Varian Associates) was constructed soon after. "Light industry will be permitted," Sterling stated to the press that October, "but nowhere would it be permitted to detract from residential values."[83]

Varian Associates, a San Carlos electronics firm with close ties to university faculty, became Stanford's first industrial tenant when it signed

a 10-acre lease on October 1, 1951, for a prepaid rent of $8,000 per acre for 99 years (until the 1970s, leases throughout the industrial park were prepaid). It was more than a nod at El Camino's nickname of "Electronics Avenue."

The Varian tenancy, like Arnold's Stanford Oaks lease, was something of a test case. Leasing policies, and other practicalities like utilities, had yet to be worked out when the leasing was discussed. Nor was attracting additional leasehold tenants to this parcel a sure thing; thousands of acres of orchard and pastureland were available for purchase in neighboring towns. Page Mill Road was a two-lane road, bordered by cow pastures and ditches seasonally filled with water. Brandin's second 1950 prospect, Stecher-Traung Lithograph Corporation of Rochester, New York, soon backed out, worried that the company would not be able to attract financing to build on leased land.[84] Varian had no such qualms. The company's engineers and physicists wanted a location close to campus and, since they could not afford to buy land, welcomed the leasing arrangement. They also benefited, in early 1951, from a $1.5 million loan for construction and equipment from the U.S. Reconstruction Finance Corporation.[85]

At this point, Stanford's concept was less high tech than low impact. "In the original planning," Brandin recalled several years later, the acres set aside were for "light industry that wouldn't be a 'nuisance.'" Varian's enthusiasm led the company to expand its proposed site to 16 acres. "This was preposterous," said Brandin, "but it made us sit up and take notice."[86]

Eastman Kodak, looking for a site for a film processing plant, became the second industrial tenant, expressing interest in September 1952 and signing its lease the following March. The original Eastman Kodak 1953 lease was for 10 acres at $12,000 per acre per year, prepaid for a term of 50 years with a renewal option for 25 years.

In 1955, Kodak's West Coast processing lab on Page Mill Road typified the utilitarian style of the original buildings that would, by 1956, be called the Stanford Industrial Park.   STANFORD NEWS SERVICE

Since subsequent industrial leases were for 99-year terms, the board extended the Eastman Kodak lease from its original term to 99 years in June 1954, when Eastman Kodak leased another parcel of 4.79 acres for the longer term.[87]

Facilitated by City Manager Jerome Keithley, Palo Alto agreed to supply utilities, through annexation, to the first, relatively small parcel leased to Varian Associates (and later Eastman Kodak site) just as Menlo Park was agreeing to annex Stanford Oaks.[88]

Keithley's cooperation had limits, however. Palo Alto and Stanford haggled over how much land the city would annex—Palo Alto wanted more acres than university officials were willing to give up. Palo Alto was also sparring over the shopping center site, refusing service there. An agreement was worked out, but Keithley made it clear that any future annexation of larger parcels, like the shopping center's Lot 1 or potentially hundreds of acres of residential developments, required considerably more time for planning and negotiation.[89] Annexation issues, like leasing policy, would take the rest of the decade to work out.

Strong personal relations existed between Varian's officers and university officials. (Three founding board members were Stanford professors, with close ties to founders Russell and Sigurd Varian.) With strong views about a park-like setting for their company, Varian Associates had already hired modernist architect Erich Mendelsohn. Plans were completed in September 1951, a month before the lease was confirmed. The design included buildings, landscaping, parking, and proposed utility needs. It appears that there was "little guidance or resistance from the University," writes historian Henry Lowood. "Practical requirements preceded rigid planning guidelines, which in fact did not yet exist." No doubt, as the favored tenant in this industrial zone experiment, Varian was given considerable leeway.[90]

Conscious of public concern about the noise, soot, smells, and the "sea of asphalt" associated with industrial zones, Brandin emphasized that at Stanford, "light" industry meant no smokestacks or elevated towers. When Varian's final design for a second building included a small stack, Brandin persuaded Varian co-founder Edward Ginzton to remove it. That this did not occur until construction was underway, however, suggests that the process was still in flux. The university would not

General Electric's Microwave Laboratory was drawn to a location near Varian's microwave research buildings. The proximity of Stanford's Microwave Laboratory, nearby on campus, was an additional attraction.   RUSSELL ILLIG / STANFORD NEWS SERVICE

interfere with tenant selection of architect or with the overall design but, Brandin now insisted, Stanford maintained the right of final approval. When it opened in 1953, Varian's nearly 40,000-square-foot building was welcomed by the *Palo Alto Times* as a "clean, smokeless much-desired plum of industry."[91]

The Business Office now enforced a low-density setting in the industrial zone. Buildings were sited with deep setbacks, with no more than 40 percent of the leased lot occupied by the building and adequate off-street parking buffered from street view by landscaping. Lawns would flow from one leaseholder to the next, uninterrupted by fences. No advertising or obstructive signs were allowed. The overall look echoed Lewis Mumford and Ted Spencer's early recommendations regarding green space and extensive use of landscaping. University staff soon called this approach "Alf Brandin's Theory of Lawns."[92]

Stanford's cautious and demanding approach to land development simply did not make good business sense to some prominent local real estate developers. William Kelley, of Hare, Brewer and Kelley, found Stanford "not particularly imaginative." He suggested to the Board of Trustees in 1955 that his firm (Portola Development Company) could better care for the university's interests than Sterling's business manager—including ways to bypass Palo Alto's City Council and Planning Commission. Sterling replied to Kelley that the university would manage its lands as it was doing. (Kelley and his sons remained unconvinced.)[93]

Nor did the esthetics of the designs represented in the industrial park always impress influential architectural critics. While its 40 percent ground coverage rule, mandatory landscaping, and green setbacks represented "higher standards than in conventional developments, very few of the structures can be described as handsome," wrote the outspoken San Francisco architectural critic Allan Temko, and "some are extremely coarse." Nevertheless, Temko admitted that those who worked in the industrial park appreciated the pleasant setting as well as the prestigious location.[94]

Buildings 4 (left), 2 (center), and 1 (a portion visible at far right) of Hewlett-Packard's new headquarters on Page Mill Road, were designed by prominent Palo Alto architect and Stanford alumnus Birge Clark. North-facing clerestory windows maximize natural light. Construction began in 1957. HEWLETT-PACKARD / STANFORD UNIVERSITY ARCHIVES

Despite warnings from realtors about design restrictions and trustee fears that leased land would be unattractive to potential industrial tenants, Stanford's site-specific criteria became a key attraction. Brandin pointed to his initial encounter with an Eastman Kodak official, then scouting a West Coast site. "He wasn't interested, but would come over," Brandin recounted in 1958. "I decided if he was going to waste my time, I'd waste his." Brandin took his time telling him the history of Senator Stanford's land grant, about the endowment and its problems. "I told him we would insist that any plant conform to our strict zoning. We would have to approve architectural plans. We would demand special parking provisions. We would be tough to deal with." The Eastman Kodak official was convinced. "If you're going to be so tough," he told Brandin, "this is what we want. We're going to be sure other people who come here will have to meet the same high standards."[95] Leases with two publishing houses, Houghton-Mifflin and Scott-Foresman, followed in 1954, as did leases with Sylvania, General Electric, and Hewlett-Packard.

When, in 1954, Hewlett-Packard Company (HP) leased a parcel up Page Mill Road for its headquarters, it became, with Varian, a flagship tenant. It was becoming clear that some tenants were a more natural fit than others, given Stanford's strong interest in electronics. David Packard, who joined the university's Board of Trustees that year, also helped promote the technology concept. Sylvania's Electronics Defense Laboratory and General Electric's Microwave Laboratory were attracted by Varian's microwave research facility, with Stanford's Microwave Laboratory nearby on campus. Lockheed also became a major tenant.

"By insisting on strict, high standards," Brandin could boast with happy hindsight in 1958, "Stanford has now attracted 19 industries in plants worth about $25 million." More leases followed. Stanford's "Industrial Park" was sufficiently successful that a model and a movie about it were exhibited that year at the Brussels World's Fair.[96]

Even as the Stanford Industrial Park was recognized internationally, the university's strategy was described as "a backward, left-handed, ridiculous approach to the highly competitive and scientifically studied problems of attracting industry," according to the *San Francisco Chronicle*'s business and finance columnist. It was a "weird success," he concluded.[97]

With such criticisms in mind, Brandin jested to an audience of realtors at a 1958 national convention in San Francisco that "about all you could say for it was that [Stanford's approach] worked—sensationally. We didn't know what the hell we were doing . . . If we knew how *hard* it was to get industry," he joked, "that you've got to give tax exemptions, cheap labor and free buildings, we probably wouldn't have tried. We were as tough as we could be and we couldn't discourage them."[98]

Although Sterling had turned over to Brandin the management details of non-academic land development in 1952, he made himself available,

even without forewarning, whenever important potential tenants were under consideration. Brandin relied on the president's charisma, and enjoyed recounting the day he asked Sterling, with a few minutes' notice, if he could bring Lockheed President Robert E. Gross to the President's Office. When they arrived, Sterling, busy working at his desk, greeted them informally in stocking feet and subsequently charmed the Lockheed lease into being.[99]

Sterling also joined Brandin at many Palo Alto City Council and Planning Commission meetings. He never objected to appearing, even when the council seemed intent on making a point of putting the university in its place by placing Stanford-related items toward the bottom of the agenda. Without Sterling, "we couldn't have gotten along as well as we did before those city council meetings," Brandin later remembered. "He had a marvelous sense of timing."[100]

Although Birge Clark was known around Palo Alto for his Spanish colonial revival architecture, his design for Hewlett-Packard's headquarters, seen here in 1963, was modern. The visitors' entrance, off Building 3, featured a stylish roof overhang.   STANFORD UNIVERSITY ARCHIVES

For the interior of Hewlett-Packard's headquarters, Clark created open-concept office and manufacturing spaces; clerestory windows and pitched roofs added a spacious feeling and ample light.

STANFORD LANDS—PALO ALTO FARM

1885	6,967 acres	Palo Alto Farm at time of Founding Grant
1893	8,448 acres	Acreage purchased by Sen. Stanford, 1876–93
1908	8,248 acres	Revised survey after boundary adjustments
1950–70	8,800 acres	Estimated acreage for land development studies
2022	8,180 acres	Current official university acreage (net of condemnations)

Adapted from Appendix A.

Fred Terman, as dean of engineering (1946–58) and provost (1955–65), played a crucial role in the industrial park's development, pointing out that the university received more in gifts and grants from technology companies on Stanford land than from actual lease income. Sterling encouraged Terman, a member of many local technology company boards, to line up possible leases for the park. "Alf Brandin saw the point very quickly," Terman later recalled, "and very soon thereafter, if you weren't a high-technology company, you had a hell of a time coaxing him to give you a lease."[101]

Much has been written about Terman's role as a "godfather" to the later emergence of "Silicon Valley" (a term not commonly used until 1972). However, as professor, dean, and provost, Terman always focused on Stanford. As an administrator and faculty voice, Terman was especially effective in promoting the specification, protection, and growth of total acreage allotted to the academic portion of Stanford lands. His interest in the industrial park was closely related to his concept of Stanford's academic development. Numerous engineering and science departments subsequently benefited directly from income from the Honors Cooperative Program (a novel program allowing local companies to send top employees to study for graduate degrees, at double the tuition rate). Companies also provided research funds, subcontracts, fellowships, and faculty salary support. This outside funding loosened up university funding that could be channeled into the humanities and social sciences. The relationships also provided a creative environment, outlets for commercial applications for faculty research, faculty consulting opportunities, and employment for graduating students.[102]

Industrial and commercial leasing remained a long-standing trustee concern throughout Sterling's presidency, and committee debates over lease possibilities and options were intense. In February 1956, Herman Phleger pressed the trustees to limit future leases to 50 rather than 99 years, as was then the custom. While more prepaid rent might be secured up front from a

99-year lease, he argued, such long leases turned control of large areas surrounding the university over to the lessees for nearly a century. "Considering that the University is only 65 years old, and the great changes in it and in this area that have taken place during this period, it must be anticipated that during the next 99 years the changes will be beyond our clear comprehension." Given the success of their recent developments and steady enhancement of real estate values, he pointed out, it did not seem necessary to offer leases beyond 50 years to induce tenants to make necessary improvements, protect them from inflation, and give them the benefit of enhanced property values.[103]

John Cushing, chair of the Special Committee on Land Development, and real estate advisor Colbert Coldwell strongly disagreed with Phleger, urging the board to continue the tradition of 99-year leases as a necessary attraction to potential leaseholders. Other members of the committee, however, agreed with Phleger after comparing income expected from investing the upfront rental proceeds with the significantly higher rental value likely at the end of the lease. The committee strongly advised a new maximum lease term of 50 years, but the board stuck with the authoritative Coldwell, voting to continue 99-year terms.

Three years later, in February 1959, board President David Packard appointed a special committee to review land use policies, particularly leasing and types of development. After a detailed nine-month financial review of the past 10 years, the review committee again strongly recommended that, with the university's *future* interests in mind as well as immediate financial gains, all subsequent leases should not exceed 50 years.[104]

Land committee chair James Crafts openly disagreed, attempting to keep the board on track with full development for immediate

gains. Sterling's staff was emphasizing current financial needs of an expanding academic program, he said, and he was convinced that land development was the answer, not extensive fundraising. Countering Brandin's optimism, he told fellow trustees that prospective tenants were not, in his view, waiting in line to lease Stanford land. Too many interested companies ultimately located elsewhere even though Brandin had experimented with shorter leasing times and more flexible leasing arrangements. (Using a simple equation of number of inquiries vs. signed leases, Crafts did not explore what other factors may have been involved in such decisions, nor whether these other companies were up to Stanford's now deliberately selective approach.)[105]

The full board wavered. Coldwell continued to promote the existing 99-year policy. But, when pressed by the now equally influential Packard, the board, in January 1960, partially reversed itself to follow the advisory committee's recommendation: Hereafter, non-residential leases were limited to 51 years, unless a special case was made otherwise.[106]

As it turned out, Phleger and Brandin proved correct: The university attracted tenants at prepaid 51-year rentals, earning an immediate income nearly equivalent to those earned from 99-year terms. Also, as Phleger, Terman, and Planning Director Ted Spencer predicted, by the close of Sterling's presidential term, there was an increasing need to both rethink industrial park space and reallocate land for academic purposes.

READJUSTMENTS TO COME

By mid-decade, the university had a master plan, keystone companies in the Stanford Industrial Park, and anchor stores nearly complete at the Stanford Shopping Center. Experiments in

This expansive 1963 view from the Hewlett-Packard Visitor Center looks south/southwest to Stanford's rolling hills, including the controversial Coyote Hill area (foreground hills at left). The Santa Cruz Mountains are in the far distance. The university's mid-1950s plans to develop large portions of its hills would be reappraised during the 1960s. STANFORD UNIVERSITY ARCHIVES

commercial residential housing were underway. Sterling, with multiple mechanisms now in place to oversee land development, turned away more than one real estate company keen on taking over construction and management of the university's rural acreage.

But the well-publicized success of these initial steps belied long-running internal debates. More challenges and difficult decisions and readjustments were yet to come. Was unaffiliated (non-faculty) residential housing truly a viable option? Was expansion of the industrial park preferable? Should the university more aggressively expand

academic reserves? Could Stanford protect its land legacy? The next few years presented defining moments.

Even the development-minded Alf Brandin had struck a note of caution when interviewed in late 1955 by Falcon O. Baker of the *Saturday Evening Post*: "If this had been a routine real estate development, the job would have been a cinch. We would have cut it up into lots, sold out fast and dashed off to Palm Springs to enjoy the profits, but Stanford can't run away. If we make a mistake, we'll have to suffer with it for ninety-nine years."[107]

6

REAPPRAISING STANFORD'S LAND DEVELOPMENT

By 1955, Stanford University's land development program was a national conversation piece. "Out in California, one of America's leading institutions of higher learning has plunged into an exceedingly unacademic role," stated the *Saturday Evening Post* in December 1955. "This is no papier-mâché tabletop affair, but a real brick-and-mortar community where some 40,000 people will work, play, shop and sleep," author Falcon O. Baker enthused. "The city is rising now on Stanford's 9000-acre property on the Peninsula," he noted, with a recently opened shopping center, noiseless and smokeless research and manufacturing in its industrial park, and families (unaffiliated with the university) already living in costly homes.[1]

Baker breathlessly described how the owner of this blue-chip property was finally giving up its horse and cattle pasturelands to house some of the San Francisco Bay Area's rapidly growing population. But if Baker was accurate about the recommendations outlined in the 1953–54 Skidmore, Owings & Merrill (SOM) master plan, he was quite wrong about how much of that model city of nine neighborhoods was, in fact, being built. Only Stanford Oaks, a small, disconnected 24-acre parcel across San Francisquito Creek begun before SOM's plan was drafted, was open to home buyers. Most of the rest of the master plan's proposed residential recommendations would be reappraised and eventually scrapped over the next decade. *(On the master plan, see Chapter 5.)*

Baker, like many watching the American suburban boom, did not reckon with the impact on Stanford property of government condemnations of land, local annexation politics, and dueling goals of neighboring cities. Nor did Baker, like SOM, understand the physical nature and extent of the university's academic ambitions.

By the time Baker's article was being read across the country, the federal government had taken land for a new Veterans Hospital and the state of California had announced its intention to run a freeway somewhere through Stanford land. Over the remainder of Sterling's presidency,

< This aerial view of a large portion of Stanford's 8,800 acres, taken in 1962 from above Stanford Stadium, looks across the main campus toward the university's rolling hills and Jasper Ridge. Portola Valley, Woodside, and the Santa Cruz Mountains' ridgeline are beyond. The Stanford Linear Accelerator Center would soon be built on the broad plain, off Sand Hill Road (upper right).

PALO ALTO AIR PHOTO CO. / STANFORD UNIVERSITY ARCHIVES

131

condemnation attempts threatened to remove hundreds of additional acres from the university's land legacy, reflecting the goals and assumptions of politicians and neighbors in stark contrast to the university's educational mission.

Annexation, like condemnation, also became a major development issue, a public relations matter as much as a technical one. Sterling's challenge remained: How to articulate—to faculty, students, alumni, trustees, and neighbors (both friendly and antagonistic)—what role the land development program played in maintaining and enhancing the university's fundamental educational mission.

How the Sterling administration dealt with government land condemnations, city and county annexations, and off-campus expectations is a significant part of the university's land development story. Many of the decisions made during his presidency are fundamental to the shape of today's Stanford campus.

CONDEMNED
ACCEPTING A VETERANS HOSPITAL AND A FREEWAY

With the Peninsula's population rapidly expanding, the university's undeveloped lands were vulnerable to demands for land by federal, state, and local government agencies exercising the right of eminent domain. By 1968, 665 acres had been condemned for "public use," more than half of the roughly 1,000 acres that would be developed for non-academic use during the Sterling administration.

The 1950 condemnation of 8.9 acres by San Mateo County for the new Oak Knoll Elementary School was a natural—it had been part of the experimental Stanford Oaks development and served those new homes and others nearby. Although the transfer to the county and school district required a lawsuit, necessary to permit

alienation of Stanford trust property, it was considered a "friendly" condemnation.

The decision to consent to condemnation rather than lease to the Menlo Park School District reflected the experimental nature of the residential development. Subsequent school sites on Stanford land (Escondido, L. M. Nixon, Gunn, and a proposed Sequoia High School District site) also would be treated as condemnations.

Two notable subsequent condemnations were neither friendly nor hostile but were simply unavoidable: 93 acres for a U.S. Veterans Administration Hospital and roughly 200 acres for an interstate freeway.

In 1954, the U.S. government instigated the first major condemnation of Stanford lands when the Veterans Administration (VA) announced its intent to take land for a 1,000-bed neuropsychiatric hospital. The agency already had a presence in the area, operating the Menlo Park VA Hospital, opened in 1924, as well as hospitals in San Francisco and Livermore. The VA's interest in augmenting its aging facilities had accelerated with news of the university's plans to relocate to the campus its own medical school and hospital from San Francisco. The agency initially had in mind a 200-acre parcel at the intersection of Page Mill Road and Junipero Serra Boulevard, well within Stanford's boundaries.[2]

With the VA announcement, the President's Office received a petition and a flurry of letters from faculty members, and Los Altos and Barron Park residents opposing a VA "insane asylum" anywhere on Stanford lands. (A significant component of the new hospital would be aimed at mental health services.) A drop in property values was one worry, but so, too, was a concern about community safety. "It will need only the raping or strangling of one coed or faculty wife anywhere on the campus community," one concerned professor wrote Sterling, "to give

The Palo Alto Veterans Hospital complex of 15 buildings, seen in 1971, stretches along Foothill Expressway. Its 93 acres were acquired from Stanford by the federal government in 1955 after two years of site negotiations. The hospital, designed by Welton Becket & Associates (architects of the Stanford Shopping Center), was opened in 1960. Horses graze on Stanford land in the foreground.   STANFORD NEWS SERVICE

Stanford an irretrievably black name among parents of potential students and affect its whole future course as a university."[3]

University trustees did not oppose the concept of a VA Hospital on the periphery of its lands. Even if they had, they probably could not prevent condemnation should the government press its power of eminent domain. It was the specific site that was concerning. They countered the agency's proposal with at least two other sites: one closer to El Camino Real, tucked in behind Varian Associates, and the one ultimately chosen, farther southeast on Junipero Serra Boulevard (Foothill Road) near Arastradero, in an area set aside in the Skidmore, Owings & Merrill 1953–54 master plan as part of the site of the next major unaffiliated residential housing development.[4]

As Sterling explained, in response to one complaint about the VA's desired Page Mill Road site, the university had no interest in creating a federal "island" in the middle of other university property. That acreage's financial value as an eventual extension for light industrial development meant the land loss would be both more costly to the university as lost potential lease income and more expensive to the federal government for condemnation reimbursement. (The price per acre had risen considerably with leases to Hewlett-Packard, Lockheed, and other industrial tenants down Page Mill Road.)[5]

In December 1954, the trustees authorized Sterling to negotiate with the VA for the friendly condemnation and sale of approximately 110 acres—ultimately 93 acres—at the alternative site along Junipero Serra Boulevard, near Arastradero Road and Matadero Creek. While the university would permanently lose this acreage, the trustees hoped to benefit from an injection of unrestricted funds at a time when these were not in plentiful supply. The university also negotiated a reallotment of services, increasing the proportion of beds dedicated to medical and surgical patients rather than neuropsychiatric or psychiatric patients as a basis for promoting interaction between the VA Hospital and Stanford's new medical school facilities.[6]

Another unavoidable government land condemnation was not so much unfriendly as it was problematic in location. With the area's postwar growth spurt, much-needed improvements to local highways followed, particularly along the San Francisco to San Jose corridor. Significant upgrades were being made to "Bloody Bayshore," the accident-prone two-lane U.S. Highway 101 that hugged the Bay along the Peninsula, with its stoplights and unprotected crossroads. By the mid-1950s, pressure was building for completion of a new four-lane interstate freeway to the west, similarly connecting San Francisco and San Jose. Work began in the City in 1955, with various proposals for a route through San Mateo and Santa Clara counties. Regardless of the route chosen, Stanford lands would be affected.

By 1957, the California Division of Highways had completed portions of the freeway into northern San Mateo County. Plans to proceed southward down historic El Camino Real had been scrapped, given vocal opposition from every city and town along the way. That April, the Highway Division finally revealed two alternative routes. (The state's plans were roughly sketched, causing city officials along the Peninsula to speculate on just what parts of their communities would be affected, but the Division's intent was clear.)

The Highway Division's favored route progressed along the western edges of Peninsula towns. In southern San Mateo County, it roughly followed Alameda de las Pulgas and Stanford's Junipero Serra Boulevard, skirting the university's growing industrial zone to meet the unused railroad tracks. Proceeding down the railroad right-of-way, it bisected Los Altos and headed down Fremont Avenue.

A more speculative ridgeline route, along Skyline Boulevard and Cañada Road, and to the west of Stanford's Searsville and Felt lakes, went through the town of Woodside. The Highway Division considered this less accessible "western"

route too far away from population centers to be cost-effective for drivers.[7]

Officials in San Mateo County cities, from Belmont to Menlo Park (Woodside excepted), were nearly united in opposing the eastern route, heavily favoring the western one as less destructive. Not so Palo Alto, largely unaffected by the physical toll of the freeway's construction down either route. City Manager Jerry Keithley argued that the freeway should be "as close as practical to Palo Alto," while Palo Alto planning commissioners stated that a Page Mill Road interchange any farther west than Junipero Serra Boulevard was simply too far away to attract drivers.[8]

A new compromise route was thrown into the mix later in 1957. Located to the east of Woodside, and Searsville and Felt lakes, it bisected the less developed hills of the town of Los Altos Hills, threatening its golf course. This rural route won strong support, especially from Menlo Park, Atherton, Woodside, and Los Altos—but not Los Altos Hills.[9]

No matter the route chosen, Stanford faced the loss of at least 200 acres along a 5-mile corridor for the roadway and three interchanges. The Junipero Serra Boulevard route impacted the campus proper, placing it along faculty housing areas and dividing the campus from additional academic reserve land on the adjacent hillsides. The compromise route ran through lands set aside in the Skidmore, Owings & Merrill master plan for development of some 1,500 residences. Throughout the public debate, university officials consistently stated that they preferred a route as far west as possible. They hoped to avoid partitioning academic lands and locating a major freeway next to faculty housing.[10]

As the Highway Division leaned toward the new compromise route, Los Altos Hills residents targeted the university in their fight to be heard by the Highway Division. In letters to the President's Office and to local newspapers, Stanford

The Peninsula's scenic, 57-mile-long Interstate 280 connects San Francisco to San Jose. Construction began in 1955 in San Francisco; one of its last major elements—San Jose's 280/101 interchange—was completed in 1981. The freeway's final siting took years of negotiation and reorientation from heavily populated areas to the hills. Stanford lost more than 200 acres to the state for the roadbed and three interchanges but avoided a major freeway adjacent to the main campus. Here it passes over the Stanford Linear Accelerator Center, ca. 1974.   PALO ALTO AIR PHOTO CO. / STANFORD NEWS SERVICE

was excoriated for exerting its influence. President Sterling's response to one such complaint, which accused Stanford of behind-the-scenes efforts targeting Los Altos Hills, was succinct:

> Stanford would not like to have the freeway on its property at all and has so stated. However, the University recognizes the importance of this road not only to the local community but to the Peninsula and the State. If it is inevitable that it cross our property, we are anxious that it be located as far west as is practicable in order to preserve the integrity of our lands.[11]

In reality, Sterling's administration was far less influential on final site selection than Los Altos Hills complaints assumed. Throughout the rest of

1957, from San Carlos to Sunnyvale, public hearings, planning commissions, expert witnesses, and civic groups like the Citizens Committee for Peninsula Highways argued against community disruption, favoring a more rural route. Relative costs to property owners and city tax bases were balanced against consumer (driver) costs; and social and environmental implications were weighed. Complaints by the much smaller, largely rural and upscale communities of Woodside and Los Altos Hills faced widespread public opposition from heavily populated cities threatened with the loss of hundreds of houses, along with schools, churches, and businesses in the path of the Highway Division's more urban path.[12]

By the time the compromise route through

Young Andrew Shilstone of Redwood City, son of a newspaper reporter, rides his tricycle across the unopened roadway south of the Woodside Road interchange for this section of Interstate 280 in late 1969. The next exit, ¾ mile away, is Sand Hill Road.
PALO ALTO HISTORICAL ASSOCIATION

this section was chosen, Stanford was reconsidering the ramifications of large-scale residential housing in the area. Given the proximity of the future highway, Alf Brandin instead attracted commercial tenants to the area along Sand Hill Road (near the future major interchange) for office buildings, including Addison-Wesley Publishing Company. These leases, in turn, established a higher value for the freeway acreage, raising the condemnation sale price the state had to pay for the freeway's right-of-way. (Sand Hill Road later became widely recognized as a major venture capital center of the United States.)[13]

Construction of this section of the freeway, with three interchanges—Page Mill, Alpine, and Sand Hill roads—finally began in late 1967. (Designated I-280 in 1964, it was dedicated as the Junipero Serra Freeway in 1967.) Meanwhile Stanford's academic reserve had expanded significantly. The new Stanford Linear Accelerator Center, constructed between 1962 and 1966, was dedicated in September 1967. The accelerator gallery ran nearly perpendicular to the freeway, with the roadway passing over it about midway on a preplanned overpass.

The 57.5-mile-long freeway, today considered one of California's most scenic, was finally completed through Cupertino in 1972, although a vital San Jose overpass linking I-280 to the 101 freeway remained, literally, in the air and unfinished until 1981.

The university continued to fight off other attempts to confiscate land. Santa Clara County attempted to condemn land near El Camino, within the industrial park, for a North County Courthouse and jail-holding facility. Instead, it was built in Palo Alto, across El Camino near Park Boulevard, not far from the California Avenue shopping district.[14] In 1961, the College of San Mateo (community college) informed the Board of Trustees that it was considering three different Stanford sites for a future campus. The sites, all near the future 280 freeway, ranged from 130 to 180 acres. The new campus, Cañada College, later was built in Redwood City.[15] The most consequential attempt to take Stanford land, the U.S. Army Corps of Engineers' campaign to take over more than 540 acres for a dam and recreational reservoir, is discussed later in this chapter.

RECONSIDERING RESIDENTIAL DEVELOPMENT

The Board of Trustees, in late 1954, was only vaguely aware of government interest in a Veterans Hospital site and a future interstate freeway when it approved, in principle, but not in detail, the plan Skidmore, Owings & Merrill (SOM) laid out for Stanford's "city in the hills." Even though immediate plans for the next non-affiliated housing development—along Foothill Road, near Arastradero—would be put on hold with the 1956 siting of the new VA Hospital, the residential element remained key to the land development plan.

Nevertheless, the trustees soon reconsidered the dimensions of Stanford's academic lands.

After discussions throughout 1955, prodded by faculty and Planning Office concerns, the board instructed SOM to set aside Areas 3, 4, and 5. Some 3,780 acres were now considered as the campus and academic reserve. This kept "the campus itself from becoming a 'tight little island' in the shadows of shopping centers and housing tracts," reported the *Stanford Daily*.[16]

The trustees, however, left thousands of acres (much of it used for hay and flower production, as well as livestock grazing) available for future development. Population studies suggested a tremendous need for housing on the Peninsula, and the university's property was eyed by real estate developers and neighboring city officials as one of the last large suitable areas. Property taxation remained a serious problem. Stanford's many agricultural leases came nowhere near the tax bill. (The 1955 lease of 2,292 acres to dairy-man Manuel Piers brought in $20,000 annually but property taxes on all Stanford lands were approaching $500,000.) It was likely, Alf Brandin told the *Daily*, that some "5,000" Stanford acres could be completely developed in 25 to 50 years. But, he assured the reporter, the results will be "esthetically, as well as commercially, first class."[17]

Indeed, the SOM master plan had recommended nine self-contained neighborhoods, each with a neighborhood elementary school, grocery and drug store, barber and beauty shops, shoe repair, dry cleaners, and laundry pickups, along with church sites, and small parks and playgrounds. Another 100 acres was set aside for garden-style apartments.[18]

Today's view across Stanford hills, looking west to the Santa Cruz Mountains, includes the Dish, a radio research facility completed in 1962. This area was earmarked by two land planning studies for residential housing of 9,000 homes—a "city in the hills"—in the early 1950s. Faculty responded that the area was needed for future academic research use. In 1955, the trustees voted to keep the campus "back drop," and other hilltops and ridges, free of any structures (they specifically granted an exception in 1958 for the Dish). In January 1960, they abandoned plans for extensive residential housing. SUNNY SCOTT

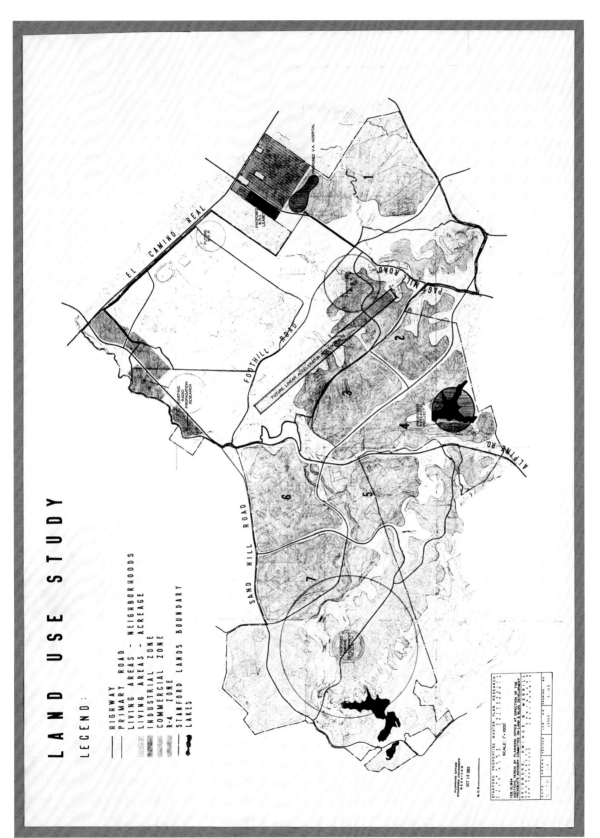

LAND USE STUDY

LEGEND:

——— HIGHWAY
——— PRIMARY ROAD
▨ LIVING AREAS — NEIGHBORHOODS
LIVING AREAS — ACREAGE
▨ INDUSTRIAL ZONE
▨ COMMERCIAL ZONE
R-4 ZONE
——— STANFORD LANDS BOUNDARY
● LAKES

After an earlier version of this 1953 Skidmore, Owings & Merrill plan recommended extensive residential housing (Areas 1 through 7), Sterling's faculty advisory committee hastened to add academic research sites in this February 1954 revision. An early proposed site for the 2-mile linear accelerator runs along Foothill Road; circles mark proposed research sites there and at Searsville Lake (far left) and Felt Lake (at bottom). Also shown is Stanford's first proposed site for a VA Hospital, in the industrial zone; the VA rejected it. The shopping center fronts El Camino (at top). The white "S" shape along Alpine Road is Stanford Weekend Acres, a non-university residential area developed in the 1920s. STANFORD UNIVERSITY ARCHIVES

Hoping to get ahead of the curve, in the 1950s, the Sequoia Union High School District decided it would condemn 40 acres near Sand Hill and Whiskey Hill roads for an additional high school to serve the growing needs of the proposed residential developments. (The courts approved the condemnation in 1961, and Stanford received $281,000. But 19 years later, when no such "city in the hills" had materialized and thus no justification could be made for a high school there, the university had to pay $1.1 million to regain its land.)[19]

The 1953–54 SOM master plan had quickly gathered influential critics even while in draft form—on campus and off. Well before the trustees approved the plan in principle, if conditionally, various portions of the plan were heavily criticized by the president's advisory Committee on Land and Building Development (CLBD) *(see Chapter 5)*. In response, the trustees in 1955 not only expanded the academic reserve but also announced a new policy: to prohibit construction of buildings in the area considered "the back drop" (the first slope) behind the campus and on the hilltops, ridges, and skylines of land within the campus boundaries. This would help "guarantee the rural and secluded atmosphere of the campus," reported the *Stanford Daily*.[20]

Faculty and alumni continued to worry about the impact of development on both the ambiance of the campus as a community and the future availability of land for academic purposes. New academic projects needing space were already underway. In April 1954, Stanford leased 11 acres at Alta Vista overlooking Lagunita (earlier, the home of Jane Stanford's brother Charles Lathrop) to the new Center for Advanced Study in the Behavioral Sciences (CASBS), funded by the Ford Foundation.[21] And serious discussions began in 1957 regarding at least two potential campus locations for a 2-mile-long, federally funded, linear accelerator proposed by the phys-

ics faculty. Also, biology and engineering faculty were busy documenting the importance of the Jasper Ridge area and the hills above Junipero Serra Boulevard for research and teaching. Strong relationships between faculty and industrial park tenants, with well-documented contributions to science and engineering programs, suggested expansion of industrial, rather than residential, zones.

Nevertheless, the university had not given up on the concept of large-scale non-affiliated residential housing. Palo Alto architect and alumnus Christopher Arnold, '53, carried out a prolonged "letters to the editor" debate with Stanford News Director Pete Allen in the *Palo Alto Times* in March 1957, sparked by the announcement of a 940-acre residential development between Alpine and Sand Hill roads. "Far-sighted planners," Arnold argued, considered SOM's proposed residential development of the foothills neither "a desirable planned community nor as a contribution to foothill landscape." He challenged SOM's proposal for large communities unaffiliated with the university and "with no focus, no balance, no reason for existence." Christopher Arnold found it difficult to believe that Stanford's supporters wanted the university to be "an enterprising real estate outfit." Would the visiting scholars tucked in at the new Center for Advanced Study in the Behavioral Sciences find themselves "in the middle of a sea of ranch style houses and grocery-loaded station wagons . . . ?"[22]

Back in 1950, university officials had welcomed the early interest of Harry Arnold's Peninsula Pacific Construction Company (PPCC). By April 1954, Arnold could boast of selling 25 of the projected 45 new houses at Stanford Oaks, now going for $35,000–$45,000 (more than three times the cost of the average Bay Area suburban home). Resistance to leaseholds was less than he expected, and he hoped to develop other parcels. While still building at the Menlo Park site, he had asked about 50-acre parcels behind the light industry area, SOM's Area 1, and, later, about 50- to 200-acre portions between Sand Hill and Alpine roads, SOM's Area 6. Stanford's persuasive real estate advisor Colbert Coldwell had been enthusiastic about residential development in these areas, especially acreage above the industrial zone. Arnold's Area 1 proposal, endorsed by SOM and Coldwell, was sidelined by the VA Hospital and ongoing interest in industrial tenants, but Area 6 offered more lucrative possibilities with higher-end homes in a foothill setting.[23]

The Board of Trustees had in hand expressions of interest from large-scale residential developers Del Webb and Joseph Eichler, among others. This interest provoked discussion of various options for residential development, from smaller ones along the lines of the Stanford Oaks development, to complex consortiums of investors that might include university funding. Other offers came in. A proposal from Utah Construction offered to remove the hazards from Stanford's idle quarry site above Page Mill Road in exchange for the remaining profitable sandstone (which it hoped to use on another highway construction project). Utah Construction also would improve the 131-acre site for residential use.[24] Negotiations on that project stalled while the

In 1955, Manuel Piers (left), who leased Stanford land for his Piers Dairy cows, and Business Manager Alf Brandin survey university acreage near Alpine Road leased to Suey Lum for aster flower growing. At the time, Stanford had nearly 3,500 acres leased for agricultural production. In the distance are the beginnings of the Ladera community. GENE TUPPER, *PALO ALTO TIMES* / STANFORD NEWS SERVICE

trustees debated who would pay for infrastructure, particularly installation of utilities.

Meanwhile, Brandin explored small sites farther up in the foothills near Searsville Lake, sites deemed too steep and inaccessible for anything but housing, and a comfortable distance from any possible academic needs of the sort suggested by Engineering Dean Fred Terman and the CLBD. Brandin targeted wooded hillside areas where rugged terrain was better suited to large lots of 2 to 4 acres, or "estate size" construction. In July 1954, Brandin set aside five such lots on about 17 acres between Mountain Home and Sand Hill roads, opposite the entrance to Searsville Lake, as a pilot project. When he offered the lots on the open market, however, he found owner/builders to be far more cautious about leasehold land there than they had been only months earlier. Brandin grew discouraged when he received only one show of interest after showing the property 32 times.[25]

Despite Brandin's discouraging experience in the more distant foothills, large estates in this area remained a part of the Sterling administration's vision. In 1956, Sterling gave picturesque presentations regarding Stanford's possible foothills developments. One enthusiastic listener was thrilled to learn of these plans, instead of the "glorified housing projects that so many of us originally feared. Probably no land in America will be more valuable for living sites twenty-five years from now than our 'rolling foothills,'" Roland Hauck wrote Sterling. "If their beauty is not conserved in some form of park it seems to me it can only be done by subdivision into estates as you have outlined."[26]

The gentle slopes of Area 6, between Sand Hill and Alpine roads, remained more attractive. Although Eichler had turned elsewhere, developing homes in the Ladera area and in Atherton, Del Webb proposed a planned community, with projected upscale residential sites surrounding

a new 125- to 150-acre private golf course with exclusive clubhouse, pool, and tennis courts. After months of deliberations and questions, the trustees decided to go small, asking SOM to break up Area 6 into multiple 50- to 100-acre development portions. (Brandin continued to discuss a major golf course–oriented residential plan as late as summer 1956; Webb gave up on Stanford after an unsuccessful bid to construct the Veterans Hospital a year later.)[27]

The Skidmore, Owings & Merrill firm continued to be particularly interested in Area 6, suggesting 1,876 home sites there. In March 1957, the university announced that the first 30 acres of a 940-acre tract laid out by SOM, to be called Stanford Hills, was underway, to be constructed by Arnold's PPCC. In August 1958, a month after the compromise route was finally selected for the interstate freeway, construction began on the first of 88 planned houses. Ultimately, 78 California ranch-style houses were built. The designs, by David Day and James Aced, passed the CLBD more easily than Arnold's earlier contributions. They were clearly meant to be upscale: the houses were laid out on three streets named for pioneer Stanford faculty members, with only one access road off Sand Hill Road. Arnold initially predicted they would cost $33,000 to $50,000.[28] Across Sand Hill Road, the oak-studded Sharon Estate had been sold to the real estate firm Fox and Carskadon, which began single- and multi-family residential development of 574 acres in spring 1958, on acreage annexed to Menlo Park.[29]

Housing closer to campus also remained tempting. While Stanford was still negotiating with Del Webb, Arnold had shifted his attention to 30 acres tucked in between San Francisquito Creek and Willow Road (later connected to Sand Hill Road and renamed). Arnold made a strong pitch in 1955 for building non-affiliated housing in this area to the west of the new Stanford

Medical Center, still under construction. He argued that a high-end single-family residential area would serve local doctors who needed to be close to the hospital, although he admitted that they would be too high-priced to be affordable to mere university faculty or staff or to Shopping Center employees.[30]

This project was vehemently and repeatedly opposed by the CLBD, which insisted that it was simply too close to the campus. Committee chair Ray Faulkner called the proposal "a serious mistake at this time," while Ted Spencer called it "bad planning and bad economics." Some trustees, however, saw Arnold's proposal as an immediate source of funds, and the proposal went back to the faculty advisory committee at least four times. The committee insisted, yet again, that officials pay particular attention to lands adjacent to the main campus; this site was "one of the critical pressure points within the University Lands." Asked for the fifth time to review the proposal, the committee refused to discuss the

matter further, remaining "adamantly opposed to the development of the 24 acres at this time, in view of the strong influence which the rapidly changing situation in this area will have upon potential uses and land values." Even Alf Brandin, who usually abstained from controversial committee decisions, urged the board to develop Areas 1 and 6 before considering non-affiliated residential housing close to campus.[31]

The Arnold proposal finally was shelved, but the area remained zoned as R-4 (multiple housing) as per the SOM master plan. Four years later, in 1959, the university negotiated with Willow Creek Corporation, a consortium, to build five 8- to 12-story luxury apartment buildings (200 apartments) on about 20 acres. Palo Alto master planner Charles Luckman had recently recommended building high-rise apartments in Palo Alto, and he was supported by architectural critic Allan Temko and influential residents like Dr. Russel V. Lee. However, after vocal protests by Menlo Park residents living across San Francisquito Creek, the plans were modified and landscape screening was planted along the creek. The first unit of the three-story Oak Creek Apartments, designed by Warnecke and Associates, was constructed instead. Additional buildings, designed by Wurster, Bernardi and Emmons, were built a decade later.[32]

Sterling with architect John Carl Warnecke (left) and an unidentified official at the 1959 groundbreaking for the Willow Creek Apartments, between Willow (later Sand Hill) Road and San Francisquito Creek. The trustees had approved a multi-family five-building complex of up to 12 stories, but Menlo Park residents across the creek staged a successful protest against the high-rise. A three-story complex, named Oak Creek Apartments, was built instead. STANFORD UNIVERSITY ARCHIVES

"A REAL HOT POTATO"
STANFORD'S ROLE IN AN EARLY FAIR HOUSING DEBATE

Still getting its feet wet as a residential landlord in 1957, and with 940 acres of residential housing planned for the future Stanford Hills development along Sand Hill Road, the university was unwillingly drawn into the increasingly public debate over racially restrictive real estate practices in California. Early that year, members of the Palo Alto–Stanford branch of the National Association for the Advancement of Colored People (NAACP) petitioned the university to insert a clause prohibiting racial discrimination in its future land development contracts.[33]

The debate about the request, and the trustees' subsequent rejection, soon spun out of Sterling's control, much to his annoyance, when it reached regional newspapers. But the dispute reflected growing regional, as well as campus, concern about racial discrimination in California housing sales and state fair housing legislation amid well-known local cases of discriminatory real estate practices and other civil rights issues. It also foreshadowed major changes to come in the 1960s when members of the Stanford community pushed the university to take a more active role in fostering social reform.

In a landmark case in 1948, the U.S. Supreme Court had ruled that the equal protection clause of the 14th amendment prohibited racially restrictive housing covenants from being enforced in court. Covenants did not disappear but became less relevant as developers and realtors now effectively self-selected which houses to show clients on the unspoken basis of race rather than income. The practice of "red-lining" (the systematic denial of home and construction loans in certain areas, usually those inhabited by people of color and low-income working-class borrowers) also continued unabated in the Bay Area. Northern California fair housing reformers had made significant

Influential Bay Area real estate developer Joseph Eichler first introduced his contemporary "Ultra California" floor plans to the Peninsula in 1949. Throughout the 1950s and into the '60s, Eichler ran afoul of the California Realtors Association, a prime mover against state fair housing legislation, with his insistence on selling homes to interested buyers regardless of race or religion.   PALO ALTO HISTORICAL ASSOCIATION

strides in opening housing in public projects in Oakland and San Francisco, but racial discrimination within the mushrooming postwar "dream house" suburban developments around the Bay Area was common.[34]

When Frank Williams, an accomplished lawyer and senior NAACP field officer, expressed interest in an Eichler development home in Palo Alto in 1950, Joseph Eichler worried about the effect on his FHA housing loans, and his business in general, if a Black family moved into one of his developments. Eichler initially solved the problem by purchasing a single lot in Barron Park and, ignoring the neighbors, built Williams a house.[35]

But Eichler was disturbed by his own actions; thereafter he and his staff became resolute in their non-restrictive sales policy. His company weathered vocal protests from a handful of white residents, most famously at a subdivision in Marin County but also in Palo Alto. By the mid-1950s, Eichler homes were noted for both their innovative designs and their marketing policy of selling to buyers regardless of race or religion.[36]

A well-known example of loan discrimination was close to home. The Peninsula Housing Association (PHA), formed in 1944, had 150 members that included Stanford professors and staff (among them Wallace Stegner and Sigurd Varian), as well as Palo Alto residents. They hoped to build Ladera, a cooperative housing neighborhood on 260 acres bordering Stanford land. At least three Black families and one Asian family were among the original members of the PHA.

Many in this progressive group wanted no racial or ethnic restrictions—written or unwritten—of any kind. Their cooperative venture should overtly exemplify democracy and brotherhood. Others, however, worried that a *de facto* interracial community would bring financing difficulties. They proved correct. The PHA was denied an important loan by the Federal Housing Authority because Ladera's bylaws proposed a racial mix that would roughly reflect California's existing demographic racial mix. The PHA went broke in the early 1950s, and realtor William Kelley and his Portola Development Company took over the development. He quickly agreed to a *de facto* racially restrictive approach, complying with an American Trust Company loan guarantee.[37]

During the 1950s, the NAACP had had little success in tackling such discrimination where public money was not directly involved. Stanford's well-advertised interest in massive non-affiliated residential housing development, although privately funded, suggested to the NAACP's Palo Alto–Stanford branch that the university could be a moral example to the wider community. "We feel Stanford should be an example to the community in ensuring democratic housing patterns," said Norman C. Howard, legal counsel and executive committee member of the local NAACP branch.[38]

Their request coincided with other local anti-discrimination and civil rights efforts. In San Mateo and Santa Clara counties, residents were calling for fair housing and fair employment county ordinances. A growing number were now taking part in a statewide push for fair housing and fair employment legislation in such organizations as the Mid-Peninsula Council for Civic Unity. In Palo Alto, the American Friends Service Committee sponsored small, mixed-race neighborhoods. On the campus, Dean of Men William G. Craig leaned on Stanford's 24 fraternities after it had been publicized that at least 13 of the local chapters had racial discrimination membership clauses in their national charters.

An ideal home in an ideal community! *Yours* at
LADERA

NOW you can afford the kind of relaxed, indoor-outdoor living you've dreamed about — thanks to Ladera's unique NON-PROFIT building plan.

PENINSULA HOUSING ASSN.
Box 248, Palo Alto, California
A non-profit corporation owned by the future residents of Ladera. H. S. Hunter, General Manager.

The Peninsula Housing Association, formed by Palo Alto and Stanford residents in 1944, hoped to build Ladera, a cooperative housing neighborhood bordering Stanford land. Openly opposing racial discrimination in housing, its membership included at least three Black families and one Asian family. The PHA went bankrupt when it could not get loans from either local banks or the Federal Housing Authority.

ONCE UPON A DREAM / EICHLER NETWORK

"The University is opposed to discriminatory racial and religious clauses and practices," he announced in early March 1957, "and will work with students to eliminate them at the earliest date."[39]

Since the beginning of its postwar land development effort, Stanford officials carefully protected the university's right, as a private landowner, to make decisions regarding its lands. But many trustees, and particularly real estate advisor Colbert Coldwell, also cautioned against placing any restrictions on potential builders. When Norman Howard met with Sterling and Brandin in March 1957, Sterling expressed sympathy with the NAACP's concern but remained noncommittal about solutions specific to Stanford, stating that the matter would have to be sent to the Board of Trustees.[40]

Sterling apparently thought the matter remained between the chapter's executive officers and Stanford officials. A *Palo Alto Times* reporter, however, read about the NAACP request in a paragraph in an NAACP chapter bulletin. Articles soon began appearing in Northern California newspapers, prompting letters to Sterling encouraging his support of the request. This was a "tough break," Fred Glover noted. Glover predicted that the situation could turn into "a real hot potato."[41]

Howard and Lester P. Bailey, NAACP field secretary for the Western United States, grew impatient with Sterling. Bypassing Sterling, on March 18, 1957, they submitted their petition directly to the Board of Trustees, asking that the university insert "mandatory anti-discriminatory clauses in all contracts wherein university property is leased, rented or otherwise conveyed to private interests for the purpose of developing housing and/or other facilities on said property." In addition, clauses should prohibit discrimination "in the employment of professional, skilled, semi-skilled and common labor engaged for the development of housing and/or other facilities on university property." While Stanford could not be expected to change neighboring community patterns, the petitioners stated, the university should nevertheless "resist the repetition of undesirable community patterns within its own estate, where its jurisdiction and authority are unchallengeable and well-defined."[42]

Before his meeting with Howard, Sterling had been briefed by legal counsel Robert Minge Brown. There was no legal reason not to include an anti-discrimination clause, should the trustees choose to do so, Brown had admitted. But, Brown noted, the trustees were reluctant to place restrictions of any kind on any developer that might cause him to go elsewhere.[43]

The petition was buried by the trustees' Special Committee on Land Development. At their March 21 meeting, the board decided to continue its current policy of non-interference. Since state law made racial covenants on the part of any developer unenforceable, they concluded, no further action on their part was needed. Sterling reported the decision to the press on their behalf, stating that after considering the request that clauses prohibiting racial discrimination be inserted in university leases with land developers, the board decided that anti-discrimination clauses would be superfluous in university homesite leases in view of Stanford's long-standing policy against discrimination.[44]

Norman Howard's response was succinct: "Dr. Sterling missed the boat . . . We are not denying that Stanford is always open to all qualified students, but we don't know what a private developer will do."[45]

"I am sorry," one alumna wrote Sterling on reading his statement, "that my alma mater does not find it worthwhile to take a strong stand in the matter of fair treatment of races other than white." Another alumnus wrote: "You muffed the chance to make a magnificent, courageous gesture." Another, a Los Altos resident, wrote:

> A Stanford professor told me last night that he regards you as one of the greatest men he knows, and that he is certain you hated to read to the press

your statement on the anti-discrimination guarantee. I'm accordingly disposed to agree with my friend—unless you correct me—that your statement doesn't represent your own views, but that you were very reluctantly forced to write it as a matter of expediency.[46]

The *Palo Alto Times* noted a "growing wave" of local protest. Stanford was, in effect, surrendering control of its lands to private builders and future house owners. Therefore, the only way to ensure non-discrimination, they said, was during the initial leasing process.[47]

Sterling had firmly supported the trustees' decision, however, believing that the NAACP was in effect asking Stanford to assume a governmental function. "There is no need under our lease procedures, to insert clauses forbidding discrimination," he responded at length to one critic. "Stanford has not been found wanting in the fight for tolerance on any front," Sterling added, "but there are choices of methods and not everyone agrees on which is the proper one. I am sure that our goals are the same and that you do not have cause to be disappointed in the results of the University's position."[48]

Law Professor John H. Merryman, then living in Menlo Park, was among the more vocal faculty who felt that Stanford was evading the larger issue: While Stanford did not condone discrimination, it appeared reluctant to admit that racial discrimination in housing existed not only in neighboring communities but also in early residential developments on university land. In housing developed earlier by Arnold's PPCC, Merryman reported to the president, "there is a well-defined, clearly understood informal policy of discrimination," not as a result of racial covenants but of the practice of real estate agents and brokers who feared "the economic consequences of integration." Thus, economically qualified members of racial minorities were not shown

John Merryman was a young associate professor of law when he questioned the university's commitment to fair housing in its residential developments. Merryman opposed racially based selectivity in marketing houses on Stanford property. STANFORD NEWS SERVICE

property in middle-class or affluent neighborhoods like those envisioned for Stanford lands.

Assuming Sterling to be interested in faculty viewpoints, Merryman wrote, he described what many of his colleagues believed to be happening. "Those who know a problem exists, and thus do not accept the University's public statement at face value, ask themselves what might have been the real reason for its stand," he wrote.

Many of them decide the only possible reason was fear that a firm position against discrimination might lose some money. They hear the voice of the Business Office in the University's statement, and to them that voice says that in a conflict between principle and expediency, principle must lose. I cannot believe that this is true, but I can accurately report that others fear that it is. They see this as merely another in a series of cases in which disproportionate weight has been given to the counsel of hucksters. The University, whether it wishes to do so or not, provides intellectual leadership in the community. Its decisions on matters of public importance become precedents for actions by other groups and persons. This position of leadership carries with it certain responsibilities, which it should acknowledge and accept.[49]

Sterling did not discount the need for reform, he answered, but would not accept what he viewed as the NAACP's politically inspired methods. Should Stanford handle racial discrimination "its own way" or "as a propaganda measure"? He had been disconcerted to find that the NAACP had shared its letters and petition to Stanford with the press, giving the university little time to consider or reply, he told Merryman. "It is a pity that they weaken a good cause by bad manners and questionable strategy, but this is apart from the basic issues."[50] (It is unclear whether Sterling knew that the young associate professor was also an active member of the board of the American Civil Liberties Union of Northern California.)

The day before, Bailey had, in fact, politely invited university staff and trustees to join him at the next Palo Alto–Stanford branch meeting for a discussion of the issue, but neither Sterling nor trustee President Lloyd Dinkelspiel saw any reason to reopen the matter.[51]

Robert Minge Brown was also inclined to see the NAACP request in terms of political pressure. Using a defense that the university would raise during the 1960s, Brown also referred to Mrs. Stanford's injunction that the university "shall forever be kept out of politics." The Council for Civic Unity and the NAACP should recognize, he concluded, "that the investment policy of a university is not a suitable vehicle for the enforcement of tolerance in housing."[52]

Bailey turned to Herbert Packer, a member of the NAACP's Palo Alto–Stanford branch and, like Merryman, an associate professor of law at Stanford. A noted liberal who believed strongly in the NAACP's goals, Packer was nonetheless unconvinced that Stanford was the right battleground at this time. What the petition proposed, he responded, was that the university enforce an anti-discrimination clause, which would require it to engage in day-to-day management of sub-

contractors and leasing. "Stanford University is not in the housing business," he advised. "It is in the business of providing an education for its students." With resources severely limited, "any diversion from that business, however laudable the purpose may seem, is a dilution of the job at hand." He continued:

> Stanford has no more of an obligation, legal or moral, to create an interracial community on its leased land than it does to enforce the corporate and tax laws with respect to the industrial concerns of that leased land in the Industrial Park. Nor, to put the issue more directly, do I think that Stanford is required to see to it that those industrial leases maintain non-discriminatory hiring practices. To hold otherwise, would be to impose an intolerable burden on the University administration. The NAACP has not taken the position that Stanford should concern itself with the internal management of its industrial lessees, and I would be surprised if it were to do so. How then can it logically call on the University to do so in the housing field?[53]

Robert Minge Brown was indeed worried about Stanford's investments since, as he subsequently told Dinkelspiel, "this represents a direct interference with the business of the real estate developer, who is already being asked to enter a somewhat unfamiliar field in marketing houses erected on property which is leased rather than purchased." Colbert Coldwell also was consistent in his opposition to any restrictions whatsoever on developers. Coldwell did not think Harry Arnold, on board to begin construction on the first 30 acres of Stanford Hills, would sign a master lease with a clause requiring the university's approval of restrictions of any nature in any subleases, Glover told Sterling. (In a rare break with Coldwell, Alf Brandin disagreed, believing Arnold would not be frightened away.)[54]

Throughout the summer, individuals and community groups, including Palo Alto's First

Congregational Church's Social Education and Action Committee, the First Methodist Church, the Council for Civic Unity, and the American Friends Service Committee, prodded Sterling for some sort of action. But while acknowledging the problem of *de facto* discrimination, Sterling refused to engage. Stanford must fight for tolerance and equality, he responded, as an educational institution and could do so only if supported by use of its endowment as the board deemed appropriate. Despite its moral authority, the university did not have the staff to police developers and lessees who were not breaking the law. When, a year later, Joseph Eichler suggested that interracial housing on university land would indeed be a worthy cause, Sterling commented to Glover that Eichler's suggestion was akin to the many other worthy but non-academic purposes suggested by outsiders for Stanford's acreage.[55]

Despite its vow to continue the battle, the local NAACP chapter was facing internal issues of declining membership and divisions over immediate goals. Of greater concern for its multiracial members and sympathizers was success of pending state fair housing legislation (beginning with the Unruh Act of 1959) and influential political opposition to such legislation by the real estate industry. However, the issues raised by the fair housing and fair employment debate influenced Stanford faculty and staff, like Merryman and News Director Robert Beyers, to take more proactive roles in local efforts to support state fair housing legislation.[56]

Students similarly began to raise questions about the university's commitment not only to the general concept of fair housing, but also to its allegedly welcoming stance toward all, regardless of race or religion. As one alumna pointed out, during her years (1948–50) at Stanford, she rarely saw a Black student, unlike her experience at the equally elite, and expensive, University of Chicago. "I remain convinced that although there may be no ironclad and stated policy of discrimi-

nation, a strong tendency to discriminate can be the only explanation for the extreme rarity of Negro students." While some fraternity members had complained about Dean Craig's interference, others put his advice into action. That April, the Interfraternity Council unanimously passed a resolution condemning racial restrictions and began to back local chapters when they clashed with their national organizations about opening membership.[57]

Ultimately, between 1963 and 1967, the Sterling administration changed its stand as a condition of receiving federal government research grants and contracts, adding comprehensive non-discriminatory clauses and internal means to enforce them. These changes were framed by the California fair housing political scene. When, in 1964, a state referendum sponsored by the California Association of Realtors—Proposition 14—overturned the 1963 Rumford Fair Housing Act, the U.S. government cut all housing funds to California; in 1967, the U.S. Supreme Court overturned Prop. 14 and reaffirmed the provisions of California's Fair Housing Act.[58]

THE DEMISE OF RESIDENTIAL HOUSING
COYOTE HILL CONTROVERSY

By 1960, campus opinions of the long-term value of residential development were decidedly mixed. The two early-1950s planning studies by outside consultants—Punnett, Parez & Hutchison (1951) and Skidmore, Owings & Merrill (1953–54)—had simply assumed that significant portions of Stanford lands could, and should, be earmarked for residential housing and that the new residential neighborhoods would be occupied largely by non-university-affiliated residents. If these plans were carried out, faculty and students faced the prospect of competing with an exceptionally large block of unaffiliated voters whose self-interest could overshadow the university's educational priorities, including decisions about use of its land legacy for academic purposes.

Large-scale residential development had also ensnared the university in the local politics of its neighbors, particularly fast-growing Palo Alto and Menlo Park, since such developments had to be annexed to neighboring municipalities to permit access to utilities.

Planning Director Ted Spencer, backed by Fred Terman (university provost since 1955), continued to stress the need to preserve significant portions of surplus lands for future academic use. "Several major universities of the world have run out of land and been forced to handicap their needs and to pay dearly for additional land on which to expand," he wrote in 1958. "In the past, Stanford's ability to attract important activities has been to some measure due to its available land. During the next century this may become increasingly true.

The triangular Stanford Hills residential development stands out in this 1958 aerial view, with only two initial roads laid out (with two stubs for future roads) and one model house constructed. At left is Sand Hill Road, while Alpine Road and Stanford Golf Course span the middle distance. Only 78 houses, on 30 acres, were constructed of the recommended 1,800 houses on 940 acres. More than 425 acres (not shown) were later devoted to the Stanford Linear Accelerator Center.

HATFIELD AERIAL SURVEY / STANFORD UNIVERSITY ARCHIVES

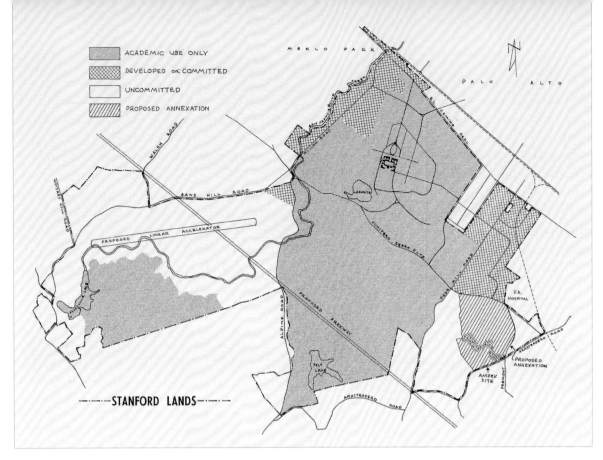

In contrast to the 1953 master plan, trustees in early 1960 set aside 4,700 acres for academic reserve and halted consideration of non-affiliated suburban housing development. This April 1960 rendering shows the Coyote Hill area that became a bone of contention to neighbors who opposed expansion of the industrial park there (note the Ampex Site and Proposed Annexation labels). It also confirms Jasper Ridge (east of Searsville Lake) as a portion of academic lands, as well as the final sites for the linear accelerator and the VA Hospital. STANFORD NEWS SERVICE COLLECTION / STANFORD UNIVERSITY ARCHIVES

It is important that land assignment be pointed toward providing a way of living conducive to the long-term goals of the University."[59]

In January 1960, after years of debate, the Board of Trustees decided to stop further residential development on outlying lands "for the time being." At this point, only 90 acres of the master plan's recommended 2,850 acres had been leased for non-Stanford-affiliated housing. As the board's Special Land Policy Review Committee pointed out, this acreage was essentially lost for the duration of the 99-year residential leases for a relatively small return. Industrial, professional, and, especially, commercial leases were far more lucrative. Such residential areas also created the need for schools, parks, and other public facilities, inviting condemnation by Palo Alto or

Menlo Park. "If the resident population becomes numerous," the review committee pointed out, "the residents could control the land use by zoning ordinances that could supersede Stanford's rights as owner of the property." The annual income from this source, their report bluntly stated, was "not enough to risk the prospect of Stanford losing permanent control of the land through this type of development." The review committee also urged the board to return to its pre-1950 policy of restricting leases for single-family dwellings on university lands to Stanford faculty and staff, a decision reinforced in 1974.[60]

This decision, in turn, prompted reconsideration of the Coyote Hill area, roughly 600 acres in Area 1 bounded by Page Mill Road, Junipero Serra Boulevard (later Foothill Expressway),

Arastradero Road, and the planned interstate freeway corridor, acreage once eyed by SOM for intense suburban development. The university's interest in gradual expansion of its industrial zone was no secret, but its request to the Palo Alto City Council in 1960 for a rezoning of 254 undeveloped acres in the Coyote Hill area from residential to a light-density industrial zone proved unexpectedly controversial.

In May 1960, the Palo Alto City Council approved Stanford's rezoning request and then unanimously approved annexation of the 254-acre parcel. Unlike the flatter, less picturesque parcels along El Camino, these were oak-studded rolling hills much appreciated as open space by residents in nearby Palo Alto, Los Altos, and Los Altos Hills. But it was not simply the prospect of development that caught public attention. Much of the protest was aimed at the area's proposed first lease: an 80-acre site for a production and warehousing facility for Ampex Corporation.[61]

Sterling had expected the usual objections to these development plans. The previous March, he had met with three directors of the Citizens Committee for Regional Planning, whose concerns largely centered on the need for Palo Alto and neighboring towns to get a handle on their own long-term development plans. Three days later, after their own March meeting, Stanford trustees issued a policy statement noting that they realized that "some persons may feel that the 'rolling foothills' should be preserved regardless of the educational and research objectives of the University," but that they hoped that these people "might be convinced otherwise if they understood the important educational and research attainments; and the objectives of Stanford and the programs designed to attain them."[62]

Later in March, Sterling had issued a "Dear Friends" invitation to the community at large to an April 2 meeting at Bowman Alumni House to discuss Stanford's development plans. More

than 100 attended the event, which followed a morning-long meeting of local city and county officials. In his introductory remarks at that meeting, Sterling emphasized the trustees' obligation to develop university lands in the best interest of Stanford's academic mission. "This by no means precludes the careful consideration . . . of how Stanford's neighbors may be affected by these developments or how their problems may relate to ours," but the trustees' fiduciary responsibilities were to the university's students and faculty.[63]

He had some good news about property taxation to report—the state legislature had recently revised the 100-acre exemption law to allow Stanford to exempt a somewhat larger portion of the campus, around 1,200 acres. However, this did not apply to most of the university's acreage or include future academic growth.[64]

Sterling also stressed the vulnerability of university lands, one of the largest blocks of open space in suburban Santa Clara and San Mateo counties, to government condemnation. "Our experience, and the experience elsewhere in the country, suggests that the continued existence of such open space is an attraction for condemnation." Sterling explained that trustees recently had again increased the academic reserve, now around 4,800 acres, adding that "with a look at the very distant future, it is quite conceivable that all Stanford land will be directly or indirectly essentially an academic reserve."[65]

Palo Alto pediatrician Dr. Esther Clark, '21, M.D. '25, a Los Altos Hills neighbor, wrote Sterling a supportive letter noting that the university had generously allowed the public to enjoy its lakes and rolling, tree-studded hills, with few restrictions for more than 60 years. "As a result of this privilege having been granted for so long a time," she said, "many have come to feel that they have 'rights' to the Stanford land and should have a voice in determining what use Stanford will make of it."[66]

Coyote
Hill

Stanford students Mary Lou McKinley, '61, and Jerry Rankin, '62, walk in the industrial park in a 1960 publicity photo. Behind is Hanover Street, approaching Hillview Avenue (out of view), and, in the far-right distance, a portion of Lockheed's 1956 buildings. An extension of Hanover, where they are walking, will become Porter Street, named for Palo Alto Mayor Noel Porter.

STANFORD NEWS SERVICE

Others assumed the extension represented the university's new preference for industrial research with university connections. Noel Stearn, '18, of Portola Valley, in a letter to the *Palo Alto Times*, wrote that the "industry" intended for the expansion was research oriented, thus "bringing into our community the cream of the nation's brain power dedicated to the discovery and exploration of technological frontiers." But the Ampex lease was more than a simple expansion of electronics research facilities—the

< Foothill Road (Junipero Serra) runs from upper left to lower right, intersecting Page Mill Road, in this ca. 1958 aerial campus view. Sand Hill Road (this part was then named Willow Road) is near the top, with Menlo Park beyond; Arastradero Road runs horizontally near the bottom. A 254-acre industrial park expansion was proposed in 1960 for a portion of the Coyote Hill area, bounded by Foothill, Fremont, and Arastradero roads and tree-lined Deer Creek, in left foreground. Under construction are the VA Hospital (right foreground) and Stanford Medical Center (between Willow Road and the Oval and bisected by tree-lined Governor's Avenue).

PALO ALTO HISTORICAL ASSOCIATION

company intended to include a significant manufacturing space and needed ample warehousing acreage and parking for large trucks.[67]

Dan Endsley, '47, editor of the Alumni Association's *Stanford Review*, reiterated Sterling's points in more than one editorial. "We are all prone to regard Senator Stanford's entailment of the land as a permanent protection," he wrote in May, but condemnations, both "small erosions" and two large ones under consideration (the interstate freeway and a U.S. Army Corps of Engineers dam and reservoir near Ladera), now amounted to more than 10 percent of the original 1885 grant of 6,967 acres. Was the university expected to deplete funds for students and faculty to keep the land undeveloped for the enjoyment of neighbors?[68]

Stanford leaders seemed "disposed to emphasize communication because, time after time, they have been accused of secrecy and poor public relations," Endsley noted. "Although in some areas they may have sinned, any objective assessment of their performance in land development would surely bring them a rather good mark." As evidence, the May 1960 *Review* included a five-page article, "The Shrinking Stanford Lands," that pointed out the numerous times Stanford's master plan land-use map had been sent out, that the proposed change for Coyote Hill had been publicly discussed since 1957, and that zoning changes due to the interstate and the Stanford Linear Accelerator had long been a matter of public discourse.

But Endsley understood that this time, this "particular fire" had deeper implications. While the university might hope to head off misunderstandings and contention, he feared that "in a head-on conflict of interest, better understanding may just make the contenders more pugnacious." He doubted that anyone who attended Stanford's April open house "left feeling any differently," adding that one man told him that "Stanford was running scared." Stanford's opponents, concluded Endsley, were fighting not over land but for a way of life. "They apparently believed Stanford's responsibility to them transcends its responsibility to its own central purposes. In the face of this powerful and fully understandable human emotion, no argument will stand. Whatever happens, the losers will be in no mood to toast the victors, and no amount of communication is going to change *that*."

Soon after Endsley's editorial, 115 unidentified "Bay Area Stanford Alumni" placed a four-page advertisement in the *Stanford Review* (including a two-page photograph of beautiful rolling hills dotted with oaks). They accused the Board of Trustees of poor planning and misunderstanding Senator Stanford's original intent to surround the university with natural beauty. They recommended that if the university wished to maintain its reputation "as a University of high degree and as a good neighbor," it should undertake a study of how to obtain financial return from its lands

without defacing its foothills, and to coordinate such a master plan with those of its neighbors.[69]

Sterling bristled at the criticism of the board's motives and the alleged lack of professionalism among university planners and planning consultants, despite years of attention to its master plan and to adjustments prompted by faculty input, condemnation threats, and changing academic needs:

I have no doubt the additional planner your petition strongly recommends that the University employ would be subjected to the same kind of criticisms if his study also revealed that restricted types of light developments are ideally suited to certain portions of the Stanford lands near Los Altos Hills. Because you disagree with our planning does not change its logic or alter the facts confronting any planner we employ.[70]

By June, opponents of the Ampex proposal, and of foothills expansion more generally, had successfully circulated a city-wide petition, sponsored by the Citizens Committee for Regional Planning, challenging the council's rezoning action with a referendum on Palo Alto's November ballot. As Endsley predicted, both sides communicated often and at length through publications, public forums, and letters in local newspapers. On November 8, 1960, the referendum against development of the Coyote Hill area was defeated. (It fell short of a required two-thirds vote, earning 57.4 percent.)

Ampex Corporation ultimately chose not to proceed with the foothills lease, finding it less troublesome to remain in Redwood City.[71] Despite the loss of this potential tenant, Sterling's administration moved forward with expansion in Coyote Hill as a low-density development with several research ventures. Today, much of the acreage remains rolling hills and pastureland.

Nevertheless, the protest was the first major salvo of growing concern about traffic, pollution,

The Syntex buildings are under construction in this 1964 view of part of the contested Coyote Hill area. The main campus is in the distance (note Hoover Tower). Foothill Expressway runs along the middle distance.
STANFORD NEWS SERVICE

urban sprawl, and the loss of agricultural and open space, forcing reconsideration of city development plans throughout the region. A group of Stanford, Palo Alto, and Los Altos Hills residents, protesting in 1960 to "keep factories out of the foothills," established the Committee for Green Foothills two years later, with Professor Wallace Stegner as its president. In 1972, Santa Clara County voters created the Midpeninsula Regional Open Space District, which later expanded into portions of San Mateo and Santa Cruz counties.

Growth of interest in widening Palo Alto's Oregon Avenue into an expressway connecting the industrial park to Bayshore Highway sparked an especially volatile public battle over urbanization and development. Palo Alto had doubled in size and population during the 1950s, with annexation of the area south of Oregon Avenue, a region that by 1960 featured Eichler neighborhoods and other large subdivisions. Many of the residents had been drawn to the area by employment opportunities at the university and the industrial park, as well as by the quality of

schools and residential neighborhoods. But the downside of California's population boom also was becoming apparent and many Palo Alto residents were increasingly interested in protecting the once-quiet, residential character of the town and the rural environment of nearby baylands and foothills.[72]

In 1961, after a major upgrade of two-lane Bayshore Highway to a freeway, Santa Clara County planners proposed a major change to Oregon Avenue. This neighborhood road was one of several cross-town streets linking the Bayshore with El Camino Real and had become a popular thoroughfare. Upgrading the now-crowded roadway was widely supported until the county unveiled its utilitarian design: a four-lane swath of asphalt, bounded by chain-link fencing, with only two cross streets. The plan called for the removal of 107 houses.

Support for the county's proposal quickly weakened. Letters, editorials, and public meetings took up the debate over the bleak design, as well as the social cost of rampant development. Oregon Expressway, writes Palo Alto historian

Ward Winslow, became "one of the city's most divisive flare-ups of the century."[73]

Stanford came in for a fair share of the blame. Mistrust of the university's ongoing plans to develop land around Coyote Hill and beyond continued to fuel warnings that the foothills would soon be covered with industry, parking lots, and a haze of auto exhaust. Supporters, in turn, staged a "traffic action," with parked cars and placards pointing out the dangers of the old road. (Their event caused a two-hour traffic jam at the avenue's busiest section.) The public outcry, pro and con, brought major changes to the county's plan: six signaled cross streets and 11 access roads, a landscaped median and side service road, a strict speed limit, and a ban on large trucks. (Ultimately, 92 houses would be removed.)

The final city referendum vote in 1962, favoring the revised plan, was very close, winning by 474 votes out of more than 18,000 cast. Nevertheless, the campaign bolstered the growing "residentialist" movement that soon changed the configuration of the city council and successfully thwarted Palo Alto urbanization projects of the early 1970s: a large downtown hospital associated with the Palo Alto Medical Foundation (on the site of today's Heritage Park), a high-rise commercial "superblock" (240,000 square feet) on Bryant, and the widening of Alma to six lanes as part of the Central Expressway.[74]

Stanford was caught up in the inevitable political reaction, recalled Andy Doty, a later Stanford director of community relations. "Once Palo Alto gained economic security, it could turn its attention to other values: traffic congestion, the loss of open space, over-development, and the overall 'quality of life.'" But over the next decades, the bitter divide between "the residentialists" and "the establishment" at times brought city government to a standstill on civic issues. Interactions with the university became all the more tense and confrontational. Alf Brandin no longer had the

opportunistic attention of city officials who had built Palo Alto city coffers and school facilities with property and sales taxes and utility income derived from Stanford's industrial and commercial ventures.[75]

LADERA DAM
FIGHTING WASHINGTON'S MOST POWERFUL AGENCY

Sterling's most prolonged battle to retain control of university lands got underway in fall 1961 when the U.S. Army Corps of Engineers announced its plan to take 542 acres of Stanford land and 42 acres from the town of Woodside for a 2,500-foot-wide flood-control dam, to be called Ladera Dam because of its proximity to the nearby Ladera community. Unlike similar local reservoirs, Ladera Reservoir was expected to be empty for much of the year. And with the lower reaches of Jasper Ridge and the 525-surface-acre reservoir site stripped bare of vegetation up to the high-water mark, it would leave not parkland but a wide rim of barren dirt during California's long dry season.[76]

The idea of an additional dam along San Francisquito Creek had been discussed more than once since the university took over Searsville Dam in 1919. Searsville's reservoir, a popular recreation site, had been silting up from the beginning. Searsville water, used only for irrigation, when possible, was yellow, muddy, smelly, and undrinkable.[77]

Flood control was less of an issue until the mid-1950s, as Peninsula housing began to spread along the alluvial plains where foothill creeks ran into San Francisco Bay. Widespread flood damage throughout the Bay Area and Santa Cruz during the "Christmas Floods" of December 1955, with about 1,000 residents evacuated in Palo Alto alone, prompted strident calls for stronger flood-control measures upstream. Further flooding in 1958,

An early view of an infrequent water release at Searsville Dam, acquired by Stanford in 1919. The lake's heavily sedimented, unpotable water provided agricultural irrigation and, until 1976, recreation. Today's lake has lost nearly 90 percent capacity due to siltation.   STANFORD UNIVERSITY ARCHIVES

This 1967 view of Searsville Lake was taken from the west side, close to the dam, facing south-southeast, with the slopes of Jasper Ridge in the background. Searsville was for many years a popular privately run recreational area. The lake, which has been silting up since its beginning (the dam was built in 1891), is part of the Jasper Ridge Biological Preserve.   STANFORD NEWS SERVICE

damaging Palo Alto's airport and golf course, both on the baylands, encouraged the U.S. Army Corps of Engineers to dust off studies from the 1940s. In September 1961, the new $8.4 million dam and reservoir project was announced, with three features: flood control, water conservation for local use, and a public recreation site.[78]

Buoyed by firm support from a unanimous Palo Alto City Council, the Santa Clara County Board of Supervisors, and U.S. Representative Charles Gubser, the Corps expected no opposition during the upcoming congressional approval process. Yet, while there had been broad interest previously in flood-control measures, there was no consensus on

In 1965, the university produced this aerial photo with overlay to show the impact of the federal government's proposed Ladera Dam. When full, the reservoir would wind under the linear accelerator and inundate the intersection of Sand Hill and Whiskey Hill roads (lower right). The recently developed Ladera community is just beyond the intended dam (upper right). Given the region's semi-arid climate, the proposed recreation area was expected to be largely denuded mud-land for much of the year. Construction of the 280 freeway would not begin for two more years.   STANFORD NEWS SERVICE

such a large dam and particularly its multiuse reservoir. Ladera Reservoir would extend, when full, nearly 2.25 miles along the base of Jasper Ridge to Whiskey Hill Road. A wider arm would abut Sand Hill Road, beneath the projected Junipero Serra Freeway–Sand Hill Road interchange. Major portions also would spread under the planned 2-mile linear accelerator. Sand Hill and Whiskey Hill roads would be relocated to higher ground, and homes in the Whiskey Hill–Bear Creek area would be submerged, as would farmland next to Ladera. A 57-acre public beachhead recreation area, bounded by the new freeway, the linear accelerator, and the reservoir, would be located near the dam, edging into the Jasper Ridge preserve.

Within weeks of the announcement, Menlo Park joined with the Ladera community, Woodside, and Stanford in vocally opposing the Ladera Dam project. Widely respected biology faculty members expressed deep concern about probable damage by unlimited public recreational use to Jasper Ridge's pristine and delicately balanced ecological setting and to scientific instrumentation located there. Stanford engineers questioned the project's site and structural engineering, cost estimates, and its hydrological analysis. The Corps had not fully considered more immediate, less expensive, and more effective ways of achieving flood control, they argued, such as smaller dams, improving creek channels, clearing creek beds, and adding bayland floodgates to control abnormally high tides and dissipate water from developed areas along the baylands.[79]

The Corps not only had ignored the value of Stanford's lands for academic purposes, but also had significantly underestimated their market value, both as part of the university's endowment and in calculating their cost to the federal government at condemnation. Regional real estate values alone doubled the Corps' estimated cost. If the Board of Trustees was asked to release "so much vitally important land to a project that will serve

no academic purpose," President Sterling challenged, "[t]he Corps of Engineers should be asked to demonstrate that the proposed project is the *only* reasonable means by which the San Francisquito Creek can be controlled."[80]

Support for the Corps' Ladera proposal from the federal Board of Engineers for Rivers and Bridges briefly wavered in the face of such protests late in 1961, but Corps representatives, backed by Palo Alto, successfully argued that neither Jasper Ridge nor the accelerator project would be affected. The university, they said, was simply being selfish. Other critics pointed to Stanford's "mercenary" attitude for expecting to determine the use of its own land. Frank J. Madison, a candidate for Santa Clara County supervisor, stated that the university was "vicious, irresponsible and dangerous" for not wanting "to sacrifice some 500 acres of revenue for the needs of the citizens of Palo Alto."[81]

Palo Alto City Manager Jerry Keithley worried that Palo Alto alone might not be able to push the project through and urged the public to "let Congress know how badly we need it."[82] Letters from lowland Palo Alto poured into California congressional offices. As one congressional aide reported, many urged: "Don't let Stanford dictate for the area."[83]

In early 1962, Sterling enlisted faculty, trustees, alumni, and friends in taking the fight directly to Washington, D.C. In the midst of a major university-wide fundraising campaign, he had at hand a newly organized staff that would prove to be a formidable team. In Washington, D.C., a few weeks after the Board of Engineers decided to support the plan, Sterling's new director of university relations, Lyle Nelson, reported: "Beyond a doubt, this is going to be a very difficult struggle." The Corps of Engineers, he added, was regarded "as the most powerful federal lobby in Washington, one almost impossible to oppose."[84]

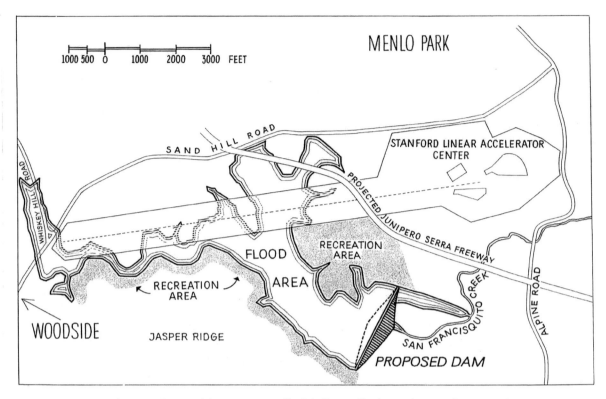

The U.S. Army Corps of Engineers' proposed dam was promoted by Palo Alto as a flood-control measure but opposed by the communities that would be affected by its construction and its use for public recreation. The university also faced the loss of 542 acres of land to the federal government, and adverse impacts on the adjacent Jasper Ridge research area and the Linear Accelerator Center, then under construction. PUBLIC AFFAIRS OFFICE / STANFORD UNIVERSITY ARCHIVES

The Corps of Engineers, however, under-estimated the opposition. Nelson was encouraged by Stanford's many supporters and felt that "the facts of the case will sustain our position." To counter Palo Alto's blanket letter-writing campaign, Stanford used its friends strategically. Alumni in Washington, D.C., as elected officials and attorneys, gave Sterling and his staff a road map of the rambling approval course the project must navigate, and helped analyze the political "line up."[85] Sterling "had a marvelous way of sizing up the situation," Nelson recalled about their visit to Washington to battle "the lobby that can't be beat." On one day alone, Sterling and Nelson juggled 11 appointments.[86]

California's delegation was crucial, not only those who represented local constituencies but also those on important House and Senate committees. At first, most preferred to avoid the controversy but some, especially those committed to supporting higher education in the state, were willing to listen. U.S. Senators Claire Engle and Thomas Kuchel initially were on the fence but began to take an interest when presented with the nature of Stanford's objections and particularly its voluminous, and growing, engineering data. Letters from the Nature Conservancy, the Sierra Club, and local conservation organizations concerned about Jasper Ridge boosted Stanford's position. Congressman J. Arthur Younger (San Mateo), once uninterested, became an important ally when he became annoyed with a poorly designed Corps breakwater project in Half Moon Bay.[87]

California Governor Edmund G. (Pat) Brown,

a strong advocate of both higher education and state water projects and whose opinion on the Ladera project could make or break it, expressed his support of Stanford's opposition. California's Department of Water Resources already had raised doubts about the alleged cost savings of the water conservation feature. It was unlikely that the water would be drinkable, something residents had already experienced with Searsville water. (Stanford residents receive their drinking water from the Hetch Hetchy water system.)[88] Local developer Joseph Eichler, asked for his opinion by Governor Brown, reported that his own engineering department and other civil engineers employed by his firm concluded unanimously that the project was "ill-advised."[89]

As the proposal worked its way through the process in spring 1962, Stanford built up documentation through additional engineering, hydrology, and economic studies. Faculty experts made themselves available for local county supervisors' meetings and public hearings in Washington. An economic-engineering analysis of the project by civil engineering Professor Ray Linsley

Stanford engineering Professor Ray K. Linsley was already an internationally known hydrologist and water resources engineer when he served as a key advisor during the 1961–71 fight to prevent the U.S. Army Corps of Engineers from building Ladera Dam and Reservoir.
STANFORD NEWS SERVICE

became an important weapon. Linsley, an internationally known hydrologist and water resources engineer, also was familiar with government agencies, having worked earlier for the Tennessee Valley Authority and the U.S. Weather Bureau.

Linsley reiterated that there was not enough annual rainfall to make the project worthwhile for water conservation or as a recreation area and that as a flood-control measure, it was overdesigned.[90] SLAC Director Wolfgang Panofsky countered the Corps' suggestion that the dam and reservoir would not affect his linear accelerator project, pointing out that the Ladera Reservoir would add considerable construction, maintenance, and operation costs to the federally supported accelerator project, and would limit future expansion at the site.[91]

The Corps was rumored to be "starving for work" in the San Francisco district, reported Don Carlson, Sterling's former assistant and now Nelson's associate director of university relations. This accounted for "the special pressure to bang the Ladera Dam through." However, "the Corps hasn't shown much willingness to get into an argument with engineers like Ray Linsley about it," said Carlson. "This is a great deal of public money to spend in order to permit the City of Palo Alto to develop the San Francisquito lowlands without requiring construction to be on filled land."[92]

University trustees quickly picked up on the Corps' reputation for "being generously low in cost estimates and generously high in estimates of potential damage."[93] David Packard, trustee and influential Hewlett-Packard president and co-founder, commended fellow-Republican Gubser for his recent opposition to other legislation that imposed federal influence over local matters. Packard insisted the congressman now have "the strength of conviction" to oppose the "monstrous boondoggle" of Ladera Dam. There were other more efficient ways to handle the flood control problem, Packard argued, while "all of the other benefits which are listed in support of this pro-

Stanford staff members walk along Jasper Ridge in 1967. Biologists have studied environmental factors in the life cycles of California plants and animals continuously here since the university's opening in 1891. Beginning in 1956, university trustees expanded protection to the Jasper Ridge area, formally designating 960 acres as a biological preserve in 1973. The preserve has since grown to more than 1,100 acres.   STANFORD NEWS SERVICE

gram, such as recreational use, water conservation, etc., are simply attempts by the Corps of Engineers to justify another empire builder project."[94]

Colonel John A. Morrison, chief of engineers in the Corps' San Francisco district, lobbied hard among sympathetic Palo Alto audiences, advocating the advantages of the dam over channel improvements, modifications of bridges, and relocated rights-of-way.[95] Despite protests by the Nature Conservancy and other conservation groups worried about damage to Jasper Ridge, and years of local protests against the possible environmental destruction caused by expansion of the industrial park into the foothills, many in Palo Alto appeared pleased when the National Park Service suggested that Ladera's lake could attract 100,000 users a year to its large paved parking area and boat launching facilities.[96]

U.S. Secretary of the Army Elvis Stahr tabled the project in May 1962. Stahr demanded further study of alternatives less damaging to Jasper Ridge and ordered more discussions with Stanford.[97] Col. Morrison, backed by the Santa Clara County Board of Supervisors and Palo Alto City Council, countered with a single-purpose flood-control dam, requiring only 400 acres of Stanford land, as a more politically viable option. Hoping to get a proposal into a later 1962 congressional omnibus bill but unwilling to discuss alternatives with Stanford and Menlo Park, Morrison urged supporters to quickly obtain statements of support from the two jurisdictions. He insisted, however, that Stanford not only agree, but repent. The university must state its reasons for supporting the single-purpose dam, in lieu of the multipurpose reservoir, said Morrison, "in terms of Stanford's understanding of the overall public interests, rather than in terms of its interests alone."[98]

Stanford, however, had already moved beyond protesting the dam and reservoir to promoting locally more expeditious, economical, and less damaging downstream alternatives, a strategy that heartened Engle, Kuchel, and Younger.[99] San Mateo's supervisors, acknowledging the firm opposition of Menlo Park and Woodside, increasingly vocal protests by conservation groups, and a growing distrust of the Corps' economic figures, decided to sit on Morrison's new proposal. Perhaps they were reassured by Sterling's insistence that any differences of opinion regarding flood control could be "resolved by mutual review of the proposed project and joint study of other possible means of obtaining common objectives."[100] Governor Pat Brown, now on first-name basis with "Wally," assured Sterling that "we will consider carefully the possible effects on future educational and research programs at Stanford," should a future evaluation be required.[101]

The Ladera Dam project languished but did not officially die for another nine years. The prospect of a large dam and reservoir in Stanford's foothills remained a heated political debate as San Mateo County and Menlo Park, as well as Stanford, continued to call for a more comprehensive approach to flood control along the entire San Francisquito flood zone, while Palo Alto leaned on its neighbors to support the Ladera proposal. For every Corps-sponsored study of San Francisquito Creek that supported the dam as the cheapest way to prevent flooding, other non-Corps studies pointed to less costly and less damaging downstream improvements.

A "Supervisors' War" broke out in 1963, when Santa Clara County supervisors held out on unrelated cooperative projects in an unsuccessful attempt to press San Mateo's supervisors into supporting the Ladera project.[102] Ultimately, the flood-control districts of San Mateo and Santa Clara counties teamed up to support channel and creek-bed improvements and a diversion scheme as an "interim" solution. In 1971, the Corps of Engineers capitulated, finally ruling the now $15 million project officially dead.[103]

A UNIQUE UNIVERSITY ASSET

The legacy of the Ladera Dam controversy, Don Carlson wrote to a *Science Magazine* journalist in 1966, was that such battles are "95 percent political." Surrounded by five municipalities in two counties, and part of two congressional districts, two state assembly districts, and two state senate districts, Stanford continued to face potential loss of control over its land legacy.[104] "Our land in its natural state is a thing of beauty," David Casto, Stanford's real estate manager, noted that same year. But with ever-increasing condemnation threats for freeways, dams, parks, utility lines, county roads, and schools, he added, "if Stanford does not develop its land, it is evident that local government bodies will finds ways to develop it for us."[105]

For the remainder of Sterling's administration, Stanford vigorously fought any further "land grabs." The attitude "here on out will be one of a great deal of stiffening," Lyle Nelson told an appreciative Alumni Conference audience of more than 1,000 that year. "It is our intention to fight vigorously any further intrusion on Stanford's priceless land endowment."[106]

By 1966, some 5,100 acres had been assigned to academic use. With the sharp increase in the university's need for space for academic programs over the previous 10 years, the trustees now assumed not only that land use on campus would intensify and academic acreage increase, but also that some of the current 800 acres of leased lands would eventually be transferred to academic use.[107]

Annexations had turned out to be as problematic as condemnations. The threats were two-fold, noted Carlson: First, it was not unusual for a new town master plan to reach beyond its established jurisdiction "to 'plan' for the future use of the University's lands" without informing Stanford. Second, annexation of contiguous lands gave local jurisdictions the power to exercise zoning regulations, land use, and taxing authority. "Up to this point," Carlson wrote, "annexations have not taken place without university approval," but this was changing. The town of Woodside, Stanford's ally in the Ladera fight, tried to annex Jasper Ridge in 1963 to "control its development." They did not inform the university of their intention, however, prompting a reminder from Thomas Ford, Stanford's director of land development, that the university's designated academic lands could not be legally annexed.[108]

In 1967, Palo Alto's Planning Commission denied zoning permission for an annexed 5-acre site off Page Mill Road for a research center on population issues, hoping to prod the university into bargaining over Ladera Dam. The center was never built.[109]

By the end of the 1960s, some 665 acres had been condemned for public use, while Stanford had developed roughly 1,000 acres—far less than originally intended. Had these lands not been leased, financial Vice President Ken Cuthbertson estimated in 1970, they would now be taxed at a rate of around $1 million a year. Instead, the tenants paid the taxes, while the properties earned the university approximately $2 million annually, and provided more than $5 million in property tax and utility income to local school districts, municipalities, and county governments. Stanford's $3 million net gain in unrestricted funds each year, he calculated, was the equivalent of approximately 160 faculty positions or student aid for 1,800 undergraduates.[110]

And, as Sterling had predicted nearly two decades earlier, land use had had an obvious influence on gift income to the university. "Our gifts come from thousands of sources and for differing reasons, but virtually all donors expect Stanford to make the best use of our own resources in order to get maximum mileage from their gift dollars," said Cuthbertson, who also oversaw fundraising. "Donors have choices. If we were not doing a thoughtful, responsible job of developing part of the Stanford lands for income, I'm sure many of our donors would choose to support other institutions and I could not fault them."

Cuthbertson mirrored Sterling's unapologetic pride in the university's proactive management of its land endowment, an attitude that remains today an ongoing source of tension with its neighbors. Stanford's lands "were put in trust for the University, not for the surrounding communities," Cuthbertson noted. "Had the founders intended the latter, they would have established a park, not a university." However, this unique university asset not only had "enabled great educational advances; it had provided the surrounding communities with just about the only large open area remaining in the mid-Peninsula."

THE PLANNING OFFICE EVOLVES

On a walking tour of the campus in November 1948, Wally Sterling had noted the toll deferred maintenance and round-the-clock wartime use had taken on campus facilities. Fortunately, the newly appointed president inherited both tools and momentum to deal with the situation, but he soon added astute fundraising, collaborative processes, and long-range planning to the mix.

Sterling's predecessor, Don Tresidder, had created a novel, if modestly staffed, campus Planning Office and the Board of Trustees was committed to revitalizing the worn-down campus infrastructure. Three unusually large personal donations, in 1948, had made possible the $3 million building projects underway when Sterling took office in April 1949. In addition to a new microwave laboratory, two student residences were nearly finished (Crothers Hall for law students and Lucie Stern Hall for undergraduate men). Planning Director Ted Spencer also recommended major renovations to Main Quad buildings, including double-decking the single-story structures, and significant upgrades to traffic circulation and expansion of a science-technology quad and a cultural quad.

But the university's proud unveiling, in July 1948, of architectural plans for Stern Hall had stirred an unexpected 12-month alumni and faculty ruckus that dampened the otherwise enthusiastic welcome of Stanford's incoming president. The new

A 1948 drawing of Lucie Stern Hall for men shows the Escondido Road entrance between the ends of two wings. The strikingly contemporary design, complete with flat roofs, sparked an outpouring of alumni and faculty dismay. A mocking homemade sign, posted near the building during the spring 1950 Alumni Conference, read, "Opening Soon at This Site: Chevrolet Body Plant, Stanford Division."
STANFORD UNIVERSITY ARCHIVES

complex was modern in design, with functional horizontal lines, large glass areas, and a distinctly utilitarian look. What quickly caught the eye of many was Stern Hall's flat, tar-and-gravel roof, with no red tile to be seen. Also of concern, the plans had already gone out to bid, and construction had been scheduled.[111]

Before Sterling had the chance to settle in on campus or visit with alumni clubs, dozens of caustic alumni letters had been published, as had a scalding letter from William Kellogg, president of the then-independent Stanford Alumni Association, to the trustees. (A *Stanford Alumni Review* survey later revealed more than 90 percent of alumni respondents opposed the fundamentally new design direction.) The Associated Students' Executive Committee worried about what might happen with a forthcoming student union building, urging a design with "traditional Stanford lines, red-tile roofs and all." Critics of these reactions, in turn, alleged that emotions had gotten the better of common-sense cost considerations and architectural progress.[112]

The trustees compromised. In March 1949, they resolved that in the future "campus building construction should harmonize as far as possible with the general architectural effect of the original Stanford buildings." But, they added, due consideration will be given to availability and cost of materials, and structural and architectural advances. They would not, however, change Stern Hall's roof. The much-needed first section, to house 240 undergraduate men, was scheduled for an August completion.[113]

The trustees' resolution "gave them time to breathe," wrote architect and influential alumnus John Carl Warnecke, '41, in his April 1949 critique of the controversy. The trustees, however, did not address the controversy's inherent design question, he added. Could architectural characteristics that, for many alumni and faculty, evoked Stanford's historic character be reconciled with newer needs of campus buildings and with architectural progress? Yes, Warnecke responded, arguing not only that modern architectural design and technological advances accommodated such elements— notably red-tile sloped roofs, buff-colored walls, and arcades and courtyards—but also that color and texture were important aspects of modernist designs.[114]

Throughout the next three decades, the university adopted modernist architectural styles and techniques, but (with notable exceptions) such key design elements as red-tiled roofs, buff-colored exteriors, and the use of arcades and courtyards remained the standard. (This understanding was not applied to science labs, nor to the many mid/late century modern buildings on the leased land of the industrial park and shopping center.)

For Sterling, however, the Stern controversy highlighted broader needs than design selections. Warnecke, too, had critiqued the decision-making process and challenged the university's commitment to thoughtful planning. For decades, "a general feeling had prevailed that the architecture of Stanford would take care of itself," he stated during the Stern Hall crisis, adding that building decisions appeared to be made as "a closed-door policy and a minority decision of a few." Without criticizing Ted Spencer directly, Warnecke urged creation of a full-time supervising architect's position and a large buildings and grounds department under the Planning Office,

Director of Planning Harry Sanders points to a roof plan in a 1960 planning discussion with Alf Brandin (left), John (Jack) Lynd, associate director of planning, Sterling, and Caroline Moore Charles, chair of the trustee Buildings and Grounds Committee. Sanders was Stanford's first full-time director of planning.
JACK FIELDS / STANFORD UNIVERSITY ARCHIVES

something Stanford could not yet afford. He also suggested more than a dozen advisory committees (including a student committee), a cumbersome bureaucracy with unclear lines of authority unsuited to the new president's managerial style.

With neither the funds nor the inclination to build up the university's administration, Sterling focused on building a planning and approval process. By the end of his first year, Sterling had established a faculty advisory committee, which would grow significantly in influence over the next four decades. He also encouraged ongoing communication between his Planning Office, the advisory committee, and the trustees' Buildings and Grounds Committee.

Sterling incorporated building needs into long-range academic planning efforts as these expanded over the next decade. Improvement of research and teaching facilities became an integral part of faculty recruiting. Ample and upgraded student housing, so that all Stanford students could live on campus, also was a priority. Between 1950 and 1969, more than 4.1 million square feet, not including the Stanford Linear Accelerator Center, were added to campus infrastructure. This compares to the 2.5 million square feet constructed in the preceding 62 years, between 1887 and 1949. Unlike Stanford's building boom of the 1920s, the Sterling expansion was fostered not by football receipts but by campus-wide planning and fundraising efforts *(see Chapter 7)*.[115]

During the 1950s, Ted Spencer never again enjoyed the independence he had had working with Tresidder. Reporting directly to Sterling, Spencer also worked as an integral part of the president's faculty advisory committee. Preferring a more gradual approach, Sterling kept the responsibilities of the Buildings and Grounds Department, under Business Manager Alf Brandin, separate from those of building planning, design, and construction, under Spencer. From 1956 to 1959, heavily focused on the new medical center, Spencer reported to then presidential assistant Ken Cuthbertson, who was closely tied to the fundraising and financial aspects of that project. The

A classic 1960 Jack Fields photograph of President Sterling, looking over the Quadrangle from Hoover Tower, meant for a *Saturday Evening Post* feature on Sterling and Stanford. Sterling holds an architect's early concept for future science buildings beyond the Quad. JACK FIELDS / STANFORD UNIVERSITY ARCHIVES

Planning Office also now included a full-time associate planner, Harry L. Sanders Jr., a 1937 graduate of Tulane (architecture) with experience at San Francisco's Redevelopment Agency, along with a small but growing staff.

In 1959, the 67-year-old Ted Spencer resigned from Stanford. His firm continued to include Stanford among its clients (notably Tresidder Union, 1962), but Spencer also continued to design private residences, including one of his favorite projects, the Carmel home of his friend Ansel Adams.[116]

That year, Sterling named Harry Sanders as full-time director of planning, an expansion backed by the trustees. Although Sanders' office now reported to Brandin, Sterling gave Sanders the means to recruit additional architects, engineers, landscape designers, and project managers to coordinate, with faculty and outside architects, the ever-growing number of construction projects brought about with the success of the PACE fundraising campaign. The number of committees grew, too, with Sanders serving on more than 20 during PACE. Over the next decade, Stanford's Planning Office became the largest such office in the country. By his retirement in 1976, Sanders had overseen 515 building projects, earning a reputation for working effectively with faculty, staff, and trustees, as well as outside architects, contractors, and consultants.[117] *(For list of important new buildings and renovations, see Appendix B.)*

Sanders' planning office of the 1960s and 1970s also worked with an advisory council of architects, including Warnecke, Gardner Dailey, Ernest Kump, and Milton Pflueger, and landscape architects Thomas Church and Robert Royston. This group is credited with influencing the character of the university's architecture. (Many of the buildings and landscape projects of this era were designed by their firms, along with that of Ted Spencer.)[118]

Alf Brandin, newly named vice president for business affairs, also changed responsibilities in 1959. The position of land management director, now reporting to Brandin, was passed to staff counsel Thomas Ford, who had joined Brandin's staff in 1955 to administer research contracts and grants. Ford advised on the 1960 Coyote Hill controversy and took a special interest in the Stanford Industrial Park and in Sand

Hill Road's commercial development. Although a Yale and Michigan graduate, Ford became a passionate supporter of Stanford and a longtime benefactor after he resigned, in 1964, to follow a career in commercial real estate development. He was followed by Boyd Smith, but the title of land development director was abandoned.[119]

Sterling took personal pride in the appearance of the campus throughout his presidency and enjoyed discussions with Spencer and later with Sanders and his planning office staff and with visiting architects and landscape architects. Until 1959, when the Planning Office moved to Encina Hall, it was located across the courtyard behind the President's Office. "Wally was in the Planning Office so many times," remembers Gene Kershner, who joined the office in 1957. "Those few years that we reported directly to the president made us all feel so important!"[120]

One of Sterling's favorites was Tommy Church, nationally known landscape designer and a Stanford consultant for 30 years. Brandin and Sanders liked to reminisce about Sterling's eye for detail. When they were planning the Escondido Village high-rise buildings, the president often walked the site alone, recalled Brandin. Looking at the plans, he told Brandin and Sanders, "We can't take away the vista from the other side of El Camino Real looking back at our hills. You've got those [buildings] too close. You have to stagger [them] so people can see the hills."

"Wally virtually placed each one of those buildings himself, because he went out and visualized them from all four sides," said Brandin. "It was remarkable. He did that time and time again with many of the new buildings on campus. But he did so from the perspective of a university president, not a land developer."[121]

[Notes for this sidebar appear at the end of the book with the notes for Chapter 6.]

MAN WITH THE MIDAS TOUCH
DEVELOPING A FUNDRAISING STRATEGY

Few features of the Sterling administration have been studied as much as the historic change in the university's financial capacity. This change in Stanford's financial base, and the equally dramatic growth of the university's academic program, was grounded in Leland and Jane Stanford's generous legacy and invigorated by strong post–Second World War interest in higher education. But the dimensions of these changes owed much to the energetic leadership, pragmatic vision, and personality of President Wallace Sterling.[1]

As early as 1960, *The Saturday Evening Post* dubbed Sterling "Stanford's Man with the Midas Touch" and, a year later, *Time* magazine would attribute to Stanford a new "California Gold Rush." Under Sterling's oversight, Stanford experienced a six-fold increase in its endowment (from $41 million in 1949 to $268 million

in 1968) and a 10-fold increase in corporate, government, and individual gifts.[2]

On arriving in 1949, Sterling took an immediate interest in fundraising. The previous November, while considering Stanford's offer of the presidency, he had made his goals clear: Stanford should make every effort "to build a faculty not merely of good men but of the best men, and to attract a student body capable of high academic performance," but this could be done only with adequate financial resources. Stanford, he told the trustees, had "ground to gain" in both areas.[3] As university chancellor 26 years later, Sterling was still active in university fundraising and his broad, pragmatic goals had remained the same: "One cannot attract an outstanding student body or hire distinguished faculty without money."[4]

While Sterling's remarkable talents, as *The Saturday Evening Post* noted, included "a built-in radar for detecting big money and a flair for sizing up balance sheets at a glance," his more notable talent was his ability, unlike his predecessors, to bring an array of people into the process and help disparate groups work together. Throughout his administration, Sterling tried to impart to each university constituency—faculty,

< Ken Cuthbertson shows off the detailed model of the campus to highlight plans for new buildings during the trendsetting PACE fundraising campaign. The scale model, seen here in April 1961, was on the third floor of Encina Hall, South Wing. (Cuthbertson points to the current Business School location on the Outer Quad; a new headquarters, white, next to Memorial Hall, had been proposed.) STANFORD NEWS SERVICE

Dubbed Stanford's "Man with the Midas Touch" in 1960, Wallace Sterling had a talent for bringing people into the process and engaging all parts of the university—alumni, students, faculty, staff, and trustees—in his efforts to build Stanford's financial base.
JACK FIELDS / STANFORD UNIVERSITY ARCHIVES

staff, trustees, alumni, and students—a sense of engagement and goodwill.[5]

The university did not make a sudden leap forward but eased ahead during Sterling's administration, guided by the president's ability to articulate clear, pragmatic goals; to access opportunities; and to work across formal and informal channels. His strategy to make clear steps toward "self-help" during the 1950s—through reenergized alumni groups, engaged trustees, experiments at land development, as well as an increase in tuition—put Stanford in a position to take risks when opportunities arose to make targeted improvements. Equally important, these efforts led to a second decade of trend-setting analysis and forecasting, a landmark fundraising campaign, and ever-expanding confidence and expectations.

STANFORD'S TROUBLESOME LEGACY

Public and private interest in higher education during the 1950s and early 1960s would be backed by new prospects for foundation, corporate, and individual gifts as well as multifaceted government support. This was especially true in California, with its booming postwar economy, dramatically growing population, and considerable taxpayer investment in three public higher education systems (the University of California, the state colleges, and the community college system).

As Sterling moved into his office in spring 1949, however, such advantages were still in the future. Although he had visited the campus periodically since earning his doctorate, Sterling was struck by the deteriorating state of the university's 58-year-old physical plant. Maintenance had been deferred during the Depression and wartime uncertainties. Heavy use by military training programs had overtaxed both permanent and temporary facilities. Student housing remained inadequate, especially at a university determined to be largely residential.[6]

Stanford's original endowment, once generous for early enrollments of 600 or 1,000, was insufficient for a 1949 student body of more than 8,300 (including some 2,970 graduate students). Tuition, implemented in 1920 to cover additional costs, now constituted an important portion of the university's operating income, but covered only around 40 percent of the cost of educating each student. While veterans could take advantage of the GI Bill, postwar scholarship support for other students remained inadequate and student jobs were few.[7]

Sterling also found faculty morale conspicuously low. Sub-par salaries for much of the past 60 years, along with severely limited funds for library and laboratory facilities, and for research, travel, and publication, were only part of the problem. Significant increases in postwar enrollment brought in tuition money but had additional stress on classroom facilities, and on the faculty, which had not grown proportionately.[8]

Determined to infuse the faculty with new blood, boost morale, and attract outstanding students, Sterling set his eyes on more than temporary fixes. He needed a dramatic increase in stable, unencumbered funding. Funds with no strings attached, Sterling believed, "are the lifeblood of a private university."[9]

Sterling understood that he owed much to his predecessors, each of whom had different strengths and successes, and who had worked in less advantageous economic times.[10] He began with some well-developed tools at hand—an energetic and independent Alumni Association, an innovative and activist volunteer group known as the Stanford Associates, and an increasingly engaged Board of Trustees.

However, previous Stanford administrators also provided examples of miscues, miscommunication, and lost opportunities. And each president had been confronted with a stubborn and long-standing image problem: Stanford, founded as a rich man's philanthropy, had appeared to become a rich boy's country club, "a rich sleepy school with rich sleepy students," as *Time* magazine described it in 1962. Well into the 1960s, Sterling and his staff would battle what one staff member called "the public's impression

of unbound riches and the prevailing idea that outside gifts were neither wanted nor needed."[11]

Stanford University had been established in 1885 with a magnificent Founding Grant of land and the promise of a financial inheritance from its founders, Senator Leland Stanford and Jane Lathrop Stanford. As a result, by its opening in 1891 as a tuition-free coeducational institution, it had already gained the reputation as America's most richly endowed university. At the beginning of the 20th century, Stanford's endowment, estimated at more than $20 million, outstripped those of Columbia, Harvard, Yale, and MIT.[12]

During the lives of Senator and Mrs. Stanford, the university's actual endowment was its new physical plant and three large ranches, and ultimately, as residual heir, Leland Stanford's railroad bonds and other investments. Just as the Stanfords had paid out-of-pocket for design and construction of university buildings, the university's operating budget was managed as part of the Stanford family's complex financial estate. During her years as administrator of the Stanford Estate following her husband's 1893 death, Jane Stanford prioritized completing construction of the physical campus. A stunning campus on a grand scale was nearing completion when Mrs. Stanford died, in 1905.[13]

The notion that the university could go it alone was a mixed blessing. Leland Stanford

Stanford's future seemed bright in 1905, with one of the largest endowments in the country and an impressive campus, complete with Memorial Arch and statue of "Faith" at center of the Oval. But the 1906 earthquake caused irreparable damage across campus (including destruction of the Arch and Memorial Church's steeple). By 1920, repairs to remaining buildings, overly conservative investments, and post–World War I inflation had dropped Stanford's endowment below those of its peers. STANFORD UNIVERSITY ARCHIVES

had foreseen a time when the university's endowment would need strengthening, thus his assumption that his California ranches eventually would prove a valuable investment (he also predicted the possibility of future tuition fees). But while Mrs. Stanford welcomed gifts initiated by family members and close friends for targeted projects—to build a favorite book or art collection, or the establishment of Hopkins Marine Station—she actively discouraged overt fundraising by those associated with the university. Even during the university's dire financial doldrums of the mid-1890s, she found it personally humiliating to concede that outside funding might be needed to improve sub-par faculty salaries or help develop research facilities. Leland Stanford Junior University, she made clear, had been established as a complete gift to the people of California by the Stanfords as a memorial to their son, and needed no financial help.[14]

The university's photogenic image, as well as its pocketbook, was hard hit in 1906 by the San Francisco earthquake, when many of its most striking buildings were badly damaged or destroyed. Over the next three decades, the frugal Board of Trustees, constrained by trust requirements, California law, and post–World War I inflation, struggled to support a gradually expanding academic program.

While Stanford remained among the top 20 American universities (it was a founding member of the American Association of Universities in 1900), by 1920 its ambitions well outstripped its income. Its once-preeminent endowment had dropped to 20th in the nation. That it remained within range of its perceived peers was a credit to President Ray Lyman Wilbur's success with

Stanford University of the present and of the immediate future

Buildings under constr
or needed immediate
1. Residence Hall for men
2. Law Building
3. Biological Building
4. Women's Gymnasium
5. New dormitories for wor
6. Dining Hall for men —
7. Mining Building
8. Anatomy, physiology and bac
9. Memorial Building
10. Laboratory for physica
    industrial chemistr

Publicity for the university's earliest fundraising campaign, the First Million for Stanford, was aimed at alumni. Their cumulative small gifts were expected to match a foundation grant that would bring faculty salaries up to par. The campaign dragged through the 1920s and was saved from missing an embarrassing second deadline extension, in 1929, by a gift from the Board of Athletic Control (BAC).
STANFORD UNIVERSITY ARCHIVES

private foundations. As a respected member of many national efforts in higher education and public health, Dr. Wilbur drew strong and ongoing interest from the likes of the General Education Board, later subsumed by the Rockefeller Foundation, and the Carnegie Foundation for the Advancement of Teaching.[15] Sterling would later focus on ways to make these ties stronger and even more fruitful.

Equally important, Wilbur's close friend Herbert Hoover, elected to the Board of Trustees in 1912, promoted major reforms in the way endowment income was monitored and invested, providing the trustees a more proactive approach to its stagnating bond investments *(see Chapter 13)*. At a time when corporate giving was legally limited, Hoover encouraged business associates to join him in making personal gifts of initial funding for creation of programs in which he was interested, such as the Hoover War Library and the Graduate School of Business. He also promoted a review of faculty salaries and encouraged faculty recruitment. However, Hoover had little faith in the capacity, much less willingness, of most Stanford alumni to make significant contributions and sought major donors elsewhere.[16]

Dr. Wilbur also had seen the need for long-range planning. By 1921, he and the trustees had in hand a 10-year plan, which proved especially useful in Wilbur's ongoing efforts to attract foundation funding. It was Wilbur's reputation with foundations that won Stanford, in 1921–22, the opportunity to earn a foundation matching grant. The university's first fundraising campaign, the First Million for Stanford, was triggered by a proposed $300,000 grant from the General Education Board to improve faculty salaries and pensions. The matching-grant drive for $700,000 was aimed primarily at alumni. After an initial rush of pledges, the trustees' new Endowment Committee outlined

two more campaigns, a Second Million (for new buildings) and Third Million (for the Medical School) to support the broad goals outlined by their 10-year plan.[17]

The campaigns turned into an eight-year slog, with more than one deadline extended. The trustee committee had turned the drive over to a consultant, then to an "endowment secretary" with little experience and unclear responsibilities. Efforts were lackluster as pledges were not converted into gifts. Financial reporting was rosy, but misleading.[18] The task ultimately fell heavily on the personal intervention of a president uncomfortable with pressing the flesh.[19]

Wilbur was saved from the humiliation of missing yet another deadline extension in 1929 by a vital $50,000 donation from Stanford's Board of Athletic Control (BAC), whose chairman, Dr. Thomas M. Williams, '97, and secretary, Professor J. Pearce Mitchell, '03, Ph.D. '09, were close friends of Wilbur. A final $16,000 to complete the match was raised in a five-day push by local alumni.[20]

The BAC's efforts were also significant as the Second Million collapsed with a mere $18,000

Professor and University Registrar J. Pearce Mitchell, a close friend of President Wilbur, was longtime secretary of the Board of Athletic Control. Here, Mitchell might have been dictating his manuscript for *Stanford University, 1916–1941* (1958), which documents many aspects of Stanford's second quarter century.   STANFORD UNIVERSITY ARCHIVES

Stanford's iconic Lagunita boathouse, seen here in 1949, along with its golf course, polo team, temperate climate, and tree-studded environs, fostered the university's country club image for decades. The boathouse was demolished in 1989, and the lake is now mostly dry. The professionally designed golf course, opened in 1930, featured a Bakewell & Brown clubhouse. Charles Seaver, '34, at left, was co-medalist in the 1931 U.S. Amateur; Lawson Little, also '34, won the British and U.S. Amateur championships in 1934 and the U.S. Open in 1940. In the mid-1930s, Stanford's polo team included a touch of Hollywood: Will Rogers Jr., '35 (second from left), son of the popular American movie star, humorist, and polo enthusiast, was also an intercollegiate debater.

The BAC, a joint faculty-student-alumni committee, had overseen athletics since 1916. Its chairman, Dr. Thomas M. Williams, a classmate and friend of Ray Lyman Wilbur, helped plug holes in faltering fundraising efforts during the 1920s and early 1930s. The BAC funded Branner Hall for men and Roble Gymnasium for women, both targets of a Second Million for Stanford Campaign. STANFORD UNIVERSITY ARCHIVES

Trustee Paul Shoup, a personal friend of Herbert Hoover and Ray Lyman Wilbur, in 1927. In taking on leadership of the Third Million for Stanford (aimed at Medical School improvements), Shoup changed tactics. By targeting San Francisco residents who appreciated access to Stanford's hospital facilities, rather than relying on alumni, he brought in a remarkable $400,000 with little help, but still fell far short of the campaign's goal. STANFORD UNIVERSITY ARCHIVES

raised. The BAC, a joint faculty-student-staff oversight committee, had taken charge of Stanford's athletics program in 1916, turning it into a self-supporting, even profitable enterprise. BAC funding built a large men's residence, Branner Hall (opened early 1924), and Roble Gymnasium for women (1931), both targets of the campaign, among many other athletic facilities and improvements.[21]

Trustee Paul Shoup, the Southern Pacific Railroad executive who led the medical campaign, took a different approach, urging San Franciscans, rather than just alumni, to support Stanford Hospital and Medical School (located in the City) as a community resource. Without the promise of a matching grant, Shoup brought in more than $400,000 for the Third Million.[22]

As the Depression hit, Stanford attracted two extraordinarily large matching grant offers, a one-for-one $750,000 Carnegie grant for the sciences, and an extraordinary $2.5 million anonymous gift with a required $1.25 million match for the Medical School. Both were doomed from the start. With Ray Lyman Wilbur in Washington, D.C., as Herbert Hoover's secretary of the interior (1929–33), caretaker acting President Robert Swain faced the severe economic downturn and budget deficit with no fundraising strategy, staff, or means to manage such an effort. It proved impossible to raise the staggering sum of $2 million needed. The anonymous donor walked away.[23]

Nevertheless, Depression-era Stanford did not suffer as much as some campuses (there were no economy-driven layoffs, for example), but faculty salaries were temporarily cut in 1933 and maintenance deferred for the duration. Ironically, as Stanford became more dependent on tuition income, the image of a "rich man's university" took on a new twist. With few scholarships available and student jobs disappearing, the campus drew a less economically diverse and more affluent student body. Given its bucolic environment and temperate climate, not to mention its boathouse and golf course, Stanford's country-club image emerged.[24]

In 1933, trustees embarked on an unexpected strategy to generate more tuition income. That year, they repealed Mrs. Stanford's 1899 limitation of the number of women who could enroll at one time, the legendary "Stanford 500." Within five years, enrollment of women had more than tripled, to 1,588.[25]

SKILLFUL HERDERS

Prompted by declining gifts and fragile tuition revenue as the Depression lingered, and by Wilbur's frustration with the personal side of fundraising, a group of alumni came together in 1934 to help. Named the Stanford Associates and led by Dr. Harry B. Reynolds, '96, they were initially interested in helping students hard hit by the Depression, but soon expanded, with Wilbur's blessing, to consider broader ways to support the university. Formally organized in October 1935 with 41 members, the self-generating group grew quickly. Many invited were successful businessmen, but others were considered men of ideas or scholarship who could draw contributions from others. It was an all-male organization until 1954. (Notably absent from the group was Herbert Hoover.)[26]

"Getting signatures on the dotted line is a good deal like herding jackrabbits on a bicycle," Wilbur wrote in his autobiography, "but the Stanford Associates turned out to be skillful herders." Two iconic programs were established: the Stanford Annual Fund Committee and a Special Gifts and Bequests Committee. Students as well as alumni were involved in committee work, programs, and annual

The extroverted Paul H. Davis, who returned to Stanford as director of the Stanford Associates Annual Fund and later became its first general secretary, skillfully bridged the gap between Wilbur and Hoover's inner circle and the founders of the Associates.
STANFORD UNIVERSITY ARCHIVES

fundraising drives. Faculty joined the group's committees, donor efforts, and programs about the university. Deeply interested in fostering student scholarship, the Associates established a "Pick of the Crop" committee to recruit outstanding California high school students. By the end of the 1930s, Stanford's gifts totaled $7.6 million for the decade, significantly more than the $5.5 million received during the affluent 1920s.[27]

In 1937, the Associates hired Paul H. Davis, '22, Engr. '23, as director of the Annual Fund. Davis, fresh from overseeing Depression-related philanthropic relief efforts in San Francisco, set a style as well as a pace. The extroverted and energetic Davis worked well with President Wilbur, despite their very different personalities.[28]

Davis also worked well with influential Associates, such as Judge Louis H. Roseberry, '03, a leading Southern California trust lawyer. Alumni had been discussing the possibilities of alumni bequests for a decade, but Roseberry had noted Harvard's success attracting bequests from individuals with no connection to the university. Lawyers, particularly those trained at Stanford, could be advised about new California tax law regarding gifts, he concluded, and in doing so, be kept better informed about the university. (It would be known as the "R Plan," in Roseberry's honor.) The Associates' second hire, David S. Jacobson, '30, LL.B. '34, "pounded the pavement" along with other R-Planners to encourage lawyers and trust officers to remind clients about Stanford's needs and opportunities when drafting wills.[29]

Roseberry's Special Gifts Committee co-chair, Morgan A. Gunst, ex-'08, focused on improving Stanford's efforts at attracting individual major gifts. Gunst, a retired vice president of the Bank of America active in San Francisco Jewish philanthropies, developed what Jacobson called the "G Plan"—an invaluable list of special prospects. Fundraising efforts during the Sterling era

Judge Lou Roseberry (second from right) and Morgan Gunst (right), the innovative co-chairs of the Stanford Associates' Special Gifts Committee, were each recipients of Stanford's Degree of Uncommon Man. President Sterling, seen here with Trustee May Chandler Goodan, presented the awards, Stanford's highest honor, in December 1954. (It is now the Degree of Uncommon Citizen.)
STANFORD UNIVERSITY ARCHIVES

would benefit greatly from the Associates' efforts to actively reach out for future gifts as well as nailing down bequests.[30]

Together Davis and Jacobson emphasized the personal and the positive, with both alumni volunteers and donors. Appeals were made personally (not by mass-produced letters from Wilbur or Hoover), and with careful attention to major donors' interests. Requests were never complaining or needy but rather reflected how the university could productively spend new money. This strategy was carried forward by the Sterling administration.[31]

Gifts during the 1940s, based on their spadework and on more active interest among trustees, were encouraging. In 1945, an exceptional individual gift of nearly $1.3 million in memory of former trustee Wallace Alexander, held the record as the largest unrestricted gift to Stanford for the next 15 years. Stanford's gifts that year (1945–46) exceeded those received by "Big Four" fundraisers Harvard, Yale, Columbia, and Chicago—a feat Stanford would not match for years to come.[32]

By Sterling's arrival, pieces of the staffing puzzle were at hand, if not quite yet in place. In 1941, President Wilbur had moved the Associates' staff into the President's Office as the General Secretary's Office (rather than as a vice president or assistant to the president). Under Sterling, the general secretary would work closely with the president and his assistants for financial affairs, Robert Wert and later Kenneth Cuthbertson.[33]

As Stanford emerged from the uncertainties of the Second World War, President Donald B. Tresidder, Wilbur's successor, increasingly focused on continuing to attract government research funding, on land-development possibilities, and on fostering relations with businesses through establishment of the Stanford Research Institute, but he appeared to be withdrawing from alumni colleagues and particularly the Stanford Associates, of which he had been a charter member.[34]

When General Secretary Davis, fed up with what he thought to be a tense and divisive administration, left Stanford in 1946 for Columbia,

Tresidder promoted the recently arrived associate general secretary, Thomas P. Carpenter, a Dartmouth alumnus and former professor at Knox College. (David Jacobson was then serving as Tresidder's assistant.) Tresidder's vice president, Alvin C. Eurich, thought Carpenter "just the right person to help Don get the program underway." Whatever the new program was that Eurich had in mind, Carpenter struggled with what was at hand, failing to connect with key players among the alumni, the Stanford Associates, and the faculty. (His only Stanford tie apparently was the unpopular Alvin Eurich—the two had worked at the Bureau of Naval Personnel's Standards and Curriculum Section during the war.)[35]

Tresidder's postwar attempts to improve academic programs and explore alternate sources of income made significant strides, foreshadowing Sterling's goals, but these were cut short by his sudden death in early 1948. The Board of Trustees, especially its new president, Paul C. Edwards, looked forward to putting a new man at the helm who could take advantage of what seemed to be a new momentum while also dealing with problems and difficulties that had been evident over the past decades. The charismatic J. E. Wallace Sterling fit the bill. "Possessed of intelligence, urbane manners, wit, and generous good sense, Sterling was in many ways the perfect choice to provide Stanford with leadership," Frank Medeiros wrote in his dissertation on the Sterling era. "No one could have possibly anticipated at the time just how far Stanford University was to progress in the years to come."[36]

BUILDING THE BASE

On arriving in April 1949, Sterling evaluated the small staff inherited from the Tresidder-Eurich administration, particularly those whose positions seemed unclear or accomplishments limited. While serving as acting president, Alvin

Eurich had created the new position of vice president of university development in late 1948 when he hired Louis Lundborg, '27, formerly manager of San Francisco's Chamber of Commerce and a busy Stanford Associate. Eurich expected him to work closely with Carpenter on the Annual Fund (which Lundborg had chaired since 1947) and other unspecified efforts, as well as public relations, although his relationship to Carpenter, or to Fred Glover, director of information, and other staff is unclear. When Lundborg left Stanford in September 1949 for a very successful career at the Bank of America, the new president did not replace him.[37] Sterling avoided the title "vice president" altogether for another 10 years.

While Lundborg's position seemed ill-defined, General Secretary Tom Carpenter seemed at sea. Sterling found the gentlemanly but unassertive Carpenter likeable but ineffective. Unlike Paul Davis or Dave Jacobson (back as associate general secretary), Carpenter avoided "going out into the field," as Jacobson put it, to build contacts and prospects, but rather focused on building extensive files.[38]

As Sterling made the rounds of alumni conferences and Associates' events throughout 1949 and 1950, Jacobson was clearly the go-to man. Sterling was quick to pick up Jacobson's cues. "Dave Jacobson has told me of your very effective work on Stanford's behalf in the San Diego area," the recently arrived president wrote a San Diego attorney and volunteer that autumn. "More power to you. I am sure you have no idea how much it means to me in these early days as President of Stanford to know that we have such effective volunteers backing us up."[39]

In 1951, after Carpenter resigned because of ill health, Sterling promoted Dave Jacobson, who would serve as general secretary until 1965. While Sterling's administrative staff thought Jacobson mercurial and given to dispensing a voluminous flow of memorandums to the president and others, he was an innovative and effective fundraiser. Ken Cuthbertson, Sterling's assistant and later vice president of development, thought Jacobson's imprint on Stanford fundraising "without compare." While presidential assistant, Cuthbertson once told Sterling that he "didn't understand Dave going off and looking into some hole someplace on this or that issue. And Wally said, 'Well, Dave is one of those people who can see a worm in an apple a mile away.'"[40]

The energetic if temperamental Jacobson later admitted he did not always see eye-to-eye with Sterling, and nearly resigned at least once. Nevertheless, the two developed an effective working relationship. Sterling found ways to help underwrite additional staff support, while Jacobson recruited and trained talented professionals, many of whom later went on to major positions elsewhere. Traveling often in his fundraising efforts, Jacobson quickly drew together the Associates' directors and standing committees to develop a plan for expanding gift support during the 1950s, while continuing to work closely with the R-Planners.[41]

In Sterling's eyes, the alumni conferences and the founding of the Stanford Associates were two significant steps that helped prepare the university to take advantage of the opportunities of the 1950s and 1960s. Each was a voluntary alumni action, he said, "acting on their own initiative and enterprise because they aspired to improve something they valued and loved."[42]

Like the Stanford Associates, the Stanford Alumni Association provided an especially welcoming environment for the congenial and articulate new president at local events and especially at its increasingly popular alumni conferences. Sterling began speaking at the annual Los Angeles conference even before moving back to Stanford, in April 1949, and spoke at seven more

Stanford-trained lawyer Dave Jacobson (seen here in 1962) joined the Stanford Associates in 1937 to help "pound the pavement" to pin down bequests. Later, reporting to Sterling as general secretary, he oversaw fundraising during the 1950s until the 1959 elevation of Ken Cuthbertson to vice president of finance, with responsibility for development. Jacobson and the General Secretary's Office continued to focus on legal issues regarding gifts, bequests, and donor relations.
STANFORD NEWS SERVICE

annual conferences across the West during his first months in office. "I sensed a genuine pride in the Stanford name," he noted 10 years later, "but also a rather wavering pride in the University's reputation for distinction," fearing that the university had reached a plateau.[43]

Even so, at alumni conferences and other events, Sterling was gratified to find strong interest among many individual alumni in helping to improve Stanford's fundraising record. Writing in 1950 to George Morell, publisher of the *Palo Alto Times* and a Stanford trustee who took special interest in fundraising, Sterling reported:

I'm just back from three days in Southern California where I've been taking soundings about the possibilities of support for an enlarged scholarship program at Stanford. I didn't bring anything back in my bag except the knowledge that donors are open. We will have to play it carefully I'm sure. I doubt that we can count on pie in the sky, but at least I returned feeling a little optimistic.[44]

His luncheon address at annual alumni conferences, bookended by faculty panels on timely topics and academic strengths, became a key conference element. Sterling used this forum and the Association's monthly magazine to promote alumni participation and support throughout his presidency, and the Association grew substantively. Under Director Jack W. Shoup, '28 (1947–58), the independent Stanford Alumni Association became the fastest growing alumni organization in the country: membership doubled and life memberships tripled. The regional Stanford Conferences, the first and best of their kind in the United States, tripled their number of cities by the end of the 1950s, while Stanford clubs and reunions, as well as the Alumni Association's monthly magazine, became important avenues to help clarify the university's financial needs and goals.[45]

Ken Cuthbertson, '40, was an active alumni volunteer before joining Sterling's staff in 1954 as presidential assistant. Looking back at an early

Tex Middleton was a strong voice among Stanford alumni in Southern California, particularly regarding fundraising and the opening of a Southern California office in 1953.
STANFORD NEWS SERVICE

meeting with the new president, he noted that he and his fellow alumni activists had been used to Wilbur's "rather formal personality" and Tresidder's distance, but Sterling was "different from anything we expected. He was warm and open. I can remember the reaction from alumni that I knew. . . . People loved him right away." Robert Pierce, Alumni Association director during the 1960s, said, "When Wally walks into the room with the Alumni Board, they all feel as if they've known him forever and they're relaxed."[46]

Southern California offered both special opportunities with alumni and increasing fundraising competition. Caltech, Pomona College, and the University of Southern California were intensifying their fundraising efforts. With many Stanford alumni in the region, a Southern California office seemed a logical step to reduce the sense of distance between the university and alumni in Los Angeles, Santa Barbara, and San Diego.[47]

Jacobson had been reluctant to support this move because of the influence of a few alumni concerned largely with recruiting and supporting football players to compete with USC and UCLA. But when Joel (Tex) Middleton, '26, became a strong voice among the Southern

During Jack Shoup's 11 years as director (1947–58), the then-independent Alumni Association became the fastest growing alumni organization in the country, with an award-winning monthly magazine and an expanding network of alumni conferences and clubs across the country.
STANFORD UNIVERSITY ARCHIVES

Californians, Jacobson backed Sterling's decision to open a small office in Los Angeles.

The Southern California office, established in 1953, was meant to be a fundraising arm, but it also served as an important outreach office to Southern California alumni and parents on other university issues. "The alumni down there were starved for attention from the university. Wilbur had never given them much, and Tresidder was seldom there," recalled Don Carlson, its second director (1954–59) and later director of university relations. "So, when we finally opened an office there, that really meant something."[48]

STANFORD'S DISTINGUISHED TRAVELING SALESMAN

Stanford's efforts during the 1950s were supported by what Sterling called "a favorable breeze" as the country, and especially California,

grew prosperous and interest in the possibilities of higher education became widespread. Federal aid to campuses like Stanford, UC Berkeley, and Caltech, with strong science and engineering programs, was especially promising.[49]

Military funding had helped keep Stanford's classrooms open during the war years, supporting faculty research and salaries as well as military training programs on campus. After a drop in the late 1940s, federal funds again became available during the Korean War for targeted faculty research, a trend strengthened by the Soviet Union's launch of Sputnik in 1957 and deepening Cold War concerns. Equally important for Stanford, however, were general funds provided by nonspecific federal aid programs, such as the National Defense Education Act (1957), which sponsored a broader base of recipients than the GI Bill, as well as supporting research in the social sciences and loans to

Donn B. Tatum (left), the class of 1934's alumni president, and John C. Cosgrove (right), 25th reunion endowment gift chairman, presented President Sterling with a $104,325 check, the largest effort to date by reunion classes. As Stanford broadened fundraising opportunities in the early 1960s, Sterling believed alumni volunteer organizations were still key.
STANFORD UNIVERSITY ARCHIVES

students. The National Research Facilities Act (1953) had contributed to construction of the new Medical Center on campus.[50]

The Sterling administration would later be criticized for depending too much on federal funding.[51] Sterling, however, remained cautious about reliance on federal aid, due to its patchwork nature and to the threat of political interference. As a member of the Commission on Financing Higher Education from 1949 to 1952, Sterling shared the commission's distrust of federal expansion into higher education and its preference for foundation, corporate, and individual gift funding. Sterling was not opposed to government aid, but he considered reliance on it, except for targeted improvements or research, to be dangerous.[52]

Sterling devoted much of his fundraising time to cultivating foundation and corporate relationships. The *Stanford Daily*, in 1956, called President Sterling "Stanford's distinguished traveling salesman," noting that he spent some 10 weeks a year on the road as he combined alumni conferences and national committee work with meetings with foundation officials. Sterling made sure the students understood that it was more than public relations. The article continued, "Dr. Sterling says he has three main objectives: meeting alumni demands, pursuing a 'man hunt' for faculty talent, and furthering the 'dollar hunt.'"[53]

The Ford Foundation, a major resource of funding for universities, had been re-created as a major national philanthropy after the war, and by 1950 had become an important force in American higher education. It would be instrumental in two major Stanford fundraising efforts during Sterling's administration: the Medical School campaign, 1956–59, and the PACE Campaign, 1961–64. The Rockefeller and Carnegie foundations also expanded their interest in academic programs and remained important benefactors for Stanford.[54]

Sterling with trustees Lawrence Kimpton, '31, M.A. '32 (center) and David Packard, '34, Engr. '39, at a Los Angeles fundraising event around 1961. Kimpton had been dean of students and a philosophy professor when Sterling arrived in 1949. Packard, a former trustee president, 1958–60, and already a noted philanthropist, headed the trustee's major gifts effort for the PACE Campaign. ROTHSCHILD PHOTO / STANFORD NEWS SERVICE

As one Stanford dean told the *Saturday Evening Post* in 1960, "the big foundations are great gamblers, and they want to bet on something big. Wally realized that Stanford was a good package to sell, and he sold it."[55] The president's calendar for a 1954 New York City trip was emblematic: John Gardner, president of the Carnegie Foundation; Jeremiah Milbank, philanthropist and friend of Herbert Hoover (regarding a gift to the Hoover Institution); Herbert Hoover, at breakfast in the Waldorf Towers; Alfred P. Sloan Jr. of General Motors and the Sloan Foundation; and Dean Rusk, president of the Rockefeller Foundation.[56]

Sterling liked to recount the advice of one major foundation head: "Don't send me any of your professional money-raisers or I'll throw 'em out. I want to deal with you or your deans or professors." By the mid-1950s, his administration budgeted travel funds for deans and faculty to visit foundation officers, most of whom were on the East Coast, to explore and develop funding ideas.[57]

While corporate support had first surfaced during the Depression, its legality was questionable until legislation in various states during the 1950s facilitated charitable corporate gifts. Stanford joined other major private universities in 1956 in establishing guidelines for corporate giving, and Sterling was a welcome speaker at an array of business meetings and corporate events.[58]

The appointment of engineering Dean Frederick E. Terman as Sterling's second provost (1955–65) marked a new administration effort at cultivating industry as well as federal government sources. Sterling and Terman were an especially effective team as they promoted stronger foundation and corporate funding, and enticed faculty in the humanities and social sciences as well as engineering and the sciences

into taking a more active role in analyzing their departmental needs and exploring off-campus resources to maintain Stanford's momentum into the 1960s.[59]

Many national studies remark on Stanford's burst of growth during this period, as it refashioned itself into a university of national prominence. Particularly after Terman's appointment, wrote John Walsh, Stanford's "transformation was an astutely conducted metamorphosis achieved through purposeful engagement of resources and particularly of its relations with industry and the federal government."[60]

Sterling, however, recognized that there were many key individuals who contributed to this effort as trustees, staff, faculty, and alumni. Often recruiting among those with strong Stanford ties, he looked for participants who also could communicate easily with faculty.

GREAT PROGRESS REQUIRES AN ENGINE

Few among Sterling's staff made as notable an impact on Stanford fundraising as Sterling's financial assistant and later vice president of finance and development, Kenneth M. Cuthbertson. "Many people refer to that remarkable period of growth at Stanford as the Sterling-Terman era, but I think of it as the Sterling-Terman-Cuthbertson era," said Donald Kennedy, Stanford's eighth president, who had participated in fundraising as a biology professor during that era. "Great progress requires an engine," Kennedy said. During this great period of growth, "the thoughtful, adroit risk-taker that provided the engine was Kenny."[61]

For more than two decades, Cuthbertson would play a pivotal role in organizing Stanford's long-range financial analysis and planning, two pathbreaking fundraising campaigns, and nearly two decades of organized fundraising programs. Equally important, Cuthbertson was

KEN CUTHBERTSON
ENGINE OF CHANGE

Kenneth M. Cuthbertson (1919–2000) was instrumental in implementing Stanford's goals of attracting top faculty and outstanding students by developing trendsetting fundraising programs that drew unusually high participation by alumni and faculty volunteers.

"Ken was wonderfully thoughtful not only about the university and its value but also about the kind of community it was," former Stanford President Donald Kennedy remarked at the time of Cuthbertson's death. "In a time of great change in the university, he was able to make everyone feel they were still part of the Stanford family. And that was a real challenge. He won and retained the respect of this faculty and was very well regarded."[1]

Cuthbertson was president of the Associated Students (his future wife, Coline Upshaw, was vice president) and captain of the soccer team when he was recruited by David Jacobson as part of a council of seniors to augment the university's fundraising efforts. The dollar results were modest, Cuthbertson later recounted, but the seniors "got a heavy indoctrination into Stanford fundraising from which Dave Jacobson expected future results." Cuthbertson remained active in alumni affairs after graduation, developing a strong interest in fundraising.

Cuthbertson, a Phi Beta Kappa economics major, graduated from Stanford in 1940. While attending Harvard Business School in 1941, he joined the Navy, serving for five years. After his discharge, he completed his MBA, in 1947, at Stanford's Graduate School of Business and then joined McKinsey and Company, management consultants. From 1951 to 1954, he was a partner of Levison Brothers, a Pacific Coast insurance brokerage firm whose

On a bicycle built for two and dressed up for Back to the Farm Day during their senior year, 1940, are student body President Ken Cuthbertson and Vice President Coline Upshaw (the future Mrs. Cuthbertson).
STANFORD UNIVERSITY ARCHIVES

Kenneth Cuthbertson, '40, began fundraising as a student volunteer. So great was Sterling's confidence in Cuthbertson that, five years after hiring him as a presidential assistant, Sterling put Cuthbertson in charge of both finance and development.
STANFORD NEWS SERVICE

founder, Robert Levison, '21, was a founding member of the Stanford Associates and on the Stanford Alumni Association's Board of Directors. Cuthbertson became Sterling's assistant for financial affairs in 1954.

As part of a 1959 administrative reorganization, Cuthbertson became vice president for finance, which also included responsibility for development. He was the principal officer in charge of the PACE Campaign, 1961–64, and the Campaign for Stanford, 1972–77, each setting a national fundraising record in American higher education. In 1971, he gave up the finance role, becoming vice president for development. He retired from Stanford in 1977 to serve as administrative vice president, then president, of the James Irvine Foundation. In the late 1980s, Cuthbertson returned as a volunteer co-chair for major gifts in Stanford's successful $1 billion Centennial Campaign.

Stanford's extraordinary success in fundraising was due, Cuthbertson said in 1980, to a long-term approach, which overcomes economic instability and outlasts the "glow of the moment" that comes with large single gifts. This approach, he added, along with "the realization that education comes from leadership and support, not administration," and the ability to develop an effective staff, were key. His successor, Joel Smith, pointed to two other factors: Cuthbertson's integrity and his commitment to Stanford and its academic program.[2]

In 1981, in his honor, several faculty families anonymously funded the prestigious Kenneth M. Cuthbertson Award to be given annually at commencement for exceptional service to Stanford. Cuthbertson was the award's first recipient.

NOTES

1. Kennedy quoted in "Kenneth Cuthbertson, Fund-Raising Strategist, Dies at 81," *Stanford Report*, May 3, 2000, 2.
2. "Cuthbertson Energized Stanford Fundraising: A Man of Integrity and Conviction," *Stanford Daily*, May 29, 1980. See also Bob Beyers, "Ken Cuthbertson: Stanford's Financial Architect," *Sandstone & Tile* 24:2/3 (Spring-Summer 2000) 14–21.

widely respected on and off campus, a modest man admired for his commitment to the faculty, as well as his integrity and rapport with fellow staff.[62]

It was Fred Glover's idea to bring in Cuthbertson to fill the position as Sterling's presidential financial assistant and budget control officer, in 1954. Two years earlier, when Glover first became Sterling's assistant, he had teamed up with Robert J. Wert, assistant to the president for financial affairs. When Wert decided to leave the university in 1954, Glover had a successor in mind. Sterling asked: "It isn't a Delt, is it?" (Glover and Wert, like Cuthbertson, were members of Stanford's chapter of Delta Tau Delta fraternity.) "Fred, people are going to think the Delts are running the university." Glover, an alumni advisor of his chapter, had been impressed with the breadth of Cuthbertson's understanding of both fraternity and university affairs. The president reluctantly agreed to see Cuthbertson for 15 minutes. The meeting lasted two hours. Glover proudly concluded: "I've always considered it to be my greatest contribution to Stanford that I recommended Ken Cuthbertson for that job."[63]

Soon after, in a long letter typed on a Sunday, Sterling welcomed Cuthbertson with a comprehensive list of items for the new assistant, including the upcoming budget, non-academic land development, and a financially troubled Stanford Press. "You really can't imagine," Sterling concluded, "how delighted I am to have you aboard."[64]

A few months after starting his work, Cuthbertson wrote Robert Moulton, '40, a Stanford friend and classmate then at the Ford Foundation:

> In my first three months I have been so busy trying to learn and at the same time shoulder problems requiring early action that I haven't had an opportunity to think. Unfortunately, this lack of time to think seems to be an occupational disease in University administration. I just hope that over a period of time I get where I can be of sufficient help to let Wally have some time for thinking, anyhow. As you can well imagine, the demands on his time are fantastic and if he is to maintain the kind of good climate of public relations he has developed, he must get involved in a good deal of non-administrative work.[65]

DEVELOPING A FUNDRAISING STRATEGY

The university's first foray into a well-organized fundraising campaign that effectively drew together trustees, staff, and alumni leaders turned into an important learning experience. The Medical Center Fund Campaign, 1956–59, enabled the move of the Medical School to campus by raising $22 million for the new facilities and the school's endowment. Like the Third Million for Stanford of the 1920s, this campaign was aimed at a more widespread appeal than Stanford alumni by engaging with those interested in medical education and research throughout Northern California, but its organization was notably different.

The proposed move of the school to the main campus was controversial, with vocal objection from some Medical School alumni and faculty *(see Chapter 4)*. Echoes of past failure loomed. The campaign received a significant kick-start contribution from the Ford Foundation of $3.1 million, as part of the foundation's program to strengthen medical school instruction but, as before, individual gifts lagged. Despite a list of distinguished leaders—topped by honorary Chairman Herbert Hoover—and several impressive individual gifts, Cuthbertson found Stanford volunteers reluctant to "approach large gifts prospects personally and carefully." When the first listing of major gift donors awkwardly included many non-Stanford donors (many of

The Stanford Medical Center fundraising campaign, 1956–59, taught the trustees and Sterling's staff important strategic and organizational lessons used in later, broader, fundraising efforts. In summer 1956, from left: Winsor Cutting, dean of medicine; W. Parmer Fuller III, Stanford Associates team leader; James Black, trustee campaign vice-chair; Herbert Hoover, trustee and honorary chair; and President Sterling.
STANFORD NEWS SERVICE

them UC alumni) but fewer than expected Stanford trustees and alumni, there were "some hasty commitments from Stanford people," he recalled.[66]

Trustee President Lloyd Dinkelspiel's ties to San Francisco philanthropists proved vital, as did staff efforts. Associate General Secretary Lyle Cook, with the help of a consulting firm, worked closely with trustees, Stanford Associates, and other volunteers to organize and complete the effort. The Associates team leaders turned out to be an impressive list; all were future trustees and leaders of two later campaigns (PACE, 1961–64, and the Campaign for Stanford, 1972–77), among them future trustee Presidents W. Parmer Fuller III, Richard Guggenhime, and Morris Doyle, as well as future GSB Dean Ernest Arbuckle.[67]

While the Medical School relocation project was underway, Sterling continued to focus on upgrading Stanford's overall academic program. "If we can't find quality in faculty in sufficient numbers, we are failing to reproduce our seed corn," he told Stanford Annual Fund organizers in 1957, emphasizing the difficulty in getting good faculty when handicapped by low academic salaries.[68] Sterling, Terman, and Cuthbertson gave top priority to improving salaries and benefits.

Pulling in funds from a variety of sources, including land development initiatives like the Stanford Shopping Center, they made the leap of faith that spending on faculty recruitment and salary improvements would attract the kind of quality that would, in turn, attract adequate permanent funding. In 1955, the Ford Foundation awarded Stanford $3.6 million toward that effort. The comparatively large size of the grant, most of which went into endowed faculty salaries, led trustee President Lloyd Dinkelspiel to joke that the university should spell its name StanFord.[69]

In 1959, on Chet Huntley's nationally broadcast *Outlook* television series, Sterling described a university president's inescapable and time-consuming task of raising money. Nevertheless, he said, there was reward in seeing the campus grow and widen educational opportunities. It offered him new opportunities to study his university, from admissions and curricular revisions to statistics and decision-making. "He showed obvious relish for his task," reported the *New York Times*.[70]

That year, as part of a major reorganization of the President's Office to help Sterling cope with the increasingly time-consuming business side of the university, Cuthbertson was appointed vice president of finance, and assigned responsibility for development as well as budgeting and financial planning. This was an unusual move, and one not favored by many advisors. But Sterling wanted Cuthbertson, as his chief financial officer, to be on top of both financial problems and opportunities.[71]

CREATING "THE RED BOOK"

With the success of the Medical School fundraising campaign, Ken Cuthbertson and Dave Jacobson were convinced that Stanford could plan a comprehensive, campus-wide fundraising campaign. The Medical School campaign had been an exhausting effort, however. It had netted significant major gifts, but it also had demonstrated the need for excellent organization, ample staffing, and more active leadership from trustees and other influential volunteers. Above all, it

Working with Sterling and Cuthbertson, Robert Moulton, '40 (seen here in 1962), initiated the long-range financial forecasting methodology behind "The Red Book." This was the first major comprehensive analysis, backed by faculty participation, of financial needs and opportunities at an American university. He also became Stanford's point man during federal negotiations for the Stanford Linear Accelerator Center.   STANFORD NEWS SERVICE

underscored the need for clearly articulated goals based on carefully studied estimates of needs and opportunities.[72]

During the first 10 years of Sterling's presidency, expenses had tripled to support significant improvement in faculty, facilities, and student programs. By 1958, Stanford was barely operating on a break-even basis. The president faced tough questioning by the trustees: How long could this continue, and by what means could the university finance such progress? Sterling "was caught between a trustee concern that we were going too fast and a faculty and student concern that we were not going fast enough," said Cuthbertson. "Stanford was in a position of having great opportunities to improve the quality of its activities; faculty recruiting was bringing increasingly able men to teach and conduct research; and our admissions pressure was such that the quality of students was rapidly improving."[73]

Beginning in 1958, Cuthbertson led a team to better understand Stanford's long-range financial problems. Bob Moulton (who joined the President's Office staff in 1957) was instrumental in initiating the long-range financial forecasting methodology that contributed so critically to Stanford's transformation. Moulton's complex analysis, elaborated by Kenneth Creighton, university controller, and Duncan McFadden, director of finance, covered 10 years of financial data on faculty, enrollment, facilities, and maintenance costs. They calculated opportunities, made preliminary estimates, reviewed assumptions, and refined their estimates.

An important element of the study was the involvement of faculty, department heads, and deans throughout the university. As they took a hard look at the challenges of the next 10 years, "we were desperately aware of the cost crisis which clouded our hopes to grasp clear opportunities to make Stanford a better university," noted Cuthbertson. "We saw critical building needs and potential operating deficits of two to three million dollars per year; they translated into what appeared to be impossible gift goals." Growth in faculty size and compensation was the largest cost component, along with student needs (financial and residential), and other physical plant improvements.[74]

The campus-wide study, *Stanford's Minimum Financial Needs in the Years Ahead*, was written principally by Cuthbertson. It summarized the "academic objectives we had in mind," said Sterling, "and how much it would cost to achieve them." Cuthbertson described it as a refinement of priorities that reflected Stanford's attempt at global thinking.[75]

The 1958–59 report, bound in red, was quickly dubbed "The Red Book." It would become the blueprint for much of the university's development during the 1960s.

Deans and department heads had carefully reviewed the study's results before they were shared with trustees, the Board of Governors of Stanford Associates, and the Executive Board of the Alumni Association. A special joint meeting of two trustee committees—Finance, and Planning and Development—was held in October 1959, to review the study's financial and fundraising implications over the next 10 years.[76]

In the study's introduction, Provost Terman wrote:

In formulating a development program for Stanford, it is not possible to compile any list of "needs" which, if satisfied, would then meet all the future requirements of the institution. In education, one can set progressively new and higher goals, without limit. In fact, when strength is added to a part of the academic structure, this does not necessarily reduce "needs." On the contrary, it often generates more opportunities which represent new needs. . . .

Briefly, education has an insatiable appetite, and no one institution can produce enough support to satisfy it. The appropriate procedure under these circumstances is to attempt to achieve a program that will over a period of years provide: (1) a strong salary structure; (2) a healthy rate of growth, and in particular a rate of growth adequate to take advantage of good opportunities that come along; and (3) physical facilities that at any time are adequate for the operation being carried on at that time.

The overall magnitude of Stanford's *minimum* needs, in terms of new dollars over the next 10 years, amounted to $346 million in potential improvements, including $91 million for salaries and additional personnel; $42 million for scholarships and fellowships; $75 million for construction and operation of libraries; and $115 million for construction and rehabilitation of other facilities. Of this total, it was anticipated that $100 million would come from predictable sources, including tuition increases and land development revenues; the remaining $246 million entailed doubling the rate of giving to Stanford as of 1960.[77]

In early 1960, three projected levels were presented—minimum needs, an ambitious estimate of maximum expenditures, and a middle ground—to the full trustee board at an all-day session. In an unusual change of procedure, the provost and academic deans joined Sterling to describe new academic work and how Stanford salaries compared with those of its peers.

As Cuthbertson later explained, as each of the projected funding levels was discussed, the trustees commented that "what was proposed was not good enough if Stanford was to meet its opportunities." The trustees, he said, were "impressed but perplexed—uncertain, even doubtful, whether the suggested gift levels were achievable." It was an intimidating challenge but looking back at a decade of unanticipated fundraising accomplishments, the trustees agreed to undertake it.[78]

A few weeks later, Sterling received an unexpected phone call from James Armsey, director of the Ford Foundation's higher education program. Armsey informed the president that he and a colleague wished to visit Stanford but went into no further details. It was quickly arranged, and Armsey and foundation treasurer Joseph McDaniels joined Sterling, Terman, Cuthbertson, a few deans, and other campus officers over dinner at the Lou Henry Hoover House.

After dinner small talk, Armsey told them that the foundation was considering a program of large general support grants and asked if Stanford had given any thought to where it might be in 10 years. "You could imagine our smugness and their surprise," recalled Cuthbertson, when Sterling produced a copy of the Red Book. Quickly skimming the pages, Armsey muttered, "Well, I'll be damned!" Armsey revealed that the Ford Foundation was considering a special program of challenge grants to be made to a handful of universities that had worked hard to improve themselves. Stanford was one of those under consideration, but Armsey would provide no further details.[79]

No other university in the country had made such a thorough study. Cuthbertson spent his 1960 summer vacation (joined by his wife and four children, in the family's new, bright red station wagon) visiting 20 leading private universities and colleges across the country to compare notes and share strategies. Indeed, none had done anything like Stanford's 10-year analysis (and only one expressed the same level of concern), but most had deeper reserves than Stanford. Soon after Cuthbertson's return, the Ford Foundation collaborated with him and his staff to develop worksheets to be used to seek long-range planning information from other universities the foundation was considering for the program.[80]

Stanford's innovative in-depth financial forecasting was handsomely rewarded. In September 1960, the Ford Foundation announced an unprecedented $25 million grant to Stanford, to be given over a five-year period on a three-to-one matching basis (one foundation dollar for every three generated from all other gift sources). Four other universities received grants, although none was more than $6 million. Ford Foundation President Henry T. Heald, in announcing the gift, said, "We sought private universities already embarked on future development commensurate in scope, imagination, and practicability to the vast needs of American society." The foundation's "Special Program in Education" grants were the first of their kind and would give Stanford the impetus to move forward with fundraising to support ambitious financial and academic goals.[81]

During the fundraising efforts to come, Sterling continued to point out that this opportunity would not have come about if Stanford had not made such efforts at self-analysis. Sterling also insisted that Stanford had earned attention because of its efforts at self-help, including significant additions to the endowment through foundation, corporate, and individual gifts, and innovative land management. Cuthbertson, too, believed the Red Book had much to do with the size of the grant. Stanford was, Sterling and Cuthbertson hoped, stepping into the first rank of prestige universities.[82]

PLAN OF ACTION FOR A CHALLENGING ERA

With the September 1960 announcement of the Ford Foundation grant, Stanford set out to raise the matching $75 million, "our boldest venture since the University was founded," Sterling announced. The campaign was known as the PACE Program, the initials for Plan of Action for a Challenging Era. This ambitious fundraising effort, wrote Frank Medeiros, became "a tangible and symbolic indication of Stanford's institutional momentum in the early sixties."[83]

This time the fundraising effort was well staffed, at a high level. Under Vice President Ken Cuthbertson's direction, Richard O'Brien became director of the PACE Campaign. Dudley Kenworthy became director of Devel-

opment Programs. Dave Jacobson and Daryl Pearson continued to work closely with Stanford Associates' volunteers. In 1961, Robert W. Beyers was appointed director of Stanford's News and Publications Service, under Lyle Nelson's University Relations office. Pete Allen now focused on an expanded program of much-needed university publications, including *Stanford Today*, a newsletter reformatted into a sophisticated magazine focused on faculty commentary and news.

Herbert Hoover, now approaching 87 and in ill health, again agreed to lend his name as honorary national chairman, but Sterling found individual trustees reluctant to volunteer to take up the job of National PACE Campaign Chairman. Initially, at Sterling's urging, trustees James B. Black, chairman of Pacific Gas and Electric Company, and Edward R. Valentine, '30, president of Robinson Building Company, agreed to serve as temporary co-chairs until the board could find someone willing to take on the job. They found their leader outside the

Trustees James Black (left) and Edward Valentine (right) agreed to serve as temporary co-chairs of the PACE Campaign. STANFORD NEWS SERVICE

board: Theodore S. (Ted) Petersen, recently retired president of Standard Oil of California, took up the challenge and was elected a trustee. Petersen, who had never gone to college, was "a fast learner" who came to love Stanford, Cuthbertson said, although he found the process of academic decision-making "a bit unwieldy." Petersen livened up formal PACE dinners with "oil field language for the sake of emphasis." Jim

Black and Thomas P. Pike (trustee president, 1960–62) continued to lend a hand.[84]

Based on the Red Book's recommendations, the campaign targeted growth in faculty size and compensation, expansion of student financial aid, expansion of graduate training and research, and a significant improvement to the physical plant (residence halls, libraries, and laboratories).[85]

Even before the campaign was formally

PACE staff and volunteers look over a portion of the campus model, in September 1963, moved to the upstairs lobby of the recently completed Donald B. Tresidder Memorial Union. Proposed science buildings stand out in white on the west side of the campus, among them what would become the Herrin Biology buildings, Stauffer Chemistry, the McCullough Building, and a Medical Center expansion.   STANFORD NEWS SERVICE

launched, Cuthbertson visited academic departments to engage faculty in the process. Newly arrived historian Richard W. Lyman, later Stanford's seventh president, thought the campaign's name "a rather ponderous way of reaching for a neat acronym," but Lyman was impressed with the thoughtfulness and clarity of the program, and with Cuthbertson's understanding of and respect for faculty. "If ever there was a fund-raising chief who understood that dollars were but a means to an end, and the end is academic quality, it was Ken."[86]

The campaign was formally inaugurated at a luncheon in the Lagunita Court dining room on April 18, 1961, the anniversary of the 1906 San Francisco earthquake. President Sterling called it "our boldest venture since the University was founded." Keynote speaker and Stanford alumnus Clark Kerr, M.A. '33, then president of the University of California system and a former chancellor of UC Berkeley, emphasized that "a strong Stanford is the best guarantee of a strong Berkeley."[87]

Sterling's strong leadership and substantial time commitment gave these efforts a crucial boost. He personally ensured that "The Case for Stanford" was heard in speeches at alumni and special events across the county, as well as for local audiences like the annual Stanford Today and Tomorrow student-faculty convocation. One of Sterling's favorite quotes was taken from Daniel Burnham, director of works of the 1893 Columbian Exhibition at Chicago: "Make no little plans; they have no magic to stir men's blood," underscoring the ambition behind the university's undertaking.

Early in the campaign, when Sterling had lunch with students at one of the eating clubs, a student asked, "How do you ask a person for a million or more dollars?" Sterling replied bluntly, "One does not do it by keeping one's mouth shut." When asked what "PACE" stood

for, Sterling explained the need for a catchy campaign title. He was delighted with the student's response: "Oh! I thought it meant People Aren't Contributing Enough." Sterling said he "found his translation very useful and put it to good use more than once."[88]

To back up Sterling's personal interactions, the university published *The Case for Stanford* (1961), illustrated with photographs by Ansel Adams, Pirkle Jones, Kenneth Reichard, and others. Wilbur Schramm, professor of communication, immersed himself in Sterling's speeches to help him craft a campaign statement included in the book.[89]

Novelist Wallace Stegner, professor of English and director of the Creative Writing Program, coined another key campaign phrase: "Stanford is a university trembling on the edge of greatness." Stegner's written contributions to the fundraising efforts were "just magnificent," recalled Glover.[90]

Sterling also played a central role in mobilizing alumni groups in major cities across the country to organize and commit to the campaign. Estimates vary, but some 5,000 to 6,000 individuals took on local leadership positions.[91]

By August 1962, less than a year and a half into what had been proposed as a five-year effort, the PACE Campaign passed the halfway mark at more than $52 million. By the end of 1963, the campaign had earned $109 million ($9 million over the target).[92]

In January 1964, Stanford reported to the Ford Foundation the progress it already had made toward faculty development: While plans had called for the addition of 125 new full-time faculty members, the university already had been able to make a net increase of 170 professors. Selective faculty salary increases averaging 35 percent were scheduled over a five-year period beginning in 1964, but its current overall increase already averaged 27 percent. Stanford, which had hoped to be among the top 10 in faculty salaries, was very close to the top five. Ten endowed chairs, including one visiting professorship, had been funded of an expected 15. Graduate enrollment increased from 3,636 in 1960 to 4,781 in 1963. The number of National Science Fellows on the faculty increased dramatically, from 44 in 1959–60 to 151 in 1963–64, while Woodrow Wilson Fellows increased from 33 in 1960–61 to 81 in 1963–64.[93]

Stanford formally closed the $100 million PACE Campaign books in April 1964, only three years from its kickoff, with a final total of nearly $114 million ($1.1 billion in 2023 dollars). The largest university-wide campaign of its time in the United States, PACE was more than a "watershed in Stanford's fundraising history," Cuthbertson later said. Stanford had moved "into high gear on the fundraising front."[94]

THE FAVORABLE BREEZE FADES

As hoped, the PACE Campaign lifted the annual rate of non-campaign giving in the years to come. For the six years before the campaign, the university had averaged $13.6 million in gift receipts a year; during the three PACE years, the average reached $30 million. The average for the six years following the campaign remained high, at $26.5 million, or nearly twice that of the pre-PACE years.[95]

Yet, despite its forecasts and fundraising successes, university expenditures were again outdistancing its income by the mid-1960s. Controller Ken Creighton worried that the university's massive efforts to build its academic prestige during the 1950s and early '60s had resulted, again, in deferred maintenance and renovations. The university's strong focus on graduate programs (graduate students now numbered nearly half of Stanford's 11,000 students, up from 37 percent in 1950) had raised the per-capita cost of educating its students due to additional faculty and research facility needs.[96]

STANFORD PACE PROGRAM

Where will the money go?

LIBRARY OPERATIONS
$6 MILLION

FACULTY SALARIES
$26 MILLION

STUDENT AID and SERVICES
$10 MILLION

CURRENT PROGRAM
$16½ MILLION
(Faculty Salaries, Student Aid, Research, Library and others)

ACADEMIC, RESIDENCE and OTHER BUILDINGS
$41½ MILLION

Three-Year Campaign Goal $100,000,000

This is one of many illustrative charts used during the kickoff of the $100 million PACE Campaign. STANFORD UNIVERSITY ARCHIVES

Five undergraduates pose for a photo to illustrate Stanford's launch of a $100 million fundraising campaign. All five were scholarship students. (One campaign goal was to increase scholarship funding.) From left, Richard W. Hall, senior, industrial engineering; Nancy Coe Carpenter, senior, political science; Paul Cocks, junior, Russian history; Robert Rader, senior, physics; and Ellen Barbara Friedman, junior, English and American literature.
STANFORD NEWS SERVICE

In addition, the favorable breeze that had benefited Stanford during the 1950s was no longer blowing. "Stanford doesn't have it made," Cuthbertson told a campus audience in 1968. Despite the university's progress, "We are a recent and insecure arrival into the first rank of the world's great universities." Cuthbertson, as an alumnus as well as a staff member, was deeply troubled. Alumni, annoyed by newspaper headlines of student protests, were turning against higher education, yet "Stanford was never so greatly in need of support rather than animosity."[97]

Ten years before, a wistful Sterling told a student and faculty audience, "Every American university worthy of the name has financial problems."[98] As it turned out, even after Sterling's retirement in 1968, he found fundraising for Stanford inescapable. As chancellor, and a member of the Board of Trustees, Sterling would serve as national co-chair of the Campaign for Stanford *(see Chapter 21)*. That $300 million drive, 1972–77, looked to lessons learned from PACE about leadership, self-examination, organization, and planning. Again, facing an initial reluctance to volunteer, campaign staff relied on Sterling's ability to inspire volunteer leaders as well as major donors.

CREATING THE STANFORD
LINEAR ACCELERATOR CENTER

Stanford scientists had been working on the frontiers of high-energy physics for a number of years before Wallace Sterling became president. When he arrived, in 1949, Stanford's new Microwave Laboratory was under construction near the Quad to house the Mark III accelerator, then 30 feet long. By the end of Sterling's presidential term, Stanford was home to the 2-mile-long Stanford Linear Accelerator Center (SLAC), on a 426-acre site along the then rural Sand Hill Road. Years later, Sterling would reflect that the construction and staffing of SLAC was one of the more challenging episodes of his presidency.[1]

Development of the linear accelerator concept at Stanford can be traced to physics Professor William W. Hansen's interest in x-ray research and nuclear physics in the 1930s. Subsequent work on campus by research assistant Russell

Varian and his brother Sigurd, collaborating with Hansen and engineering graduate student Edward L. Ginzton in the late 1930s, led to local development of a klystron tube, the necessary high-energy source for a linear electron accelerator.[2] At the end of World War II, Hansen and Ginzton, now an assistant professor, with John R. Woodyard, examined the use of klystrons to accelerate electrons at high energy. With federal funding, they built the Mark I and II accelerators in the Physics Department (Building 380) basement on the Quad. After Hansen's death, in 1949, Ginzton carried on as director of the new Microwave Laboratory, west of Physics Corner, which housed the ever-growing Mark III electron accelerator.[3]

BIRTHING AND BUILDING THE MONSTER

In 1954, a visionary memorandum titled "A Large Linear Accelerator for Stanford" was sent to President Sterling by professors Ginzton, Robert Hofstadter, Wolfgang K. H. (Pief) Panofsky, and department head Leonard I. Schiff.[4]

The idea of building a much larger machine had been a "matter of common discussion,"

< This January 1965 aerial view of SLAC's east-end building complex and under-construction research yard looks toward the main campus, marked by Hoover Tower. In the middle distance, the triangle of houses to the right of Sand Hill Road is the experimental Stanford neighborhood, Stanford Hills. In the foreground, note the structural components for the future Interstate Highway 280 roadbed.   SLAC ARCHIVES

Stanford's 1949 Microwave Laboratory housed the original 30-foot-long Mark III linear accelerator. The ever-expanding Mark III, a workhorse machine used throughout the 1950s for Nobel Prize–winning experiments, hit the end of the building at 300 feet in 1960. Two earlier accelerators had been set up in the Physics Department's basement, then on the Outer Quad.   STANFORD NEWS SERVICE

High-energy physicist Wolfgang K. H. (Pief) Panofsky, seen here in 1961, had been recruited from UC Berkeley 10 years earlier and soon after became director of the High Energy Physics Laboratory. He took over, in early 1961, from Ginzton as director of Project M, renamed the Stanford Linear Accelerator Center.   STANFORD NEWS SERVICE

Professor Edward Ginzton was director of the Microwave Lab and first director of the 2-mile accelerator project, dubbed Project M for "monster." Here, he stands alongside the Mark III linear accelerator in 1952.   STANFORD NEWS SERVICE

Ginzton later recounted, as soon as Mark III proved its utility, in 1952. Hofstadter was deeply engaged in research with the Mark III. Panofsky, who had been recruited in 1951 by Schiff and physicist Felix Bloch, was head of the High Energy Physics Laboratory (HEPL). HEPL joined with the Microwave Laboratory to make up the new W. W. Hansen Laboratories. Hofstadter and Panofsky, along with Ginzton, were especially interested in building a much larger machine, at least 10 times bigger than the Mark III.[5]

After reviewing recent developments at Brookhaven in New York and at Harvard-MIT, the memorandum continued:

> If we at Stanford are to remain in the high-energy field, it is necessary to start making preparations now for the construction of a new large accelerator to take place in the next five years or so. . . . It is not surprising that some thinking along the lines of developing a large (25–50 BeV) [billion electron volts] electron linear accelerator has already been carried out at Stanford. The present linear accelerator has been a success even though it has proved more costly than originally estimated.
>
> One consideration which might prove appealing to the AEC [Atomic Energy Commission] would be the availability of land on the campus, since a linear accelerator of this size would probably require a straight path approximately two miles long. . . .
>
> We believe that an accelerator project of the sort outlined above, properly implemented with personnel and research facilities, would keep Stanford in the forefront of physics during the next decade or two and would firmly establish the University as a center of high-energy physics. . . .
>
> We would resist all attempts by the AEC or other contributing agencies to impose security restrictions on this project. Moreover, we would like to keep this [facility] not only unclassified but open to visitors, regardless of clearance and citizenship.

A few weeks later, after a visit to the AEC in Washington, D.C., and Baltimore, they reported to Sterling:

> The AEC considers it very important that Stanford participate financially in the project. This might consist of long-term use of land, building construction, certain faculty salaries, and some contribution to operating cost. The main reason given for this is that it will make it possible for Stanford to handle the project without undue control from the AEC. If Stanford were not to participate to a considerable extent, the S.F. AEC office would have to assume full responsibility for construction, with Stanford serving merely as a consultant. In this case, there would probably be an AEC area office at Stanford, and arrangements would not be negotiable by Stanford. Another reason for Stanford's participation is that this would provide a tangible expression of Stanford's interest in the project. . . .
>
> The question[s] of construction cost, operating cost, and performance are very hazy at present. It seems likely that some set of overall cost figures will be imposed on the machine, and that the performance to be expected will deliberately be left vague, the hope being that interesting results will be obtainable with the funds available.[6]

The AEC agreed to fund a small, 20-foot, two-klystron (80 MeV) (million electron volts) test-bed accelerator, called the Mark IV. The Mark IV also was used in preliminary studies of electron beam cancer therapy under the direction of Henry Kaplan, professor of radiology, with Ginzton and Schiff consulting. Their work led to the first commercial medical linear electron accelerator, in 1956.[7]

The details for a truly large accelerator remained speculative, however, until early 1956, when a nucleus of professors and Hansen Laboratories staff agreed on the basics of a formal proposal for a facility to be administered separately from both the Hansen Labs and the Physics Department. The result was a 100-page formal proposal that President Sterling submitted in April 1957 to the Atomic Energy Commission, the National Science Foundation, and the Office of Naval Research within the Department of Defense for their consideration.[8] For the time being, it was called Project M; opinion was divided whether M meant "Multi-GeV" or "Monster."

Early in the 1956–57 meetings, the Stanford group agreed that "the primary objective of the proposed large accelerator was declared to be basic physics research. There should be no security measures except to protect personnel and property, no classification [classified research], and freely published results; the facilities should be available to qualified research visitors." Ginzton would serve as director through design and construction, with Panofsky as assistant director, and Schiff and Hofstadter as consultants. Hofstadter, however, objected to sharing access. He later withdrew from project planning, and joined Felix Bloch, another original supporter, and Walter Meyerhof in opposing the project.

The proposal was the most comprehensive scientific project submitted to date to the federal government. At the time, it was the most expensive non-defense research venture in the United States, as well as the largest single project yet undertaken by Stanford University: Project M's proponents requested $114 million to build a linear accelerator center on Stanford land, with an annual operating budget of $14 million. (Stanford's endowment at the time was $61 million, and its annual operating budget was $22 million.)[9]

Stanford's efforts seemed to be moving slowly, but successfully, with consistent scientific support and strong endorsements by the National Science Foundation and the president's science advisor. In a nationally broadcast speech in New York in May 1959, President Dwight Eisenhower announced that he would recommend to Congress construction of a linear accelerator at Stanford. Eisenhower, however, had not observed the usual courtesy of informing the Joint House/Senate Committee on Atomic Energy of his endorsement of this expensive federal project prior to his announcement. Over the course of nearly two years of congressional hearings, the Democratic chairmen of the committee, Senator Clinton Anderson and, later, Representative Chet Holifield, posed many hostile questions and interjected various obstacles to the project's approval.[10]

During one hearing, Anderson unexpectedly accused Ginzton, as the newly appointed president of Varian Associates, of profiting from the project. Varian's board subsequently agreed to withdraw from participating, despite the company's importance in developing the klystron technology that was integral to the project. Stanford's Board of Trustees agreed to waive patent royalty payments to the university that might result from the use of klystron tubes in the construction or operation of the accelerator. (Stanford had been assigned the patent for the inventive klystron work of Hansen, the Varians, and Ginzton.)

To avoid conflicts, Ginzton would later withdraw as director of the project and be replaced by Panofsky, in early 1961. In his 1995 autobiography, Ginzton, a co-founder of Varian Associates, said that he left the project for several reasons, among them his election as chairman and CEO of Varian following Russell Varian's death, in 1959. Although he played an important role in the development of the linear accelerator's engineering, he also realized that, as an engineer, he could build the SLAC accelerator but not use it. Much to his annoyance, Ginzton's loyalty also had been challenged due to his Russian birth.[11]

While the Congressional Joint Committee haggled with Stanford's representatives, initial architectural and engineering studies revealed that the original site for the project was geologically unsuitable. It had been Ginzton's idea to build the accelerator in the foothills, originating near the golf course and the abandoned "Isolation Hospital" near Alpine Road, and running southward underground roughly parallel to Foothill Road (today's Junipero Serra Boulevard). The accelerator was to emerge and bridge over Page Mill Road and end in the undeveloped Coyote Hill area, to the west of the Stanford Industrial Park.[12]

The Board of Trustees had reserved 125 acres in that area for the project in 1956, but a 1960 study by John Blume and Associates of San Francisco determined that the soil conditions were unsuitable for tunnel construction, and recommended a new site near Sand Hill Road, running west to Whiskey Hill Road, as offering the greatest flexibility for future phases, acceptable earthquake risk, and proximity to existing campus scientific facilities. The trustees were assured that all design parameters had been chosen "such that radiation levels produced by the accelerator beam outside the project boundaries will not exceed that of natural sources of radiation [such as cosmic rays and local sources of radioactivity] which occur normally in this area." Convinced, the trustees allocated 480 acres of land adjoining Sand Hill Road that year to Project M. (In recent years, this has been reduced to 426 acres.)[13]

As the work of the Congressional Joint Committee got underway, the team learned confidentially that AEC chairman John McCone planned an unannounced visit to scout the proposed site, after which he planned to declare it unsuitable. McCone, a highly successful California industrialist in steel and shipbuilding, was on the board of the Stanford Research Institute and several of his business colleagues were Stanford trustees. As a fixture in Republican national political circles, McCone also associated with David Packard, co-founder of Hewlett-Packard and trustee president from 1958 to 1960; and with Packard's successor as trustee president, Thomas Pike. McCone was already acquainted with Sterling from his years as a Caltech trustee.[14]

When McCone became head of the AEC, "we felt greatly favored," said Robert Moulton, Sterling's presidential assistant for SLAC and man at the center of the storm. "As it turned out, his appointment only intensified our problems. McCone was unimpressed by basic research and favored applied research. Equally important, he wanted the accelerator, if built at all, produced in its entirety by private industry."[15]

The team had no idea when McCone would visit, or how they would "deal with this new bit of intrigue." Sterling guessed that McCone would combine such a visit with the upcoming Bohemian Club encampment (both men were members). Sterling "innocently" asked McCone if he would be coming out for the encampment, Moulton recalled, and then boldly invited him to the campus for a project update. McCone and the AEC director of research came to campus on July 18, 1959, and were given a tour of the proposed site as well as the latest work with the Mark III. Although McCone no longer publicly opposed the project, his real concern—who would control planning and construction—continued to come up in the ensuing tense Stanford–AEC negotiations over the operating agreement.[16]

Initially, the AEC tried to write a contract stipulation requiring the university to agree to any regulation imposed by the government for purposes of national security, including requiring the lab to undertake security classified research. Panofsky strongly opposed this, and made it a "do-or-die" issue. Sterling and Packard agreed, and the AEC ultimately backed down.[17] The ongoing concern remained preservation of the basic academic character of research activities associated with the new accelerator. Panofsky and Ginzton had had to convince Sterling, and in turn the Board of Trustees, that Project M would follow university academic policies, and that the university, not the federal government, would set policy and determine research priorities, including whether the project would pursue or allow security classified research. Having the linear accelerator project on campus, they argued, would not only strengthen Stanford's ability to preserve university management but also avoid creating a separate administrative staff, other than that needed to monitor high-energy physics research.

With the trustees, many of whom incorrectly believed it was the government that was imposing the project on Stanford, prepared to discontinue negotiations if a satisfactory agreement with the AEC could not be reached, Sterling maintained his strong support of the project and carefully watched the negotiations.[18]

The Joint Congressional Committee and the AEC both continued efforts to sever the project from Stanford, proposing other sites in California and elsewhere in the United States. During congressional hearings, one suggestion was a site on the East Bay end of the Dumbarton Bridge. One senator suggested an abandoned train tunnel in his state of Washington; another offered an

abandoned silver mine in his state of Nevada. Panofsky and Ginzton made it clear, however, that this was Stanford's project, and it would be built at Stanford, where qualified scientists could use it, or not at all.[19]

In October 1959, Ginzton learned that the AEC was exploring Moffett Field in Mountain View as an alternative site in an attempt to retain responsibility for scientific and technical decisions as well as construction. An AEC staff paper suggested prohibiting institutions like Stanford from being responsible for planning, designing, and constructing any projects like Project M. Ginzton sensed that the resolution of this Stanford–AEC conflict would affect the fate of Stanford's role.[20] He urged Sterling to again insist that Stanford must have complete jurisdiction over *all* architect/engineering work on the project, as well as administration, and not tolerate any arrangement under which government officials reviewed scientific and technical decisions. Neither he nor Panofsky, Ginzton warned, would participate

In April 1962, university officials signed the federal government's contract, initiating site work for the 2-mile linear accelerator. Morris M. Doyle (seated, left), vice president of the Board of Trustees, and Ira S. Lillick, board secretary, signed for Stanford. Standing (left to right): Dwight B. Adams, Stanford business manager; Professor Panofsky, director of the accelerator project; and Robert Minge Brown, university counsel.
STANFORD NEWS SERVICE

in the project if the university did not take a stand on this issue.[21]

Sterling remained involved in crucial discussions with McCone. Sensing that the AEC director viewed him as a mere academic incapable of discussing the practical side of the proposal, he especially appreciated the help of Packard, who also chaired the trustee's Special Committee for the Stanford Linear Accelerator.[22] Packard included on his committee other influential Pacific Coast industrialists with the clout to talk to McCone as equals, including McCone's former business partner Stephen Bechtel, president of the world's largest construction company, who joined the board in November 1959; Paul R. Pigott, oil and steel magnate; and Edmund Littlefield, grandson of a founder of Utah Construction Company.[23]

McCone, scheduled to present to Congress and President Eisenhower estimates of the construction and operating costs of pending high-energy physics proposals, called for a December 9 negotiating meeting at AEC headquarters in Washington. Sterling joined Ginzton, Moulton, and Frederic Pindar, the project's administrative director, in discussions with McCone, AEC General Manager Maj. General A. R. Luedecke, and AEC Assistant Manager R. E. Hollingsworth. Stanford representatives were told that inept handling of several construction projects at other universities had recently embarrassed the AEC. When Sterling responded that he would defy any other university or government department to equal the value Stanford got from its dollars, the cynical reply was that Sterling was referring to Stanford's own funds, not government funds. Refusing to be baited, Sterling replied that project scientists must be given authority over the project they would be responsible for using. Nevertheless, Hollingsworth stated, the AEC intended to contract with a third party for overall management. Ginzton replied "quite bluntly,"

Construction of the 2-mile tunnel, completed in June 1966, that would carry the perfectly straight, extremely powerful beam. Engineers were able to build the tunnel with a gradual drop of one-half of 1 degree to accommodate natural terrain and minimize some earth moving.   STANFORD NEWS SERVICE

Moulton recorded, that neither he nor Panofsky would have anything to do with the project under such an arrangement.[24]

Panofsky urged Sterling and Packard to join the project team in a March 1960 showdown with the AEC held at the Naval Air Station in Alameda, to reconcile, if possible, opposing views about division of responsibility for the project. Robert Minge Brown, the university's general counsel, also joined the group. Ginzton and Panofsky agreed to compromise by proposing that some nonscientific elements, such as earthmoving, roads, and buildings, could be contracted out, but insisted that Stanford build the actual accelerator. They assured the AEC that although Stanford felt it must assume direct responsibility for the project's engineering and design, including architect/engineering services and construction or procurement of components, the AEC would retain fundamental fiscal and legal control. Packard spoke strongly of his conviction from personal experience that Stanford's scientists must retain control over the architect/engineering aspects.[25]

As Moulton recorded the exchange, McCone prodded Packard, asking whether Stanford would refuse to proceed, as the others had insisted, if the AEC insisted on private contracts for the entire project. Packard affirmed this. McCone accepted this point for the time being, but went on to say that he would have a final discussion about the project with President Eisenhower, where he would stress the project's cost. McCone said it was time to decide whether "to marry the girl," and, if the decision was affirmative, the government should "buy a ring" and get on with it. Moulton recorded in his notes, "We left with the feeling that Mr. McCone not only fully understands our management philosophy but there is good reason to hope that he will actually accept our view in this matter."[26]

Looking back on these meetings, Moulton later wrote: "McCone was never reconciled to the SLAC project. He could not foresee practical applications coming from our project, and he resented our having reserved a large part of the work to ourselves. Although McCone supported SLAC publicly, it was well known in Washington circles that privately he did everything he could to kill it." In 1961, President John F. Kennedy replaced McCone with nuclear chemist and UC Berkeley Chancellor Glenn T. Seaborg, a change much welcomed at Stanford.[27]

In September 1960, the AEC agreed that the prime construction responsibility for the project could rest with Stanford, provided the university employ as a subcontractor a private architect/engineer/management contractor; the AEC and Stanford would jointly select the subcontractor, and AEC approval was required for all prime and subcontracts. A joint Stanford–AEC Selection Board was established, which ultimately chose the joint venture group of Aetron, Blume, and Atkinson as the architect/engineering/management subcontractor. Even so, Sterling had to reassure the Congressional Joint Committee in its final hearings in May 1961 that Stanford was fully qualified to administer such a facility. He again confirmed its cost estimates and explained the relationship of the proposed project to Stanford's research program.[28]

In addition to completing an operating agreement, Stanford and the AEC finally settled on lease terms for the 480-acre parcel Stanford made available. In a December 30, 1960, letter to Bob Moulton and Tom Ford, director of land development, General Counsel Robert Minge Brown summarized the basis for the lease:

- A 50-year term, $1 per year rental
- Lessee to pay all taxes assessed against the property
- Lessee to bear the costs of bringing utilities to the premises
- Stanford to be indemnified against all claims for injury to person or property
- Lessee to have the option of terminating the lease upon prescribed written notice
- At the termination of the lease, Stanford had the option of requesting the restoration of the premises to their original condition or of accepting the leased premises in their then condition[29]

There was extensive discussion regarding the AEC's responsibility to restore the premises at the termination of the lease, but all of these terms were ultimately accepted by the AEC.[30]

End station and beam switchyard construction, late 1965, with the klystron gallery, atop the accelerator tunnel, heading into the distance.
STANFORD NEWS SERVICE

The end stations and beam switchyard under construction in January 1966. The trustees had set aside 480 acres of land for the complex (later reduced to 426 acres), along Sand Hill Road.
SLAC ARCHIVES

Final congressional hearings were held in May 1961, when the SLAC project nearly got entangled with legislation on the nuclear facility at Hanford, Washington, but the bill approving Stanford's project was finally signed that September. In December, the Board of Trustees formally replaced "Project M" with a new name, the Stanford Linear Accelerator Center.[31]

After continued lengthy and difficult negotiations, the SLAC contract was finally signed by the AEC on April 30, 1962. Groundbreaking took place in July 1962.

Major construction was essentially complete by late 1966, more than nine years after Sterling submitted the Project M proposal. The most difficult part of the project was construction of the 2-mile linear accelerator, delegated to Professor Richard Neal, whom Panofsky credited with completing construction on schedule, within budget, and in accordance with performance standards exceeding the original goals of the project.[32]

On the morning of May 21, 1966, an electron beam traveled the full 2 miles to the beam-switchyard area for the first time. By November, SLAC's formal experimental program was underway. During the first nine months of operation, 26 particle-physics experiments had been submitted and reviewed (at least half from physics groups based at Stanford). Five experiments had been completed, and another six set up before SLAC's formal dedication by President Sterling in September 1967.

The Mark III, near the Main Quad, had continued as the workhorse throughout the 1950s, growing from 30 to 300 feet long in 1960, when it "hit the wall," just inches short of the inside wall of the building in which it had been built. Hofstadter would be awarded a Nobel Prize in 1961 for his pioneering studies of electron scattering using the Mark III to determine the size and structure of the nucleus.[33]

WOODSIDE CHALLENGES POWER LINES CONSTRUCTION

Stanford's officials might have assumed that construction of SLAC would avoid further political battles, but that was not to be.[34] The accelerator required a 220,000-volt power source, budgeted in the proposal. A string of tall steel towers had been envisioned for the project, running down a 100-foot-wide swath from the Pacific Gas & Electric Company (PG&E) trunk line along Skyline Ridge, by way of Searsville Lake, through the foothill woods and meadows to the accelerator.

Sterling had been alerted to a looming dispute even before the final lease and contract were signed. A prescient note to the president from executive assistant Fred Glover was attached to an article from the June 28, 1961, *San Mateo Times*. "We are going to be involved in a ding dong over the SLAC power lines cutting through Woodside. This is the opening gun. I don't know what we can do about it," wrote Glover, "but when you run power poles through an area like Woodside, it is hard to keep people happy, science or no science."[35]

Selection of the final site for the accelerator had already raised protests by the Menlo Park City Council and at a public meeting at the Ladera Community Club. But local concern would become national headline material in 1963, when the planning commission of the town of Woodside refused to grant PG&E a use permit to build the 3 miles of high-voltage power lines needed to operate the linear accelerator. When the Woodside Planning Commission in September 1962 deferred a decision because of strenuous local objections, Stanford officials became concerned about a possible project delay.[36]

Residents, environmental groups, and others opposed to overhead high power lines for aesthetic as well as environmental reasons hired

Palo Alto attorney Pete McCloskey to represent them.[37] In June 1963, he won a 30-day delay to prepare a report to the AEC on alternatives, promising engineering studies of economically feasible alternatives that would be acceptable to Woodside, if not Stanford.[38] Fred Terman, as acting president while Sterling was recovering from surgery, responded, informing the commission that Stanford would accept either of two alternative routes offered to Woodside by PG&E, but the "costs of placing underground lines to carry greater voltages than 12 kV [kilovolts] were so high that we could not reasonably expect allocation of public funds to cover such costs." Nevertheless, the Woodside Planning Commission denied the use permit application.[39]

PG&E appealed to the Woodside Town Council that December, proposing a compromise design of "trim, tapered" steel towers half as tall as those originally planned, with a single-circuit instead of the dual-circuit system. The appeal was denied.[40]

McCloskey continued to lobby for a single-circuit underground line, suggesting a complex formula for cost sharing, to avoid federal concerns, with a $500,000 payment by Stanford. The Committee for Green Foothills, a local environmental group that had been formed in 1960 to oppose the extension of the Stanford Industrial Park, added its voice. Its president, English Professor Wallace Stegner, wrote Sterling to condemn the plan, insisting that the lines run underground, whatever the cost. The Board of Trustees, however, refused to use university funds for undergrounding, and passed the problem back to the AEC.[41]

The AEC estimated the cost of the preferred double-circuit overhead lines, as originally proposed, at $668,000, while placing comparable lines underground would be $6.4 million. (The probable cost of less adequate single-circuit overhead lines on the tubular steel poles proposed as a compromise was $922,000, as compared to placing an equivalent, but less reliable, line underground at a cost of $3.6 million.)

In addition, undergrounding would add a significant delay in completion time of the project and thus the start of research use of the accelerator. "At this point the schedules of the laboratory are being jeopardized by this problem," Panofsky wrote U.S. Senator Thomas Kuchel, who had pressed the Joint Committee on Atomic Energy to review the power-line situation. "I hope that you appreciate the threat of further delay to this unique scientific venture, which you yourself helped to initiate. There are only ten miles of transmission line of this voltage underground in the entire United States, and these are placed in the center of densely populated metropolitan areas."[42]

The AEC was well aware that no transmission lines had ever been placed underground in Woodside. "Anyone familiar with the maze of poles and wires in Woodside and along many of the thoroughfares in Palo Alto and other neighboring communities," Panofsky pointed out, "would appreciate Stanford's policy of requiring the undergrounding of campus electrical lines up to a voltage of 12 kV."

Senator Kuchel, a Woodside ally, was among the many attending the Joint Commission hearings. Commission Chair Chet Holifield placed on display 4-by-6-foot photographs of Woodside's existing above-ground 12 kV lines. The photos, wrote eyewitness Bob Moulton, "were damning indeed, showing ugly, multiple lines strung all over the beautiful Woodside landscape. Whatever Woodside's good intentions, the revelation of past sins was devastating to Woodside's cause, particularly since, in past years Stanford, by comparison, had placed 12 kV lines within its own boundaries underground, absorbing the cost." Kuchel, embarrassed, left the meeting.

Local delegations had, in fact, not been able to make a convincing case to the Joint Committee

As construction got underway, Woodside residents, environmental groups, and others opposed, for environmental and aesthetic reasons, the prospect of large overhead high-power lines running down from Skyline Ridge. Stanford and federal officials balked at the high cost of putting high-voltage lines underground, pointing to the town's own unaesthetic lower-voltage poles (like these).   SLAC ARCHIVES

on Atomic Energy that federal funds should be used to place a line underground when lines in the same area of much lower voltage and involving much lesser cost had not been placed underground. "It is difficult for me to see how a request for undergrounding as the only alternative can still be supported if the objective is truly the preservation of the hillsides and the skyline in our area," Panofsky said.[43]

The AEC had the option of condemnation, in which case local communities would lose all control over the acreage in question. The U.S. Court of Appeals for the Ninth Circuit blocked this action in May 1965, but Congress then passed a bill permitting the AEC to override such local ordinances. President Lyndon Johnson signed the

bill in August, but asked Laurance Rockefeller, chair of the White House Conference on Natural Beauty, to look into the matter. "Rockefeller was particularly stunned by the huge power substation in the Woodside Town Center adjacent to what was then the Pioneer Hotel," Doug Dupen, SLAC's associate director for technical and public information, reported to Panofsky.[44]

By this time, the AEC had adopted a new design: simple, green tubular, single-stanchion steel poles rather than the originally planned steel grillwork towers. Both poles and wires were to be installed by helicopter, recorded Bill Kirk, Panofsky's right-hand man, in his *Informal History of SLAC*, "to minimize the clearing of trees and shrubs, and to soften the general

In a compromise with neighbors, simple tubular, single-stanchion steel poles, rather than steel grillwork towers, were proposed. A model pole, designed by Herman Halperin, is seen here on the green in front of SLAC's Administration and Engineering Building in 1964. Halperin, right, shows his plan to Larry Mohr, the Atomic Energy Commission's Palo Alto manager.   STANFORD NEWS SERVICE

impact on the landscape." After Rockefeller viewed the area, Johnson told local conservation groups he would recommend that the AEC "should agree to replace the overhead transmission line with an underground line some time between five and seven years—assuming that the local area has made reasonable progress in its own efforts to underground the power lines in the community." In September 1965, Woodside's mayor announced that the town would end its legal opposition.[45]

Sterling later noted that the dispute was ultimately resolved by the redesign of the towers.[46] Today, the green-painted tubular poles are so

After the town of Woodside withdrew its legal opposition in 1965, both poles and wires were installed by helicopter to minimize tree clearing and soften the impact on the landscape. Helicopter is seen here at a pole staging area, spring 1966.   RICHARD MUFFLEY / SLAC ARCHIVES

inconspicuous in the densely wooded route from Skyline Boulevard to SLAC that it is difficult to identify them.

Even with this four-year controversy subsiding, Stanford officials were concerned about getting the power delivered on schedule. At one staff meeting, Sterling recalled, the tension was lightened by Bob Moulton, with a tribute to Panofsky's energy: "Don't worry, Wally! If the lines don't bring in the power, we can always plug in Pief!"[47]

THE PHYSICS DEPARTMENT–SLAC TURF BATTLE

Wolfgang Panofsky, SLAC's director since early 1961, already had played a principal role in creation of the project. With Ginzton, he had firmly insisted that the university be responsible for the design, construction, and management of the project, and that research results remained unclassified and unregulated by government agencies. He was determined that the facility

At a June 10, 1966, press conference announcing completion of both the linear accelerator and the laboratory's controversial power lines are, from left: David Packard, Stanford trustee; nuclear physicist Glenn Seaborg, head of the Atomic Energy Commission; and Pief Panofsky, SLAC director. Three weeks earlier, the first electron beam had traveled the full 2 miles from the accelerator trigger end to the beam switchyard.   STANFORD NEWS SERVICE / SLAC ARCHIVES

be open to all qualified users, a position that would not satisfy all at Stanford. The accelerator would only become a tool for excellent research, however, if Stanford created a strong in-house research staff, which, he felt, could happen only if the leaders of this staff were members of Stanford's regular faculty.[48]

Before SLAC construction got underway, conflict emerged with the Physics Department over recruitment and responsibilities of the Stanford scientists who would be working with the 2-mile accelerator. Early in 1962, key members of the Physics Department insisted that SLAC physicists, including Panofsky, should not be permitted to hold appointments on the Physics faculty.[49]

Many of Stanford's physicists had been enthusiastic about developing the next big machine to follow the Mark III. Professor Richard Hofstadter had first thought up the idea of a machine 10 times bigger than the Mark III, recalled Ginzton. "We wanted to push the technology further," Ginzton said, remembering the enthusiasm of the mid-1950s. "With a bee in our bonnet

and with Mark IV under construction, ideas took form in 1955–56."[50]

In 1957, however, Hofstadter openly dissented with the Project M proposal to open research to non-Stanford scientists. Hofstadter, realizing he would not have first claim on the new accelerator's beam time, joined other campus physicists who were concerned that SLAC's large budget and large staff would overwhelm non-SLAC faculty influence on department policies and teaching and research agendas.[51]

At its meeting on February 26, 1963, the Advisory Board of the faculty's Academic Council accepted the principle that SLAC could make a reasonable number of faculty appointments carrying, when appropriate, tenure and membership in the Academic Council. The Academic Council adopted a more general policy, and procedures for appointments at university research laboratories and institutes, an action meant to impose more faculty control over appointments that involved faculty status. The 1963 policy was meant to clarify this for SLAC in particular, but in counteraction, the Physics Department denied that SLAC was in any way related to the department and cut off the possibility of joint appointments.[52]

The Advisory Board also recommended acceptance of the principle that the Physics Department would control graduate training in physics, in particular admission of graduate students, establishment and supervision of graduate coursework, and the granting of degrees. In good faith, the Board assumed that the Physics Department would utilize the unique scientific opportunity afforded by SLAC and its staff, but strong voices in the Physics Department, including its department head, theoretical physicist Leonard Schiff, took the position that SLAC was a separate academic unit of Stanford. They believed SLAC should have no degree-granting authority and no say in undergraduate curriculum or teaching, nor in graduate admissions, curriculum, or research supervision, including for those graduate students specializing in high-energy physics.[53]

Celebrating the September 9, 1967, dedication of the new accelerator center, from left: AEC Chairman Seaborg, SLAC Director Panofsky, President Sterling, U.S. Presidential Science Advisor Donald Hornig, and Edward Ginzton, first director of the original Project M.   STANFORD NEWS SERVICE

Other campus faculty members, concerned about the growing influence of government-sponsored, extra-departmental research labs and institutes at Stanford, lent their support to the contrarians in the Physics Department. By mid-1963, SLAC was already a virtually independent organization, separate from the Physics Department, with nearly 500 physicists, engineers, and technical staff. SLAC administrators had the sympathy of much of the university administration, particularly Sterling, Provost Fred Terman, Graduate Dean Albert Bowker, and Vice President for Business Affairs Alf Brandin, who had all worked with Panofsky and his associates since 1957 to build the Monster.

Leonard Schiff captured the support of powerful faculty members in chemistry, including Arthur Kornberg, Henry Taube, William Johnson, and Paul Flory. Also, 11 members of the Mathematics Department wrote Sterling regarding recent approval of several professional appointments to SLAC: "It seems to us that serious problems are implicit in the assignment of regular faculty privileges and responsibilities to a large group whose interests overlay those of an existing strong academic department."[54] Sterling was especially annoyed when the conflict was reported in the magazine *Science,* where it was obvious that physics faculty were lobbying extensively outside the department. He warned Schiff to stop the lobbying and the inequity against pro-SLAC graduate students.[55]

Actions of the Physics Department, and counteractions by SLAC's leadership, required Sterling's ongoing involvement. The Physics Department not only refused to consider joint appointments, but passed increasingly restrictive resolutions, causing an internal split with a minority of professors sympathetic to SLAC.

View of SLAC's main "quad" area, with the Auditorium and Cafeteria Building to the left and the Central Laboratory to the right, in 1967. The budget called for strictly utilitarian buildings. Panofsky was proud to note that the project was on time, on spec, and on budget.   RICHARD MUFFLEY / SLAC ARCHIVES

Sterling agreed with Terman and Bowker that the protesting physicists—led by Felix Bloch, Walter Meyerhof, Robert Hofstadter, and Leonard Schiff—were not only inconsistent, but also unjust to their former colleagues now at SLAC.

Terman and Bowker urged Sterling to issue an ultimatum, but he chose instead the course of patient persuasion.[56] He wanted to avoid open revolt and perhaps significant resignations in the department or at SLAC, and he continued to meet individually with Schiff and Panofsky to reconcile differences. He had great respect for Schiff, who was widely esteemed on campus as a brilliant scientist as well as a gentleman. He also admired Panofsky and had been a staunch supporter of Ed Ginzton. He would not sympathize with the intransigent attitude shown by Schiff and his colleagues toward Panofsky and the team of physicists he was trying to assemble at SLAC. Sterling also felt that it was irrational for the department to deny eminent former colleagues, as well as new recruits to the department, the opportunity to teach, work with graduate students, and even to access the Hansen Labs.[57]

In spring 1964, however, over the objection of Provost Terman, the Physics Department limited to 10 percent the number of second-year graduate students who could be supervised outside the department, that is, the number of dissertations in physics using SLAC facilities and working with SLAC faculty. Sterling informed Schiff that "a fixed percentage suggests 'quota' and, as I have told you, I am uneasy about quotas of any kind—not least of all because they are negative toward flexibility."[58] Panofsky, in turn, proposed establishment of a graduate program in elementary particle physics under the immediate supervision of the SLAC faculty.[59]

The SLAC–Physics Department controversy became so emotionally charged that in April 1965, Hugh Heffner, associate provost for research, told Schiff he was "seriously concerned personally that we would be headed for a direct collision between SLAC and Physics," and that he feared "a resolution of the problem would involve a serious blow-up in one or the other of the two groups." Heffner suggested two small steps to be taken by Physics: removal of the quota

Physics Professor Robert Hofstadter, seen here after winning the Nobel Prize in 1961 for his work using Stanford's Mark III accelerator. In 1954, Hofstadter had dreamed of a much longer accelerator, 10 times the length of the Mark III. He later withdrew from project planning, however, objecting to the concept of sharing access with non-Stanford faculty.   STANFORD NEWS SERVICE

Professor Leonard I. Schiff, chair of the Physics Department and widely esteemed physicist, believed SLAC should be separate from the Physics Department, with no degree-granting authority, and no role in curriculum decisions, graduate admissions, or research supervision, including supervision of students in high-energy physics. Sterling intervened to quiet the resulting SLAC–Physics Department discord and work out a compromise.
STANFORD NEWS SERVICE

the SLAC–Physics controversy would be over by Christmas 1964. Heffner feared that the remaining SLAC faculty would resign if Sands left, which would jeopardize the future of SLAC's program. In addition to the problems Stanford was already experiencing in attracting top physicists to SLAC, Heffner warned "we could run the danger of a complete review of the SLAC program by the AEC with a view toward separating it from the University and making it a national laboratory separate from academic activities."[62]

Frustrated by the impasse, Panofsky had privately recommended to Sterling the appointment of "an Advisory Board of some kind to conduct a study within the University to explore how the work of the various academic units in pure and applied research should be coordinated such that they would best serve the educational purposes of the University."[63] He was impressed, he wrote Sterling a month later, by the contrast between the deliberations of the National Academy of Sciences' Physics Survey Committee, "which are focused on the problem of providing graduates education commensurate with the expanding needs, and the current procedures which involve blocking of increased educational opportunities at Stanford."[64]

Later that year, Sterling proposed a more direct course, a joint Physics Department–SLAC meeting. The Physics Department refused to attend, Virgil K. Whitaker, dean of the graduate division, reported to Sterling. "I repeatedly emphasized to Professor Schiff that I felt the basic difficulty lay not in specific issues but rather in the fact that the Physics Department and the SLAC faculty were facing each other like Americans and Russians across a conference table," wrote Whitaker, "and that so long as such an attitude of distrust prevailed no memoranda or guarantees would get us very far because they would always be subject to argument about interpretation." He added that "this was the flattest

for graduate students working at SLAC, and an invitation to a SLAC faculty member to teach a course in the Physics Department.[60] "The answer to both of these suggestions," Heffner reported to Sterling five days later, "was an impassioned, elaborated, but definite 'no.'"[61]

Heffner had already pointed out that, ironically, SLAC's associate director, Matthew Sands, was co-author of "the most exciting and most widely employed new text for undergraduate physics, and yet we cannot make use of his talents in teaching." Sands had rejected the offer to head the Physics Department at the University of Minnesota because Sterling had promised him

but the friendliest defiance of my authority that I have ever received. I propose to let the call for meeting stand, and the refusal of the P[hysics] D[epartment] representative to attend will become a part of the record."[65]

In a confidential September memorandum to Sterling, Whitaker added in part:

> I would be the first to admit that Panofsky can be irritatingly persistent. He gets under my skin at times, as he has no doubt got under the skin of his former colleagues in Physics. But this is part of the energy that makes him so effective. And he is subject to terrible tensions. He must complete the project despite unexpected hazards (it is wonderful to imagine the Physics Department having to deal with the Town of Woodside), and he must so design his great machine that it will produce commensurate results in the ten years or so that are its effective life. Under these tensions, almost beyond human endurance, I think it is possible that Panofsky is overestimating the help he needs and the troubles he faces, as any human being in his position would. But I have encountered in the members of Physics to whom I have talked no glimmer of understanding of Panofsky's plight let alone the sympathy due to any

human being in a tough spot in which they put him. This lack of elementary human consideration I find incredible.[66]

Bob Moulton summed up the issue to Sterling this way:

> The anti-Big Business Science people are indulging their prejudice in a way that injures education and contributes needlessly to an increasing antipathy between Big Science and education. . . . [T]he attitude of the Blochs and Schiffs will help make real the Big Science they fear because if their position prevails Big Science *will* tend to be devoid of academic content and academic types. It is ironic that they will contribute in a major way to the development they are so anxious to prevent.[67]

As a result of the dispute, Panofsky and Sidney Drell resigned from the Stanford Physics Department in May 1962 to become faculty members at SLAC. Sterling's forbearance was later partially rewarded with a compromise of sorts. The Physics Department grudgingly agreed to allow SLAC faculty to teach courses and to supervise graduate student work, but the former only at the department's discretion, and the latter only in conjunction with a member of

Fastest way to travel the 2-mile long klystron gallery was via bicycle, as seen in 1967. The combination modulator-power supply units (large boxes) provide pulses of power to the klystron amplifiers (striped cylinders), which then deliver intense bursts of microwave radiation through a waveguide system to the accelerator below. The penetrations, located every 20 feet along the floor, carry down the piping which connects the microwave, water, and vacuum systems to the accelerator.
WALTER ZAWOJSKI / SLAC ARCHIVES

The experimental program at the Stanford Linear Accelerator Center, seen here in February 1967, was well underway months before its September dedication. Five experiments had been completed, six set up, and 26 experiment proposals submitted in the preceding nine months. Beams are launched from a small building near the intersection of Sand Hill and Whiskey Hill roads, top of photo. Note the future Interstate 280 overpass. STANFORD NEWS SERVICE

the campus department. By the time the Stanford Linear Accelerator Center was formally dedicated in September 1967, 11 of its senior staff had faculty appointments at SLAC. Interestingly, at least half of the initial 26 proposals for use of the linear accelerator were from Stanford physicists, including members of the Physics Department.[68]

In September 1966, Sterling gave his file on the SLAC–Physics Department dispute to his secretary, Jessie Applegarth, with a handwritten note: "I guess this can go to file now. May it R.I.P." Applegarth was more skeptical. Her note to an assistant secretary said: "Jane—watch this carefully—It may not R.I.P.—Jessie."[69]

9

EMBARKING ON
OVERSEAS CAMPUSES

In June 1958, 63 Stanford undergraduates flew in a chartered plane to Stuttgart, Germany. The final destination was Landgut Burg, on a hill overlooking Beutelsbach, a village of 2,000 inhabitants 12 miles east of Stuttgart in southwest Germany. Their arrival inaugurated Stanford's newly established and innovative study-abroad program, which became an important component of undergraduate education during Sterling's second decade as president. At the program's peak, near the end of his administration, some 800 students and 20 faculty families a year were going to Stanford campuses in Germany, France, Italy, Austria, and England, a total of more than 50 percent of undergraduates.[1]

Accompanying the students to Beutelsbach were the two men who played principal roles in the program's initiating and planning: Professor Robert A. Walker, first director of Overseas Campuses, and Professor Friedrich W. (Willi) Strothmann, the Landgut Burg's first academic

director. They were joined by political science Professor Kurt Steiner, known on campus as "Mr. Austria."[2]

President Wallace Sterling later described the overseas campuses as the "brain children" of Strothmann and Walker, who believed that the international perspective students would gain was an essential part of a liberal education.[3]

Strothmann had come to Stanford as an instructor of Germanic languages in 1930 after receiving his doctorate in German philology at the University of Cologne. He later served as head of his department from 1949 to 1970, including periods when it was combined with Romanic Languages and a decade (1958–68) when it was named Modern European Languages. Despite a heavy teaching load, he promoted language studies generally, as well as German studies, and co-authored important language textbooks.[4]

Walker had joined Stanford's political science faculty in 1949, becoming chair in 1958. An expert in public administration and urban planning, and a strong-minded, practical administrator, he was called on by Sterling and Provost

< The October 1960 dedication of Stanford-in-Italy was trumpeted by Florentine musicians wearing Renaissance-style costumes at Palazzo Vecchio, the Florence town hall and museum. STANFORD UNIVERSITY ARCHIVES

Students, faculty, and administrators on their way to inaugurate the first overseas campus, at Beutelsbach, Germany, posed with their chartered Air France turboprop plane in June 1958.   METRO NEWS PHOTOS, CHICAGO / STANFORD NEWS SERVICE

Frederick Terman to serve on many important advisory committees, including a broad study of undergraduate education.[5]

In 1954, Sterling had initiated the Stanford Study of Undergraduate Education, the first review of undergraduate curriculum in 35 years. Walker chaired two committees that devised a new set of general required courses for under-graduates outside their major. The Committee on General Studies saw this as a way to develop well-rounded students. Sterling also urged the committee to consider more foreign language opportunities, believing that postwar America's educated citizens should master at least one non-native language.[6]

Walker and Strothmann sold Sterling on the idea that a program sending students to Europe for two quarters (including chartered travel to Europe) could be paid for from the usual tuition and room-and-board charges. Stanford could increase enrollment with students who would take their places on the home campus. Ken Cuthbertson, Sterling's senior financial man, initially wasn't sold on the economics of the program but said to Sterling, "If it's good for the University and you want to do it, go ahead."[7]

Political science professor Robert Walker, first director of Stanford's Overseas Campuses, in 1962. Walker strongly believed Stanford undergraduates would benefit from international experience.
STANFORD NEWS SERVICE

Professor of German Friedrich (Willi) Strothmann, here in 1969, a popular teacher and author, partnered with Walker in making the case for overseas study opportunities.
STANFORD NEWS SERVICE

genuine educational visionary, as well as a very effective political infighter at the university," recalled Professor Norman Naimark, one of Walker's successors as program director. "One needed both traits to start a program like Overseas Studies from scratch."[9]

"Willi's background, linguistic ability, and societal understanding suited his role, and Bob's tough questions, demanding answers, and foreseeing problems were also indispensable," said G. Robert Hamrdla, an early Beutelsbach student and later Overseas Campuses administrator.[10]

SEARCHING FOR SHANGRI-LA IN GERMANY

Selection of the first campus was partly opportunistic, but also reflected the importance, at the time, of studying German for students in engineering and science, as well as the humanities. Germany in 1957–58 was also comparatively pro-American and inexpensive.

Strothmann spent summer 1957 crisscrossing Germany, using a free rail pass provided by the German government, and found a suitable facility at Landgut Burg, above Beutelsbach, in buildings that once housed a branch of the Goethe Institute. The 30-acre estate, surrounded by vineyards, held commanding hilltop views of the Rems Valley. According to Sterling, Strothmann cabled Walker that he had found "Shangri-La." That same summer, the Sterlings had taken their two daughters to Europe. Sterling knew nothing of Strothmann's travels until he returned home and was informed by Fred Glover that Strothmann's expenses had been paid from the "President's Gift Fund."[11]

Strothmann and Walker hoped to locate facilities in European countries and to have these facilities constitute a part of Stanford. Walker argued strongly for smaller towns in rural, provincial sites, where he thought residents

"The idea was so compelling and so suitable to our effort to improve general education and particularly to get rid of the sophomore academic slump," wrote Cuthbertson once the program was well underway, "that we simply had to figure ways to make financial reallocations so that the program could be undertaken."[8]

Walker and Strothmann investigated sites, negotiated contracts, and designed the programs, with Walker as administrator. Walker "was a

In war-torn Germany, Strothmann in 1957 searched for a potential campus facility. He finally found his "Shangri-La," a 30-acre estate, Landgut Burg, above Beutelsbach. The large manor house included dining room, living room, and accommodations; two buildings added later completed the campus. STANFORD UNIVERSITY ARCHIVES

were more welcoming; the degree to which local language was "pure" also played some role. He also thought Stanford students would not survive well in European student dormitories, and worried about moral issues if students had their own apartments independently in town.[12]

According to Naimark, Walker opposed home stays based on his own experiences as a Fulbright scholar in Belgium. "Our students could not count on the good graces of European landladies, who, he thought, might exploit them in a variety of ways." Also, Naimark added, Walker's concerns about European student dormitories "turned out to hold true in early experiments in Berlin."[13]

Glover, who spoke German and French fluently, helped with the searches. It was a conscious decision, he later recalled, to have separate Stanford facilities rather than placing students in established European universities.[14]

Stanford provided its own teaching staff, supplemented by local instructors in language and, later, in other fields as well. "The contacts between the faculty and the students when they're living together and traveling, doing all of this stuff, was a marvelous experience for them," Glover explained. This approach also helped Stanford students holding California State Scholarships, which were valid only in California institutions. Course work would apply to programs back at Stanford, and students could graduate on time.[15]

The university paid the students' transportation to Europe and provided board, lodging, and a 10-day group field trip, each quarter, for the same cost as for study on campus. Students were expected to pay their own way home, and many took the opportunity for more travel, especially during the three-week break between quarters. Only undergraduates already enrolled at Stanford were eligible to attend, and only after they had completed freshman year. Selection was based primarily on academic standing, but with strong attention paid to the applicant's qualifications for leadership, stability, and capacity to live in a small group. At first, only one quarter of language preparation was required.

Similar centers were established in 1960 in a former hotel in Tours, in the Loire Valley in France, and at Villa San Paolo, in Fiesole (an elegant suburb northeast of Florence), Italy. A center opened in Semmering, about 50 miles

southwest of Vienna, in fall 1965, and the following January at Harlaxton, Lincolnshire, just over 100 miles north of London.

EUROPEAN POMP AND POLITICAL CIRCUMSTANCES

Openings of the Stanford campuses abroad were carefully arranged affairs. At Beutelsbach, Glover and his wife, Nini, served as interpreters. Glover also was in charge of protocol and the German press, and news conferences were held in German. The German representatives were the Bürgermeister (mayor) of Beutelsbach, the Oberbürgermeister of Stuttgart, and the president of the State of Baden-Württemberg. President Sterling, who flew in with his wife after commencement and

Officers of Germany's second group play at stuffing skis into a small flight bag as they prepare to depart in late December 1958. Kneeling is William Sterling, son of President Wallace Sterling. Standing, from left, are G. Robert Hamrdla, Robert Moore, Robert Capron, and Marcia Millu. STANFORD NEWS SERVICE

Students from the first group at Stanford-in-Germany gathered outside what was then the most popular tavern in Beutelsbach, the Krone (Crown). HEINZ A. BENDER / STANFORD NEWS SERVICE

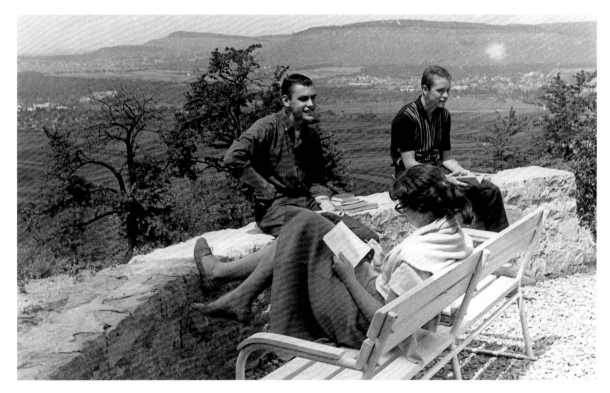

Students relax at the rural Landgut Burg, overlooking villages of the Rems Valley in southwestern Germany. Stuttgart is out of view, 12 miles west.   G. KESSELBACH / STANFORD NEWS SERVICE

other duties, was deferentially referred to as "Your Eminence" by German officials. When the Glovers teased him about it, Sterling jokingly put them in their place by calling them "Untereminenz" or "Eminenz Zweiter Klasse."[16]

In October 1960, the Sterlings and Glover flew to Europe for the next two campus openings, France and Italy. Students and faculty, meanwhile, took a nine-day voyage aboard a Cunard liner, with Walker hosting faculty-staff cocktail parties almost every evening and Bob Hamrdla serving as bartender. Faced with the significant expense of transporting 160 students, plus faculty families, by air to the French and Italian campuses, the university experimented with the less expensive, but more time consuming, journey by steamship. This, however, introduced new itinerary complications that involved gathering

students in New York (121 of the 160 flew in from San Francisco), sailing to Le Havre, then making cross-country train connections to Tours and Florence. The trial run was not repeated.[17]

For Stanford-in-France, a former hotel had been found in Tours, near the banks of the Loire, 145 miles from Paris. To Glover's dismay, he quickly learned that dedication plans were already causing "a bitter struggle" between officials of the local Université de Poitiers, and the city and departmental government, over which group would preside at the event. University officials wanted to welcome the Americans with a *"séance académique,* an academic meeting, while the civil service people wanted it to be a state affair," Glover recalled. More important to Glover, "At stake was where the [Stanford] students would sit, and where the American

President Sterling speaking at the 1960 dedication of the French campus in Tours. Despite diplomatic haggling about seating arrangements, the event was convivial and well received.

In the end, students sat near the front and faculty sat on the stage with government officials. The dean of the university presided, however.[18]

At the October 8 dedication, Sterling spoke about the founding of Stanford. "Wally gave an excellent talk and the ambassador spoke in halting French," Glover recalled. As at later dedications, there was no translation because everyone was presumed to speak English. "They didn't, but that's the way it was."[19]

The provincial governor hosted an elaborate luncheon after the dedication. He spoke no English, Glover realized, while Sterling, though he spoke German, did not speak French. Glover hoped to sit near Sterling, but local protocol was strict, placing the presidential assistant at the end of the table. "I was puzzled as I watched Wally, for he and the governor seemed to be engaged in a lively discussion," Glover remembered. "Later I asked Wally what they were talking about, and [he] said it was about higher ambassador and [Stanford] faculty would sit." When he told Sterling of the current plan—with either the French faculty or the politicians prominently seated on the stage, and students seated at the back of the audience, Sterling gave Glover "very specific instructions."

> I relayed these [in French] to the university and government officials who were seated around a big table . . . in the basement of the elegant city hall. . . . "*Messieurs*," I told the group, "President Sterling has asked me to give you his specific instructions. He did not bring our students 6,000 miles to have them sit in the back of the room. He wants them to be in the front row and he'll leave it up to you to determine where the faculty and government officials should sit. The American ambassador should sit where the President of France would sit if he were here. Thank you very much and *bonjour, messieurs*."

The campus in Tours, France, opened with 80 students in this former hotel near the banks of the Loire in fall 1960. The program moved to a different Tours building in the mid-1970s, then closed in 1991.   STANFORD NEWS SERVICE

education. When I queried the governor, he said that they'd had a most interesting discussion of juvenile delinquency." Glover added that the constantly replenished wines must have helped the discussion.[20]

From France, the Sterlings and Glover journeyed to Florence for the October 12 dedication of Stanford-in-Italy, held in the town hall, the famous Palazzo Vecchio. The first home, Villa San Paolo, was formerly a school run by the Barnabiti Brothers, a Catholic order. Sterling asked Glover to talk to Padre Rienzi, the senior father, to explain the provision in the Founding Grant forbidding close ties to any sectarian religion. (All of the brothers, Glover was relieved to discover, spoke fluent French.) Sterling wanted it clear "that the first time the Barnabiti tried to convert any of our students, there was going to be a lot of trouble." When Glover raised the issue, Padre Rienzi called the other fathers to join them. Glover was standing with the five black-clad brothers making his point when Sterling walked by, calling to Glover, "Do you need five priests in order to confess, Fred?"[21]

With three programs underway, more than 30 percent of undergraduates would have the opportunity to study overseas.

Stanford-in-Austria, opened in September 1965, was first located in a former tourist hotel, Panhans, at Semmering, about a 90-minute drive southwest from Vienna. Austrian Chancellor Josef Klaus and U.S. Ambassador James Riddleberger were among those at the dedication. In his speech, Sterling reminisced:

> When I was a schoolboy, I knew little more about the Austro-Hungarian Empire than that it occupied a large and central place on the map of Europe. It was only later that I learned something of its history, and still later that interest led me to select one of its crises as the subject of my doctoral dissertation. But my love affair with Austria began before I developed

Sterling, with Italian officials, spoke at the Florence dedication, held off-site at the Palazzo Vecchio, a building steeped in Renaissance history. In the 16th century, Cosimo I de Medici redecorated and restructured it, for a time, into his ducal palace. STANFORD UNIVERSITY ARCHIVES

Villa San Paolo, formerly a Catholic school, was the first of several locations for Stanford-in-Italy. Located in Fiesole, an elegant suburb of Florence, the villa was once site of famous salons for Florentine intellectuals. The program put students in the middle of the Italian Renaissance. STANFORD NEWS SERVICE

an interest in her history—it began when I first heard her music, and I may have been at a particularly sentimental age when I head Richard Tauber sing *Wien, Wien nur du allein*, but I knew that one day I must come to that city of my dreams. And so I did, years ago, and it is always a joy to return.[22]

Sterling also explained the rationale for establishing overseas campuses: After World War II, the United States had emerged as a world power but that "in its long period of so-called isolation, had paid inadequate attention to the languages, literature, and culture of other nations. It seemed to some, therefore, that in this particular, the U.S. was less well equipped than it might be to discharge the responsibilities which accompanied its new position as a world power."[23]

Stanford-in-Britain located in Harlaxton Manor, near Grantham, Lincolnshire, was dedicated on April 16, 1966, three months after it opened. The massive stone manor house, built between 1837 and 1845 combining elements of Jacobean and Elizabethan styles, was an unusually extravagant setting. Harlaxton was even more difficult to reach than Semmering. Located 23 miles south of Nottingham, it was connected to London by way of a complicated series of train routes.

At the dedication ceremony, the Sterlings were joined by Lord Willoughby de Eresby, the Lord Lieutenant of Lincolnshire, as well as Sir Robert Aitken, vice-chancellor of the University of Birmingham. Other dignitaries were the Duke and Duchess of Gloucester *(see also*

Stanford-in-Britain opened in January 1966 at Harlaxton Manor, Lincolnshire, 110 miles north of London, but very challenging to reach by train. After three years, the Stanford program was transferred, first to Cliveden, later to Oxford.   AEROFILMS & AERO PICTORIAL LTD. / STANFORD UNIVERSITY ARCHIVES

Chapter 17), the Bishop of Grantham, and U.S. Federal Ninth Circuit Judge Ben C. Duniway (a member of the Stanford Board of Trustees) and his wife, Ruth.[24]

AFFILIATED AND SPECIALIZED PROGRAMS

An affiliated program managed by Stanford Overseas Campuses was the Intercollegiate Center for Classical Studies in Rome, established in 1965 and opened in February 1966. Originally a consortium of 16 American colleges and universities, it was the brainchild of Stanford Professor Brooks Otis, an expert in Latin literature, with significant involvement by Walker. It has evolved into North America's premier undergraduate center in Italy for the study of the Roman classical world. Thirty students attended during its first semester. Sterling could not be present for the dedication on April 23, 1966. Graduate Dean Virgil Whitaker representing Sterling was joined by the esteemed Frederick Reinhardt, ambassador to Italy.[25]

Also by the late 1960s, smaller language programs had been created in Nantes, Salamanca, and Hamburg. Stanford tried a different approach with Japanese and Chinese studies centers, which were organized by other departments and not connected to the Overseas Campuses Office.

The Stanford Center for Japanese Studies got underway in 1961 with 4 graduate and 13 undergraduate students in temporary headquarters at Waseda University in Tokyo. Professor John Goheen, head of Stanford's Philosophy Department, organized the program and was its first director. He had been fostering

exchange initiatives since spending summer 1950 in Japan leading seminars for Japanese scholars. The Stanford center would provide educational opportunities for a select group of graduate and undergraduate students specializing in Far Eastern affairs, especially the language, institutions, and cultural traditions of Japan.

For Goheen, a key goal was to train students for the U.S. Foreign Service. Unlike the residential European campuses, these students were housed in Japanese dormitories and stayed for a full year. Sterling, who spoke at the opening on April 12, 1961, was awarded the Imperial Order of the Rising Sun, Second Class, from the emperor for "efforts at promoting Japanese Studies at Stanford, his help to Japanese students and scholars, and his efforts in helping Japanese universities establish American study programs." Goheen was awarded the Japanese Order of the Sacred Treasure for his contributions to U.S.-Japanese cultural and educational relations.[26]

Philosophy Professor John Goheen (left) and Sterling were entertained during the 1961 opening of the Stanford Center for Japanese Studies in Tokyo. Not part of the Overseas Campuses program, this year-long immersive curriculum was aimed at graduate students and undergraduates specializing in Japanese language and Far Eastern affairs. STANFORD UNIVERSITY ARCHIVES

The Stanford Center for Chinese Studies in Taipei opened in September 1962, when 12 undergraduates and graduate students traveled individually to Taiwan to begin a full year of intense Mandarin study. A few months later, Peking (Beijing) Radio included Stanford's new Chinese Center in an indictment of "the intensification of the cultural aggression in Taiwan by the American imperialists," accusing educational exchange programs of operating as "cultural secret agents." Students in Taipei made their own living arrangements, usually either rooming in a dormitory with Chinese students or living with a Chinese family, although some chose to live alone in apartments.[27] A special committee of the departments of History and of Asian Languages initially organized and administered the program.

In 1964, the two Asian centers, renamed the Inter-University Center for Japanese Studies in Tokyo and the Inter-University Program for Language Studies in Taipei, expanded to serve a consortium of universities, administered by Stanford's Office of Graduate Overseas Centers and Special Programs. When the Ford Foundation in 1966 renewed its support for the Taipei program, it was hosting 41 students from 14 U.S. institutions.[28]

EXCITEMENT, THEN CRITICISM

In an era when airline fares were heavily regulated, and relatively costly, few young people had traveled extensively outside the United States. The *Stanford Daily* reflected students' early excitement about the overseas campuses, with front-page coverage, and occasional banner head-

No details are available, but Sterling's private discussion with a Japanese official certainly had a beautiful Tokyo backdrop. He did not travel to Taipei for the 1962 opening of a study center there.   STANFORD UNIVERSITY ARCHIVES

lines (including, in 1964, a huge, all-caps, two-line banner at the top of page one announcing "CAMPUSES APPROVED IN AUSTRIA, ENGLAND").[29]

When 33 men and 30 women were chosen from 167 applicants for Beutelsbach's first session, the *Daily* published names of the lucky ones (including two *Daily* staffers) and reprinted, in German, an excerpt about the anticipated Stanford campus from the *Stuttgarter Zeitung*.[30] Of the first overseas campus, the *Daily* editorialized in 1957:

> Forward-looking Stanford administrators have investigated and are now in the process of completing a fantastic Study Center in Germany. The mere dream of Stanford flying 120 students off to Germany each year to study under a plan which will fit directly into our General Studies Program is daring. The fact that Stanford is actually on the brink of accomplishing this feat is commendable—no, it is downright exciting!
>
> The University as a whole is on the brink of a change which cannot help but cause us to graduate better-educated, broader-viewing men and women.[31]

A group photo of Austria VIII, during spring-summer 1969 (picture taken at the Hofburg complex, headquarters of the Hapsburg Empire). Officials in 1967 moved the campus to downtown Vienna, easy walking distance to the Opera House, the Hofburg, and many other cultural attractions.   FOTO WINKLER, WIEN / STANFORD UNIVERSITY ARCHIVES

As an illustration, one student from Beutels-bach in 1960 described in four long paragraphs to his parents what he learned about the refugee situation during a trip to Berlin: "Germany has a present population of about 54 million; of these, 13 million are refugees from somewhere behind the iron curtain—i.e. 25% of the whole popula-tion! That is a lot of people to absorb especially when three-fourths had another language, customs, etc. . . ." He added that the "psycho-logical importance of [W]est Berlin as an escape valve for refugees from Communism cannot be exaggerated!"[32]

When students were accepted for the new French and Italian programs, in 1960, the *Daily* again published their names. It also ran a letter to the editor from a civil engineering student expressing regret that so few in his engineer-ing cohort went overseas. In fact, university officials had been struggling to accommodate students whose four-year curricula lacked flex-ibility. Stanford-in-Britain became the campus where budding engineers, pre-meds, and science majors could engage with the humanities and social sciences, without the burden of learning a foreign language. The Overseas Campus Office produced sample programs showing the best timing for such students. Completing any of the two-quarter programs automatically fulfilled the General Studies area requirements in Humani-ties and Social Sciences.[33]

However, it did not take long for critics to

question Stanford's European enclaves, where students interacted more with Americans than with the people whose countries they were visiting and where some said academic standards were not sufficiently rigorous. In an October 27, 1964, edition of "The California Weekly People" of the *San Francisco Examiner*, Sterling said, "We want to avoid the mechanics of transferring credits between institutions. We don't want the experience to be restricted to language specialists. And we want the experience to occur before the student decides his major subject."

Criticism continued, however, and by the late 1960s the validity of going overseas was being challenged, as part of questioning fundamental aspects of society and the university, Norman Naimark, director of overseas studies from 2004 to 2009, has written.[34]

By 1967, the overseas experience was "no longer a novelty," according to Bob Hamrdla, a member of the second group in Germany. From 1960 to 1966, he served as an administrator at the Beutelsbach campus, after which he was assistant director of overseas campuses until 1970. In addition to being viewed as Eurocentric, he said, the program was "disdained as an entrenched part of the establishment rather than an educational innovation." Student interest dropped sharply.[35]

The first serious review of the program came in 1967–68, as part of the Study of Education at Stanford. Its report, issued just months after Sterling left office, recommended "substantially greater flexibility" in the program, giving each campus more autonomy to adjust its activities and curriculum, and providing greater budgetary support. It also advocated greater demands on students "both in prior preparation and in academic standards at the overseas campuses."[36]

Evolution and change had occurred during Walker's years as director. Responding to criticism of the rural settings and distances from cultural centers, the Austrian campus moved from Semmering to Vienna in 1967 (the campus closed in 1973 and a separate program was launched with the University of Vienna; that program closed in 1987), the British campus from Harlaxton to Cliveden in 1969 (then to Oxford in 1984). For several reasons, including better access to German culture and politics, the program in Germany was moved to West Berlin in 1976 and is still in Berlin. The Tours Center closed in 1991, when its undergraduate program was combined with a more specialized program in Paris. The Italy program remains in Florence but has been located at several different sites.

In the wake of a 1972 Presidential Commission on Overseas Campuses, Walker resigned, and the program was extensively reorganized. Under its second director, history Professor Mark Mancall, Overseas Campuses became Overseas Studies, in 1973, and the process of establishing smaller programs around the world accelerated. In 2005, Helen and Peter Bing endowed the overseas program.[37]

Over the program's six decades, despite its flaws, "few aspects of a Stanford undergraduate education . . . have meant so much to so many," according to Hamrdla. With approximately 55 percent of undergraduates going overseas in the late 1960s, he said, "No other institution of higher education in the world had mounted, much less sustained, a comparable effort to send large numbers of its undergraduate students away to learn in other settings, in other nations, in other cultures."[38]

10

BUILDING PARTNERSHIPS
STERLING AND HIS PROVOSTS

Wallace Sterling launched his administration in 1949 by jettisoning what he viewed as his predecessor's cumbersome layers of administrative staff. Concerned about faculty morale, Sterling resisted the vice-president option while increasing faculty participation on advisory committees and administrative roles. A pivotal step in this integration was his creation, in 1952, of the office of provost.

Stanford's presidents had long utilized the position of vice president, right-hand men drawn from senior faculty ranks, as a back-up during their own absences from campus. One vice president, geologist John Casper Branner, also had unusual influence over academic affairs during David Starr Jordan's administration, including the firing of faculty members. Another vice president, chemist Robert E. Swain, played a four-

year caretaker role when President Ray Lyman Wilbur simultaneously served as U.S. secretary of the interior. In 1944, Donald Tresidder went a step further. He granted his newly appointed vice president, Alvin C. Eurich (a new hire not drawn from Stanford's faculty), full responsibility for all things academic, placing this administrative position between himself and the faculty. This step freed Tresidder's hands to deal with the implications of a wartime campus and the financial needs of post-Depression and postwar recovery. However, his choice of Eurich, an academic better known for his government work and prone to micromanagement, was disorienting for a faculty accustomed to independence and direct access to the president.

Unlike Tresidder, Sterling was experienced with faculty governance and was comfortable with Stanford's earlier tradition of strong department heads and deans without a vice presidential intermediary. Preferring a hands-on, open-door style, Sterling and his small staff of assistants worked directly with faculty on academic affairs and budgets. He increased faculty participation through new university advisory committees, such as the university's Land and Buildings

< The partnership of Sterling and Provost Fred Terman became legendary for strengthening Stanford's faculty and student body through targeted fundraising, aggressive recruiting, and improved research facilities. Bay Area photographer Jack Fields captured their congenial relationship in this 1960 photograph for the *Saturday Evening Post*.
JACK FIELDS / STANFORD UNIVERSITY ARCHIVES

Development Committee (1951), and was comfortable calling on the Advisory Board and appearing before the faculty's Academic Council.

By 1952, however, Sterling had his hands full. As he worked through yearly budgets line by line with department heads, he also was fully engaged with revamping the Medical School, renovating old facilities, taking front stage with alumni and public relations, sorting out the implications of the Korean war draft, and working with the trustees to find alternative funding sources. He needed to add someone to his team who could focus on academic affairs and who could serve as evaluator, advocate, and expeditor. He did not want someone who would create the impression of an impenetrable wall between faculty and president.

In moving forward that year, he purposefully chose a different sort of title, one with an academic ring and without prior associations: "provost." His choices for the post, notably Frederick Terman and Richard Lyman, molded the position into the influential office it is today.[1]

THE BIOLOGIST
DOUGLAS M. WHITAKER, 1952–1955

Sterling's first appointment as provost, in March 1952, was close at hand: Professor Douglas Merritt Whitaker, dean of the reorganized School of Humanities and Sciences, Stanford's largest single academic unit, and former vice president to acting President Alvin Eurich.[2]

Whitaker had been executive head of the Biology Department when, in 1946, President Tresidder had appointed him dean of a new School of Biological Sciences. Two years later, when that school was folded into the School of Humanities and Sciences by acting President Eurich, Whitaker briefly stepped into Eurich's old shoes as vice president (acting). On Sterling's arrival and dissolution of the vice presidency,

Whitaker became dean of Graduate Studies, then, in 1951, dean of Humanities and Sciences.

Whitaker, A.B. '26, Ph.D. '28, an esteemed biologist, had been on the faculty since 1931. His work in experimental embryology and cell physiology led to better knowledge of fertilization and organ formation in embryos. In 1947, he served as chief biologist on the U.S. Army-Navy study of the effects of atomic radiation on marine and animal life on Bikini Atoll, the nuclear test site bombed as part of "Operation Crossroads."[3]

Whitaker was already familiar with many of Stanford's academic departments. In addition to his deanships, Whitaker had been broadly active in university affairs, and had remained well liked among the faculty despite serving in the Tresidder-Eurich administration. He was also a second-generation faculty member who had grown up on campus. His father, economics Professor Albert C. Whitaker, '99, served on the Stanford faculty from 1902 to 1942, and played an important role in building his department. The editors of the 1952 yearbook, *Stanford Quad,* called Doug Whitaker the "worthy and popular Dr. Whitaker."

Mary Tresidder, recalling her husband's long hours as university president, congratulated

President Sterling introduced the position of provost in 1952 with his appointment of biology Professor Douglas M. Whitaker, former dean of Biological Sciences, then of the expanded School of Humanities and Sciences. He grew up on campus, the son of economics Professor Albert Whitaker. STANFORD NEWS SERVICE

Doug Whitaker (left) was chief biologist for the 1947 U.S. Army-Navy Bikini Scientific Resurvey of Rongerik Island in the Bikini Atoll. Working with him on the study of the effects of radiation on marine and terrestrial flora and fauna following atomic bomb testing were (from left) P. M. Brooks, Lawrence Blinks (director, Hopkins Marine Station), and Gilbert Smith (botanist, Biology Department). U.S. NAVY / STANFORD NEWS SERVICE

Sterling on making the appointment: "I hope that Dean Whitaker will be . . . successful . . . and will free you for some of the long-range problems that must haunt the thinking of a university president. As a one-man job there isn't world enough and time."[4]

There was little fanfare when Sterling announced this appointment to the Academic Council. Whitaker had no particular job description for the new post other than to assist Sterling with academic affairs and to serve as acting president in his absence. Sterling left it to Whitaker to define his own role.[5]

In 1953, Whitaker oversaw a self-study of departmental needs in the behavioral sciences, which revealed little improvement since an initial department review by Sterling in 1949. Depart-

ments reported ongoing problems with lack of space, poor salaries, and staff shortages. Low morale was not helped by a budget freeze and rising enrollment. Stanford was in danger of losing recently acquired faculty "stars" because of low salaries. And with some departments seriously at odds over faculty differences, it remained difficult to recruit new faculty from outside.[6]

Whitaker struggled to deal with such problems. It is unclear why he did not participate in Sterling's review of the Medical School, or in faculty recruiting for the school. Nor did Whitaker take a leading role in Sterling's university-wide curriculum review, begun in 1954 (Sterling chaired its major committees). Nevertheless, Whitaker eased faculty into accepting the concept of a provost.

Sterling, who continued to review departmental budget line items himself, thought highly of teamwork, but he also valued decisiveness and results. In 1955, Provost Whitaker resigned to accept the post of vice president of administration at the Rockefeller Institute for Medical Research. Sterling later stated that the parting was amicable, but he had encouraged Whitaker to take the position as soon as possible. He already had a replacement in mind: Dean of Engineering Fred Terman.[7]

THE ENGINEER
FREDERICK E. TERMAN, 1955–1965

The high point of his presidency, Sterling later told an interviewer, was when Fred Terman became provost. "Sterling had been drawn to Terman's philosophy and ambition for Stanford, so similar to his own," observed Terman biographer Stewart Gillmor, "but he was also drawn to proven results displayed in Terman's School of Engineering."[8]

Sterling had a favorite story about his July 1955 visit to Dean Terman's office to invite him to become provost. After some discussion, Terman responded by asking what Sterling would be doing at 10:30 a.m. two days later. Sterling responded that he hoped he'd be listening to Terman's answer to Sterling's invitation. At the appointed time, the dean came to Sterling's office with a small stack of 3-by-5 cards. On each was a question, and Sterling answered each to the best of his ability. When the last card had been turned, Terman said, "Well, that's that!" Sterling replied, "What's what? You haven't said yes or no." Terman said, "Oh, I'm sorry. It's yes!" Sterling later observed, "For the next ten years I had the great good fortune of working with that remarkable man."[9]

Sterling's recognition of Terman's abilities and their successful collaboration made the period from 1955 to 1965 the most productive period of

Stanford's second provost (1955–65), electrical engineer Frederick E. Terman, also grew up on campus, the son of psychologist Lewis M. Terman. He was active on campus as a professor, department head, and then dean of engineering. He was a reluctant candidate for Stanford's presidency in 1940 and 1948.   STANFORD NEWS SERVICE

Sterling's 19-year presidency. Despite, or perhaps because of, their very different personalities, Sterling and Terman were well suited by intellectual assumptions and values to work together effectively. "Fred didn't give a damn what people thought about him or whether he stepped on toes," remembered Ernie Arbuckle, dean of the Graduate School of Business. "Wally was perfectly willing to accept that from Fred, because Wally could come in afterwards and clean up the messes with his wonderful personality and sense of fairness."[10]

"I struck it rich," said Sterling. "Never have I worked more harmoniously with an extremely able colleague. He *did* take responsibility. He had an extra sense for spotting younger men of real ability. Work was his hobby, and it was after his appointment as Provost that Stanford really began to make headway."[11]

Terman, like Whitaker, had grown up in a faculty family on the Stanford campus, moving there as a child when his father, Lewis Madison Terman, joined the faculty, in 1910. Lewis Terman, a pioneer in educational psychology, headed Stanford's Psychology Department, 1922–45, and served as an influential advisor to university presidents and trustees.[12]

After earning his bachelor's degree in chemistry at Stanford, in 1920, Fred Terman continued on for his engineer's degree (roughly equivalent to a master's degree) in electrical engineering, in 1922.[13] He worked with Harris J. Ryan, head of the Electrical Engineering Department, on his thesis on high-voltage power transmission. Encouraged by his father, he took Ryan's suggestion to pursue graduate study at MIT. His electrical engineering Sc.D. degree, received in 1924, was only the eighth awarded by MIT. "A few people may have thought me crazy," Terman said later. "Nobody got doctorates in engineering in those days. It turned out to be one of the smartest things I ever did."[14]

MIT offered Terman an instructorship, which he accepted, but when visiting home that summer, 1924, he was diagnosed with tuberculosis. He spent the next year recuperating, frustrated that his reading time was limited to a short period each day. Because of this, Sterling later remembered, "Time became extremely important to Fred, and he always crammed in as much work as he possibly could."[15] Terman's capacity for work and his attention to detail became legendary. Fred Glover recalled that Terman would come back from Christmas vacation with a caddie full of dictation rolls. "He just worked constantly." Glover remembered getting a telephone call from Terman at 11 p.m. on New Year's Eve. "He wasn't aware it was New Year's Eve."[16]

When an opening came up at Stanford's Electrical Engineering Department, Terman accepted a post as a part-time instructor, allow-

ing him to recuperate in California's warmer weather. Named an assistant professor in 1927, he was a full professor by 1937, when he was appointed head of the Electrical Engineering Department.

Although he had worked on high-voltage power transmission, Terman, an avid ham radio operator as a teen, now focused his energy on the up-and-coming field of radio technology, or "electronics." As a young department head, Terman found fellowship and salary support despite the Depression. Attracting talented graduate students to the department, he also often found them jobs and postgraduate positions. In 1932, he published his seminal textbook, *Radio Engineering*, a long-standing authoritative text in the field, and followed it in 1943 with an important handbook for radio engineers. In 1941, he was elected president of the Institute of Radio Engineers, the first who lived farther from New York City than Rochester, New York. Terman, a polished and prolific writer, also sought to improve his students' communications skills by broadening the engineering curriculum.[17]

With the outbreak of World War II, Vannevar Bush, then director of the U.S. Office of Scientific Research and Development, and Lee DuBridge, the physicist then directing MIT's Radiation Laboratory, asked Terman to establish the National Defense Research Committee's Radio Research Laboratory (RRL) at Harvard University. As director of the RRL from 1942 to 1946, Terman supervised development of radar countermeasures. His staff of 800 included 75 to 100 professors. Terman worked extensively with government officials, Harvard and MIT administrators, and industry contractors, managing a budget larger than that of Stanford University.[18]

Terman returned to Stanford in 1946 as President Tresidder's chosen dean of engineering. His experiences at RRL, with government officials like Bush, and within Harvard-MIT circles, convinced him that Stanford's academic prominence in engineering could be built upon the ability of faculty members to attract research funding from both government and corporate sources. He also had concluded that Stanford engineering training at both undergraduate and graduate levels was inadequate, and he resolved to develop the quality of the school's faculty as well as its student body.[19]

In 1948, Terman's name was among those seriously considered by Stanford's presidential search committee, although he was not enthusiastic about taking that step. He also had been nominated by faculty colleagues, and by President Ray Lyman Wilbur, as a candidate to follow Wilbur in 1940.[20]

"I most enjoy helping to build something up, taking an unformulated enterprise and making it into what it could become," Terman later told an interviewer. When Sterling asked Terman to become provost in 1955, Terman happily accepted, but he also remained dean of engineering for another three years. During this period, it was awkward for other deans to report to a fellow dean, and some non-engineering department heads balked until they came to know him better. Terman relinquished the engineering deanship in 1958. Vice president was added to his title in 1959 as part of a broader reorganization.[21]

Biographer Gillmor emphasizes that Terman focused on engineering and medicine during his first three years as provost largely because there were more outside funding opportunities. After 1958, he turned increasingly to the humanities and sciences, especially to the departments of biology, biochemistry, chemistry, English, history, mathematics, physics, psychology, political science, and statistics.[22]

Terman was known for his tough-minded selectivity in faculty recruiting, and its importance in building academic excellence. "In education there is no substitute for faculty quality," he

wrote in 1968. "While faculty committees may play checkers with the curriculum, and administrators may look for neglected areas, the reputation of an engineering school is dependent almost entirely on the caliber of the faculty. Likewise, the soundest programs in sponsored research are those that are based upon the demonstrated productivity of the faculty, rather than upon the grantsmanship of the administrators."[23]

Terman's approach to the search process introduced a new level of rigor to faculty recruiting and hiring throughout the university. Like Sterling, Terman hoped to "get the sights at Stanford raised as high as possible. We had a little bit of an inferiority complex that we really couldn't afford the best."[24] As provost, Terman expected a higher level of organization as well as analysis from search committees, often instructing department heads and faculty committees how to conduct their search. "When I got going, I was turning down a third of the [recommended] appointments that came to me," he recalled. "There was an attitude 'Who are you to turn these things down? You're supposed to sign them and send them on to the Advisory Board.'"[25] Sterling often tempered the instructions, and kept his own door open to complaints, but the end product was a team effort.

Sterling and Terman were as focused on the attraction and retention of top students as they were of top faculty. Both were essential to improving Stanford's academic program. Lyle Nelson, Sterling's director of university relations during the 1960s, described the symbiotic relationship of building faculty and students by paraphrasing Sterling:

> "Now that we've built up the faculty, we've got to put more money into students so that we have the quality of students the faculty deserves." And then [Sterling] turned around sometime later and said, "Now that we've got these quality students, we've got to build up the faculty."[26]

Since the 1930s, Terman had encouraged active recruiting of graduate students across the country. As provost, he encouraged departments to use their teaching assistant positions as recruiting tools. Top-quality graduate students in turn became a pool of strong candidates for faculty positions at Stanford and elsewhere.

Much has been written about Terman's support for two engineering students, David Packard and William Hewlett, who thought they'd like to go into business together. After graduating, in 1934, Packard went to work for General Electric and Hewlett worked on his master's degree at MIT. With suggestions from Terman, Hewlett built an audio oscillator; with a patent on the invention in Hewlett's hands and a gradu-

Stanford alumni David Packard (left) and William Hewlett (center) greeted their mentor, engineering Dean Fred Terman, to celebrate the 1951 construction of an electrical engineering student instruction wing of the Electronics Research Laboratory. The unpretentious building was made possible through a gift from Hewlett-Packard Company.   STANFORD UNIVERSITY ARCHIVES

ate research stipend from Stanford for Packard, they started a company. With Terman's help, the Hewlett-Packard Company was launched in 1939 in Palo Alto in a one-car garage workshop at a house on Addison Street.[27] The company later became a centerpiece of Stanford's Industrial (Research) Park.

Terman was well known for linking graduate students with faculty interests and research projects that, in turn, led to notable collaborations among physics and engineering faculty. He had played an important role in the development of Stanford's Microwave Laboratory, an interdisciplinary physics and electrical engineering lab, which evolved from the work of Bill Hansen, a physicist, and Ed Ginzton, a Terman student of electrical engineering. Stanford became a center for microwave technology, holding an important patent for klystron microwave tubes and traveling wave tubes of various kinds. Varian Associates, first occupant of what became Stanford's Industrial Park, and Stanford's Linear Accelerator Center, were stellar outcomes of this early collaboration.[28]

In 1959, Provost Terman articulated the Sterling administration's comprehensive, and challenging, strategy to build Stanford's academic prowess. As part of the administration's efforts to persuade the Board of Trustees to support a major university-wide fundraising campaign, Terman warned them that during this dynamic period in higher education, "Stanford cannot stand still." To develop a truly national stature, and "to establish Stanford securely as one of the small group of leading universities in the country," he argued, the university must have a progressively stronger salary structure, healthy growth of departmental faculties, rehabilitation of campus infrastructure as well as additional buildings, and improved student housing. "If we keep our sights high, we can satisfy our needs for improved salaries, our need for reasonable

President Sterling and engineering Dean Fred Terman flanked influential early trustee Judge George Crothers, '95, at the October 1954 groundbreaking of Crothers Memorial Hall (honoring his mother), for engineering graduate students. (Crothers already had funded Crothers Hall for law students.) Sterling selected Terman as his second provost the following summer.

growth in the size of the faculty, and our needs for physical plant, then the very successful past and present of Stanford is as nothing compared to what the future will bring."[29]

Sterling and Terman worked closely to determine university academic needs and priorities. Terman carefully evaluated the faculty of each school or department they had targeted, determining what additional strengths or fields were needed. He personally scoured the country for top-flight talent, seeking the judgments of those highly respected in the field, often drawing Sterling into negotiations.

A notable example of the flexibility of their strategy and symbiotic nature of their interaction was the development of the Chemistry Department when an unexpected windfall check from Procter & Gamble for $25,000 allowed Sterling and Terman to strengthen the department. Backed by a committee of influential scientists, they focused on William S. Johnson of the University of Wisconsin, an outstanding organic chemist. Johnson, however, would not come unless Carl Djerassi of Wayne State University came as well. Each man was eminent in research, had a team of younger researchers financed by government grants, and required adequate laboratories for both of their research teams.[30]

At that time the university's operating budget was $14 million, with the General Fund (the uncommitted portion of the operating budget) only a little over half a million dollars. According to Sterling, the situation called for "a rather bold stroke." Sterling proposed using almost all of the General Fund to provide space for the Johnson and Djerassi research teams. "With some arching of eyebrows and understandable doubt, the Trustees granted our request."[31]

Meanwhile, Terman approached John Stauffer, director and son of the founder of Stauffer Chemical Company, and Stauffer's flamboyant niece, Mitzi Stauffer Briggs, ex '50, with the proposition that they finance construction of a new chemistry building. During the Bohemian Grove encampment that summer, Sterling decided he would call on Stauffer at his camp. The Bohemian Club's "Weaving spiders come not here" motto was intended to discourage business dealings at the Grove, but this was a social call. When he reached Stauffer's camp, however, he found Terman and Stauffer, on their hands and knees, poring over blueprints for a new chemistry building. Sterling paid his respects and hastily retreated. By early fall 1959, Terman had "closed the deal with Stauffer and Briggs, and we had the

great pleasure of handing back the half-million dollars to the general fund," noted Sterling. "The Chemistry Department went on to become one of the top three in the country." (The John Stauffer Chemistry Building, the first of three Stauffer buildings, was completed in 1960 and dedicated, at a major conference, in 1961.)[32]

Newsweek in 1961 featured a photograph of 13 new Stanford professors brought from Eastern schools, including Harvard, Yale, Dartmouth, Princeton, and Columbia. "For academic larceny," the article concluded, "Stanford is past matching the University of California at Berkeley, the only other western U.S. campus that cares or dares to compare itself to Harvard." Noting that Easterners would enjoy the mild Bay Area climate, Sterling was quoted: "It is the intellectual climate which is significant, and this, we hope, is vital and stimulating at Stanford."[33]

Time magazine also took note in an article the same year: "The hottest stock on the academic market these days is Stanford University which said it wants to be the 'Harvard of the West.'... Stanford is raiding blue chip faculties all over the East."[34]

Sterling enjoyed teasing his provost (center) when Terman became too serious. At right is presidential assistant Robert Wert; man at left is likely E. Howard Brooks, then provostial assistant. JACK FIELDS / STANFORD UNIVERSITY ARCHIVES

"Faculty raiding is a two-way operation," Frank Taylor noted in his 1960 *Saturday Evening Post* article about Sterling. As faculty salaries rose some 60 percent during the 1950s, Stanford needed to fight off other "talent hunters." A "Fighting Fund," derived from uncommitted sources such as unrestricted gifts and grants, and income from land development, provided what Taylor called an emergency war chest to match offers from other institutions for Stanford's top professors, without waiting for yearly budget allocations to be confirmed. It was also used to help deans negotiate when recruiting professors to Stanford. "We used to offer salubrious climate and living conditions as part of a professor's reward," Sterling was quoted as explaining. "Not any more. Now we meet the competition with dollars and throw in the sunshine."[35]

Faculty raiding between Stanford and the University of California was softened by an informal but firm understanding. As a professional courtesy, it was assumed that each would alert the other when interested in pursuing a member of the other's faculty, with direct communication between the president and chancellor if an offer was to be made. The arrangement, worked out initially between Chancellor Edward W. Strong at UC Berkeley and Terman at Stanford, was explained by Terman to newly arrived Dean Robert Glaser of the School of Medicine, in 1965.

> The primary purpose of these procedures is not to prevent recruiting from each other's campuses, but rather to insure that what recruiting is done is carried out in a gentlemanly manner, and to insure that candidates are considered in addition to those on the faculty of our neighbor institution. Thus we should not ask to negotiate with a UC faculty man until we have made a national search and have found that the UC man comes out on top of the list.[36]

The non-raiding agreement included all campuses of the dramatically growing University of California. In 1963, Sterling wrote to his friend Clark Kerr, now president of the UC system, complaining that UC San Diego had invited one of Stanford's senior faculty members for a visit and had commenced "genuine negotiations" without contacting Stanford. He asked that Kerr clarify the non-raiding agreement with all of the newer UC campuses.[37]

The requests, whether refused or accommodated, were always taken seriously. Sterling did his best to encourage such candidates to remain. Writing Kerr about UC's request to approach Stanford's economist Kenneth J. Arrow, in 1965, Sterling wrote, "You have our permission to negotiate with him, but I do not wish you any success." Arrow stayed, at least for the time being. (Arrow, at Stanford since 1949, left for Harvard in 1968, but returned to Stanford in 1979.)[38]

By the early 1960s, the tremendous growth of research activities under Sterling and Terman was provoking criticism that massive federal research support had produced institutional imbalance at Stanford.[39] "The common idea that the large government programs in science and engineering create imbalance with a university is something of a myth," Terman argued in a 1964 defense of this kind of growth.

> The government programs are self-supporting and hence do not subtract from the resources available to other university activities. Rather, without government funds for research in science and engineering, there would be irresistible pressures for the support from university funds of research laboratories and graduate programs in the sciences and engineering. As a result, government support for science and engineering has resulted in there being *more* rather than *less* money for the humanities.[40]

"Terman was so precise and methodical," Fred Glover later recalled. "His searches for new faculty were so spectacularly successful. . . .

Despite their differences, Wally appreciated Fred Terman's strengths."[41] Similarly, Terman appreciated Sterling. At the conclusion of a five-page letter to Sterling, then in Germany, updating the president on Stanford happenings, Terman wrote in 1964, "In conclusion, let me say that I am increasingly becoming acutely aware of your absence from the campus. Presiding over Commencement, opening the Shakespeare Festival with a few well-chosen remarks, etc. comes more naturally to Sterling than to a Terman."[42] Terman later called the years 1955–65 as "the happiest ten years of my life."[43]

"According to some on campus, the provost's assessments were cold and calculating," wrote Terman biographer Stewart Gillmor, "while to others, Terman's approach was welcomed as astute, wonderfully flexible, and exhilarating. In either case, Stanford was a far different place in 1965 than it had been

While Sterling was in Germany, Provost Terman filled in as host of the June 1964 commencement and later delivered opening remarks at the Shakespeare Summer Festival, both in front of a temporary stage set in Frost Amphitheater. Such tasks come "more naturally to Sterling than to a Terman," he wrote in an update to his boss. STANFORD NEWS SERVICE

Fred Terman's impending retirement was commemorated in May 1965 with the dedication of Building 500, which housed his office before World War II. The ceremony capped renovation of the original 1902 engineering lab across the street from the Quad's Engineering Corner. Engineering Dean Joseph Pettit (left), Terman, Sterling, and trustee President Richard Guggenhime posed after the unveiling.   STANFORD NEWS SERVICE

in 1955." Sterling clearly chose Terman for his counterbalancing strengths. As Ernie Arbuckle, dean of the Graduate School of Business, noted, "He recognized in Fred Terman a person who could get the job done that needed to be done, while Wally was attending to things that he did best."[44]

Fred Terman retired on August 31, 1965, having reached the then-mandatory age of 65, passing on to his successor a well-organized office with substantial authority and a budget four times what it had been in 1955. The provost's staff worked well together, and with Sterling's presidential staff. The Provost's Office, however, now faced a period of more moderate growth of undergraduate and graduate academic programs and a more challenging funding climate.[45]

The new provost would not only actively participate in fundraising, faculty-administration relations, and ongoing academic reviews, but also take on a new responsibility: to help the president navigate dramatic changes in American higher education with increasingly hostile student and faculty protests and growing public distrust.

THE HISTORIAN
RICHARD W. LYMAN, 1967–1970

Before Terman's projected retirement in 1965, Sterling had begun looking for a replacement, knowing how difficult it would be to fill the position after his excellent working relationship with Terman. Sterling's national search would be patient and broad-reaching, but he ultimately found, from within Stanford's faculty ranks, a talented provost to help him steer through the difficult final two years of his administration.

This time, Sterling worked closely with a search committee, appointed in early 1965. The committee, chaired by economics Professor Kenneth Arrow, included Gabriel Almond (political science) and John K. Vennard (civil engineering).[46]

Terman himself suggested philosophy Professor Patrick Suppes as a candidate in an August 3, 1965, memorandum to Sterling. (At Stanford since 1950, Suppes was director of the Institute for Mathematical Studies in the Social Sciences, and an expert in the philosophy of science.) Another suggested candidate was physicist Wolfgang Panofsky, the dynamic director of the Stanford Linear Accelerator Center. Sterling received numerous other suggestions of possible candidates, among them Al Bowker, former dean of the Graduate Division and head of the Statistics Department (since 1963 chancellor of the City University of New York); Ed Ginzton, professor of physics, busy as chairman and CEO of Varian Associates; and Herb Packer, the highly respected Law School professor. It was not clear, however, that this time the provost would have strong Stanford ties.[47]

After more than a year of searching, the committee recommended President Johnson's science advisor, Donald F. Hornig, a Harvard-trained chemist and explosives expert who had taught

Sterling with Richard Lyman, history professor and provost-designate, at the December 1966 Stauffer Chemical Engineering Research Lab dedication. Shortly before, Sterling had pushed Lyman's appointment through the Board of Trustees, coupled with that of law Professor Herbert Packer as vice provost.
STANFORD NEWS SERVICE

at Brown University and Princeton after serving on the Manhattan Project. In 1966, Sterling offered Hornig the position of vice president and provost, as well as a professorship in chemistry. Hornig was concerned about the future, however, questioning whether Sterling's eventual successor would wish to have him continue as vice president and provost. He would accept the offer only if the trustees committed to continuing his appointment in these positions under a new president. After talking to several trustees and colleagues, Sterling concluded he would not recommend that the board make such arrangements, and turned to a now-more appealing candidate, David Truman of Columbia University. (Hornig went on to serve as president of Brown, 1970–76.)[48]

David Bicknell Truman, a professor of political science at Columbia since 1951 and dean of Columbia College (1962–67), was a distinguished scholar with federal government experience. Truman met with the trustees in July 1966. Following his campus visit, he asked Sterling for more information regarding budget responsibilities, the provost's responsibility for relations with alumni, and Stanford's financial situation. Sterling thought highly of Truman, but Truman declined the offer later that year after negotiating with Columbia. "The proposals made to me [by Columbia] were such that I could not do other than to allow my long attachments to Columbia to be decisive," he wrote Sterling. (He subsequently became vice president and provost there. After a tumultuous year of student unrest, during which he was praised as a university administrator who retained student respect, he left, in 1969, to become president of Mount Holyoke College.)[49]

Sterling, who had known Columbia's president, Grayson Kirk, for years, congratulated him on keeping Truman. "I tried very hard to persuade Dave to accept my invitation to become vice president and provost here. I did so because, after a really hardheaded search, he was the one man I wanted to have here."[50] As Sterling later recalled, it was cold comfort to know that he was searching among the major leagues.[51]

Months had passed since Terman had left office. Relying heavily on his two vice provosts, Robert Wert and Howard Brooks, Sterling felt pressed to make a good selection. (Wert, who also served as dean of undergraduate education, left Stanford in 1967 to become president of Mills College. Brooks served as a vice provost until 1971, when he became provost of the Claremont Colleges.)

Ultimately, Sterling concluded that he had good material inside Stanford.[52]

In April 1966, dean of Humanities and Sciences Robert Sears had reported to Sterling that his associate dean, Professor Richard Lyman, had just returned from a trip to Seattle where he discussed the possibility of going to the University of Washington as dean of arts and sciences. As both Sears and Sterling knew, Lyman was close to accepting the presidency of Haverford College, and had been informally approached about a dozen other administrative positions in the past three years. "I think you might find it worthwhile to consider Lyman himself!" Sears concluded. "*Please* do what you can to hold him."[53]

Lyman had earned his bachelor's degree from Swarthmore (1947), after a three-year stint in Asia with the U.S. Army Air Force, and his Ph.D. in history from Harvard (1954). As a Fulbright scholar at the London School of Economics, 1951–52, he wrote for *The Economist*, but chose to finish his dissertation and teach (he had been offered a post at Washington University, St. Louis) rather than continue as the magazine's Washington correspondent. His dissertation, *The First Labour Government, 1924*, had just been published in England to critical acclaim when he was recruited as an associate professor in 1958

As vice provost for academic planning and programs, Herb Packer reviewed student disciplinary procedures and fostered a new approach to racial diversity. Sterling welcomed Packer's leadership of the Study of Education at Stanford, including his work launching the Faculty Senate.   STANFORD NEWS SERVICE

by Stanford's History Department to replace the retiring Carl Brand, Stanford's British history scholar. Lyman was attracted to Stanford by the exceptional British Labour Party history collection at the Hoover Institution, the best outside of Britain.

Known as a demanding teacher, Lyman was also as supportive as he was challenging. "He was curtly intolerant of empirically unanchored assertions, lax logic, and imprecise or needlessly ornamental language," his colleagues remembered in 2012. "He was also unstintingly generous with merited praise, and with incisive, detailed, and always constructive criticism." He became a full professor in 1962 and began his administrative career in 1964 as associate dean of the School of Humanities and Sciences. Sterling felt strongly

that this exacting scholar and inspirational teacher also had the proven administrative abilities necessary to take over from Terman as provost.[54]

Lyman, however, insisted that he would accept the position of provost only if Herbert L. Packer, professor of law and a member of the Academic Council's executive committee, was appointed his vice provost for academic planning. Sterling, who considered the Yale-trained Packer a brilliant man of great moral courage, agreed. Packer, at Stanford since 1956, had also worked well with Law Dean Carl Spaeth, a friend of Sterling, in rebuilding the Law School.[55]

"Wally was very fond of Herb," recalled Fred Glover, but "the trustees were very mistrustful." Packer, an expert in criminal law, had been under attack by conservative journalists and alumni for his study of the veracity of key ex-Communist witnesses used during the House Un-American Activities Committee investigations into communist infiltration. Packer's *Ex-Communist Witnesses: Four Studies in Fact Finding*, published by Stanford University Press in 1962, had focused on the controversial case of alleged Communist Alger Hiss. This book, and later works on criminal justice and penal law reform, established Packer as an imposing scholar and helped Stanford's Law School grow in prestige.[56]

Sterling supported Packer's proposed appointment, but the trustees did not. Trustee David Packard objected "fiercely to Herb's appointment," Lyman later recalled. "Herb had been under fire from Fulton Lewis Jr., a right-wing radio commentator, and others for allegedly being a left-winger, which was pretty ridiculous, but it wasn't funny when the board said no."[57]

Sterling, who hoped to announce his retirement plans soon, had not taken his usual steps in working with individual trustees to gradually build up support for his selections. His recommendations did not go as smoothly as he expected. While the trustees in November accepted Sterling's appointment of Lyman, they tabled Packer's appointment. Although Lyman already had turned down the Haverford offer, he stuck to his guns about his terms of accepting the provost's position with Packer as vice provost. Sterling felt he could turn the board around at its next meeting, but a delegation of all seven university deans, led by Bayless Manning, law, called on Sterling at home to insist that waiting another month was unacceptable. They urged him to call an emergency board meeting. Sterling moved quickly, calling the special meeting at Hoover House for the following Sunday,

where he won approval of both appointments, effective January 1967. Now free to consider his retirement plans, he announced three months later that he would step down no later than September 1, 1968.[58]

As it turned out, Lyman and Packer would take the brunt of heavy criticism during Sterling's final tumultuous 18 months in office. Lyman served as Stanford's provost until 1970. Packer became vice provost for academic planning and programs. Some of the events of the year and a half they served Sterling are explored elsewhere later *(see Chapters 19 and 20)*. These include reviewing student disciplinary procedures, formulating a response to stu-

Provost Dick Lyman, in November 1968, with members of the Mexican-American Student Confederation, including its chairman, law student Luis B. Nogales (center). They met to discuss Hispanic student recruiting and inclusion of Hispanics in administrative offices. Nogales became the first university officer for minority affairs. He served on the Stanford Board of Trustees, 1978–88. STANFORD NEWS SERVICE

dent and faculty antiwar protests, and fostering a new approach to racial and ethnic diversity. Sterling also welcomed Packer's leadership of the sweeping Study of Education at Stanford, 1967–69, and his essential role in the creation of the Faculty Senate of the Academic Council in 1968.

In 1969, Packer suffered a near-fatal stroke, but overcame extreme physical difficulty to return to the Law School later that year. He was named Jackson Eli Reynolds Professor of Law in 1971 but died the following year. Remembered as an unusually creative, productive, and influential scholar and colleague, Packer had an enormous influence on the university, the School of Law, and the field of criminal law during his 16 years at Stanford.[59]

Provost Lyman's reserved, seemingly severe and even combative nature was, for some trustees and influential alumni, a stark contrast to Sterling. But during the brief tenure of Sterling's successor, Kenneth Pitzer, Lyman remained key to Stanford's stability.[60]

In 1970, the trustees became aware that Lyman was being seriously considered for the presidencies of Wesleyan and Harvard. After Pitzer's resignation in late June (effective August 31), the trustees in September chose Lyman as Stanford's seventh president. Lyman "employed candor and occasional bluntness to build a more civil community," recalled Professor Donald Kennedy, his presidential successor. "Those of us who served him grew soon to respect his

Provost Lyman was selected as Stanford's seventh president in September 1970, serving until 1980. After a subsequent eight-year presidency of the Rockefeller Foundation, he returned to campus as founder and director, until 1991, of the Stanford Institute for International Studies.   STANFORD NEWS SERVICE

values and then to share them, as we watched him accomplish an extraordinary 10-year feat of gradual, steady institutional resurrection."[61]

Lyman left Stanford, in 1980, to become president of the Rockefeller Foundation, but returned in 1988 to found and direct its Institute for International Studies (today's Freeman Spogli Institute for International Studies). He retired in 1991 and died in 2012.

11

TAKING THE LEAD
IN SELECTING DEANS

Sterling's participation in faculty recruiting was vital, but he took special pride in finding good deans. Leadership qualities and team building took equal weight. In his searches, he sought not only evidence of forceful academic leadership and the ability to advocate for an individual school, but also a willingness to perform as an officer of the university and the potential to advance Stanford's overall objectives, including successful fundraising.

Ideally, he once said, he sought deans who are "predisposed to vigorous action and radiant good cheer." While some of his favorite deans were more congenial than others, those he viewed as successful were energetic, creative, and, ultimately, as dedicated to Stanford's overall success as its president.[1]

Stanford University had opened, in 1891, as an amorphous and incomplete academic program made up of independent departments, based on the strengths and interests of the faculty that President David Starr Jordan could attract to the new institution. With little connection to one another, or to the University Council (which oversaw degree granting), departments had little reason to cooperate regarding requirements, curriculum, or interdepartmental studies. Rivalries often emerged over budgets, space, and academic expectations.[2]

The university's first deanship, in 1913, was simply a title change for Ray Lyman Wilbur, executive head of the Department of Medicine. When the Board of Trustees upgraded the department's title to Medical School, Wilbur became its dean.[3] Perhaps this was a nod to Stanford's rival medical campus in San Francisco, the University of California's Affiliated Schools, consolidated on Parnassus Heights in 1898, which had had a dean of medicine since 1882.

When Wilbur became Stanford's third president five years later, he turned his organizing talent to upgrading professional as well as academic programs. Over the first 10 years of his administration, he corralled the university's 26 independent departments and tamed rivalries to upgrade

< When President Sterling arrived in 1949, administrative offices had recently dispersed across campus to provide space for the Law School (left) in the former Administration Building (Building 160) on the front of the Quad. This 1950s photo shows the Law School next to the original Assembly Hall (Building 120), remodeled in 1937 for the Graduate School of Business. KEN REICHARD / STANFORD UNIVERSITY ARCHIVES

professional standards, streamline curricula, and rationalize course requirements. Following Medicine, the next two schools created, Education (1917) and Law (1923), were undergraduate programs upgraded to meet professional expectations of California state teacher requirements and accreditation by the American Bar Association, respectively. The School of Nursing (1922), similarly upgraded, was formalized within the School of Medicine. A new graduate level professional school, the Graduate School of Business, was established in 1925. The School of Engineering (1925) brought together departments that already had a pattern of cooperation, while four other new schools were an attempt to bring together like fields: Biological Sciences (1922), Social Sciences (1923), Physical Sciences (1925), and Letters (1925). Wilbur wrapped up his efforts with creation of the School of Hygiene and Physical Education (1928).[4]

By the time Wallace Sterling arrived on campus in spring 1949, these groupings had been modified once again. A new school of Mineral (later Earth) Sciences had been created in 1947. The following year, acting President Alvin C. Eurich made another major consolidation: the schools of Biological, Physical, and Social Sciences were brought together with Humanities (recently renamed from "Letters") into a new School of Humanities and Sciences.

Sterling took time to get to know the deans he inherited. Some soon became good friends, like Carl Spaeth (law) and Frederick Terman (engineering), on whom he would rely after they stepped down from their deanships. Some, like GSB's J. Hugh Jackson, he patiently prodded into retirement or, like Clarence Faust (H&S) and Loren Chandler (medicine), he politely nudged toward other settings.

Initial deanship changes were made with little input—he chose biology Professor Douglas Whitaker to succeed Faust in 1951, and then Ray Faulkner, professor of art and architecture, to take over after Whitaker's promotion to provost in 1952. (The reluctant Faulkner insisted on remaining "acting dean" throughout the four years he served.) On Chandler's resignation, in protest of the Medical School's move to campus, in 1953 Sterling selected pharmacology Professor Windsor Cutting as Chandler's successor. By the mid-1950s, however, as faculty recruiting went well beyond Stanford's borders, Sterling spent considerable time vetting candidates and began following a more inclusive strategy, with considerable faculty and trustee input. He later credited members of the Academic Council's Executive Committee, and especially the university's Advisory Board, made up of senior faculty well versed in university-wide affairs, with wise counsel. The ultimate choice, however, rested with the president.[5]

Of the 14 changes in deanships during Sterling's administration, three searches are particularly illuminating. His patient search for the right leadership for the Graduate School of Business revolved around securing a man much admired in business, alumni, and trustee circles, Ernest (Ernie) C. Arbuckle. For the School of Medicine, a nationwide search circled back to campus to Robert H. Alway, a faculty member brought to Stanford to upgrade its pediatrics programs, but who had proven himself a diplomatic catalyst for change and who could work with vocal and impatient young faculty and administrators. And with Law Dean Carl Spaeth a hard act to follow, Sterling took a chance on a highly respected young Yale man, Bayless Manning, whose negotiating tactics presaged a more contentious relationship with the administration, but whose voluminous correspondence with President Sterling reveals much about Stanford in the second decade of Sterling's administration.

TRANSFORMATIONAL DEAN FOR
THE GRADUATE SCHOOL OF BUSINESS

Sterling's search for a new dean for the Graduate School of Business turned into a time-consuming affair, lasting nearly three years until early favorite Ernest Arbuckle agreed to return to Stanford, in 1958.

J. Hugh Jackson, an expert in the field of accounting, had been GSB's dean since 1931. The Harvard-trained Jackson was a prolific writer, a popular teacher, and a mentor who insisted on high standards of teaching from his faculty. During his administration, the school, founded in 1924–25 with the encouragement of West Coast business leaders (and only the second business school in the United States to offer a graduate degree curriculum), had gradually attained national stature and a degree of respect from the business community. During his 25 years as dean, Jackson had been active in community affairs, including service on the Palo Alto School Board, as an advisor to many local banks, and as president of Kiwanis International.

During Ernest Arbuckle's 10 years as dean, 1958–68, GSB's faculty more than doubled in size, its curriculum was significantly strengthened, and the student body shifted from its regional character to one of national and, eventually, international importance. Arbuckle was a Stanford trustee from 1954 to 1958 and, after his deanship, from 1968 to 1976.
STANFORD NEWS SERVICE

Sterling found Jackson affable but unimaginative and unaggressive; he was determined to find a leader for the school who would place it within America's booming postwar economy. As Jackson approached retirement, in 1956, Sterling began looking for a successor, a move Jackson endorsed.[6]

Sterling turned first to a Stanford school friend, businessman Ernest Arbuckle, '33, MBA '36. Arbuckle had been entirely self-supporting as a student, working as an assistant dean of men and spending summers as a section hand on the Sierra Railroad in his native Tuolumne County. He earned his Block S on the Stanford track team and served as president of the Men's Council. During World War II, Arbuckle commanded a PT boat squadron, earning a Silver Star and Purple Heart. He had remained active in Stanford alumni affairs and, in 1954, was elected to the Board of Trustees as part of Sterling's injection of younger community leaders onto the board.

With a strong reputation for both leadership and compassion, Arbuckle was a down-to-earth man with a strong sense of integrity and an infectious sense of humor. He and Sterling had kept in touch during Sterling's Caltech years and the first years of his presidency. Yet, while flattered by

J. Hugh Jackson, the Business School's dean for 25 years, was a prolific writer, popular teacher, and mentor to many.   STANFORD NEWS SERVICE

Sterling's 1955 recruiting, Arbuckle declined. He had just assumed new corporate responsibilities, which he felt obliged to continue. He also had just been made campaign chairman of the United Bay Area Crusade and felt strongly that he must continue the campaign's organization.[7]

Sterling subsequently appointed a committee of the Business School faculty to assist in finding a successor to Jackson, whose tenure as dean would conclude at the end of the 1955–56 academic year. Professor Herbert Dougall, an expert on corporate finance and investment, chaired the committee. Dougall, like Sterling a Canadian-born alumnus of the University of Toronto, had come to Stanford in 1946 and had been the first GSB faculty member named to an endowed chair.[8]

During its first year, the committee considered at least 80 candidates, including Robert McNamara, then vice president of Ford Motor Company. When Sterling personally approached McNamara, he expressed interest but had reservations about the timing.

As the search committee struggled on, Sterling resisted Dougall's suggestion of retaining a consulting firm to conduct the search.[9] On Jackson's retirement in June 1956, Sterling appointed Carlton W. (Bud) Pederson, professor of business management, as acting dean. Pederson would hold the position for two years while the search continued, organizing and leading the school's first long-range planning committee. (Later, while serving as associate dean, he helped create and direct the school's Sloan Program.)[10]

Sterling sounded out presidents of major institutions and corporations. "There is no need of my commenting to you regarding the lack of leadership over the past years that the Business School has had at Stanford under Hugh Jackson," Paul L. Davies, chairman and CEO of Food Machinery and Chemical Corporation (later renamed FMC Corporation) in San Jose, wrote Sterling in 1957.

I do not know what the solution at Stanford is. I know that if leadership is not provided for the Business School soon, there is going to be a further deterioration in the School amongst both the faculty and the students. I believe it would be very sound to have an Advisory Board for the School, consisting of prominent men in the Bay Area, and have them available to discuss the problems of the Business School with the faculty and you.[11]

Sterling agreed an outside advisory board would be useful, "and not only for the Stanford School of Business. This sort of relationship between the University, including the professional schools, and the community is one that I have been promoting here for some time. Frankly, the brake on it is faculty attitude and inexperience," Sterling wrote to Davies.[12]

Later that year, Sterling hosted a group of influential Bay Area business leaders at the Pacific Union Club in San Francisco. These were not only influential businessmen, but individuals with a clear interest in Stanford's welfare. In addition to Davies, the group included Laurence W. Lane Sr. of Lane Publishing Company, publisher of *Sunset* magazine, whose headquarters had moved to nearby Menlo Park in 1951; his family would retain a long-standing connection to Stanford. Also in attendance were E. C. Lipman, president of Emporium Capwell Company, who, in 1953, had been the first retailer given a lease at the new Stanford Shopping Center; Herbert Carr, vice president of finance, California Packing Company; and Fred H. Merrill, vice president of Fireman's Fund, and a future Stanford trustee. Rounding out the group were Stanford trustees and businessmen Charles R. Blyth, Ernest Arbuckle, and Donald J. Russell, president of Southern Pacific Company. (Invited but not in attendance were T. S. Petersen, president of Standard Oil of California, and trustee David Packard of Hewlett-Packard.) Although the candidate they had gathered to meet was ultimately not selected, Sterling used the occasion to strengthen the connection between these business community leaders and both the business school and the university.[13]

By the end of 1957, the committee had reviewed more than 160 names. Dougall was clearly frustrated. After two years, he had come to believe "that we shall probably not be successful in getting a very prominent business person in the age group, 45–55, of the type we like," he wrote Sterling. "The ones that 'have everything' are not available. They already have big jobs, big salaries, big commitments." And while a number of fine academics "would enjoy being the Dean of the school, few would be willing to come here as strangers to undertake a job that involves a very significant money-raising assignment as well as academic administration."[14]

Sterling, too, was frustrated. This dean's search experience was "as traumatic an academic one as any I care to go through. I have in turn been disappointed, frustrated, angry, and embarrassed," Sterling candidly wrote a colleague in March 1958.[15]

At least four candidates participated in intense campus visits and meetings with trustees and faculty. When the last of the strong candidates was on the campus, Sterling was away and unable to attend the candidate's meeting with the trustees. When he telephoned the next morning, each trustee he talked to told him to keep looking. Later that day, trustee Edmund W. Littlefield, '36 and MBA '38, agreed they should keep looking, but added that he had had lunch with Arbuckle that day (Arbuckle and Littlefield were trustee members of the search committee). Sterling should ask Arbuckle again, he advised.[16]

Arbuckle recalled later: "I thought we'd found a dean, a man from General Motors, who I thought was pretty good. But the faculty didn't support him, and that was when they decided to ask me." After talking about the hazards,

Littlefield "persuaded me that any affiliation with a university like Stanford would be a plus for anyone, especially if they were working with Wally. That's what really turned the tide as far as I was concerned."[17]

Sterling, in New York, called Arbuckle early the next morning. Arbuckle hemmed and hawed, Sterling later recalled, as the president pressed his case. When they met back in California, Arbuckle agreed to take the post. Sterling credited Littlefield's opportune lunch, and his strong endorsement of Arbuckle, with influencing him to renew his appeal. Sterling also noted that their

Dean Ernie Arbuckle, class of '33 Stanford athlete, was voted 1967 *Red Hot Prof* in an annual campus fundraiser popular in the 1960s. The prize: leading a cheer at a football game. Arbuckle guided the student cheering section with gusto at the November 11, 1967, game against University of Oregon. Proceeds were donated to an international student agency.
STANFORD NEWS SERVICE

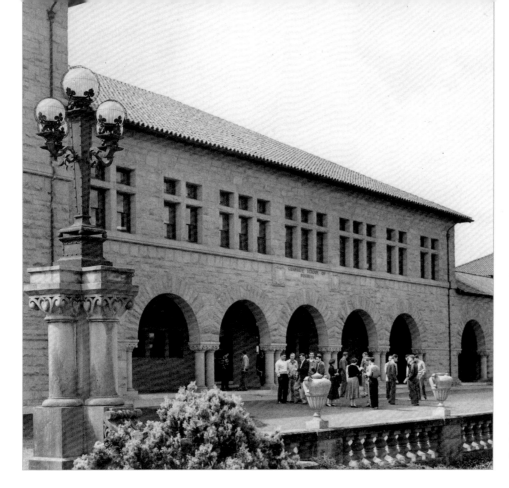

With completion of large new auditoriums in Memorial Hall (1937) and the Education Building (1938), the Assembly Hall (Building 120) could be gutted inside and repurposed as the Graduate School of Business. Seen here in 1951, Building 120 would be home to the GSB until 1966.
STANFORD NEWS SERVICE

Dean Arbuckle led the planning, fundraising, and construction of the new $5.5 million GSB headquarters between Memorial Hall and the Oval. (The cantilevered building suffered significant damage in the 1989 earthquake, but was repaired. In 2011, the school moved to a new complex of 360,000 square feet; the 1966 building has been put to other uses.)   STANFORD NEWS SERVICE

mutual friend John W. Gardner (then president of the Carnegie Corporation of New York) told Arbuckle to take the job because he was in a business rut and needed to be "repotted."[18]

The 45-year-old Arbuckle accepted Sterling's offer in March 1958 but stipulated that he would serve for only 10 years. He would not have said yes if Sterling had not been the one who asked him, he later said, and Sterling had reassured him that he, too, would be at Stanford for another 10 years. He also remembered an early meeting when he asked Sterling what the president's ideas were for the school and what he wanted the new dean to do. "And I'll never forget it—he looked at me and he said, 'It's here,' putting his hands on the table, 'and we want it here,' putting his hands over his head. 'Take it there.' I said, 'Thank you very much.' And he never once second-guessed me on anything I was doing."[19]

Later Arbuckle recalled Sterling pointing out to him that during his first years as dean he would need more funding than tuition to "get this thing going." The new dean made a deal. If, after two or three years, he could keep 75 percent of the Business School tuition income, he would assume responsibility for raising the rest of the money for the Business School program. As he stated it, Sterling encouraged the principle of self-sufficiency at Stanford or "putting a tub on its [own] bottom." Arbuckle said, "That made all the difference in the world to me. . . . I couldn't really do this job without the incentive system behind it. And the incentive system is that you can do as much as the money you raise will let you do."[20]

At a 1960 Business School Affiliates luncheon at the Bohemian Club, Sterling commented:

> One function of any university president is to find good deans—assuming that is not a contradiction in terms—deans who are predisposed to vigorous action and radiant good cheer. Ernie Arbuckle is, as many of you know, just such a man. Whether

or not he can adapt to the rigors and unpredictabilities of academic life after the relative calm and composure of business remains to be seen, but the weight of a year and a half's evidence is all in his favor.[21]

He jokingly concluded about his friend, "If I have one regret about his appointment, it is that I got more action than I bargained for, with the result that I'm having to work harder than I find congenial."

Ernie Arbuckle is credited with creating today's internationally prominent Graduate School of Business. During his 10 years as dean, he set in motion the school's dramatic expansion and improvement. The size of the faculty doubled and the number and quality of MBA and Ph.D. applicants rose sharply as the school broadened its curriculum and research. The budget increased seven-fold, faculty salaries increased significantly, and endowed professorships went up six-fold. Arbuckle energized

Celebrating the October 1966 GSB dedication were (from left): trustee President Richard Guggenhime; U.S. Secretary of Health, Education, and Welfare John Gardner; Dean Arbuckle; President Sterling; and George G. Montgomery, chairman of the Business School's Advisory Council. Gardner and Arbuckle were close friends from their MBA days at the Biz School. STANFORD NEWS SERVICE

the school's alumni and played a central role in fundraising for the school's enlarged quarters, completed in 1966.[22]

"He was one of the most naturally gifted leaders I ever met," said John Gardner. "His achievement in setting the business school on the path to greatness still stands as a model of leadership at its best." Future Dean Robert K. Jaedicke considered Arbuckle the model of the businessman dean. "I believe Ernie will be most remembered for his personal style—his emphasis on the individual. He never lost sight of his belief that people are more important than organizations. He was a friend, mentor, and counselor to all who knew him."[23]

Arbuckle and Sterling both retired in 1968. As Sterling became chancellor of the university, Arbuckle became chairman of Wells Fargo Bank. Arbuckle also served a second term on Stanford's Board of Trustees, 1968–76.

ANOTHER ARDUOUS SEARCH
THE MEDICAL SCHOOL DEAN

In 1953, Dr. Windsor C. Cutting had replaced longtime Medical School Dean Loren Chandler, who opposed Sterling's proposed move of the school from San Francisco to the campus. Much had happened during Cutting's four years as dean, as Sterling pressed for an intensive review of the school's facility needs, faculty accomplishments, and curriculum. A major volunteer-driven fundraising campaign was underway as the university's Planning Office worked with architect Edward Durrell Stone on plans for the new Medical School site on campus.[24]

In January 1957, while searching for the Business School dean, Sterling also launched a nationwide search for a new dean of the Medical School. Sterling hoped to develop the school's faculty with broader recruiting. After asking Cutting to step down, Sterling met with the

school's department heads, telling them that Cutting's successor likely would not be from Stanford and would want a free hand in potentially replacing them. The president expected each of them to tender their resignation on the new dean's arrival. In theory, appointments

Yank Chandler's 20 years (1933–53) as Stanford's widely respected dean of medicine spanned the Great Depression, World War II, and the decision—which he opposed—to move the Medical School from San Francisco to the Stanford campus. Chandler later reconciled to the move and was involved in planning the Palo Alto Veterans Administration Hospital and serving as its first chief of surgery. EDGAR HOLCOMB / STANFORD UNIVERSITY ARCHIVES

Windsor Cutting, chair of the Pharmacology Department, succeeded Chandler in 1953. During his four years as dean, the program continued in San Francisco while planning and fundraising for the new Medical Center complex got underway. Cutting resigned, in 1957, to become the founding dean of the University of Hawaii Medical School. STANFORD MEDICAL HISTORY CENTER

were one-year posts, so no one objected. Few thought the resignations would actually be accepted.[25]

In March 1957, Sterling appointed Dr. Robert Hamilton Alway, professor and chair of the Pediatrics Department since 1955, as acting dean. Alway had joined Stanford's faculty as an associate professor in 1949, but had left in 1952 for a full professorship at the University of Colorado. He was persuaded to return, he later said, by Stanford's "silver-tongued" president.[26]

Bob Alway, Henry Kaplan (radiology), and Avram Goldstein (pharmacology) were the three executive heads most associated with the school's new focus on research in medicine and related fields. Kaplan, unhappy with the decaying facilities in San Francisco, was a strong voice for the interdepartmental research possibilities of the school's move to campus. Goldstein, who had left Harvard in 1955 for Stanford, was active in recruiting leading scientists like Joshua Lederberg. Pondering his own selection as dean over these two colleagues, Alway later commented: "I had the feeling that Avram and Henry were considerably more pointed, shall we say, in their criticism, whereas I could talk with Windsor [Cutting] and express my concern without his feeling worn down." They were not wrong in what they were fighting for, he added. Alway, too, was dissatisfied, "but I wasn't so pyrotechnic about my dissatisfaction."[27]

Sterling himself chaired the faculty-alumni search committee for a permanent dean. Alway and Kaplan were members, as was clinical faculty member Dr. Dwight Wilbur, a distinguished San Francisco physician and son of the late Stanford President Ray Lyman Wilbur. Sterling received hundreds of letters proposing candidates, some proposing themselves.[28]

In November 1957, after eight disappointing months of searching, the committee agreed that Sterling should write deans of leading medical schools for suggestions. Alway advised Sterling: "Stick to your statement that the next dean should not be a Stanford man."[29]

Three months later, the search committee narrowed the search down to two candidates, one from New York and the other from Illinois, both deans of medical schools. The New York candidate was frequently referred to as urbane and the Illinois candidate as youthful and earnest. When Sterling asked for a brief note from each of the 24 Medical School faculty members who had met with the two candidates, opinions were decidedly mixed. Neither candidate "has sufficient personal weight and professional understanding to justify such an appointment," one professor summarized. "As far as administrative duties are concerned, I presume either one would be competent. But I believe that the dean of university faculty should be a man who has already made his mark in the field of learning proper to that faculty and has in this way earned the respect and trust of those over whom he is placed. Neither of these men has done so, as far as I have been able to find out."[30]

Sterling concluded to the committee, "I should say that we owe it to ourselves, to the School and to the University not to stop with visits from only two possible candidates. I suggest, therefore, that we determine what other persons we might invite for a period."[31]

After more months of screening and checking, trustee President Lloyd Dinkelspiel found the situation "a bit discouraging." He wrote to Sterling: "I am persuaded now that no one we can attract here, however good he is, will win anything like the enthusiasm that, blessedly, is and will be in store for Arbuckle. In this situation I see no alternative but for the President to move, and that rather quickly, because time is awasting."[32]

A strong majority of the search committee, as well as a comparable majority of executive heads of departments in the Medical School, favored the selection of Alway as dean.[33] "I have been very much impressed with the way Bob Alway has carried out the duties as Acting Dean," concluded one professor after evaluating candidates.

> He has, in my view, dealt very successfully with the Executive Committee and the other members of the medical faculty, as well as with the practicing physicians on the Peninsula. With each group he has shown firmness and decisiveness without attempting to be dictatorial. I don't think that Christ himself could get a unanimous vote of confidence from the local practitioners, so one should hardly expect any medical dean under the present circumstances to do any better. . . . I would suggest, therefore, that if Alway could be interested in accepting the deanship, I believe I would favor him.[34]

Alway had already turned down the position at least once. Asked again, he wavered but again answered no. After another round of visits by yet another candidate, however, "as I settled into the task of re-checking all we had done on this matter, I re-checked him as well as others," Sterling later wrote to the outside candidate, a fellow Canadian and friend. "This time I had an affirmative answer. In consequence, I had to 'process' him as a candidate for whom there had always been substantial local support." He added:

> The Committee has never been unanimous about any candidate; nor has there been unanimity on the matter among heads of departments in the Medical School. Nor do I expect ever to get unanimity among the M.D.s on any such matter. But the weight of judgment—in which first-hand knowledge of and experience with our local situation and problems weighed heavily—was that I should offer the position to Alway. It was a judgment in which I concurred, not least of all because of the pressure of time to get decisions made that have been too long pending. Alway has accepted. . . .[35]

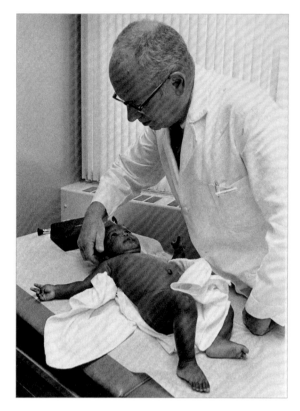

Appointed acting dean in 1957 and finally agreeing to be dean in 1958, chair of pediatrics Robert Alway was known for his passion about improving the school and for his directness. He worked well with Sterling to attract new medical faculty leaders, tripling research funding while smoothing the transition to new facilities. He resigned, in 1964, to return to teaching and community medical affairs, later serving as director of Stanford University Hospital until his retirement, in 1977.   STANFORD UNIVERSITY ARCHIVES

In announcing Bob Alway's appointment as dean in May 1958 to the Medical School's department heads, Sterling reminded them that they had agreed, at the time of Cutting's resignation in January 1957, to let the new dean have the privilege of recommending to him such changes in the appointments of executive heads "as and when we" might see fit. As a result, all department chairs were vacated by August 31, 1958, and Dean Alway "began his deanship with a clean slate."[36]

Alway, who planned to serve as dean for only five years, resigned in 1964 after an eventful seven years as acting dean and dean. In addition to planning and implementing the 1959 move, he smoothed the way for many faculty and curriculum changes to the school, doubling the size of the medical faculty and tripling research funding during his seven years. He was known for his ability to scout new talent, and for his diplomacy in developing a working relationship with community medical agencies and local physicians suspicious of Stanford's new medical presence on the Peninsula. Alway also instituted a new and innovative five-year curriculum and guided the school's academic development.[37]

After stepping down from the deanship, Alway served as acting chairman of pediatrics, associate dean for clinical affairs, and later as medical director of Stanford University Hospital until his retirement, in 1977.[38]

The nationwide search for Alway's successor was an eight-month affair, resulting, in February 1965, in the appointment of 46-year-old Harvard-educated Robert J. Glaser, president of Affiliated Hospitals Center and professor of social medicine at Harvard. Glaser, as dean and vice president for medical affairs, dealt with new issues regarding the hospital and Palo Alto relations *(see Chapter 4)*. In 1968, Glaser served as acting president of the university, bridging the departure of Sterling and the arrival of incoming President Kenneth S. Pitzer *(see Chapter 21)*.[39]

TRANSITIONING A LAW SCHOOL DEAN

In 1962, Carl B. Spaeth stepped down as dean of the Law School to build and lead Stanford's newly established, university-wide multidisciplinary Committee on International Studies, backed by a major Ford Foundation grant.

Spaeth, a noted internationalist, was a difficult act to follow. Over his 16 years as dean, Spaeth had transformed the school from a regionally to nationally respected one that valued both teach-

ing and scholarship. He had introduced Stanford to international law and governmental affairs and had established its *Stanford Law Review* and the *Stanford Journal of International Law* as highly respected publications. He was also a very successful fundraiser, who had brought in five endowed professorships and a number of new endowed student scholarships as well as foundation, corporate, and private funding. Equally significant, Spaeth was a convivial, patient, and effective member of the Sterling team, highly respected as a university diplomat as well as a scholar, teacher, and administrator.[40]

The Law School's 1963 yearbook noted that the size of the school was "deliberately being kept small." Since 1950, it had admitted about 150 students each year in the face of an annual increase

Noted international law expert Carl B. Spaeth transformed the Stanford Law School from a regional to a nationally respected program during his years, 1946–62, as dean. A talented fundraiser as well as administrator, he developed the school's distinction in international law and government relations. The convivial dean and his friend Wally Sterling also enjoyed a good poker game. STANFORD NEWS SERVICE

in applications from 300 (1952) to 750 (1963). By 1963, the student body of about 375 had become international in character.

While Professor John R. McDonough served as acting dean, the search for Spaeth's replacement was much easier than the earlier searches for new deans of the Graduate School of Business and the Medical School, although subsequent negotiations may have made it one of the more frustrating transitions.[41]

Beginning the search in May 1963, Sterling, backed by strong support from Law School faculty, was able to report his selection to the Board of Trustees for approval at its June 20 meeting.[42] His choice, Yale law Professor Bayless Manning, was expected to take up where Spaeth left off: to build the school's faculty, improve the quality of the student body, expand the school's programs, and raise money for faculty salaries, scholarships, and new facilities.

Manning's curriculum vita was impressive. After receiving his B.A., Phi Beta Kappa, at Yale in 1944, he completed his Yale LL.B. in 1949, with election to the Order of the Coif. He had been editor-in-chief of the *Yale Law Journal*. After a year as a law clerk for Justice Stanley F. Reed, he practiced law for six years with Jones, Day, Cockley & Reavis in Cleveland. He returned to Yale as an associate professor of law from 1956 to 1960, then full professor during 1960–62. Like Spaeth, Manning had considerable government experience. He had been on leave from Yale as a special assistant to the undersecretary of state when he was added to Stanford's list of prospective candidates. At the time, he also was a member of the President's Commission on Ethics in Government and a consultant to the U.S. Department of Commerce. He also helped to organize the Peace Corps program in Latin America and worked for NATO on multinational nuclear issues.[43]

Eugene V. Rostow, dean of the Yale Law School, considered Manning "one of the shini-

est fish to come out of the sea. He has the drive, charm, and quickness, which permit him to do anything and everything superlatively well. But he also has depth and sitzfleisch, insight and imagination. His work is more than a clever synthesis. It is invariably marked by originality and power."[44]

Manning was enthusiastic after his first Stanford visit in May 1963. "The whole university is vibrant, alive and moving ahead at an astonishing rate," he wrote in the first of many letters to Sterling. "I am convinced from what I saw that this dramatic development, which has already begun to work in the Law School, will soon bring within reach the possibility of making the Stanford Law School one of the truly first-rate law schools in the nation."[45]

Members of the Law School faculty were equally enthusiastic. "Manning is so good, could be such a fine dean," wrote Professor John Merryman, "that I think we should do everything possible, and a little more, to get him."[46]

After expressing reservations about the move from one coast to the other, Manning accepted the position that summer, "subject to agreement on a few open points." He sent the president a 10-year projection for the Law School outlining the kind of program he had in mind and the scale of expenditures.[47] His appointment, to take effect in June 1964, was announced at the Stanford Law Alumni Association in San Francisco on September 25, 1963.

Manning had been a popular and winning candidate, but after his appointment was approved by the trustees, negotiations between Sterling and Manning continued to be challenging, particularly about the Law School budget.

Manning must have known that Spaeth had recently attracted five leading legal scholars from Columbia and Cornell, and he was intent on putting his own mark on faculty growth. He had been happy to find that Sterling understood the extra pressure on universities to compete with the corporate world and government to retain "first rank professional talent." He was impatient to get started on faculty and student recruitment, development of the school's library, building up the visiting professor program, and funding a new law school building to support a growing faculty and student body.[48]

Manning was soon at loggerheads with Provost Fred Terman, however. During a December visit, the dean-to-be was frustrated when Terman informed him that the Law School and Law Library would receive only a modest increase in general funds for 1964–65. As he looked at the "budgetary facts" of the allocation, Manning wrote to Sterling in December 1963, the "allocation fails completely to achieve the Provost's intentions." Manning felt undermined. His was not a "routine budgetary disappointment that is the occupational complaint of all deans," he wrote Sterling. This was "a fundamental misunderstanding on the part of the Provost of the agreements reached and the principles decided upon between you, the Trustees and me last summer."[49]

The interior of Building 160 in September 1948 was being stripped to the four walls for reconstruction as the Law School. Its elegant stained-glass windows, polished marble wainscoting and door frames, copper balcony railings, and other ornamentation were removed. They had previously adorned the reading room of the Thomas Welton Stanford Library (1900–19) and survived as the lobby of the longtime Administration Building (1919–48). STANFORD UNIVERSITY ARCHIVES

In 1949, much of Building 160's demolition was done, but some roof remnants could be seen through the window frames. The new interior would maximize the space with five floors. LEO HOLUB / STANFORD UNIVERSITY ARCHIVES

This popular image of the Law School and its students was taken shortly after the school's move from various Inner Quad buildings to its newly renovated quarters on the Outer Quad in 1950. The school would remain here until 1975. Statues of Benjamin Franklin and Alexander von Humboldt, removed from their pedestals near the entrance during the renovation and subsequently lost, were replicated and replaced in 2013. STANFORD NEWS SERVICE

It fell to Sterling to caution Manning without discouraging him, and Manning carefully documented their meeting at the Hoover House. As Manning later interpreted their discussion, Sterling had said that university receipts would not increase more than 5 to 6 percent in the 1964–65 fiscal year, and that Manning would need to spend the next three or four years building up relations with alumni, trustees, and foundations (as had Spaeth) to further develop financial support for the school. Manning could not be expected to generate major financial support for the Law School immediately, but they agreed that during this period he must be free to work on forward development without the worry of losing current faculty to raiding.[50]

Sterling concluded, according to Manning, that the Law School needed a substantial "blood transfusion" not only to initiate the new stage of development but to preserve the situation, at least until the school's programs could pay for themselves. Manning was delighted that Sterling said he would go to the trustees' Finance Committee for permission to transfer to the Law School, for use at the dean's discretion, between $250,000 and $500,000. This would be available as though it were a foundation grant, with both principal and income to be spent over a three- to five-year period, and would be over and above the regular budget and regular budgetary increases. Sterling would make no further commitment but mentioned that he had discussed the situation with some of the trustees. They, too, wanted a first-rate Law School, matching the best in the country.[51]

Sterling also agreed with Manning that the Law School, then housed in cramped quarters on the front of the Quad, needed its own building. Manning calculated that a new building would likely cost $7 million, requiring at least two to three years to fund. Manning thought that they could expect to raise only $2 million with an alumni group of only 2,800, but Sterling

Time magazine reported new law Dean Bayless Manning's arrival from Yale as another success for Stanford, that "ferocious raider of Ivy League faculties." Also mentioned were his black Porsche, a worn set of Shakespeare volumes, an Egyptian statue, and "a rapidly expanding reputation as one of the busiest young legal scholars in the business."
LEO HOLUB / STANFORD UNIVERSITY ARCHIVES

reassured him that the funds could be raised and recalled the decision to build the Medical Center at a time when the university only had $750,000 available for the purpose. He advised Manning not to discuss the matter of funding any further with the provost. He would "like to think on the matter for a bit," he told Manning, and discuss it further with members of the Trustee Finance Committee.[52] (The new Law School building, dedicated in 1975, cost close to $30 million.)

A week later, back in New Haven, Manning apologized for confronting Sterling with Terman's memorandum. He was now proudly committed to fending off the wolves who were raiding top universities, he wrote, adding that he had persuaded two Stanford faculty members to not accept attractive offers elsewhere.[53]

Sterling responded reassuringly that the situation looked "less bleak" than when Manning visited Hoover House. But he again cautioned that they must "take the measure of what is possible for the Law School to do within a regular budget before I can appropriately or effectively discuss with the Trustees anything by way of a booster shot."[54]

No doubt Manning was reassured at the news of Stanford's successful conclusion of its university-wide PACE fundraising campaign. Reflecting Sterling's own infectious enthusiasm, he sent Sterling his congratulations: "How justifiably proud and gratified you must have been when last week you announced the $109 million. Potentials are always so much greater than most men can see. You are among those born with the gift of sight and the energy to translate the vision into reality."[55]

Nevertheless, Manning's disagreement with Terman on fundamentals continued. Still four months before arriving, Manning wrote Sterling, "it appears to be Fred's fundamental view that financing for the Law School's forward jump should in largest measure be derived from increased tuition income. I cannot possibly see how this can be the case." Echoing Sterling's well-known distrust of relying on tuition and student body growth for financial support, Manning argued, "it is far from clear that increase in the size of the student body of the Law School will generate extra net income if, at the same time, the new program for the improvement of the School is put into effect; increased demand for student aid, faculty and other items will offset the tuition increment to a substantial extent—perhaps entirely." No incoming dean, Manning said, who was charged with lifting the School to a position of national prominence "could agree that his entire program would be *conditioned* upon an increase in the student body."

Within days of arriving on campus, in June 1964, Manning wrote a foundation president: "As I view it, Stanford's Law School, already excellent, is the law school that today has the greatest combination of potentials for becoming a national school of the very first rank in the next few years." His own choice to leave Yale was emblematic: "I am sufficiently persuaded of it and sufficiently convinced of the national importance of expanding the small company of national law schools that I am leaving Yale to do what I can to contribute to this development."[56]

To the outside world, Manning himself personified what *Time* magazine, later that year, would call Stanford's record "as a ferocious raider of Ivy League faculties." *Time* went on to report colorfully:

> Yale's bright, articulate Bayless Manning, 41, rolled into Palo Alto last summer completely equipped with wife, four children, a black Porsche sports car, a worn set of Shakespeare, an Egyptian statue, a dagger that had been used in a Philippine murder and a rapidly expanding reputation as one of the busiest young legal scholars in the business.[57]

Manning remained at Stanford until 1971, when he was named president of the Council on Foreign Relations. He is credited with groundbreaking curriculum changes, including interdisciplinary studies and creation of the joint graduate law and business degree. He diversified the school by attracting international faculty and students, and he encouraged students to engage in pro bono work. "He uniquely understood that the study of law could no longer be confined to a single discipline—that the law influenced and was influenced by economics, history, medicine, and the arts," remembered John Merryman, "and that law graduates should be and would be, like him, capable of many great things."[58]

SCHOOLS AND DEANS DURING THE STERLING ADMINISTRATION, 1949–1968

President Sterling, seen here with his deans in November 1967, emphasized a university-wide perspective among his team, encouraging them to stay abreast of university affairs while keeping each other posted regarding their schools. The deans (from left): Education, H. Thomas James; Humanities and Sciences, Robert Sears; Medicine, Robert Glaser; President Sterling; Engineering, Joseph Pettit; Earth Sciences, Richard Jahns; Law, Bayless Manning; and the Graduate School of Business, Ernest Arbuckle. STANFORD NEWS SERVICE

Medicine (organized 1913, acquired by Stanford in 1908 as its Department of Medicine)
> Loren R. Chandler (1933–53)
> Windsor C. Cutting (1953–57)
> Robert H. Alway (acting 1957–58, dean 1958–65)
> Robert J. Glaser (1965–71)

> *School of Nursing* (created in 1922, was formerly the Lane Hospital Training School for Nurses, founded in 1895 and operated by the School of Medicine until it was closed in 1974)

Education (organized 1917 from the Department of Education, created in 1891; renamed the Graduate School of Education in 2013)
> John Bartky (1945–54)
> James Quillen (1954–66)
> H. Thomas James (1966–72)

Law (organized 1923 as a graduate program from the undergraduate Department of Law, created in 1893; the department renamed itself the School of Law in 1908, but did not function as such until 1923)
> Carl B. Spaeth (1946–62)
> John R. McDonough Jr. (acting 1962–64)
> Bayless Manning (1964–71)

Engineering (organized 1925 from departments created in 1891)
> Frederick E. Terman (1944–58)
> Joseph M. Pettit (1958–72)

Graduate School of Business (created 1925)
> J. Hugh Jackson (1931–56)
> Carlton A. Pederson (acting 1956–58)
> Ernest C. Arbuckle (1958–68)

Earth Sciences (created 1947 as School of Mineral Sciences, including some departments from 1891; renamed Earth Sciences in 1962; renamed the School of Earth, Energy and Environmental Sciences—Stanford Earth for short—in 2015)
> A. I. Levorsen (1947–50)
> Charles F. Park Jr. (1950–65)
> Richard H. Jahns (1965–79)

Humanities and Sciences (organized 1948 from four previous schools: Biological Sciences, 1922; Social Sciences, 1923; Physical Sciences, 1925; and Letters, 1925, renamed Humanities in 1943, including many of the university's earliest departments)
> Clarence Faust (1948–51)
> Douglas M. Whitaker (1951–52)
> Ray N. Faulkner (acting, 1952–56)
> Philip H. Rhinelander (1956–61)
> Robert R. Sears (1961–70)

Sources: *Stanford Annual President's Reports* (1903–04) through (1947–48); J. Pearce Mitchell, *Stanford University 1916–1941* (Stanford: Stanford University Press, 1958); Ray Lyman Wilbur, *The Memoirs of Ray Lyman Wilbur, 1875–1949* (Stanford: Stanford University Press, 1960); *Stanford Daily; Campus Report; Memorial Resolutions.*

GRANT

Founding and Endowing

THE LELAND STANFORD JUNIOR UNIVERSITY

12

STERLING AND THE TRUSTEES
PROMOTING STRONG RELATIONSHIPS

From the outset, Wallace Sterling recognized in Stanford's Board of Trustees the potential for vital support for his administration and his ambitions. Sterling considered the board an asset, recalled two-time trustee Ernest Arbuckle, as "another arm, and he used it that way."[1]

The trustees bear legal responsibility for the university's future by guarding its assets, controlling its expenditures, and selecting its president. While the university president is granted unusual authority over university affairs and management, the board's opinions serve as guiding principles. The trustees' relationship with the university president depended on confidence, noted board President Richard Guggenhime. "When you're lucky enough to get a man like Wally Sterling, then you rely on his judgement in many areas."[2]

Sterling brought to Stanford years of productive interaction with trustees of Caltech and the Huntington Library and Art Gallery. He also was acquainted with many board members of philanthropic, civic, educational, and cultural institutions throughout Southern California. During his 19-year administration, he worked closely with Stanford's board in a way none of his predecessors had envisioned, encouraging its expansion in size and activity, respecting its responsibilities, yet maintaining his own authority. He carefully developed personal relationships with many trustees and effectively used the board, and especially board committees, to bolster his goals while building faculty participation through university committees. After his retirement as president, board members found it difficult to imagine continuing their work without him; in 1969, Sterling became the only former Stanford president to serve as an elected member of the Board of Trustees.

Established by the university's Founding Grant of 1885, the Board of Trustees of Leland Stanford Junior University was initially "a shadowy body," as first registrar Orrin Leslie Elliott called it.[3] Jane Lathrop Stanford kickstarted it

< Cover page of the 1885 Founding Grant of Leland Stanford Junior University. Although the grant created the university and outlined its goals, the trust's properties and income were not conveyed to its trustees until surviving founder Jane Stanford relinquished her powers over the trust in 1903. The grant has been clarified and supplemented through legislation and judicial decrees. STANFORD UNIVERSITY ARCHIVES

269

Trustees Morris Doyle (left) and Judge Homer Spence conversed with Ann and Wallace Sterling at the trustees' 10-year celebration of Sterling's administration, 1959, at San Francisco's St. Francis Hotel. President Sterling developed a productive and cordial working relationship with his Board of Trustees.   CHRIS KJOBECH / STANFORD NEWS SERVICE

not only to manage university investments, but also to find means to recover from the 1906 earthquake's extensive damage, and to facilitate President Jordan's ambitions for academic growth. Key agenda items included balancing academic departments, assimilating Cooper Medical College, and, eventually, transitioning from Jordan's administration to those of his successors.

In the ensuing years, the board slowly adapted its once-narrow 19th-century legal interpretation of its duties—to manage the university's assets as provided by the founders—to explore new ways to invest, nurture, and increase the endowment. (This included the controversial establishment of tuition in 1920, and new investments and major gifts and grants in the 1920s and 1930s.) By 1948, the university could announce a record year of new gifts and grants, due in part to exceptional donations by individual trustees.[5]

With the academic program and organization left in the hands of Stanford's president, the board oversaw important changes to the student body, often with financial implications. They framed as a moral responsibility their 1933 elimination of Mrs. Stanford's 1899 limitation on the number of women enrolled at one time, claiming a return to the original wishes of the founders as embodied in the Founding Grant, but the move was, in fact, a financial strategy to build the student body and, thus, Stanford's tuition base during the Depression.[6]

While President David Starr Jordan had spent much of his administration appeasing Mrs. Stanford and negotiating with a handful of trustees who were among her closest advisors, President Ray Lyman Wilbur largely held the trustees at a distance. Confident and proactive, Wilbur had the long-standing backing of one of the board's oldest and most esteemed members, Timothy Hopkins (an original board member from 1885 who died in office, in 1936). At his

into action in 1903, when she formally relinquished her powers as "surviving founder." (She died two years later.) Mrs. Stanford had already named some of her most trusted advisors as board officers, removed three she considered disloyal, and set up executive and financial committees. Earlier that year, she had created a new organizing committee, chaired by a former president of the University of California, to establish the board's bylaws, and to develop means to exercise its powers and conduct its business. By 1904, the board had moved forward, with President Jordan's cooperation, to recast the university's administrative system and supported creation of the Academic Council.[4]

After 1908, with final probate of Mrs. Stanford's will, the board swung into full operation,

Trustee President Leland Cutler spoke in front of Memorial Church at Stanford's 50th anniversary celebration, 1941. (Sharing the stage were trustee Herbert Hoover and university President Ray Lyman Wilbur.) Cutler, who joined the board in 1920, remained active and supportive until his death, in 1959.
STANFORD UNIVERSITY ARCHIVES

1916 inauguration, Wilbur famously refused to wear academic dress because Hopkins, who had not graduated from college, would not be able to do so. His real reason was more telling: Board President William Mayo Newhall had insisted on the dress code. "I knew that if I let the president of the board decide this question for me," Wilbur later wrote, "he would try to decide other more important questions, not through action of the Board but by pressure on me."[7]

Even more important than the backing of Hopkins was Wilbur's relationship with his old friend from Encina Hall, Herbert Hoover. Wilbur's personal relationship with Hoover loomed large. Elected to the board in 1912, the formidable young businessman Hoover had an immediate impact on financial decisions, particularly relating to tuition, fundraising, broader investing, and faculty recruiting. Hoover did not step down from the board during his four years as U.S. president (1929–33), nor did he allow the board, despite campus pressure, to force Wilbur to choose between his cabinet post and his university presidency. Wilbur's long-distance

management while secretary of the interior put Stanford in an awkward caretaker situation early in the Depression, demonstrating the board's unwillingness to clash with either Wilbur or Hoover.[8]

Hoover, who had orchestrated then Dean of Medicine Wilbur's selection as university president in 1916, also was instrumental in the election of Dr. Donald B. Tresidder to the board.[9] When the 44-year-old Tresidder had joined the board in 1939, at the recommendation of trustee Harry Chandler, he was then its youngest member. His appointment to the board's presidency, in 1941, was strongly endorsed by Hoover and Wilbur. In accepting the presidency, Tresidder presented a list of conditions, including a reorganization of board committees, limitation of terms, and an age limit for future trustees (70). The board accepted these unanimously.[10]

Tresidder led an energetic but ultimately fruitless search for a successor to President Wilbur, who had been asked to serve through 1941, the year of Stanford's 50th anniversary

Six trustees in 1934, during Wallace Sterling's graduate-student days, were still on the board when he became president 15 years later (five were present for this photo: Cutler, Fuller Jr., Hoover, Lillick, and Miller). From left: W. M. Alexander, H. C. Hoover, F. B. Anderson, T. Hopkins, A. E. Roth (comptroller), J. D. Grant, R. L. Wilbur (university president), L. W. Cutler (board president), W. M. Newhall (former board president), I. S. Lillick, C. O. G. Miller, W. P. Fuller Jr., F. P. Deering, and J. T. Nourse. MORTON PHOTOGRAPHS, SF / STANFORD UNIVERSITY ARCHIVES

celebration. Due to wartime conditions and the difficulty attracting suitable candidates, Wilbur reluctantly agreed to stay until 1942, then again, until September 1943. Facing their dilemma, Tresidder's board colleagues, with Wilbur's endorsement, prevailed on to him accept the job as Stanford's fourth president. (Tresidder side-stepped the Founding Grant's stipulation that the university's president "shall not be one of their number" by resigning from the board before his appointment.)[11]

As university president (1943–48), Tresidder worked well, and often, with the board, leaving academic matters previously tended to by Wilbur to his newly established academic vice president, Alvin C. Eurich. Tresidder's moral authority paid off with strong trustee support for war-time mobilization, and such postwar changes as studying campus land development as an income source, establishing the Stanford Research Institute, and encouraging federal support for research. Tresidder's growing distance from the faculty, however, and his reluctance to interact with faculty leaders led to problems, which Sterling later sought to address by serving as a faculty advocate and bridge between the trustees and the campus.

Sterling, ever pragmatic, sought balance through a cooperative and non-confrontational style. "Wally was wonderful at handling the board," recalled presidential assistant Fred Glover. "He would bring up controversial issues at one board meeting; get a feeling of how the board stood; then lobby by phone prior to the next board meeting when he would bring the issue to a vote. There were few 'no' votes. The board tended to hammer things out before com-ing to a vote."[12] As Ken Cuthbertson noted of Sterling's careful strategy: "He didn't want to have split votes. If there was a possibility of hav-ing it unanimous, he wanted it unanimous—and never over the dead body of any of the board."[13]

THE TRUSTEES WHO WELCOMED PRESIDENT STERLING

At Sterling's arrival, in 1949, the 15-member Board of Trustees included some of Northern California's most eminent legal and corporate names. What was once a board of trusted business associates of Leland Stanford had become, by the 1930s, a self-selecting group of largely (but not exclusively) Stanford alumni with strong credentials of university service as Alumni Association officers, Stanford Associates, and/or campus community volunteers.

The oldest trustees, 80-year-old Judge M. C. Sloss and 83-year-old Pacific Gas & Electric executive Christian O. G. Miller, would soon retire after some 30 years of board service. Other long-standing members, however, remained particularly active for another decade. The 64-year-old Leland W. Cutler, '06, an insurance executive and president of San Francisco's Chamber of Commerce, was trustee president through the Depression and early war years, 1931–42. He had joined the board in 1920 at age 35—the third youngest appointed to the board before 1961. Cutler had a long history of campus contributions, beginning with his organization of the Stanford Band as an undergraduate. While on the board, he also served two terms as Alumni Association president and 10 years on the Board of Athletic Control.[14]

The Board of Trustees at their San Francisco headquarters in December 1956, reviewing a plan for science and engineering buildings. Seated (from left): Caroline Moore Charles, Leland Cutler, Ruth Fesler Lipman, Arthur Stewart, May Chandler Goodan, Lloyd Dinkelspiel (board president) at table's head, Charles Blyth, Donald Russell (sitting back), George Ditz, Homer Spence, W. P. Fuller Jr., and Ira Lillick. Standing (from left): Edmund Littlefield, Ernest Arbuckle, George Morell, James Black, Monroe Spaght, David Packard, and James Crafts. (Absent: Herbert Hoover, Tex Middleton, Neil Petree, and Herman Phleger.) MOULIN STUDIOS / STANFORD UNIVERSITY ARCHIVES

Sterling's first board included two former trustee presidents, Leland Cutler, '06 (left), and W. Parmer Fuller Jr., '10. Both were long-standing advocates for undergraduates and athletics, and each served as an important connection between Sterling and older alumni.
STANFORD UNIVERSITY ARCHIVES

During the board's early decades, few trustees were alumni. Cutler had been only the fourth alumnus appointed to the board. In 1923, Ira Shell Lillick, '97, was the fifth. Lillick was an expert on maritime and shipping law with a strong interest in legal ethics. As a trustee officer and member of many board committees, Lillick chaired the presidential search committee that selected Sterling. Like Cutler, he served as an important intermediary for the new president, introducing him to fellow trustees and influential alumni.

Three trustees had UC Berkeley connections: C. O. G. Miller had attended Cal before going into business in 1885; on his 1950 board retirement, he was replaced by Cal graduate James Byers Black, '12, retired chairman of Pacific Gas & Electric. Herman Phleger, Cal '12, an international law expert, was a classmate and friend of UC President Robert G. Sproul. Phleger and Lloyd Dinkelspiel, '10, earned their law degrees at Harvard, as had Judge Sloss. Seeley Mudd had left Stanford to finish at Columbia and then earned a Harvard medical degree; investment banker Charles R. Blyth was an Amherst graduate. Throughout Sterling's years in office, however, most trustees would have strong Stanford connections.

In 1949, few of the trustees lived beyond the Bay Area. George Ditz, '11, a prominent Stockton lawyer who had served as Alumni Association president, was an important tie to Central Valley alumni. Like current trustee President Paul Edwards, Ditz was a founding member of the Stanford Associates. Along with significant fundraising experience, Ditz brought to the board a strong interest in student recruiting and financial support. May Chandler Goodan, '14, another strong voice in alumni affairs, was the first woman on the board since Jane Stanford. Goodan had joined in 1942, when her father, Harry Chandler, publisher of the *Los Angeles Times* and a powerful Southern California real estate developer, stepped down. Chandler had been the board's first Southern California appointee, and Goodan continued his role. Like her father, she would serve two 10-year terms and, in 1954, would be among the first women asked to join the Stanford Associates.[15]

Only two other trustees lived beyond Northern California. The 74-year-old Herbert Hoover, '95, had long attended only one meeting a year, but influenced board decisions largely through correspondence and trustee visits to his New York City residence. Dr. Seeley G. Mudd, eminent cardiologist and cancer researcher, and briefly USC's dean of medicine, lived in Southern California. As a Caltech professor, Mudd was one of the few trustees who had known Sterling before his 1948 candidacy.

Sterling's first board included two past board presidents. Like his predecessor Leland Cutler, W. Parmer Fuller Jr., '10, was a well-known presence on campus and an advocate for student athletics. A close friend of Don Tresidder, Fuller had stepped down as trustee president in 1948 following Tresidder's death but remained active on the board for another 10 years. His successor, Paul C. Edwards, would reinforce the pattern of mutual trust between the board and the university's president.

PAUL C. EDWARDS
THE BOARD IN TRANSITION

Paul C. Edwards was among the many trustees and Stanford Associates who had counted Donald B. Tresidder as a friend, and who considered the Tresidder administration the beginning of Stanford's revitalization. Edwards' voice was influential in finding an energetic successor similarly ambitious for Stanford's future and creative in dealing with problems and opportunities. His early interactions with Wallace Sterling provided an important connection to those trustees still mourning Tresidder's death and regretting faculty opposition to acting President Alvin Eurich. Sterling soon appreciated Edwards' quiet but effective diplomacy.[16]

Edwards, '06, had taken over as board president in May 1948. He was an accomplished and articulate newspaper editor with more than 40 years of experience with the Scripps-Howard organization. During his student journalist days, his interests were more literary (he was a prize-winning writer and editor of the literary magazine, *Sequoia*, and an English Club member), but he also delved into current issues such as the problems faced by working students at Stanford. Four years out of Stanford he was in the thick of newspaper editing, becoming founding editor of the *Dallas Dispatch* (1910) and then of the *Houston Press*

Paul Edwards, trustee president from 1948 to 1953, took on board leadership amid the unpopular acting presidency of Alvin Eurich, easing the transition to Sterling. A veteran news editor who had faced down the Ku Klux Klan in Texas, he helped Sterling navigate controversies during the McCarthy era.
STANFORD ASSOCIATES / STANFORD NEWS SERVICE

(1911). After seven years (1925–32) as editor of the *San Diego Sun*, Edwards became associate editor of the *San Francisco News*. Deeply interested in civic affairs nationally as well as locally, he became a trustee of the Rosenberg Foundation and served as president of the Commonwealth Club. He also became actively involved in Stanford alumni affairs. He was a founding member of the Stanford Associates (and elected its president in 1941) and chairman of the Stanford Annual Fund. When he was elected to the Board of Trustees, in 1943, he was one of the youngest board members at the time, at 66.[17]

Edwards appreciated the need to smooth the transition from Eurich's acting presidency to Sterling's very different administrative style. Before Sterling's campus arrival in April 1949, Edwards made clear at alumni conferences from Seattle to Bakersfield that Stanford would continue its long-range policy to maintain, as Leland Stanford had asserted, a university of highest degree, and to build on its recent successes at fundraising, faculty recruiting, and campus planning. "To assure that, we must steer away from bigness and toward giving superlative education to a body of highly selected students," he said. "By my many talks with him and by what I have observed of his character and personality, I am confident Stanford has another great intellectual leader at its head," Edwards reassured his audiences. "Dr. Sterling takes over the direction of a University not only of high degree but of sound condition. . . . Stanford, I confidently believe, faces a future of greater and greater accomplishment."[18]

Edwards was known for his attention to detail, the soundness of his decisions, and his ease working with others on controversial subjects. He and Sterling shared a deep interest in the written word, and in the principles Edwards described in 1961: "To print the truth and defend the rights of the public without regard to the effect of such policy on advertisers, and to publish the news faithfully, fearlessly, and fairly."[19]

"Paul had a very special place in my life because he was President of the Board of Stanford University when I returned to Stanford to assume this office," Sterling wrote years later to the editor of *The Houston Press*. "It will be no surprise to you to have me say that working with Paul was one of the most agreeable and constructive experiences I have ever had." Their working relationship quickly developed into a "strong and welcome friendship," Sterling said at Edwards' 1962 memorial service. "He brought much to friendship."[20]

The modest Edwards displayed an unassuming style of leadership that belied the vigor of his convictions and firmness of his principles. As a young editor in Texas, he had faced down powerful local politicians and angry Ku Klux Klansmen. In 1949–50, Edwards similarly backed Wallace Sterling when off-campus Communist hunters and some alumni attacked Sterling as a Communist sympathizer for refusing to denounce Stanford faculty protests against the loyalty oath at the University of California. During the turbulent times of McCarthyism, Edwards (who considered himself a moderate Republican) continued his eloquent and timely editorials against "emotionalism, ideology, prejudice, and hate" until his retirement from the *San Francisco News*, in 1956. He was the first recipient, in 1953, of Stanford's Degree of Uncommon Man.

When Edwards retired after 10 years on the board, he could look back at five busy years as president. He had helped push the momentum begun under Tresidder and now continued by the Sterling administration. New special board committees were busy with the challenges of land development and dealing with new fundraising expectations, to alleviate heavy reliance on tuition and to support faculty recruiting. One of Edwards' final accomplishments was to persuade the board to approve the Medical School's move from San Francisco to the home campus.

LLOYD DINKELSPIEL
MASTER FUNDRAISER

Lloyd Dinkelspiel, a partner in the San Francisco law firm of Heller, Ehrman, White and McAuliffe, and past president of the San Francisco Bar Association, followed Edwards as president of the board.

As a Stanford undergraduate, Dinkelspiel, '20, had been editor of the *Daily* and the *Quad*, as well as an associate editor of *Chaparral*. He earned a Block S varsity letter as a sprinter. His friendship

Lloyd Dinkelspiel, board president from 1953 to 1958, became good friends with Wally Sterling and was especially effective at fundraising. Dinkelspiel was well known in San Francisco Jewish philanthropic circles.
STANFORD NEWS SERVICE

with teammate Fred Terman, '20, a long-distance runner, would be lifelong. Dinkelspiel went on to earn his LL.B. from Harvard in 1922 and returned to San Francisco to practice law.[21]

During World War II, Dinkelspiel had served as a lieutenant colonel in the Army Air Force and was awarded a Legion of Merit for his service. Like his merchant father, Samuel, who had served as president of Temple Emanu-El, Lloyd Dinkelspiel was a highly regarded community leader and philanthropist active in local and national Jewish organizations. He served as vice president of the National Jewish Welfare Board and president of the National Jewish Welfare Fund of San Francisco. Like fellow alumni and Stanford Associates Robert Levison and Morgan Gunst, and trustees Leon and M. C. Sloss, both Dinkelspiel and his wife, Florence Hellman, were from pioneering California families with ties to Gold Rush San Francisco. All were influential members of the Emanu-El congregation.[22]

Dinkelspiel and Sterling first met in 1948 when the candidate dined at the Dinkelspiels' San Francisco home with several trustees and was unofficially "looked over" for the presidency. Their congenial professional relationship, which

quickly evolved into a strong friendship, was an enormous boost for Sterling in guiding the university during the 1950s.

Dinkelspiel's board presidency, 1953–58, helped provide momentum behind Sterling's ambitious plans, much of which involved active trustee participation in development and financial planning. Dinkelspiel's enthusiasm motivated the trustees to make even greater efforts as they oversaw such initiatives as development of the Shopping Center and Industrial Park, a campus-wide land development master plan, and evaluation of the curriculum and facilities needs of the Medical School. "They were two risk-takers who had a lot of personality," remembered Ken Cuthbertson, "but they also had a good sense of which risks to take."[23]

Sterling and Dinkelspiel enjoyed traveling together on Stanford business. Their sense of humor was notoriously disarming, and both enjoyed writing humorous poetry for various public occasions. Sterling's poem honoring Dinkelspiel at a 1953 Stanford Associates dinner reads, in part:

> If I sat down to make a rhyme,
> Assuming that I had the time,
> I really don't know how I'd feel
> About conjuring with Dinkelspiel. . . .
>
> I met him first five years ago.
> As a new trustee he had to throw
> A dinner so the brass could see
> Whether they liked the looks of me.
>
> On face, they were most polite
> And some of them seemed even bright.
> The food was good, the cocktails strong
> And that was how they done me wrong.
>
> Right then I learned about our guest,
> Who sits here now demurely dressed,
> That when he's acting as your host,
> That's when you have to watch him most.[24]

"The relationship between Wally and Lloyd was just a marvelous thing," Glover recalled, referring to annual holiday dinners given by the Dinkelspiel family for Sterling's presidential staff: "We were each asked to put on a stunt, and I think that was one of the most demanding things that I ever had to do, was to do something for Wally and Lloyd Dinkelspiel, who were such clowns themselves."[25]

Dinkelspiel and Hellman family members and friends underwrote Dinkelspiel Auditorium, in memory of Lloyd's wife Florence, who had died of cancer in 1954. Opening night, May 23, 1957, at the Florence Hellman Dinkelspiel Auditorium featured a professional opera cast in the West Coast premiere of Douglas Moore's *The Ballad of Baby Doe.* The new hall was "so advanced in design that it has been called the theater of tomorrow," announced the *Stanford Daily*.[26]

Dinkelspiel, aged only 60, died in May 1959, a year after he stepped down as president.[27] "He made his troubles and his sorrows his problem and no one else's," eulogized Sterling at the

funeral service at Congregation Emanu-El in San Francisco. "His joys he generously shared."

It was not his energy that impressed me as uncommon, though he had it in great abundance; nor was it his remarkable ability to bring the power of a gifted mind into regular concentration on the task at hand. It was rather the range and depth of his emotion. He *felt* injustice with indignation that could bring fire to his eyes. He *felt* as something

The lobby of Florence Hellman Dinkelspiel Auditorium was filled to overflowing as opera devotees and Stanford donors and friends attended the theater's grand opening: the West Coast premiere of Douglas Moore's opera *The Ballad of Baby Doe*, May 23, 1957. Lloyd Dinkelspiel and others donated the facility in memory of his first wife.
STANFORD NEWS SERVICE

profoundly personal the responsibilities of good citizenship, and gave expression to his feelings in ways and in a degree that brought blessings to his country and community. He *felt* the joys of deep affection and warm companionship and revealed the fact in his transparent pleasure in having fun. He *felt* and conveyed that unspoken assurance which stems from a pledged word freely given and loyally kept.[28]

Lloyd Dinkelspiel Jr. wrote Sterling the day after the funeral thanking him for his remarks: "I think I can truthfully say that of all the people Pop was associated with, you were the one whom he respected most and to whom he was devoted. I know that he never enjoyed any opportunity more than he did his years as a Trustee and particularly the ones as president. You and Mrs. Sterling were primarily responsible for this great enjoyment."[29]

Mrs. Thompson, Dinkelspiel's secretary, also wrote to Sterling:

He told me one day when I was admiring one of the letters you had written, that he thought you had the finest mind of anyone he had ever known, and also that rare thing—a love for your fellow man—two attributes which he said seldom went hand in hand. (Actually, I thought at the time that it sounded almost like a description of himself.)[30]

The Stanford Associates, in late 1959, paid tribute to Dinkelspiel for "exceeding every standard of loyalty and service to Stanford" when they posthumously named him the fifth recipient of Stanford's Degree of Uncommon Man.[31]

A WORKING BOARD

Jane Stanford had found the original 24-member board cumbersome, made up as it was of many men who had little experience with university affairs. In 1899, no doubt on the recommendation of the few who were willing to devote time

to the effort and unhappy with several members selected by her husband, she set its number to a more workable 15.[32] However, with the board playing a more active role in subsequent years in land development, fundraising, and the review and expansion of the academic program, board committee work had grown accordingly.

By 1954, it was clear that there were too few trustees to get the work done. The board, encouraged by a study done by Sterling's presidential assistant Robert Wert, increased its size from 15 to 23 to better distribute its workload. In addition to 20 regular members selected by the board, three (serving five-year non-renewable terms) were to be recommended by the Stanford Alumni Association.[33]

Equally important to broadening the workload was a broadening of the board's geographic base, particularly through greater representation from Southern California. "The money," Fred Glover quipped, "was in Los Angeles."[34]

The incoming nine trustees (eight new slots and one vacancy) included some of the board's most dynamic members of the era. Among them were Ernest Arbuckle, '33, MBA '36, a vice president of W. R. Grace & Co., who would later become dean of the Graduate School of Business; David Packard, '34, co-founder and president of Hewlett-Packard Co., who would succeed Lloyd Dinkelspiel as board president four years later; and Caroline Moore Charles, '27, a Rosenberg Foundation member and former president of the League of Women Voters.[35]

Sterling and his staff appreciated the special expertise provided by key board members. "Most people underestimate the work and contributions made by trustees," recalled Glover, a keen observer of administration-trustee relations from 1952 until his retirement, in 1977.[36] Some trustees worked particularly closely with business manager (and later vice president of business affairs) Alf Brandin, and presidential assistant (and later vice president for finance) Ken Cuthbertson. Glover, initially in charge of board minutes and publicity arrangements, came to know many of the board's leaders. Several already were his friends, having been his colleagues during their World War II military service.[37]

Caroline Moore Charles, active with the World Affairs Council and with the Alumni Association, worked especially effectively with Sterling's administration. Charles had Stanford degrees in mathematics and in education, and dove into financial figures enthusiastically and effectively. As chair of the Buildings and Grounds Committee, she climbed ladders and got "into the muck." Charles would be remembered for her intelligence, energy, and commanding presence during her two decades on the board, 1954–75.[38]

Fellow trustee Morris Doyle considered Charles "remarkably open-minded," experienced, and unusually perceptive. She was willing to take a chance on changes in student lifestyles—such as coeducational dormitories—if she thought the change "well-grounded and well-thought out." When "many trustees would be a little uptight about innovations of that kind," Doyle recalled, "she wasn't." One of her strengths was her willingness, without much encouragement from other trustees, to stay in touch with the undergraduates, allowing her to serve as a bridge between the board and the student body.[39]

Caroline Moore Charles and May Chandler Goodan both served for more than 20 years as active and respected members of the board. Another long-serving member was Lilian Force Fletcher Nichols, 1963–76, who, like Charles, tried to be an advocate for student interests.

Three other women joined the board during Sterling's administration as five-year alumni trustee appointments. Best known was Ruth Fesler Lipman, 1954–59, a member of the Alumni Association Executive Board and a

Caroline Moore Charles, a dynamic trustee and chair of the Buildings and Grounds Committee, played an influential role in construction oversight and was an advocate for student interests.
STANFORD UNIVERSITY ARCHIVES

recent recruit, with Charles and Goodan, to the Stanford Associates. Lipman's father, Bert Fesler, had been master of Encina dormitory when it opened in 1891, and she had served as First Lady Lou Henry Hoover's secretary during Hoover's White House years. Lipman was followed by Alfrida Poco Teague, 1959–64, a Santa Paula rancher and community activist whose husband, Milton Teague, was president of the Alumni Association in 1959. She, in turn, was followed by Emilie Dohrmann Cosgrove, 1964–67, a leader in alumni affairs in Southern California. A Phi Beta Kappa economics major, she had been president of the Associated Women Students and was a student leader in Pan Hellenic. Her husband, John C. Cosgrove, was a Stanford Associate.

George Morell, on the board from 1944 to 1956, chaired the Buildings and Grounds Committee for 10 years and also was an influential voice on land-development issues. Morell, a self-made man, was president of Peninsula Newspapers Inc., and publisher of the *Palo Alto Times*, which he had purchased in 1919. He attended Stanford intermittently between 1904 and 1910, paying his way by working with a pick and shovel and as a teamster, ranch hand, placer miner, seaman, sawmill hand, and advertising solicitor. He left to go into agricultural real estate in the Central Valley. (He was granted a B.A. in 1930.)[40]

When he arrived at Stanford in 1904, Morell was struck by the beauty of Black Mountain, a 2,800-foot peak in the Santa Cruz Mountains, not far from Palo Alto. In 1940, he fulfilled a long-held dream when he started acquiring land there for a cattle ranch. During 1961–72, he donated his Black Mountain Ranch to the university, with the idea that it would be used for educational purposes. (In 1978, Stanford sold the 694 acres for $475,000 to the Midpeninsula Open Space District to add to its Monte Bello Open Space Preserve. The controversial low price honored his wishes that the land not be developed.)[41]

Morell was firmly against condemnation of any Stanford lands, friendly or otherwise. "He thought the university charged the trustees with holding onto the land, Stanford land, without any exceptions," Glover recalled. Morell opposed several condemnations that Sterling and his staff thought advantageous for Stanford, particularly that of the Veterans Administration Hospital location off Foothill Road.[42]

Despite his differences of opinion with Sterling and his staff, Morell remained a supportive advisor. "Before the swift march of events makes the hassle over the Veterans' Hospital a matter of ancient history," he wrote Sterling in 1954, "let me rise and give three cheers. First—for your courage in making the decision regarding the hospital. Second—for the timing of your presentation to the various groups concerned. Third— for your superb presentation to the Board."[43]

Herman Phleger, a founder of the San Francisco law firm Brobeck, Phleger and Harrison, was given special mention as a trustee by Brandin, Cuthbertson, and Glover. Phleger was involved in the earliest discussions of land development. "He would ask more questions about financial matters and land development policies than I thought could be possible," Glover remembered. "He was a man with an amazing knowledge of real estate, so you had very, very professional questions. He wanted everything all wrapped up." Glover thought this approach a delaying tactic, and Brandin, often the target of Phleger's questions, could become frustrated. Cuthbertson, however, disagreed. He believed Phleger was asking the right questions.[44]

Although his manner was not always appreciated by staff members making presentations to the board, Phleger was astute and made innovative recommendations, among them the suggestion that they shorten long-term commercial

Congenial and entrepreneurial George Morell, here in 1944, became a Peninsula newspaper tycoon in the 1920s and 1930s. He donated his beloved ranch in the nearby mountains to Stanford.
KELLOGG STUDIO / STANFORD NEWS SERVICE

International law expert Herman Phleger, a Cal alumnus, had been among those vetting Sterling in 1948. He was an active and exacting trustee who played a strong part in monitoring land development.
STANFORD NEWS SERVICE

land leases from 99- to 51-year terms, in order to generate millions of dollars in extra income. He also argued that trees be planted in the extensive parking areas surrounding the Stanford Shopping Center. (Phleger, like Morell, had large land holdings in the foothills. Phleger's Mountain Meadow estate, more than 1,000 acres of Santa Cruz ridgeline, is now part of the Golden Gate National Recreation Area.)

Cal grad Jim Black, of PG&E, had joined the board in 1950. Throughout his 10 years as a trustee, he worked diligently on improving Stanford's fundraising efforts, including as vice-chair of the Medical Center Fund campaign (1956–59) and as co-chair of the PACE Campaign as an emeritus trustee (1961–64). He often functioned as a foil to Herman Phleger's critiques, and at the end of his term, as a peacemaker between fellow trustee Hoover and the administration.

Donald Russell, president of the Southern Pacific Railroad, took a keen interest in budget matters and was an effective chairman of the trustee Finance Committee at a time of great change on campus. Fred Glover, reflecting on Russell's business influence, said, "When he hiccupped at breakfast, it could be felt along the tracks as far as Los Angeles." Russell had been a Stanford undergraduate when, in 1918, he enlisted in the Canadian Air Force during World War I. He returned to Stanford to study engineering but left again, in 1920, to join the Southern Pacific, working his way up through management positions.[45]

For years, Sterling had tried to interest the trustees in sitting down early each year to have a look "at the budget pie that had to be cut, and to discuss with us how the cuts should be made, given the current financial situation of the University," as he wrote in October 1963 to his friend Lawrence Kimpton, a trustee since 1961. When Russell began to visit the campus to go over budget estimates, an encouraged Sterling told

Donald Russell left Stanford to fly for the Royal Canadian Air Corps during World War I. He started working at the Southern Pacific Railroad as a timekeeper and became the company's president in 1952.
SOUTHERN PACIFIC RAILROAD / STANFORD NEWS SERVICE

Kimpton: "I hope that this will mean that Trustees will feel a deeper participation in the broad lines of budget preparation . . . otherwise, they're almost driven into a position of accepting the pie as we cut it, because, as you know the cuts have to be made in time for faculty recruiting to begin."[46]

Russell was among the many who urged Sterling to take care of his health. "Please slow down," Russell wrote Sterling in early 1964, suggesting he "delegate some more and let somebody else worry and do some of these jobs you have been trying to carry on your broad shoulders."[47]

In mid-1964, while Sterling, whose problems with diverticulitis dated back to the 1940s, was recovering from surgery for acute peritonitis, Russell became disgruntled on learning that Stanford had rejected the application of a Southern Pacific executive's daughter. Russell, his 10-year term about to expire, decided to withdraw his name from consideration for re-election to the board. From home, Sterling wrote Russell:

I have learned from Morris Doyle that you are deeply upset and annoyed with the decision concerning [the candidate's] application for admission to Stanford. The reports that I have about the case indicate that it wasn't a simple one; other applicants from the same school, with better records and school recommendations, were not admitted, and several of these were daughters of parents both of whom were Stanford graduates and some of whom have worked for Stanford. The preparatory school involved was aware of this situation. . . . So were the parents of the other applicants. These circumstances combined to make [the applicant's] case anything but simple and to involve really the integrity of our decisions about admission.

Morris Doyle also reported to me that your reaction to the decision was such that you were considering resigning as Trustee. If the doctors did not have me still under restrictions, I would come to see you to ask you not to do so. I would ask this not only out of friendship, which I treasure, but also out of profound appreciation of your services and value to Stanford as Trustee. Please accept this letter in lieu of a visit and believe that I want very much to have you continue as Trustee. I hope with all my heart that you will see your way clear to do so.[48]

Russell responded, "I am very sorry, but I think after serving ten years that a younger and perhaps a more persuasive and effective person should replace me."[49]

DAVID PACKARD AND THOMAS PIKE

By the late 1950s, Sterling's staff and faculty expectations were high. As the staff completed a 10-year forecast and financial analysis, Cuthbertson felt that he and his colleagues moved "too far in front" of the board and perhaps had not kept trustees well enough informed when, for the first time, the board was asked to think in terms of hundreds of millions, rather than thousands, of dollars for dramatic program improvements. Sterling, in the middle, "was beautifully able to play the game of keeping the campus encouraged that there was forward motion, and then bringing the board along at the same time."[50]

When David Packard, '34, Engr. '39, was named president of the board, in 1958, the

trustees were still "heavily undergraduate oriented," according to Cuthbertson. The staff did not believe the trustees had the same sense that Sterling and his faculty had of "a great research university unfolding and developing." Cuthbertson and his colleagues credited Packard's leadership for smoothing the way for such efforts as the PACE (Plan of Action for a Challenging Era) fundraising campaign and the Stanford Linear Accelerator Center. "He understood what that potential was, and he carried a lot of weight with the board in bringing it about. Dave urged the board to go ahead with these research opportunities, the development and interim financing of those inexpensive buildings in the Science Quad and all."[51]

David Packard, president of what was then described as "a Palo Alto manufacturing firm," Hewlett-Packard, and a director of Varian Associates, was well positioned to foster Stanford's academic ambitions.[52] Packard and classmate and co-founder William Hewlett, mentored by Professor Fred Terman, chair of electrical engineering, had maintained close relations with Terman and the School of Engineering. Packard and his wife, Lucile Salter Packard, already were generous donors to the university, including engineering scholarships, an endowed chair in English, and a joint gift, with Hewlett, for engineering laboratory expansion.

Packard also was active in local civic affairs, including the presidency of Palo Alto's Board of Education, and had helped negotiate the 1956 friendly condemnation of 51 acres of Stanford land near Arastradero Road to the Palo Alto School District for later construction of the district's third high school (opened in 1964 as Gunn High School).

In addition to overseeing campus, medical center, linear accelerator, and shopping center construction projects, Packard served as board spokesman during the controversial Coyote Hill

David Packard (here with Sterling, 1959) was trustee president from 1958 to 1960 and a major supporter of Sterling's goals to develop the faculty, research facilities, graduate studies, and fundraising capacity.   ROBERT COX / STANFORD NEWS SERVICE

the board's presidency had grown considerably over the previous decade, and Packard's load had been heavy. Recognizing the implications, the board expanded its number of vice presidents, and Packard continued on the board as one of Pike's most influential vice presidents, along with Doyle and Guggenhime. Packard also became head of the major gifts section of the PACE Campaign.

Pike was instrumental in the establishment of the Petroleum Investments Committee, a special board committee encouraging gifts of, and university investments in, oil and gas (the industry was heavily represented on the board). As a resident of San Marino, he took special interest in promoting fundraising in Southern California.[55] Working with PACE Campaign trustee co-chairs Ted Petersen and Jim Black, he traveled extensively on Stanford's behalf, made many speeches, and marshaled volunteers for major solicitations during the early years of the campaign.

Pike, however, had taken on the demanding board presidency while juggling dramatic changes in his family's business interests and his own increased political responsibilities: He was California chairman of Richard Nixon's 1960 presidential campaign. Pike had known Nixon since 1946 and had helped with fundraising and publicity in Nixon's controversial 1950 campaign for the U.S. Senate against Helen Gahagan Douglas. In 1953, Pike had resigned from his company to become chairman of the Republican Party Finance Committee. He served as deputy assistant defense secretary in 1953, assistant defense secretary in 1954, and a special assistant to President Dwight Eisenhower from 1956 to 1958.[56]

expansion of the Stanford Industrial Park. He also had to contend with frosty town-gown relations and changing attitudes about development of Stanford lands, as well as the growing importance of university relations with government.

In 1959, four men who would later become board presidents joined the board: Morris Doyle, Richard Guggenhime, W. Parmer Fuller III, and Thomas P. Pike.

In a quick turnaround, board newcomer Tom Pike, '31, a former student body president, was chosen board president only a year later, in June 1960, when his Alpha Delta Phi fraternity brother David Packard stepped down. (Packard remained on the board until 1969, when he resigned to join the Nixon administration.) Pike, founder of the large California oil drilling contracting firm that bore his name, was a cousin of Parmer Fuller.[53] Packard invited Pike to become a trustee just one year after he had added Pike to the Hewlett-Packard board.[54]

The responsibilities and time commitment of

Following Nixon's defeat in 1960, Pike had the unusual duty of stopping rumors that Nixon was to be appointed president of Stanford, with Wally Sterling allegedly kicked aside by the trustees to a ceremonial position. Pike, as board president, quickly and vigorously denied the rumors and confirmed the board's full confidence and trust in President Sterling, a denial made all the more believable given his relationship with Nixon.[57]

Pike became a magnet for letters trustees often received from concerned alumni and others—most often fellow conservative Republicans—complaining that the university and its faculty were too liberal. In October 1961, in the midst of Stanford's PACE fundraising campaign, Pike heard from former trustee Joel (Tex) Middleton:

> You know the feeling of uneasiness that I have had the last few years about the growth of socialism on our Campus. Marcia and I had dinner with Ken Cuthbertson recently and our conversation with him that evening was anything but reassur-

Thomas Pike, a former student body president and fraternity brother of David Packard, was elected board president just as the university geared up for its groundbreaking PACE fundraising campaign.
STANFORD NEWS SERVICE

ing. We did not have any great arguments but it was factual statements by Ken which caused Marcia (who hates all controversial questions) to say after he left, "Is there any real reason why we should continue our financial support to Stanford?" A luncheon with Wally, which you had attended, did nothing to ease my mind.[58]

Presumably Pike forwarded the letter to Sterling, but there is no record of a written reply by Pike or the President's Office. A phone call or personal meeting was more often the strategy for responding to such an influential letter writer.

Pike also helped deal with increasingly vitriolic letters from Ralph (Big Jim) Reynolds, who originally had been a great supporter of Sterling. After hearing Sterling at a Stanford Associates event soon after he became president, Reynolds wrote effusively, "I would like to have you know that I want to play on your team."[59] Although primarily interested in athletics, especially in improving Stanford football, Reynolds was virulent in

Trustees Packard and Pike, seen here with Herbert Hoover, were active in Republican Party affairs and served on the Hoover Institution Board of Overseers. Pike was California chairman of Richard Nixon's 1960 presidential campaign while serving as president of Stanford's Board of Trustees. STANFORD NEWS SERVICE

his hatred of communism and socialism, and sent Sterling many letters expressing his views. He had been incensed when, in 1949, some 245 Stanford faculty members publicized their support for UC faculty who refused to take a recently revised state-mandated loyalty oath. From then on, Reynolds bombarded the President's Office and selected trustees with letters about individuals he was convinced were spreading communist beliefs on campus.[60]

In October 1961, Pike responded diplomatically to one such letter from Reynolds, echoing a position taken by Sterling at his first presidential press conference back in 1949:

> It is my earnest conviction that Stanford students should be taught *objectively* what Communism and Socialism really are, because they can't successfully combat something they don't thoroughly understand. I like the old Chinese proverb that says: "It is far better to light one candle than curse the darkness." It would help me immeasurably in achieving what you and I both want for Stanford if your suggestions and criticism could be positive and constructive, i.e., candle lighters instead of "darkness cursers."[61]

Although Pike often softened blows from Republican critics, he did not develop the same kind of effective working relationship with the President's Office typified by earlier board presidents Edwards, Dinkelspiel, and Packard, or by Pike's successors, Morris Doyle, Dick Guggenhime, and Parmer Fuller III. As the Sterling administration reorganized and planned for a major fundraising campaign, Fred Glover expressed concern that Pike seemed to have difficulty understanding the board's role as a policy-making body rather than one of administration. "Wally is aware of the danger," Glover added, "and we will be on the watch for it; I am sure Wally will not be silent if the problem becomes of any real concern."[62]

Sterling kept his concerns out of the public

eye, but he kept his friends among the trustees posted. "As soon as occasion permits, I think it might be well if I put my feet on the desk alongside yours and had a chat with you about the current President of the Board of Trustees here," Sterling wrote confidant and trustee Lawrence Kimpton, former dean of students at Stanford and former chancellor of University of Chicago, in 1961. Pike, who later admitted to approaching hero worship of Herbert Hoover, took a narrowly partisan approach to Hoover Institution matters relating to the university *(see Chapter 13)*. His "passion to broadcast a credo is, I think, symptomatic of something which may create a number of awkward circumstances," Sterling alerted Kimpton. "It wouldn't surprise me if there was discussion about this sort of thing one day at the Board of Trustees. I certainly am not going to prompt or initiate such discussions, but some Trustee tempers are a bit edgy at the moment so that discussion may result from Trustee initiative."[63]

Nevertheless, Pike and Sterling's relationship remained cordial and productive. The two shared a strong interest in music, and teamed up at the piano for songfests of old favorites. Pike later described Sterling as charismatic, a "master fundraiser, administrator, and raconteur par excellence" who he had been delighted to work with during his two years as board president. Pike remained on the board until 1979.[64]

BOARD LEADERS DURING CAMPUS TURMOIL

Morris (Morrie) Doyle, '29, followed Tom Pike as president in 1962–64, during the heady days of the PACE Campaign and the dramatic improvements it would bring to the academic program. As a 6-foot-3 undergraduate from Bishop, California, he towered over teammates when he played football for Glenn (Pop) Warner at

Stanford. After receiving his Harvard law degree in 1932, he joined a prominent San Francisco law firm, where he became an expert in antitrust law and environmental protection. (In 1958, his name was added to the firm, McCutchen, Doyle, Brown & Enersen.)

Doyle, a member of the Board of Trustees from 1959 to 1979, also served on the boards of the Alumni Association, the Stanford Research Institute, and the Hoover Institution, as well as the Law School's Board of Visitors. He served as one of Tom Pike's vice presidents, along with Packard and Dick Guggenhime, 1960–62, and was co-chair of the PACE Campaign's San Francisco Bay Region when he was selected as trustee president. Doyle also had a long-standing association (1962–89) with the James Irvine Foundation, as it became the largest private grant-making foundation focused on California.[65]

"There are people who look perfectly the part that they are called upon in life to play," Richard Lyman said of Doyle. "Morrie looked the part and acted the part—stalwart, steady, sensible and wise. It was as if he was a classical figure in the middle of whatever turmoil was going on."[66]

Ken Cuthbertson appreciated Doyle's broad perspective, particularly in terms of fundraising. Doyle long served as chair of the Stanford Associates Special Gifts, Trusts and Bequests committee, that quiet part of fundraising that produces the most results in the long run, and then he presided over the Board of Trustees at the peak of the PACE Campaign. His steady hand "not only kept consensus on the board but reassured and enthused the alumni and friends of the university," Cuthbertson noted, adding:

> To keep up with the rapid development of the university, the character of the board had to be changed from a custodial style to one of active participation, particularly in fundraising, but also in interpreting the new challenges in higher

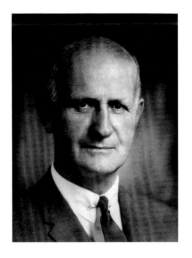

Morris (Morrie) Doyle took over as board president in 1962 during the heady days of the PACE Campaign. Doyle remained an influential advisor through the 1960s and 1970s. STANFORD UNIVERSITY ARCHIVES

education. Morrie's leadership in the sensitive nomination process brought about such changes and produced an effective and appropriately diverse board able to face successfully Stanford's opportunities.[67]

Doyle died in 1997, just two weeks after receiving Stanford's Degree of Uncommon Man.

In 1956, the *Stanford Daily* wrote admiringly about the trustees who, despite being 23 of the most successful men and women in the country, willingly gave their time, without compensation, to Stanford. Ten years later student leaders deemed the board to be "falling short." In their view, the trustees were too old (average age 58), too inbred (21 of 22 were Stanford alumni), too local (18 were from California), too distant (none lived on campus), and too many from the same profession (business and law).[68]

Into this setting, Doyle was succeeded by his Harvard Law School roommate, Richard E. Guggenhime, '29, and Harvard law LL.B., '32. Guggenhime would serve on the board from 1958 to 1978. Guggenhime, a San Francisco native, had returned to the City to practice law, joining the firm of Heller, Ehrman, White and McAuliffe in 1939. (He led the firm from 1959 to 1973.) He also served as president of the Rosenberg Foundation, and was active with the

Stanford Associates, as well as a chair of major gifts efforts of the PACE Campaign.

Guggenhime's term as president, 1964–67, spanned some of Sterling's most difficult years. Student activism, initially urging reform of social regulations and student judicial procedures, expanded to antiwar protests and campus disruptions. At the same time, the university increasingly was criticized by alumni and the public for taking too lenient an approach to student discipline.

Even when student leaders attacked the integrity and purpose of the board itself, Guggenhime earned grudging respect for his frankness. "The Board of Trustees of a university serves as a bridge between the university community and the university constituency," he emphasized in a 1966 *Stanford*

Sterling shows a PACE fundraising progress chart to Theodore S. Petersen, PACE Campaign chair, and Morrie Doyle, board president. As of September 1963, the campaign had reached $90 million of its $100 million goal.   STANFORD NEWS SERVICE

Daily interview. "It interprets the university to the outside, and also it provides within the university itself an independent view of the community by someone who is outside of the faculty

Trustee President Richard Guggenhime (far right) and fellow trustees (from left) Judge Homer Spence, George Ditz (emeritus), and W. Parmer Fuller III at a barbeque, September 23, 1966, to celebrate the recent completion of the Stanford Linear Accelerator Center. (SLAC would be dedicated a year later.) Fuller succeeded Guggenhime as board president in 1967. Recently retired Provost Fred Terman can be seen behind Spence and Ditz.

STANFORD NEWS SERVICE

The Board of Trustees in 1967, several months after Sterling announced his retirement. From left: Robert Minge Brown, Richard Guggenhime, Caroline Moore Charles, Lawrence Kimpton, David Packard, William (Lefty) Rogers, Edmund Littlefield, Homer Spence (emeritus), board President W. Parmer Fuller III, President Sterling, Charles Ducommun, William Hewlett, Roger Lewis, Morris Doyle, Lilian Force Fletcher Nichols, James Crafts, and Thomas Pike. (Absent: Ben Duniway, Fred Merrill, Richard McCurdy, Arthur Stewart, Gardiner Symonds, and Dean Watkins.)   STANFORD NEWS SERVICE

but who still understands higher education." Nor did he hesitate to challenge student tactics to instruct the administration. "We need to have everybody—students, administration, faculty, and trustees—make an effort to understand the others' position," he told the *Daily*, adding that he thought the trustees were trying harder than the students to do so.[69]

W. Parmer Fuller III, '34, great-grandson of the founder of the Fuller Paint Company, took over from Guggenhime shortly after Wally Sterling announced, early in 1967, his intention to retire the following year. Fuller's father, W. Parmer Fuller Jr., had been Tresidder's board president. Like Guggenhime, Fuller III had been

a Stanford Associates director. He had chaired the university's Medical School fundraising drive, and later co-chaired the PACE Campaign's San Francisco Bay Region.

Fuller oversaw the search for Sterling's successor, and, after Kenneth Pitzer's brief tenure and resignation, the transition to Richard Lyman as Stanford's seventh president.

Fred Glover, musing on his years working with trustees Doyle, Guggenhime, and Fuller III during difficult times, noted that he had worried that the university was going to fall apart when they retired. "That didn't happen, and it doesn't happen, but we were blessed with some wonderful trustees at this time."[70]

THE PRESIDENT AND THE CHIEF

STERLING AND HERBERT HOOVER

Throughout Wallace Sterling's tenure, as he forged important alliances among Stanford's Board of Trustees, one relationship remained special: his connection with the university's most influential alumnus, former U.S. President Herbert Hoover.

Elected to the board in 1912, Hoover was the only trustee ever appointed to five 10-year terms. (Other trustees stepped down to make way for younger members but retained influential emeritus status. Only founding trustee Timothy Hopkins, a life member, served longer.) During the 1920s and '30s, Hoover played a leading role in stabilizing the university's finances, maintaining its momentum, and encouraging its growth. By the time of Sterling's return to Stanford, in 1949, Hoover Tower, housing the Hoover Institution on War, Revolution and Peace, was the most imposing landmark on campus. Herbert Hoover had also been instrumental in construction of the

university's first student union and in establishing both the Graduate School of Business and the Food Research Institute.[1]

Hoover, '95, and his wife, Lou Henry Hoover, '98, had put their roots down on campus. In 1919, while living on Dolores Street, Mrs. Hoover began overseeing construction of their new home at 623 Mirada, near the top of San Juan Hill, with views to the Quadrangle, the bay, and the foothills. Although they had lived in many places during Hoover's international mining, public service, and political careers, this house, completed in 1920, was their favorite. In 1945, the year following Mrs. Hoover's death, Herbert Hoover gave the house to the university in her memory for use as the official residence of the university president *(see Chapter 17)*.

When Wally and Ann Sterling first arrived at Stanford, in December 1930, Herbert Hoover was president of the United States. Sterling had been attracted to Stanford's graduate history program by the research collections of the Hoover War Library. His advisor, the university's esteemed professor of modern European history, Ralph Lutz, served as the Hoover War Library's chairman and library director. As the Depression

< President Wallace Sterling and former U.S. President and Stanford trustee Herbert Hoover enjoyed the campus celebration of Hoover's 75th birthday, in August 1949. Their congenial relationship was periodically tested by Hoover's increasing preoccupation with the independence of the Hoover Institution.   STANFORD UNIVERSITY ARCHIVES

deepened, Sterling was fortunate to land a job there as a research assistant, working closely with another popular professor, Harold H. Fisher, Lutz's right-hand man and assistant director.

The strong connection between Sterling and the Hoover Library continued through the 1940s. Sterling, now a scholar of modern European history and influential faculty leader at Caltech, was nearly enticed to return in 1946 to take over as the Institution's director. Although he did not take the position, Sterling remained in close touch with Lutz and Fisher. He also became acquainted with a number of Herbert Hoover's staunch friends on Caltech's Board of Trustees and faculty. Several also were on the board of the Huntington Library and Art Gallery and were active in Southern California philanthropic circles.

By 1949, Hoover's success story as engineer, humanitarian, statesman, and U.S. president no longer singularly dominated Stanford's evolving self-image, but he remained a leading voice among alumni, and particularly among trustees, until his death, at 90, in 1964. "The Sterling-Hoover relationship was warm, deep, respectful and, at times in Hoover's last years, difficult," recalled former presidential assistant Don Carlson.[2]

Looking back at his university presidency in 1974, 10 years after Hoover's death, Sterling spoke fondly of Hoover, stating that getting to know him well was one of the rewards of his office. Sterling respected this talented but shy man, so unlike the buoyant young university president, and admired his accomplishments, his personal values, and his wit. Hoover was "a great *raconteur*, full of stories out of his own experience, frequently with himself as the butt of the joke," recalled Sterling. He believed that Hoover's strong will had been indispensable in his achieving so much as a humanitarian and administrator. Sterling and his staff also had no illusions about Hoover's determination.[3]

Ralph Lutz, esteemed professor of modern European history, was Sterling's History Department advisor in the 1930s. Lutz served as Hoover War Library chairman and director from 1922 to 1943.   STANFORD NEWS SERVICE

When Hoover set his mind to accomplish something, Sterling later recalled, "those who stood in his way were in for a contest."[4]

Differences between the university president and the former U.S. president were accentuated during the last years of Hoover's life, particularly by Hoover's friends, who felt Sterling was disloyal whenever he resisted greater administrative independence for the Hoover Institution or defended the academic freedom of his faculty. At the same time, Sterling was criticized by influential members of the faculty, and by some of his senior staff, for not confronting the aging and increasingly disengaged trustee who disparaged Stanford's "fuzzy headed academics" and campus "left-wingers." Ultimately, Sterling walked his own middle path, hoping gradualism and conflict mediation would prevail. Stanford's president had much to do on behalf of the university, on and off campus, as his administration, not Herbert Hoover, became the driver of Stanford's growth and change.

THE QUINTESSENTIAL STANFORD MAN

Herbert Hoover, born in 1874 of Quaker parents in West Branch, Iowa, had a solid background in hard work and hard-scrabble living by the time he enrolled at newly opened Stanford University as a member of the Pioneer Class of 1895 (he would graduate with a degree in geology). Hoover's Stanford experiences were formative and his friendships lifelong, including that with Lou Henry, whom he married in 1899.[5] Among his closest friends was fellow Encina man, and future Stanford president, Ray Lyman Wilbur, '96.[6]

Seemingly inexhaustible, Hoover worked his way through school at a variety of jobs. He was equally energetic and resourceful after graduating. Hoover was the first Stanford alumnus to make what Wilbur called "really big money" as a mine manager, investor, speculator, and organizer of men. Dubbed the "doctor of sick mines" for his work in Australia, China, Burma, and later Russia, Hoover played an important role in early 20th-century development of the international mining industry.[7]

By August 1914, Hoover had set up mining consultancy offices in San Francisco, London, New York City, St. Petersburg, Paris, and Mandalay. Living in London at the outbreak of the Great War, Hoover quickly organized an effort with 500 volunteers to help some 120,000 Americans there return home, distributing food, clothing, steamship tickets, and cash.

Within months, a serious food shortage in occupied Belgium threatened the population with starvation. Hoover organized the Commission for Relief in Belgium (CRB), a nongov-

ernmental volunteer organization supported by private donations and government grants. The CRB obtained, imported, and guarded food supplies, which were distributed by the Belgian Comité National de Secours et d'Alimentation. By 1918, the CRB had distributed more than two million tons of food to nine million war victims, having successfully negotiated permission to distribute with both the occupying Germans and with British officials worried that a relief effort would conflict with their war effort.[8]

At the end of the war, Hoover headed the American Relief Administration (ARA), which organized shipments of food for millions in

Herbert Hoover, seen here with his dog King Tut (a Belgian shepherd) during the 1928 presidential campaign, was then Stanford's most conspicuous alumnus. By the late 1950s, his influence was waning among young alumni and faculty drawn from across the country. (This photograph, widely circulated at the time, was credited with helping Hoover win the election.) HERBERT E. FRENCH / LIBRARY OF CONGRESS

Central Europe. The ARA also helped feed many in Germany, and in famine-stricken areas of Russia in 1921–23. Many Stanford friends helped with both the CRB and ARA efforts.[9]

Throughout his world travels, Hoover had retained a strong interest in the university's welfare. While working as a young mining engineer in Western Australia, he wrote a friend that "Stanford is the best place in the world." Within a few years of graduating, he was "looking out for friends," recalled Wilbur, channeling funds through a classmate who was told to give them where they would do the most good, often anonymously paying the incidental fees and other educational expenses of students he knew.[10]

In 1912, the 37-year-old Hoover was the first addition to the board selected by fellow trustees rather than founders Leland and Jane Stanford and was the board's second alumnus. He was soon instrumental in negotiating the change in presidential leadership from David Starr Jordan, who in 1913 was given the new and largely ceremonial post of chancellor, to that of John Casper Branner, Jordan's 63-year-old vice president and Hoover's former geology advisor, while the board searched for a successor. Jordan was delighted with Hoover's impact. "Almost every reform we have dreamed of," he wrote Branner, "has slipped through as if oiled." The board's president told Jordan that Hoover had more ideas in 10 days than the board had had in 10 years.[11]

Hoover then urged the selection, in late 1915, of Ray Lyman Wilbur as Stanford's third president, to take office January 1, 1916. Wilbur had been appointed executive head of the medical department in 1911, and two years later was named dean. Hoover's views on Stanford's management were made clear in his campaign on Wilbur's behalf. He stressed the importance of getting a Western man, preferably one who had experienced what he viewed as Stanford's unique ideals, and who

Lou Henry, '98, the first woman to earn a geology degree at Stanford, married her classmate Herbert Hoover, '95, and worked with him on mining projects in China and, during the Great War, with the Belgian Relief Commission. She preferred her campus home to Washington, D.C., and New York. This photograph was given "To Mrs. Wallace Sterling, With the Kind Regards of Herbert Hoover." STANFORD UNIVERSITY ARCHIVES

preeminently would be an administrator, not an orator or Ivy League–trained academic.[12]

Herbert and Lou Henry Hoover were catalysts for targeted fundraising for several campus projects. They were determined to create a meeting place where the rapidly expanding student body could gather with faculty, alumni, and trustees on common ground. They prodded friends and alumni to join them in contributing to construction of the original Stanford Union, exclusively for men. (To build an accompanying Women's Clubhouse, the undergraduate Women's Club raised funds with the help of female faculty, faculty wives, and alumnae. The buildings were completed in 1915.) Hoover also was behind creation of the Food Research Institute in 1921 and the Graduate School of Business in 1925.[13]

Hoover also helped establish the Stanford Research Institute, first conceived by his friend, chemistry Professor Robert E. Swain, '99, in 1925, and finally implemented under President Donald Tresidder, in 1946. While Swain envisioned an interdisciplinary academic-based research institute, Hoover, by that time a two-term U.S. secretary of commerce (1920–28), discouraged "pure" research dominated by faculty interests in favor of an industry-driven agenda.[14]

Hoover backed Wilbur's attempt to mobilize the university's first major fundraising campaign in 1922, the First Million for Stanford, by composing a personal message to alumni as part of the appeal. He later accepted a similar role for President Sterling in the 1956 campaign to fund the new Stanford Medical Center, and with Stanford's PACE Campaign, in 1961. While Wilbur (like Sterling) adeptly leveraged foundation funding, Hoover preferred to focus on successful business associates rather than on soliciting from alumni, thinking they did not have the financial capacity to make significant contributions. (He did not participate in fundraising efforts of the Stanford Associates, established by influential alumni during the Depression.)

During his first 30 years as a Stanford trustee, Hoover was responsible for significant improvements in university financial procedures, trustee investment policies, and the organization and accountability of board committees. He pressed trustees to pull Stanford's endowment away from low-yield railroad bonds to a diversified portfolio, in 1935 personally shepherding this change through a legally required Superior Court petition and court decision.

Hoover also was interested in raising faculty salaries, notoriously low since Stanford's financially difficult years of the 1890s. In 1913, after three months of study, he concluded that low salaries made it difficult for the university to hire or retain preeminent senior faculty, while current faculty, in general, were finding it hard to keep up with the rising cost of living. "Money is the basis of reputation," David Starr Jordan had written to him in 1912. "Strong men make the institution." Hoover agreed that the university must grow at the top, and over the ensuing decades encouraged a "steeples of excellence" strategy later credited to Provost Fred Terman. Hoover was equally concerned about cutting out "dead wood," and was disappointed to find faculty members he considered lazy or incompetent protected by the "sacred garment of perpetual tenure." In 1914, after a discussion with friend and history Professor E. D. Adams, he reluctantly agreed that tenure was necessary to recruit outstanding professors in this generally underpaid profession. His alternative was to oppose automatic salary increases, hoping that holding some salaries low would encourage the "dead wood" to go elsewhere.[15]

One of Hoover's income-raising strategies changed Stanford forever: tuition. Instituted by the trustees in January 1920 at his suggestion, it became an important new source of funds for faculty support.

STANFORD IN WASHINGTON
SUPPORTING A FAVORITE SON

In 1928, Stanford University's president and Board of Trustees deliberately and enthusiastically set aside the university's nonpartisan policy on behalf of Hoover's campaign for the U.S. presidency. It was Wilbur's idea that Hoover emphasize his modernity that August by delivering a major policy speech while accepting the Republican nomination before an audience of some 70,000 spectators at Stanford Stadium, as well as millions of listeners through a trendsetting, live national radio broadcast.[16] The Stanford Alumni Association board formally endorsed

In August 1928, the Hoovers were driven into Stanford Stadium, where Mr. Hoover accepted the Republican Party nomination with a major policy address broadcast on national radio. The Alumni Association, formally endorsing Hoover, hosted Hoover booster clubs and many faculty and administrators, including President Ray Lyman Wilbur, campaigned for his election. STANFORD UNIVERSITY ARCHIVES

When the Hoover entourage returned home on November 5, 1928, the day before the election, thousands greeted them at the Palo Alto train station and lined Palm Drive. As demonstrated by this crowd at the Quad, the Stanford community had set aside all pretense of nonpartisanship to support the candidacy of its most famous alumnus. STANFORD NEWS SERVICE

Hoover for the U.S. presidency, and encouraged formation of the California Committee of Stanford-for-Hoover. Committee members included university trustee Leland Cutler, '06, chair, and future trustees W. Parmer Fuller Jr., '10, and George Ditz, '11, men who remained influential well into Wallace Sterling's presidency. Wilbur was the keynote speaker at the organizational meeting of Hoover's California delegates to the Republican convention, and throughout the fall quarter he actively campaigned for his friend.

After an energetic national campaign, Hoover was welcomed back home at a student rally. "I would rather have a greeting from Stanford men and women," he told them, "than any other group." After voting at their election precinct on campus on November 6, the Hoovers were at their house on San Juan Hill when he learned he had been elected president. A great rally of students, campus residents, and Palo Alto townspeople surrounded the house, and the "Stanford Hymn" was heard around the world on broadcast radio.[17]

At the outset of his administration, President Hoover called on many Stanford colleagues for help. None was more important than his best friend, Ray Lyman Wilbur, whom he tapped to be his secretary of the interior. Management of the university slowed considerably during acting President Robert Swain's four years as caretaker, since Wilbur, dubbed Stanford's "president by mail," remained directly involved in routine university affairs. More than once, the trustees asked Hoover to release Wilbur, but Hoover, facing severe public scrutiny as the Depression deepened, refused to let his friend return to Stanford. The board acquiesced but eventually suggested that Wilbur take unpaid leave.[18]

Even the University of California considered successful presidential candidate Hoover to be California's "favorite son." During Big Game at Berkeley's Memorial Stadium, November 25, 1928, the Cal rooting section's card stunt featured Hoover's image, complete with stiff collar, for the entertainment of a packed crowd. (The thrilling game ended, appropriately, in a 13–13 tie.)   STANFORD UNIVERSITY ARCHIVES

Four years later, in January 1933, after his defeat by Franklin D. Roosevelt, the Hoovers returned to live in their San Juan Hill residence. They were home among friends, but the university also was a welcome respite from the "smear campaign" by the New Dealers. Even after he was out of the public limelight for many years, Hoover faced "a constant campaign of misrepresentation," said Wilbur.[19]

First called the Chief by miners and CRB volunteers, Herbert Hoover was still the Chief to some fellow trustees, administrators, and many alumni. "I think that no man ever inspired more intense loyalty or a finer sense of team work among his co-workers than has Herbert Hoover," wrote Wilbur in his memoirs. "No man ever attracted greater groups of devoted volunteers in times of emergency, even though he could not offer them salaries. He simply offered them the opportunity to serve. . . . To us he will always be

Ray Lyman Wilbur and Herbert Hoover shared a deep love of the outdoors, especially fishing. Hoover often joined a small group of Stanford friends at their remote and rugged Wooley Camp, deep in California's Siskiyou Mountains. Seen here, in 1934, from left: Palo Alto businessman Fred H. Smith; 20-year-old Ray Wilbur Jr. (behind his father); Wilbur; Hoover; Dr. Tom Williams (in back); and University Registrar J. Pearce Mitchell. STANFORD NEWS SERVICE

'The Chief.'" Stanford was a safe-haven where Hoover's opinions were rarely openly challenged.[20]

With Ray Lyman Wilbur's impending retirement as university president, in 1941, the Board of Trustees again tackled the difficulties of a wartime presidential search. Hoover was instrumental in selection of the board's own recently elected president, Donald B. Tresidder, '19, M.D. '27, as Stanford's fourth president, in 1943. Hoover admired Tresidder's business sense and appreciated his lack of pretense about academic credentials. Tresidder, like Hoover, also was uncomfortable with faculty politics and academic expectations, and later in his presidency endured a smear campaign—a personal attack by a handful of faculty critics who instigated an anonymous postcard protest drive.[21]

Following Tresidder's sudden death, in 1948, Stanford's trustees considered it important to let Hoover, a member of the presidential search committee, vet the university's next president. Hoover's insistence that the candidate be interrogated on his political views, particularly his opinion of the New Deal and of President Franklin D. Roosevelt, was not openly questioned. Unlike acting university President Alvin Eurich—a known "New Dealer" who had Washington, D.C., experience as a naval attaché—Sterling, a Canadian citizen during the Depression, had no personal political history other than being a recently registered Republican when naturalized as a citizen, in 1947. He was on record, however, in interviews and as a CBS news commentator, as criticizing aspects of the New Deal and FDR's personal political style. The Chief became personally invested in Wallace Sterling's selection later that year.[22]

STANFORD'S FIRST CITIZEN AND STANFORD'S NEW PRESIDENT

In July 1949, within months of Sterling settling into his new office, Hoover visited to consult with him and Harold Fisher, now chairman of the Hoover Institution and director of its Library. Sterling then joined Hoover at the Bohemian Grove encampment. While Sterling later liked to speak of first meeting Hoover at the Grove's summer encampment, he already had met and conferred with the Chief in New York the previous January, four months before taking office.[23]

Like Ray Lyman Wilbur and University of California President Robert Sproul, Sterling had been elected a member of the Bohemian Club. At the Grove, Sterling joined the Cave Man camp, which included many corporate and governmental leaders—including Hoover—as well as the leaders of California's major universities. In the relaxed environs of the redwoods, Sterling later said of Hoover, "it was a great experience for us to know him in private and off-stage."[24]

Sterling's inaugural year as president also saw Stanford's gala celebration of Herbert Hoover's 75th birthday and the zenith of his campus-wide popularity. In August 1949, Hoover delivered a major address in Frost Amphitheater, part of birthday celebrations organized by Fisher and the Hoover Institution staff.[25]

That day, August 10, 1949, was filled with many honors. With Sterling as master of ceremonies, Hoover (then the only living ex-U.S. president) was presented with a joint resolution of birthday greetings from the U.S. House and Senate. The day before, Governor Earl Warren, a guest at the day's events, had sent birthday greetings on behalf of the state of California. A Birthday Fund, made up of private gifts to support the Hoover Institution and Library, also was announced.

The *Stanford Daily* was filled with photographs, interviews, and anecdotes about Hoover. A banner stating "Hoover Slept Here" was hung from Encina Hall. As Stanford's "most honored graduate," Hoover was elected a "permanent member of the student body" by ASSU's Executive Committee and was named Stanford's "first citizen." The City of Palo Alto granted Hoover honorary lifetime city citizenship and set the day aside as Hoover Day to acknowledge his humanitarian efforts and bipartisan service to the country.[26]

In his overtly political address, "Think of the Next Generation," Hoover decried federal government spending as "collectivist." Speaking to an audience of more than 12,000 in the shadow of Hoover Tower, as well as to a national radio audience, he argued that the "confiscation of savings" by government through taxation lowered the nation's standard of living, and exposed independent colleges like Stanford and

Hoover, Sterling, and other members of the Bohemian Club enjoyed an annual July get-together at its private wooded campground, the Grove, on the Russian River in Sonoma County. As a prominent leader of one of California's major universities, Sterling was elected to the all-male club; Chancellor Ray Lyman Wilbur was instrumental in having Sterling join him and Hoover in the Cave Man camp.
STANFORD UNIVERSITY ARCHIVES

Sterling hosted Stanford's celebration of Hoover's 75th birthday, August 10, 1949, introducing him to an overflow crowd at Laurence Frost Amphitheater. In a nationally broadcast speech, Hoover decried federal taxation as "collectivist," and warned that private universities were in danger of becoming too dependent on government support. Hoover Tower and the fly loft of Memorial Auditorium can be seen in the distance.

STANFORD NEWS SERVICE

other privately supported institutions to the risk of becoming dependent on the state. He accused "fuzzy minded people" of fostering "the foolish notion that a collectivist economy can at the same time preserve personal liberty and constitutional government," and called for a dramatic reduction in government costs.[27]

While some complained that Hoover's remarks (and a subsequent university convocation speech by Philippine President Elpidio Quirino, a staunch Chiang Kai-shek ally, who appeared to use his speech as part of his re-election campaign) violated the university's regulations against political partisanship, there was little fuss. The *Daily* noted the complaints but urged students to take better advantage of the full range of speakers now appearing on campus to "find out what's going on in the outside world," pointing out, presumably as alternatives, recent visits by United Nations representatives Dr. Ralph Bunche and Madame Vijaya Lakshmi Nehru Pandit.[28]

AN AGING HOOVER AND THE POSTWAR UNIVERSITY

Sterling's presidential files contain many "Dear Wally" letters from Hoover. "I always knew where I stood with Hoover by the signature on his letters," Sterling recalled years later. "If things were going well, the letter was signed 'Herbert.' If they were just sort of in balance, it was signed 'HH.' And if they weren't going well, it was 'Herbert Hoover.' "[29]

Hoover, the only trustee at the time not residing on the West Coast, continued to visit the campus each summer, while his health permitted, usually staying with the Sterling family at the Lou Henry Hoover house. (Since World War II, a suite at the Waldorf Astoria Towers, New York City, served as his permanent residence.) A trip to the annual Bohemian Grove encampment would follow. Each year, the Board of Trustees moved its July meeting to campus from its San Francisco headquarters to accommodate him, and each year he provided them with a "state of the union" message, briefing the board on what was happening in Washington, D.C.[30]

Hoover remained publicly supportive of Sterling's drive to improve Stanford's academic program, particularly the Medical School and other professional schools, and applauded the university's growing prestige in American higher education. Although he had become distant from routine trustee undertakings, notably the board's increasingly activist roles in land development, fundraising, and planning and expansion of the academic program, he continued to offer advice and comment.

In 1956, the 81-year-old Hoover took the stage at a Stanford press conference as honorary chairman of the Medical Center fundraising campaign, announcing the start of the largest effort of its kind undertaken in the Western United States. Long interested in public health issues, Hoover strongly believed medical advances relied on university research, and supported Sterling's conclusion that the Stanford Medical School needed to be revitalized and moved from San Francisco to the main campus.

Sterling's assistant Fred Glover told a revealing anecdote about Hoover's forcefulness. Pete Allen, Stanford's news director, had prepared a detailed three-page news release for the reporters waiting at the trustees' headquarters for the formal announcement of the controversial move. Glover and Allen, both experienced newspaper editors, felt strongly that it was in Stanford's best interest to provide as much accurate information as soon as possible. During the board's discussion that day, Hoover asked to see Allen's press release, took out his pen, and cut the lengthy text down to one page. "Pete and I were just horrified," recalled Glover, "because we knew that you had to say some of these things."

A group of most of the 1954 Board of Trustees, including a rare appearance by Herbert Hoover, at the front door of the Lou Henry Hoover House, then President Sterling's residence. The board was significantly expanded that year to make up for absentees and a more complex workload. Front row (left to right): Charles Blyth, Paul Edwards (emeritus), Ruth Fesler Lipman, Caroline Moore Charles, board President Lloyd Dinkelspiel, Herbert Hoover, May Chandler Goodan, W. Parmer Fuller Jr., and Ira Lillick. Back row: Neil Petree, Ernest Arbuckle, Donald Russell, Leland Cutler, John Cushing, Homer Spence, James Black, Arthur Stewart, and George Ditz. (Absent: George Morell, Herman Phleger, James Crafts, Tex Middleton, and David Packard.)   STANFORD NEWS SERVICE

In a rare act of insubordination, Glover began to argue with Hoover in front of the trustees. "I just couldn't stand it anymore," he later recalled. Trustee President Lloyd Dinkelspiel quickly ended the interaction, saying, "Fred, let's talk about it later." After the meeting, Hoover made the formal announcement while Glover distributed the abridged press release as instructed. Dinkelspiel then verbally filled in the deleted information to the reporters. Subsequent news coverage was detailed, lengthy, and accurate. Glover admired the way Dinkelspiel accomplished the administration's goal without upsetting Hoover. "Lloyd said to me, 'Fred, you can never win an argument against a former president of the United States.'"[31]

Like many older alumni, Hoover found changes to the physical campus disconcerting. When Edward Durell Stone's architectural plans for the medical center were unveiled, Hoover protested to fellow trustees that its modernistic architecture was "a complete departure from the Romanesque." He was not against construction on campus but continued to point out "sorry departures" such as the new Post Office and Bookstore, with their modernist, concrete-heavy design, that would be typical of many buildings going up across campus in the late 1950s and 1960s.[32]

Vigorously urging his colleagues to maintain a uniform architectural design, and discounting trustee concerns about building costs, he wrote Dinkelspiel in 1957, "I only want a record that

I did not approve of this grave departure from the spiritual and historical background. There are others among the trustees who have agreed with me." Stanford, he argued, was among the few American universities having "a distinctive and consistent architecture," one appropriate to California and an essential part of its inheritance from Senator and Mrs. Stanford. (No reference was made to 1941 campus criticisms of the new 285-foot-tall Hoover Tower as a purposeless departure from the Quad's traditional architecture.)[33]

While the Chief strongly supported President Sterling's goal to attract accomplished faculty through improved salaries, research facilities, and infrastructure, his long-standing distrust of academics in general grew increasingly bitter as close friends like Ray Lyman Wilbur, Robert Swain, and Ralph Lutz died or stepped away from academic work. Faculty members of the 1920s and 1930s were being replaced by individuals who had not attended Stanford; many were unaware of, or unimpressed by, the pre-war Stanford-Hoover relationship. During the 1950s, this changing demographic scene would be complicated by the Cold War, with its shadow of Congressional anti-communist probes and by vocal anti-communist, anti-academic syndicated columnists.[34]

The Board of Trustees, too, was changing. In 1954, it was expanded from 15 to 23. This made it easier to deal with the much-increased workload, as well as to gain a quorum. A number of influential newer board members were closer to the charismatic university president than to Stanford's "first citizen." Board presidents Paul Edwards, Lloyd Dinkelspiel, and Morris Doyle developed especially close friendships with Sterling and were adept at mediating on his behalf. Much of the board's work now took place in standing and special committees as Sterling drew the trustees into major efforts to develop and reorganize the university. After 1957, Hoover's Stanford activities would take place largely from a distance and within the realm of a new special advisory committee on the Hoover Institution.

Trustee Hoover regarded much of Stanford's post–Hoover Tower construction (1941) as deviations from the original Romanesque-inspired Quadrangle. Particularly upsetting, in his view, were modernist, concrete-heavy designs typical of many structures going up across campus in the 1950s and 1960s. This included the 1959 Medical Center and the 1960 Bookstore and Post Office (right, in distance).
STANFORD NEWS SERVICE

MR. HOOVER'S LIBRARY

Herbert Hoover's contributions to the university had been many, but he maintained a unique level of personal control over only one. By the mid-1950s, his heartfelt interest was housed in Hoover Tower. Officially a branch of the university, the Hoover Institution had long enjoyed a special status, backed by Hoover's unusual influence as a respected public figure, as well as the close friend of Stanford presidents and fellow trustees. Herbert Hoover took responsibility for much of its outside funding as its primary fundraiser, but the institution named for him continued to rely on the university for space and staffing. Hoover spent much of the last decade of his life urging its independence while fighting any decrease in university support.

Decades earlier, Hoover had resolved to undertake a systematic collection of contemporary documents about the causes and implications of the Great War, before they were lost to history. Much of the initial documentation emerged from the activities of the Commission for Relief in Belgium and the American Relief Association. Several Stanford faculty members, among them history professors E. D. Adams and Ralph Lutz, worked with Stanford alumni to gather records—archives, pamphlets, newspapers, posters, government documents, and other ephemeral materials—to document the war, as well as the revolutions and upheavals that followed. With encouragement from President Wilbur, the ever-growing Hoover collection was established at Stanford in 1919 as a special archival collection, directed by Adams. It was housed in Stanford's new Main Library building, just off the Quadrangle, with a $50,000 contribution from Hoover and funds remaining in the CRB Trust. In 1922, Hoover's collection was renamed the Hoover War Library.[35]

In 1924, President Wilbur presented to the Board of Trustees an organization plan for the Hoover War Library. The plan provided for appointment of a 10-member Hoover Library Board of Directors, to be appointed annually by the university president, and to include the president, university librarian, and representatives of several academic departments. The directors were required to submit an annual budget for Wilbur's approval, but were free to determine their other functions as they chose.[36]

Initially, the university librarian appointed staff for this special collection, as with all of the library's special collections, while President Wilbur retained ultimate control over the selection of its director, advisory board, and budget. Hoover, however, wanted the War Library's board to have veto power over the university librarian's staff appointments. Wilbur agreed, granting the university librarian merely the power to nominate staff, subject to the approval of the War Library's director, Ralph Lutz, who had succeeded Adams in 1922.

University Librarian George Clark, and especially his successor, Nathan Van Patten, grew frustrated by the growing strain on library space and funding, and attempted to monitor the Hoover directors' efforts to expand the collection, but to little effect. Lack of adequate outside funding, however, left the War Library largely dependent on the university for operating funds and space. By the time Wallace Sterling began his graduate studies in January 1931, the now widely respected Hoover War Library collections were overflowing into hallways and crannies of the University Library's first floor. In 1938, the ever-expanding collection was renamed the Hoover Library on War, Revolution and Peace.

At one point, Hoover contemplated, as a last resort, using the family's house on San Juan Hill for the War Library. Finally, funds from two foundations controlled by Hoover—the ARA and the Belgian American Educational Founda-

History Professors Ralph Lutz (left) and E.D. Adams with an early shipment of war-related documents they helped gather from across Europe for the new campus archive. These scholars played key roles in creating and building the Hoover War Library, with Adams as first director and Lutz succeeding him.   STANFORD NEWS SERVICE

tion—were used to support design and construction of the imposing 14-story Hoover Tower, dedicated in 1941.[37]

With the new building completed and the Hoover Library now beyond the control of the university librarian, Hoover pressed for the Hoover Library's director to report directly to the university president alone, rather than to a university committee that would include faculty. After Lutz had to step aside in 1943 because of health problems, Hoover also worried that his library's director and curatorial staff, especially if granted tenure or joint appointments, might be subject to faculty influence.[38]

The War Library's first directors were drawn from Stanford's History Department faculty and continued to teach and advise. Their loyalty to Hoover was unquestioned. E. D. Adams and Ralph Lutz had worked closely with Hoover in the early days of gathering the war library's col-

lections, and they remained strong Hoover supporters. Harold Fisher was also a familiar figure, personally selected by Hoover. While working on ARA food relief in Russia in 1922, Fisher searched out tsarist and Bolshevik documents for the War Library that became a foundation for the library's Russian and Soviet collections. In 1924, the Chief had asked the young scholar and ARA staff member to write a history of the ARA. Fisher quickly became a popular professor of Russian and Soviet history as well as Lutz's right-hand man at the library. In 1943, he succeeded Lutz as acting chairman and director of the Hoover Library, becoming director in 1946.

Fisher lost Hoover's confidence, however, with the 1946 publication of *America and Russia in the World Community,* in which he argued that American and Russian aims were not irreconcilable. Fisher also joined other academic figures that year in publicly criticizing the American

The 285-foot-high Hoover Tower was dedicated in June 1941, in conjunction with Stanford's golden anniversary. The Main Library (1919) is behind and Memorial Hall (1937) is at center, with the Quadrangle beyond, at right. STANFORD NEWS SERVICE

government's support for the Chinese nationalist government of Chiang Kai-shek and urging an international effort to terminate the Chinese civil war. Hoover and his friends were incensed to see Fisher among those blatantly stating this view in the *New York Times*, where Fisher was identified as Hoover Library director.[39]

Hoover proposed a new reorganization of the Hoover Library's Board of Directors, with a life membership for himself, his son Allan, a few close friends on the faculty, and several non-Stanford friends. Fisher, who had only reluctantly taken the directorship when Lutz retired, disagreed, arguing that the library benefited from an advisory board that included academics interested in the welfare and use of the collections. He also believed that the director, as a scholar, should function like the head of an academic department. Hoover responded to Fisher's opposition by prevailing on Edgar Rickard, a close friend and member of the current Hoover Board, to propose a gift of $30,000 for the library, but only if Stanford's Board of Trustees appointed the administrative (non-academic) board, as Hoover suggested, which "shall have an active part in determining the policy of the Library."[40]

Then-President Tresidder stepped in with a compromise, which the Board of Trustees approved in 1946. Changing the library's name to the Hoover Institution and Library on War, Revolution and Peace, they confirmed it to be "a separate division of the University," not merely a library. (The name was shortened to Hoover Institution on War, Revolution and Peace in 1957, and more recently, simply the Hoover Institution.) Also in 1946, an advisory, not solely administrative, board was created consisting of Hoover (as a life member), the president of the university (ex officio), and others to be appointed by the president. This body would advise the university administration on general policies as well as library acquisitions and development. The president would continue to appoint the board's chairman (who served as the library's director), who would function in a manner similar to academic department heads throughout the university. Hoover was satisfied, and subsequently told Rickard to move ahead

The reading room of the Hoover Library and Archives, in Hoover Tower, in 1962. At the end of the room is an antique Belgian tapestry depicting a queen and her court.   LEO HOLUB / STANFORD UNIVERSITY ARCHIVES

with his $30,000 donation. This agreement would serve as President Sterling's operating document until 1959.[41]

LEADERSHIP IN TRANSITION

By Sterling's return to Stanford in 1949, Hoover Tower was busy with visiting researchers while its accomplished curators and research associates promoted active collecting programs around the world. Before long, however, Sterling had to serve as a mediator between the Chief and the Hoover Institution's senior staff.

A self-proclaimed, independent-minded "Vermont Republican," Fisher did not share Hoover's narrowing conservative political philosophy. Nor did he agree with Hoover's increasingly vocal suspicions of campus Communists

Hoover Institution Chairman Harold Fisher (right) and Easton Rothwell, director of the Hoover Library, examining a box of Communist propaganda documents received from a library representative in Malaya, in 1954. STANFORD NEWS SERVICE

and other "left-wingers." Fisher continued to talk at conferences, public lectures, and other academic events, often speaking against anti-communist attacks by newspaper columnists and state and federal legislative committees on colleges and universities at a time when Stanford was heavily criticized for harboring Communists. He was not only an influential scholar and articulate public speaker, but also a popular news commentator on San Francisco radio station KNBC, where he was often asked for his views, as an expert on Russian and Soviet affairs, of U.S.-Soviet relations.[42]

Hoover's friends were equally suspicious of Fisher's vice chairman, Easton Rothwell, who, with Sterling, had earned his Stanford Ph.D. in history in 1938 and had worked with Lutz and Fisher as a research assistant. Rothwell had worked at the U.S. State Department during the war, and then on establishment of the United Nations. These connections led to accusations that he was a "fellow traveler" and a proponent of world domination of the United States. Also suspect were curator and China scholar Mary C. Wright, whose work in China and ongoing connections there were the foundation of the Library's strong Chinese collections; and research associate Robert North, the highly decorated veteran who had returned from the Pacific to study Russian-Chinese relations. None of them hid their associations with the Hoover Institution when publicly encouraging international mediation in the Chinese civil war, or when warning against domestic red-baiting.[43]

In protest, a number of Hoover's affluent friends, encouraged by Hoover, withheld contributions to the Hoover Library, placing the university in the awkward position of having to increase its subsidy at a time of significant financial pressure on the university's general funds. With the library yet again dependent on university allocations, Hoover once more insisted

China scholar and curator Mary C. Wright and library director Easton Rothwell in 1957 examining materials received from Communist China. Wright's wartime experience in China and ongoing connections there were the foundation of the library's strong Chinese collections. She left Stanford in 1959 to accept a position as the first female tenured faculty member at Yale; she later was its first female full professor. STANFORD NEWS SERVICE

on greater independence for the institute and a shorter leash on Fisher and other Hoover staff.

By 1951, Fisher concluded that Hoover and the Hoover Institution Advisory Board members wanted his resignation, on the grounds that his opinions on public questions harmed the library and embarrassed Mr. Hoover. Fisher told Sterling that Hoover had not questioned his right to hold his opinions; nor was academic freedom an issue, he assumed, because he had tenure as a history professor. Now, however, Herbert Hoover's friends were openly questioning his personal loyalty to the Chief. Congressional investigations of alleged communist influence in American government, academia, libraries, and churches made such confrontations front-page news. Regardless of their differences of opinion, Fisher wrote President Sterling, he respected and had great affection for Mr. Hoover. The Chief, he felt, was entitled to have it his way.[44]

Easton Rothwell, on leave teaching at the National War College, wanted Fisher to reconsider. He understood Fisher's personal feelings and the financial threats being made, but he feared that Fisher's resignation would be seen as capitulation to the concept that the Institution's chairman and staff must comply with the beliefs of Herbert Hoover, as founder, and to its financial supporters.

Rothwell felt strongly that objective inquiry must prevail, with honest, scholarly consideration of all viewpoints. "On controversial issues, as on all issues, we must avoid pleading a special case or cause, but work towards conclusions which represent the most measured judgments available on the basis of all the facts that can be dug up," he wrote.[45]

Sterling agreed but hoped they could ride out the controversy with compromises.[46] In 1952, Rothwell assumed administrative responsibility for the Library, and Fisher was given a heavier load of teaching and writing in an effort to distract him from public appearances. Yet while Fisher stepped down as Library director, he retained the title of chairman of the Hoover Advisory Board and continued his many activities. "Harold Fisher is still anathema and the old gent is really unhappy about the Library and Institution," Lloyd Dinkelspiel wrote Sterling in 1954, after a breakfast visit with Hoover in New York. "Doesn't want anybody fired but I don't think a resignation would offend him."[47]

Fisher retired in 1955 from the Hoover Advisory Board; Sterling appointed Easton Rothwell to succeed him as chairman. Hoover did not protest this action, which was the university president's to make, but the appointment of someone he considered Fisher's man rankled. Hoover again asked financial backers to hold off contributions. He terminated a major fundraising drive, launched in 1950 but as yet not very successful. Donors were affronted, Hoover said, by Rothwell's attempt to broaden the Institution's publishing policy to include not only publication of edited primary sources but also scholarly analytical texts by Hoover staff. The threat worked. The publishing program returned to the publication of documents and bibliographies.[48]

Equally galling to Hoover was Sterling's appointment in 1952 of a faculty committee to investigate conditions between the Hoover Institution and the university, an approach Sterling increasingly used to review important university programs. The committee, chaired by psychology Professor Paul Farnsworth, an experienced university citizen, found relations in "a deplorable" state, aggravated by the Institution's growing reliance on university general funds despite its "extreme autonomy" and "separatist tendencies." The faculty committee urged university oversight and faculty interaction.[49]

STERLING AND TRUSTEES TACKLE ISSUES

With the Hoover Institution falling into a severe financial crisis, in March 1958 the trustees formed a new special committee, chaired by the influential James B. Black, to oversee matters.[50] Easton Rothwell presented the new committee with a comprehensive program review. More strapped than ever for funds, he worried that the Institution was losing academic credibility and fundraising potential as research and teaching interests once centered on the Hoover Institution were now moving elsewhere on campus. Rothwell proposed fundamental changes to help meet costs, among them joint appointments (salary sharing) with academic departments for curatorial positions. He recommended that the university assume full responsibility for the Hoover Institution's budget.[51]

Hoover responded directly to Black, urging him to retain the Institution's "independent identity within the frame of Stanford University." He was not opposed to seeing what he called the "teaching staff" transferred elsewhere in the university since he did not see teaching as a primary function of the Institution. This had already been done with research assistant Robert North, who in mid-1958 transitioned to a full-time tenured faculty position in the Political Science Department. (The previous year, Hoover had asked Sterling to disassociate North, who received his Ph.D. that year, from the Hoover Institution if another campus opening became available.)[52]

Hoover based his argument on what he referred to as an agreement with President Wilbur assuring the independence of the Hoover Library. Over the years, said Sterling, Hoover had talked about the relationship between the university and the Institution during his stays with the Sterling family, but his accounts were inconsistent, and no documentation could be found to support them. Rothwell could find no evidence of such an agreement. Sterling set in motion thorough searches through Stanford's presidential office files as well as Hoover's files at the Tower and in New York, but with no result. Wilbur, who had died in 1949, left no record of such an agreement in his presidential or autobiographical files. As a last resort, Sterling conferred with Stanford professors Robert E. Swain and J. Pearce Mitchell, both old friends of Wilbur and of Hoover. Both were now in their 80s. Neither had an answer, suggesting only an oral agreement.[53]

Sterling was determined not to pass on to Stanford's next president this unfinished Hoover Institution business, now seemingly based on a 1946 compromise that Hoover deplored and a decades-old, undocumented verbal agreement that could not be confirmed. He suggested to the Board of Trustees that it ask Herbert Hoover to compose a statement of purpose.[54]

Hoover provided a lengthy memorandum, which included a notable paragraph. He declared that the purpose of the Hoover Institution must be, "by its research and publications, to demonstrate the evils of the doctrines of Karl Marx—whether Communism, Socialism, economic materialism, or atheism—thus to protect the American way of life from such ideologies, their conspiracies, and to reaffirm the validity of the American system."[55]

In March 1959, the board revoked the 1946 compromise on recommendation of the special committee, and declared its consensus that "the relation of the Hoover Institution to the University should revert to the initial relationship that obtained in the early Twenties." Rather than a "separate division," the Hoover Institution was now deemed "an independent Institution within the frame of Stanford University," with a line of authority directly through the president to the trustees.[56]

Hoover was annoyed, however, when President Sterling insisted that the director of the Institution must continue to be recommended to the Board of Trustees by the university president, rather than independently by the trustees. Sterling compromised by agreeing that the president's recommendations did not require approval of the Advisory Board of the university's Academic Council (but he did not relinquish his right to ask for faculty opinion). The trustees' resolution also noted that the director would no longer have academic tenure but "administrative tenure" (similar to that of the university president and senior officers), thus keeping the position away from procedures and protections regarding tenured faculty. The final wording did not include Hoover's controversial paragraph.[57]

"The resolution had been put together from texts written by the Chief, by me, by [trustee president] Dave Packard, and with the counsel of Jim Black," Sterling reassured Robert Swain, Wilbur's vice president, soon after.

> My central purpose in the whole enterprise was to get the matter on paper in a way that would spell out as clearly as possible the relationship of the H.I. to the University, and in a way that the Chief would welcome. I think that this

has been done, and the Board resolution was most enthusiastically approved by all present. I suspect that, with the resolution thus approved, the way is cleared for action in the search for a Director.[58]

"All left-wingers are out," Hoover wrote a Palo Alto friend that June.[59] Months before, in January 1959, Rothwell had accepted the offer of the presidency of Mills College. He was tired, he told Sterling, of defending the Hoover Institution to its founder and the university against one of its trustees.[60] Other changes were already underway among the Institution's staff. North had taken his faculty position, on his way to a highly respected academic career. Curator Ruth Perry died in 1958 in Africa on a collecting trip. In mid-1959, Mary Wright and her husband, history Professor Arthur Wright, both accepted tenured faculty positions at Yale. The Japanese and Middle-Eastern collections had changed hands as well. Curatorial appointments remained fluid for several more years.[61]

Hoover had also won a skirmish over the Institution's subsidy. In the midst of a university-wide review of departments and programs as part of its 10-year budgeting forecast, Sterling told Hoover that the university would have to trim the subsidy, in balance with other university needs. The Institution continued to be a financial drain while Stanford's budget was squeezed tightly to cover faculty recruiting and growing costs for the new Medical School and hospital. An angry Hoover threatened that if cuts were made, he would inform donors that they were free of any obligations they may have made. Board President David Packard stepped in to reassure Hoover that the trustees would not reduce the allocation, although there would be no increase in the foreseeable future. The tempest dissipated, but Hoover remained annoyed by what he deemed Sterling's "disloyalty," while some of Sterling's administration and key faculty

members were concerned about the precedent of outside influence on university decisions and diversion of attention from larger financial problems and opportunities facing the university.[62]

With Rothwell's projected departure, Sterling, in April 1959, appointed Humanities and Sciences Dean Philip Rhinelander, an accomplished administrator, to serve as the Institution's acting director and caretaker until a new director was named. Sterling reassured Mr. Hoover that Rhinelander, as his designate, would report through him to the Board of Trustees, without faculty oversight. Hoover, however, had expected the appointment of his favorite curator, Witold Sworakowski, a strong Hoover supporter.

Former Hoover Institution research associate Robert North was a highly decorated veteran who had returned from the Pacific to study Russian-Chinese relations. North's views on American involvement in China, like those of curator Mary Wright, were unpopular with Mr. Hoover. STANFORD NEWS SERVICE

Both Mr. Hoover and curator Witold Sworakowski, a Hoover confidante and assistant director since 1955, expected Sworakowski to be appointed as Easton Rothwell's successor. The curator's dislike of both Rothwell and President Sterling was well known. STANFORD NEWS SERVICE

Sterling did not think him qualified.[63] A few days later, a story was leaked to the national press from West Branch, Iowa, that Hoover's personal and professional papers (but not the war and peace library) would be transferred to a presidential library and museum to be established there.[64]

THE SEARCH FOR A NEW DIRECTOR

In November 1958, well before Rothwell's official resignation, Hoover wrote Sterling a "My Dear Wally" letter to recommend a candidate known to be "a 'gentleman,' a man of fine personality, quiet demeanor, always well groomed." By March 1959, the Chief had identified an additional six such possible candidates.[65] Sterling was not impressed with Hoover's initial list. "As a group," he responded, "they represent a strong emphasis on the 'librarian' as against the 'historian.'"[66]

Ray C. Swank, Stanford's director of university libraries, told Sterling, "I can't figure how Mr. Hoover could have come up with a list that is slanted so far afield from the interests of the

Hoover Institution and that contains so few distinguished names."[67] Sterling also shared Hoover's list of candidates with Dr. Louis B. Wright, director of the Folger Shakespeare Library in Washington, D.C., and Sterling's predecessor as director of the Huntington Library and Art Gallery. Wright was a well-respected scholar and prolific author as well as a highly successful director of special libraries. Wright suggested, "Have you considered a search for a live and imaginative young historian and putting him in charge of the Hoover Library?. . . The Hoover Library needs a statesmanlike historian with imagination."[68]

Hoover remained distrustful of mixed loyalties, however. "I know you are still concerned about faculty domination," wrote trustee President David Packard. "I am certain Dr. Sterling will support your position in this matter with the greatest vigor. You may be sure that the Trustees will give continuous attention to insuring the Institution is handled in the spirit, and to the letter of the pledge we have already made."[69]

That August, Hoover added another name: economist Wesley Glenn Campbell, research director of the American Enterprise Association for Public Policy Research in Washington, D.C.[70] Sterling responded that he could find only skeletal information on Campbell, and suggested the name of a highly respected academic librarian, Douglas W. Bryant, '35, a Stanford graduate who was then associate director of the Harvard University Library. (Bryant went on to a distinguished career as head of Harvard's University Library system, the country's largest and most influential.)[71]

Hoover had fixed on Campbell, however. Raymond Moley, the nationally known neoconservative *Newsweek* columnist, had first recommended Campbell.[72] Colby Chester, former chairman of the board of General Mills and currently chairman of the American Enterprise Association, added: "We believe that Dr. Campbell is ideologically sound as a dollar."[73] After meeting with Campbell in New York later in September, Hoover wrote Sterling, "I told Dr. Campbell that his appointment must be made by you and the Trustees of the University, and that I would recommend it to you."[74]

Campbell, like Sterling, had been born in Ontario, Canada. He had received his bachelor's degree at the University of Western Ontario (1944) and went on to earn his master's (1946) and Ph.D. in economics (1948) from Harvard. After several years of teaching there in an untenured position, he joined the U.S. Chamber of Commerce as a research economist in 1951, and then became research director of the American Enterprise Association (later Institute). Having received Hoover's verbal approval, Campbell, like Hoover, was anxious to move the board ahead on the appointment.[75]

The board's Special Committee was now chaired by David Packard, a strong supporter of Campbell's candidacy, and someone who would become an important donor to the American Enterprise Institute. The committee met soon after and recommended to the trustees "that if President Wallace Sterling recommends appointment of W. Glenn Campbell as director of the Hoover Institution, the President be authorized to extend the appointment to him following Dr. Campbell's pending visit to the campus and upon notice from Mr. Hoover that the appointment has his formal approval."[76]

Sterling had yet to formalize the recommendation to the full Board of Trustees when it became plain that Campbell's appointment was not well received on campus. Sterling had invited Campbell to visit Stanford, scheduling meetings for him with members of the Advisory Board, the Academic Council's Executive Committee, and deans, a procedure followed for any serious candidate for a deanship or major university officer position. The collective judgment, he later recalled, was clearly unfavorable.[77]

Many on the faculty considered the Hoover Institution to be a great asset. Its collections continued to be an attraction in faculty recruitment. Gordon Wright, a preeminent historian of modern France and then executive head of the History Department, wrote Dean Rhinelander of his department's hope to better integrate with the Institution, building on joint strengths to create one of the country's best places for graduate training in modern history. "I have no doubt at all that both you and Wally feel as strongly as I do about this matter—probably more so, indeed, for nobody likes to run a university with small men in big jobs. I imagine, too, that Wally's long association with the Hoover makes him particularly concerned to see it in good hands."

Wright also had no doubt that Sterling had been "caught in an impossible situation here and that he has put up the toughest fight. I am writing this letter only in the desperate hope that it may contribute to blocking a weak appoint-

In April 1959, Sterling appointed Humanities and Sciences Dean Philip Rhinelander, an accomplished administrator, as acting director and caretaker during the search for Rothwell's successor.   STANFORD NEWS SERVICE

ment in that court of last resort, the Board of Trustees. I suppose that the Board is in the same bind as everyone else, but I would rather not give up all hope until the final whistle blows."[78]

On the final evening of Campbell's visit, Sterling informed Campbell that he could not recommend his appointment to the Board of Trustees. Campbell told the president that the deal already was done: Mr. Hoover had offered him the job and he had accepted. As Campbell later confidently told Stanford News Service Director Robert W. Beyers, "The [appointment] had to first be approved by Mr. Herbert Hoover. I was the only candidate Hoover would approve."[79]

On university business in New York soon after Campbell's visit, Sterling told Hoover that he could not recommend Campbell for the directorship. Campbell had told him that the Chief already had offered him the job, he continued, but Sterling could not believe that Hoover would do such a thing behind his back. This forthright conversation was uncomfortable for both men,

Sterling later recalled. Sterling felt that Hoover now recognized the awkward position in which Hoover had placed him. But it was Sterling who relented, concluding that compromise was required when Hoover came near to pleading with him to reconsider.[80]

Bowing to the inevitable, Sterling made the formal offer to Campbell on November 6, 1959, clarifying that the position had administrative tenure only, that is, the same as Sterling, Provost Terman, and other senior administrative officers who served at the pleasure of the trustees, without tenure and with an expected retirement age of 65. (In 1988, approaching retirement age, Campbell unsuccessfully challenged the Board of Trustees on this requirement.)[81]

Rhinelander believed that Sterling took the position that Hoover had dictated Campbell's appointment and that he couldn't resist it. The controversy took a toll on Sterling's relationship with the faculty at a time when Stanford was building its academic ranks. "The fact that so important a post should be dictated from outside," said Rhinelander, "was something that a good many people regretted." Rhinelander feared that Hoover wanted to control all international programs at Stanford and, as a result, Hoover resented competition for foundation support that the university might present during upcoming major fundraising efforts. Stanford continued to make strong faculty appointments in this area, however, and in 1962 further developed its International Relations Program, chaired by Law Dean Carl Spaeth.[82]

In his memoirs, Sterling expressed both relief and regrets. Campbell was a better director than he anticipated. Sterling had established at Stanford the principle, noted Business School Dean Ernie Arbuckle, of "putting a tub on its own bottom," that is, encouraging deans, department heads, and directors to take an active role in locating funding for their units so that they could

Herbert Hoover Jr., former Russian leader Alexander Kerensky, and Hoover Institution Director W. Glenn Campbell at the dedication of the Lou Henry Hoover Building, October 1967. Campbell's 1959 appointment had been strongly supported by trustee President David Packard, later an important donor to the American Enterprise Institute, and his successor, Thomas Pike, simultaneously trustee president and California chair of Richard Nixon's 1960 presidential campaign.   STANFORD NEWS SERVICE

become more self-reliant. Over his 30 years as director, Campbell did just that, successfully raising operating funds and building the Institution's endowment. Two new buildings were added to the Institution, adjacent to the Tower. Campbell later claimed credit for creating joint appointments between the Institution and academic departments, and for a strong publishing program of academic scholarship, initiatives that Rothwell had previously been unsuccessful in persuading Mr. Hoover to approve or support.[83]

As predicted by campus leaders, Campbell never became comfortable with faculty or administrators, choosing to remain academically aloof and socially isolated from the university at large. Unlike Sterling and the most effective members of his team, Campbell enjoyed being confrontational and on the sidelines of the university's

dynamic overall expansion in the 1960s, although during Sterling's presidential tenure he largely refrained from outright sparring with the administration and the faculty, of whom he remained contemptuous.[84]

THE FIGHT AGAINST MARXISM CONTINUES

With his chosen director in place, Herbert Hoover launched a new drive for contributions. Without conferring with Sterling or the trustees, in 1960 he approved publication of a fundraising brochure that included his blunt statement of purpose about the fight against the evils of communism, socialism, economic materialism, and atheism. Since the Hoover Institution was part of Stanford University, this implied that the Board of Trustees endorsed the concept that research at

Stanford would begin with an established conclusion and proceed to find evidence. Sterling later admitted that he had previously missed the paragraph's significance. He knew Hoover too well, he said, and the Chief's own scientific approach to research, to think Hoover would place the conclusion before the investigation.[85]

"All hell broke loose," said Fred Glover, when the publication was circulated on campus. On March 29, 1960, the *Stanford Daily* made the issue a public one when it printed a copy of Hoover's brochure. Its editorial precipitated an avalanche of letters to the *Daily,* largely hostile to Herbert Hoover and to the Hoover Institution. Sterling, who agreed that Hoover's original statement appeared a violation of academic principles, was deeply upset. Tired, and suffering a recurrence of a serious stomach ailment, Sterling contemplated a letter of resignation during a sleepless night. By morning, Glover recalled, the president had concluded that the university was worth more than the Hoover Institution.[86]

Sterling convened a contentious meeting of the Academic Council, on April 1, 1960, and admitted his oversight. He shared their apprehensions, telling them that "the well-established and honored principle is that no research that is bona fide and worthy of the name can be undertaken with predetermined conclusions." He felt that Hoover, the trustees, and the new director agreed with this view. In a close vote, the council set in motion an Advisory Board committee to draft a new statement of purpose for the Hoover Institution to be submitted to the trustees.[87] A month later, the Advisory Board asked the trustees for a positive statement reaffirming Stanford's dedication to scholarship, academic freedom, and freedom of inquiry.[88] The board responded ambiguously. Hoover's statement was a nonbinding one, the trustees said. They had not contemplated that the statement would be interpreted as university policy.

Hoover was incensed with this faculty interference, complaining that Sterling, Packard, and Black had all read his statement before it was submitted to the board in 1959, and they had made no objections at the time. They had decided to stop him, he argued, only when the faculty complained. Hoover could only conclude, he wrote Ralph Lutz, that the faculty's "real feeling is objection to the American way of life."[89]

Sterling, again in the middle, subsequently submitted to the trustees in June 1960 a four-paragraph statement of the Hoover Institution's aims and purposes. Sterling's document was more technical than philosophical, he said, and reiterated that the director would not have academic tenure; that the director should nonetheless be a member of the Academic Council; that joint appointments between the Hoover Institution staff and university departments should be encouraged; and that the Institution's budgets should be reviewed in the context of other university budgets. The trustees relabeled his statement as simply a report on the principles by which President Sterling would administer the trustee resolutions of 1959 and 1960.[90]

When asked at the January 1961 Academic Council meeting why the trustees had not repudiated Hoover's statement, Sterling reported that they considered the principle of free inquiry to be secure, and that they did not wish to cause Hoover, now 86 and in poor health, "personal hurt." Sterling deemed the business closed.[91]

REMOVING PRESIDENTIAL RECORDS TO IOWA

The business was not closed for the Chief, however. For some years, and at his own expense, Herbert Hoover had maintained his own papers, including his personal and presidential papers, in Hoover Tower. In 1955, when the U.S. Congress enacted legislation permitting the creation of federally funded presidential libraries, Rothwell suggested that the Hoover Presidential Archives be placed on certain floors of the tower. It could be designated the Hoover Presidential Library, which would make it eligible to receive perhaps $100,000 a year in federal money. Hoover rejected the suggestion, fearing that federal financing would subject his library to political influences.

In 1959, Hoover promised Sterling and the board that his personal and presidential archives would stay at Stanford. Despite the earlier leak that they were headed to Iowa, he turned over title to the papers to the board. However, on December 15, 1960, without prior discussion with Stanford officials, Hoover formally offered his extensive presidential and post-presidential papers to the National Archives for deposit in a new library-museum to be built in West Branch, Iowa. Hoover appealed personally to the trustees to return to him title to the recently donated presidential archives, explaining that he would donate the papers to the West Branch presidential library, but they would remain physically in the tower, housed at the expense of the National Archives. The trustees unconditionally complied.[92]

Hoover then offered his remaining non-presidential archives, including the records of his numerous relief efforts, to the Stanford trustees on the condition that they amend their 1959 resolution to flip the appointment process: After his death, any director of the Hoover Institution recommended by the university's president must first receive the approval of the Hoover Foundation, a New York corporation composed of various family members and friends. When, in May 1962, the trustees again accepted his offer and terms, the disposition of his vast collection seemed to be complete.

However, the Hoover presidential archives did not remain, as promised, at the Hoover Institution. The following August, after Hoover for-

mally dedicated the Herbert Hoover Presidential Library, he arranged to have this vast collection moved from Stanford to West Branch, Iowa.

THE AMETHYST PENDANT

Hoover resigned from the Board of Trustees in January 1961 and subsequently was elected trustee emeritus. With his attention drawn to West Branch, says his biographer, George Nash, Hoover "suppressed his feelings for the greater good of Stanford University." He agreed to serve as honorary chairman of Stanford's upcoming PACE fundraising effort, helping to open the campaign with his public endorsement. In April 1961, he joined former trustee President David Packard and current board President Thomas Pike in co-hosting the campaign's opening dinner at the Mark Hopkins Hotel in San Francisco.[93]

Emeritus trustee Hoover was responsible for steering a number of major donations to other university targets, including an Alfred P. Sloan gift fund to the Business School, and an unrestricted bequest from William M. Keck to fund the sciences. The Hoover Institution, in turn, benefited considerably from the PACE Campaign.[94]

Despite their "toe-to-toe skirmishes" in later life, Sterling did not believe that Hoover held a grudge. Nor did Sterling. Throughout the remainder of his life, Sterling refrained from commenting on issues that had divided them, preferring to praise Hoover's accomplishments and good intentions.[95]

Herbert Hoover died, at 90, in New York on October 20, 1964. Flags flew at half-mast on a campus awash with new student and faculty expectations, new clashes between the student body and the administration, and old confrontations with neighboring towns about Stanford's relentless growth.[96] On October 23, the campus paused for an academic procession of trustees and a memorial service to honor the man the *Stanford Daily* called "Stanford's greatest alumnus."[97]

President Wallace Sterling paid tribute to Hoover as an engineer, a humanitarian, a public servant, and a champion of peace, speaking of his contributions in terms of initiative, vision, enterprise, and persistence. He recalled the man who read and wrote books, who defended children, and who loved lakes and trout streams. Hoover had devoted to his alma mater "an incomparable measure of attention and devotion," Sterling said. "That he should have done so out of a life which was so busy, which took him so often to so many lands, and which brought to him great public responsibilities is eloquent testimony to the high value he placed on education and to his affection for Stanford."

Sterling made headlines, however, by recalling a talk given by Hoover years before at Stanford. "Calling names is not debate," he quoted Hoover. "It is a confession of defeat by logic and fact. It is more—it is the infallible sign of intellectual dishonesty."[98]

Looking back years later, both Wallace Sterling and Fred Glover made a point of recording a poignant story of the Chief's final interaction with President Sterling. After Sterling's serious illness and hospitalization in spring 1964, he and Mrs. Sterling took a much-needed vacation to Europe. Since they were passing through New York, the nearly 90-year-old Hoover, himself seriously ill, insisted they have lunch with him. Hoover gave Mrs. Sterling an exquisite amethyst pendant. He and Mrs. Hoover had collected several while they had lived in China, Hoover told them, where they were considered something like a St. Christopher's medal or safe-travel talisman. This was his last one. The Sterlings were deeply moved by the gesture.[99]

Sterling's staff had worried about his health as the Hoover-related difficulties arose during the exceptionally busy years of 1957–64. "I think that was the most painful experience I've ever had, watching Wally going through the struggle about the organization of the Hoover Institution when the Chief really had the leverage on him hard," recalled Ken Cuthbertson, Sterling's presidential assistant who became vice president for finance in 1959. "Wally simply wasn't going to damage a person who was such a friend of the University and had been for such a long time." Others saw the periodic skirmishes as merely a distraction from the work at hand. "We certainly didn't have the perspective he did," concluded Cuthbertson. "Who's to know whether it was right or wrong, but he went with his view."[100]

A favorite photograph of Herbert Hoover, with pipe, is preserved in the J. E. Wallace Sterling personal papers in the University Archives. It is inscribed: "To Wally and Ann Sterling With the affection of Herbert Hoover." STANFORD UNIVERSITY ARCHIVES

14

EDUCATIONAL REVIEWS AND ADMINISTRATIVE REORGANIZATION

Stanford's rise to national academic prominence is often attributed to a 1960s burst of growth to its financial base and research facilities based on new industry and government connections. Add to these the opportunities of being in the right place at the right time. Wallace Sterling's objective—academic improvement—was firmly grounded, however, on careful study and analysis begun during the previous decade.

Two notable studies bookended Stanford's 1950s: an examination of conditions at the Medical Center, then in San Francisco, that led to its move to campus and a major reorientation toward research (*see Chapter 4*), and a campus-wide financial analysis of academic needs and opportunities that would fortify a major fundraising campaign of 1961–64 (*see Chapter 7*). Two other studies, however, also proved consequential. One analysis would impact undergradu-

ate studies and intellectual life, while the other would remodel the administration. Similarly, Sterling would end his presidential years with a major reconsideration of the university's educational model.

THE UNDERGRADUATE IN THE UNIVERSITY
HOOPES-MARSHALL STUDY, 1954–1956

In the mid-1950s, Sterling guided the university through a revision of undergraduate curriculum more extensive than any during the preceding 35 years. A curriculum review committee had been at work since 1948 and made its report to the faculty during Sterling's first year as president. Despite the lively discussion it provoked, a large majority of the faculty rejected its recommendations. On making inquiries, Sterling found that the committee had not consulted very widely, and that the faculty was more interested in curricular review and reform than the report suggested.[1]

In August 1954, Sterling set out to review the entirety of Stanford's undergraduate program. Unlike earlier studies of general education, or of targeted areas or schools, this study, Sterling said,

< This Inner Quad arcade view, with Buildings 1 (with open door) and 10 (right foreground), is one of the many exquisite campus photographs by law Professor Moffatt Hancock taken between 1953 and 1966. The tile drinking fountain was a gift of the Class of 1925.   MOFFATT HANCOCK / STANFORD UNIVERSITY ARCHIVES

Freshmen gather in a crowded History Corner classroom for a Western Civilization class during the 1940s. The three-quarter course, required since 1935, was phased out by 1971. (Sterling was a Western Civ instructor in the mid-1930s.)
LISETTE FAST ROBINSON / STANFORD UNIVERSITY ARCHIVES

"would embrace problems deemed important to all undergraduate education," curricular and extracurricular, concentrating on teaching and learning. Its aim was to improve the effectiveness of undergraduate teaching at Stanford as well as to improve the intellectual motivation of Stanford students. The first year of the study was supported by a grant from the Ford Foundation's Fund for the Advancement of Education, the second by the Carnegie Foundation. Both the process and the results of the study were documented in its report, *The Undergraduate in the University: A Report to the Faculty by the Executive Committee of the Stanford Study of Undergraduate Education, 1954–1956.*[2]

Its range of study was wide, from admissions policy and the usefulness of the lecture system and of campus libraries to undergraduate intellectual life, students' relationships with the world beyond the campus, and the impact of faculty research on undergraduate teaching.

Two faculty committees—an executive committee of eight and an advisory committee of 23—worked closely with Sterling on the research and preparation of recommendations. Two additional subcommittees were formed, one on university curriculum and the other on requirements to obtain a bachelor's degree. Both subcommittees were chaired by Robert A. Walker, professor of political science, who also was a member of the executive committee. Walker had joined the political science faculty in 1949, serving as its chair from 1958 to 1963. As an expert on public administration and governance, and as an able administrator, he was often asked for advice by the Sterling administration.[3]

Sterling promoted widespread participation and invited input from interested faculty through various informal means. Aiding the faculty was a committee of 19 undergraduates selected by the Associated Students of Stanford University. Even the *Stanford Daily* was squarely behind the new study, applauding its inclusion of both student and faculty comments from across campus, as well as its ambitious purpose.[4]

President Sterling chaired both the executive and advisory committees, with the assistance of Provost Doug Whitaker, in 1954–55, and Whitaker's successor, Fred Terman, in 1955–56.[5] The study process was directed initially by psychology Professor Donald Taylor, who was succeeded in 1955 by the assistant director, Robert Hoopes of the English Department. Hubert Marshall, an assistant professor of political science, then filled in as assistant director.[6] The president appreciated the leadership, "spiced with an appropriate dash of prodding," of the successive directors of the study, and he made sure they were ably staffed.[7]

Over the two years of the review, the directors arranged many discussions, usually at lunches for 10 or 12 faculty members who were not on either the executive or advisory committee, as one means to broaden discussion and a sense of involvement. An "outline of problems of investigation" was also circulated to all faculty, including instructors, for comment, as were two questions: "What are the goals of the university?" and "What education goals should be common to all Stanford students?"[8]

In early 1956, a sweeping revision of the undergraduate curriculum recommended by the study was presented to the faculty's Academic Council. Sterling began the meeting by inviting full discussion. He was ready, if decisions could not be reached during the meeting, to convene a second meeting. Within half an hour, however, a motion to accept the recommendations of what came to be called the Hoopes-Marshall Report was seconded and carried with a nearly unanimous vote. Two years of grassroots work had paid off, Sterling recalled, and the report, published in 1957, received national attention.[9]

An unusual aspect of this report was its acknowledgment that readers might be interested in the how and the why. "In hope that the sum of our experience might be of service to similar enterprises, undertaken here and elsewhere in the future," said the authors, their report documented the process and discussions, as well as recommendations, and also "sought to isolate and define those areas of study that remain as yet unsolved." No doubt echoing their president's perspective, they expected self-study to become a permanent "habit of mind" at Stanford.[10]

The Stanford Study of Undergraduate Education replaced the Lower and Upper Divisions,

Sterling's 1954–56 sweeping review of Stanford's undergraduate program, the Study of Undergraduate Education, was directed by two assistant professors, Robert Hoopes of English (left, who took Professor Donald Taylor's place in 1955) and Hubert Marshall of Political Science. A key recommendation was the introduction of overseas campuses.
STANFORD NEWS SERVICE

created in 1920, with an integrated four-year approach. A new General Studies Program was created, devised by Walker's committee (Walker became the first director). The program was intended to give students greater freedom and variety in selecting courses outside their major. At the same time, the new requirements increased the range of "general education" courses each student must complete, thus assuring exposure to a wider field of knowledge. Among the new requirements were a full year of freshman English (composition and literature) and a senior colloquium outside the student's major department. All undergraduates were still required to take the year-long History of Western Civilization track, as they had since fall 1935.[11]

Years later, in his Stanford memorial resolution, Walker's colleagues noted:

Bob vigorously argued that all students should be exposed to areas of knowledge beyond their fields of concentration and that the faculty had a solemn obligation to agree upon a relatively restricted list of courses open to students in meeting the new general education requirement. His views prevailed. Thus all students, without exception, were required to take History of Western Civilization (History 10, 11, 12), giving the entire student body a common intellectual experience. His committees approached the science requirement with equal certitude, requiring that students who had not had biology in high school take three quarters of the subject at Stanford. Other requirements did offer students

President Sterling and Professor Robert Walker, chair of political science and first director of the Overseas Campuses program, spoke at a press conference during the opening of the Stanford-in-France campus in Tours, 1960. Walker was an enthusiastic advocate for breadth of undergraduate learning and for overseas studies, promoting its mid-1950s creation during the undergraduate education study.
U.S. INFORMATION SERVICE / STANFORD NEWS SERVICE

Humanities honor students were required to take a seminar in their field directed by a senior faculty member, such as the noted John Dodds, seen here in 1959 with his students. The Humanities Honors Program had started in 1946 while Dodds was dean of humanities.   STANFORD NEWS SERVICE

a greater range of choices. The new requirements were summarized on the famous "green sheet" that guided several generations of Stanford undergraduates in course selection outside their majors.

Sterling later reflected on the success of two of the reforms. The senior colloquia, small seminars taught largely by senior faculty on topics of their choice (not necessarily in their primary field), quickly became popular with students and faculty alike. Sterling himself taught one titled "The Making of Decisions." Another recommendation led to the establishment of Stanford's ground-breaking Overseas Campuses program. Sterling had argued for more language instruction generally, and the concept of a study abroad program located at Stanford-sponsored and -managed sites took off under the enthusiastic leadership of committee members Bob Walker and Friedrich Strothmann (*see Chapter 9*).[12]

RETHINKING STANFORD'S MANAGEMENT
THE CORSON REPORT, 1957–1958

By 1957, as the university continued to grow in size and complexity, it was overdue for a major reorganization of administrative and other functions.

During his first years as president, Sterling kept his personal staff to a minimum to avoid isolating himself from faculty and students. Initially, it was a way to better understand the university, but he was also sensitive to faculty criticism of a growing administrative staff. "He didn't want to build up that service end of the University," explained Ken Cuthbertson.[13] He had quickly gotten rid of three vice-presidential positions inherited from the Tresidder administration. Public affairs and development had been absorbed by staff within the President's Office, and Eurich's position as vice president with oversight of academic affairs had been discontinued, then was reformulated on a smaller scale, in 1952, as the Provost's Office.

For years, Sterling scrutinized every line of the budget himself, an unprecedented practice among most university presidents. This changed only as presidential assistants Robert Wert, then Ken Cuthbertson, and, in 1955, newly appointed provost, Fred Terman, gradually took on much of the budget work. By 1956, some decision-making also had shifted to academic units.[14]

The Board of Trustees, especially members of the board who were in executive positions them-selves, had been pressing Sterling to rethink how he managed his ever-increasing workload with only a small presidential staff. Although by this time each of his assistants—Fred Glover, Ken Cuthbertson, Don Carlson, Bob Moulton—had a portfolio of sorts, "Wally had everyone in the University reporting directly to him for a long time," recalled Cuthbertson. He did that "until he understood what was going on pretty well." Only then was he willing to delegate some of the tasks. He was also comfortable moving the academic leaders over to Terman, something he had hesitated to do with Terman's predecessor, Doug Whitaker.[15]

In late 1956, Sterling acknowledged the increasingly heavy load on his shoulders and the natural limits of one man's participation in the entire range of Stanford affairs. Already under-way were a major fundraising campaign for the new Medical Center, the significant study on undergraduate curriculum, and a major rethink-ing of Stanford's land use. It was time for a review of the administrative structure itself, he told the Academic Council.[16]

Stanford needed an outside management consultant, Sterling wrote to a colleague, to determine "whether our organization was adequately designed to keep off the president's desk all that might be handled by other offi-cers of the University; to maximize faculty participation—or at least the sense of participa-tion; to determine what changes of administra-tive organization and/or additions to personnel would be needed to achieve the two purposes previously stated."[17]

The university invited three prominent management consulting firms—McKinsey & Co.; Booz Allen Hamilton; and Cresap, McCormick & Paget—to make proposals. Each firm sent a team of three or four men. After interviewing them, Sterling felt that only one man on each team was clearly the one for Stanford. Each firm was asked to suggest one man, their top man, to do the Stanford study. All agreed, and in 1957, Sterling selected John J. Corson of McKinsey & Co. Corson had an extensive career in government social services and was an authority on public admin-istration. The study, in its many drafts, became known as "The Corson Report."[18]

Later in 1957, Corson interviewed faculty and university officers across the campus. Sterling and Corson immediately "hit it off," said Ernie Arbuckle, then a university trustee, who would take over as dean of the Graduate School of Busi-ness the following year. Corson, he added, was a "low-key fellow who appreciated Wally and his approach."[19]

While the initial pretext was organiza-tional, the review had far-reaching implications beyond staff reorganization, suggesting means to improve communication among faculty (as well as between faculty and administrators), to refine faculty participation in administration and academic policy, and to suggest more effective means of student self-governance.

In February 1958, Sterling arranged a two-day retreat to review a first draft of the Corson Report with an ad hoc committee at the Bohe-mian Club in San Francisco. In addition to Pro-vost Fred Terman and the deans of each school, the group included Bob Walker, director of

View from Hoover Tower looking west across the Quad, around 1960. A major renovation and double-decking in 1956–57 facilitated growth of the offices of the president and the provost in Building 10, on the Inner Quad. A covered walkway connected Sterling to the Planning Office on the back side of Building 160.   STANFORD NEWS SERVICE

general studies; Don Winbigler, dean of students; Al Bowker, graduate dean; and presidential assistants Carlson, Glover, and Cuthbertson.[20]

The discussion was unusually broad, covering such topics as:

- Tenure policies
- Access to the president
- Proper procedures for faculty recruiting
- Faculty participation in academic policy formulation
- Appropriate size of student body
- Whether some departments should be eliminated
- Whether professional school deans should report to the graduate dean
- Deterioration of the Graduate School of Business
- Problems with the Business Office
- Student behavior (especially freshmen in Wilbur dining room)
- Priorities for physical plant improvement

"I've been marinating in Stanford juices for nearly seven years, but no single experience of mine was ever so penetrating as the Bohemian meeting," Don Carlson wrote Sterling two days after the meeting. "The really wonderful thing about it for me was that it opened doors to attitudes and ideas in the University that I didn't even realize were there. Most immediately important, perhaps, it changed some of my rather adolescent opinions about a few of the men around that table."[21]

Two months later, Sterling made a detailed report to the Academic Council based on Corson's third draft.[22] The Corson Report classified the organizational units comprising the university into five groupings: academic affairs, student affairs, business affairs, development affairs, and financial administration. Among its recommendations were increased responsibility for the provost and the creation of two vice presidents—one for finance and administration, and one for planning and development. It also recommended extending the scope of responsibility of both the dean of students and the graduate dean (as principal aide to the provost); more involvement of faculty and university officers in decision making; and improvements in internal communication (such as the creation of a Committee on University Policy).[23]

After listing two pages of serious deficiencies in the university noted by Corson, Sterling wryly observed: "You will be relieved to know that, despite these criticisms, he regards Stanford as a great institution."[24]

Regarding the role of faculty in governance, Corson stated:

The existing machinery of faculty committees, which provide an opportunity for individuals to make known their views and to participate in the decision making processes of the University, does not enlist a major portion of the faculty in the concerns of the University, has made few noteworthy contributions, and fails to bring to the President and Provost a continual understanding of the views of the faculty as a whole. There are noteworthy instances in which appointed committees have worked hard and effectively when assigned clearly defined problems. But the consensus is that a majority of the statutory standing committees get little important work done, and that too little use is made of junior faculty members on committees, and that the whole structure needs overhauling.[25]

"Provost, President and Deans must all be in the business of stimulating better teaching and more research and better analyses," Sterling responded to Corson, "but somehow they must contrive to do this without leaving the impression that all this sort of thing comes from on top, because such impression sits badly with the faculty." Noting Corson's suggestion that faculty members be more involved in decision making, Sterling also observed: "They [the faculty]

Encina Hall transitioned to an administrative building in 1960. Built in 1891 as the men's dormitory, it briefly housed women in 1956. The center section was gutted in 1958 and extensively renovated in 1959–60 to house growing staff offices such as Business and Finance, Development, and News and Publications Service. In recent decades, Encina has become home to academic programs related to international relations.   STANFORD NEWS SERVICE

will buy what you have suggested, but I am not certain they have carefully considered the purchase price that is involved." Sterling would later point out that while the faculty was reluctant about adding to the size of the administrative staff, it was also reluctant to accept additional burdensome administrative duties.[26]

John Corson submitted his final report to President Sterling in May 1958. Some actions (such as a review of committee structures) were already underway. Sterling and his staff were deep into a review of the university's budget with 10-year forecasting, and with a time-consuming review by faculty and staff of every academic program. This effort benefited from Corson's recommendations, which in turn supported the

upcoming university-wide PACE fundraising campaign (*see Chapter 7*).

In June 1959, the Academic Council established a Committee on University Policy (COUP), advisory to the president. Sterling and senior university officers joined academic deans, the dean of students, and the nine members of the Academic Council's elected Executive Committee. COUP was intended to provide a broad-based forum for discussion of a wide range of university issues, and enabled Sterling to communicate more effectively with the faculty. This was especially useful during budget negotiations. The process gave Sterling opportunities to advocate broader university values. The group's collaborations facilitated work on the Red Book

(Stanford's 10-year financial forecast) and on goal setting for the subsequent PACE fundraising campaign.[27]

In addition, the president was to request the committee's advice on any matter the Executive Committee of the Academic Council requested him to submit to COUP.[28] The group began meeting monthly, but by 1962 it met quarterly or at the request of the president. Although it was not long lasting (it did not survive the 1960s), it served as an important conduit of information during the turbulent decade because a summary of its deliberations was distributed to faculty and staff as a means of improving internal university communications.[29]

Corson had recommended to Sterling that he not only delegate, but also group some functions together. Sterling, however, continued to resist the connotations of the title of vice president. "A provost he could understand," said Cuthbertson, but the notion of non-academic vice presidents was disturbing to him. ("Provost" is an academic term, while "vice president," a political or corporate term; this brought back memories of Tresidder's problematic top-down approach.) Sterling ultimately concluded that the reorganization would work if the provost also was made a vice president, in keeping with the post's broadened responsibilities.

The titles of vice president for business and vice president for finance also were established, but instead of creating new posts and job descriptions, Sterling moderately redefined the range of responsibilities of key men he trusted—Terman, Brandin, and Cuthbertson—while granting them considerably more authority. With approval of the Board of Trustees, Provost Fred Terman became vice president and provost; Business Manager Alf Brandin became vice president for business affairs; and presidential assistant Ken Cuthbertson became vice president for finance, but also with respon-

sibility for development and associated public information efforts. Fred Glover was named executive assistant to the president, acknowledging the expanding range of duties he had already taken on.[30]

Another important addition to the Sterling team occurred with the arrival, in 1961, of Lyle M. Nelson as director of university relations, taking on general public relations tasks Cuthbertson and other presidential assistants had been handling. Nelson's approach would bring widespread respect from other educational institutions and the news media. Stanford succeeded in getting not only Nelson from the University of Michigan but also Andy Doty, who became director of community relations, and Bob Beyers, director of the News and Publications Service.

Although Sterling was credited with recruiting Nelson, it was Ken Cuthbertson who had persisted for two years to persuade Nelson to join Sterling's administration. Nelson arrived just in time to deal with new pressure on town-gown relations, changing land development plans, and construction of a major federally funded science research facility. Government relations also were tense due to the U.S. Army Corps of Engineers' intention to take nearly 600 acres from Stanford and Woodside to construct a dam and reservoir.

On arriving at Stanford, Nelson asked to be named director of university relations, not vice president (his previous post at U-M), a request that no doubt pleased Sterling. Nevertheless, he, too, reported directly to Sterling. He had no idea what his salary was going to be until he got his first paycheck. Nelson placed his trust in his colleagues, said Beyers, and quickly earned their trust. Seemingly tireless in approaching university goals, the unpretentious Nelson was quick to credit others: "I think we all became over achievers because of Wally," he recounted in 1985.[31]

Building on a tradition begun by former news-

The Stanford Union

In 1966–67, the Old Union—seen here in 1938—was remodeled for Admissions, Registrar, Student Affairs, and Financial Aid, among other units. The Spanish colonial revival Stanford Union, built in 1922, originally had four dining halls on its first floor, and housed 120 men on the second and third floors. In 1933, men moved out and women moved in. (It was renamed Old Union with the opening of Tresidder Memorial Union in 1962.) STANFORD UNIVERSITY ARCHIVES

paper editor Glover and promoted by Sterling—a former CBS news commentator—Nelson advocated full and honest reporting of campus events and issues. Nelson and Beyers championed press ethics, informative coverage, and good relations with news media colleagues, over traditional notions of public relations. As an era of campus protests and national unrest unfolded during the 1960s, Nelson and Beyers set a standard of presenting unvarnished news of campus events. "The minute you try to gloss it over and present it in a distorted light, you're in for long-run trouble," said Beyers (*see sidebar, Chapter 19*).[32]

Under Beyers, the News Service became a respected news source, interacting with news outlets around the country. In 1966, Stanford's News Service started the *Stanford Observer*, an external monthly newspaper for alumni, parents of students, and high school guidance counselors, with a circulation of 160,000. In 1968, *Campus Report* (later *Stanford Report*), a campus weekly newspaper aimed at faculty and staff, began publication. Both newspapers became models for direct communication and "tell it like it is" reporting at dozens of other major colleges and universities.

LYLE NELSON
PROBLEM SOLVER AND CHAMPION OF PRESS ETHICS

When Lyle M. Nelson left the University of Michigan in 1961 to become Sterling's director of university relations, he became an important buttress to the team: a wise advisor, strategist, and problem solver. A champion of press ethics and institutional integrity, he was also a popular journalism professor and internationally known mentor to journalists from around the world.

"He was a man of acute vision and great expectations," recalled a Stanford colleague. "He wanted Stanford to be a great, honorable, and humane university, and he told every Stanford president, from Wallace Sterling on, the hard truths he thought were necessary to reach that goal."[1]

Nelson, born in 1918 in Yamhill, Oregon, received his B.A. from the University of Oregon in 1941. While a student, he was editor of the campus newspaper, the *Oregon Daily Emerald*, and there he met his future wife, Corrine Wignes, a fellow student journalist. They married in 1941. Service with the U.S. Army Ordnance Department during World War II interrupted his budding career as a reporter in Portland. In 1947, he returned to the University of Oregon as associate professor of journalism and assistant to the president.

In 1953, he left Oregon for Ann Arbor as assistant to the president of the University of Michigan. He also became general secretary of U-M's Educational Television and Radio Center (precursor to the Public Broadcasting Service), beginning a lifelong interest in national and international issues encompassing public educational television. He became director of university relations at U-M in 1957, and was named vice president in 1960.

At Stanford, Nelson quickly gained respect across campus for his astuteness in dealing with political problems, local and national, that were affecting the university, including the proposed Ladera Dam. He worked well with Sterling's team, where his wit, his generosity, and his thoughtfulness fit into Sterling's collegial style. Like Sterling, he was a master of thank-you notes, especially to staff. And, like Sterling, he valued humor, agreeing with the president that a person who couldn't laugh at himself

Lyle Nelson, seen here in 1994, was admired as a wise advisor, strategist, and upbeat problem solver as Sterling's director of university relations and later as director of the Knight Journalism Fellowship Program. Nelson also was a popular journalism professor.
STANFORD NEWS SERVICE

had no sense of humor, and those with no sense of humor lacked good judgment. Nelson recalled Sterling saying, of a recently appointed university president, "I notice he can always laugh at others, but I've never seen him make any others laugh at him. I just don't think he'll make it." And, Nelson added, "he didn't."[2]

Nelson, appointed lecturer in the Department of Communication on his arrival in 1961, rose to full professor by 1969. He retained a strong interest in development of the department during his busy years as university relations director. The year following Sterling's 1968 retirement, Nelson moved full time to the Communication Department, serving as chair (1969–70 and 1972–79). He was named the first Thomas M. Storke Distinguished Professor of Communication in 1973.

Also in 1969, he became director of Stanford's Professional Journalism Fellowship program, which provides mid-career sabbaticals to American and international journalists. Nelson nurtured the program academically and through his fundraising, securing its permanent endowment, in 1984, with a $4 million grant from the John S. and James L. Knight Foundation. The renamed John S. Knight Journalism Fellowships program is one of the premier programs of its type.

Nelson was a highly creative and productive fundraiser. In retirement he continued to seek support for the journalism fellowships, particularly for international fellows. Hoping to assist any journalist who was trying to tell the truth against difficult odds, Nelson helped Solidarity union journalists in Poland and reporters for the *China Daily*, among many others. Linking to his interest in freedom of information internationally, the Lyle and Corrine Nelson International Journalism Fellowship was started in 1994 with seed money from former international Knight fellows.

Nelson's "bedrock concern was individual integrity," said Robert Beyers, who followed Nelson from Michigan to Stanford in 1961. When a student who had been caught cheating argued that "everyone does it," Nelson asked: "Isn't there room for one honest person who says, 'but my standards won't permit *me* to do so'? What happens to a democratic form of society if all citizens say, 'I have no obligations to rules and standards of decency and honesty'?"[3]

NOTES

1. James Bettinger at Lyle Nelson memorial service, 1997, reproduced in *Remembering Lyle M. Nelson* (Stanford: privately printed, 1997) 6. See also "Knight Fellowship Program Founder Dies," *Stanford Daily*, September 19, 1997; *Memorial Resolution: Lyle M. Nelson (1918–1997)* Stanford University.

2. "A Session on Wally: Transcription of an Oral History about J. E. Wallace Sterling, Recorded for the Stanford University Archives" (1985) 35, 51, SUA.

3. Bob Beyers, in *Remembering Lyle M. Nelson* (1997) 3.

A MASSIVE REVIEW
STUDY OF EDUCATION AT STANFORD, 1967–1969

The "habit of self-study" promoted by the 1956 Hoopes-Marshall Report continued to bear fruit in the 1960s. Follow-up studies beginning in 1961 included a four-year, three-part study by the Committee on General Studies and a broader study of undergraduate life by a 25-member, widely representative presidential advisory Committee on Undergraduate Education, chaired by Vice Provost Robert Wert. Both committees haggled with an increasingly vocal ASSU legislature about student representation.[33]

In spring 1964, the *Stanford Daily* leapt in with its own poll, asking a third of the freshman class their reactions to their first year. Their report underscored undergraduate criticism of curriculum offerings and teaching assistants.

The General Studies Committee, based on extensive surveys of seniors, issued similar findings that fall, vowing to revamp required first-year courses, freshman advising, and the use of first-year graduate teaching assistants. Meanwhile, the Committee on Undergraduate Education juggled such issues as residential living and student judicial reform as the advisory arm to a new office, the Dean of Undergraduate Education. (In late 1963, Wert was named dean.)[34]

An altogether separate faculty committee, led by Professor Albert J. Guerard, created the popular Freshman Seminar Program. This small-group study experience taught by senior faculty was introduced in fall 1965. (The committee had been created to study possible uses for an anonymous gift.)[35]

By 1965, Sterling was thinking of an even

As part of a new General Studies requirement, most seniors working for B.A. degrees were required to take a senior colloquium outside their field of study. President Sterling joined other faculty in leading quarter-long seminars, each limited to 15 students. His oversubscribed winter 1959 course was titled "The Making of Decisions." ROBERT COX / STANFORD NEWS SERVICE

Sterling appreciated law professor and Vice Provost Herb Packer's leadership during the broadly conceived Study of Education at Stanford (SES), 1967–69, and especially Packer's proactive interest in creating a faculty senate. Packer chaired the SES Steering Committee.
STANFORD NEWS SERVICE

broader examination of the university when he initiated a series of informal discussions about Stanford's future direction. In fall 1966, he established and chaired an eight-person planning committee to plan a comprehensive review of educational programs. Sterling also created the position of vice provost for academic planning and programs, selecting law Professor Herbert Packer to fill the post, effective January 1, 1967. (Packer was a member of the early planning group.)[36]

In early 1967, a decade after the Hoopes-Marshall Report, Sterling launched the Study of Education at Stanford (SES). The SES review produced major changes in graduate and under-graduate programs, residential education, and the overseas campus program, as well as advising, extracurricular activities, teaching, research, and faculty governance.[37]

SES got underway winter quarter with Packer as chair of its Steering Committee. Faculty members included James Gibbons, electrical engineering; Albert Hastorf, psychology; Joshua Lederberg, genetics; Mark Mancall, history; and Leonard Schiff, physics. Its three student mem-

bers were undergraduate Norton Batkin III, philosophy (who had been deeply affected by his freshman seminar experience); and graduate students Michael Menke, physics, and Anne Osborn, medicine. The Packer appointment turned out to be crucial. He shared Sterling's commitment to a comprehensive review of all of Stanford's educational programs and of its structure of governance. (Jim Gibbons took over the final phases of SES in early 1969, when Packer suffered a near-fatal stroke.)[38]

The character of the university's faculty and student body had changed substantively since the Hoopes-Marshall study. Equally important, by 1967 new academic disciplines were being created while others were dramatically changing. "The times appeared to demand re-examination of the nature of education and of the university, self-appraisal and change," the Steering Committee noted.[39]

The multi-year examination actively involved more than 200 faculty, staff, and students. It yielded 10 volumes, comprising more than 900 pages of analysis and recommendations, and represented one of the most comprehensive self-studies ever undertaken by an institution of higher education. (The first two volumes were issued in November 1968, two months after Sterling's retirement.) The 10 volumes are:

I: The Study & Its Purposes
II: Undergraduate Education
III: University Residences & Campus Life
IV: Undergraduate Admissions & Financial Aid
V: Advising & Counseling
VI: The Extra-Curriculum
VII: Graduate Education
VIII: Teaching, Research & the Faculty
IX: Study Abroad
X: Government of the University

Some reforms went into effect before the study was complete, including the introduction of

Provost Richard Lyman and President Kenneth Pitzer are seated, in alphabetical order, among the senators at the September 25, 1969, meeting of the Faculty Senate's second year. Photo taken from the vantage point of Senate Chair William Clebsch.   STANFORD NEWS SERVICE

interdepartmental majors, efforts to attract and admit minority students and faculty, improved computer access, and creation of a faculty senate. The Steering Committee also noted that it would be "irresponsible" to advocate programs that required vast new funding "at a time when financial pressures are painfully acute." Therefore, most curricular recommendations "cost nothing or call for a reordering of priorities rather than incremental expenditures."[40]

Sterling later observed that the study's reforms affected undergraduate more than graduate education. It reduced the number of required courses (notably, the History of Western Civilization series was phased out by 1971) and introduced new courses that were intended to offer subjects of broader interest and value (such as human biology, 1970). The reforms also offered students an opportunity to introduce courses, a move that Sterling thought unwise but that pleased the students. Among the suggestions not adopted was a return to the pre-1916 semester system.[41]

Other reforms included a dramatic shift of university teaching resources to the freshman year, major revisions in grading practices, and student opportunities to design their own majors. The study advocated continuing educational reform, with a standing committee and an administrative officer. Reforms also were proposed in other areas, including housing, advising, admissions and financial aid, overseas campuses, graduate education, faculty matters, and university governance. An Academic Planning Office was organized to assist students, faculty, and administration in obtaining data for rational planning. In 1970, the academic advising system was strengthened with a residence-based freshman advising program, and the Academic Information Center was created to help students define and achieve their academic goals.[42]

Sterling and Packer shared a strong interest in faculty governance, and particularly in finding a way to improve faculty participation through the Academic Council. Sterling had long worried that the council, which included all tenured and tenure-line assistant, associate, and full professors, was too large and cumbersome; he also favored a broader representation of faculty than through the council's nine-member Executive Committee. Promoting such a major step had been sidetracked by his efforts to reorganize fundraising and oversee the PACE Campaign, improve budgeting, and search for a new provost and vice provost in 1965–66. His 1964 illness also diverted his attention. Sterling's selection of Packer as vice provost and as SES chair proved to be pivotal,

since Packer had a similar idea, a faculty senate of perhaps 40 elected members, with the president and provost serving ex-officio.

The Senate of the Academic Council, commonly known as the Faculty Senate, came into being, with 53 members, in fall 1968, after deliberations of the SES Committee on Government of the University, which Packer also headed. Leonard Schiff, professor of physics, served as the senate's first chair (1968–69), and William Clebsch, professor of religious studies, as vice chair (and chair of the second senate, 1969–70). Sterling was delighted to be able to attend an early meeting. The change in faculty governance was well received: "Although the Senate is only in its first year of operation it has clearly demonstrated its superiority as [a] deliberative and decision-making body over the Academic Council," the study's final volume stated in 1969.[43]

The Study of Education at Stanford was completed after Sterling's retirement, and much of the credit would go to Packer for his pivotal role, overshadowing Sterling's efforts to get the study going and the work he and Packer did together to plan a strategy. Praise of Packer's contributions was well deserved. Nevertheless, Sterling was proud of his part setting in motion the study and its dramatic reforms.[44]

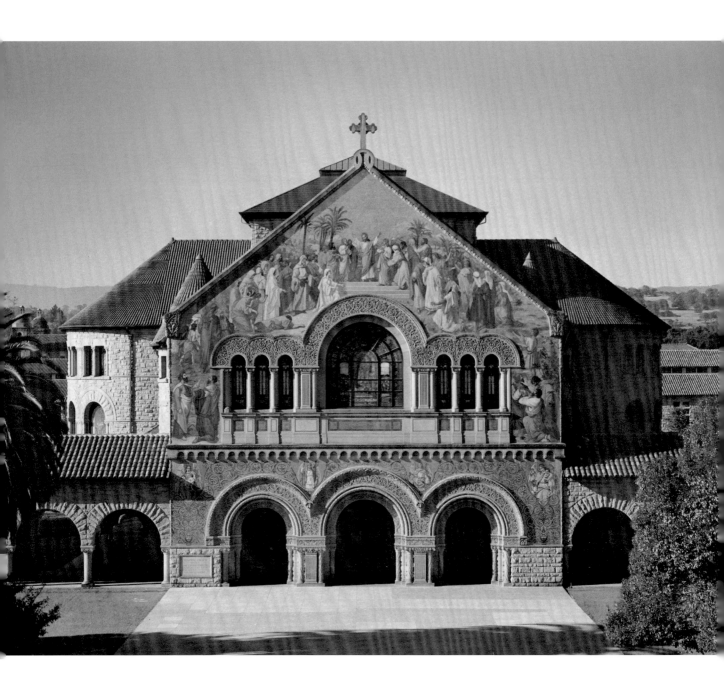

15

RELIGION AT STANFORD

THE INTERSECTION OF
MEMORIAL CHURCH AND ACADEMIA

Wallace Sterling, son of a Methodist minister—and a former Stanford graduate student—appreciated the special place Memorial Church held on campus. The physically imposing structure rarely fails to impress visitors, yet this church has a very personal history as a legacy of Jane Lathrop Stanford and was meant to fit comfortably within an informal and friendly campus community.

Arriving back on campus amid faculty and student complaints regarding the recently appointed new chaplain, the new president quickly saw that the larger issue was the functioning of Memorial Church as a viable segment of Stanford's academic community. Would it be possible to develop a religious studies curriculum and faculty on par with other academic programs?

Sterling gave his support to the creation of a religious studies program, setting the process in motion with a notable 1950 appointment and thereafter backing selection of individuals with both strong academic credentials and community service. Recruitment of a highly regarded religious studies faculty, in turn, stimulated a sense of social justice among Stanford's student body as Sterling's era closed. The 1966 appointment of scholar and Vietnam War critic B. Davie Napier as dean of the chapel gave Memorial Church a dynamic new role in Stanford campus life unseen since the days of its first chaplain. That same year, the trustees endorsed a two-year student campaign to reorient church services to be more truly embracing of students of differing Christian beliefs, reinforcing growing interest in the study and practice of all religious faiths represented on campus.

Sterling's initial task, however, was a personnel issue. On the surface, the question of retaining the Rev. Paul Covey Johnston was one of conflicting expectations, but it also exposed significantly different perspectives of the community to be served by the church and on the role of Memorial Church within Sterling's vision of a top-ranked academic institution.

< Unusual photo of Memorial Church (the skylight, seen here, is not visible from the ground in front) taken by George Gould and Ted Off, both '49. They climbed atop the Inner Quad's pointed arch to record the sun's pattern on the façade at 6:30 a.m. one day in May 1949.   STANFORD UNIVERSITY ARCHIVES

PICKING THE RIGHT MINISTER
FOR THE STANFORD COMMUNITY

Although Paul Covey Johnston's year-long clash with Sterling is barely a footnote in the era's history, the chaplain challenged Sterling's authority, as well as his patience.

Johnston, appointed by Alvin C. Eurich, outgoing acting president, had assumed his post in January 1949, only three months before Sterling took office. By March, evidence of the mismatch between the overbearing chaplain and Stanford's students and faculty was already filling the presidential inbox.

At the university's opening, a chapel was provided in one of the smaller Quadrangle buildings. Visiting clergymen often presided (with faculty members supplementing the service), and a volunteer student-faculty choir used a small organ provided by Mrs. Stanford. Attendance, too, was voluntary.[1]

The original Quadrangle's architectural plans had set aside a central location for a church of substantial size and design but it was not until after Senator Stanford's death, in 1893, that Mrs. Stanford focused her attention on the new church structure. Design and decoration evolved over her years of involvement to include magnificent Venetian mosaics, elaborate stained-glass windows, carved wood architectural touches, and white marble statuary. Memorial Church, begun in 1899, was dedicated January 25, 1903.

But this large and elegant church belied the informality and originality of Leland and Jane

Postcard view of the ornate interior of Memorial Church, after its 1903 completion but before significant destruction caused by the 1906 earthquake. The chancel included 12 marble statues of the apostles, which, when delivered, turned out to be too large for their niches. Two upper bands of mosaics represent the glory of angels and biblical prophets.   STANFORD UNIVERSITY ARCHIVES

Stanford's vision for its use. Mrs. Stanford is usually credited with establishing the nondenominational nature of the church, but Leland Stanford was equally adamant. (Neither Leland nor Jane Stanford claimed any denominational affiliation, attending various neighborhood churches while at the Palo Alto Farm and during their travels.) In addition to the 1885 Founding Grant, which clearly prohibited "sectarian instruction," Senator Stanford, in a newspaper interview two years later, reiterated, "The Church is to be regularly used for the benefit of the students. No creed or dogma will be permitted to be taught within its walls, but ministers of all denominations will be invited to deliver lectures on the fundamental principles of religion."[2]

In her "General Revision of the University Trusts," October 3, 1902, a few months before the formal opening of Memorial Church, Mrs. Stanford firmly stated:

> The services in the Memorial Church must be simple and informal in character, and the theological questions, services, and observances upon which the sects differ should not be entered upon, so that members of every church may worship and receive instruction therein not inconsistent with their individual beliefs. . . . Attendance at religious services shall be entirely optional, and no profession of religious faith or belief shall be exacted of any one for any purpose.[3]

Mrs. Stanford's first church appointment was R. Heber Newton, a prominent Episcopalian priest and writer, as "Select Preacher to the University and Pastor of the Memorial Church." Newton arrived on campus from New York City in late 1902, after a long career as rector of a large urban church. He and Mrs. Stanford soon clashed over his expectations of a traditional congregation, with services backed by a formally attired, professional choir (she preferred a student choir), and a light workload. He resigned five months later.[4]

Mrs. Stanford and the Board of Trustees decided no one was needed to replace Newton as "pastor." They had at hand Dr. David Charles Gardner, the young minister of All Saints Episcopal Church of Palo Alto, who, as "university chaplain," was working as Newton's

assistant. Gardner's less ostentatious style and widespread rapport with the community made him an integral part of the campus for the next 34 years.[5]

Overseeing what he called "an undenominational church," Charles Gardner began a longstanding tradition of varied services, simple and spiritual in character and meaning. Like the Stanfords, he sought to "avoid the things that divide, and exalt the principles upon which we can all agree," he said. "Thus, we say no creed. We know nothing of the ceremonial—except the necessary rule of reverence and dignity." Since he found that many students didn't care for church services of any kind, he visited "these delightful drifters" in the dormitories, fraternity houses,

The Rev. David Charles Gardner, an Episcopalian, began the church's long-standing tradition of simple and varied services, seeking to avoid "things that divide." During his 34 years as chaplain, he developed a strong rapport with students and faculty, and encouraged public service.
FRANK DAVEY / STANFORD UNIVERSITY ARCHIVES

or infirmary, and invited them to his home. "The parson is the friend of all—not alone of the pious," Gardner said.[6]

Gardner also fostered a tradition of public service. He cooked for Stanford's volunteers working at relief sites in San Francisco following the earthquake and fire in 1906. He later inspired creation of the Stanford Home for Convalescent Children (precursor of today's Lucile Packard Children's Hospital) not only for patient recuperation but also as an outlet for social service involving Stanford students. Gardner was remembered fondly as someone who represented the university to the public "in a way always to elevate and to dignify, and he did much to perpetuate the ideas of the founders of the university."[7]

Gardner and his successor as university chaplain, D. Elton Trueblood, who took over in 1936, welcomed individuals of all faiths. Jewish and Catholic guest speakers were invited to campus along with ministers of various Protestant denominations. Trueblood, a Quaker with lifelong friendships among Stanford's Quaker community, also met regularly with Jewish students in the vestry, and hosted Friends meetings at his home. Trueblood had a faculty appointment as a professor of philosophy (he had received his Ph.D. in philosophy from Johns Hopkins) and

Like his predecessor, second chaplain and professor of philosophy D. Elton Trueblood, a Quaker, welcomed all faiths, inviting Jewish and Catholic speakers as well as those from various Protestant denominations. He worked to build a religious studies curriculum across multiple departments. STANFORD UNIVERSITY ARCHIVES

was a prolific author and well-respected scholar. Trueblood left Stanford in 1945 to establish the Earlham School of Religion (a Quaker seminary in Richmond, Indiana).[8]

In 1947, Robert (Rabb) Macfee Minto was appointed associate chaplain, while the search for a new chaplain or minister to replace Trueblood took an unexpected turn. Minto, born in Scotland, had received his A.M. in 1929 from the University of Glasgow and his master of sacred theology degree from Union Theological Seminary in 1933. After he was ordained in the Church of Scotland, in 1934, he served in Scotland and Malaya before coming to Stanford.[9]

During the difficult year following President Tresidder's January 1948 death, acting President Alvin C. Eurich accepted the recommendation of Clarence H. Faust, then library director, to consider appointing Paul Covey Johnston, whom Faust had heard preach. (The appointment was at the discretion of the president, with the approval of the Board of Trustees.) Faust, an ordained evangelical minister, had a personal interest. He had received a bachelor's degree in divinity from Evangelical Theological Seminary (Myerstown, Pennsylvania) before getting his University of Chicago Ph.D. in English. He was especially interested in the intersection of theology and education.[10]

Johnston was then head minister at Immanuel Presbyterian Church in Los Angeles, which Johnston claimed had a congregation of some 4,500 members and a staff of 25. Johnston also was president of the Council of Churches of Greater Los Angeles. The Nebraska-born Johnston was a graduate of Bellevue College and McCormick Theological Seminary (1916). In 1938, after holding pastorates in Indiana and Nebraska, he moved on to Rochester, New York. By the late 1940s, he was minister at Immanuel Presbyterian Church, with its monumental Wilshire Boulevard building, modeled on a

French Gothic cathedral. He had no professional experience in an academic setting.[11]

After a meeting in the spring of 1948, the enthusiastic Johnston wrote Eurich a seven-page letter to set straight his understandings regarding the post of chaplain. He would be head of a Department of Religion, he stated, with a salary of $9,600 and his usual two months of vacation. He understood, he added, "that tenure would depend upon my competency as preacher, counselor and director of the Department; or until the retirement rules of the University would operate in my case."[12]

Johnston assumed that the Stanford chaplaincy would support his projected elaborate expansion of courses on religion. "At the earliest possible moment, one, and another, and possibly more, individuals should be found and established as teachers of religion." A school of theology was not far from his thinking. "I imagine we should look toward the erection of a building which could be somewhere near the Church and would house all the religious functions," he wrote.

He concluded his comments by telling Eurich that his friends had warned him against accepting the position until Stanford's new president had been selected "and his inclinations known."

Eurich attempted to clarify Johnston's impressions. "In stating to you that the Stanford University Memorial Church ranks as a department of the University, I did not intend to create the impression that a Department of Religion exists apart from the Church," he explained (that is, there was no academic department of religion and Johnston's was not to be an academic appointment). The "future development of additional instruction in religion would be in accordance with the development of our program of general education, which, as you know, will be under the direction of Dr. Faust" (whose appointment as dean of Humanities and Sciences began the following September). Nor did Eurich

In seeking to fill the vacant chaplaincy, acting President Alvin Eurich warned of Stanford's limited financial resources but equivocated about the campus community's preference for a broadly conceived religious experience, rather than a membership-based, Protestant congregational practice. PHILIP FEIN / STANFORD NEWS SERVICE

"look forward with any assurance to the development of an additional building." He offered only some space in the church basement "which we can perhaps put to better use."[13]

Eurich went on to explain that some things suggested by Johnston (such as "affiliated memberships," free-will offerings, raising church funds) would need to be studied, just as the details of a program of religion would "await the course of events which will follow wise leadership." For the moment, the appointment of additional staff to Johnston, Minto, and one full-time secretary "must necessarily await the development of the program and the augmentation of our resources." His conclusion was, nonetheless, ambiguous:

> I cannot extend to you any positive assurance regarding the views of the President of the University who will be appointed as a result of the search now being conducted by our Board of Trustees. I believe, however, that I can write with all confidence that our Trustees will designate a President who will be in sympathy with the present policies of the University.[14]

Johnston, undaunted, responded that although he would suffer a loss of $4,000 annually in pay, and inadequate working facilities and staff, these facts "are overcome in my mind by the vision of the future of the work we may build . . . and by the glowing desire to immerse myself in student life." Eurich confirmed Johnston's appointment that July, to commence January 1, 1949.[15]

Following Wallace Sterling's appointment in fall 1948, Johnston visited Sterling and came away "a very happy man." He subsequently wrote Sterling, "I felt that our minds met at once over basic matters pertaining to the work at Stanford."[16]

Johnston was not long to remain a happy man. And Sterling soon found Johnston neither sympathetic nor cooperative.

HIGH HOPES UNFULFILLED

Johnston came to Stanford in January 1949 "with high hope," Sterling wrote an alumnus a year later. "This hope was widely shared by members of the Stanford family. The hope was not fulfilled."[17]

Even before arriving on campus, Johnston enjoyed fielding letters from those ready to complain about the untraditional nature of Stanford's Memorial Church. He passed one such letter about his future associate chaplain to Eurich, who responded: "I am at a loss to understand the letter you received [about Minto]. . . . Less than three months ago [the professor] was strongly urging that we appoint Minto Chaplain."[18]

It quickly became apparent that Johnston was not accustomed to a campus setting. Even before Sterling's arrival at the beginning of April 1949, student complaints about Johnston had led both Trustee President Paul Edwards and University Chancellor Ray Lyman Wilbur to question Clarence Faust, acting president as of Eurich's December departure. Edwards also confirmed with Wilbur that the trustees had taken no action that would change the original concept of the place and function of Memorial Church, despite Johnston's suggestions, "nor have I discerned any desire for a change on the part of board members."

Paul Covey Johnston, hired by acting President Eurich in 1948, had been head minister at Immanuel Presbyterian Church of Los Angeles, with a large congregation and professional staff housed in a building styled after a French Gothic cathedral. CURTIS STUDIOS / STANFORD NEWS SERVICE

Library Director Clarence H. Faust, an ordained evangelical minister, recommended Paul Covey Johnston to Eurich after hearing him preach. But, as acting president for four months before Sterling's arrival, Faust unsuccessfully tried to get the chaplain "on the right beam." STANFORD NEWS SERVICE

Faust reassured Edwards that he would get the new chaplain "on the right beam."[19]

A letter from a freshman was typical of the kinds of complaints leveled against the new chaplain. In a letter to the editor of the *Stanford Daily*, Thomas F. Grose wrote that Johnston's Easter sermon said little about Jesus Christ and much about politics. "I learned that our Chaplain disapproves of high taxes, militarism, swimming pools, cocktail parties, etc.," especially in Hollywood. "If the University hired Dr. Johnston as an exponent of the Republican Party, I think they could have had the respect for the Church in not placing him in the position of Chaplain." Sterling's Easter greeting was better suited to the spirit of the occasion, he concluded.[20]

As Sterling later described the situation to an alumnus:

> Dr. Johnston had not been long on the campus before it was clear that he was antagonizing the main body of students interested in the church and religious affairs here. He seemed strangely impregnable to suggestions made to him with good will and in good faith by those members of the faculty with whom he consulted about the Memorial Church and the religious program at Stanford.[21]

During his busy first months in office, Sterling looked into the situation, talking to student leaders and faculty interested in the church program. He also kept the trustees fully informed. In June, he told Johnston that he appeared to have "gotten off to a very bad start and that I was uncertain as to whether the damage could be repaired under his chaplaincy."[22]

Johnston was clearly surprised at the negative performance review. "Your remark that I had made a pretty complete bad start on this campus knifed me to the quick, of course, much as I appreciated your kindness in sharing with me your great concern, and letting me have both barrels. It was not easy for you to do."[23]

In his own defense, Johnston responded with

a lengthy indictment of Stanford. "The first item that I care to call to your attention is the set of mind pervading the Campus," he wrote Sterling. He recalled a remark that startled him, delivered at an early meeting of the Chaplains' Advisory Committee. History Professor Edgar Eugene Robinson told him that if the faculty had been given "the chance to vote on whether they cared to have a Chaplain on the campus—any chaplain—the answer would have been a resounding 'no'!"[24]

Just as he was unaware that many of the faculty had been supportive of the broader approach of Gardner and Trueblood, Johnston was confounded by the emotions still festering about the Tresidder and, especially, Eurich administrations. He was proud of the support he had received from Clarence Faust, who came to church frequently, but singled out Eurich: "The fact that I was chosen and brought here by Dr. Eurich has not helped me any. At the very least he was not popular with scores of the Faculty because of his directives and his non-sharing of administrative decisions."

As for his preaching, Johnston said, "where you have heard twenty detractors, I have had scores and scores which have come to say that they have been helped. You yourself have never heard me preach in the Church. You therefore have no personal and first-hand knowledge of my offerings." With a clear, if poorly informed, slap at his predecessors and his associate chaplain, he added, "but if what the Faculty want is simply an easy-going good fellow, who will marry their living and bury their dead; say a prayer at the proper time, and needle the conscience of his hearers, then I am not your man." Johnston concluded with an ill-advised threat, with a bit of emotional blackmail thrown in:

> After a number of able men have turned down the opportunity of being chaplains here, and so many more have their fingers crossed as to the possible

success of the work, it would not work much good for the University if a man who has made something of a national reputation and who has been willing to risk his neck, is turned out to grass. I am writing, you see, just as candidly and bluntly as you have opened the way for me to do. . . . I have not shared any of this with my wife. I trust that I will never have to. In her physical condition I fear she could not take it.[25]

A month later, Johnston attempted to go over Sterling's head by directly contacting board President Edwards "about Stanford matters which are our mutual concern." Edwards made it plain that the trustees would not interfere in administrative questions; he referred Johnston to President Sterling.[26]

Sterling again studied the matter carefully, perhaps longer than he had originally intended, consulting widely now with students, alumni, and faculty. Again, the responses confirmed that despite its formal, conservative appearance, the church's appeal to the Stanford community was quite different from what Johnston had experienced at his Immanuel Presbyterian Church. The director of the Stanford Research Institute told Sterling of his disappointment: "I sense a coldness and lack of spirituality in the service which to me is quite disturbing. . . . A week ago last Sunday the Chaplain made more than twenty quotations from various sources with few original thoughts and little constructive thinking of his own."[27]

An alumna, now at Union Theological Seminary in New York, worried about the impact on students, writing:

Despite the excellent work of the Reverend Robert M. Minto, the Church has to struggle with the policies of a head Chaplain whom the students had no voice in selecting, and who has incurred the disfavor and antagonism of both students and faculty alike. As a result, the student attitude has become one of increasing apathy, antagonism, and ignorance toward the Church and its work in an age when educators throughout the country

The size and elegance of Memorial Church belied the simple nature of its services and staffing. This timeless view, likely taken in the 1930s, is from the choir loft.

BERTON CRANDALL / STANFORD UNIVERSITY ARCHIVES

are realizing that life in an atomic age must be grounded upon a Christian allegiance strong enough to morally control an amoral science, which may be used for good or evil.[28]

Sterling terminated Johnston as chaplain in March 1950, generously giving him full pay through August 31 (the end of the university's fiscal year), with a paid leave of absence for six more months. In addition, Johnston was free to spend the summer quarter as he saw fit. "I realize, as do the members of the Board, that the decision which led to this official action has not been easy for any party concerned," Sterling wrote Johnston after the trustees approved the action. "I explained to the Board my deep appreciation of your effort during these past eighteen months, of the respect I have for your great sincerity and abiding convictions, and of your conduct under heavy disappointment."[29]

In late June, Johnston responded in a lengthy public speech, covered extensively by the *Palo Alto Times*, at an off-campus farewell luncheon in his honor arranged by clergy of the Mid-Peninsula. The heart of the problem, Johnston said, had to do with the relationship between Memorial Church and Stanford's student body and faculty. His criticism of the university was scathing:

> The precious idea exists that that beautiful building stands at the focal point of the University equipment; it is non-sectarian, it is available to all, and when a student pays his matriculation fees he buys its privileges. All that is excellent; but the connection of persons with it is unrealistic. The Church is not a Church in any true sense. It is mainly a preaching station. It has no membership, no boards, no service organizations, no opportunities for people to support its work by their giving, and scarcely anything that is tangible whereby anyone can feel he shares its ongoing life. This condition is the basis of the judgment of one of your distinguished citizens that the Stanford Memorial Church is but a "hollow shell!"[30]

To fix this, he argued, Memorial Church should have at least an associate membership for students and a regular membership for resident faculty members. This membership should elect a board to govern its affairs, and the chaplains, rather than "having their fortunes completely and solely in the President's office," should be chosen by and report to this board—"with, of course, final approval by the executive head of the institution, in accord with regular University practice."

Johnston had lost hope in Stanford. "High morals and fine manners are contingent upon real religious literacy and conviction, and Stanford must soon or late realize this truth," he stated. "The aura of intelligent but specific religious devotion must come to envelop the entire educational process; or we are lost, and Stanford—for all its marvelous equipment and traditions—is lost. 'Education without religion will create a race of clever devils' is still an axiom."[31]

While the philosophic points that Johnston raised were a matter of debate, he then raised the question of the university's integrity on the matter of his employment. According to the *Palo Alto Times,* Johnston stated that he had a written agreement with the Stanford administration "for the establishment of an adequate student religious organization and program, and of chairs of religion in the various departments," as the *Times* paraphrased, "with himself having the status of dean," and that these agreements "have not been kept."[32]

Sterling, ill with the flu, did not attend the luncheon, but others were quick to report back. The Rev. Edward L. Parsons wrote to Paul Edwards that although Johnston spoke in a friendly way about Stanford and Sterling, he definitely gave the impression that his large scheme for development of the chapel and religious work had been previously approved. Parsons thought Johnston's notion of church memberships and a church board separate from university authorities

Chaplain Paul Covey Johnston (left) and Assistant Chaplain Robert Minto flank the Memorial Church Committee, a student-faculty group that helped them direct the church's religious activities. A key project was the Inter-Faith Committee, which included all organized denominational groups on and off campus. Johnston wanted to build a congregation based on church membership rather than seeking to encompass the entire student body and faculty; he also wanted a professional choir. His brief tenure tested how Sterling would handle serious personnel issues.   STANFORD UNIVERSITY ARCHIVES

unwise, "far from the kind of place in the university life which the Stanfords planned," and believed that Johnston intended an exclusive, congregational church.[33]

Both Sterling and Johnston were immediately aware of the negative news coverage.[34] Johnston wrote to Sterling the following day, enclosing a copy of his remarks to show that his transcript merely said: "It was *understood* that the contemptuous neglect of the presentation of religion on the academic level should be overcome, and that, as the way was made plain, there should be established chairs of religion in each of the major departments of the University."[35]

Sterling, perhaps more savvy about press cover-age than Johnston, remained suspicious of Johnston's intentions. The allegations that Stanford had acted in bad faith was one Sterling would not let go unchallenged. After reading the press report of the luncheon, Sterling wrote Johnston that he could see that an "understanding" could evolve into a "written agreement" in the reporter's eyes. "I understand that a speaker may be misquoted. I understand also that a misquotation when printed in the press, has an effect which, however regrettable, may be difficult to correct." Nonetheless, "this report amounted to a public impeachment of the University's integrity."[36]

Sterling, having also reread all of the correspondence between President Eurich and

Johnston preceding his appointment, continued: "The correspondence provides no ground for concluding that Stanford University has breached a 'written agreement.' The indictment of Stanford embodied in the press report of the luncheon is erroneous. I shall do what I can, in ways that I consider most effective, to rectify the error," he told Johnston.[37]

The National Association of College and University Chaplains, learning Johnston's side of the story, asked Sterling for a statement of the university's position. He responded bluntly:

> The terms of Dr. Johnston's appointment were particular in that they did not embrace the usual forms or terms of faculty tenure. His tenure of office as Chaplain was entirely dependent upon the competency with which he discharged his responsibilities as Chaplain, this competency to be judged, naturally, by those who bear the high responsibility for guiding the destinies of the University. In the judgment of these persons, Dr. Johnston's chaplaincy here was not a success and we felt it necessary to terminate

the appointment. Each of us in his own way very deeply regretted that such termination was necessary, for we admired Dr. Johnston for his courage and convictions and his deep religious faith.[38]

When Johnston sought a new position at First Presbyterian Church in Wichita, Kansas, later that year, the congregation's search committee chairman asked Sterling in October for "a very frank opinion." Sterling frankly responded. About his preaching ability, Sterling wrote, "I was not favorably impressed. I felt a certain arrogance of tone, disposition to denounce, fascination with words, in short, his sermons rubbed me the wrong way."

As for his personality, "Dr. Johnston is a man of considerable energy and vigor; he makes a good appearance and an initial impression of warm friendship." However, the president told them, "vigor can easily turn into aggressiveness. Whether or not this is a good or bad thing, I leave to your judgment."[39]

A student lights candles in this 1954 photograph of Memorial Church. Students continue to play an important role at the church. STANFORD NEWS SERVICE

Sterling was especially disappointed with Johnston's inability to work within Stanford's collegial community environment:

I am sure Dr. Johnston would be the first to express surprise at my opinion that he was not cooperative. I'm sure he intends to be, but he lacks the facility. Our experience here was that he found it difficult to accept the suggestions of those who were trying to help him to adjust to a new situation. He had his own ideas as to what should be done at Stanford and these ideas we welcomed, but he did not indicate at any time that he possessed the instinct and sensitivity and technical skill of winning broad support for those ideas; rather did he attempt, so to speak, to shove his ideas down Stanford's throat. That Stanford resisted this approach of Dr. Johnston's may be a criticism of Stanford. I simply state the experience for what it is worth to you as a guide.[40]

The Kansas church subsequently appointed Johnston as its senior minister. Johnston, now a happy man, wrote Sterling jubilantly to advise him of his appointment, and boasted that the church had purchased a $30,000 residence for him and his wife. "This is the most aggressive church in the mid-west in our Presbyterian

In 1950, Robert (Rabb) Minto took over as university chaplain. Unlike his predecessor, Minto continued Stanford's practice of attracting speakers from across religious divides and carried on the tradition of service and student involvement. He retired in 1973.   DANIEL ZIMM / STANFORD NEWS SERVICE

denomination," he added, "and our beginning-days augur well for the future."[41]

Stanford, too, was happy. Associate Chaplain Rabb Minto already had been promoted to university chaplain. "The scheme now is to have Rabb carry on as the splendid pastor he is, and provide some continuity in the pulpit," Sterling wrote a ministerial friend. "I hope, however, that we may attract to the pulpit the best that the US and perhaps some other countries have to offer." This would prove to be the case, as Minto carried on the service tradition of Gardner and Trueblood until his retirement, in 1973.[42]

EMERGENCE OF RELIGIOUS STUDIES AT STANFORD

In his 1950 comments to the National Association of College and University Chaplains, Sterling had noted that Johnston's termination should not be interpreted as meaning that Stanford was "indifferent to or unaware of the great role that religion can and should play in an academic community and curriculum. Our plans for the future and the budgetary appropriations underlying these plans are, I think, evidence of our intent to develop into greater strength the whole religious program of the university."[43]

In his parting luncheon speech, Johnston had complained that "Stanford does not enjoy an enviable reputation as to its religious interests. It is known far and wide as an exceptional institution in the sciences and in the arts, but that it has given itself to the rational, humanistic culture to such a degree that religion has mighty little chance here." Ironically, it was within the Special Program in the Humanities that Stanford's Religious Studies Program was born, in 1950, and nurtured.[44]

Sterling thought that religious studies had a place among the humanities programs, as did another preacher's son, John W. Dodds, former

Sterling often conferred with another preacher's son, John W. Dodds, about building up religious studies as an academic pursuit. As founder and first director of what would become Humanities Special Programs, Dodds oversaw expansion of religious studies.
STANFORD NEWS SERVICE

dean of humanities and founder and director of what became Humanities Special Programs.[45] Over the years, religious studies, as an academic pursuit, had depended on the personal efforts of the university's chaplains. Gardner had given a course in biblical history. Trueblood had gone a step further, not only teaching his own courses in the philosophy of religion and church thought, but also gradually building up a curriculum by encouraging other faculty to participate. (In 1941, the university's course catalog listed 21 religion-related courses, ranging from biblical studies to early Mediterranean and Egyptian religion and Hindu studies, taught by other professors.)[46]

However, after Trueblood left, in 1946, the faculty had lost interest. It worried Sterling, Dodds later recalled, that these courses did not seem to come together as a program. Eager to get things moving, Sterling suggested to Dodds that they begin searching for someone to teach at the undergraduate level. Initially, they were disappointed to find that those they interviewed were looking toward futures as teachers at seminaries or theological schools—this was not what Stanford wanted. In 1950, they found what they were looking for in Alexander Miller, a young activist preacher from New Zealand. Miller, an ordained minister in the Presbyterian Church of New Zealand, had received his Ph.D. from Columbia University while at Union Theological Seminary. Dodds described him as "a terrific shot in the arm."[47]

Alexander (Lex) Miller, a man known for his kindness, humility, and sense of humor, came to Stanford with "an impressive jail record," his colleagues noted with some amusement, having picketed in New Zealand for workers' rights and pacifism during the 1930s. "He felt keenly the necessity for Christians to be committed to secular work out of a high appreciation for the dignity of human labor, and a passion for the integrity of human society." Miller had served in London's East End during the Blitz (1940–41), making a name for himself among the working class along the bombed-out waterfront, and later in Scotland. He brought to Stanford "a vitality of a theology concerned with the real affairs of real men, seeking to illuminate all of human life by the affirmation of the Christian gospel."[48]

Miller was an excellent teacher, as well as a prolific author, a sound scholar, and a respected academic colleague. He was energetic in finding others to teach undergraduate courses, but, more significantly, he took the lead in raising money for salaries of new appointments. Within a few years, Stanford added two more professors to the program, Edwin M. Good and H. Jackson Forstman. Good, like Miller, had received his Ph.D. from Columbia, and his master's in divinity from Union Theological Seminary. He came to Stanford in 1956, remaining until his retirement.[49] Forstman, also a Union Theological Seminary graduate, served as an assistant professor from 1960 to 1963.

In 1953, Miller drafted a pamphlet titled *The Teaching of Religion at Stanford*. Sterling sent Miller his thoughts, which would influence the continuing evolution of religious studies on campus: "I take the liberty of suggesting that, given the broad based nature of our program and hopes here, together with the spirit of the founding

The 1950 recruitment of Alexander (Lex) Miller, a young activist preacher from New Zealand, was an important step in developing an undergraduate religious studies curriculum. Miller, a respected scholar and popular teacher, attracted funding for additional faculty appointments and stabilized religious studies as a program.
STANFORD NEWS SERVICE

grant, that such phrases as Christian tradition, Christian inheritance might be broadened to be more inclusive than the adjective implies."[50]

As later published, the pamphlet, with a note by Sterling, made it clear that "It is not planned to build a School of Religion or a Department of Religion at Stanford. Our program is more modest and, we believe, more strategic than this. Our prime concern is not to train specialists in religion, but to bring a greater understanding of the issues of religion to the whole student body."[51]

Miller died of a heart attack in 1960, but he had set in motion the growth of a sound Religious Studies Program. By 1968, the program had eight full-time faculty members. Its expanded offerings now included Catholic, Jewish, and Buddhist studies. Undergraduates could major in the humanities in the field of religious studies, and the program also offered a selective graduate program, including the Ph.D. (In 1973, the program became the Religious Studies Department.)

In 1961, Sterling wrote with confidence of the university's vigorous steps to add faculty to the Religious Studies Program. "Where Stanford ten years ago had no full-time faculty members in the field of religion, we now have two men in the field and we are adding still a third," he

responded to a letter from concerned parents of an undergraduate. "Professor[s] Henry J. Forstman and Edwin M. Good are currently on the faculty, Professor Robert [McAfee] Brown, formerly Auburn Professor of Systematic Theology at Union Theological Seminary in New York City, will come to Stanford next year. And, of course, we have a Chaplain and Associate Chaplain whose special strength lies in religious counseling."[52]

Lex Miller had exposed the campus to a new kind of ministerial activism on behalf of social justice. Robert McAfee Brown, a leader in civil rights and social justice causes who joined the faculty in 1962, followed in Miller's footsteps.

Brown, the son and grandson of ministers, had been ordained in 1944, shortly after he earned his bachelor's degree from Amherst. He received a second bachelor's degree, in divinity, from Union Theological Seminary in 1945, and served as a Navy chaplain. His Ph.D. in philosophy of religion from Columbia followed, in 1951. An organizer of Mississippi Freedom Riders in 1961–62, Brown, then a professor at Union Theological Seminary, was in jail in the Deep South when Stanford's Board of Trustees approved his appointment.

Brown would become an international leader

Robert McAfee Brown, one of many clergy active in the civil rights movement, was in jail in the Deep South when Stanford's Board of Trustees approved his appointment. He later became a vocal critic of American intervention in the Vietnam War.
STANFORD NEWS SERVICE

in ecumenical and social justice causes during his 14 years teaching at Stanford. He took an active part in protests against U.S. involvement in the Vietnam War, and was a co-founder of the group Clergy and Laity Concerned About Vietnam. Considered an inspiring and empathetic figure, Brown offered classes on religion and ethics in contemporary life and literature that were among the most numerically popular on the Stanford campus. "Brown was an immensely popular teacher," recalled political science Professor David Abernethy. "He was just one of the most articulate people I ever met. He combined eloquence with a marvelous sense of humor." Brown left Stanford in 1976 to join the faculty of the Pacific School of Religion.[53]

In 1964, William A. (Bill) Clebsch arrived at Stanford to replace Forstman. Clebsch played a key role in development of Humanities Special Programs and later of the Religious Studies Department. He also was a highly respected university citizen who would influence faculty governance, two university presidential selections, undergraduate admissions and financial aid, and university fundraising.

The Tennessee-born Clebsch had served in a number of ministerial and theological seminary positions in Michigan, Virginia, and Texas before joining the Religious Studies Program as a professor of humanities. Like Miller, Good, Forstman, and Brown, he had studied at Union Theological Seminary, in New York, receiving his Th.D. in 1957.[54]

A man of wide learning and endless curiosity, Clebsch became a prolific scholar active in numerous academic societies as well as a challenging and energetic teacher. In 1976, he received one of the first Dean's Awards for Distinguished Teaching in H&S.

When, in 1967, John Dodds stepped down as Humanities Special Programs chairman, Clebsch took his place, while continuing to help the

William Clebsch, prolific scholar, distinguished teacher, and first chair of the Religious Studies Department, was a respected university citizen, with wide influence in academic governance. A long-standing Advisory Board member, he chaired the Academic Council's second Faculty Senate. STANFORD NEWS SERVICE

Religious Studies Program mature. "By his work with Stanford's Department and in the national organizations," his colleagues later recalled, "he led in identifying Religious Studies as a discipline of the Humanities, which has cut the apron strings to the theological tutelage of religious bodies and traditions."[55]

In 1973, the program became the Religious Studies Department. Clebsch served as its chair, 1973–80, as he continued to teach courses in other Humanities programs. "Bill wished only that the Department be the best small Religious Studies Department in the country. Such fiscal and structural responsibility made him welcome in the offices of Deans—and the fact did not escape his notice."[56] He also was energetic and creative in pressing the cause of the humanities. He recruited colleagues from across the campus to create the American Studies Program, which he chaired from 1975 to 1980, and he helped

organize the Values, Technology, Science, and Society (VTSS) program.

Clebsch's strong interest in and commitment to faculty governance paralleled that of President Sterling. As deputy chairman of the first Senate of the Academic Council (1968–69) and chairman of the second (1969–70), Clebsch set the pattern for future senate operations, playing a central role in the formulation of the senate's rules and definition of committee functions. He served as an elected member of the senate for most of 1968–80, and was selected as a member, vice-chair, and chairman of the Advisory Board during 1976–80.

MEMORIAL CHURCH AND THE 1960s

Student interest in the church grew markedly during the 1960s, though not necessarily in a direction that Sterling would have predicted.

In February 1966, responding to growing student complaints, the Board of Trustees approved sectarian worship services in Memorial Church, overturning a long-standing practice of allowing only nondenominational Protestant services. This followed an ardent two-year campaign by the *Stanford Daily,* led by editorial staff members Ilene Strelitz and Bruce Campbell, and a subsequent study by the student legislature (LASSU) confirming that students who attended off-campus churches and synagogues had difficulty with transportation and often felt out of place among older congregations.

The trustees' February resolution opened the church, but only the church, to all religious groups on the grounds that Mrs. Stanford had intended to provide a pan-sectarian religious experience relevant to student life. The move was welcomed by campus Catholics, but Memorial Church's iconography still made it an inappropriate site for some faiths and some Christian denominations. When university officials denied requests to hold a Jewish Sabbath and a Unitarian service in the unadorned Women's Clubhouse, the outcry—and a threatened lawsuit—led to yet another change. Three months after their landmark church decision, university trustees backtracked, supporting use of the Women's Clubhouse (renamed the Clubhouse) as a venue accommodating religious worship.[57]

Sterling retained a keen personal interest in Memorial Church and in the religious life of Stanford's students, and supported vigorous steps taken to bring outstanding preachers to the church pulpit. Guest preachers often reflected

President Sterling and Chaplain Rabb Minto preparing for an event in Memorial Church in 1960. Sterling and Minto shared a keen interest in how the church could relate to undergraduate life. JACK FIELDS / STANFORD UNIVERSITY ARCHIVES

‹ A timeless arch at the front of Memorial Church. STANFORD NEWS SERVICE growing campus interest in social and ethical issues, especially civil rights and concern about the escalation of American involvement in Vietnam.

Not all were pleased. Following a February 1966 sermon by well-known civil rights and peace activist Chaplain William Sloane Coffin of Yale University, Mary Wilbur, wife of Dr. Blake Wilbur (a son of former President Ray Lyman Wilbur), wrote Sterling indignantly: "Yesterday I attended the Memorial Church service and I was never before so angry at a sermon. I was alone and so do not know how it affected others except for the squirming around me. I shall certainly never go to hear Mr. Coffin again."[58]

Sterling wrote a sympathetic response:

> The pulpit of Memorial Church is no place for a political speech, although I must say, judging from press reports, that there is a national—even international, tendency to link religion to all aspects of life today. Ann and I were away last Sunday. When I read Monday morning's press account of Coffin's "sermon," I called Rabb Minto. He feels as you do. Indeed, he reported that Coffin himself feels that he went too far in this sermon. Fine time for such judgment![59]

In 1966, the Rev. B. Davie Napier, a biblical scholar and Holmes Professor of Old Testament Criticism and Interpretation at Yale, was offered the positions of dean of the chapel and professor of religious studies. Napier, born in China to missionaries and himself a Congregational minister, was deeply influenced by his high school and undergraduate years in Alabama, which forged his interest in civil rights and social justice.

Napier had a strong interest in undergraduate life. (He had served the previous year as master of Yale University's Calhoun College.) "Gifted as a preacher as well as a jazz pianist, Napier turned the chapel into what some regarded as Christian theater—the introduction of jazz and other types of experimental worship as well as provocative preaching," according to Van A. Harvey, who

Dean of the Chapel B. Davie Napier engaged undergraduate student interest when he introduced jazz music in church services and used provocative preaching to relate Christian scripture to the turbulent events of the era. His opposition to the Vietnam War drew off-campus criticism.
STANFORD NEWS SERVICE

joined the Religious Studies Department in 1978. "Suddenly a jam-packed Memorial Church became the fashionable place for undergraduates to congregate on weekends." Like Brown, Napier was a vocal critic of U.S. intervention in Vietnam. He gained fame among students for his efforts to relate scripture to the turbulent times of the late 1960s.[60]

In the months before his retirement, Sterling continued his role as mediator. In early 1968, Lowell Berry, '26, a successful businessman and devout evangelical, complained about the chapel to Provost Richard Lyman, with a copy to the president. Berry, whose foundation was created to strengthen Christian ministry at the local church or parish level, had given several gifts to Stanford's chapel program, including a scholarship. (Berry was also one of the organizers of the New Founders League of Stanford, launched in 1970 by Stanford alumni, which advocated, among other things, the return of the Stanford Indian mascot, the return of ROTC to campus, admission of "qualified students only" with no recognition of affirmative action, and reestablishment of Memorial Church "as a sanctuary which instills a faith worth living as specified by Mrs. Stanford.")[61]

In 1951, the Lowell Berry Foundation had given $10,000 "to be used in stimulating student interest in Stanford Memorial Church Services."

Chemistry professor and two-time Nobel laureate Linus Pauling received a standing ovation in Memorial Church following his October 15, 1969, address calling for an end to the war during Stanford's Vietnam Moratorium. Sterling, now chancellor, continued to defend use of the church for events of campus community concern, and praised Dean Napier's rapport with students.
STANFORD NEWS SERVICE

Berry had offered additional funds for a scholarship for a student doing preparatory work in religious education, preferably an athlete. At Sterling's suggestion, it became a scholarship for "students who have demonstrated and are demonstrating an active interest in the works of the Stanford Memorial Church," and "that preference be given to students of second year or higher standing whose academic work and appetite for leadership make them worthy in the eyes of the [selection] committee."

Referring to a *Stanford Observer* article about student doubts about traditional Christian worship, Berry wrote:

> This and other reports of the religious philosophy that is being expounded there, are such as to lead me to feel that our gift has been the means of initiating a program of religious training at the Chapel, which is about as foreign to the basic tenets of the Christian faith as we could imagine. This leads me most reluctantly to the conclusion that we must respectfully solicit from the Board of Trustees permission to make these funds available to some other department of the University.[62]

Sterling was sympathetic but stood his ground. "I acknowledge that judgments about Dean Napier—or any other clergyman for that matter—may differ. But the development of the Church program has been considerable. It has attracted increased numbers of students and has involved ministries other than Dean Napier's."[63] Napier remained at Stanford another four years, leaving in 1972 to become president of the Pacific School of Religion.

WESTERN
AIRLINES

FLIGHT
155

STERLING, FOOTBALL, AND THE COLLAPSE OF THE PACIFIC COAST CONFERENCE

Introducing Stanford's new president during Big Game weekend, November 1948, seemed especially meaningful. Wallace Sterling had impressed university trustees and alumni as a three-sport athlete and college and professional football coach in Canada who went on to a successful academic career. Aside from the character qualities many ascribed to that early experience, Sterling's clear love of sports held the promise of a new injection of traditional Stanford spirit and a longed-for end of Stanford's headline-grabbing football doldrums.

At his first press conference after taking office the following spring, Sterling—described by one reporter as looking like a "line-crushing

< "No Stanford president had closer personal ties to Stanford football than Wally Sterling, former player, collegiate and pro Canadian football coach," wrote Don Liebendorfer. Sterling expended much time and political capital on football, especially the Pacific Coast Conference's collapse over compliance issues. Here Sterling is en route to a PCC meeting with Assistant Athletic Director Chuck Taylor (left) and Faculty Athletic Representative Rix Snyder. STANFORD UNIVERSITY ARCHIVES

full back"—was peppered with questions about potential changes to the struggling football program. Memories of Stanford's glorious Vow Boys teams of the mid-1930s and Wow Boys of 1940 were still fresh. So, too, were the three years when Stanford's football program was discontinued, a "casualty of war" as Chancellor Ray Lyman Wilbur put it. The heavy presence of the U.S. Army on campus, 1943–45, with only a few athletes left among the remaining male civilian student body, had ended the university's competitive athletics for the war's duration. (The Army would not allow intercollegiate sports to interfere with physical training of their soldier-students at wartime campuses; the Navy, by contrast, encouraged team competition, and the Navy's presence at Stanford's rivals allowed them to field strong wartime intercollegiate teams. As a result, some Stanford players had transferred to UCLA or to Cal to continue playing competitive football.)[1]

While other sports had recovered quickly after 1945, Stanford was only gradually rebuilding a

Alumni, including Sterling, had strong memories of Stanford's Vow Boys (above) and Wow Boys. Sports reporters in 1933 goaded varsity sophomores about their freshman vow to never lose to USC, then on a 27-game winning streak and victorious against Stanford since 1928. The Vow Boys kept their promise, earning a boisterous parade back on campus. They went on to beat the Trojans—and Cal—three years running (1933–35), winning three PCC championships and three Rose Bowl appearances. Later, the Wow Boys won the January 1941 Rose Bowl and a #2 national ranking.   STANFORD UNIVERSITY ARCHIVES

winning football program. Its greatest rivals—Cal, UCLA, and USC—continued to field powerful teams, and go to the Rose Bowl, through the decade. Now, their experienced teams dominated league competition. As the campus transitioned to an ambitious, postwar academic recovery, rumors had flourished that then-President Donald B. Tresidder was interested in following the University of Chicago in giving up football altogether. The question lingered: Would Sterling ultimately do away with football?[2]

Some of Stanford's Southern California alumni had notoriously rebelled against Tresidder's temperate approach to postwar football recovery. Following Tresidder's January 1948 death, several were on record as willing to "buy" a new round of football players, and to pay the

university's way out of potential Pacific Coast Conference (PCC) financial penalties. "The Old Reds are right now in the midst of an extensive, all-out recruiting campaign unmatched on the Western slope," alleged one well-known Bay Area sports columnist.[3] Many of these alumni were now vocal supporters of Sterling's selection as president. Stanford, they believed, had considerable catching up to do, and this new president had the right background to do the job quickly.

During his well-publicized April 1949 news conference, Sterling happily answered questions about his views on communism in academe but was evasive with reporters' second favorite topic: changes to the football program. Asked if there would be an increased emphasis on sports during his presidency, he said: "Stanford already has the emphasis."[4]

"Like every alumnus, I want to see Stanford teams win," Sterling added. "We're going to try to improve the quality of our teams, but there'll be no great drive for winning teams as such."[5] When Sterling suggested that the football team was doing all right, "somebody exploded, 'What?'" reported the *San Francisco Examiner*, adding that Stanford's

> Canadian-born, ex-University of Toronto letterman and onetime University of Alberta football

coach laughed and explained: "We were speaking of emphasis—what we want, of course, is quality all along the line." The general impression was that Doctor Sterling knows a winning football team when he sees one. And when a woman reporter asked what his "chief likes" are in sports, he grinned: "victories!"[6]

The football program did indeed turn around during the first two years of Sterling's administration. Stanford won the PCC football title in 1951 and was headed to the Rose Bowl. The transition, however, did not "signal a cavalier

Three war years (1943–45) without football weighed heavily on Stanford; U.S. Army officials replaced intercollegiate sports with physical training of soldier-students. PCC rivals Cal and UCLA, where the U.S. Navy held sway, continued to field strong teams, beefed up by Stanford transfers. STANFORD UNIVERSITY ARCHIVES

In 1921, Stanford fast-tracked construction of a major new stadium to open at Big Game in November. Designed by three engineering professors (Charles B. Wing, Charles D. Marx, and William F. Durand), Stanford Stadium, seen here ca. 1950 when it accommodated nearly 90,000, was among the largest U.S. collegiate football stadiums. (Its 2006 reconstruction dropped capacity to 50,000.)

disregard for PCC rules," observed Glenn Seaborg, a Nobel Prize–winning chemist and Cal's PCC faculty representative through much of the 1950s: "When J. E. Wallace Sterling became Stanford's president in 1949, he brought a shrewd understanding of the need to be both a winner in sports and a paragon of virtuous compliance."[7]

Throughout his presidency, Sterling's support for athletics was unflinching, but he also insisted that intercollegiate athletics not interfere with his overall goals of both improving the university's academic program and developing the good character of its students. Despite considerable pressure from influential alumni, he made no special arrangements to drop entrance requirements—what one alumnus called "silly aptitude tests"—or to condone under-the-table payments for athletes.[8]

As the rise of money-driven collegiate football spread across the country during the 1950s, and as pay-for-play scandals hit the Pacific Coast Conference, Sterling navigated Stanford through the long and painful collapse of the conference and creation of a new one. Throughout the heavily publicized discord, Sterling continued to emphasize his belief that college athletes, in all sports, should participate in intercollegiate competition as amateurs. "In all of this I thank heaven that I was brought up in an atmosphere where the game was the thing," he wrote a colleague.[9]

MANAGING ATHLETIC POLICY
REVIVING THE ATHLETIC BOARD MODEL

As elsewhere in his administrative duties, Sterling confronted this balancing act with patience, a dash of humor, and a fundamental conservatism. Throughout his 19-year presidency, Sterling worked closely with his athletic director (he had only two). He was careful not to feed speculation about the future of any individual coach.

And despite the ongoing interest, and potential interference, of alumni and the public, he maintained a consistent perspective: The athlete was, above all else, a student.

Sterling's first athletic director not only shared this perspective but had built up considerable moral authority with Sterling's two predecessors. Alfred R. Masters, '24, a tough-minded manager who had overseen the university's financially stable athletic program for more than two decades, was an uncompromising foe of "free-rides" for star athletes. Only a few weeks before Sterling's campus arrival, Masters bluntly told a large alumni audience in Los Angeles that he strongly opposed suggestions that Stanford reduce its entrance requirements for athletes. "It would not only hurt the University's academic prestige," he said, "but 99 percent of this type of athlete would flunk out anyway."[10]

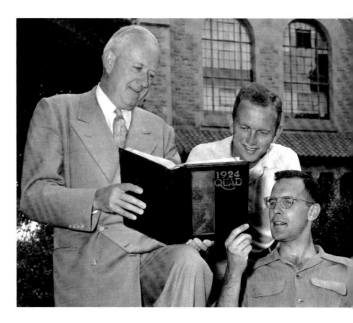

Portland-born Alfred R. Masters, '24, the tough-minded manager of Stanford athletics for more than 38 years, with fellow Oregonians Keith Beekman, senior class president, and Wayne Alley, student body president (right) at commencement in 1952. Masters, a former ASSU president and varsity soccer standout, firmly believed that athletes were students first and strongly opposed professionalism in intercollegiate sports. STANFORD NEWS SERVICE

The new president had more than a sympathetic athletic director. Masters had extensive experience as the efficient manager of Stanford's Board of Athletic Control (BAC), the governing body of the university's athletic program, created in 1917. The BAC became an effective collaboration of faculty, alumni, students, and administrators that operated the athletic program and cared for its sports facilities. It turned a flailing, often bankrupt student-run operation into a profitable, as well as accountable, enterprise. When the BAC was disbanded for the duration of the war in 1943, it turned over $80,000 to the university.

President Tresidder's tentative restoration of an athletic program in 1946 did not restore the BAC, however. Instead, he set up a Stanford Athletic Council as an advisory committee only, with no budgeting, accounting, management, or policy role. This new council had little, if any, purpose in Tresidder's rebuilding plans.

More significantly, he appointed Al Masters as director of physical education and athletics. Masters' experience with the BAC system had been long and fruitful. Masters, a former Associated Students of Stanford (ASSU) president and co-captain of the varsity soccer team, had also served as a student representative on the BAC. He had been brought back to Stanford in 1925, only a year after graduating, as the BAC's new "graduate manager." Under a succession of titles and expanding duties within the BAC, he had overseen sports facilities and programs from 1925 to 1943. (When intercollegiate sports were suspended during the war, he served as an assistant controller in the university's Business Office.) Through the BAC, Masters had come to know influential faculty members and alumni, and the backing of the BAC made Masters an authority to be reckoned with. But during his first three years as athletic director, he missed the solid backing of the BAC as he fended off strong alumni pressure on policy and personnel changes.

The Board of Athletic Control, formed in 1917, brought faculty, alumni, students, and administrators together to manage men's athletics and care for sports facilities, quickly turning a bankrupt student-run operation into a profitable enterprise. The 1939–40 board: top row, Al Masters, Stanley Hiserman, Walter Ames, Hampton Pool, Larry Livingston (*Daily* editor), and Ken Cuthbertson (future Sterling assistant and VP); bottom row, Wesley Howell (chair), Dr. Thomas Storey, Prof. William Owens (PCC rep), Judge Louis Weinmann, and Prof. J. P. Mitchell.   STANFORD UNIVERSITY ARCHIVES

Card stunts, seen here at Stanford Stadium around 1950, were a rooting-section feature of both sides at Big Game for decades.
STANFORD QUAD / STANFORD NEWS SERVICE

President Sterling, at least initially, recognized the potential of the BAC model, with its broad representation and broad public relations shoulders. He reproduced it in May 1950 with a new name: the Stanford Athletic Board (SAB). "The BAC, sorely missed since Stanford resumed intercollegiate athletics after the war, is functioning once again, and the sports outlook on the Farm is far brighter," editorialized the *Stanford Daily*, which called the revival under a new name "perhaps the greatest single contribution that could be made to Stanford athletics."[11]

Like the BAC, the SAB's nine voting members consisted of three faculty (appointed by the president), three students (appointed by the ASSU president), and three alumni (appointed by the Alumni Association's president). Masters was an ex-officio member, but as manager of the board—a role similar to his prewar status—he was essential to the board's operation.

The SAB's portfolio during its first years was large, although limited to men's athletics; it supervised men's physical education as well as men's intramural and intercollegiate sports

Students distribute cards and instructions before a 1955 football game. During the heyday of card stunts in the 1950s, creating the elaborate, multicolored, and animated displays required hundreds of students in planning and execution. At Stanford, computers were first used in fall 1962.
STANFORD QUAD / STANFORD NEWS SERVICE

teams. Women's athletics remained a separate department until 1975, and although the university had strong women's club teams, women's competitive sports were unrecognized by the NCAA and the Pacific Coast Conference, and largely ignored by the Sterling administration. Even so, Stanford women had made a strong showing among Olympic swimmers and divers as early as 1924, and more recently at the U.S. Amateur Golf Championships and on the national tennis scene.[12]

The SAB initially appointed coaches for the men's teams, subject to approval of President Sterling and the Board of Trustees. Equally important, like the BAC, it had jurisdiction over the intercollegiate athletics pocketbook, including receipt and disbursement of funds, budgeting, and accounting, accomplished by its own distinct accounting personnel. It operated the campus athletic plant and retained all income from athletic events. Unlike the BAC, it received a modest subsidy allocated by the trustees, at Sterling's suggestion, from general university funds.

Any annual excesses of income over expenditures were allotted to capital additions or improvements recommended by the SAB. "In other words, the SAB has a solid grip on the reins, and can plow profits right back into athletics," crowed the *Daily*, hoping that this pointed to better facilities, better training, and ultimately better intercollegiate teams.

But the SAB was also intended to play a key role in formulating policy on athletic competition, strongly supporting Sterling's perspective of the student-athlete. "Stanford, with its high academic requirements, must have a high degree of student, alumni, and faculty support of its athletic program if it is to continue to compete with other universities in a favorable light, as all these groups wish it to do," noted the *Daily* editors. "In return for this support, the students, faculty, and alumni have the right to a voice in athletic policy. The SAB provides this."[13]

The SAB quickly began juggling competing requests to fund major sports (football, baseball, and men's basketball, track and field, swimming, golf, and tennis) and petitions for allocations from several unsupported "minor" sports (particularly the men's crew team). Also on the agenda were the tasks of tending to delayed maintenance of gym facilities, upgrading Stanford Stadium, and dealing with alumni unhappiness over allocations of Big Game tickets. None of its deliberations, however, would compare with the commotion over the contract renewal of the current football coach.

THE FIRST TEST
THE FATE OF COACH MARCHIE SCHWARTZ

Before the year 1950 was out, Sterling and Masters would be put to the test by vocal on- and off-campus pressure to fire football coach Marchmont (Marchie) Schwartz.

Schwartz had replaced coach Clark Shaughnessy for the 1942 season, but football was suspended one season later when the U.S. Army took control of Stanford's athletic facilities and coaches. When intercollegiate sports were partially revived, in 1945, Al Masters asked Schwartz, who had returned to the Midwest, to come back to Stanford, signing him to a five-year contract. A full football program did not get underway until 1946, however, and even then, its progress was slow.[14]

Schwartz had been a two-time all-American halfback for Knute Rockne's undefeated Notre Dame squad of 1930 and 1931. After graduating, he was a popular assistant coach at Notre Dame, then became an assistant coach for Shaughnessy at Chicago (1934), then head coach at Creighton University. He first came to Stanford to again assist Shaughnessy (1940), helping him coach the undefeated Wow Boys all the way to a victory over Nebraska at the January 1941 Rose Bowl. He was considered an outstanding coach, popular with players and colleagues, and was resoundingly welcomed back to campus in 1946.[15]

Wow Boys coach Clark Shaughnessy (right) was a hard act to follow. Anticipating the shutdown of Stanford football by the U.S. Army, Shaughnessy left after the 1941 season. Shaughnessy's assistant coaches (from left) Marchmont Schwartz (Notre Dame), Jim Lawson (Stanford, '25), and Phil Bengston (Minnesota) were former All-Americans. Schwartz succeeded Shaughnessy as varsity coach; Lawson and Bengston later became NFL coaches.   STANFORD UNIVERSITY ARCHIVES

After a disappointing postwar reboot (in 1947, the team had a 0–9 record), Schwartz was gradually turning the program around with winning seasons in 1949 and 1950, but progress was not fast enough for some exasperated critics. It did not help that arch-rival Cal went to the Rose Bowl following dominating 1948, 1949, and 1950 seasons. During his first 18 months in office, Sterling was confronted with questions about the coach at alumni conferences and events.

In early November 1950, Sterling announced, on behalf of the SAB, that Schwartz had been offered a five-year contract renewal. The SAB met "its first big test," reported the *Daily* approvingly, and it had faced down outside pressure from students, alumni, and "certain sports writers." Sterling pronounced his confidence in the board's deliberations and his appreciation of its work. The decision, however, quickly turned into a public relations battle for the university and an ordeal for Schwartz and his family.[16]

Student support wavered. The *Daily* noted some general dissatisfaction, particularly among older undergrads, given the football team's failure to live up to early sports press predictions of success that year. It also noted, however, that "the majority of alumni and friends of the team gave the contract their blessing" and sportswriters were "unanimous in their approval" (or so the editors were told by Athletic Information Director Don Liebendorfer). When a group of some 200 students, apparently prodded by anonymous phone calls to several dorms, met at the Post Office chanting "Down with Marchie!" they were soon dispersed by football players, who widely supported the reappointment.[17]

"A number of our alumni and some of our students were out to get said coach," Sterling wrote a colleague, "and the announcement has brought down on our head the wrath of the disappointed. We shall ride it through."[18] Sterling set aside time to hear student opinion on the contract, but soon concluded that there was nothing more to say.[19]

So, too, did the *Daily*'s editors, who decided to stop printing letters to the editor on the subject after a few days because the letters tended to say the same thing, and because "further discussion would only result in low morale among team members, students, and all concerned with Stanford."[20]

The debate, however, was not over.

Vocal Southern California alumni wanted a coach more in the mold of UCLA's new, and increasingly controversial, win-at-all-costs coach Harry (Red) Sanders—soon to be embroiled in Pacific Coast Conference payment scandals. "Alumni morale in this area is low over the proposed Schwartz contract," one prominent Southern California alumnus urgently telegraphed Sterling. "Keep him but in some other capacity. Stanford support in all fields can be impaired by this move. Please consider carefully."[21]

"I am replying to your request for donations to the Stanford Fund; unfortunately, I cannot possibly contribute due to the sums of money I have lost wagering on our 'Big Red Machine' this season," wrote a young alumnus from Southern California. "I will be more than happy to do my share as soon as we field a winning football team or one that lives up to its potential. As I see it, this will only be possible when we replace Marchie Schwartz with a football coach." Others wrote of their intentions to stop donating to Stanford and to drop their membership in its booster group, the Buck Club, an important, and comparatively accountable, source of legitimate scholarships for student-athletes.[22]

A more public attack was made by a number of San Francisco alumni. A group calling itself

the Executive Committee of the Stanford Jr. Alumni Association of San Francisco, an unchartered group unrecognized by the Alumni Association, began a campaign reminiscent of recent state political battles. In addition to the usual letter to the *Daily*, they distributed mimeographed petition blanks among the student living groups, encouraging students to sign and send them to the Board of Trustees and the SAB. They also were suspected of being behind the "Down with Marchie" protest.[23]

Strong support for Schwartz continued from Sterling, Masters, and the SAB, as well as by players, coaches, and faculty. "Hearty congratulations upon the admirable way the football situation has been handled," Everett Dean, Stanford's widely respected head basketball coach, wrote Sterling:

> Your action will surely encourage other college administrators to tighten their grip on the control of college athletics. I have a firm conviction that only college presidents can effectively keep this problem under control. It is reasonable to believe they would have the full support of all athletic departments and all faculties, a large majority of the alumni, most of the student bodies and all fair-minded people. I believe the thinking public all over the country has been waiting for such action. Again, Stanford takes the lead in right thinking.[24]

Sterling's decision also was warmly approved by some sports commentators. The influential *Football Digest* dedicated its most recent edition to Sterling for "his superb stand in backing a deserving coach, and an admirable leader of young men, Marchie Schwartz. . . ."[25]

Schwartz tried to stay aloof, all while guiding his team to three significant "victories"—a startling come-from-behind win against favored Washington State; a moral victory in keeping the top team in the nation, Army, scoreless for 45 minutes (Army finally pulled off a last-minute 7–0 win); and keeping greatly favored Cal to a tie

Marchie Schwartz, Knute Rockne's two-time All-American halfback at Notre Dame, was considered an outstanding football coach by Stanford players, colleagues, and presidents. But after five difficult postwar rebuilding years (1946–50), and harassment from hostile sports columnists and some alumni, he declined Sterling's contract renewal offer. STANFORD ATHLETICS

in the Big Game. Schwartz was selected to coach the West for the December 30, 1950, East-West Shrine Game, to be played in San Francisco. The West, considered a clear underdog, won a decisive victory.

Schwartz surprised the sports writers gathered around him in the locker room after the Shrine Game by announcing that he had decided to step down from coaching. "I feel like I have gone as far as I can go," the 41-year-old coach announced. Few outside Stanford administration circles knew of the personal harassment and humiliation Schwartz and his family had been suffering.[26]

"He ended the season in a virtual blast of glory," concluded the *Daily* sports editor. "At the conclusion of the season, his wolves were dead silent, and he left the coaching scene a bigger man than any one of his critics."[27] In the end, Schwartz left with a 28–28–2 record and a revitalized football program.

"Schwartz's sudden but graceful bow-out seemed to be the main topic of conversation in yesterday's elongated registration lines," reported the *Daily* in January. As surprise mixed with both regret and relief, the campus applauded Schwartz as a character-building coach, a gentleman, and a man of integrity.[28]

CHUCK TAYLOR, THE YOUTHFUL DYNAMO

Some worried that the pressure was on for Stanford to dive into the pay-for-play habits of its southerly rivals. "We have only to look at [the University of] Southern California, where a group of win-hungry alumni with dollar bills as mouthpieces forced Coach Jeff Cravath to resign," noted the *Daily* a few days after Schwartz's announcement.[29] The *Daily*'s editor backed the opinion that Schwartz had meant more to the university than football field tactician; he seemed to embody the notion that

San Francisco 49ers quarterback Frankie Albert, '42, who had led Stanford's Wow Boys team of 1940, was considered an enticing possibility to replace Marchie Schwartz in 1951. Albert retired as a player in 1953, and later coached the 49ers, 1956–59.
STANFORD UNIVERSITY ARCHIVES

Stanford was, somehow, different from the "machine-like" grid giants craving national attention.[30]

Other students and alumni, eyeing the possibility of a repeat of wartime draft worries and an Army presence on campus as the Korean conflict heated up, feared that the administration would again temporarily suspend football.

Surprisingly, despite these concerns and an abundance of rumors about possible successors— a return of Clark Shaughnessy or attracting former Stanford football stars turned professional, like Frankie Albert or Chuck Taylor— there seemed to be no "noise" or pushback from critics demanding the best coach money could buy. Masters moved quickly during the month following Schwartz's announcement, interviewing some 30 candidates. "The Stanford Athletic Board, like the Marines, have the situation well in hand. . . . There have been no pressure groups, alumni or otherwise, telling the Board who to choose and who not to choose," reported the *Daily*, speculating, correctly, that a choice would be made fairly quickly.[31]

Charles A. (Chuck) Taylor, '43, Wow Boy guard and consensus All-American, is one of only two men to participate in the Rose Bowl as a player, coach, and athletic director. Taylor was the backbone of football during much of Sterling's administration. After a well-respected 11-year Stanford coaching career (1947–57), Taylor modernized the athletic program as assistant athletic director and later director of athletics until his retirement in 1972.

Track star Bob Mathias, '53, who had won his first Olympic decathlon gold medal before his freshman year, was a football walk-on as a junior running back in 1951. His rough season start was forgotten after a spectacular 96-yard kickoff return against USC. He was Stanford's only 1953 NFL draft selection, a year after winning his second Olympic gold medal. He later served four terms in Congress and was first director of the U.S. Olympic Training Center. STANFORD UNIVERSITY ARCHIVES

Stanford stars Paul Wiggin, '57, defensive end (left), and quarterback John Brodie, '57. After 11 seasons with the Cleveland Browns, Wiggin became an NFL coach and administrator; he served as Stanford's head football coach, 1980–83. Brodie, 1956 consensus All-American, also played on Stanford's golf team. After leading the San Francisco 49ers for 17 years (1957–73) with notable passing records, he became an NBC football and golf analyst. STANFORD UNIVERSITY ARCHIVES

The February 5, 1951, selection of Charles A. (Chuck) Taylor, '43, was supported enthusiastically by Sterling, Masters, and all nine members of the SAB. This unanimity of administration, faculty, alumni, and students was noteworthy, given the ongoing public conflicts among corresponding constituencies at USC, UCLA, and Cal.[32]

The Portland-born Taylor had been a star guard for Shaughnessy's 1940 Wow Boys team and an All-American his senior year. After serving in the Navy during the war, he played a year of professional football with the Miami Seahawks. He then returned to campus to coach postwar freshman football teams to three undefeated seasons, 1947–49, impressing players and colleagues with his energy and upbeat nature. In addition to his football duties, he had volunteered to coach rugby and wrestling, and had inspired the same level of hard work and commitment from players and assistants across all his teams. In 1950 he briefly returned to the NFL as a line coach for the San Francisco 49ers.[33]

The red-headed, always-smiling Taylor seemed "a youthful dynamo . . . restoking the latent fire of school spirit" by appearing at alumni gatherings not only on campus but, unusually, as far away as Seattle and Los Angeles, and by making the luncheon circuit at campus dorms and fraternities. While working on spring drills with his current team, he and his assistant coaches began to actively check out prospective football talent.[34]

Taylor's youth (he was 30 when hired) was a concern for some, but not for long. He quickly took the team Schwartz built to a PCC championship the next fall, and on to the Rose Bowl in January 1952. (Stanford lost badly, 7–40, to Illinois.) He was named Coach of the Year by the American Football Coaches Association, at that point the youngest so honored. Taylor had been appointed to a one-year contract as director

of football; after the Rose Bowl game, Sterling happily reported to the Board of Trustees that the young coach had accepted a five-year contract.[35]

After a winning 1957 season (with notable victories against Cal, UCLA, and USC), Taylor's seven-season record was 40–29–2, but he had had enough of coaching. Public scrutiny of PCC coaches during scandals dogging the 1956 and 1957 football seasons may have factored into his decision. But Taylor did not go far afield. Through much of 1957, he had been assuming athletic director administrative duties to help Al Masters, then recovering from two major surgeries. Just before the 1957 Big Game, Sterling named Taylor assistant athletic director. He had not lost faith in Taylor, Sterling said, and still considered Taylor the ideal football coach, "combining technical proficiency with high character and the qualities of a fine teacher." But Taylor was now needed elsewhere. "Much as we will miss Chuck as a coach, he is made to order for his new job and will be a great help to our program."[36]

Al Masters, battling cancer, was reluctant to retire, and Sterling did not press him. Taylor was later credited with patiently easing the long transition from the nearly four-decade-long Masters' era to a new age of athletics administration. (It would be more than five years before Taylor inherited Masters' position.) Even as assistant director, Taylor brought a more contemporary outlook to the athletic program with his approach to the public as well as to alumni and students. He explored such innovations as television coverage, including doing his own TV show, and stadium ticket packages, and he encouraged bringing professional (anathema to Masters) as well as amateur tournaments to campus.[37]

Significant management changes also took place throughout the transition. Sterling returned the athletic director's reporting line to the President's Office, and gradually stripped the SAB

Don Liebendorfer, seen here in 1968 with the Stanford Band, was *Stanford Daily* sports editor in 1924 when he was appointed the nation's first college sports publicity director, a post he held for the next 45 years. He retired to complete his history of Stanford sports, *The Color of Life Is Red* (1972). STANFORD NEWS SERVICE

of financial as well as policy authority. By the early 1960s, even the SAB's advisory role had been replaced, initially by separate student, alumni, and faculty committees. In 1964, Sterling created a new iteration of the Stanford Athletic Board, an advisory group of 24 prominent alumni capable of interacting productively with trustees and management, as well as with Athletics Department staff.[38]

With Taylor's new assignment, the department grew significantly, with its own business manager and financial staff, along with the usual director/managers of physical education, intramural sports, operations, ticket sales, and coaching camps. Mainstay Don Liebendorfer continued as director of publicity—later, sports information—until 1969. (Liebendorfer, '24, was sports editor of both the *Stanford Daily* and the *Stanford Quad* when he became the first full-time college sports publicity director in the country during his senior year.) Liebendorfer was joined, in 1965, by former baseball star pitcher Robert W. (Bob) Murphy Jr., '53, as manager of athletic relations.

Meanwhile, Taylor continued some off-field football tasks at which he excelled, particularly helping with football recruiting and developing relations with alumni and prospective supporters. "For the most part, all the new coach will have to do is coach," he optimistically told the *Daily* on stepping down as coach. As it turned out, that new coach did not have it so easy.[39]

THE TALE OF "CACTUS JACK"

Reminiscing years later, Sterling said he had made only one mistake vetting coaches during his presidential years. Although he refrained from naming the man, his correspondence and the recollections of staff members make clear that Taylor's coaching successor, "Cactus Jack" Curtice, was the mistake Sterling coped with for five years.[40]

Jack Camp Curtice, the 50-year-old football coach and athletic director at the University of Utah, was considered a plum choice. His Utah teams had won four league championships during his eight years there, and he was deemed a highly successful passing-game strategist. Curtice's appointment was announced in January 1958, shortly after he had coached the victorious West in the Shrine Game, beating the heavily favored East. Curtice, a three-sport collegiate athlete who went on to coach in Texas and Utah, was described as "one of the most colorful and astute coaches in the game." He appeared at many football clinics nationally and was in constant demand as an after-dinner speaker. He was also a member of the NCAA Football Rules Committee and a trustee of the American Football Coaches Association.[41]

Curtice was Chuck Taylor's favored candidate (the opportunity to work with Taylor had been one of Curtice's reasons for coming), and Sterling was a strong supporter of Taylor. "We have chosen him because he coaches the sort of imaginative football we like," Sterling said in announcing the appointment, "and because we are confident that he believes in and teaches the ideals we have always sought to embody in Stanford's athletics program."[42]

By the end of 1960, his third year, however, serious doubts were being raised on campus about Curtice as a coach. That year, he had been elected president of the Football Coaches Association of America, but Stanford's football program was on the road to disaster: The team

STANFORD UNIVERSITY ARCHIVES

"Cactus Jack" Curtice, Utah's outstanding football coach (here at a Big Game rally), was a colorful speaker and national coaching figure when he arrived at Stanford in 1958. But his career stalled when he had difficulty connecting with players and made little effort to become part of the campus community. In 1962, after his five-year contract was not renewed (he was not fired), he began a successful career as head coach, later athletic director, at UC Santa Barbara, retiring in 1973.

STANFORD NEWS SERVICE

lost 10 consecutive games, including a humiliating defeat by San Jose State. Curtice had not yet pulled off a winning season (2–8, 3–7, and 0–10 thus far). "There was considerable opinion as to why he did not have a winning season," recalled Liebendorfer, including several costly injuries (involving the loss of important receivers) and lack of speed.[43] But the distress was more widespread than it had been with Schwartz, and Curtice had not won the level of campus-wide respect that either Schwartz or Taylor had enjoyed.

Once again, students and alumni, not to mention some sports writers, questioned Stanford's willingness to stay in the Big Football ranks. Comments were often sarcastic: Since academics were now more important than athletics at the university, perhaps it was time to throw in the towel and schedule less rigorous competition against teams more "like us." Sterling's reluctance to lower admission and eligibility standards, the complaint ran, came at a high price—initially to football success but, ultimately, to student spirit, that highly valuable, if intangible, asset that tied many alumni to the campus.[44]

After the disastrous no-win 1960 season, Sterling met with Curtice, telling him that he talked too much and spent too much time away from campus making speeches. Perhaps Taylor's love of campus involvement had suggested to coach Curtice that that role was already in Taylor's able hands, but Curtice also did not communicate well with Sterling, Masters, or faculty members. The coach's first meeting with the president, in 1958, had been emblematic. Curtice talked the whole time, presidential assistant Fred Glover later recalled, and never asked a single question. Another former presidential assistant, Ken Cuthbertson, added: "Chuck was pretty enthusiastic about getting Curtice here. I guess he was quite a tactician, but Wally was kind of shaking his head after that first meeting."[45]

Sterling resisted pressure after the 1960 season to fire Curtice, despite advice from his Presidential Advisory Committee on Athletics and the Stanford Athletic Board. But while he continued to publicly support the coach, he warned Curtice that his performance was under review.[46]

After another dismal season in 1961 (4–6), the 1962 season unfolded as what was clearly Curtice's final contract year. Sterling insisted that it was not Curtice's record that raised a red flag, although fan attendance at Stanford Stadium had dropped precipitously. Prompted by complaints from the players themselves, the Presidential Advisory Committee, along with several trustees, had been gathering evidence of Curtice's failings. Fred Glover confirmed Sterling's suspicion that the team lacked confidence in the coach, who often "cussed the boys out." Also, Curtice reportedly could not convey a pre-game strategy, made play-calling mistakes, and was overly excitable on the sidelines.[47]

Equally important to Sterling, Curtice appeared to make no effort to become a part of Stanford, as a community or a university. "With his 'corn pone pleasantries' and barnyard philosophizing, Curtice had established a reputation as the Will Rogers of college football," wrote one San Francisco reporter. His style was popular on the national lecture and after-dinner circuit, but it did not sit well with Stanford faculty, alumni, or players. "We tried with little success to get rid of the nickname the new head man brought with him, and which never was popular with Stanford people," said Liebendorfer. "Each side did some readjusting, but a mutual understanding was never really achieved."[48]

Taylor may have been a hard act for Curtice to follow, but other new coaches also presented an unflattering comparison. Track and field coach Payton Jordan, the former USC sprint star who had come to Stanford in 1957, quickly made a strong favorable impression on students, fellow

Arriving a year before Curtice, track and field coach Payton Jordan—a former USC track star—was, like Chuck Taylor, a model against whom Curtice was measured. Jordan (right) quickly became a respected campus community advocate. He is seen here with Olympian Jesse Owens and *Palo Alto Times* Sports Editor Walt Gamage at the pathbreaking July 1962 USA-USSR Track and Field Dual Meet, which Jordan spearheaded. PALO ALTO HISTORICAL ASSOCIATION

never really learned anything about Stanford University. He made no serious or sustained effort really to identify himself with Stanford." During the coach's five years, Sterling noted, "I could count on the fingers of my two hands the occasions which . . . he attempted to spend time with students in their living groups."[50]

Although newspapers, including the *Stanford Daily*, often assumed that Curtice was fired, Sterling simply did not offer him a contract renewal at the end of the 1962 season. Masters made it very clear that the Stanford Athletic Board had no role in the decision, cutting off any complaints sent in that direction, but also revealing the SAB's weakened responsibility in sports management.[51]

coaches, faculty, and staff as well as on his track teams. Jordan also was clearly in the Sterling mold. Writing to the president in summer 1962 on the upcoming challenge of the Soviet-American international track meet, Jordan told Sterling, "I believe in our University and the things for which it stands, and I assure you that my energies, heart and thoughts will always be directed toward the development of the kind of track and field teams that are in keeping with the high standards of Stanford University and of which all of us may be proud."[49]

By contrast, Sterling found Curtice's talk "interesting, and often witty," but the coach's nonstop banter was often unproductive. "I argue that a man who talks incessantly has no time in which to listen, and in failing to listen, he lacks the opportunity to learn," Sterling explained to a Santa Barbara alumnus in 1962. "Mr. Curtice

Despite Curtice's failure to execute a single winning season on the Farm (ultimately, his teams went 14–36 over five years, and 5–19 in conference play), the decision confused some students—was winning the only measure after all?—and angered some alumni.

One acrimonious letter to the president stated: "I believe sports in general as well as Stanford University would probably be better off if it were you and Mr. Masters leaving instead of Mr. Curtice." Sterling responded: "Thank you for your blunt letter. I hope that you can accept a blunt reply: You don't know what you're writing about." The decision "did not rest on the win-loss record; nor was it in response to alumni pressure. Nor was it a decision reached in haste. I am confident that it is in the best interests of the University."[52]

With rumors, as usual, flying around in the

Bob "Horse" Reynolds, '36, an All-American tackle and distinguished Vow Boy, was the only athlete to play *every* minute of three consecutive Rose Bowl games, 1934–36. Reynolds, later a highly successful radio broadcasting executive and co-owner of the California Angels and the Los Angeles Rams, was an influential voice among Stanford's Southern California alumni and served on Sterling's athletics advisory board.   STANFORD UNIVERSITY ARCHIVES

press about possible replacements, alumni advised the president to spare no expense to find the "very finest man available." Sterling reassured the president of the Stanford Junior Alumni Association of Southern California that the administration would make every effort, but balked at the concept of high salary compensation. "Our resources are not unlimited. In addition, there is the matter of being politic and wise in establishing for one man a salary and expense which would place him in inequitable relationship to other men doing essentially the same kind of service to the University. . . . We shall go after the very best man that we can attract."[53]

Masters again claimed primary responsibility for finding a new coach, one of his last major

tasks. Updates came from his or Sterling's office, not from the Stanford Athletic Board.[54] Masters and Taylor gathered considerable information on dozens of candidates, but their work was, in fact, supplemented by a six-member alumni committee appointed by President Sterling and by the Presidential Advisory Committee. A long list was reduced to 12 men, and each of these candidates was interviewed jointly by Sterling, Masters, Taylor, and, representing the advisory committee, Professor of Law John Hurlbut (a former PCC faculty representative and NCAA vice president).[55]

Even before the university formally announced it would not renew Curtice's contract, some predicted that Bud Wilkinson of the University of Oklahoma would be the new coach.[56] Sterling and Masters had indeed approached Wilkinson as early as the previous August. As the University of Oklahoma's head coach and athletic director (1947–63), Wilkinson compiled a remarkable 145–29–4 record, including a 47-game winning streak, 14 conference titles, and three national championships. Wilkinson thought "the opportunity to be a part of Stanford is a rare and wonderful opportunity," but the possibility of his coming boiled down to authority. While Sterling thought he could meet Wilkinson's salary, he would not promise him appointment as athletic director—what would surely be seen as a slap down of Masters' presumptive heir, Chuck Taylor. Wilkinson declined Sterling's coaching offer. He retired from collegiate coaching a year later, becoming an ABC sports broadcaster and Republican politician.[57]

Masters and Sterling also were turned down by Wayne (Bud) Hardin, the impressive head coach at the U.S. Naval Academy since 1959, who was considered one of college football's brightest young strategists. Hardin, a College of the Pacific alumnus (1948), previously had several coaching positions in California, and was now bringing national attention back to the Navy Midshipmen. Stanford alumni had approached Hardin unofficially in early November. Hardin initially was uninterested, and by the time he reconsidered, in part because of his admiration for Sterling, Stanford had moved on. With Sterling's approval, the job had been offered to John R. Ralston.[58]

Ralston, like Hardin, had been among the Athletics Department's early favorites. The 35-year-old Ralston, Utah State's highly successful head football coach, had taken a struggling program to a 31–11–1 record in three years. By 1960, his Aggies were co-champions of their conference and national rushing offense leaders; the following year, they were national leaders in scoring and rushing defense. Taylor liked Ralston's approach to football fundamentals and strategy, but Ralston was also recognized as an able administrator. He was articulate and communicated well with players and prospective players' parents, coaching staff and administrators, alumni, and the press.[59]

But Ralston was no shoo-in, and his coming to the Farm was clouded by what some influential alumni considered a serious flaw. The Oakland-born Ralston, Cal '51, was not only a Golden Bear, but a notable former linebacker on two of Cal's Rose Bowl teams. He had then served as an assistant coach under California's highly respected coach Lynn (Pappy) Waldorf. On the day he was to be offered the job, United Press International reported: "Stanford's hunt for a new football coach bogged down in a sea of confusion yesterday." Former Vow Boy Robert O'Dell Reynolds, '36, a prominent member of Sterling's alumni athletics advisory committee, was perhaps the most influential of a large segment of Stanford alumni from Southern California who allegedly opposed Ralston. Reynolds (no relation to the well-known booster "Big Jim" Reynolds) had made a last-minute attempt to press Bud Hardin to change his mind, and may have succeeded, but Ralston had been offered— and accepted—the job.[60]

Ralston had his own Stanford connections.

Golden Bear John Ralston, a linebacker on two Cal Rose Bowl teams and protégé of Cal's influential coach Pappy Waldorf, had to overcome significant alumni distrust as Stanford's new head coach in 1963. His teams went on to win seven of nine Big Games against Cal, along with two conference championships and two Rose Bowls. DAVE BITTS, *STANFORD QUAD* / NEWS SERVICE

Ralston quickly made himself a campus presence, stimulating student enthusiasm for Stanford football during the 1960s. He also pushed the Admissions Office to accelerate Stanford's recruitment of minority-student athletes and fostered a strong staff of future collegiate and NFL coaches, including Bill Walsh, Dick Vermeil, Jim Mora Jr., Mike White, Rod Rust, and Jack Christiansen in the NFL; and Roger Theder, Tony Knapp, Ed Peasley, and Rubin Carter as college coaches.   STANFORD NEWS SERVICE

Earlier in his career, he had worked with James W. Lawson, '25, another college football legend as a stand-out tight end, two-time team captain, and three-time All-American (Stanford's first). Like Al Masters, Jim Lawson had been a student representative as a senior (1925) on the Board of Athletic Control. He subsequently was a popular Stanford assistant football coach for more than 20 years, moving on to the San Francisco 49ers, and was well known in Bay Area coaching circles. Lawson was a significant supporter of Ralston's hiring, as was Chuck Taylor, whom Ralston had gotten to know when he began his coaching career at two Bay Area high schools.[61]

Seemingly cast from the Taylor mold, Ralston

quickly became a part of the university community. He was soon speaking at student and alumni gatherings, emphasizing the need for their vocal fan support, and he faced inquisitive press conferences at Big Game time with strong messages about Stanford's ability to not only compete but to win. Ralston's teams would go on to win seven of the next nine Big Games against his alma mater.

Ralston was also an exceptional recruiter, looking well beyond Stanford's usual list of selective California high schools. He was not the first to enlist an African American player—Eddie Tucker was recruited to the basketball team in 1950, and, in 1961, Jack Curtice had attracted Morrison Warren, a three-sport high school star from Phoenix as well as class salutatorian, with an Alfred P. Sloan academic scholarship. (Running back Tom Williams had preceded him as a walk-on addition to Taylor's 1955 team.)[62]

Ralston took a broader approach, however, prodding the Admissions Office to expand its

Gene Washington, '69, began his legendary Stanford football career as a quarterback, but changed to wide receiver as a junior after an injury, backed by his suspicion that the NFL would not welcome a Black quarterback. Aware that Black athletes were role models, he and teammate Mike (Ron) Miller, '67, co-founded Interact, precursor to the Black Student Union, to bring together Stanford's small Black community. STANFORD ATHLETICS

Coach Ralston (bottom left) joins Stanford's new manager of athletic relations Bob Murphy, '53, in a whimsical 1965 football publicity shot. Assistant coach Bill Walsh (top left) looks on as Ralston and (left to right) assistant coaches Dutch Fehring, Mike White, and Leon McLaughlin give Murphy the scoop. "Murph," whose lighthearted and personal touch endeared him to generations of players and alumni, became the "radio voice of Stanford football." STANFORD ATHLETICS

perspective. He also headed to regional high schools that had helped make UCLA's and USC's long-integrated football teams among the best in the country. By 1965, his varsity squad included Roger Clay, '66; Dale Rubin, '66; John Guillory, '67; Al Wilburn, '67; Dave Lewis, '67; and Michael (Ron) Miller, '68. Gene Washington, '69, joined them the following year.[63] In 1969, Ralston also hired Bill Moultrie, then football and track coach at Ravenswood High School (East Palo Alto), who became Stanford's first African American assistant coach. In 1971, Moultrie was among top candidates to replace Ralston.[64]

During his nine years on campus, Ralston created a strong rapport with his players and his coaching staff, compiling a 55–36–3 record and two conference championships. Sterling had retired by the time Ralston brought Stanford's football program back into national prominence, with two successful trips to the Rose Bowl against heavily favored Ohio State in 1971 and Michigan in 1972.[65]

Ralston also earned a reputation for his relentless work ethic, innovative play calling, and organizational skills. Known for his outgoing personality, positive attitude, and unfailing politeness, Ralston, like Schwartz and Taylor, was recognized as a "true gentleman." "He was as perfect for Stanford as perfect can be," recalled Dick Vermeil, who, in 1965, joined other future NFL coaches Bill Walsh and Mike White as one of Ralston's young assistant coaches.[66]

BREAKUP OF THE
PACIFIC COAST CONFERENCE

While Stanford's football program regained competitive standing, much of President Sterling's first decade would be shadowed by conflicts within the Pacific Coast Conference. As scandals erupted on the West Coast during the mid-1950s, Sterling was drawn deeply into the debate about the implications of the PCC's stringent conference rules and the effectiveness of its self-enforcement measures. For Stanford's president, at issue was the notion of institutional accountability as much as it was the growing influence of professionalism and commercialism in collegiate sports. Many of the issues raised at that time have yet to be resolved.[67]

The collapse of the PCC in 1956–57 and its reformulation in 1958–59 became one of Sterling's toughest administrative confrontations. The PCC controversy turned into what sports historian John R. Thelin has called "one of the most bitter incidents involving the politics and philosophy of intercollegiate athletics." From the rubble, a new conference eventually would be formed, the Athletic Association of Western Universities (nicknamed the Pacific-8), consisting of all but one of the previous partners. Code enforcement power shifted to the National Collegiate Athletic Association (NCAA).[68]

Sterling's insistence that professionalism should play no role in collegiate athletics and his strict interpretation of accountability earned him a reputation, particularly in Southern California, for a "holier than thou" attitude. He took on his counterparts at UCLA and USC over code enforcement, yet also worked diligently to allay alumni fears that he would remove football from campus life, carefully framing his responses in terms of integrity and fairness to all students. Stanford University, he insisted, could be a model of a sound and competitive football program at an academically ambitious university where the athlete was essentially a student.

The Pacific Coast Conference had been

Stanford's first Pacific Coast Conference team—basketball, not football—started in the new league in February 1917, winning the PCC championship three years later as it became a basketball powerhouse. While taking part in other conference sports, Stanford did not play PCC football until 1919, after reverting from rugby rules (agreed to by Cal and Stanford in 1906) to American-rules football to reinstate the Big Game with California. (Cal had switched back in 1915.)
STANFORD UNIVERSITY ARCHIVES

formed in 1915 by four charter institutions: California (Berkeley), the University of Washington, the University of Oregon, and Oregon Agricultural College (later Oregon State). Stanford turned down a charter invitation that year, due to its reluctance to eliminate freshmen from competition, but officially accepted in December 1916. Its first conference contest, the following February, was a basketball game with Washington State; baseball, then track and field soon followed. It would take two more years of negotiations between Cal and Stanford regarding scholarship standards and eligibility to convince Stanford to follow Cal's 1915 action giving up rugby-rules football for American-rules football. The two universities celebrated their reunion with the 1919 Big Game.[69]

By 1950, the conference consisted of nine institutions. Washington State also had joined in 1917, the University of Idaho and USC in 1922, and the newly established UCLA in 1928. Montana, a member since 1924, dropped out in 1950.

Throughout much of its 42 years, the PCC would be recognized nationally as a model conference based on continuing reform efforts and adjustments. Faculty members—not coaches, students, or college presidents—had drawn up its constitution and strict code of conduct. (Stanford law Professor William B. Owens co-authored the PCC conference bylaws and its system for checking eligibility.) The PCC Code was one of the most detailed and complex in the country, with a seemingly effective oversight mechanism reliant on self-reporting and self-enforcement. Power was vested in the council of faculty representatives, backed by a council of presidents of member universities, and, since 1944, a commissioner tasked with investigating infractions, but without the power to impose penalties.[70]

Sterling had articulated his philosophy regarding professionalism in collegiate sports as early as 1951, following the Marchie Schwartz reten-

tion controversy. Shortly after, scandals broke out nationally over Midwestern basketball and football teams. These scandals, and subsequent accusations emerging among several PCC members, drew attention to the willingness of team booster clubs to pay unrecorded bonuses and to offer fake jobs to talented athletes, and also the practice of some universities to lower academic requirements for select athletes or to overlook grading and exam irregularities.

"The public and alumni must recognize that insofar as they encourage a student athlete to sell his services to the highest money-bidder, they are contributing to the malaise which has produced 'fixed' games. Honest jobs are available to needy athletes. These should suffice," Sterling told an alumni audience that year, adding: "Any university permitting any academic advantage or privilege to an athlete is culpable and delinquent." His stern words were so unusual that they were quoted in the passionate heart of Southern California football by "Mr. Rose Bowl" himself, Rube Samuelsen, famed sports editor of the *Pasadena Star-News*.[71]

Football, both collegiate and professional, was flourishing in the affluence and commercialism of postwar America. The old question of how sports influenced higher education had given way to questions about how colleges could boost their revenue stream through football stadium enlargements, radio and TV broadcasting contracts, and bowl game compensation. Few Pacific Coast universities exemplified this lucrative strategy better than USC and UCLA.

As Sterling began to articulate his ambitious plans to improve Stanford's academic program, he was especially sensitive to the need to comply with scholastic eligibility requirements. Reporting on an eligibility debate during a PCC meeting in 1950, Dean of Students Lawrence Kimpton reassured Sterling that "every athlete has to meet our [PCC] minimum standards, so

Major changes came to the Stanford Band, seen here in 1953, when Arthur P. Barnes became director 10 years later. Military uniforms were exchanged for a distinctive contemporary look (blazers, black slacks, and white canvas hats). Barnes also brought a contemporary new sound and less formal field movements to the LSJU Marching Band. In the post-Sterling era, the Band has grown untidier.   DICK KEEBLE / STANFORD NEWS SERVICE

Dancing with the Band in the 1950s and '60s, the pom-pom girls, later called the Dollies, were selected following rigorous tryouts for only five positions. The 1964–65 team, (from left) Peg Eaton, Suzy Janss, Lynne Williams, Freddie Baumstark, and Winki Belz, is seen here early in the football season with Band members Jon Erickson (left) and Frank Robertson with their field cannon, then used to celebrate each Stanford score.   STANFORD NEWS SERVICE

from that point of view we do not admit anyone irregularly." However, he said, it was the case "that occasionally we drop below our [Stanford's] competitive standards in order to admit an athlete, but never below our minimum standards."[72]

Among those who, throughout the 1950s, urged Sterling to lower admission and scholarship requirements for athletes was Ralph H. (Big Jim) Reynolds, '10, an influential Southern California alumnus. Big Jim had played football (as did his two sons) and had rowed on crew, and although he did not graduate, he remained intensely loyal and generous to the university throughout his life. Reynolds had become a pivotal figure among alumni focused on athletics, particularly among those Southern Californians aggravated by the domineering presence of USC and UCLA football.[73]

For years, Big Jim had been on the radar of PCC watchdogs as a transgressor. For decades he had been raising funds and allocating them to self-selected Stanford athletes. Robert Johnson, UC President Robert Gordon Sproul's special assistant for athletic affairs, kept an eye on Reynolds. "The activities of Jim Reynolds should be investigated in complete detail as the Stanford people are quite boastful of the programs he and his cohorts are making, especially in the manner in which they are flagrantly violating PCC rules," Johnson told Cal's PCC faculty representative in 1948.[74]

Less than a year after he'd taken office, Sterling shared with Athletic Director Al Masters a letter from Reynolds, one of many he would receive over the years. Reynolds, an enthusiastic advocate for Sterling's presidency, was now eager to see progress on the football field. After hearing Sterling speak at an alumni event in early 1950 on the university's academic aspirations within its tight budget, he told the president that Stanford's $800,000 budget deficit could be best ameliorated by "a very successful football season."[75]

Masters responded bluntly: "You know, of course, what Jim Reynolds wants is for us to go out and get ourselves a football team by special inducements and by lowering our admission requirements," he wrote Sterling. "It would be no trick at all to go out and get a championship team if we threw caution to the winds and broke down our long-established policies." Masters said that Stanford "should give a prospective athlete every break we can and still be consistent with University policy as far as admissions are concerned." But he hastened to add, "I am not a bit interested in the program which Jim Reynolds would like to set up, because I know it involves the elimination of policies which have kept our intercollegiate athletic program on a high plane."[76]

Sterling agreed: "As you have repeatedly said to me, we must keep our standards high."[77]

When, in 1953, a round of accusations and penalties erupted, first at the University of Oregon, then with infractions reported at every other member institution, the presidents of the nine conference members seemed determined to make a stand against what was seen as growing commercialism in collegiate football. They met in San Francisco to discuss better enforcement of the PCC code. At this signature meeting, the members recommitted to full and rigorous self-enforcement of the code.

To emphasize the seriousness of their enforcement commitment, a formal letter was composed that would be signed and sent by each PCC university president or chancellor to their respective athletic director, coaches, athletic staff, and all university officers charged with administering the code. The letter reaffirmed, "in the most emphatic terms," not only that each institution would conduct its intercollegiate athletic program "in complete compliance with the rules, policies, and objectives of the Conference" but that "I must hold you personally and individually responsible for your participation, directly or indirectly, in any activity involving the offer or grant of illegal subsidization to athletes."[78]

Enforcement, however, remained a matter of interpretation by coaches, administrators, and alumni and booster organizations. From time to time, reports of minor infractions landed on Al Masters' desk. As if to prove a point, in spring 1954, his hammer fell on two students, a noted swimmer and a standout rugby player, after they appeared in the *Stanford Daily* in a men's clothing ad. Neither was paid in cash, but each received $100 in clothing. The infraction was reported to the PCC, and both athletes were ruled ineligible from further intercollegiate competition. Stunned, the *Daily*'s business manager claimed he did not know they were athletes—one was junior class president, the other head of the Prom Committee—and neither was identified as an athlete in the ad. Masters was unmoved. "It's the fault of the students. We constantly warn the players against taking money or goods from commercial firms."[79] Throughout the coming "pay for play" debate, penalties fell far more heavily on individual athletes than on coaches, directors, presidents, or affluent "old grads" among the booster clubs, a situation that did not go unnoticed by student commentators.

Professor Rixford Snyder, Stanford's director of admissions who also served as faculty representative to the PCC and subsequently to the Pacific-8 Conference (1952–69), later recalled the deepening uneasiness about the influence of alumni money. In January 1956, as Snyder put it, "one might say the lid blew off of the pot."[80]

That year, a new round of scandals broke out in West Coast newspaper exposés, largely concerning under-the-table "slush fund" payments given directly to football players by local booster organizations. Initially, University of Washington players were reported receiving illegal aid, well over and above the level prescribed by the NCAA and PCC, from a group of Seattle businessmen (through the Greater Seattle Advertising Fund). Accusations quickly spread to UCLA, where both the coach and chancellor knew of ongoing infractions involving nearly the entire team (from the Bruin Bench and the Young Men of Westwood organizations), then to USC (from its Southern California Educational Fund), which allegedly fostered a sophisticated system of under-the-table payments. UCLA representatives, in turn, blew the whistle on Cal and its Southern Seas organization and the San Francisco Grid Club.[81]

Conference sanctions, as determined by its faculty council, were harsh: In addition to substantial fines, USC and UCLA received three years of probation, Washington two years, and Cal one year. Players who had violated the rules by accepting money or fake jobs were ruled ineligible to play. Significantly, during their probation, the teams were ineligible for conference titles (the highly lucrative Rose Bowl game) and any other bowl games. Television coverage, then in its infancy but already notably profitable, was also affected. Four other campuses, including Stanford, received small fines for minor infractions.

History Professor and Director of Admissions Rix Snyder served as Stanford's Pacific Coast Conference and Pac-8 faculty representative, 1952–69, and as a two-term PCC president. He succeeded two law professors: William B. Owens, who co-authored the PCC conference bylaws, and John Hurlbut.
DICK KEEBLE / STANFORD NEWS SERVICE

Stanford appeared in the first Rose Bowl game, in 1902. Optimists considered the team's 0–49 defeat something of a success since they kept "point-a-minute" Michigan to under 60 points. The game was not played again, for all that, until 1916.
STANFORD UNIVERSITY ARCHIVES

The January 1925 Rose Bowl was a clash between the best collegiate coaches of the era, Knute Rockne and his "Four Horsemen" of Notre Dame against Glenn (Pop) Warner and Stanford's already legendary Ernie Nevers. Seven Farm men, including Nevers and star end Jim Lawson, played the entire game, both offense and defense. Although Stanford lost (10–27), it won the battle of statistics.
STANFORD UNIVERSITY ARCHIVES

Stanford sent a float to Pasadena's Tournament of Roses Parade on January 1, 1952. Later that day the team lost badly, 7–40, to Illinois. After Cal and Stanford appearances early in the decade, USC and UCLA assumed proprietary rights over the PCC's "Pasadena affair" through the rest of the 1950s and 1960s.
STANFORD UNIVERSITY ARCHIVES

Washington and Cal accepted their severe punishment, but USC and especially UCLA went down swinging. As one sportswriter put it, "the Pasadena affair [Rose Bowl] had been practically their own private enterprise."[82]

The finger-pointing quickly became as controversial as the infractions themselves, revealing serious friction within the University of California (between Cal and UCLA) and, more obviously, between the Southern California schools and all those to the north except Washington. Conference meetings themselves became hostile environments of mutual recrimination. The tension among the presidents surfaced in July 1956 at the PCC Presidents' Council special meeting in San Francisco, chaired by University of California President Robert Sproul. Following the revelations and subsequent punishments, the PCC members had agreed to conduct self-studies of each campus and to share the results at this meeting as a means of revealing the depth of the problem and, it was hoped by some, to spread the blame.

With the tempting rewards held out by booster groups in the PCC spotlight, Sterling and Al Masters kept a careful eye on Stanford's Buck Club, founded in 1934 as a private organization of both alumni and non-alumni (preferred stadium seating had been an early inducement). Dues went to scholarships for student athletes but, unlike the funds raised and independently doled out by booster clubs elsewhere, the Buck Club's funds were managed and distributed by the university. Investigative reporters as well as Stanford administrators made more than one deep dive into mid-1956 rumors about possible Stanford infractions. Ultimately, Masters confidently announced that while some individual violations had been uncovered (and reported to the PCC), they had found no organized attempt to create and distribute "slush funds similar to those at the four penalized schools."[83]

At the July PCC meeting, Stanford, Oregon, Oregon State, Washington State, and Idaho were given clean slates, as no evidence of slush funds or organized alumni payoff systems and no organized or wholesale pattern of subsidization was revealed. The meeting soon unraveled.

Earlier, UCLA Chancellor Raymond Allen and USC President Fred Fagg Jr. had asked for reconsideration of the harsh sanctions. After a stormy debate, they lost a reprieve in a 5–4 vote, along predictable lines. Allen then dramatically held up a briefcase, alleging that it was full of affidavits by Stanford football players implicating Stanford boosters for similar infractions. When Sterling asked for them, in accordance with PCC policy, so that the affidavits could be passed on and guilty parties punished, Allen refused to let anyone see the contents of the case. Rix Snyder, among others, was convinced that the briefcase was full of blank paper. "It was finally clear to most of us that each of the institutions was trying to blow the whistle on the others so that we all would be guilty and therefore start over again," recalled Snyder.[84]

"Strife-torn from Seattle to Southern California, the Pacific Coast Conference lurches uncertainly into the current football season," Sports Illustrated reported in September 1956. Unlike earlier rounds of reviews and penalties, the 1956 scandal was now driven by public accusations and counter-accusations by senior administrators and fueled by influential alumni. Noting the sparks flying, driven by an "ill wind" across California, the article recognized the coming of the real rift: "Thus far, Pullman [Washington State], Corvallis [Oregon State], Eugene [Oregon], Palo Alto [Stanford], and Moscow [Idaho] have not been touched. Truthfully, these seats of learning are in no way sympathetic to their suffering brethren, particularly those in the Los Angeles area."[85]

STANFORD INDIAN MASCOT, EXPLAINED

Timm Williams (Yurok), here in 1967, first danced as Prince Lightfoot at the 1951 Big Game rally, then at all home football games starting in 1952. For two decades, he personified the Stanford Indian mascot for delighted alumni. The student body in 1892 had chosen cardinal red as the university's color, but sportswriters in the 1920s demanded animate identifiers to describe the battle, prompting trojans, huskies, and cougars to join such older mascots as golden bears and beavers. Stanford alumni pushed an Indian-warrior concept, but students remained indifferent until 1930, when the ASSU Executive Committee ostensibly endorsed it. During the 1940s and '50s, the heroic motif degraded into a bulb-nosed, dim-witted caricature, as in this 1959 football program. Eventually,

STANFORD NEWS SERVICE

STANFORD UNIVERSITY ARCHIVES

SAN JOSE STATE
STANFORD

OCTOBER 31, 1959
STANFORD STADIUM

PRICE 25¢

BOY SCOUT DAY

Williams' eclectic costume and reinterpretation of other tribes' religious dances, as well as stereotypical racial portrayals by non-Indian undergrads at games and rallies, offended newly recruited indigenous students. In 1972, Native American students and staff successfully petitioned for removal of the "Indian" as a motif, mascot, or symbol of Stanford and its sports teams. Despite sporadic loud alumni protest, a series of student referendums sorted through more than 130 alternatives (the Athletics Department ruled out the popular Thunder Chickens and Robber Barons) until a 1981 student referendum, endorsed by the Mascot Advisory Committee and President Donald Kennedy, concluded that the long-standing cardinal red tradition would suffice, along the lines of Alabama and Harvard.

"THE HALOS"

DEFENDING STANFORD'S HONOR

Through much of the next year and a half, more rounds of votes would be taken on whether, and how, to limit or lift various sanctions, lower code requirements, or raise limits for outside funding (grants-in-aid) of players. The possibility of eliminating both the PCC's enforcement process and scheduling obligations with fellow members also was now considered. Alliances continually shifted, especially when the smaller schools began to worry about losing their connection to their traditional opponents, but a line was clearly drawn between, on the one hand, the "aggrieved"—UCLA backed by USC—and the "purists"—Stanford backed strongly by the University of Oregon and Oregon State. Even Cal's faculty representative Glenn Seaborg found Sterling's "self-assessment of virtue a bit excessive."[86]

In a response to a Los Angeles radio station query, Fred Glover framed the split among the PCC presidents and faculty representatives as between one group who wanted the PCC rules loosened so its teams could compete with the football giants of the Midwest and East (such as Notre Dame and Oklahoma) and those, like Sterling, who believed the object of the PCC was to regulate its own affairs so conference teams could compete among themselves without paying much attention to cross-conference and cross-country rivalries. Others boiled it down to Raymond Allen of UCLA versus Wallace Sterling of Stanford.[87]

At that notable July 1956 PCC meeting, some on the Presidents' Council wanted to press the faculty governing body to soften the blow on football seniors, many of whom wanted a showcase final year of play before possible professional careers. (Those not seniors were ineligible for leniency.) Some of the best-known seniors, like USC's All-American Jon Arnett, were threatening to drop out to play a professional year in Canada. The presidents' vote to reprieve sanctioned seniors (allowing them to play in five consecutive 1956 season games) was nearly unanimous (8 to 1): The dissenting vote was that of Stanford's president. Sterling also opposed lowering the probation periods to one year.[88]

Sterling and Stanford now took the brunt of Southern California protestations as newspaper headlines, prodded by UCLA and USC alumni, shouted "unfair" and "them, too." Raymond Allen's unsubstantiated allegations would surface in Los Angeles over the '56 and '57 football seasons with various reasons given for not providing details and names, among them a dubious concern for the future of coach Chuck Taylor. An unidentified group of UCLA sleuths claimed to have unearthed evidence at each PCC campus. Only at Stanford, they said, would their witness not put the evidence in writing because it might get Taylor fired. "If they have anything on us," replied Masters, "let them speak up. We're ready to take our medicine if we have done anything wrong."[89] No evidence was forthcoming.

As the accusations swirled in Southern California that the southern schools were simply scapegoats, Sterling underscored his views in a lengthy letter to alumnus Norman Chandler, '22, the powerful publisher of the *Los Angeles Times* whose sister, May Chandler Goodan, '14, was a Stanford trustee. Sterling was responding to a letter Chandler sent shortly after the July PCC meeting, along with the July 12, 1956, *Times* editorial praising Presidents Fagg and Allen for protecting their defenseless schoolboys. "The present circumstances in the Pacific Coast Conference are regrettable and stem, in my view, from a distorted evaluation of the place of athletics in higher education and from an almost pathological emphasis on winning games," Sterling wrote Chandler.

It is worthy of note that the advocacy of "more realistic" Code provisions—by which I infer is meant more generous subsidy for student athletes—comes in the main where the agreement of

1953 was either ignored or flaunted. A breach of faith is a shabby and unreliable basis from which to advocate change. And as to "realism," I am deeply concerned about the realities of the true educational responsibilities of institutions in honorably discharging the trust which founders, foundations and other supporters and legal charters of statutes have expected them to discharge. I do not believe that the discharge of this trust includes subsidies for student athletes whose interest in getting an education may be dubious. . . .

The charge has been repeatedly made from Los Angeles County that Stanford is as guilty of violations of the P.C.C. Code as any institution in the conference. Yet [I have] not taken a sort of smug, holier-than-thou attitude. I do not say, nor have I said, that Stanford is "pure." I do say that we have tried hard to live up to the provisions of the Code and that we invite evidence to the contrary so that we may make corrections. Apparently, I am not believed when I say this. It would seem that some of Stanford's accusers cannot or will not comprehend that I have meant exactly what I have said. I have been told that some persons have in their possession affidavits evidencing Stanford violation of the Code. When I have been told of this, I have asked that this evidence be placed in the hands of the Conference Commissioner and that copies be sent to me. I continue to hope and request that it will be submitted in this way so that it will be utilized by the Conference. It gets no one anything or anywhere to resort to threats, veiled or otherwise.[90]

That November, in the midst of football season, Sterling extended these thoughts into a long commentary aimed at alumni in a major article in the *Stanford Review*, "The President Speaks on Athletic Policy." In it, he elaborated on his vote during the heated PCC meetings earlier that year.

I voted as I did because I could not agree that a student, guilty of violating the Code, was entitled to special consideration because he was a senior. A university is honor-bound to hold students to

accountability for obligations they assume as students, whether or not they are athletes. . . .

A university is measured most exactly by its educational standards and performance, by the training which it affords to young men and women who seek to improve their minds by acquiring knowledge and wisdom, and by the examples it sets for them in matters of character and conduct. In the whole educational enterprise, which is measured by these standards, there is an important place for intercollegiate athletics. But this place cannot be justified if such importance is attached to victory on the athletic field as to produce practices which lead to cheating. . . .

It is the concentration of assistance to athletes and the history of dubious practices in connection with such aid which so strongly suggests that interest in a student's opportunity for education may be secondary to interest in a student's ability to win games.

Contrary to frequent allegations, Sterling reiterated, Stanford was not engaged in whistle-blowing on other conference schools, nor was it being self-righteous. Stanford made no claim to be blameless in the matter of code violations. "What we have claimed is this: that we have worked hard and faithfully to honor the provisions of the code."

In sum, Sterling said, "our concern has been to make our word as good as our bond by doing our best to live up to the obligation of our conference compact with our sister institutions as well as to Stanford's own Fundamental Standard of honesty and good conduct by which our students govern themselves."[91]

The finger-pointing, Sterling told *Sports Illustrated,* was "a misdirection of energy and animus which placed under additional strain such good faith as existed among the conference institutions." It was unfortunate, he said, "that equal energy was not expended in seeing to it that the provisions of the code were lived up to."[92]

Working themselves up for their fall 1956 games against Stanford, USC and UCLA coaches, players, and alumni piled it on. "The game will cap a vendetta" against the one PCC member to consistently refuse to vote for any allowance to seniors, wrote Rube Samuelsen, noting the "deep-seated desire for revenge" expected at the upcoming Stanford-USC game in Palo Alto. Samuelsen had been told that several thousand Trojan fans had a sign ready for the train that would take them north: "Halo Alto Special." USC's basketball coach wanted banners printed with just "8 to 1" for team motivation (referring to Sterling's lone vote against the senior reprieve). UCLA's *Daily Bruin* ran a classified ad: "Wanted: Halos. Must fit over football helmet. Apply Chuck Taylor, Palo Alto, Calif."[93]

Stanford beat USC 27–19 at home, but lost to UCLA 13–14 in Los Angeles.

As the controversy plodded into its second year, Sterling's position received widespread campus support. In 1956, UCLA's Academic Council had backed Chancellor Allen's aggressive defense of its football program; the following January, Stanford's Academic Council countered with an equally aggressive defense of Sterling's moral stand. To "strengthen the hands" of the university's PCC representatives, it unanimously passed a resolution commending Sterling, Snyder, and Masters for their efforts to defend "the principles of amateurism and administrative integrity in intercollegiate sports." Sterling was given a standing ovation with the vote. (The resolution was written by six faculty members, all current or former department heads, who were alumni and notable football fans: Thomas Bailey, John Mothershead, Robert Sears, Hugh Skilling, James T. Watkins IV, and Virgil Whitaker.)[94]

Surprisingly, Sterling also had strong support from the *Stanford Daily*, and generally among the student body. A quick survey by the *Daily*

after the PCC voted to liberalize financial aid to athletes found Stanford students differing widely about the pragmatism of staying or leaving the PCC, but little opposition to maintaining academic standards and considering financial support only in terms of the entire student body's needs. "Although Stanford's athletic emphasis is far from perfect," the *Stanford Daily* editorialized, "we can be proud and thankful that the university's name spreads further than" the football stadium and newspaper sports pages.[95]

By the end of 1956, Stanford alumni also were beginning to close ranks, even in Southern

Speedy, agile, and arrogant, "Tricky Dick" Hyland, '27, was a star of Stanford's 1925 Rose Bowl team. A colorful and temperamental playmaker at rugby and, later, football, Hyland delighted in stirring public indignation during his 40-year career as an *L.A. Times* sportswriter and columnist. He mocked Sterling's backing of PCC self-regulation, and alienated alumni with his open support of UCLA.

GEORGE R. BOGUE / STANFORD UNIVERSITY ARCHIVES

California. Comments that summer by Governor Goodwin J. Knight, '19, earned mixed reviews among fellow alumni when he was quoted blaming the PCC "mess" on "the professors running the show. They're just a bunch of spindly-legged runts who resented athletes back in their college days, and still resent them." He, too, had heard of players with fake jobs, he said, but offered no evidence. Whether or not he was quoted correctly, the colorful governor went on record supporting dissolution of the PCC. Months later, however, when the outspoken *Los Angeles Times'* sportswriter Dick Hyland, '27, a former Stanford football star and Olympic rugby gold medalist, called Sterling and Masters "phony bastards" at a December Santa Monica Junior Chamber of Commerce dinner, Stanford trustee Tex Middleton, '26, took direct action. Middleton, who had played football with "Tricky Dick" Hyland, confronted *Times* publisher Norman Chandler about the remarks; as Middleton reported to Sterling, Chandler subsequently called Hyland "on the carpet."[96]

Even the *Daily* was impressed with alumni, for without their support, Sterling "would be a prisoner of his own moral convictions, and his demands for a sound athletic program, accepted and practiced by all schools in the PCC, would be futile."[97]

The defense of UCLA and USC had long since moved from PCC's council rooms, campus discussion, and newspaper editorial columns into political circles. In mid-1956, the Los Angeles City Council had passed a resolution alleging that UC President Robert Sproul was "working against the development of UCLA" and accusing the rest of the PCC of trying to wreck UCLA and USC.[98]

In January 1957, a controversial bill, AB2275, was introduced in the California State Assembly by Charles Wilson and eight other assemblymen representing Los Angeles constituencies to create a California Intercollegiate Athletic Commission to regulate intercollegiate activities in all sports. The commission's five salaried members would be appointed by the governor, and have oversight of all scheduling, including post-season games, championship play-offs, and athletic aid and scholarship programs, with the ability to enforce rules and impose penalties. The bill swept in private institutions (as recipients of property tax exemptions) as well as state campuses. "Every college and university in this state and the officers, faculty, students, student organizations, and alumni organizations thereof are subject to the provisions of this chapter, and all rules issued by the commission."[99]

Few paid much attention until October, when an initial hearing by a State Assembly Subcommittee on California Intercollegiate Athletic Activities, chaired by Frank Bonelli of Huntington Park, began its investigation with testimony by UCLA and USC athletics staff. Bonelli's opinion was firm: The commission was meant to investigate unfair and perhaps illegal penalties against UCLA and USC brought about by vindictive fellow members; he was incensed that the Southern California schools had been "kicked around," and had no interest in investigating original infractions or illegalities.[100]

Hearings in San Francisco and Los Angeles did little but publicize the discord. Southern California witnesses, largely coaches and athletics department staff, highlighted the unfairness to UCLA and USC of PCC penalties. UCLA coach Red Sanders painted a picture of a conference "climate of jealousy, intrigue and venom."[101] Northern witnesses were equally strong in defending the PCC as an effective means of allowing members to monitor their own collegiate athletics. Greg Engelhard, Cal's athletic director, who attended all of the hearings and testified, was hardly alone in concluding that the hearings were rigged, since subcommittee member questioning appeared intent on discrediting the PCC in order to eliminate punishments levied on UCLA and USC.

State Attorney General Edmund G. Brown deflated the effort, issuing an opinion that, counter to Bonelli's contention, the fines levied by the PCC were indeed legal and had not been paid by taxpayer money. Bipartisan opposition argued that state intervention was hardly an appropriate approach to managing what were, in fact, student-faculty affairs, and that such a state commission was just another step down "the road to collectivism" (communism) by placing politicians in charge of football schedules and scholarships. Despite protests that the hearings were a waste of taxpayer money, the "probe" plodded along for three months.

Edwin Pauley, Cal '23, Beverly Hills oil magnate, a co-owner of the Los Angeles Rams, UCLA philanthropist, and chair of the University of California's Board of Regents, took more direct action. Pauley pushed fellow regents to force withdrawal of both University of California campuses from the PCC if conference members did not agree to UC's new five-point program. (Among other code and penalty changes, the resolution held that UCLA must be permitted, after the 1957 season, to drop any PCC opponent it considered "unworthy"—that is, the smaller Pacific Northwest schools.) With this regents' June 1957 ultimatum in hand, UC President Sproul was in the unenviable position of underscoring university unity by forcing one campus to accept, however reluctantly, the infractions and reprieve of the other. It was especially awkward for Cal Chancellor Clark Kerr, who had often sided with Sterling on the issue of institutional

During the Depression and war, it was hard for out-of-state fans to travel to California. UCLA and USC pushed to dissolve the PCC partly to end obligations to play Pacific Northwest schools, which did not send enough fans to boost ticket sales (stands at this 1939 Stanford home game against Washington State are an example). But the Southern California schools relished gate receipts from well-attended home games against the despised Stanford Indians. STANFORD UNIVERSITY ARCHIVES

integrity. USC's Board of Trustees passed a similar resolution a month later.[102]

Provost Fred Terman reported to Sterling, then in Europe, on UC's position. "Enjoy things while you can," Terman told Sterling. "You cannot predict what crisis may arise when you are back to stir up trouble."[103]

Sproul's announcement of UC's five points, including the claim that UC had higher academic standards, embellished the breach. "Admissions and academics have little to do with the withdrawals," A. L. Strand, president of Oregon State, wrote Sproul. The driving force was profit, not admission standards or grades, and political expedience within the University of California. The smaller schools were not a draw for Los Angeles stadium attendance, nor could their fans travel easily to Los Angeles. And, while the conference victor received a winner's take for attending the Tournament of Roses, each of the PCC campuses also was allocated an equal share, spreading the funds beyond California.[104]

Sterling was disappointed to find what he thought had been common cause between Cal and Stanford had fallen through. The opportunity had been lost, he wrote his friend Clark Kerr, "in one of the sorriest cases of misrepresentation that I have ever experienced in university life. I doubt that I can ever forgive what then happened; I can only struggle to forget."[105] It would take another year, and Kerr's intervention, to get Stanford and UC back at the same conference table.

Sterling's frustration was underscored in his reply to a request from Rube Samuelsen, the sympathetic sports editor of the *Pasadena Star-News*, that he again issue a statement responding to the continuing vituperative attacks in the Los Angeles press. He declined, saying:

> There are times when it is wise to be silent, and I am sure that this is one of them. There is little that we could say at this point that would not be misinterpreted as a direct attack on UCLA or

other Conference colleagues, and this would not contribute to our efforts, being carried on several fronts, to reach a sensible solution of Conference problems.

Despite claims in the Los Angeles press, Sterling added, Stanford had seen no impact on either enrollment applications or gifts to the university. Indeed, he said, his mailbox revealed strong support, as a matter of dignity and even of indifference to the criticism's source.[106]

By the end of 1957, the Pacific Coast Conference had fallen apart.

USC had followed on the heels of the University of California, formally announcing in December that it would sever ties with the PCC. Frank Bonelli was delighted with the "forthright action" of UC and USC. He called off the Assembly inquiry into the PCC, commenting that he expected the president of Stanford University, the last California school in the PCC, "to see the light and take similar action."[107]

Sports Illustrated editorialized: "It is quite clear that—regardless of the stigma resulting from the scandals—USC, UCLA, Cal, and Washington have been able to use them as a very convenient excuse for ridding their schedules of three unprofitable opponents. Neither Oregon, Oregon State, nor Washington State drew well in the Big Four stadiums."[108]

The future of the Rose Bowl was also in doubt as a PCC contractual arrangement. Aside from the confusion over whether the bolting universities would retain the contract with the Rose Bowl management after the January 1, 1958, Oregon–Ohio State game, the Big Ten conference faculty council overtly backed Stanford and Oregon. Well into 1959, they remained leery of contracting with universities willing to break up their own conference in order to avoid penalties, holding off to see if Stanford would join the other California schools. It turned into an 18-month wait.[109]

At their December 1957 meeting, Stanford's

The Stanford Axe has symbolized Stanford-California rivalry since an 1899 baseball rally, on campus, and game, in San Francisco. After defeating the Cardinal, Cal rooters grabbed the Axe and escaped. For the next 31 years, Cal used the Axe to mock Stanford until an elaborate 1930 theft brought it home. Soon, officials of both schools agreed to award it annually to Big Game's football winner. Here, after six straight losses, the Axe is going into storage in 1955 while an alarmed case is built in Stanford's Cellar eatery. Sure enough, it was purloined after a week in its new case. *PALO ALTO TIMES* / STANFORD UNIVERSITY ARCHIVES

John Ralston's third Big Game victory, 1965, was assured when running back Ray Handley, '66 (#48), scored the winning touchdown in Stanford's narrow defeat of Cal, 9–7, as Cal fans and band looked on. Handley later became an assistant coach at Stanford, West Point, and the Air Force Academy, and won two Super Bowls as offensive backfield coach of the NFL's New York Giants.   STANFORD NEWS SERVICE

Board of Trustees followed Sterling's wait-and-see strategy, voting to stay in the Pacific Coast Conference as a matter of institutional obligation to its fellow members but confirming that Stanford would not support any more watering down of the code. In a subsequent press release, Sterling announced that the university would honor its existing conference schedule commitments through 1960, including any Rose Bowl invitation, should there be one. "Beyond that, Stanford will, I think, have to consult its own interests as these are determined by its educational program and the place of intercollegiate athletics therein.

I personally look forward to a vigorous continuation of such athletics here."[110]

As Sterling confided to Bob Reynolds, of his alumni athletics advisory committee, "I could not bring myself to recommend [to the trustees] something which would align Stanford with three universities who had violated the code after the presidents of those institutions, with Sproul in the lead, had, in 1953, argued and agreed that the code should be honored and those who are trying to make departure from the conference look virtuous." He was dubious of the proposed new alliance. Because "of their failure to honor

During pre–Big Game revelry in 1967, a replica of Oski (Cal's mascot since 1941) was chased and "killed" by an "Indian" near Engineering Corner. The Bearial procession, led by Stanford pom-pom girls (from left) Ellie Watkins, Sue Beck (behind), Nancy Kerr, Sue McCann, and Susie Phillips, along with the "Indian," then made its way to White Plaza's Claw fountain.   STANFORD NEWS SERVICE

agreements voluntarily entered into, I could have little confidence that the new principles (self-policing to mention only one), would be honored in the future."[111]

But Stanford was simply too profitable an opponent for the "Big Four" to let go. The Big Game had always been a mainstay of the athletic programs at both Stanford and Cal. In Los Angeles, games against Stanford filled the Coliseum, home to USC Trojan football since 1923 and the UCLA Bruins since 1928.[112] Yet, despite repeated prodding by Sproul and Allen, Sterling would not bolt the old conference and would not, as yet, negotiate joining a new one.

Sterling again spoke directly to his alumni. Members of the university's athletic teams would continue to be students first and athletes second, he wrote soon after in the January 1958 *Stanford [Alumni] Review*. In terms of financial aid, there would be no discrimination, in favor of or against a student, because he happens to be an athlete. Sterling had no intention of de-emphasizing the athletic program, he said; indeed, he viewed it as being strengthened. Thus, the university would explore scholarship options and work opportunities, but would provide no free rides for athletes. "Stanford has maintained that the old PCC code in some instances discriminated against athletes by barring certain work opportunities and forms of financial aid available to other students," he noted, but free-ride proponents put athletes in a separate class by giving them aid not available to other students. Both approaches were wrong.[113]

In the end, however, he emphasized, "one thing can be stated with complete assurance:

Big Game Bonfire, like the Axe, was rooted in the Stanford-Cal baseball rivalry. Built at various locations through the years (here in an open field across from Encina in 1910), the Bonfire had been part of pre–Big Game activities since 1898. The giant structure— a freshmen responsibility—often blazed 200 feet high. In 1940, the "Burn the Bear" event was relocated to Lagunita's lakebed. Due to environmental and safety concerns, as well as student apathy, the last giant one burned in 1992.   STANFORD UNIVERSITY ARCHIVES

One of Stanford's highest priorities is maintenance of good relations with the University of California."

After the University of Washington also formally left the PCC, in mid-1958, Sterling saw little hope of preserving the old conference. In his December 1957 statement on the trustees' decision, Sterling had already mentioned an interest in going Ivy League for football. Sterling and Kerr discussed this possibility for both of their campuses, and each made overtures among Ivy League colleagues. Interest was modest, at best, and at least one key Ivy League member shut down the idea altogether. More importantly, travel costs would have been prohibitive and the question of competition in other sports remained.[114]

Stanford also was rumored to be a potential member of a proposed league of independents—to also include Army, Navy, Notre Dame, Oklahoma, UCLA, and USC (a notion that first appeared in press coverage in 1956). Dubbed the "Airplane League," due to the obvious reliance on air travel, it never got beyond speculation in United Press reports.[115]

Sterling regained his faith in UC's intentions when, in June 1958, Clark Kerr succeeded Sproul as president of the University of California system, beating out UCLA's Ray Allen for the post. "We have not made up our minds yet just what we plan to do about this new conference," Sterling wrote a Southern California alumnus in September, "but my present mood is to stand by and watch developments." Clark Kerr, he hoped, "may be able to make some sense, in the long run, out of what has been difficult North-South relationships, but I am not unaware of the difficulties confronting him."[116]

AND THEN THERE WERE FIVE
THE ATHLETIC ASSOCIATION OF WESTERN UNIVERSITIES

In July 1959, Stanford took up its place as the fifth member (with Cal, UCLA, USC, and Washington), a "charter member" position that had been held in reserve, in the new Athletic Association of Western Universities (AAWU). "The luring of Stanford into the fold consti-

tutes a major diplomatic victory for the other four schools," noted the *Stanford Daily*. Aside from scheduling, "the Big Four gains greatly in respectability." Other major football schools, suspicious that the new organization might be a cover-up for shady recruiting, were watching: If Stanford joined, "the new league must be on the up-and-up."[117]

Despite an allegedly hearty welcome, Stanford had been in no hurry.[118] Football scheduling had been no problem—Stanford was the only former PCC institution to continue to play the former "round robin" of PCC teams, along with scheduling major Midwest teams like Notre Dame and Wisconsin. As an independent, it had also been eligible for a range of bowl games beyond the Rose Bowl. The Board of Trustees had no intention of approving the new league membership without Sterling's firm endorsement.

Clark Kerr and Wallace Sterling's personal relationship, enhanced by former labor arbitrator Kerr's negotiating skills, brought reconciliation. According to Kerr, he was delegated by the other university presidents to persuade his good friend Sterling to reconsider. "He was particularly offended by the conduct of the representatives of UCLA," Kerr later recalled, "and refused to accept UCLA as a voting member. He did trust me, however."

Kerr agreed to represent both Cal and UCLA even though, he later wrote, it went against his policy of decentralizing campus governance—and against the wishes of Glenn Seaborg, his successor as Cal's chancellor. However, Kerr stated, "I thought that no West Coast conference would be complete without Stanford, and that it was very important to Berkeley to maintain its cherished relationship with Stanford above all else. . . . The new conference could not have been solidly built and have maintained its integrity without Stanford."[119]

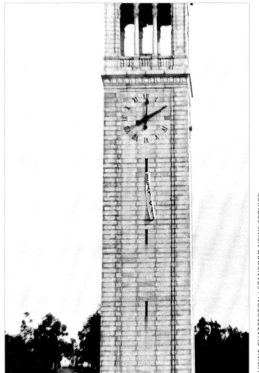

Stanford students sometimes took their Beat Cal banners off campus during Big Game week. Clockwise from top left, the leaning Tower of Pisa (1960); Cal's iconic Campanile (1960); San Francisco's Coit Tower (1963); and outside the Spanish Riding School in Vienna (1965). The efforts in Italy and Austria, along with a later banner hanging from London's Tower Bridge, were the work of overseas campus students.

When Big Game, November 1963, was postponed a week by the assassination of President John F. Kennedy, the memorial events honoring the fallen president included this half-time American flag display as the Stanford Band played "America the Beautiful." Before the game, the Band's haunting new rendition of the Star-Spangled Banner, starting with a drum roll then fading to a lone trumpet for half the piece, triggered many tears in the crowd of 82,000 and earned special notice in news coverage. The arrangement, by Band Director Art Barnes, has been played ever since at home games. STANFORD NEWS SERVICE

Kerr met Sterling's two conditions: 1) the *president* of each institution in the new conference had to take direct control of and responsibility for enforcing scholastic requirements, and 2) each school had to furnish its member colleagues with scholastic records of all of its players. Responsibility for the policy and conduct of intercollegiate athletics now rested in the hands of each university president. Stanford's own academic standards, Sterling announced, would

remain "exacting," and it also would continue its long-established policy of faculty-administered financial aid to needy and qualified students without regard to participation in intercollegiate sports.[120]

The forced resignation, in June 1959, of UCLA's Chancellor Allen also was a factor. Allen had earned UC regent Pauley's disfavor for his handling of the PCC crisis, and he was replaced as UCLA chancellor shortly after Kerr's presidential promotion. Kerr and Seaborg were relieved when Sterling then agreed to work with Seaborg and UCLA's new chancellor.[121]

Other important administrative changes that had taken place also eased the way. USC's president, Fred Fagg, had resigned in 1956, stating that he no longer had the energy and health to meet the demands of his position. Washington, Cal, USC, and Stanford all had new coaches, as did UCLA. Bruins coach Red Sanders, once the center of UCLA's bitter fight to maintain its football domination and its revenue stream, had already been testing the waters for more lucrative positions, without strings, in Texas, but died of a heart attack in August 1958 at age 53.[122]

Professor and Admissions Director Rix Snyder, who had chaired the PCC Faculty Council during its devolution, became Stanford's faculty representative to the new AAWU conference. Snyder, like Chuck Taylor, concluded that joining the new conference was the right decision, since "our lot was really with these three other California institutions." They had been worried about scheduling other sports without a league structure. Rose Bowl revenues were also an enticement.[123]

Not long after Stanford joined, the AAWU was nicknamed the Big Five. Washington State was admitted in 1962. When Oregon and OSU joined two years later, the conference—now minus only Idaho—was dubbed the Pacific 8. (The conference name was formally changed to the Pac-8 in 1968.)[124]

In 1960, not long after the dust settled, writer and Stanford alumnus Frank Taylor composed his flattering feature article on Sterling for *The Saturday Evening Post*, just in time for the kick-off of Stanford's landmark campus-wide fundraising campaign. During the past four years, Sterling had won acclaim for building the university's academic program, strengthening its faculty, raising student academic requirements, and stimulating long-range campus planning. He had overseen a major curriculum review and had revitalized and rebuilt the Medical School. But PCC scars remained and, even in this upbeat profile, the consuming nature of football had to be addressed, although from a distinctly Stanford perspective. "Former Coach Sterling has had some rough going on the football gridiron despite his liking for the game and his habit of lunching now and then at the training table with the Stanford varsity," Taylor wrote, adding sardonically: "It happens that he holds strictly to the philosophy that 'intercollegiate games should be played by bona fide students.' Some loyal old grads who have scouted long and hard for ball-carrying talent feel that the president is entirely too demanding of proof of bona-fideness, so to speak."[125]

"Sterling took a drubbing in the sports pages of the newspapers for this heresy, and for a time it seemed that Stanford might be the only member of a Pacific Coast Ivy League. Fortunately, the other presidents came around," wrote Taylor. "Dr. Sterling's wounds have been salved somewhat by the record, not of glittering Stanford victories on the gridiron but a more erudite score which reveals that more than half of all Pacific Coast varsity athletes who won Phi Beta Kappa keys last year wore the Stanford Block S."[126]

A WARM WELCOME FOR ALL

From their arrival in April 1949, Wally and Ann Sterling were at the center of an extended and congenial Stanford community of faculty and staff, alumni and students, trustees and friends. Sterling and his first lady quickly began spreading confidence in the university's future through personal charm, hospitality, and an enthusiasm for social interaction on campus and off.

The Sterlings were often the honored guests at campus lunches, dinners, and receptions, and on the alumni conference circuit, or as they traveled across the country and around the world. They also quickly established themselves as welcoming hosts. Visitors became a constant in the life of the university president and his family. The Sterlings adeptly used the Lou Henry Hoover House to entertain members of the Stanford community, as well as a wide array of those whom Sterling called "the great and near great," from a handsome Belgian king to a laconic English duke who cheered up only when he could talk of his dairy cows.[1]

ENTERTAINING AT THE LOU HENRY HOOVER HOUSE

The success of the Hoover House as the site of hundreds of receptions, luncheons, teas, and dinners each year depended upon Ann Sterling and her small staff. Her husband always gave special credit to her for her diligence, effort, and special talents as organizer and hostess.

As the university's first lady from 1949 to 1968, Ann Sterling earned "a reputation for graciousness, wit, elegance, and total dedication to the institution and everyone associated with it." Her job, Sterling later said, was all the harder because she had to work from no job description or guidelines, and had to establish methods and rules of thumb along the way. The house was ready to receive guests at any time of day and well into the evening. Overnight accommodations were also in the mix.[2]

Within months of moving into the Hoover House, they welcomed former U.S. President

< Wallace and Ann Sterling with their golden retriever, Heidi, on the back lawn of the Hoover House, early 1960s. Heidi, who had the run of the campus, once got caught in a roundup by the county dog catcher. A faculty spouse recognized her when she went to the pound to retrieve her own dog.
STANFORD QUAD / STANFORD NEWS SERVICE

403

Settling into the Lou Henry Hoover House in April 1949, Wallace and Ann Sterling enjoy the sitting room (originally Herbert Hoover's study). Early fears the house would be unsuitable for their three children quickly gave way, and it became a center of university hospitality as well as the family's home for the next 19 years.
MOULIN STUDIOS / STANFORD NEWS SERVICE

Herbert Hoover to his former family residence for the first of many weeklong summer visits. Later that year, Ann Sterling organized a reception for 750 guests as part of her husband's inauguration. Sixteen years later, the Sterlings hosted the Duke and Duchess of Gloucester and their entourage of eight (including aides, a lady in waiting, and a security man from Scotland Yard). Equally important to them was the 1968 party for the university's maintenance staff and their families, to thank them for their upkeep of the president's house during the family's 19 years there.

Ann Sterling's goal, she once told an interviewer, was to keep the house "gay and welcoming." Keenly interested in antiques, especially 18th-century English furniture and porcelain, she decorated the house like an English country home. With a lifelong interest in historic gardens and gardening, she also made most of her own floral arrangements for university functions at the house, using flowers raised by her husband on the Hoover House grounds supplemented

by others donated from the gardens of friends. (She was a member of the Woodside-Atherton Garden Club, and a director and show judge—decorative arrangements—of the Garden Club of America.)

"She was such a wonderful hostess," remembered presidential assistant Fred Glover. "She had a great sense of humor, and she was completely irreverent." Glover also appreciated her ability not only to provide an elegant atmosphere, but also to soften the stiffness of formal events. "She would unstuff a stuffed shirt as quick as anybody I ever saw. She was fun to be with. She was a great tease."[3]

As a measure of their entertaining, Sterling told a favorite story of the time their income tax returns were challenged. The Sterlings had not shown as income, the auditor claimed, the value of living rent-free at the presidential residence. Sterling explained that the Hoover House was an institutional responsibility, used on behalf of the university as part of the functioning of his

Judy, Ann, and Susan Sterling, at home at the Hoover House, apparently planning a trip, in 1959. Herbert Hoover in 1945 donated the house to serve as the official presidential residence.   JON BRENNEIS / STANFORD NEWS SERVICE

office. As evidence, Ann provided her records, including menus, guest lists, and evaluations of each event (for future reference) of her nearly daily entertaining on the university's behalf. These records revealed that some 12,000 to 15,000 people were entertained at the Hoover House that year, from luncheons, dinners, and cocktail parties to afternoon teas, after-dinner desserts, and coffee gatherings for student and faculty groups. The challenge was dropped.[4]

Ann Sterling was also credited with making the Hoover House a comfortable home. Here the Sterlings raised their three children, William, Susan, and Judy. The children were often included in social events, brightening the atmosphere and helping to further "unstuff" the formalities. Sterling later expressed concern that he and Ann had to be away many nights during the week, or away on university business, and praised the children's resilience in growing up in such a busy household.

At Stanford, Ann Sterling continued her interest and involvement in the arts and other civic organizations. She helped found the Stanford Museum's Committee for Art, which played a vital role in the museum's revitalization, and the Stanford Distaff Club, an association of female staff members. She also was a trustee of the San Francisco Symphony Association, and on the boards of the San Francisco Museum of Modern Art and the Palo Alto Chapter of the American Red Cross.

WELCOMED BY BORIS AND CHEERIO

When moving into the Lou Henry Hoover House, the Sterling family had been welcomed by Kosta and Essie Boris. "Boris" and "Cheerio" had strong ties to Herbert Hoover and, in essence, came with the house. They became an important part of the Sterling family.[5]

Serbian-born Kosta Boris had first met Herbert Hoover in 1918 when he was assigned by the U.S. Army as an orderly to Hoover's U.S. Food Administration headquarters in Paris. Boris was fluent in French, Serbian, and English, and got things done. After the war, he became Hoover's valet and aide for more than 25 years, in Washington, D.C., and at Stanford.

Known popularly as just "Boris," he was tall, handsome, and dignified. One White House staff member said, "He looked more like a diplomat than a valet." Hoover's friend, journalist Will Irwin, '99, described Boris in 1932 as "guardian of the children, handyman, factotum of the guests, an indispensable cog in the machinery of the household" of then-U.S. President Herbert Hoover. The Hoover family dubbed him their "Factum Factotum" and "Domestic Maestro."[6]

After Mrs. Hoover's death, in 1944, and Mr. Hoover's decision to take up permanent residence in New York City, Boris and his wife, Essie, stayed on at Stanford to aid Presidents

Tresidder (in residence, 1944–48) and Sterling (1949–68). And for many summers during the Sterling years, they welcomed Hoover back to his former house.[7]

Essie Paul Boris served as Mrs. Sterling's aide throughout the 1950s and 1960s. She had met and married Boris, then working for President Hoover, in Washington, D.C., not long after emigrating from Northern Ireland. For the Sterlings, she not only helped plan and execute social events, but also played an important role in the lives of the three children. Susan Sterling Monjauze later remembered her greeting them when they came home from school, celebrating their successes, and lifting their spirits. "She emanated joy and love." Friends turned her "Cheerio!" farewell into her popular nickname.[8]

Kosta and Essie Boris retired in 1968, when

In 1978, Kosta (center) and Essie (Cheerio) Boris, at the front door of the Lou Henry Hoover House when it was designated a California Historic Landmark. Palo Alto architect Birge M. Clark (left) had supervised construction and assisted his father, Professor A. B. Clark, and Mrs. Hoover, who worked together on the design.
CAROLYN CADDES / STANFORD UNIVERSITY ARCHIVES

Ann and Wallace Sterling left Hoover House. Kosta died in Palo Alto, aged 89, in 1979, and Essie in 1994, just before her 90th birthday.

HOSTING DISTINGUISHED GUESTS

Before becoming Stanford's president, Sterling had met a number of prominent academic, diplomatic, and military figures through his scholarly work, as a CBS commentator, and while teaching at the National War College. As head of Stanford, he met others through his work on international committees, as president of the American Association of Universities, and through Stanford's negotiations for its overseas campuses. The Sterlings took pleasure in reciprocating the hospitality they enjoyed when traveling around the world, but he was also especially interested in drawing Stanford students into the experience of extending hospitality to prominent and important figures, and in providing means for faculty to interact with visitors relevant to their work or their personal lives.

The imposing university president enjoyed enlivening formal events at Hoover House with a songfest, gathering guests around the piano. "After dinner at Stanford affairs, Wally loved to sit down at the piano to play and sing," recalled Stanford trustee President Tom Pike. "Although he was a much better pianist than I, he generously tolerated my amateurism, and we had great fun teaming up as a piano duo and beating the familiar rhythm and harmonies of the old favorites of the twenties and thirties."[9]

The Sterlings delighted in mixing the ceremonial and stately with informal family and community life. Fred Glover and Don Carlson recounted

Sterling enjoyed livening up formal events by gathering guests around the piano. Here, in the early 1960s, Delta Kappa Epsilon fraternity brothers Cameron (Cappy) Hurst III, '63 (left), and Jeff Gaylord, '63, stand by the piano as President Sterling and an unidentified man play a duet for four hands.
STANFORD UNIVERSITY ARCHIVES

While in Great Britain in June 1963, Sterling discussed the interest of Prince William of Gloucester in attending Stanford for a year of postgraduate study. (William was the eldest son of Prince Henry, Duke of Gloucester, and first cousin of Queen Elizabeth; at the time, he was sixth in line to the British throne.) The Sterlings were in England as part of a delegation of the American Association of Universities, joining British vice-chancellors to celebrate the 50th anniversary of the Association of British Commonwealth Universities. Sterling and Sir Henry Willink, master of Magdalene College in Cambridge, had been corresponding about Prince William. Sir Henry arranged lunch for them two days later at York House, in St. James's Palace, with the Duke and Duchess of Gloucester, their younger son, Richard,

one "sensational" dinner as illustrative of their style. After a long day of meetings, a group of distinguished British university vice-chancellors was treated to a Sterling barbecue, with hamburgers and hot dogs, corn and beans, served on the lawn of the Lou Henry Hoover House on a beautiful California evening. Ken Cuthbertson, Alf Brandin, and other senior officers and faculty served as waiters.[10]

Given their family backgrounds and personal interests, as well as Sterling's academic pursuits, Wally and Ann Sterling especially relished visits by British scholars, diplomats, and other dignitaries. Among those that stood out for Sterling were guests Lord and Lady Halifax and visits at Stanford and in England with the Duke and Duchess of Gloucester.

Sterling greeted Prince William of Gloucester, who arrived in fall 1963 for a year of graduate study. He had earned an engineering degree at Cambridge; at Stanford he studied political science, American history, and business. Queen Elizabeth's stylish cousin was listed in Stanford's directory simply as William Gloucester. STANFORD NEWS SERVICE

and others. Although the duke was a quiet man who avoided conversation, Sterling described the lunch as a happy one, with much talk about William and his prospective attendance at Stanford.[11]

Prince William made a good impression while pursuing a year of study in Humanities Special Programs, in 1963–64. Vice Provost Howard Brooks enjoyed serving as advisor to the young man as he studied political science, American history, and business. (William intended to join the British Diplomatic Service.) The prince set two precedents: He was the first British royal to attend a coeducational university (he had earned an engineering degree at Cambridge), and the first to study at an American institution.[12]

In Stanford's *Student Directory,* Prince William Henry Andrew Frederick was listed simply as William Gloucester. He lived in Crothers Hall on campus. Known in England as "the most democratic and politely rebellious member of the royal family," he wanted to make his own way in life, reported the *Stanford Daily* discreetly, in its only article on Prince William's year at Stanford.[13]

Fred Glover was charged with keeping intrusive news reporters at bay. When a reporter from *Time* magazine came to the campus and inquired about Prince William, Glover told him there was nothing particularly newsworthy to report. The reporter replied, "If there isn't any news, we're going to make it." When Sterling learned of this comment, he called the magazine's owner, Henry Luce, whom Sterling had known for years. The reporter was called back to New York.[14] (Prince William died in 1972, while piloting a plane.)

When the Sterlings hosted the duke and duchess at Hoover House in March 1965, they took the royal couple to their rustic cabin in La Honda for a barbecue lunch. With a warm fire in the large stone fireplace on this overcast day, Sterling remembered that they had "a fairly merry time." Fred Glover later was amused that the duke called the cabin a "hut." Sterling had given Glover a tough assignment, seating him next to the duke. The accomplished interviewer tried to make conversation, but "I just couldn't get anything out of him."[15]

When, in April 1966, the Sterlings were in England for the dedication of Stanford's overseas campus at Harlaxton, Sterling learned the secret to conversing with the duke. He and Ann were his guests at Barnwell Manor, near Peterborough, where the duke and duchess had their farm and country home. Sterling mentioned that he was a country boy, with fond memories of growing up in farm country, and the duke was delighted, sharing his intense interest in farming, particularly his livestock and crop

In 1963, the Sterlings had been guests of the Duke and Duchess of Gloucester; they returned the gesture by hosting the couple at Hoover House in 1965. The quiet royals attracted British publicity to dedication of Stanford-in-Britain when, in 1966, they came to Harlaxton to see the Sterlings and mingle with students. STANFORD NEWS SERVICE

Junior Craig Tate, an economics major, visited with the Duke of Gloucester during the dedication reception for the Stanford campus in England, at Harlaxton Manor.   STANFORD UNIVERSITY ARCHIVES

GLOVERS ON CALL

On campus, Fred Glover was often on hand to help Sterling with visiting dignitaries, foreign and domestic, just as he was vital to the smooth opening of Stanford's overseas campuses. Educated in France and Germany before and after attending Stanford, Glover spoke fluent German, French, and Spanish. He also was expert at the intricacies of protocol and security, and knew how to deal with the curiosity of the press. "It was an enormous advantage in the President's Office to have a linguist," he recalled, because when the visitors came through, not always with much prior notice, "Wally could say, 'My assistant, who speaks French (or German), will take you on a tour of the campus.'"[17]

breeding. He gave them a personal tour of the dairy he had designed.

Glover and his colleagues were having difficulty at the time (it was the week before Easter) getting any mention in British newspapers of this first Stanford-in-Britain campus. When the duke and duchess appeared at the opening ceremony, however, they got the press attention Stanford officials hoped for. "All it takes in England is to have a duke and duchess, any royalty at all," Glover mused. The couple "came to see Ann and Wally," recalled Don Carlson. "It was a very personal, warm thing. That made it all the better a [news] story." Even more, Glover added, the duke and duchess enjoyed mingling with the Stanford students. This sort of interaction was an important part of university activities, said Glover, because Sterling always wanted to involve students as well as faculty in such events.[16]

Glover and his wife, Nini, were also always on call to fill in as hosts, using their own house, as well as to stand in at the last minute at Hoover House. They kept formal clothes at the ready. At one dinner, Fred Glover later recalled, Nini (who was fluent in German but not French) pulled off an animated dinner party for a noted Italian visitor who spoke French but no German and little English. "Wally and Ann just expected us to do that."[18]

The congenial Glovers also filled in at the last minute at formal dinner parties. One of his most "terrifying experiences," Glover recalled, was at a dinner for Earl Warren, chief justice of the U.S. Supreme Court and former California governor. Glover was seated next to the chief justice at the Hoover House dinner following Warren's 1964 commencement address. As a journalist, Glover was an adept interviewer, but each topic he raised with Warren turned out to be one the chief justice felt he should not discuss. "I had a heck of a time," said Glover.[19]

WELCOMING FOREIGN DIGNITARIES

The Hoover Institution, with its extensive collections, often was a magnet for international visitors. In 1953, Baron Robert Silvercruys, the debonair Belgian ambassador to the United States, visited Stanford to formally donate a tapestry expressing Belgium's gratitude for American contributions to Belgium in the First World War (in addition to directing wartime relief, Hoover sponsored fundraising to rebuild the renowned Louvain Library). This was one of five tapestries illustrating important chapters in Belgian history that had been woven in 1939 for the Belgian Pavilion at the New York World's Fair (1939–40). The five had been sent to Stanford in 1940 for safekeeping, as war again broke out in Europe. The Hoover Institution returned four in 1953. The fifth remains at the Hoover Institution.[20]

The baron, a guest at the Lou Henry Hoover House, was treated to a faculty luncheon at the Menlo Country Club, and another at the Bohemian Club in San Francisco. Sterling felt it important to draw Stanford students into the mix and hosted a Hoover House dinner for more than 30 guests, including students working in international studies.[21]

In May 1959, King Baudouin of Belgium made a carefully organized and highly publicized three-hour visit to the campus. Protocol arrangements were intricate, covering such details as who would walk with the king after the group left Memorial Church and the form of address to use with the king and his 17 accompanying dignitaries.[22] After leaving the church, Sterling took the group to the Hoover Institution for a reception, a view of the area from the tower's observation deck, and a look at materials relating to Belgium in the institution's extensive archives. This was Baudouin's only college visit during his three-week tour of the United States. While much of the time was taken up with his Hoover

President Sterling and Baron Robert Silvercruys, Belgian ambassador to the United States, at the 1953 formal donation of a Belgian tapestry woven in 1939 for the New York World's Fair. This one honors American efforts, including Herbert Hoover's leadership, on behalf of Belgium in World War I.
STANFORD NEWS SERVICE

Sterling and King Baudouin, the 28-year-old king of the Belgians, crossed the Inner Quad in 1959 to visit Memorial Church where they viewed flags carried by Stanford ambulance volunteers in Europe during World War I. At the Hoover Institution, they looked at archives of the Commission for Relief in Belgium.   STANFORD NEWS SERVICE

visit, he took a few minutes to chat with some of the 200 students gathered to see him. "I would like to stay here and study. You are all very lucky," the 28-year-old king told them. Enjoying the relative informality of the students, he invited one student headed for Oxford to visit him in Belgium.[23]

A few weeks before the king's visit, Herbert Hoover wrote Sterling that "the Belgians have had a considerable part in the [Hoover] Institution," and he requested that the king be given a full hour to visit the Hoover Archives to see its Belgian documentation. Hoover, however, also was under the impression that a visit made by

Baudouin's father, former King Leopold III, the previous November had been unusually brief due to mishandling by the university, complaining that Leopold had been "hustled" in and out of Hoover Tower in a few minutes. Sterling reassured Hoover that arrangements for Baudouin's visit were extensive, and carefully made; he also set the record straight regarding Leopold's quick visit. Leopold had arrived incognito for a very brief and private visit, simply to sign the guest book and pay his respects to Mr. Hoover, who was not there.[24] (Leopold, unpopular in Belgium because of his capitulation to Hitler in 1940 and nearly 10 years in exile, abdicated in 1951.)

The Hoover collections were a deterrent in one notable case. When French President Charles de Gaulle visited the area in April 1960, he declined to come closer to the main campus than the Medical School, and spent only 30 minutes of his two-day tour of the Bay Area at Stanford. De Gaulle's main interest, the public was told, was to see the Stanford Industrial Park (he spent considerable time at Hewlett-Packard). The President's Office learned, however, that another reason was the presence at the Hoover Institution of the papers of Pierre Laval, head of France's Vichy government during the German occupation. De Gaulle, leader of French resistance during the war, would have nothing to do with Laval. "He didn't want to be within a hundred yards of those Laval papers," recalled Fred

French President Charles de Gaulle made a quick visit to Stanford's Medical Center (and a much longer one at the Industrial Park's Hewlett-Packard headquarters) on April 28, 1960, during a two-day tour of the Bay Area.
PALO ALTO TIMES / PALO ALTO HISTORICAL ASSOCIATION

Glover.[25] (The French government executed Laval in 1945 for collaboration with the enemy.)

Nonetheless, the President's Office arranged for Sterling, joined by 78 students who were soon leaving to open the Stanford-in-France campus in Tours, as well as several French students and teaching fellows, to greet President de Gaulle at the Medical School. All did not go as planned. The French security agents accompanying the president were particularly brusque. Despite the rush, shouting security men, and a mob of newsmen being pushed out of the way, the crowd of 200 to 300 students and others gave de Gaulle a warm welcome, and he acknowledged them with a smile. De Gaulle spoke briefly with President Sterling and Palo Alto Mayor Noel Porter, as well as one or two of the French students. His entourage then headed to San Francisco.[26]

Another planned visit of a world-famous figure did not happen at all because of security issues. Soviet Premier Nikita Khrushchev came to California in September 1959, as part of an unprecedented 13-day tour of the United States. "We had all kinds of plans to meet him at Stanford," Glover recounted. As the former head of naval intelligence in Berlin in 1945, including keeping track of Russian activities there during the occupation, Glover was amused to now find himself working with two KGB agents. "It was interesting that these Russian secret service people didn't want the car to be anywhere where it had to turn around. You had to keep moving the whole time, and that's kind of difficult at Stanford, as there are a number of places where you'd want to stop and turn." In the end, Khrushchev visited IBM in San Jose (where he showed little interest in IBM's computers but greatly admired the company's self-service cafeteria). "We'd done an awful lot of work," said Glover, but like the premier's much-anticipated visit to Disneyland, his tour of Stanford was cancelled for security reasons.[27]

Hoover House, from the north, probably in the late 1920s. Located near the crest of San Juan Hill, its setting and grounds were enhanced in 1952, when the late Professor and Mrs. Elwood Cubberley's home, directly below on Cabrillo (out of view to the left), was razed and the space added to the presidential mansion's lawn and gardens. BERTON CRANDALL / STANFORD UNIVERSITY ARCHIVES

THE PRESIDENT'S RESIDENCE
LOU HENRY HOOVER'S HOUSE

The Lou Henry Hoover House, official residence of Stanford presidents since 1945, was built in 1919–20 on the slope of San Juan Hill by two of Stanford's most famous alumni, Lou Henry, '98, and Herbert Hoover, '95, and served for more than two decades as their family home.

The three-storied structure of stacked cubes and flat roofs defies easy architectural categorization. In his book *Mrs. Hoover's Pueblo Walls: The Primitive and the Modern in the Lou Henry Hoover House* (Stanford: Stanford University Press, 2004), Paul V. Turner concludes that the house was inspired by Native American Pueblo architecture of New Mexico and Arizona. Turner, the Wattis Professor of Art, Emeritus, at Stanford, trained as an architect and art historian.

The house belonged to Lou Hoover, who willed it to their sons, Allan and Herbert Jr. After her death, in January 1944, her husband bought it from them to donate to the university, in 1945. Then-President Donald Tresidder originally suggested that the house be used as Stanford's presidential residence.

A deceptively simple exterior hides an elegant interior, and its large size encompasses intimate, cozy spaces as well as dramatic public rooms. Its view of the campus and San Francisco Bay is spectacular, and hardly accidental. It was designed to be a home as well as a place to entertain friends and dignitaries, often in large numbers.

In the foreword to Turner's book, then-President John Hennessy and his wife, Andrea, wrote that they found the house to be "pleasantly livable, although not without challenges, as one would expect of an older house of this size." They surmised that Mrs. Hoover "would delight in the knowledge that the home she took great care in planning has met the varied needs of its occupants for many years, and we hope she would be pleased to see the delight on the faces of the thousands of visitors who come to the house each year."

As benefactors and influential alumni, the Hoovers had become increasingly involved in campus affairs in the early 20th century. Their decision to choose the campus as their permanent residence initially aided Herbert Hoover's work on Stanford's Board of Trustees. Before they built their dream house, the Hoovers lived in a succession of rented and purchased houses in Palo Alto and on campus, among them a large Mediterranean-style house at 746 Santa Ynez, which they sold in 1920.

Early aerial photo shows the exterior 17,500-square-foot Hoover House. Not including its two garages (one was added at left after this photo) and very thick walls, the net (interior) square footage is 13,600.
STANFORD UNIVERSITY ARCHIVES

This 1920s photo of the living room, with coved, gold-colored ceiling and view of the library alcove's leaded glass doors, displays the elegant European-style interior touches preferred by Lou Henry Hoover. (Sterling's successor, Kenneth Pitzer, had the gold ceiling painted white during his brief tenure; that remains.) Off this room to the right is the main terrace, often used for entertaining.
STANFORD UNIVERSITY ARCHIVES

Looking north from the upper terrace, off the second-floor bedrooms of the Hoover sons, one could see nearly to San Francisco Bay in the 1920s. The many terraces appealed to the Hoovers' love of the outdoors. BERTON CRANDALL / STANFORD UNIVERSITY ARCHIVES

Herbert Hoover had three requirements for their new house: a good view, useful roofs, and fireproof construction. His wife played a far greater role than he in the design. She began sketching ideas for the house in 1912.

After the Great War, Mrs. Hoover turned for help to Arthur Bridgman Clark, a family friend, neighbor, and Stanford professor of art. Clark, who had designed a number of faculty houses in the area, also knew local building conditions. He was discreet (her first architect had boasted of his commission to newspapers, resulting in his firing) as well as receptive to the Hoovers' ideas, and was already familiar with Mrs. Hoover's designs. She would be the architect-in-chief, he declared, while he served as a "sort of architectural 'secretary.'" The sketches she sent to Clark, Turner writes, "reveal careful thought and an ability to conceptualize rather complex forms and spaces."

Birge Clark, '14, helped his father with the assignment on his 1919 return to Stanford from graduate work in architecture at Columbia University and war service overseas. He supervised construction.

The Hoovers' passion for outdoor living led to a design featuring spacious terraces and outside stairways. Although they loved to entertain, they preferred a casual, rather than ostentatious, environment. They had originally envisioned a smaller house and were somewhat embarrassed by its final size.

Completed in 1920, the modern structure housed not only the Hoovers and their two sons, but also several live-in employees. It offered ample room for house guests and daytime staff.

While negotiating the offer of the presidency with trustees in late 1948, Wallace Sterling expressed reservations about raising his three young children in the Lou Henry Hoover House *(see Chapter 1)*. But soon after his appointment, his wife, Ann, enthusiastically began planning the move.

The Lou Henry Hoover House has been a registered California Historic Landmark since 1978 and National Historic Landmark since 1985.

SELECTED CAMPUS CONTROVERSIES
PARTISAN POLITICS TO LITERARY EX-CON

During his 19 years as president, Wallace Sterling faced many controversies that filled his mailbox with letters from his campus and alumni constituencies. Some issues were overtly political; others, while not rooted in politics, had political overtones. One was simply embarrassing. All had an impact on Stanford's image, often pitting faculty and students against alumni. A selection of these controversies, documented in the files of the President's Office, follows.

ADLAI STEVENSON ENDORSEMENT
PERSONAL OPINION OR PARTISAN POLITICS?

Sterling had been questioned about Communists on campus since his arrival in 1949. Public interest was high because Sen. Joseph McCarthy and others were calling for investigation of Communist influence in an ever-broadening circle

< Commenting on Fred Glover's 1952 appointment as Sterling's assistant, staff member Joseph Jedd noted that "for 16 years thereafter Sterling wore a worried look on Fred Glover's face." Together they tackled challenging and embarrassing controversies, starting with faculty endorsement of presidential candidate Adlai Stevenson.
JACK FIELDS / STANFORD UNIVERSITY ARCHIVES

of American institutions. Public criticism of universities escalated during the 1952 presidential campaign between Dwight Eisenhower and Adlai Stevenson.

On October 24, 1952, more than 150 Stanford faculty and staff signed a petition, which became a letter published as a full-page advertisement in the *Palo Alto Times*, supporting Adlai Stevenson for president. (The next day the list of faculty and staff was up to 223.)

The letter was inspired by a similar action by faculty at Columbia University in the October 16 *New York Times*, and by a "Dear Colleagues" form letter sent out in early October to colleges across the country by eminent historian Richard Hofstadter, secretary of the Executive Committee of Volunteers for Stevenson of the Columbia University Faculty. (The Stanford petition, the second in a nationwide drive, initially was circulated by Arthur Wright, associate professor of history.) Many teachers across the country were attracted to Stevenson's condemnation, in a recent speech to the American Legion, of McCarthy's witch-hunt for anti-American subversives in American schools and colleges. The individuals signing the petition stated that they did so as individual voters and as citizens, emphasizing that they in no way represented Stanford University.[1]

The advertisement made headlines across the country, and stirred feelings beyond campus boundaries, among those with no connection to Stanford, as well as among alumni who filled the *Palo Alto Times* letters-to-the-editor page. President Sterling's mailbox was also inundated with irate letters that would consume a good deal of his time.

Sterling saw two issues involved. He felt strongly that the U.S. Constitution guaranteed the right of every citizen, including teachers, to hold and express views on public affairs. However, he was also concerned that "the use of the Stanford name in this connection was improper and the impropriety is being drawn to the attention of those who misused the name. It would have been equally improper had the endorsement been for Eisenhower instead of Stevenson."[2]

The Stevenson advertisement brought strong reactions at a time when Stanford was trying to invigorate alumni giving. An alumna in Ross (Marin County) concluded that these professors were simply too partisan to give well-rounded views of all arguments, that is, to be objective as teachers. She returned empty the envelope soliciting her contribution to Stanford. Sterling took very seriously any intimation of withdrawal of financial support, but he also bridled at the notion that faculty members were to hold no political opinions whatsoever. He responded:

> Because we have men and women on our faculty who hold differing political views, it follows that, insofar as the Stanford student comes into contact with these views, they do encounter different aspects of a problem. The criteria in judging the objectivity of a teacher must be what he does in the classroom and not what he does as a free citizen. I myself hold rather strong partisan views about the current election. I have not made and shall not make them public. But according to your reason-

ing, I would be disqualified as a teacher merely because I hold these partisan views. I do not feel that this is a just disqualification, and I say this after more than twenty years of teaching history. I urge you as strongly as I can to re-think the issue that you have posed, whether or not your rethinking leads you to change your mind about support of Stanford University.[3]

Some who objected to the Stevenson endorsement recognized the right of faculty members to express their opinions on political matters, but felt it was improper for them to do so collectively under the rubric of Stanford Professors. "Stanford as an academic institution is and must remain above partisan politics whether Democratic, Republican, Socialist or Communist," as one Stanford alumnus of the class of 1940 from Southern California wrote to Sterling. "Stanford must be respected for what it is—a great institution, wholly and objectively devoted to the study and the teaching of the humanities and sciences in the common good of all mankind. It cannot exist without this respect and this respect will certainly be short lived if the Stanford name is continuously allied through policy or indiscretion by any of its family in fields foreign—as in politics—to its true purposes." The signing faculty had "betrayed this respect and along with it their strongest friends the alumni, their employers the Board of Trustees and yourself, the student body and themselves by their indiscretion."[4]

"The group was careful to point out in the publicity that they did not speak for Stanford University," noted a Carmel alumnus, "but they were sufficiently unsophisticated to hope that this qualification would be carried on the press wires. They should have known that this would not be the case. The press wires are interested only in news. The qualification was not news, but the fact that a group of people identified with the University had made such an endorsement was news."[5]

As predicted, the news, without the qualification, quickly spread. "This group of professors," wrote a physician from Pasadena, "obviously is an immature group intellectually, if not biologically. Your disposition of this case will be awaited with great interest." Professors were incapable of making sound, real-life decisions, an alumnus of the class of 1933 wrote the editor of the *Palo Alto Times*, "insulated as they are from the realities of the outside world and the problems of making a living in a competitive society" and exposed only to "the immature minds of adolescents."[6]

One writer concluded that those who signed the endorsement letter wanted to turn the country into a welfare state by indoctrinating students. Another thought the F.B.I. should investigate "the bunch." Sterling wrote the latter, "I am in no sense disturbed about the loyalty of the people who participated in this endorsement, or by the fact that their political sympathies differ from mine. Their right to differ I shall defend. Any suggestion of disloyalty I shall condemn."[7]

The Stevenson endorsement had criticized Eisenhower's reluctance to challenge McCarthy's often-unsubstantiated attacks, charging that the Republican presidential candidate had sold out to "undesirable elements." An alumnus of 1938 from Santa Monica wrote a one-sentence letter to General Secretary David Jacobson: "I'm one of those 'undesirable elements.'" Another 15 wrote vitriolic letters, attaching empty Annual Fund solicitation envelopes.[8]

The possible financial threat to the university was real enough. An alumna from the class of 1909 wanted the professors dismissed, or she would remove Stanford as a $10,000 beneficiary of her will. Sterling responded:

> I hope very much that you will rethink the issues that are involved in this case, and that when you have done so you will reconsider your attitude toward the support of Stanford, which support

your Alma Mater so greatly needs. Because if you take the position that you withhold support because of certain views expressed you are quite within your right, but in a sense you are also attempting to dictate what views should be expressed. That would not at all accord with the motto and spirit of the University, which Dr. Jordan did so much to establish.[9]

General Secretary Jacobson expressed his concerns to Sterling about the difficulties Stanford would experience if seen as a politically active university. San Francisco attorney Morris M. Doyle, '29, had just reported to Jacobson that he had prepared a will in which Stanford was to be a beneficiary to the extent of $1 million for a student loan fund, Jacobson told Sterling. Recently that client had asked Doyle to report to the university "that in view of action of a group of faculty in connection with the Stevenson candidacy, he was excluding Stanford as a beneficiary under his will."[10]

Not all reactions were antagonistic. Sterling received an encouraging letter from a Fresno man, whose son had graduated from Stanford in 1930, that reflected the perspective of those who had endorsed Stevenson. "I have observed in my lifetime, as you have in yours, one society or another, such as Hitler's Germany and Mussolini's Italy, slip into an authoritarian system because the citizens of those societies did not defend those civil liberties which are guaranteed by our own

General Secretary Dave Jacobson, who oversaw donor development, warned Sterling that faculty political views could have a negative impact on fundraising. He was especially suspicious of alumni football boosters living in Southern California. STANFORD UNIVERSITY ARCHIVES

Constitution," he wrote Sterling. "One of the first moves of an authoritarian state is to deny differences of opinion on public affairs and then to introduce a tight kind of control. It is this above all that we must avoid in this country, because the right to hold different views is the fulfillment of a free people." He was changing his will to give his estate to Stanford.[11]

History Professor David Harris was among those who signed the endorsement letter. After pondering for a week, he explained his reasoning to Sterling:

> Just precisely why the others felt it appropriate to sign I should leave to their explanations. As for myself, my original hesitations, as I told you the other day, were overcome by recollection of how the German professors, indoctrinated in political neutrality and passivity as no other group, sat immersed in their several "ologies" and allowed themselves to be swept, one by one and group by group, into that maelstrom of bestialities and obscenities which was National Socialism. It may well be that a band of university professors can

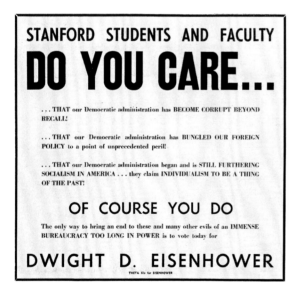

There was no public protest when, on election day, November 1952, the *Stanford Daily* printed this explicitly political but pro-Eisenhower ad by Theta Xi fraternity. This contrasted with the outcry against a faculty endorsement of Stevenson. *STANFORD DAILY*

exert no moral force on public opinion, but, as I look uneasily into the future, I think it might be injurious to the common weal to close the door to their trying. Politics—whether for good or evil—has gone beyond Rousseau's concept of two poles, the individual and the general will, with nothing in between, and if we are to guard the best of our American ideals against the onslaughts of both Communism and "Americanism" we can ill afford to cripple ourselves by the kind of atomization that made the German intellect so vulnerable.

> I am ready to recognize that, from the point of view of publicity, the issue becomes more complicated when several people, for purposes of identification, name their own common employer even though they take pains to point out that no one is committed but themselves. Yet I believe there is a valid argument in favor of considering both individual action and political action of a group as being essentially similar as a problem. In both cases the source of the trouble is in the misconstructions perpetrated by the press and by persons other than the employees and employer concerned. I do not suppose that many people on sober reflection would desire a restraint of political freedom on the ground that its exercise might be misconstrued.[12]

Professor Bernard Haley of the Department of Economics, another signatory, urged Sterling "to put *all* of the cards on the table" at the upcoming faculty meeting, to "endeavor to do so without rancor and without attempting to apportion the blame for the situation with which we are confronted. Give the faculty a *full* picture of the pressure to which you have been subjected— reading some of the letters you have found most disturbing because they were most intelligent."

Sterling initially responded with a broad stroke. At the next Academic Council meeting, January 9, 1953, he reported on the issue as one of university-public relations, at both local and national levels. The faculty pressed for more pragmatic assurances. A new faculty advisory

History Professor David Harris (left) was one of many faculty members who publicly expressed disappointment in Dwight Eisenhower's initial unwillingness to confront McCarthyism. Bernard Haley (right), head of economics, urged Sterling to tell the Academic Council of public and alumni pressure he faced defending academic freedom. Haley, like Harris, publicly supported Adlai Stevenson in 1952.   KEE COLMAN / STANFORD NEWS SERVICE; STANFORD NEWS SERVICE

committee was created to help him formulate relevant university policy. This soon evolved into the Special Committee on Academic Freedom and Responsibility, which clarified university procedures on faculty review and retention.[13]

Even after the election of Eisenhower, Sterling continued to receive complaints fielded by university officers. Gene Walker, chairman of the Stanford Annual Fund, sent Sterling the complaint of a '12 Bakersfield alumnus stating that any faculty member who supported Stevenson should not be a member of the Stanford faculty. Sterling responded:

> The point of view you raise is this, as I understand it: That those who supported Governor Stevenson were really supporting a move for a form of government which would be inimical to the best interests of the United States. I did not vote for Stevenson. At the same time I question the assumption that a vote for Stevenson was a vote for the subversion of free enterprise in this country. I know for a fact that among the Stanford group that were in favor of Governor Stevenson there were many who are bitterly opposed to the suggestion that our government should move

toward authoritarianism. Several of them have some investment in companies whose vitality is dependent upon the continued success of the free enterprise system. I do not regard these people in any way [as] disloyal to the United States and I do them the honor of respecting their integrity, even when their political judgments disagree with mine. If the support of our institutions of private education is to be dependent upon a program which will insist upon conformity of thought, and which will accept, as a condition of support, dictation as to what should be thought and taught, then we enter upon a period of thought control. This, I believe, is greatly to be feared and opposed.[14]

FIFTH AMENDMENT COMMUNIST
THE VICTOR ARNAUTOFF AFFAIR

When pressed for his views on communism, Sterling consistently made two points. Communism, historically and as a political theory, was a valid subject for study and debate on a college campus; but an active Communist, or anyone committed to the overthrow of the U.S. government and constitution, he believed, would be lacking in objectivity and therefore was not qualified to be a member of the faculty. His views were put to a test in the mid-1950s in the case of Victor Mikhail Arnautoff of the Art Department.[15]

The Russian-born Arnautoff, a former Czarist army officer who had escaped Bolshevik Russia, had arrived in the United States in 1925 to study art after years of exile in China. He became a naturalized citizen in 1937. Arnautoff was a talented sculptor, printmaker, and muralist. He was well known for his *City Life* fresco mural, decorating the interior of San Francisco's Coit Tower, and for several murals at the Palo Alto Medical Clinic. (His work, like that of many other Depression-era muralists, was underwritten by the Public Works of Art Project of the Works Progress Administration.)

Arnautoff taught at the California School of Fine Arts from 1932 until 1938. In 1936, he also began teaching part-time at Stanford; he became a full-time assistant professor in 1942.[16]

In September 1955, Arnautoff's name hit the headlines. After many citizen complaints, lithographs by Arnautoff were removed from public art exhibitions in Los Angeles and San Francisco. The image in question was one Arnautoff called "a composite and symbolic characterization of McCarthyism." Titled *DIX McSmear*, it was a caricature of Vice President Richard Nixon wearing a black mask, holding a pumpkin in one hand, and a paintbrush and bucket labeled "smear" in the other.[17]

The caricature decorated the cover of *The Nation* shortly thereafter. As Arnautoff's employer, Stanford was quickly drawn into the controversy. A Southern California alumnus wrote Sterling:

> I simply want to make known to you that my wife and I as members of the Life Alumni and givers to the Stanford Fund, find that we and many of our friends are *MOST* concerned about the laxity of the Stanford faculty administration that either does not investigate nor care if a Communist such as Victor Arnautoff is allowed on the Stanford staff. . . . We are going into our fund drive for Stanford in Southern California and our group of friends would appreciate your comments on this important matter of Stanford policy.[18]

Sterling replied, as he would to many such letters, defending free speech. "The first issues involved relate to the right of free expression," he wrote. "You no doubt have read the statement by Vice President Nixon in which he defended the right of a person to use this means of criticizing people in public life. . . ."

> Another issue revolves around the question of good taste or judgment. Opinion as to what constitutes good taste differs widely—more so in

Russian sculptor and muralist Victor Arnautoff, an assistant professor of art, never admitted to Sterling, the Advisory Board, or a federal investigating committee that he was a Communist (although he had joined the Party in 1937). Protected by Stanford's academic freedom procedures, he retained his faculty position.
STANFORD NEWS SERVICE

a free society than in others. It is our hope here that the freedom which makes possible differing opinions and the exercise of differing judgment will not be abused. This would be the ideal. It is not always attained, here or elsewhere.

> In connection with Stanford's position on the question of Communists on the faculty, I believe you should know that it is University policy that no proven Communist should hold a position on our faculty.[19]

Arnautoff resided in San Francisco, home to a large Russian émigré population. He headed the Russian-American Society and played a central role in the Russian War Relief organization, both located in the City. Toward the end of World War II, he also began teaching painting and printmaking at the California Labor School. After the war, both the Society and the Labor School were labeled "subversive" by the U.S. attorney general.

When Arnautoff met with Sterling, he answered in detail the president's questions about his public activities and his university work but declined to answer any questions about his political views.[20] Sterling, following procedure, referred the matter to the Advisory Board, elected by the Academic Council to handle faculty appointments and discipline. The Advisory

Arnautoff included a self-portrait in his 1934 *City Life* mural inside San Francisco's Coit Tower. He did not express political views while teaching but his viewpoint was reflected in his art, often emphasizing working men and women of all races. The newsstand in his mural includes the *Daily Worker* (the Communist Party newspaper). WIKIMEDIA COMMONS

Board also questioned Arnautoff, and concluded that it would not recommend termination, nor would it go on record as wishing to do so when Arnautoff's contract expired.

When he learned the result, Robert Minge Brown, Stanford trustees' general counsel, had an extended telephone conversation with presidential assistant Fred Glover. Brown, Glover reported to Sterling, was "very disturbed."[21]

The 1954 Communist Control Act, Brown noted, stated that although membership in the Party was not a crime, the Communist Party itself was illegal and membership in the Party subjected the member to certain penalties, such as not being able to run for public office or work for the government. Since it had been judicially

determined that the Communist Party advocated the overthrow of the government by force and violence, Brown argued, this gave the faculty and the university the right to ask whether Arnautoff was a member of the Communist Party. Arnautoff's refusal to answer "relates not to a criminal act, but to his moral fitness to teach, for otherwise we are putting the faculty opinion over the law of the land," Brown said.[22]

Brown contended, according to Glover, that if an organization has been legally established as dedicated to the overthrow of the government by force and violence, "it is not a question of political views that are at stake when a man is questioned as to his membership in the party." When word of the faculty's refusal to act to expel

Arnautoff became known to those interested in the welfare of the university, he argued, this case "is going to be a very damaging one."[23]

The Arnautoff matter was quiescent until December 1956, when he was subpoenaed to appear before a three-man subcommittee of the U.S. House Un-American Activities Committee, then meeting in San Francisco. When asked by subcommittee counsel Richard Arens if he was a Communist Party member, eligible to attend cell meetings, Arnautoff refused to answer, invoking the Fifth Amendment. The subcommittee, in turn, labeled him a Communist Party member, not by his own testimony but by the accusations of others. The subcommittee recommended that the Department of Justice begin denaturalization action against him on the grounds that he had been identified as a Communist.[24]

Stanford issued the following news release after Arnautoff appeared before the subcommittee:

> When a member of the Stanford academic personnel is called for questioning before a congressional or state investigating committee and chooses to stand on his constitutional right to refuse to testify on grounds of possible self-incrimination, he is not subject for this reason alone to dismissal or other disciplinary action. . . .
>
> Dr. Sterling [who was on the East Coast at the time] has stated many times that in his opinion a card-carrying Communist has foresworn [sic] any objectivity in learning and thus has no place on a college campus. At the same time he has said that in cases of this kind, the University will hold to the traditional view that an American is innocent until proved guilty.[25]

Brown again warned Sterling and Glover that Arnautoff's refusal to say whether he was a Communist provided the perfect defense of silence to what was a reasonable question, under the circumstances. He cautioned that Stanford would never, under its present academic procedures, be able to get rid of a known Communist who merely remained silent on party membership.[26]

The Advisory Board met again, and again concluded that while there was reason to question Arnautoff's judgment about political matters, there was no evidence that he had permitted his political beliefs to affect his teaching of art. Although the board was deeply divided over the issue, Arnautoff was therefore retained on the faculty.[27]

But the Arnautoff matter was not quite closed. Nearly a year later, the *San Francisco News* printed Donald Canter's exposé of the Russian-American Society and its president, Victor Arnautoff. Canter had visited Arnautoff at the society's San Francisco headquarters. After mentioning the accusation of a witness at the subcommittee hearing, he then asked Arnautoff if he thought this might put the label "Communist" on the entire Russian-American Society. Arnautoff replied simply: "I don't see what my political ideas and affiliations have to do with the Society."[28]

The article provoked yet more letter writing. "Due to the disclosure presented by Mr. Canter's article," wrote one man from Petaluma, "my daughter and son plus the two sons of my brother will not be permitted to enroll at Stanford. We do not care for Communists or their benefactors."[29]

Glover crafted a now well-rehearsed response:

> Stanford's policy is that no proven Communist should hold a position on the faculty. It must be remembered that a professor has tenure, and that in order to dismiss him, charges must be proven and not just alleged without evidence that would stand up in court.
>
> There is no such evidence in the case of Professor Arnautoff, although there is no question but what he is intensely interested in Russia and its problems. This, however, is not illegal. None are views which are unorthodox or unpopular.
>
> The right of free speech and free thought is

a very important part of a strong democracy; it is easy to lose this privilege if we do not defend the right of people to hold views which differ radically from those held by most of us. And I am sure that we can leave up to the government the job which is properly theirs of identifying and prosecuting those whose actions threaten the security of the nation.[30]

Arnautoff maintained his silence; the strategy paid off. Most academics who invoked the Fifth Amendment when testifying during HUAC proceedings lost their jobs. The label of "Fifth Amendment Communist" was grounds enough at most colleges for dismissal. Arnautoff retained his position at Stanford.[31]

He apparently never admitted to his Stanford faculty colleagues who supported him that he

Robert Minge Brown, general counsel to Stanford's trustees, was disturbed by the faculty's refusal to expel Arnautoff. He cited the Communist Control Act to Fred Glover, to pass on to Sterling. Brown became friends with Glover during their World War II service in Naval Intelligence. (He was elected to the board in 1965.) STANFORD NEWS SERVICE

had, indeed, joined the Communist Party in 1937, the same year he became a naturalized citizen. In 1955, he and his wife, Leda, had been granted permission (after repeated petitions) by the Supreme Soviet to return to Russia and become Soviet citizens. Arnautoff retired in 1962, following the death of his wife, in San Francisco, and the next year he returned to his hometown of Zhdanov, Russia.[32]

THE TALENTED MR. STRUCINSKI
STANFORD'S LITERARY EX-CON

In early 1957, a convict named Mitchell J. Strucinski, then serving a five-year term for mail theft and forgery at McNeil Island Federal Prison in Washington state, applied to Stanford for a fellowship in the graduate program in creative writing. He was turned down the first time but reapplied, bolstering his new application with letters of reference from the editors of the *Atlantic Monthly* and *Harper's*.[33]

Professor and novelist Wallace Stegner, director of the Creative Writing Program, took an active interest in Strucinski's application, and solicited more information. "Both Edward Weeks and I have tremendous faith in this author's talent as a writer of fiction, and we have already committed ourselves to two stories of Strucinski's in the *Atlantic Monthly*," Seymour Lawrence, director of the *Atlantic Monthly Press*, wrote Stegner. "He is a humble person, who knows his own faults and drawbacks, and it would mean so much to him to have this fellowship and honor as offered by the University."[34]

When Stegner asked Strucinski about his "extensive prison record," Strucinski replied:

Prison and crime have formed a great part of my adult life. While I do not consider myself a professional criminal, in the sense of being a person whose life is basically and predominantly extra-legal, this may be a nicety of definition designed to salvage my conscience, for the truth is those whose prerogative it is, class me as a professional mail thief and bad check artist. . . .

After nearly a decade behind bars I am convinced the general impression of prisoners is essentially correct. As a group, we are the most selfish, ruthless and unstable in the nation. . . . One can find good men in prison, if one looks for them. They are rare, of course, and of the six or eight thousand I have seen, I can think of only two I met. . . .

One thing prison has assuredly contributed to my writing, and that is a twisted kind of security to tide me over the dangerous period of starting out. . . . Writing has given me something I have not possessed in a long time. Call it direction, purpose, or whatever you will, for the first time in many years I look forward to the future with anticipation instead of apathy.[35]

Stegner asked prison authorities in Washington about Strucinski's stability, and his capacity

Professor Wallace Stegner in a 1963 portrait taken as part of a PACE Campaign commission by professional photographer Pirkle Jones (assistant to Ansel Adams). Stegner recommended Mitchell J. Strucinski, then serving a five-year term in federal prison, for a Creative Writing Program fellowship in 1958. (Images of Strucinski cannot be found.) PIRKLE JONES / STANFORD UNIVERSITY ARCHIVES

to adapt well to an academic community. "In the history of many offenders there appears a point when their attitudes and habits are so oriented that there is an optimum chance they will commit no further crime and achieve an adequate social adjustment. It is our opinion that Strucinski has nearly, but not quite, reached this point," the warden of McNeil Island Federal Prison replied.

> From the strong motivation which he has, we believe Strucinski can adapt himself to an academic community. Our experience with recidivists leads us to speak with caution at all times. Although the possibility exists that he may embarrass the University, the probability is that he will not.[36]

Stegner, satisfied, went to President Sterling. As Fred Glover later recounted, Stegner said he had an applicant for a graduate fellowship who was in federal prison "and that man was a genius." Sterling respected Stegner's judgment and told Glover that if Stegner wanted to do it, "let's do it."[37]

Strucinski was awarded the fellowship and was admitted as a non-matriculated student to the graduate Program in Creative Writing. (He was paroled for travel to Stanford.)

As Glover recalled, at a subsequent meeting of the Board of Trustees following the news, one of the trustees said to Sterling, "Mr. President, I just noticed that you are now admitting felons to Stanford when the children of Stanford alumni are getting rejected." Sterling said, "Well, I'll ask Fred to explain." Glover did not record his response, but recalled that at the end of the meeting, board President Lloyd Dinkelspiel turned to him and said, "Never again, Fred."[38]

Strucinski's creative writing fellowship began in fall 1958. Not long after, Dean of Students Donald Winbigler received a call from a Palo Alto Police Department sergeant, advising him that Strucinski had been apprehended under suspicious circumstances on the grounds of the

Stanford's rare books division, housed in the Main Library's Bender Room, was among several book collections in California and Nevada experiencing major thefts during and shortly after Strucinski's time in the Creating Writing Program. The FBI was on the hunt by November 1960. Strucinski ended up in San Quentin.   STANFORD NEWS SERVICE

Foothill Tennis and Swimming Club in the Stanford Industrial Park. The Police Department later concluded that the evidence was not sufficient, and they released him.

Nonetheless, Winbigler checked with Wallace Stegner, who continued to defend Strucinski and pointed out that he had cleared the award with the President's Office. Glover, however, told Winbigler that he had not been aware of Strucinski's long career in crime.[39]

Strucinski completed his Stanford fellowship, and was still living in Menlo Park when a theft of rare books was discovered at Stanford in fall 1960. Former San Francisco Mayor Elmer Robinson, who had donated his collection of rare books to Stanford the year before, was thumbing through a Carnegie Book Store (New York) rare books catalogue when he found one of the books he had given to Stanford offered for sale.

Robinson contacted Elmer Grieder, acting director of the Stanford Library, but there were no leads until Warren Howell, owner of John Howell Books in San Francisco, telephoned

Grieder in late October. Strucinski, who had been working at Howell Books, might have handled some of the missing documents, he suggested. Earlier, Strucinski had brought to Howell a number of medical and scientific books. Howell had noted cuts in the title pages and erasures, which he believed to be obliterated library markings, which led him to call Grieder. (Some 33 rare European medical texts were found to be missing from the Lane Medical Library at Stanford's School of Medicine.)[40]

By November 3, the FBI was hunting for Strucinski, Stanford's "literary ex-con," who was suspected of stealing and transporting across state lines valuable rare books and documents worth thousands of dollars. Initially, Strucinski admitted only to selling a volume of presidential letters and signatures to the New York dealer, but he claimed he had bought them before reselling them. He then disappeared, only to turn himself in five days later. The Stanford charges against Strucinski, brought in Santa Clara County Superior Court, were dismissed because of insufficient evidence, but also because the previous week a more effective case had been made regarding his theft of valuable historical maps and other documents from the San Mateo County Recorder's Office. Strucinski pleaded guilty to the San Mateo thefts at his December 28 trial, and in January 1961 he was sentenced to 1 to 15 years in San Quentin, still claiming his innocence about the Stanford thefts.[41]

A year later, a friend of Strucinski's was caught during a burglary. In his pocket was a letter, written by Strucinski from San Quentin, describing a warehouse location in Redwood City. There, the police found additional priceless documents from San Mateo, the rare books stolen from Stanford, and additional books from San Francisco, Stockton, and the Nevada State Library.[42]

How did Stanford admit a known felon and give him a $2,500 fellowship, Professor David Faville, Graduate School of Business and chair of the Advisory Board, asked Admissions Director Rix Snyder. "I have no answer for you to give to people who are asking," Snyder, who was clearly annoyed, responded. "I do not approve of such acts, and I would have refused him admission had I any authority. Graduate admissions are handled entirely by the individual departments and schools, and character is not always of interest to those admitting at the graduate level."[43]

On the day Strucinski surrendered to the FBI, Glover had pressed Stegner about the thoroughness of his investigation into Strucinski's record prior to the awarding of the fellowship grant. "We did investigate," Stegner replied, and "were persuaded by the testimony of literary people (Seymour Lawrence and Ted Weeks of the *Atlantic*); by our own readings of his manuscripts and letters; and by the prognosis of the Warden at MacNeil [*sic*] Island Prison, that we were justified in thinking Strucinski a reasonable risk." Stegner still did not believe that, "on the evidence we

had, we were unjustified" in giving Strucinski the fellowship. "I know that Stanford is not a rehabilitation center; I am not myself a natural-born probation officer or welfare worker. And yet I think we ought to keep the outside chance open for the man of talent, even this sort of a man of talent."[44]

Strucinski, Stanford fellow and "Literary Ex-Convict," was subsequently featured in a *Time* magazine article, "Writer with a Talent."[45]

STUDENT INVOLVEMENT IN FACULTY SELECTION
THE SIBLEY CASE

In the first half of 1958, a faculty matter would initially take on the appearance of an academic freedom issue, but it would soon reveal itself as a matter of who should participate in the selection of Political Science Department faculty.

Mulford Q. Sibley, a visiting professor from the University of Minnesota, was popular with his students, some of whom hoped he would win a permanent place on the faculty. James T. Watkins IV, executive head of political science, strongly recommended that Sibley be appointed to a position as full professor in the field of political theory, to fill the place of Professor Arnaud Leavelle, who had died in 1956.

The department's faculty had unanimously supported the proposed appointment, which also was initially supported by Dean Philip Rhinelander.[46] Provost Fred Terman, however, exercised his veto. When the news broke that Sibley had not won the appointment, many assumed that it was because Sibley had been a conscientious objector during World War II.[47]

Unlike the Political Science Department faculty, who had done little background checking, Terman and Sterling had thoroughly researched Sibley's qualifications and scholarship at the University of Minnesota and elsewhere before making the decision that Sibley was not the best-qualified candidate, particularly as the future departmental head they were hoping to recruit. They intended to strengthen the department, which they thought needed vigorous leadership.[48]

According to an eminent economist at the University of Minnesota, Sibley was not regarded there as a very strong member of the faculty, and he was surprised that Stanford would be considering him. As another Minnesota reference told Sterling, "He is a good teacher but not likely to make significant scholarly contributions. He is a very pleasant person but likely to confuse his role as a citizen with his role as a scholar."[49]

Another colleague at the University of Minnesota wrote to Rhinelander: "Quite obviously he is identified with social reform movements, especially socialism and pacifism. He works actively at both these causes and I believe does not attempt to be 'objective' in his advocacy of these two positions in his teaching."[50]

Rhinelander meanwhile wrote to Watkins, criticizing the department for not adequately vetting Sibley:

When the Department's formal recommendation for Mr. Sibley was first submitted to this office, I looked for a critical analysis by the Department of his scholarly work, but it turned out upon inquiry that none of the senior members of the Department had troubled to read Mr. Sibley's chief work before making the recommendation. Secondly, the initial recommendation did not contain any systematic statement of the specific grounds upon which Mr. Sibley was judged superior to the other candidates under consideration.[51]

Sterling and Terman not only had made inquiries but also had visited universities where Sibley had taught. "The tenor of the answers that we received," Sterling later recalled, "was that none of these universities would welcome him back."[52]

"When we compared notes it was clear to us

that Sibley did not meet the requirements as we visualized them," Terman wrote to the dean of the University of Minnesota Graduate School, "and our decision was made accordingly, based strictly on professional qualifications needed in our position. Quite a storm arose among certain students, aided by a few faculty members. Echoes of this may have reached Minneapolis; they are now subsiding, however."[53]

After meeting with five students, Sterling issued a press release on May 9 stating that the Sibley case was closed and that if Mr. Sibley's political views were a factor, they would have been considered when he was invited to Stanford as a

When visiting Professor Mulford Q. Sibley, a political historian, was not appointed to a permanent position, his undergraduate students alleged it was because he had been a conscientious objector during World War II. Here, he rests hands on the book he co-authored, *Conscription of Conscience*.
STANFORD UNIVERSITY ARCHIVES

visiting professor.[54] Although Sterling did not believe students should be involved in the faculty appointment procedure, he spent a great deal of time personally responding to correspondence and communicating with the various constituencies, on and off campus, who were angered by the decision. On May 12, he also met with a selected group of faculty and students to discuss the relative merits of teaching versus research in reaching such decisions.

"I am sorry that many students sincerely disagree with the University in this decision. This is, of course, their right," he wrote one student protesting the decision. "And it is equally our right—in fact, our responsibility—to make decisions which we believe in the long-range interests of the Department and the University."[55]

"I must confess to being puzzled and disappointed by the fact that other long-standing evidence of the University's forthright positions on matters of freedom of inquiry and free speech is now overlooked or scorned by those interested in this one professor," Sterling wrote an Oakland attorney who contended that Sibley was not appointed because of his political views. "Perhaps the fact that we go rather quietly about the business of defending and championing these principles makes for inadequate publicity. Even so, I prefer to proceed quietly in these matters, because it does the least harm to the individuals involved."[56]

To an alumnus, a San Francisco attorney, who wrote him complaining about the administration's "less than frank statement concerning the reasons of its action," Sterling wrote: "I do not propose to release to the public all facts relating to decisions affecting Stanford personnel. More often than not, the individual involved would be adversely and unfairly affected. In consequence, newspaper reports are usually and regrettably confused and inadequate."[57]

Sterling and Terman received considerable support from others on the Stanford faculty.

Historian Thomas Bailey (seen here in 1951) was among the faculty who considered Sibley unqualified, and supported the president and provost during the controversy. STANFORD UNIVERSITY ARCHIVES

Thomas A. Bailey, of the History Department, wrote Sterling, "You are to be commended, in connection with the Sibley matter, in placing the larger and long-run interests of the University above what appears to be an organized student claque." Bailey was an expert on the history of American politics. "I had a published interchange with Dr. Sibley ten years ago, in *American Perspective*, and so unreal was his pacifist approach to international affairs that I then tabbed him a fanatic. Developments since then have merely confirmed this judgment. While we certainly need differing points of view on our faculty, a University of high degree has no place for fanatics, however popular or stimulating they may be. A Hindu swami would no doubt attract a considerable following among the students, but we do not need swamis either." (The History Department, unlike the Political Science Department, welcomed the help provided by Provost Terman, backed by their own rigorous recruiting, in building up its faculty.)[58]

As campus controversies normally do, the uproar over not selecting Sibley for the new position began to subside. One of the students with whom Sterling had met to discuss the Sibley affair wrote Sterling on May 15: "I wanted to thank you, once again, for your generosity and patience with us. Uninformed or self-righteous student opinion can so easily become irresponsible and misdirected—I think I speak for others as well as myself in saying that we have gained a new appreciation of the enormity of the task of administering a university—and an even greater respect for those whose responsibility it is."

Nevertheless, a student petition vociferously demanding the appointment, prepared before Sterling's meeting with students, was submitted to the president. Jim Messinger, president of the Associated Students of Stanford University (ASSU), wrote Sterling on May 26 advising him of a resolution passed by the student legislature on May 8 urging the administration to reconsider its action in not reappointing Sibley, and to furnish the student body its explanation in this matter. He also advised Sterling of a petition signed by 388 registered students. Sterling replied to Messinger on June 2: "The larger implication of the petition and the resolution is that students feel that they are entitled to a voice in faculty appointments and promotions. There are many of these each year. Do you honestly think it would be practicable or appropriate for students to share in the discharge of the responsibility which is involved in decisions concerning appointments and promotions?"[59]

Later that summer, Sterling received an apology from a student who had helped circulate the petitions of protest, saying he now realized he had been guilty of "closed-mindedness, insincerity, and hasty conclusions. . . . I unfairly assumed that you were guided only by the university's fiscal interests." Sterling replied, "An apology takes courage, and I commend you both

for the spirit of your letter, and for the fact that it shows that you are thinking about complicated issues constructively."[60]

The following year, the department swung the other way, inviting as its visiting professor Willmoore Kendall of Yale, a conservative. Kendall, too, was an undergraduate favorite, and equally unsuccessful, allegedly panicking at large classes. "He improved," said Sterling, "but we're not keeping him."[61]

Terman biographer Stewart Gillmor concluded: "As elsewhere at Stanford, changes in approach and methodology in the field of political science, rather than personal political agendas of either Terman or Sterling, brought about reassessment of the effectiveness of the department's teaching and place nationally in the field." Their first key move had been the hiring of Heinz Eulau, from Antioch College, who joined the department in 1958 and twice served as department chair, 1969–74 and 1981. Their next, several years later, was to find a departmental leader: Professor Gabriel Almond,

Sterling and Terman, intent on finding academic leaders, recruited two dynamic academics to revitalize the Political Science Department. Heinz Eulau (left, in 1970), a pioneer in political behavior research, arrived in 1958, and would serve twice as department chair. Gabriel Almond, who came in 1963, was credited with modernizing the department during his chairmanship, 1964–69.
STANFORD NEWS SERVICE

appointed in 1963, came to Stanford after serving on the faculties of Yale and Princeton. He's credited with modernizing the department during his chairmanship, 1964–69.[62]

CLOSING A ONE-MAN SHOW
THE HISPANIC AMERICAN INSTITUTE

Just before leaving for Europe in summer 1963, Sterling received a letter from a visiting professor of Latin American history calling attention to serious inadequacies in Stanford's program:

> My considerable affection for Stanford leads me to refer to one seriously defective situation within the university. At this time, when Latin American studies are increasingly important in the United States, it is an unfortunate fact that Stanford's Hispanic American Institute falls shockingly behind the intellectual level of the university. . . . Should you have the time and the desire to discuss with me the reasons for my concern, I would be delighted, for my part, to do so![63]

Sterling was aware of problems in this area. Professor Ronald Hilton, on the faculty since 1942, had founded the one-man Institute of Hispanic American and Luso-Brazilian Studies at Stanford in 1948. The Oxford- and Berkeley-trained Hilton, a professor of Romanic languages in the Department of Modern European Languages, seemed to have little interest in language or literature. His real interest was in current affairs. Through the Institute, Hilton edited the *Hispanic American Report*.[64]

The *Report* was recognized as filling a critical need at a time when there were not many sources of information about Latin America, but few realized that it was produced with the help of unpaid undergraduates and graduate students and was part of a program that had not earned much respect. In addition to the controversial use of student free labor for his journal, Hilton himself tended to attract publicity, often at his university's expense.

In November 1960, Hilton made a name for himself by providing information to a news outlet about a planned U.S. invasion of Cuba to overthrow Castro. The attempt, dubbed the Bay of Pigs invasion, failed in April 1961 because of Castro's advance knowledge.

As Richard W. Lyman, at the time a fellow professor and associate dean of humanities and sciences, later unsympathetically recalled: "A charismatic figure—tall and broad shouldered with a leonine head and penetrating gaze—Hilton was also notoriously difficult to deal with administratively, and fierce in the defense of his little empire."[65]

Lyman and assistant dean Raymond F. Bacchetti undertook a study of the Institute of Hispanic American and Luso-Brazilian Studies in early 1964. Stanford was about to apply to the Ford Foundation for a massive grant, across the School of Humanities and Sciences, to improve its international studies programs. The H&S Dean's Office was concerned that a single professor had such degree-granting power, especially when it was reported that he gave academic credit to football players for clipping newspaper articles. Aware of the "accumulation of serious criticisms concerning various aspects of the institute's performance," they also hoped to provide suggestions for reform and to give Hilton a stake in improving academic standards.[66]

In April 1964, they reported the program's academic standards were found to be the lowest in the School of Humanities and Sciences. "Virtually all applicants are accepted and the individual quality of applicants has sometimes been extraordinarily low. . . . It seems apparent that the exigencies of staffing the *Report* take undue precedence over admission standards."

Although some of the work done for the *Report* by students—particularly first-year graduate students—was deemed educationally worthwhile, they concluded, "the nature and extent of the work appears to be determined more by the demands of the publication than by academic considerations." Teaching was left to unpaid lecturers, "some of them superbly equipped with firsthand knowledge of the area in question, but not necessarily qualified in any academic discipline." Not surprisingly, the attrition rate in the program was very high.

"Put in a nutshell," the report concluded, "the situation is one of which students

Professor Ronald Hilton taught a popular Hispanic world affairs seminar, here in 1953. He had launched the Institute of Hispanic American and Luso-Brazilian Studies in 1948, but his one-man program failed to earn respect. Outsiders said it lacked academic rigor (he granted credit to some for clipping newspaper articles for him). STANFORD NEWS SERVICE

receive some valuable training, but in an ill-defined and under-staffed program, unbalanced and uneven as to instruction and content, and including unspecified work for which no financial return is made."

Lyman and Bacchetti recommended that, for the time being, the undergraduate and doctoral program be eliminated but that the master's program in Hispanic American and Luso-Brazilian Studies should continue. Recognizing that the *Report* performed a unique and important function and provided valuable information in the English language, they recommended that production of the *Hispanic American Report* also continue, but that the university should accept responsibility for producing the *Report* on a professional basis, without relying, as Hilton did, on unpaid student help. The master's degree candidates would serve

as writers on the *Report*, but they were to be paid research-assistant stipends and would be eligible for tuition waivers.[67]

Ronald Hilton protested by resigning both as editor of the *Report* and as director of the Institute for Hispanic Studies, telling reporters that he resigned because of the university's decision to remove undergraduates and doctoral candidates. (Hilton remained as a professor of Romanic languages, and Professor Bernard Siegel of anthropology was named acting director of the institute.)[68]

According to Lyman, Hilton first had asked for a bigger portion of the Ford Grant for international studies. He resigned when told no but was surprised when his resignation was accepted. Lyman and Bacchetti predicted this would cause "some uproar," but had decided it was worth it "to clear up this long-standing source of trouble and academic embarrassment."[69]

Hilton continued to claim to reporters that the university had been pressured to suspend his work because of "ultra-right-wing elements who are so powerful especially in Southern California." He did not address the issues of unpaid student labor and questionable academic standards. Lyman, in turn, emphasized to the press that the *Report* had been suspended, not discontinued, pending finding an editor with the necessary qualifications.[70]

Hilton's comments generated a letter-writing campaign on his behalf by former students. Meanwhile, on campus, "word of Bacchetti's and my having dared to brave the lion in his den soon

Professor Richard Lyman, in 1963, while serving as associate dean of humanities and sciences. Lyman undertook a study of Hilton's institute, triggering a war of words while earning kudos from across campus.
STANFORD NEWS SERVICE

Raymond Bacchetti (here in 1972) worked with Lyman as assistant dean and was heavily involved in the Hilton matter. He went on to a distinguished career, retiring in 1993 as vice president for planning and management.
STANFORD NEWS SERVICE

got around." Lyman was invited to a president's staff meeting to "describe how we had done it," and soon found on campus a tone of "bemused admiration; all of a sudden I had an unsought reputation at the highest level of the Stanford administration for having the courage of my convictions."[71]

Hilton subsequently sent a flyer to *Report* subscribers advising of the suspension and telling them to direct correspondence to Lyman, but he did not give up control so easily. He was still the responsible officer of the "Hispanic American Society," he told Bacchetti, and demanded that the society be reimbursed for society funds that had been used for "routine academic purposes." Lyman, however, contended that "the Society" consisted only of subscribers to the *Report*. He asked Sterling to demand Hilton return the Addressograph label maker and address plates for the *Report*, which Hilton also claimed belonged to the "Society."[72]

Another issue was legal title to the *Report,* which Stanford hoped to resume, but by another university entity. In December, Lyman and Bacchetti gave up the idea of restarting the *Report*. They had been unable to recruit anyone of stature to come to Stanford as its editor.[73]

"Undoubtedly Professor Hilton would *like* the debate to focus on the irrelevant issue of political persecution," a Harvard historian wrote to Lyman, "and I suspect this is the reason why all the talk about the editor's unorthodox political opinions has been introduced. As an academic program, the institute was not a place I could advise any of my graduating seniors to consider as a place for graduate work on Latin America." Lyman forwarded a copy of this letter to Sterling, who wrote the professor: "Need I say that your letter made my Christmas a bit brighter."[74]

Lyman sent Sterling a hostile news clipping with the following message: "When we began dealing with the Hilton resignations, I recall your saying that 'Dick Lyman is on the firing line!' Enclosed is a small sample of enemy fire for your delectation! It looks as if the weapon used was a 12-gauge shotgun, and the aim distinctly careless. . . ."[75]

Sterling replied: "If need be—dig a deeper trench, but hang on and keep shooting. The enemy's technology is, I suspect, obsolescent and its product prone to deterioration from over-use."[76]

Lyman and Hilton continued to carry on an extensive and at times acrimonious correspondence about the transfer of the *Report* to another academic institution. In March 1965, Lyman told Hilton that university legal counsel had concluded that the Hispanic American Institute was a part of Stanford and its assets, accordingly, belonged to Stanford; similarly, the *Report*, produced through the Institute, and its assets belonged to Stanford; and that the *Report* subscription accounts could be used to refund prepaid subscriptions. The "Hispanic American Society" was probably an independent association, but the university could use funds held for the society to refund prepaid subscriptions to the *Report*, and to defray the expense of settling the affairs of the *Report*.[77]

Hilton did not back down, presenting his view of the dispute five days later in a memorandum to Benjamin Page, chairman of the Academic Council's Executive Committee: "The salient factors should be noted: The first is that certain decisions regarding the Institute were reached without consulting me by unidentified administrators who clearly have no technical competence. The second is that these decisions were enforced despite my repeated warnings of the consequences. The result was the tragedy of which we all know."[78]

Ronald Hilton at the renovated Mediterranean-style house on Santa Ynez Street that he bought in 1942. Here he lived until his death at 95 in 2007. His greatest claim to fame was his role as a source for the advance story about CIA plans to overthrow Fidel Castro during the 1961 Bay of Pigs invasion.
STANFORD NEWS SERVICE

Problems from the *Report* continued to surface. Late in 1965, the widow of a former president of Panama threatened to sue Stanford for libel. Objectionable statements had been printed in the *Report*, alleging that the widow was a narcotics courier, while implying she was associated with the group that had assassinated her husband. Evidence for these statements was very thin: interviews with individuals who claimed they overheard the widow's conversations with conspirators. President Sterling exonerated the university with a letter of retraction and a personal apology to the widow.[79]

ROCKING THE BOAT

STUDENT GOVERNANCE AND
ACTIVISM EVOLVE, 1960–1966

hroughout his 19 years as president, Wallace Sterling warmly welcomed the incoming freshmen class with convocation speeches and receptions at the Lou Henry Hoover House. Well into the 1960s, he would encourage them to make full use of their abilities and to enjoy their college years. "Keep your faces to the wind, your feet on the ground, and your eyes on the stars." But he also stressed their obligations. Stanford offered students the opportunity to pursue knowledge, wherever it might lead, but it called upon them to use responsibility and judgment in the pursuit. Humility and gratitude were part of the bargain. "What is here for you is made available by the interest, generosity, and love of others. Remember this and respect this at all times."[1]

As the 1960s unfolded, however, historic shifts were taking place in the university's relationship to its students, individually and as a whole. These changes reflected national trends and the

impact of national events, but the last six years of Sterling's administration were also framed by a gradual but distinct change in student-body demographics and leadership.

By 1960, the injection of more mature students through the GI Bill in the late 1940s and early 1950s had been overshadowed by a new student and faculty profile brought by Stanford's accelerating rise in academic standing. The student body now included significantly more graduate students, rising from 25 percent during Sterling's graduate school years of the 1930s to roughly 40 percent of the student body in 1960 (and expanding to 50 percent by 1970). Undergraduates, like graduate students and faculty, now came from across the country. Fewer students had family connections to the university. Stanford's popular Overseas Campuses Program also introduced a large percentage of undergraduates to a new level of social freedom and experience, as well as international exposure. Social regulations and a web of judicial councils, legislative bodies, and deans set up in the 1910s and 1920s were ripe for reform, particularly those that singled out women for more restrictive oversight.[2]

Stanford's student body, shaped by Sterling's

Students crowd Memorial Auditorium's entrance to attend the April 23, 1964, campus speech by Dr. Martin Luther King Jr., the highlight of the three-day All Western States Civil Rights Conference, organized by Stanford's new Civil Rights Secretariat.
STANFORD NEWS SERVICE

437

Stanford Peace Caucus protesters, advocating that "Men Refuse Military Service," march at the May 28, 1964, officer commissioning from Stanford's ROTC cadet corps. Debate about ROTC classes on campus had been slowly growing since at least 1960.   STANFORD NEWS SERVICE

drive to raise expectations for academic excellence, began to "rock the boat" (as one student body president put it) as early as 1960. Reform and readjustment came, but still largely at a pace dictated by the Sterling administration. Trustees and administrators felt the sting of parental criticism when any student behaved in ways deemed socially unacceptable or when they thought their child was placed in an unsafe situation. *In loco parentis* remained an important, if increasingly debatable, policy throughout much of the decade.

Most Stanford students of the early and mid-1960s may not have considered themselves politically active, but their growing discomfort with the limitations of student self-governance paralleled their growing concern about America's foreign policy and the country's domestic racial

divide. As it turned out, reforms of student regulations and judicial policies were, of necessity, tied to university policy regarding campus political activity.

PARTISANSHIP OR CIVIC ENGAGEMENT? 1960

The university's policy against partisan political activity was codified not in the original 1885 Founding Grant but in Jane Stanford's 1902 amendment to the grant. "The university must be forever maintained upon a strictly nonpartisan and nonsectarian basis. It must never become an instrument in the hands of any political party or any religious sect or organization," she warned, adding:

> I desire that the University shall forever be kept out of politics and that no professor shall electioneer among or seek to dominate other professors or the students for the success of any political party or candidate in any political contest. I hope that every voter, whether professor or student, will always thoroughly inform himself upon every principle involved, and as to the merits of every candidate seeking his suffrage, and then vote according to his own best judgment and conscience, irrespective of any importunity of others. And in order to freely do this he should not be subjected to any importunity, since it is possible that cases might arise where a mere suggestion might be understood to be a covert demand.[3]

Although her comments were aimed primarily at current faculty members, Mrs. Stanford stated in that same address that the trustees themselves should be "free from possible political or partisan influence."

The Board of Trustees reinforced Mrs. Stanford's policy in 1911 when they resolved: "None of the assembly halls, buildings, or grounds of the University shall be used for partisan political addresses or gatherings."[4]

The rules were ignored at the highest level

for the 1928 U.S. presidential campaign of the university's most conspicuous alumnus and trustee, Herbert Hoover. President Ray Lyman Wilbur, a delegate to the Republican Convention, allowed Hoover to use Stanford Stadium for his acceptance speech following his nomination by the Republican Party. Numerous trustees, administrators, and faculty, as well as the Stanford Alumni Association, were involved in his campaign. Wilbur subsequently joined Hoover's cabinet, while also retaining the Stanford presidency *(see Chapter 13)*.

Until the 1960s, active political debate took place mostly during presidential election years. With most undergraduates under the legal voting age of 21, straw polls taken since 1924 around voting day revealed undergraduates' strong inclination toward the GOP. Voting reports from

Straw polls, held since 1924, recorded student political choices (most undergrads were under then-legal voting age of 21). Until the 1960s, undergrads strongly favored Republicans. In contrast, voting precincts reported eligible voters favoring Democrats (exceptions: Hoover and Eisenhower). Lyndon Johnson won this 1964 poll, despite the *Daily* endorsing Barry Goldwater.
STANFORD QUAD 1965

local precincts, however, revealed a more mixed view after the 1928 and 1932 Hoover campaigns, often favoring Democratic presidential contenders but not necessarily down-ballot local Democratic candidates.[5]

Faculty and particularly student interest in less traditional political candidates remained marginal. In January 1948, the Executive Committee of the Associated Students (ASSU), backed by Dean of Students Lawrence Kimpton, denied approval of a student chapter of the Progressive Citizens of America (which supported the third-party presidential candidacy of Henry Wallace, considered a left-wing candidate). Kimpton reiterated: "Student organizations espousing partisan political doctrines or advocating political action in light of them are forbidden on the campus of Stanford University." Nothing prohibited them from affiliating with such an organization off-campus, he said, as long as they did so without recognition of their Stanford status. Nevertheless, the Stanford Area Young Republicans, and a Stanford Young Democrats counterpart, were active as elections neared, albeit meeting in Palo Alto and Menlo Park, to organize ways to get voters to the polls. Their Stanford affiliation was clearly identified.[6]

The Cold War revived faculty political expression, particularly in response to McCarthy-era attacks on American educators. Critics could easily use Stanford's nonpartisan policy as a bludgeon when hundreds of Stanford faculty advertised their 1949 support of UC colleagues during the loyalty oath crisis *(see Chapter 3)* or endorsed the Democratic presidential candidate in 1952 *(see Chapter 18)*, but Sterling backed his faculty each time on the grounds of academic freedom, civic duty, and free speech.

Growing faculty and student insistence that they be allowed, as American citizens, to examine and discuss local and national political issues led the Board of Trustees, in March 1952, to make

The April 1958 protest against hydrogen bomb testing at Eniwetok Atoll was praised for being well planned, dignified, and informative. Some 300 participated, in front of the Main Library, and organizers contacted more than 3,000 with leaflets, stirring considerable campus discussion. PALO ALTO TIMES / STANFORD UNIVERSITY ARCHIVES

a significant policy change, opening up public discussion on campus:

> Persons who are candidates for or hold public office, notable persons in public life, persons in partisan politics, may be invited to speak at meetings to be held at Stanford University subject to the following conditions: (a) That such meetings and the speakers to appear at them shall be approved by the Committee on Public Exercises, giving due consideration to the Founding Grant [1902 amendment]. (b) That, if the subject matter discussed is controversial, a sufficient number of meetings and variety of speakers will be arranged in order to ensure the presentation of all aspects of such controversial subject, and that the various speakers will be of high competence.[7]

This 1952 policy was methodically implemented on April 17, 1958, when students protested ongoing U.S. hydrogen bomb testing at the Pacific Proving Grounds site of Eniwetok Atoll in the Marshall Islands. The quiet demonstration at the fountain in front of the Main Library (today's Green Library Bing Wing) numbered around 300, but organizers claimed to have interacted with some 3,000 people across campus. Signs carried by protesters included quotes attributed to Albert Einstein ("On what people do about the bomb the fate of civilization must rest") and Albert Schweitzer ("We must muster the courage to leave this folly and face reality") along with "H bombs lead nowhere" and "Peace Talk, Not Eniwetok." A petition to President Eisenhower garnered 335 names.

The effort had been carefully organized, with President Sterling's approval, by 67 students who made it clear they were unaffiliated with any established group and held varying political views. They circulated a three-page handout, quotes by various scientists, and a fact sheet presenting both sides of the issue, intent on stimulating individual thinking and discussions in living groups and classrooms. The event was later reported as "well organized and in good taste," perhaps because the coordinators made no speeches in order to, as they said, keep the event "dignified, in keeping with the university's atmosphere." Although environmental implications of nuclear fallout were not well understood at the time, the protest succeeded in fostering early campus discussion of related health issues as well as of U.S.-Soviet relations and other political implications.[8]

The Committee on Public Exercises' Policy Manual—a key university document regarding public expression on non-campus matters—underscored the university's responsibility. If campaign issues were to be discussed, differing views had to be covered at the same meeting, and only Stanford students, faculty, and staff should be allowed to attend.[9] The student-run Political Union was revived in 1953 (an earlier version had been popular in the 1930s). Patterned after similar student clubs at Yale and Oxford, it sponsored influential speakers—carefully balanced across both mainstream political viewpoints and the less well-known—on an array of topics and offered a forum for debate among its student members and interested faculty.[10]

In 1960, the Political Union scored its most notable successes to date with campaign stops by two major U.S. presidential candidates: Senator

Massachusetts Senator John F. Kennedy, candidate for the Democratic presidential nomination, outside Memorial Auditorium, February 1960. Kennedy was on a West Coast tour to make amends for ignoring California. He delivered a major policy address on the need for a new Latin America policy.   STANFORD UNIVERSITY ARCHIVES

To counter Kennedy, Vice President Richard M. Nixon, a Republican presidential candidate, rushed a visit to Stanford during his April 1960 San Francisco Bay Area campaign tour. He, too, spoke to a capacity audience in Memorial Auditorium, but was less prepared for student questions. STANFORD NEWS SERVICE

John F. Kennedy, a candidate for the Democratic nomination for president, in February, and, in April, Vice President Richard M. Nixon, campaigning for the Republican nomination. Both spoke to overflow crowds at Memorial Auditorium.[11]

Kennedy used the opportunity, his only stop in the Bay Area, to give a major policy speech. Despite being early in the campaign, the event attracted an unusually large and animated audience (some 1,500 outside on top of an estimated 2,000 inside). The Political Union had worked hard to attract Kennedy's attention, but had not predicted the level of last-minute interest since equally important speakers rarely drew significant audiences from the often-apathetic student body. The organization was better prepared for Nixon's more extemporaneous presentation, which also drew a large audience.

Later that spring, political activism by a very small number of Stanford students who joined a Bay Area–wide protest at San Francisco's City Hall raised a fuss among alumni and unaffiliated conservative critics. On May 13, 1960, the U.S. House of Representatives Un-American Activities Committee (HUAC) met there to question and hear testimony from 110 public school teachers subpoenaed on allegations of communist influence. (Some of those subpoenaed had already lost their jobs due simply to the implications.)

Outside the 1960 U.S. House on Un-American Activities Committee hearing in San Francisco, an arresting officer pulls a female protester, wet from fire hoses, down City Hall's marble stairs. In 1965, law Dean Bayless Manning advised that "a single photograph of a female student being forcibly dragged out of a building may do irreparable harm to the University's position and public image." BOB JONES, SAN FRANCISCO NEWS-CALL BULLETIN / SF HISTORY CENTER, SF PUBLIC LIBRARY

In January 1964, student interest tables at registration outside the Basketball Pavilion are a study in contrast: Students from the Goldwater committee look askance at the senior class table advertising a concert by prominent African singer and civil rights advocate Miriam Makeba. Encina Hall is in the background. LEO HOLUB / STANFORD UNIVERSITY ARCHIVES

The meeting attracted hundreds protesting HUAC's lack of due process, including teachers, church leaders, and professors and students from the University of California, San Francisco State, and San Jose State. Protesters were denied access to the second-floor meeting room, but not to public spaces in the hall and outside. The ensuing sit-in was nonviolent until a police inspector turned a fire hose on those standing and sitting on the slippery marble stairway, causing significant property damage and sending four to the hospital. Sixty-eight protesters, among them one Stanford student, were then arrested (charges were dropped for all but one, who was later acquitted). The event was widely reported in news coverage as a "riot."[12]

Two Stanford professors—Otis Pease (history) and Sidney Drell (physics)—had listened to radio coverage of the events and, with physics postdoc Marshall Baker, subsequently interviewed a group of students who had been involved. They wrote an open letter to San Francisco Mayor George Christopher, co-signed by 86 other faculty and staff members. Printed in the *Stanford Daily* as well as other newspapers, the letter stated that "contrary to a wide misinterpretation in the press, the demonstration was for the most part a responsible protest by mature college students against what they deeply felt to be the committee's intolerable infringement on civil freedom." The mayor refused to open an investigation, stating that the incident was closed.[13]

Sterling called in Pease, Drell, and Baker after receiving a phone call from a Stanford alumnus employed by the San Francisco Police Department, complaining of bias. "He gave us a little lecture," recalled Drell, but they responded with information from credible eyewitnesses. "It was apparent that Wally felt duty bound to talk to us, but his heart wasn't in the pro-forma lecture." No judicial charges were brought against any Stanford participant.[14]

Before joining Sterling in Europe that fall quarter to dedicate overseas campuses in France and Italy, Sterling's executive assistant, Fred Glover, continued to reply to critical letters written to the president, downplaying Stanford student and faculty participation in the protest. (Apparently, his office had identified only two students who had been at the City Hall.) "We have 9,400 students, and I can assure you that they are by and large a conservative group," Glover wrote one critical alumnus:

> There is a small group of militant nonconformists, many of them extremely bright, even precocious, some might say, who create "noise" far beyond the level warranted by their numbers. Educationally they make their more conservative student colleagues think and defend their viewpoints; they play a provocative intellectual role which is in the end constructive, although I must agree with you that there are times when this small group tries my patience as they do yours. Stanford students have no illusions about Communism; but many of them are concerned about the Un-American Activities Committee because they believe that people accused of crimes should be tried in court, and with the benefit of legal counsel, and not brought to the public bar before a congressional committee.[15]

More liberal political views that emerged in the later 1960s were not yet evident in undergraduate political preferences of 1960. In the Political Union's student straw vote that November, Richard Nixon won 58 percent of the student vote, with a strong showing among freshmen, and John Kennedy took 37 percent, heavily favored by graduate students. But nearly half of the 5,600 undergraduates did not bother to participate in the straw poll. On election day, the four Stanford voting precincts reported that Kennedy won by a small margin.[16]

ROCKING THE BOAT
THE YEAR OF ROSENCRANZ, 1962–1963

In April 1963, in response to the Cuban Missile Crisis of late 1962, civil defense signs dotted the campus, identifying basement areas newly stocked as nuclear fallout shelters. The sudden appearance of the shelters, part of a federally funded civil defense program, sparked the first major postwar political protest on campus.

Stanford's Peace Caucus protest vigil was an unexpected offshoot of the already controversial term (1962–63) of ASSU President Armin Rosencranz, the first graduate student and first lawyer to serve in the office. Charismatic and highly articulate, Rosencranz succeeded in undermining the "don't rock the boat" attitude of both students and administrators, and unintentionally set the standard for ASSU presidents for the remainder of Sterling's term.[17]

ASSU President Armin Rosencranz, nicknamed "Charmin Armin," at the door of his office. Rosencranz's humor belied his serious intent to update student regulations and housing policy and encourage student interest in civil rights and civic participation. *STANFORD QUAD 1963*

Rosencranz, a popular political science teaching assistant, ran for the office reluctantly. He would consider abolishing student government if he won, he said, and reportedly commented that "it takes a pompous person to deal with pompous people. That is why I should be elected." Famously facetious campaign posters saying "Send a man to do a boy's job: Vote Charmin Armin" were not his idea, however.[18]

But his irreverent take on the responsibilities of ASSU president, which incensed both his predecessor and his opponent but delighted voters, highlighted widespread student cynicism about the relevance of student government. He was quite serious about what student government could, or should, be doing, and urged fellow graduate students to take more active roles in governance. In a record turnout, he won, due at least in part to an unusually large turnout of graduate students.[19]

Rosencranz clashed almost immediately with President Sterling during fall 1962 orientation events. Speaking at the Friday night rally and picnic as the incoming freshmen waited for cheerleaders, the Band, and a songfest, the new ASSU president spoke out for students' freedom to "emerge out of our apathy and take our rightful place of leadership in the world student community. While others are starving for lack of food and for lack of freedom, here our major concern seems to be the lack of alcohol." Radios barked out the Stanford-Tulane football game broadcast from New Orleans as he spoke of academic freedom, particularly the right to dissent, and about student participation in university policy deliberations that affect student lives. "You have heard some perplexing talk of rights and responsibilities," he said, alluding to President Sterling's welcome to them earlier that day. "The rights that I have spoken about are not given to us by the President's office or by the Administration. They are ours by birth."[20]

Sterling rebuked Rosencranz the following day in his own speech to transfer students, accusing the student body president of expecting the university to betray its founding documents, especially the prohibition of partisan political activity on campus. Not to be outdone, Rosencranz told the *Daily*, "Senator and Mrs. Stanford had no desire to make Stanford archaic by tying the University to policies which were appropriate for 1891 but are considerably less appropriate for 1962."[21]

Rosencranz challenged Sterling, in the midst of the PACE Campaign, to allow students to show why they were the best and the brightest, but he took a page from Sterling's administrative style. He assembled a strong team, many of them graduate students and founding members of GRIP (the Group with Real Inside Power). He built coalitions of faculty, university officials, and students. And he acknowledged their contributions. Even the "tradition-bound" Sterling administration, he said, was more tolerant than he had expected, giving him space to influence student affairs. He included President Sterling among those he thanked in his May 1963 final address.[22]

Outright victories were few, but even defeats had their noteworthy aspects. By the end of fall quarter, Sterling had added students to 9 of his 16 all-faculty advisory committees, among them the influential Student Affairs and Activities Committee (then reviewing social regulations and sectarian activities on campus) and the Committee on Public Exercises. Student members, ultimately chosen by Sterling, came from a list of nominees submitted by Rosencranz.[23]

Sterling met often with student leaders, but the issue of nonpartisanship dogged ASSU-administration interactions. The administration's all-encompassing definition of nonpartisanship was reinforced when, in January 1963, Rosencranz sent a letter on ASSU stationery to

U.S. Senator Thomas Dodd expressing "grave concern" over a congressional committee investigation of alleged Communist infiltration at Berkeley radio station KPFA. Dean of Students H. Donald Winbigler reprimanded Rosencranz for violating the university's nonpartisan policy. Rosencranz responded with a lawyerly analysis of the definition of nonpartisanship (political party related, not election or issue related) as apparently used by Stanford the previous fall, when the university had publicly appealed to voters to support a bipartisan state ballot proposition that benefited higher education.[24]

The legislature of ASSU (LASSU) subsequently passed three resolutions, supporting the rights of students to speak out on public issues, supporting Rosencranz's actions, and expressing concern of their own regarding the targeting of KPFA. The KPFA letter controversy produced more *Daily* editorials, articles, and letters to the editor (pro and con) across a three-week interval than any single ASSU presidential action to date. It earned Rosencranz more than one administrative rebuke, a public censure by the Inter-Fraternity Council, and the admiration of some influential new faculty members.[25]

But the timing of the KPFA controversy was inopportune. The trustees' approval of the new and much anticipated ASSU constitution, approved by the student body the previous November, now bogged down.[26]

A compromise was reached with Sterling's help: The new constitution was approved, but university policy forbidding LASSU from speaking about off-campus issues was reinforced, jeopardizing the ASSU-sponsored Political Union. However, university facilities were opened to voluntary student organizations that could take partisan stands on public issues. The new legislature finally met April 12, 1963.[27]

To fill a potential void, in April 1963 Rosencranz, Nick Wessel, and some 40 interested students quickly formed a new voluntary organization unaffiliated with ASSU: the Stanford Student Congress (SSC). The group's goal was to host structured debates exploring off-campus issues and to publish statements that reflected both majority and minority opinions. The SSC encouraged both conservatives and liberals to join. Interestingly, the Political Union, modestly funded by ASSU, also continued to host a wide array of political speakers and debates on all sides of current political issues. After an enthusiastic and busy first year (April 1963–June 1964) led by Dennis Sweeney, '65, the SSC went dark. The Political Union, however, survived well into the 1970s.[28]

Rosencranz described this transformative year as a "revolution of moderates." He and his team aimed at mutual tolerance and patience, he said, and believed deeply in the integrity of their cause and the dignity of nonviolent action. "We assumed always that we were dealing with reasonable men, even if at times some of us wondered whether the assumption was reciprocated," he added. Even during the KPFA controversy, he expressed his high regard and esteem for Sterling.[29]

"Any criticisms which we have leveled against the University," Rosencranz asserted, "have been predicated on the assumption that Stanford is one of the finest universities in the nation." The improved dialogue between students and the administration, and between students and the larger world must continue, he said, even when "our speaking is labeled 'immature and irresponsible,' even when the questions we raise in what we feel to be the best interests of the university and the student body are construed by some as condemnation of the university." New student leaders, he warned, must choose their issues carefully and act pragmatically, not simply for the sake of harassing intransigent officials.[30]

An unforeseen consequence of the partisan

policy modification—and certainly an unexpected event—was the anti-fallout shelter protest by the relatively new Peace Caucus in late April 1963. Established within the Political Union the previous November, the Peace Caucus objected to recently completed nuclear fallout shelters on campus as a symbol of university cooperation with aggressive U.S. military policy and the danger of nuclear war represented by the U.S.-Soviet missile crisis in Cuba.

One of the first events sponsored by the Stanford Student Congress was a debate on April 15 regarding the efficacy and morality of nuclear fallout shelters. Ira Sandperl, a noted Bay Area pacifist, and Dick Weinig, a conservative student, were preceded by News Service Director Bob Beyers, who outlined the technical facts on outfitting the shelters, along with their limitations. Those present voted overwhelmingly to resolve that federal funding for shelter development should be refused, that the university should remove all shelter signs from campus, and that it should fund research on peaceful methods of conflict resolution.[31]

As the Student Congress moved on to its next topic—apartheid in South Africa and U.S. desegregation—the Peace Caucus was not satisfied that the university had answered the moral and political questions involved. They met with Sterling, insisting on public debate with university officials. Sterling felt the official interaction and opportunity to question had already happened with Beyers' appearance and turned them down. In response, the Peace Caucus announced a peaceful vigil to be held outside the President's Office during the day and at the President's House on San Juan Hill by night until such a public meeting was arranged.[32]

The vigils began April 25, with a small group at Building 10. That evening, two students stood in the rain at the end of the long driveway of the Lou Henry Hoover House, at the roadside.

The administration may have been unconcerned about peaceful vigils at Sterling's office, but the notion of a vigil at the Lou Henry Hoover House was clearly unnerving. The night before the vigils began, Dean of Students Don Winbigler, along with the deans of men and women, met with the members of the men's and women's judicial councils. They would later be accused of attempting to prejudice possible future judicial cases, but more surprising was the dean's announcement of a new university policy stating that protests in the residential areas would be considered a violation of the Fundamental Standard, punishable by suspension. The result was a five-day stand-off that no one really wanted.

Winbigler had informed the students involved that "vigiling at private homes is not to be permitted," Sterling wrote his friend and former Dean of Students Larry Kimpton: "So, fasten your seatbelt, as I will do mine." Winbigler had just returned from heavy storm conditions traveling in Illinois. "I tried to persuade him that a cyclone is nothing as compared with the winds of freedom when they really start to blow," added Sterling.[33]

On learning of the deans' preemptive action,

Professor H. Donald Winbigler, Stanford's second dean of students (1950–67), viewed his role as student advocate. He was a good-humored mentor, with an unflappable personality. He also was committed to the *in loco parentis* model and was the first line of defense against student protest—and often its target.
STANFORD NEWS SERVICE

Nuclear fallout shelters, part of a federal civil defense program, sprung up across campus in spring 1963. Their appearance sparked the first major unapproved campus protest of the postwar era, followed by a crackdown on protest vigils in campus residential areas.   *STANFORD QUAD* 1966

the night vigil that began with two students grew to 16. LASSU condemned the deans' meeting with the judicial councils and countered with a resolution that the judicial councils would not consider peaceful demonstrations to be violations of the Fundamental Standard. Initially, campus security officers at the night vigils had simply collected student body cards (which students could fetch the next afternoon at the police station). When the vigils did not stop, the acting dean of men countered with the threat of suspensions. Four days into the vigiling, Director of University Relations Lyle Nelson published an explanatory statement through the *Daily*, emphasizing that the shelters were a low-budget project meant to help provide some general disaster protection to the community.[34]

A means to nonviolent conflict resolution finally appeared with a suggestion by John Fromeyer, head of the Stanford Today & Tomorrow (ST&T) program, a now-annual spring forum where students could question faculty and administrators about important issues of the day. After a five-day deadlock, the Peace Caucus ended the vigil "in the spirit of non-violence" on May 1. "The students have taken the first step," noted Nelson. He hoped the university would respond in kind, he told the *Daily*. No judicial cases against the protesters were later reported.[35]

Two weeks later, public discussion took place during a special session of the ST&T program. Winbigler and Nelson were joined by Alf Brandin, vice president for business affairs, and physics Professor Wolfgang Panofsky, director of the new Stanford Linear Accelerator Center and an expert on nuclear deterrence, to answer pre-submitted questions and those from the floor. At this unusually crowded ST&T event, the panelists defended the trustees' sense of a "moral obligation to protect its community members from disaster." But the panel also revealed considerable doubt about the efficacy of the shelters, disagreed among themselves on whether federal funding had been a key factor, and admitted that the trustees had not expected opposition.[36]

The shelter protest had a longer lifespan than its outcome might suggest, fostering not only a more stringent university policy on vigils but also ongoing discussion of the efficacy of civil disobedience and the definition of nonpartisan activity. Nearly two months after the peace vigil ended, Sterling received a lengthy, philosophical letter from a Palo Alto resident and recent graduate supporting a student's right to demonstrate at the president's residence. In an equally lengthy, philosophical response, Sterling wrote: "I suppose that anyone who is alert to and active about the desirability of change is, in a sense, a 'rebel,' in that he is protesting against the existing order of things.

In these terms, I would qualify for having been a 'rebel' many times in my life." He continued:

> For "rebels" who act for reasons of "self-gratification" I have little patience and less respect. I dislike the element of self-gratification that is involved, but beyond that, it has been my observation that they do not serve well the cause they think they are trying to advance.
>
> You mention our recent "vigil." I had no hesitancy whatever in recognizing the "right of peaceful protest." Nor was there any thought of penalizing individuals for the exercise of that right, so long as it did not extend to any harassment of others or interfere with the regular curricular work of the University. In my judgment, it is just as important to protect a private home from harassment, however slight, as it is to recognize the "right of peaceful protest."
>
> It fell to my lot to make the distinction between these two aspects of individual privilege, or, if you please, liberty, and I made it in good conscience. As to the person whom you describe as a person of conscience, who feels that he cannot achieve his objective by working within the "rules," I should say that he has a responsibility to his conscience. If his conscience dictates that work within the "rules" is not adequate and therefore drives him to work outside the "rules," again he must be prepared to accept the consequences.[37]

The Palo Alto alumnus responded with additional questions: Can men of conscience bring about change by always working within the rules? What should one do when he feels he has made every effort to work within the rules but without success? "To those persons who genuinely believe that they must demonstrate in order to attract worthy attention to their cause: This would seem to me to be a matter of personal decision," Sterling replied.

> If a person decides that demonstration is necessary, then he must be prepared to accept the consequences. These may be deleterious; they may involve a violation of the law; they may involve

hazards. But let us assume there were no such hazards. In that event, the demonstrators would be well advised to be prepared to support their cause with cogent reasons and argument. Demonstrations, by and large, appeal to, and frequently reflect, emotions. In the long run, there must be positive and effective appeal to reason based on fact.[38]

WHO CAN OPPOSE CIVIL RIGHTS? 1962–1964

Civil rights protests were distant to Stanford when a small notice in the May 4, 1962, *Stanford Daily* called for an organizational meeting for those "interested in forming a civil rights group concerned with local and national race relations problems. All interested students, faculty and staff are encouraged to attend." Glover sent a clipping of the notice to Sterling, with a handwritten note: "More 'activism' on what I suspect may be partisan matters. But who can oppose civil rights?"[39]

Glover was right on the last count. By November 1962, a Civil Liberties Caucus had joined similar groups under the umbrella of the Political Union where it could disseminate information, stimulate discussion, and encourage off-campus participation. As the group admitted, however, student interest was hard to mobilize. Calling attention to James Meredith's attempt to gain admission to the all-white University of Mississippi, Armin Rosencranz told incoming freshmen in September 1962, "We must empathize with students in our country who are conducting sit-ins and boycotts merely to attain human dignity." At the end of his year in office, he chided Stanford students for their "lack of concern with suffering and deprivation" and the burning issues of social justice.[40]

A striking early contribution of the Civil Liberties Caucus was the appearance of essayist and novelist James Baldwin in May 1963. The Caucus and the Breakers Eating Club, a co-sponsor, hoped to use the event to help raise funds for civil rights organizations fighting segregation in Mississippi, Alabama, and Tennessee. More than 1,800 attended Baldwin's talk at Memorial Auditorium, and 250 more listened outside in a light rain via loudspeakers. Baldwin focused on the situation in Birmingham, Alabama, deploring the federal government's quiescence to state-sanctioned white violence against protesters, and giving an unsparing description of segregation as an American way of life.[41]

Outside, members of the Breakers began collecting funds to be sent to the Congress of Racial Equality (CORE), until ASSU Student Financial Manager Fred Nelson arrived to confiscate the collection boxes (and $120). ASSU bylaws disallowed the solicitation of funds from students by anyone for any purpose, however worthy, he stated. He took the collection boxes away, but unsolicited contributions continued. Additional donations, adding up to more than six times the original amount, were gathered at a Tresidder Union rally and a booth at the university's main entrance on Palm Drive, then sent to CORE.[42]

In fall 1963, a dozen Stanford students traveled to Mississippi, on their own and at their own expense, to help local Black voting rights workers set up a mock state election. This project quickly revealed the large number of eligible and interested Black voters who were denied access to vote in state primaries and elections. The students also learned much from both their Black hosts and antagonistic white Mississippians. One parent "raised hell" with Dean Winbigler because his son was "subject to 100-mile an hour car chases, bullets, bodies, etc.," reported Glover to Sterling. Other parents were angry that the administration did not physically prevent the students from going.[43]

As ASSU president, Rosencranz was a hard act to follow, particularly when administrators appeared to conclude that one year of "Rosencranzism" was enough. His equally idealistic

successor, junior history major Bud Wedin, '65, envisioned a reworking of the growing university community where students were not "guests-in-residence." Wedin, however, found it difficult to communicate with, and challenge, President Sterling, beginning with Sterling's decrease of student membership on the important Student Affairs and Public Exercises committees and his insistence on selecting some student members not from Wedin's list.[44]

For many students, the 1964 *Stanford Quad* recorded, it was something of a relief that LASSU's activities now "were wisely confined to subjects of direct interest to Stanford students," including reinterpretation of Stanford's nondenominational policy regarding church services. Wedin and his supporters, particularly *Daily* Editor Ilene Strelitz, '64, and those involved in the Student Congress, also turned their activism to the civil rights movement.[45]

In the first of two Student Congress presentations in January 1964, Bruce Gordon, field secretary for the Student Nonviolent Coordinating Committee (SNCC), bluntly told a Tresidder Lounge overflow audience to leave theories, foggy notions, and fuzzy political labels behind. "If you think you're going to hop in your Volkswagen with a guitar and take a vacation south to help the Negro, don't come," he warned. A week later, a faculty panel (sociology Professor Sanford Dornbusch, acting Law Dean John McDonough, and religion Professor Robert McAfee Brown) reiterated that white student involvement in civil rights activity in the South that year carried little glamor.[46]

In February 1964, national civil rights leaders selected Stanford to serve as West Coast coordinator for students planning to engage in a massive Mississippi voting-rights drive organized by the Council of Federated Organizations (COFO), the Southern Christian Leadership Conference (SCLC), the Congress of Racial Equality (CORE), and the National Association for the

On January 30, 1964, a well-attended faculty panel (top) warned that student involvement in civil rights activity in the South was hard, dangerous, and complicated. The panel was one of many presentations of the short-lived Stanford Student Congress. At the table, left to right: John McDonough (law), Student Congress speaker Dennis Sweeney, Robert McAfee Brown (religion), and Sanford Dornbusch (sociology). *STANFORD QUAD* 1964

Stanford Daily Editor Ilene Strelitz, '64, championed reinterpretation of Stanford's nondenominational religious policy and spurred interest in civil rights as West Coast Coordinator of the 1964 Mississippi Freedom Summer project. Her reports from Jackson, Mississippi, that summer had a national audience. *STANFORD QUAD* 1964

Advancement of Colored People (NAACP).[47] Wedin's sponsorship of a Civil Rights Secretariat directly under ASSU rather than the Political Union created something of a sensation.[48]

Initially described as an effort to "stimulate student interest" in civil rights projects in the South, the Secretariat as an ASSU-supported organization raised the inevitable campus debate about the appropriate umbrella and funding for student advocacy of what some viewed to be a non-campus, and even irrelevant, political issue.

"The specter of KPFA and Armin Rosencranz immediately came to the minds of the

The Rev. Dr. Martin Luther King Jr. spoke at Memorial Auditorium, April 23, 1964, asking Stanford students to volunteer that summer in a national effort to register eligible Black voters in Mississippi. He earned a standing ovation from his mostly white audience. Behind King is ASSU President Bud Wedin, one of the event's organizers. The 40 students and several faculty and staff from Stanford who participated in Freedom Summer made up the largest group from any single university. STANFORD NEWS SERVICE

Legislature, whose memories, like their debates, are often frightfully long," wrote *Daily* political editor Justin Beck. A subsequent LASSU campus survey taken at campus living groups revealed sharply divided opinions on the Secretariat, and it became a hot topic during the spring student-body presidential campaign.[49]

The Secretariat's organizers (Strelitz, Sweeney, and Carolyn Egan, '64) rebranded the effort as simply a clearinghouse to provide information to students interested in the subject of civil rights and moved ahead with the work of informing and coordinating student interest in the Mississippi Summer Project.[50]

The April 23, 1964, campus speech by Dr. Martin Luther King Jr. was a highlight of the three-day All Western States Civil Rights Conference, organized by the Civil Rights Secretariat.[51] Speaking to an overflow crowd in Memorial Auditorium, King asked for help. Even though its modest ASSU funding was frozen in late May, the Secretariat was able to organize for the Mississippi project the largest group from any single university—40 students and 10 faculty and staff. This group would spend several weeks as part of the 1964 Mississippi Summer Project helping with various aspects of voter registration. Professors Otis Pease, William McCord, and Wilfred Stone taught in the Freedom Schools. McCord, a sociologist and former assistant dean, went on to do fieldwork there, interviewing thousands of locals and students. His *Mississippi: The Long Hot Summer*, published the following year, was one of the first scholarly examinations of the situation.[52]

Sterling's administration kept a relatively low profile on the issue, refusing to prevent students from participating in civil rights activities despite campus and off-campus letters of concern. This business in the South was not Stanford's fight, argued some: "The University is left vulnerable to damage suits filed by parents who had no knowledge, much less given consent, of their

The Political Union, co-host of numerous civil rights speakers, including Martin Luther King Jr., was obliged to present an array of speakers. Thus, in November 1964, they hosted George Lincoln Rockwell, founder of the American Nazi Party and Holocaust denier. Rockwell received a very cool reception.
STANFORD NEWS SERVICE

child's presence in Mississippi." And, the university was inviting legal action by allowing faculty and staff to promote student participation in civil rights activities.[53]

Moreover, faculty and staff members who participated in the Mississippi project were accused of being given fully paid time off from their campus duties "with the active encouragement of their superior to participate in a partisan political campaign, regardless of how desirable the ends they seek must be."[54]

News Service Director Robert Beyers, one of the more visible faculty-staff volunteers, drew

BOB BEYERS
CANDOR PAYS

A succession of student protests kept Stanford University in national headlines during the last two years of Wallace Sterling's administration. Sterling, a former CBS radio news analyst, stood by his belief that "the great principle of freedom of the press should operate just as strongly on campus as elsewhere." At the heart of this approach was his young news director, Bob Beyers, who firmly supported President Sterling's adage that "you serve the administration best by serving the faculty and students first."[1]

When he took the post of News Service director in 1961, the 30-year-old Beyers brought to Stanford a reputation for energetic and reliable reporting. Covering Stanford's accomplishments and difficulties with equal candor, Beyers acquired a national reputation for aggressive, forthright, and reliable news coverage, earning Stanford the benefit of the doubt among most national media sources.[2]

As Beyers supplied facts about antiwar demonstrations on campus, some complained to the president that it was bad for Stanford's image to describe the disruptions for a national audience or to detail student demands. Others claimed that his coverage of any subjects other than campus protests suggested that he was blindly pro-administration. Some protesters, determined not to let the News Service document events, threatened his staff. But Beyers, whose professional career had been shaped by the McCarthy era and the civil rights movement, was accustomed to walking a tightrope.

Bob Beyers in 1963, a year before he took part in the Mississippi Freedom Summer.
STANFORD NEWS SERVICE

Robert W. Beyers was born October 10, 1931, in New York City, and earned a bachelor's degree from Cornell, where, as a senior, he was the crusading editor-in-chief of the *Cornell Daily Sun*. He had not intended a journalism career, but he was a born observer and communicator, in part, he later said, because he had lived in 16 states and attended 20 schools before arriving at Cornell in 1949. As an undergraduate, Beyers joined the Cornell chapter of the NAACP. Its young president, fellow undergraduate James L. Gibbs Jr. (later Stanford's first tenured African American professor), befriended the budding journalist. Gibbs later commended Beyers for helping to persuade Cornell's conservative school government and university administration to end racial discrimination in surrounding Ithaca.

While still at Cornell, and with McCarthyism in full swing, Beyers' insistent search for the truth led him to attend, as a reporter, two campus meetings of the Labor Youth League, a group labeled as communist. He truthfully noted this when filling out a loyalty oath questionnaire, but regardless of his explanation, his life changed. After four highly commended years in Cornell's ROTC program (he ranked first nationally), he received no commission at graduation. He faced years of job uncertainty, unaware that the FBI had started a file on him. His experience gave him a keen appreciation of problems faced by the marginally employed, but it also solidified his perspective: Don't let anyone scare you away from doing what you believe in.

After several years with small-town newspapers in Texas and Michigan, he joined the University of Michigan News Service. Five years later, he followed his Michigan mentor, Lyle M. Nelson, to Stanford. Beyers leapt into the job just as Stanford, enjoying dramatic success at faculty recruiting, was embarking on a landmark fundraising campaign. The university also faced a tough battle with the U.S. Army Corps of Engineers over a proposed flood-control dam in its foothills and often-hostile government negotiations about the 2-mile-long linear accelerator, Stanford's largest research project to date. Beyers documented Stanford's busy academic life as assertively as he did its relations with neighbors over competing land development goals or the changing interests of its student body.

As editor of a weekly newspaper near Ann Arbor, Michigan, Beyers balanced a portable typewriter while recording the latest news in February 1956. BEYERS FAMILY

Soon after arriving, Beyers also took part in community efforts to fight housing discrimination along the Peninsula. As member of the Fair Housing Committee of Palo Alto's Unitarian Church, he joined a movement to change Palo Alto's racial covenants and red-lining, and to improve infrastructure and housing conditions in African American–majority neighborhoods. He later served as news consultant for the Mid-Peninsula Citizens for Fair Housing Committee to support statewide fair housing legislation.

In 1964, Beyers, along with 40 Stanford students and several other volunteer staff and faculty, enlisted in the summer's voter registration campaign in tension-torn Mississippi. He arrived just as news broke of the disappearance (later revealed to be murder) of three volunteers. Beyers brought a talent for inspiring colleagues as well as his skill as a newsman. He quickly became unofficial director of media and of police relations, creating a means to get the news out of Mississippi to a national audience. At a time when threats faced by volunteers were news-making, Beyers consistently highlighted the courage of their hosts, who faced daily risks and potential violence, and, back in California, emphasized the obvious: Racism was not confined to the South.

Like many of his colleagues—educators, clergy, journalists, lawyers—Beyers put his livelihood on the line. Throughout the summer, Sterling's administration was pressed for confirmation of Beyers' volunteer status. University officials were less concerned about partisanship than about liability, particularly after parents wrote to Sterling about discovering through national news coverage that their students were not on the peaceful Stanford campus but experiencing "100-mile an hour car chases, bullets, bodies, etc.," in Mississippi. Legal counsel had to confirm that no official effort by any university officer or representative had been made to persuade students to volunteer. Beyers, who had been granted an unpaid leave of absence, continually clarified that his work in Mississippi was not a university assignment.

Throughout his professional career, Beyers referred to his volunteer work in 1964 as the experience of a lifetime. He became more determined than ever to stand for—not against—something: democracy, justice, human rights, individual dignity, access to education, and, ultimately, the value of cold-hearted facts and freedom of the press. It also reinforced his belief in a straightforward news style: provide the facts—good and bad—without spin.

Unlike his experience during the McCarthy era, Beyers came home to a job, the support of Sterling's team, and campus-wide respect. "Bob Beyers never saw himself as engaged in public relations, always as a journalist," said one of those team members, Sterling's provost (and Stanford's seventh president), Richard W. Lyman. "He lived by the highest standards of that profession: unflagging energy, total integrity, insatiable curiosity and unsparing candor." That candor gave Stanford credibility in the difficult years to come. "After Mississippi," Beyers said, "Stanford's trashings seemed almost a piece of cake."

"Bob was the best university spokesman in the country during the years he was at Stanford," recalled *Stanford Daily* reporter and 1969 editor Philip Taubman (who later had a long career at the *New York Times*). "He never flinched from telling the truth, even when it was embarrassing to Stanford, and the university was always better for it."

NOTES

1. Bob Beyers, "*Stanford Daily* Speech," November 19, 1995 (Beyers biographical file, Stanford News Service); Bob Beyers, "Colleges Should Remember: Candor Pays in Public Relations and Fund Raising," *Chronicle of Higher Education*, August 8, 1990.
2. This profile was adapted from Roxanne L. Nilan, "Why They Went South: Stanford Newsman Bob Beyers and Mississippi Freedom Summer," *Sandstone & Tile* 38:2 (Spring-Summer 2014) 3–17, and "Bob Beyers, Longtime Stanford News Service Director, Dies at 71," *Stanford Report*, October 23, 2002.

In the midst of the 1966 sit-in at the President's Office, Bob Beyers busily gathered and disseminated information. As news director from 1961 to 1990, he covered the university's accomplishments and difficulties with equal candor.
LEO HOLUB / STANFORD UNIVERSITY ARCHIVES

attention to this criticism in order to refute it. Beyers persistently made it clear that he had carefully arranged for unpaid leave from his university duties, and that his unofficial contribution was his choice and purely voluntary.[55]

Looking back years later, Sterling emphasized the significance of this growing campus interest as more Stanford students, Black and white, participated in the political battles leading to the Civil Rights Act (1964) and Voting Rights Act (1965). One had to be insensitive, Sterling later said, not to see the changing mood.[56]

FUELING JUDICIAL REFORM
THE MORSE CASE, 1964

Frank Morse, '66, was one of six undergraduates who worked in Mississippi later that fall, making headlines when he was abducted and badly beaten. Morse had already become collateral damage in the university's slowly evolving student judicial reform effort.[57]

In March 1964, Morse, a sophomore, and two others admitted to kicking in door panels at the Stanford-in-Italy campus in Florence on the last night of their stay (alcohol may have been involved). The Florence student judicial council recommended sentences of work hours back home at the campus Corporation Yard. But when Morse returned to campus to register for spring quarter, he was told he had been suspended. He was given no written statement of charges, nor was he offered recourse to appeal Dean Winbigler's decision. (The two other students were not suspended.)

What gradually became clear was that the dean had upheld the request of Dr. Guelfo Frulla, director of studies at the Italian campus, for suspension, presumably backed by the unanimous support of the four Stanford faculty members then in Florence. But one professor had dissented, clouding the unusual proceedings.

On Morse's request, the Men's Council retried the door panel case two weeks later and assigned all three defendants double the work hours at the Stanford Convalescent Home. Before proceeding, the council tried twice, unsuccessfully, to engage Winbigler. The case was closed, he told them. Morse would not be allowed to enroll that quarter. He also lost his scholarship and had to move out of his room at Sigma Chi.[58]

"Student Resentment High" ran the April 23 *Daily* headline as the dust settled. A random poll concluded that "student opinion was running strongly and unanimously against the administration on the Frank Morse Case." (Morse, now a celebrity, also was voted "King" in the Convalescent Home King and Queen contest—a pay-for-vote fundraiser—with 10,030 votes to 1,485 for his nearest competitor.) A week of investigative journalism revealed hasty proceedings at the Florence campus, poor communication with the home campus, and bypassed procedures. A KZSU program on "the irregularities of the Morse case" highlighted these problems, among others, and disclosed that the suspension decision in fact had been made by Robert Wert, vice provost and dean of undergraduate education, who oversaw the overseas campuses as an academic operation. Although Wert's role as a "court of last resort" was not itself challenged, it appeared that the decision had been made without a review of evidence or interviewed witnesses. Morse had had no opportunity to defend himself. "Here [on campus] the student defendant must have a true last appeal on the basis of evidence," concluded station manager Hal Williams, "or a channel of final appeal is a farce."[59]

The Sterling administration may have expected a certain flutter among students, but student backlash against attending the Florence campus was unanticipated. Some students worried that the Florence staff were overly suspicious of Stanford students, and minor disciplinary infractions could easily result in suspensions. It

Frank Morse, '66 (looking over his shoulder, with Senior Class Executive Committee), had an eventful Stanford career, including a controversial run-in with Dean Winbigler, a one-quarter suspension, and civil rights work in the South. At right, Bernadine Chuck (Fong) and Class President Ira Hall; both became university trustees.   *STANFORD QUAD* 1966

would later come out that the Florence campus had already suffered from vandalism problems with two previous groups, and the owners of the historic Villa San Paolo were having second thoughts about leasing to Stanford. "If the decision in Frank Morse's case was a mistake, blame should be placed, not on any single person [Frulla], but on the absence of judicial process at Stanford," commented sociology Professor Morris Zelditch Jr., who had been on the faculty review board at Florence that quarter and opposed the suspension.[60]

Nor did they anticipate a letter from Ernest Besig, executive director of the ACLU of Northern California, inquiring whether Stanford students subject to disciplinary proceedings received due process. Darrell Halverson, chair of the Men's Council, had referred the case to the ACLU and to Judge Ben Duniway of the U.S. Ninth Circuit Court of Appeals, a Stanford trustee. Asking for comments from Dean Winbigler on six legal points, Besig copied in Halverson and ASSU President Bud Wedin. (A response, if any, was not made public.)[61]

The ACLU did not intend to get involved unless Morse requested assistance. Nor did the ASSU carry out its own review. Instead, Morse did construction work at SLAC during spring quarter while living at the campus home of Dr. John Black, director of the Counseling and Testing Service. Morse got back on track, reregistering summer quarter. His last two years were busy ones, including civil rights work in Mississippi in October 1964 and the March 1965 Selma to Montgomery march. He also ran (unsuccessfully) for ASSU vice president in spring 1965, served on the Fundamental Standard and Honor Code Commission, chaired the senior class Heritage Fund campaign, wrote an honors paper on Vietnam, and was elected to Phi Beta Kappa, completing his bachelor's degree in history on time in 1966.[62]

If it seems that this was an opportunity missed, steps would be made during the following academic year toward reforming Stanford's cumbersome, and at times arbitrary, student judicial procedures. This took place, however, as part of a review process on Sterling's terms—

an academic study committee—and the administration's timetable. The "sound and fury" of 1962 to 1964 also ran into ongoing student distrust of claims by LASSU to represent the full breadth of student body opinion.[63]

In late spring 1964, Bud Wedin was followed as president by Scott McBride (1964–65), a junior industrial engineering student and former chair of the Political Union. McBride's decided victory (in a low-turnout election) represented an ebb in the flow of 1960s student activism. He had campaigned in opposition to the trend, arguing that the ASSU executive branch should speak out less on student involvement in off-campus issues and favoring closer, but more informal, ties to the administration. McBride's candidacy was greatly aided by massive fraternity support (he was a Kappa Sigma), which expected him to squash LASSU's anticipated attack on rush policy. "Many students thought things were going too fast," one observer told the *Daily*. "It was time to slow down a bit."[64]

Even the *Daily* seemed to have taken a step back from Strelitz's "Tabasco and kerosene editorial policy" of the previous year. Commenting on an unusually complimentary *Daily* article about Sterling as the school year opened, the wry columnist and "Fearful Spectator" Art Fisher—not a member of GRIP—noted cynically:

> What if Wallace Sterling is not an incompetent reactionary? What if he is actually interested in student welfare? What if he's kindly? The tragic implication is obvious. . . . For it is well established that the primary function of student government at Stanford is the protection of innocent undergraduates against the civil ravagings of the administration. ASSU leaders must act as the "conscience of the University," they must fight for the right to be heard, and the right to be followed implicitly and the right to herd.[65]

But McBride had also noted the significance of the Morse case. He argued for an investigation of the entire judicial process, and possible creation of a supreme court of appeals made up of students, faculty, and administration. Perhaps because McBride leaned more toward offering student ideas and suggestions to the administration, and less toward protest and reform committees, a review of student regulations and judicial procedures moved quietly, if slowly, forward. McBride was also able to win back student membership numbers on 10 faculty advisory committees.[66]

A substantive review of the layers of deans involved with student affairs and the judicial process was another matter. Again, unforeseen events and unexpected consequences resulted in reorganization of the Dean of Students Office and clarification of the interactions with student judicial councils.

Scott McBride was head of the Political Union when he successfully ran for 1964–65 ASSU president. He had considerable support from fellow fraternity members and from those who wanted less conflict in student governance.
STANFORD QUAD 1964

FUELING ADMINISTRATIVE REFORM
THE DEAN ALLEN AFFAIR, 1965

Much about the university's organization appears to be an intrinsic part of its legendary founding, but neither the deans of men and women, nor the concept of *in loco parentis*, were an inheritance from Senator and Mrs. Stanford.

During Stanford's pioneer days, it was assumed that those "fit to be in college are fit to look after their own affairs." As an 1891 circular (bulletin) explained: "The university is not a reform school. Its bounty is intended for the earnest and industrious student, and the indolent and unworthy will not be retained in the institution." Little was needed, President David Starr Jordan believed, beyond the laws of the state of California.[67]

This philosophy was enshrined in Stanford's Fundamental Standard, as written by Jordan in 1896: "Students are expected to show both within and without the University such respect for order, morality, personal honor, and the rights of others as is demanded of good citizens. Failure to do this will be sufficient cause for removal from the University." Working without written regulations, the original all-faculty Student Affairs Committee—serving as both judge and jury—interpreted the Fundamental Standard as it saw fit. Jordan authorized the committee to expel any student "whose presence for any reason seems undesirable." As a result, individual punishments could be arbitrary. Stanford's first major student protest occurred in 1908, not against Jordan's two-person administration but against Student Affairs Committee efforts to curb excessive drinking by the men living in Encina Hall.[68]

Enrollment had tripled since 1891 when, in 1908, Jordan created the post of dean of women to bail out both the faculty and his overworked registrar. Stanford's first dean of women, Evelyn Wight Allan, '96, stepped into the role of counseling and advocacy that faculty could, or would, no longer sustain, and took on housing issues, admissions, scholarship, student loans, and other duties that swamped Jordan's right-hand man, Orrin Leslie Elliott. A men's dean was also planned, but due to hiring problems the position was given to recent graduates as "student advisor" until the first dean of men was appointed in 1918.

The Fundamental Standard remained in the hands of the Student Affairs Committee, but Jordan now envisioned a council of five students, selected by the student legislature. Such a council would take over from the faculty, and from house mothers and dormitory managers, the first level of student discipline. The women stepped up first, in 1911, by organizing their own Women's Council of five students selected by the Women's League, thus avoiding what would most likely have been an all-male general student council. (Largely ignored by the men dominating ASSU, Stanford's women had organized the Women's League in 1900. This precursor to the Associated Women Students represented all female students well into the 1960s.) The Men's Council was created a year later, also elected by the students. Deriving their authority from the Student Affairs Committee, the Women's and Men's Councils took over the faculty committee's judicial role, to the relief of the faculty. Each council had original jurisdiction regarding infractions of the Fundamental Standard.

For nearly two decades, the Jordan administration fended off pressure from some trustees to set up the university in the role of parent. The administration's reluctance to act *in loco parentis* changed abruptly in 1916 with the presidency of Ray Lyman Wilbur, a no-nonsense organizer who aimed to rid the campus of the "side-shows" of college life and reorient undergraduates toward scholarship. Wilbur's administration codified new student regulations and stiffened up old ones. He dismantled the faculty's role altogether by eliminating its Student Affairs Committee. The Men's and Women's Councils now derived their authority directly from Dr. Wilbur, as university president.[69]

Many of the regulations students of the 1960s found most objectionable had been instituted during the Great War, 1917–18. Some 28,000 U.S. Army troops were stationed at nearby Camp

Fremont, with some billeted on leased Stanford land only a few hundred yards from Roble Hall and the women's gymnasium and field. Rules were expanded to protect the women, particularly curfew and lock-out rules and those regarding chaperones at social events, on walks in the hills, or when out "motoring." (The university also wanted to protect Stanford coeds from the harsh reach of the U.S. Army, which had strict regulations devised to protect the soldiers from predatory women.) The Women's Council agreed to the protective measures, assuming they would go away at the end of the war, but most of the rules did not disappear with demobilization.[70]

The list of regulations grew longer and more complicated over the next three decades. Wilbur did not need much urging from his deans of women, Harriet Bradford (1916–21) and Mary Yost (1921–46), to keep Stanford's coeds tightly regulated during the heady, post–19th Amendment days of the roaring 1920s and thereafter. During his long administration (1916–43), Wilbur also oversaw construction of new dormitories to house as many students on campus as possible, particularly the coeds. The residential-campus concept, along with Stanford's new tuition policy (first charged January 1920), reinforced his commitment to parental accountability.

Well into the 1960s, little of this structure had changed. Adjudication of student behavior was in the hands of a now complex system of influential student councils with overlapping jurisdictions based on sex, age, and residence. Punishment for infractions, backed by sketchy knowledge of due process and civil liberties, often fell much harder on female students. In addition to the Women's and Men's Councils, fraternity men were also accountable to the Interfraternity Council and male freshmen to the Freshmen Men's Judicial Council. Students living in dormitories were answerable to resident assistants, who reported to the deans, and the overseas campuses had their own councils.

The position of dean of students was established in 1945 to oversee the offices of the deans of men and women, and the increasing number of staff in the offices of Admissions, Registrar, Financial Aid, Career Planning and Testing, Foreign Students, and Student Housing. Former Registrar Don Winbigler, a professor of speech and drama, was handpicked by Sterling for the post, and served as dean of students for most of Sterling's administration (from 1950 to 1967). Like Sterling, Winbigler leaned toward pragmatic problem-solving when intervention was necessary. Like Sterling, he also was committed to Stanford's long-standing residential-campus model.[71]

In addition to his administrative responsibilities,

Nora Crow (Women's Council chair, fall 1964) and Darrell Halverson (Men's Council chair, spring 1964) co-authored a scathing report on student judiciary-administration relations. The Crow-Halverson report, and the earlier Morse case, led to elimination of separate deans of women and of men and a new Student Judicial Council. *STANFORD QUAD 1965*

Lucile Allen, formerly dean of women at Cornell, came to Stanford, in 1961, as dean of women. She resigned in 1965 after allegations of interference with Women's Council member selection and judicial procedures, as well as her attempted investigation of eroticism in English Department coursework. STANFORD NEWS SERVICE

Winbigler saw his role as advocate for individual students, and for this he would be remembered by many alumni for his sympathetic and good-humored mentoring and unflappable personality. Nevertheless, since the Morse case, his position was growing "increasingly uncomfortable, being seen more and more as someone carrying bad news for the central administration and less and less as the students' advocate in the higher councils of the University," colleagues recalled.[72]

In May 1964, Dean of Women Lucile Allen asked the Women's Council to secretly investigate the English Department, apparently based on allegations by some female undergraduates that they were embarrassed by the sexual content of Freshman English class readings. Allen also believed that there had been inappropriate sexual behavior between department faculty and students.[73]

The Women's Council refused to become involved on the grounds that this was an issue the dean should take directly to the English Department. But council chair (fall 1964) Nora Crow, '65, and two other council members saw a deeper problem. The result was a highly critical and detailed report outlining major issues with the student judicial system, including its misuse and manipulation by Dean Allen, written by Crow and Darrell Halverson, '65, former chair (spring

1964) of the Men's Council, who had worked on the Frank Morse case the previous spring.

The account was submitted to LASSU on February 3, 1965, and published in its entirety the following day in the *Stanford Daily* by its new editor, Nancy Steffen. A scathing editorial concluded that Allen disrespected the intelligence and dignity of students, faculty, and administration alike.[74]

By the time the campus controversy burst into the public press—*Newsweek* covered the story under the suggestive headline "Sex at Stanford"—a three-member ad hoc committee of the Academic Council, created at Sterling's instigation, already had investigated and made its recommendations, with issues of academic freedom in mind. The committee found no evidence of excessive or inappropriate attention to sexual matters in English class assignments or discussions, nor that there had been any misconduct between teachers and students. But, equally

Influential *Daily* Editor Nancy Steffen strongly supported reform of student regulations. Among her first steps as editor (spring 1965) was full publication of the Crow-Halverson report, against administration wishes. Throughout her *Daily* career she wrote insightful articles on student-administration relations. STANFORD QUAD 1965

important, they urged the current student-faculty-administration committee effort to clarify and revise the Stanford judicial process.[75]

Noting the ineffective communication and mutual distrust between the dean of women and the Women's Council, the committee also urged Allen to resign. When University General Counsel Robert Minge Brown warned Sterling that Dean Allen might sue the university for libel, Sterling sought another opinion from law faculty members Gerald Gunther (an ad hoc committee member), Marc Franklin, and Bayless Manning. They downplayed the libel concern and backed the recommendation calling for Allen's immediate resignation.[76]

The dean soon after handed in her resignation. Smoothing the waters, Sterling wrote one of her lawyers, John Bennett King, to soften the blow: "Dean Allen has my gratitude for her service to Stanford and my sympathy for recent events. Those put her under very great strain; even so, she retained her dignity and composure—no mean accomplishment! I'm sure that you and Chuck [Charles F. Jones] helped her immeasurably to do so . . ."[77]

Following Allen's resignation, the Dean of Students Office was reorganized to enhance counseling and eliminate the separate offices of dean of men and dean of women. But more fundamental changes were already underway. The previous fall, Sterling had asked Vice Provost Bob Wert and the faculty-student Student Affairs and Services Committee to study social regulations. The advisory committee, backed by the Women's Council and LASSU, worked closely with students from the more conservative Associated Women Students (AWS) Social Regulations Committee to recommend rules changes. The AWS committee took on much of the information-gathering load, surveying parents as well as women students, interviewing faculty and staff, and studying 35 other institutions.[78]

This review took more than four months in early 1965. After discussion at many student and administrative levels, Sterling backed their resolutions in what some student leaders considered a surprise move. Among other things, the review liberalized (but did not eliminate) check-in hours for junior and senior women and closing hours for freshman dorms and ended the need for chaperons. As Sterling explained to the trustees, these new regulations placed more responsibility on the individual consistent with the Fundamental Standard and permitted increasing freedom of decision as students matured from freshmen to seniors. "In approving these changes, the University is expressing its confidence in their maturity and good judgement," he said.[79]

That same spring of 1965, the Student Judicial Council (SJC) was created to replace the separate Women's and Men's Councils as judge and jury of the Fundamental Standard and all applicable university regulations and policies governing student conduct. An appeal board, made up of faculty and students, was still under negotiation. In the meantime, a temporary all-faculty Interim Judicial Board (IJB) was set up to hear individual cases on appeal or to consider a case if the SJC concluded that it could not enforce a university policy because, in its view, it conflicted with the ASSU constitution or by-laws. No one expected the negotiations on how this mixed board would be selected to continue for three years, nor that differences between LASSU and the administration over university policy regarding demonstrations would become a fundamental stumbling block.[80]

Students saw this loosening of social regulations for upperclassmen as a modest reform, but Sterling parried parent complaints that university officers had gone too far, abdicating their responsibilities.[81] Dean Winbigler sent a carefully worded, two-page explanation to parents of all female students, trying to reassure them that this was not a precipitous effort. Recognizing "the maturity and good judgement of the overwhelming majority of Stanford women," he said, the changes would be reviewed annually and refined, a recommendation of both faculty and student committee members. He also quoted Professor Eric Hutchinson, chair of the Student Affairs and Services Committee: "We believe it is important for the university to encourage such reasonable proposals as these and others arrived at through such a commendable blend of self-government and student leadership." Such gradualism was, after all, the hallmark of Sterling's administration.[82]

But gradualism was not to be the mark of a new round of incoming student leadership. In the spring 1965 elections, the opposite of the previous year happened: Sandy Mackenzie, '65, of the earlier Rosencranz-Wedin coalition, was elected president. A new injection of graduate student activism, the Graduate Coordinating Council (GCC), had coalesced in the wake of the Free Speech Movement at Cal, and saw itself as the forefront of reform of social

regulations and of the student judicial system. Ironically, the student body also approved an amendment to the ASSU By-Laws barring LASSU from getting involved in off-campus issues.[83]

A FUSE WAITING TO BE LIT
STUDENTS, FACULTY, AND THE VIETNAM WAR, 1965–1966

Sterling believed that the ongoing discussions regarding judicial tribunals illustrated constructive student efforts to participate in university governance, but these discussions—and the slow and not necessarily steady pace of reform—also revealed the growing tension among and between students, faculty, and administrators. The civil rights struggle by itself would have fueled student activism, although likely without resort to violence, Sterling had concluded. The concurrence of that movement and the escalation of the war in Vietnam, however, made it difficult to foresee how the unrest would play out. The fuse, he said, was "waiting to be lit."[84]

In February 1965, some 400 Stanford students and faculty rallied to express their opposition to increasing American involvement in the war in Vietnam. The following month, a petition urging the end of U.S. military participation was signed by 144 Stanford faculty members and sent to President Lyndon Johnson. Petition drives and rallies continued through April, winding down with a May campus "teach-in." The teach-in led to the founding of the Stanford Committee for Peace in Vietnam (SCPV), a faculty-student group. In 1966, a Stanford chapter of the Students for a Democratic Society (SDS), a national organization opposed to America's involvement in Vietnam, was founded.[85]

But the campus community, like the rest of the country, was more divided on how to deal

ASSU President Sandy Mackenzie (left), with Biff Barnard, Axe Commission president, showing off the Axe during halftime of the 1965 Big Game. Mackenzie brought student government back to "rocking the boat," 1965–66. *STANFORD QUAD 1966*

Banners (complete with typo) and horns drew attention at an anti–Vietnam War protest in Stanford Stadium's end zone during the Stanford–Air Force football game, November 1966. Some 80 members and sympathizers of the Stanford Committee for Peace in Vietnam also released six white doves at halftime.   STANFORD NEWS SERVICE

In response to a Red Cross call for donations, the Walter Army Society set up this November 1965 blood drive in support of the U.S. commitment in South Vietnam. The group, a Stanford Army ROTC honor society created in 1956, proudly attracted more pints than a competing—antiwar—blood drive.   STANFORD NEWS SERVICE

Among student interest groups that set up tables outside the Basketball Pavilion (now Burnham Pavilion) during fall 1966 registration: the recently formed Stanford chapter of Students for a Democratic Society (SDS).

LEO HOLUB / STANFORD UNIVERSITY ARCHIVES

with the war effort. Spring 1965 saw a rally and petition drive by the Viet-Nam Defense Committee, and, in November 1965, another petition collected an estimated 1,600 signatures; both were in support of U.S. intervention in Vietnam. A week later, however, 500 Bay Area faculty and staff signed an open letter asking for an immediate halt to bombing. On January 31, 1966, following an announcement by President Johnson that the U.S. would resume bombing in North Vietnam, the SCPV attempted to organize a university-wide strike. Although only a half-dozen professors canceled their classes, that night a torchlight parade of more than 700 people wound its way from Cubberley Auditorium to downtown Palo Alto. By contrast, in April, 135 volunteers donated blood "in physical and moral support" of the U.S. war effort in Vietnam.[86]

The SCPV was only a part of the larger May 1966 protest against local production of napalm, a controversial munition (jellied gasoline) used by the U.S. military in Vietnam. Local clergy and Peninsula peace groups representing all ages, along with the SCPV and other regional student groups, picketed United Technology Center plants in Coyote (15 miles south of San Jose) and Redwood City. Citizen petitions and court cases of middle-class mothers arrested for trespassing attracted attention from across the country, helping to stir national debate.[87]

It was the draft, not napalm, however, that ignited on-campus protest. President Johnson's acceleration of American military intervention in Vietnam depended on a dramatic increase in troop deployment not seen since the Korean War (from around 120,000 in mid-1965 to nearly 400,000 in 1966). Local draft boards once again depended on drawing from the ranks of male college students, 18–21, to fill growing monthly quotas.

PRESIDENT'S OFFICE SIT-IN, MAY 1966

In 1966, full-time, currently registered male students normally qualified for the II-S student deferment, but a student's low college grades could threaten that status. To equalize class ranking issues across America's wide range of colleges and universities, in the spring of 1966 the Selective Service System reactivated its "College Qualification Test," originally created during the Korean War but discontinued in 1963. In some states, test locations were a problem, with some students having to travel considerable distances. Stanford felt fortunate to secure a campus testing location for the convenience of its students and those at nearby colleges. The national test, scheduled for four dates in May and June, was not mandatory, but college students and high-school seniors were encouraged to take it to help them confirm deferment status.[88]

The May 14 test was uneventful, with members of the SCPV handing out leaflets, produced by the national SDS, to test takers at the door.

For the May 21 test, the SCPV was better prepared. On Thursday, May 19, 1966, having already contacted news media about a possible disruption at both the President's Office on the Quad and during Saturday's test, the SCPV held a noon rally to protest university involvement in Selective Service student deferment testing and then headed to Building 10. Leaders of the protest made their demands to Bob Wert in the Provost's Office, vacant since Fred Terman's retirement, while some 40 students gathered in the sedate office reception area.[89]

The protest was one of many across the county, of varying sizes and success, meant to challenge the Selective Service System as Congress took up debate about the inconsistencies and inequalities of the draft. Student deferments gave affluent young men an unfair advantage

Stanford's first antiwar sit-in followed a May 19, 1966, noon rally to protest Stanford involvement in Selective Service testing for student draft-deferment status. Below: After covering the rally, *Daily* Managing Editor Joe Rosenbloom entered Building 10 to cover the occupation.

LEO HOLUB / STANFORD UNIVERSITY ARCHIVES

LEO HOLUB / STANFORD UNIVERSITY ARCHIVES

STANFORD NEWS SERVICE

in avoiding the draft and leaving, as Stanford's protesters said, "minority groups, the poor, and the badly educated" to be drafted. Stanford's willingness to host the exam, they added, equated to outright support for the war effort.[90]

The protesters demanded an immediate, last-minute moratorium on Saturday's Selective Service test, which could affect the deferment status of some 850 men who were expecting to take it. They refused to leave Building 10 until they received a "meaningful reply" from the adminis-

tration. As routine office hours ended on Thursday and office staff went home, an estimated 30–35 students settled in, with books, food, pets, and a few sleeping bags, for what would turn out to be a 50-hour sit-in. Flowers were handed out to other demonstrators, counter-demonstrators, administration mediators, and policemen alike. No effort was made to forcibly remove the protesters.

Sterling, then in San Francisco at a regularly scheduled Board of Trustees meeting, had already agreed to meet with group representa-

Protesters had contacted local news media, which arrived in time to cover a group of counter-protesters supporting the draft test. Their signs urged students to Speak Out, Don't Sit In; Support President Sterling; and Liberate Bldg. #10, among others.
LEO HOLUB / STANFORD UNIVERSITY ARCHIVES

Ken (Keni) Washington, '68, one of the protesters, talks with counter-protesters outside the President's Office during the Selective Service testing sit-in, May 1966. Washington later was active in the Black Student Union.   STANFORD NEWS SERVICE

tives in private. His acceptance of their invitation was rejected, however. The group insisted that Sterling meet with them in public; he declined. Wert kept the lead as administration negotiator.

A noisier counter-protest arrived outside Building 10 on Friday morning, quickly organized the night before. Some in the crowd carried such signs as "Support President Sterling," "Down with Mob Rule," and "Academic Freedom and Responsibility," and engaged in heated exchanges with protesters. By Friday afternoon, the crowd (at one point reaching an estimated several hundred) had waned. "Most of the people outside the office said they were against the sit-in," reported the *Daily*, although their random sample of bystanders also found little support for the confrontational tactics of the counter-protesters.[91]

The 50-hour sit-in was the first student take-over of a Stanford office space that successfully disrupted university business, and perhaps the first to invite media attention to itself beforehand. Notable restraint was reported on all sides. Just as no physical force was used to evict the students (unlike at other universities), the students took time to clean up behind themselves when they decided to vacate the building around 3 p.m. on Saturday. Some 33 protesters voluntarily gave their names as they left the building.

The protest was not quite over. About 100 marched through White Plaza and up Lasuen to the President's House. There they were met by Fred Glover, at the end of the circular drive off Mirada. Sterling was away for the weekend, but Glover accepted their formal statement as they filed past the home.

Saturday's exam took place with no interruption. Anti-draft protesters again handed out leaflets to those entering the various exam locations. Perhaps they heeded the advice of ASSU President-elect David Harris, on record as supporting the "lobby-in" but who warned of playing with the lives of those trying to pass the test. The

Daily's editorial staff supported public discussion of the draft, but like Harris concluded that "the choice should be left to the individual student; the dissenters are unjustified in demanding that the university foist their moral code upon the entire male segment of the student body."[92]

Given the lateness of the school year, the Student Judicial Council acted quickly, holding a series of public hearings for 36 students who pleaded *nolo contendere* to charges of violating the Fundamental Standard. The Judicial Council placed the defendants on probation, with the added requirement that they take part in a series of seminars with select administrators and faculty to explore recommendations for improving the existing decision-making structure at the university. Neither the leniency of the punishment nor its basis in the Fundamental Standard (rather than the university's demonstrations policy) went over well with either the President's Office or senior trustees, but the deadline to appeal was allowed to pass. The seminars were never held.[93]

Instead, the Committee on University Policy reaffirmed the university's policy on campus demonstrations.[94]

In the end, Stanford did not serve as a site for the fall 1966 and spring 1967 Selective Service exams. The national exams were discontinued in 1967, when President Lyndon Johnson ordered a blanket II-S deferment for all full-time, currently registered undergraduates.

A week after the May sit-in, the *Daily*'s editorial staff looked at both sides of the issue. By their own admission, the protesters had used the wrong tactic, and had prompted little popular support to end the Selective Service qualification test at Stanford or in general. But the administration, too, had failed, by showing little effort to understand a broader and growing discontent of many with the escalation of the war.[95]

Sterling was guilty simply of "not listening," they argued, reminiscing about earlier years when the popular president appeared unannounced for dinner in dormitories, and stayed to play the piano or pool. But as the demands on his time became heavier with the PACE Campaign (1961–64), Sterling's contacts with students, they claimed, had dwindled. Now, when students talk to him, they were met with "little genuine understanding and—when the attempt is made behind closed doors—often not a little anger." (The *Daily* editors were unaware of the seriousness of Sterling's 1964 illness and surgery.)

"Few issues on the Stanford campus have the potential for both arousing widespread and active student resentment and embarrassing the University," the *Daily* staff concluded. To date, "all the ingredients necessary to cause a full-scale flexing of the student muscle have not been found in any single issue. But in 1966, with student activism at Stanford gaining more and more self-confidence, it is no longer safe to say that 'it can't happen on The Farm.'"

DAVID HARRIS
ASSU PRESIDENT AS CELEBRITY PROTESTER, 1966–1967

In an informal 1965 address to the American Society of Mechanical Engineers, President Wallace Sterling talked about some of the problems of America's "restless generation." Contrasting them to the earlier generations, he noted that today's students looked not only for intellectual interest but also for moral commitment. Pointing to the Peace Corps and civil rights organizations, he also noted that such moral commitment was now aimed at national organizations rather than student government. That pull would be personified by the ASSU presidency (1966–67) of David Harris.[96]

Like Armin Rosencranz, Harris was elected on a wave of student apathy and cynicism about student government and he, too, would be boosted by the enthusiasm of a core of student activists similar to those who had helped three of the last four presidents get elected. By the end of his abbreviated term, Harris, a well-known

Sterling praised Stanford students of the 1960s for seeking moral commitment, noting the influence of national organizations such as the Peace Corps and civil rights organizations. Stanford provided one of the largest per-capita cohorts of volunteers to the Peace Corps and contributed many to the Volunteers in Service to America (VISTA). STANFORD NEWS SERVICE

Student body President David Harris was an outspoken critic of the Vietnam War. A founder of the Resistance, an anti-draft organization, he told a January 1967 rally that he would choose jail over military service. True to his word, he later served 20 months in federal prison for draft evasion.
STANFORD QUAD 1967

his perspective was dramatically changed by his experience working with the voting rights effort in Mississippi during fall quarter of his sophomore year. By his senior year, he was still debating, but it was now as an articulate and idealistic student leader comfortable with a microphone and a crowd.[98]

Harris reluctantly agreed to run for office. He did not expect to win but saw the campaign as an educational effort to stir discussion of broad reforms of higher education. More sardonic than humorous, he purposefully exaggerated his platform to avoid getting elected, calling for the option to take all classes on a pass-fail basis (something he was genuinely interested in) along with elimination of the Board of Trustees and of fraternities, and legalization of marijuana, as well as the end of university participation in the war effort. He had assumed that conservatives would rally to vote against him.[99]

During his campaign, the *Stanford Daily* labeled him "too radical to win," and, "if he were to win, too unrealistic and dogmatic to accomplish anything." Coming closer to Harris' true interests, the *Daily* also reported that Harris asserted "that the ideal university is a pure 'democracy with freedom bordering on anarchy. There should be so many things going on that the place is constantly running the risk of exploding.' "[100]

But Harris and his vice president, Michael Collins, defeated their opponents, Bob Klein and Frank Morse, in a runoff election that saw the largest number of votes cast (4,296) to date, similar to three of the previous four elections. (This was not a record turnout, however, representing only about 40 percent of the student body—the 1955 election saw a 60 percent turnout.) On learning of his election, he made it clear that he thought little of university administrators, considering them the chief obstacles of

antiwar and anti-draft student leader, now symbolized Stanford student activism, particularly for off-campus critics. Unlike Rosencranz, he even looked the part with his longer hair, facial hair, and jeans.[97]

Harris, a political science major from Fresno, California, was a resident assistant at Wilbur Hall when he ran for student body president for the 1966–67 term. At Fresno High School, he had played center and linebacker on the football team and had won state laurels as a debater. He was, he said, "an All-American frosh type," but

reform. "Virtually all of them are staid, and their thoughts about education have stagnated in their own perspective," he told the *Daily*. This, too, was hardly new.[101]

Harris' unconstrained public statements, however, coupled with his appearance, quickly brought him celebrity status off campus more than on. A week after the election, the *San Jose Mercury* reported that his "new left" platform appeared to be "a revolt against conformity, injustice, social prejudice, materialism, and the Protestant ethic, and a search for individuality in a society that molds people like [a] cookie cutter." His election was a call for "far reaching university reforms, in which students would, in effect, become virtual equals to their teachers, with the administration serving in the same role as a public utility, keeping the place running." After expressing his doubts about all faculty committees, Harris added: "We want to eliminate the general studies requirements in foreign languages, science and other fields demanded of all students by Stanford. We think students should be able to make these decisions on what they take, themselves."[102]

Glover passed the *Mercury* article to Sterling with the note "interesting reading." Even before Harris took office, letters began to flood into the President's Office from alumni, parents, and other critics. A Stanford parent from Southern California blamed the faculty:

> It is unfortunate that too many professors go down the line for socialism, instead of remembering that capitalism was the system which made our country strong. This instruction to impressionable young minds has had its effect, and those who are sent to college by the efforts of their parents' labor, are becoming socialists, beatniks, free and dirty speech advocates, and will one day tear our system down until we are sharing poverty, not wealth. We are now changing our wills so nothing will be left to the University, as we had planned.[103]

To a caustic postcard from a Santa Barbara alumnus objecting to Harris' election, Sterling remained optimistic in his reply:

> Having had experience in dealing with student activist groups, I can attest that they produce a variety of headaches for university officers. In some cases, I am sure, the production of headaches in the President's office is their real objective. On the other hand, there are students within these groups who leaven the educational process. Their appearance and manners may leave much to be desired, but their questions provoke thought. They direct their questioning not only to university officers and members of the faculty, but also to their fellow activists.[104]

Sterling wrote Harris on May 11, congratulating him on his election and requesting a meeting before the end of spring quarter. There is no record that such a meeting took place.

To his student allies, Harris would soon reach near heroic status.[105] To other students, he needed a lesson in college traditions. In fall 1966, Harris targeted fraternities, "small worlds functioning around pre-conceived ideas," as among the unnecessary sideshows of university life. (He simply favored complete re-evaluation, he told incoming freshmen, not immediate dissolution.) On October 20, 1966, he was seized by more than 20 masked Delta Tau Delta fraternity members as he was leaving a student legislature meeting, pinned down, and his head shaved. The Delts photographed the result and sent the photo to local newspapers, including the *Daily*. Campus reaction to the assault was largely negative, including condemnation by 23 fraternity men in a letter to the *Daily*. Associate Dean of Students Joel Smith called it a "despicable act," describing Harris as a conscientious, sensitive student leader. "He neither gets nor obtains automatic approval for his ideas but his right to express these ideas is fundamental."[106]

Dean of Students Don Winbigler placed at

The strain of the presidency, added to health issues, is evident in this June 1967 image of Wally Sterling, 60. He had worked without a provost from August 1965 until January 1967, when he welcomed Richard Lyman to Building 10. Sterling relied heavily on Lyman as campus protests ramped up. STANFORD NEWS SERVICE

alumnus in rural Gridley, California, stated: "I have been observing the left-wing trends at Stanford for some time now and I feel that as an alumnus it is high time that I now voice my protest. Inordinate persecution of the lads who sheared Harris can only be construed as University approval of the left-wing and amoral philosophies of Mr. Harris."[108]

To a wealthy Oakland donor who chided Sterling ("A lot of Stanford folks here were happy and delighted to hear that the president of the student body had gotten a free haircut"), the president stood his middle ground, replying: "Your delightful letter of 1 November has just the touch of whimsy we needed in the coldly serious atmosphere both the students and alumni have created over the haircutting incident."[109]

THE TRANSITION BEGINS

"Today's students are an exceedingly able and idealistic and energetic group—thank goodness—and universities must respect their right to express controversial opinions," Wallace Sterling responded to yet another angry Stanford alumnus, in 1967.[110]

But he gave no ground in his assertion that reform—on campus and off—must be carefully deliberated, without violence or threat, and that the university must ensure a climate of free speech for all constituencies while also ensuring their physical safety.

David Harris saw an educational revolution on the horizon. The administration he targeted, however, changed profile when, at the end of 1966, Sterling selected Richard W. Lyman as his new provost.

least 22 Delts on probation until the end of spring quarter and required each to submit, after probation, a written account of how he exercised his rights and responsibilities of citizenship in the Stanford community during this period. They were not asked to apologize. "I've often thought something like this might happen," said Harris calmly. "I've wondered what makes people do things like that."[107]

The haircutting incident delighted many alumni, indignant after Associate Dean Smith's support of Harris. It was rumored that a Delt alum treated the entire Delt house to a steak dinner. A typical letter to Sterling, from an

20

THE PRESIDENT'S
FINAL CHALLENGE
STANFORD IN TRANSITION, 1967–1968

In January 1967, Wallace Sterling set in motion the final segment of his long administration, allowing him to move forward with his retirement plans. That month, his newly chosen provost, history Professor Richard W. Lyman, took office. Equally important, with law Professor Herb Packer on board as vice provost, Sterling's plan for a comprehensive Study of Education at Stanford (SES) kicked off with Packer as chair of the SES Steering Committee. After more than 17 years guiding Stanford, Sterling notified the trustees in March that they had until September 1, 1968, to find his successor.[1]

Lyman, responsible for the academic program, and Packer, as SES chair, became the face of the administration and key campus negotiators during these 20 months. Sterling remained at the helm, however, and continued to take the brunt of off-campus wrath as well as the symbolic contempt of vocal student critics.

< As protesters sat in at the Old Union in May, Provost Richard Lyman defended President Sterling on proposed suspensions and rejected a suggested student-dominated judicial process. With him in Memorial Auditorium were, from left, Dean of Students Joel Smith, law Professor William Baxter, and political science Professor Hubert Marshall, chair of the Committee of 15.
STANFORD NEWS SERVICE

As the trustees struggled to select Stanford's sixth president, the administrative transition was shadowed by the explicit hostility of student political protest groups. Demonstrations during 1967–68 presaged targets and tactics that would become more violent under Stanford's next two presidents. Even so, student government continued its course of reform despite its own mixed messages and unusual turnover: four student body presidents in two years.

Students had been challenging Stanford's *in loco parentis* policies since the early 1960s, hastening reform of student regulations, governance, and judicial procedures. The influential ASSU presidency of Armin Rosencranz (1962–63) had set a pattern for student-body leaders who, with varying success, were determined to use student government to do more than allocate university subsidies for various approved student activities. Rosencranz and his successors gained student membership on influential faculty advisory committees and a significant loosening of the strict definition of nonpartisan campus activity. They questioned the social and gendered constraints of the residential-campus model as well as the goals of Stanford's traditional educational framework.

475

These leaders did not always represent mainstream student opinion. Indeed, the likelihood that Stanford students would engage in issues beyond their classwork remained an ongoing debate. But the direction they took student government was clearly toward influencing elimination of Stanford's longstanding *in loco parentis* model and broadening student political awareness.

The supporters of Armin Rosencranz, Bud Wedin, and Sandy Mackenzie may have thought of their battles with the administration in terms of "good" versus "evil," but these interactions had been conducted within the parameters of Sterling's vigorous promotion of intellectual maturity and academic freedom. The consensus among campus constituencies—students, faculty, and administration—generally held firm until 1966: The university provided a special privilege, one to be gratefully accepted and cherished by students, enjoyed by faculty, and carefully managed by university officials, both academic and administrative.[2]

Shortly after his election as ASSU president in spring 1966, David Harris had stated that he was willing to use force, if necessary, to bring about his vision of the student-centered university, where students were coequal to faculty and administrators, and trustees were irrelevant. What that meant in practice, however, would remain unclear, particularly since Harris would resign four months before the end of his term.

Branner women, here in 1966, enjoyed meals in a high-ceilinged dining room. Built in 1923 as a men's dormitory, Branner Hall became a women's residence in 1944. It was among Stanford's first coed dormitories. STANFORD NEWS SERVICE

Nor was it clear that Harris spoke for the student body, but rather for a subset of politically engaged activists from the School of Humanities and Sciences.[3]

The university, Harris told Branner Hall freshmen during orientation, should ideally be a four-year leave of absence from society. Grades "make education an external realization instead of an internal one," and getting a degree was "strictly a business proposition. It has nothing to do with education."[4]

What became plain was that Harris, who saw himself as a man of ideas, had no ambition to be an executive or a politician. He shied away from the idea that "Dave Harris was going to make things exciting at Stanford," and warned that he was not going to lead crusades. "My job should be more of an 'input' of ideas and suggestions." Student initiative, he argued, was more important. "Where students organize themselves to get what they want, it will come."[5]

Remarkably, during this era destined to be known for its forceful antiwar student protests, notable efforts at campus reform were accomplished through pragmatic, constructive work with faculty and administrators. Student initiative prodded the university into rethinking the gendered basis of student living arrangements; the racial make-up of its student body, faculty, and staff; and the very nature of the modern residential university.

WOMEN WANT OFF! 1966–1967

At the outset of his term, Harris encouraged the student referendum process to involve the entire student body. In October 1966, a target was provided by Janet Howell, '67, leader of the OFF! campaign. The effort had originated in a petition, ultimately signed by more than half of female undergraduates, advocating the end of a university policy requiring all women under the age of 23, who were not living with parents, to live on campus. In a two-day November ASSU referendum, students voted 10 to 1 in favor of giving junior and senior women the option of moving off.[6]

Two years before, in fall 1964, ongoing letters to the *Stanford Daily* and petitions by Branner and Union residents had helped fuel a reassessment of women's social regulations. Despite the breadth of that 1964–65 review, one significant request had been dropped from the Associated Women Students (AWS) study: providing women the choice to live off campus.

Through much of Stanford's early history, many women had lived off campus due to inadequate on-campus housing. This gradually eased with construction of new Roble Hall (1918) and Lagunita Court (1934, 1937) and the transitioning of other dormitories to women's use, including the Stanford Union (1933) and Branner Hall (1944). Into the late 1940s, female graduate students had been allowed to live off campus. Sterling's administration continued to upgrade campus housing to fulfill the commitment to the contemporary residential-college concept—that is, providing a common experience by housing

As leader of the 1966–67 OFF! campaign, Janet Howell, '67, challenged the university's gendered housing policy that allowed men, but not women, to live off campus.
STANFORD NEWS SERVICE

Trustee President Richard Guggenhime, a firm ally of Sterling, was reluctant to change Stanford's *in loco parentis* policy. STANFORD NEWS SERVICE

all students on campus. Not everyone could be accommodated, however, so the administration allowed men—and only men—to live off.

The student referendum tactic did not lead to smooth sailing for reform. While the ballot stated that "University policy in this matter should be revised immediately," and the resolution was subsequently approved by the student legislature, its passage was merely an expression of student opinion. Despite its overwhelming student support, the issue would take months to gain traction among administrators and faculty.

Howell initially tried to sidestep Sterling by demanding trustee action, but board President Richard Guggenhime declined to even consider the change without Sterling's recommendation. He replied with a defense of "custom and tradition":

When you chose to come to Stanford, you must have known its longstanding policy in respect to residence requirements and you were free to

choose Stanford or another institution where the rules are different. In other words, I cannot frankly see whatever may be the merits of your position that you can logically expect from your personal standpoint a precipitous change in a condition which has prevailed for many years.[7]

Guggenhime's response fell flat. The *Daily* ran Howell's rejoinder on its front page: "To ask a person to avoid the sort of involvement in the university which results in his trying to better the institution is to ask him not to use his education."[8]

Sterling's response was more pragmatic. Meeting with Howell later in November 1966, he told her that the change raised serious questions about the costs and implications of operating campus residence halls if they could not be filled, but he also admitted that he was concerned about Stanford's image. Warning her that little would be accomplished by a student protest, he nevertheless committed himself to raising the issue with the trustees. Howell was optimistic that "the lines of communication" were now open.[9]

Harris and other ASSU leaders, however, demanded Sterling immediately issue a statement agreeing to a change of policy, permitting women to live elsewhere by the next fall quarter. If Sterling did not agree, they threatened, there would be a campus housing rent strike on upcoming residence bills. Harris also sent the trustees a telegram on December 7, demanding (unsuccessfully) a meeting to discuss the off-campus ultimatum.[10]

Sterling responded on the trustees' behalf a week later, reiterating what he told Howell. "This policy will be reviewed, and appropriate University procedures will be conscientiously employed in so doing," he said, adding, "I hope that the opportunity for objective review of this matter will not be jeopardized by actions which might be considered coercive." The trustees, at their mid-December board meeting, backed

Sterling's recommendation that the issue be thoroughly studied.[11]

Howell maintained her own negotiating leverage, overriding Harris to suggest that supporters merely delay paying room and board until January 4—the last day that bills could be paid without penalty—as an expression of support. Only about 10 percent (some 350 women) did so, but this succeeded in grabbing positive on- and off-campus media attention to the issue. Unfazed by the numbers, Howell stated: "We are asking for equality with the men or a reason why not."[12]

With Sterling's support, the question now moved through various university advisory committees including the Committee of 15 and the Study of Education at Stanford, as well as a subcommittee of a busy new ASSU Housing Commission. On May 4, 1967, Sterling announced an experiment: a change in university residence policy under which up to 100 senior women, chosen at random, would be permitted to live off campus. That fall, 56 of those preselected by the university chose to do so, but there is no data showing how many of the women who wanted to move off campus were not selected among that random 100. A year later, all but freshmen women could live off, a change brought not by student protest but by the severe on-campus housing shortage. (Ironically, students choosing to live off campus were cautioned that they might not be able to return to campus housing until space was available.)[13]

RETHINKING THE RESIDENTIAL UNIVERSITY
THE ASSU HOUSING COMMISSION

The off-campus-living situation was the more boisterous part of a quieter and much broader review underway of Stanford's modern concept of the residential university. As a *Daily* editorial pointed out in October 1966, the OFF! campaign's quest for equal rights and recognition of the maturity of Stanford women raised a larger question: What was lacking in on-campus residential living that made it less attractive?[14]

That same October, Harris created the ASSU Housing Commission to examine all university housing "critically within the context of Stanford as an educational community—as a community with the responsibility and obligation to carry education from the classroom, from the library to the residence halls and houses." The year before, Harris' predecessor, Sandy Mackenzie, had insisted that the administration clarify its residential-university philosophy after the controversial announcement of closure of the popular Union as a women's residence. It appeared that Stanford was more concerned about office space, he said, than in fostering the Union, seen by many as the best example of Stanford's "hazy idea" of a full residential-academic experience for women. Housing decisions appeared ad hoc and student options a "hodge-podge." (Amid a housing shortage, rooms went empty at run-down dorms like Stern and Wilbur.) Mackenzie also insisted that students be added to the Academic Council's Undergraduate Education Committee, but that committee proved ineffectual.[15]

During four months of study by various subcommittees, the commission, led by Jan Jacobi, '67, and John Trimbur, '68, asked broad questions as well as the mundane, premised on the idea that housing students was not a landlord or parental relationship but part of the overall educational process. In what was considered an unprecedented move, an advisory committee set up by Associate Dean of Students Robert Gordon dissolved itself, accepting Jacobi's invitation to become part of the commission. Original commission co-chair Barry Ramsay became a member of the new SES subcommittee on Residence Programs & Policies.[16]

As early as 1962, ASSU President Armin Rosencranz had called for a coeducational

Senior Jan Jacobi (left) and junior John Trimbur co-chaired the ASSU Housing Commission, shepherding an influential four-month study of student housing options and goals for an ideal residential university. The report was published in full in the *Stanford Daily*, February 15, 1967.   STANFORD NEWS SERVICE

option on campus. The idea was based on more than wishful thinking. Students and faculty returning from Stanford's popular overseas studies centers had long praised their coeducational, academically inspired living arrangements. The overseas campuses also mixed lowerclassmen with older students and provided informal interaction among students, faculty, and guest scholars in what was essentially a theme-oriented house setting. (It is worth noting that Jacobi and Howell each attended the Stanford-in-Germany campus; Trimbur went to Stanford-in-France.)

On February 15, 1967, after months of study, the ASSU Housing Commission's 62-page report recommended a major reshuffling of university housing to allow freshmen to reside with upperclassmen, to offer numerous coeducational housing opportunities, and to encourage faculty-student interaction through residence-based seminars and theme-centered housing groups. With one notable exception, its recommendations were well received. Newly named Dean of Students Joel Smith, Robert Gordon, and Assistant Dean John Hanson were supportive. The SES Residence Programs subcommittee strongly endorsed specific dormitory rearrangements outright and encouraged submission of other student-initiated proposals.[17]

Even Jacobi, the commission's demanding co-chair, was pleased with the cooperative spirit represented in the months of hard work of students, faculty, and administrators who had produced the review. "I think all of us who have been involved in this process have been inspired by the vision of how significant change can be achieved at Stanford," Jacobi said. They had made a dramatic step, he concluded, toward more enjoyable, exciting, and academically inspiring residential living.[18]

The pragmatic details worked out by the university for the upcoming school year were not as all-encompassing as the commission hoped for—in part due to the cost of adapting dorms and the complexity of a new student "draw" system—but there was broad consensus on the direction.[19]

The university already had an experiment underway, echoing the size of overseas campus residences. In January 1967, 31 men and 12 women began to share the newly coeducational Grove House (the former Phi Delta Theta house, vacant after the fraternity was suspended) as an experiment in home-campus coeducational living.[20] By fall 1967, more than 520 students (of some 6,000 undergraduates) lived in coed housing, in Branner Hall (freshmen men and women lived in separate wings but shared lounge and dining facilities) and in two houses in Wilbur and two in Stern for students of all four classes.[21]

By spring 1968, the university's new housing draw offered coeducational opportunities in houses in Stern, Wilbur, Lagunita Court, and Roble for all class levels, for freshmen in Branner, and for upperclassmen in Lambda Nu. The non-residential eating clubs were already coeducational. Coed "thematic" houses, on international studies, community service, and creativity, also were offered. Single-sex options remained, in both dorms and fraternities, but coed living became the most popular choice.[22]

The bulk of the Housing Commission's February 1967 report met with enthusiastic reviews. The confrontational report of the subcommittee on fraternities was more difficult to process. This

Students at Grove House, after its January 1967 opening as Stanford's first campus coed housing unit. (The overseas campuses had been coeducational since 1958.) Seated on the floor is Phil Taubman, later editor of the *Stanford Daily*, a writer and editor at the *New York Times*, and a Stanford trustee.
STANFORD NEWS SERVICE

report, drafted by a firmly anti-fraternity member, called for an immediate official investigation by the Santa Clara County District Attorney into hazing incidents, accusing the Dean of Students Office of doing little to curb hazing, rush, and other anti-social behavior except when scandal was involved. It called for an independent board, appointed by the university president and Academic Council, to examine each fraternity over the next three years to decide if it should be allowed to stay on university property based on scholarship and faculty interaction, exclusivity of membership, and hazing. Also, all fraternities must immediately and publicly repudiate all racial and religious restrictions (at least 7 of the 24 fraternities remained all white). And, most controversial, it proposed that the next housing draw should fill 25 percent of each fraternity house with non-fraternity members.[23]

The report raised important questions, as even its fraternity-affiliated members and the Interfraternity Council (IFC) agreed. The 25 percent draw proposition seemed unlikely to make anyone happy. The tone of the report, however, hit a nerve. Letters to the *Daily* in response were unusually colorful. The *Daily*'s editor was counted among the "tireless soreheads, hippies, *Daily* writers, imbecile do-gooders" whom one Theta Chi member accused of trying to institute social conformity in the name of democracy. Others noted the impracticality of placing draw students in houses where they would likely not be welcome.[24]

The process behind the report had already raised questions when Jacobi dissolved the first committee. (The Interfraternity Council representative was accused of disagreeing with examination of fraternities from "our intended objective and thorough point of view.") On the report's presentation, some committee members complained that fact-finding questions were subjective, and the initial draft was rushed and not shown to all members. Opinions and draft edits not supported by the commission's anti-fraternity leadership had purposefully been left out, they said.[25]

The Interfraternity Council was already conducting its own study, backed by Joel Smith and

In fall 1968, Lambda Nu made headlines when it became the first Stanford fraternity to go coed, with 20 women accepted through the university's draw system. Lambda Nu, formerly Alpha Kappa Lambda, renounced its national affiliation in 1965.
STANFORD NEWS SERVICE

REFLECTIONS ON QUOTAS AND ANTISEMITISM AT STERLING'S STANFORD

In February 1953, Admissions Director Rixford Snyder noted his concern, in a conversation with presidential assistant Fred Glover, about the growing number of applications from two distinguished Southern California public high schools, Beverly Hills and Fairfax, known to have large numbers of Jewish students. Glover's background memo on this conversation was the impetus for a 2022 Stanford task force, led by Professor Ari Kelman, questioning Snyder's intent, and President Sterling's possible involvement. Given themes raised elsewhere in this book, the context of this era is worth a closer look.

The task force highlighted a sharp drop in male enrollment at Stanford from these two schools between 1952 and 1955. Whether this was due to a lack of recruiting visits (Snyder's intended plan) during those years, or to major expansions of nearby UCLA and USC, is unknown. The report also took Stanford to task for not recruiting directly at several elite New York high schools known to have large numbers of potential Jewish applicants, although at that time the university rarely recruited beyond the West Coast.

The impact of the drop in enrollees, modest from Beverly Hills but sharp from Fairfax, has been difficult to quantify. Stanford stopped asking for religious affiliation on application forms after 1950, making it difficult to compare later applications to acceptances. Estimates of Jewish student numbers at the time, based on self-identification of religious observance on campus questionnaires, ranged from around 5 percent in 1947 to 6.1 in 1952 and 6.8 in 1967. A 1965 survey estimated 9.2 to 10 percent of the freshman class were Jewish. (Jews within California's population, as in the U.S., remained around 3 to 4 percent.) This slight increase in Jewish enrollment occurred as the number of all applications mushroomed fivefold. As Stanford's undergraduate acceptance rate began its significant decline, complaints by disappointed parents increased dramatically.

Snyder appears to have left no documentation about his actual intent regarding Jewish admissions.

Whatever it was, the number of enrollees from Fairfax plummeted. Although no other public schools with significant Jewish student populations suffered the same effect, a long-standing and well-documented impression evolved within the Jewish community, particularly in Southern California, that Stanford had established a "Jewish quota" similar to those of its Ivy League role models. This belief lasted well into the 1970s. In response, three Anti-Defamation League investigations (in 1954, 1961, and 1966) were conducted, but no evidence of anti-Jewish bias was reported. Trustee President Richard Guggenhime (1964–67) unofficially raised the issue in 1966, but neither he nor predecessor Lloyd Dinkelspiel (1953–58), both prominent figures among San Francisco's Jewish community, suggested further action. While individual alumni registered concern, formal discussion among administrators, trustees, or relevant faculty bodies regarding the student body's religious and ethnic-racial makeup did not take place until the later 1960s.

Nor has documentation surfaced that Sterling responded to, encouraged, or discouraged Snyder's strategy of discontinuing informational visits to these or to any other public high schools. Glover's hastily written 1953 background memo was meant for a president heavily engaged elsewhere. At the time, Sterling was formulating the controversial move to campus of Stanford's medical school, including key faculty changes; overseeing the university's budding shopping center and industrial zone projects, mired in disagreements with Palo Alto; working with a new provost, Douglas Whitaker, who was floundering with Sterling's first curriculum review; and dealing with Academic Council demands for his attention on academic freedom issues as influential alumni pressed him about alleged Communists in the faculty ranks.

Sterling was no micromanager, relying on a small, trusted administrative team to carry out his overall goal for the university: to build an elite faculty and student body. Snyder, a friend from graduate student days, was just such a trusted team member. Sterling's instructions were simple, Snyder later recalled: he was to expand the number of applicants from *private* high schools while the president worked to increase Stanford's financial ability to attract top students and faculty.

Critics seemed surprised at Sterling's persistent contention that Stanford had no quota, or fixed proportion, for Jewish admissions. Yet Sterling generally opposed quotas. "A fixed percentage suggests 'quota,'" Sterling wrote, when the Physics Department placed a quota on graduate students at SLAC. "I am uneasy about quotas of any kind—not least of all because they are negative toward flexibility" *(see page 214).*

Stanford *did* have an admissions quota: for females. When enrollment of women had dropped to 14 percent in 1933, the Board of Trustees lifted Jane Stanford's 1899 "Stanford 500" numerical limitation. To regain balance, the board then set a 60:40 percent male to female quota (mimicking the estimated 1899 ratio). Despite this target, the percentage of women remained closer to 30; the official reason was the lack of housing for women on campus. (In 1973, with coeducational housing now providing more space for women, the trustees received court approval to end any female admissions quotas.)

Well into the 1960s, scholastic qualifications remained notably higher for female than male applicants and acceptance rates lower; selection standards were rigorous but confusing. Stories of angry parents of daughters, and at least one trustee incident *(see page 282),* were part of Admissions Office lore. So, too, were protests on behalf of star athletes left behind by increasingly selective male admissions.

It is doubtful Sterling would assume that suspending visits to public schools would discourage truly interested applicants, particularly in California, where Stanford had already built a strong reputation. As it turned to private school recruitment, Stanford continued to rely on alumni to promote interest in many suburban districts and left behind rural areas and less affluent urban school districts. Snyder, and Dean of Stu-

dents Donald Winbigler, reflected a prevailing consensus that emphasized "motivation, attitudes, character, and future potential as citizens" as essential attributes for potential admission. They shared with the university's generally conservative alumni, trustees, and donors a vision of America based on individualism, self-motivation, and a quantifiable meritocracy.

Stanford's selective self-promotion, particularly to private high schools, did, however, neglect another public-school demographic: Black and other minority students. The number of Black students, male and female, remained extremely low (two freshmen in 1960, seven in 1962), limited by narrow recruiting, geography, hesitancy to apply, and by racial bias in residential housing and extracurricular activity choices. This situation was fundamental to the Black Student Union protests explored in this chapter.

From the outset, the university was conceived as a residential (that is, not commuter) institution. As a residential campus, it was important, Snyder argued, "that students fit into our community environment." Since the 1920 start of undergraduate tuition, it was also a predominantly conservative, white, middle-class student community. Jewish undergraduates had historically played active roles at Stanford, and many, as influential alumni, strongly supported the residential concept. (Dinkelspiel, '20, for example, had been a popular student athlete and edited both the *Daily* and the *Quad.* He was a proud "Encina man" and member of the venerable Breakers Eating Club.) Sterling supported this alumni base who, as trustees, fundraising volunteers, and donors, worked to further improve Stanford's caliber. He also found long-standing friendships among them.

During the Sterling years, Jewish students were influential campus leaders, especially as ASSU officers, *Stanford Daily* editors, and residential advisors. As student activists during the 1960s, they influenced an awakening campus interest in civil rights, free speech, and the Vietnam War. They also compelled a major change, in 1964–66, in university policy regarding religious services *(see page 355),* recognizing for the first time that Jewish students desired specific religious facilities and other means of cultural support. These students, including ASSU President Armin Rosencranz and *Daily* Editor Ilene Strelitz, represented an array of Jewish identities, some secular, some observant, but they took action as part of the larger residential student community *(see Chapters 19–20)*.

For decades, men of the residence halls, not the fraternities, had the edge on campus political power. The attraction of the residential community model was reflected in the reluctance of influential Jewish alumni leaders to back establishment of a local chapter of the Jewish fraternity Alpha Epsilon Pi when, in the 1940s, chapters were being established elsewhere. Stanford Associates founding member Robert Levison, '21, recounted that he, Dinkelspiel, and Leon Sloss Jr., '20— all Encina men—viewed fraternities as "half baked" and discouraged the effort. (A chapter was established later, in 1989.) In 1944, after years of debate among women students, Stanford had disbanded its nine sorority chapters as divisive and undemocratic (there also were accusations of antisemitism). Stanford's 24 fraternities continued, but not without challenges.

By the 1950s, several Stanford fraternities, including Phi Sigma Kappa, Theta Delta Chi, Sigma Phi Epsilon, Sigma Nu, and Alpha Tau Omega (ATO), were pledging small numbers of non-Christian, non-white students, earning these Stanford chapters maverick reputations. The struggles of Stanford's ATO and Sigma Nu chapters to change their national organizations' membership bias, however, reflect the Sterling administration's reluctance to engage in broader social reform.

Earlier, ATO's few Jewish pledges went unnoticed, but four were pledged in 1960. In January 1961, ATO's national president stated his concern that the Stanford chapter soon would be composed entirely of non-Christians. The Stanford chapter was warned: depledge the four Jewish students or lose their charter. ATO's members refused. Determined to fight the national, they expected university backing. Years before, in 1957, the Interfraternity Council had condemned

discriminatory membership restrictions in national fraternity constitutions and bylaws, emphasizing the university's opposition (formalized by the Board of Trustees) to discriminatory racial and religious clauses and practices *(see pages 144–45)*. With 13 of 24 campus fraternities still abiding by "bias clauses," Dean of Men William G. Craig had leaned on local chapters to challenge their nationals, stating that the university "will work with students to eliminate them at the earliest date." However, Stanford's anti-discrimination policies, like its pledge to help its fraternities, had no review mechanism or means of enforcement.

Instead of backing the ATO chapter's protest, Sterling issued a January 31, 1961, statement complimenting the ATO chapter for defending its principles and encouraging members to remain active on campus as a local. If the chapter "must discriminate against members of the Jewish faith in order to keep its national charter in force," he wrote, "the chapter has no choice but to give up its charter." Although disheartened, ATO refused to back down, but two months later, the national revoked its charter.

The reluctance of the Sterling administration, and especially of Stanford trustees, to engage in broader antidiscrimination reforms had been highlighted by the 1957 controversy over NAACP requests that development contracts on Stanford lands include fair housing and fair employment clauses *(see pages 143–48)*. Despite support from faculty and local fair housing reform groups urging this moral stand, Sterling and the trustees refused to intervene where state and federal legislators, as yet, feared to go. While acknowledging the problem of *de facto* discrimination in surrounding towns, Sterling declined to engage in a public debate. The university must fight for equality as an educational institution, he responded. "Stanford has not been found wanting in the fight for tolerance on any front," Sterling wrote a disappointed faculty member, "but there are choices of methods and not everyone agrees on which is the proper one." (Trustee President Dinkelspiel supported this view.)

Without university cooperation, local fraternity

chapters like ATO had little leverage. In late 1962, Stanford's Sigma Nu chapter voted unanimously to withdraw from their national, following years of internal debate. Their chapter had been pledging Jewish students while trying, with alumni support, to convince its national to remove discriminatory membership clauses. In November 1962, the chapter went independent (as Beta Chi) and, like ATO (now Alpha Tau Omicron), continued to pledge Jewish and Black students.

ATO and Sigma Nu's actions were soon overshadowed by the more widely publicized efforts of Sigma Chi (1964) and Delta Tau Delta (1965), both interested in pledging talented Black student-athletes and both able to enlist more university support through long, but eventually successful, struggles with their nationals. As late as 1966, however, seven local chapters remained effectively segregated.

Leaving admissions to Snyder, Sterling and Provost Fred Terman took advantage of prevailing Ivy League antisemitism as early as 1955 to attract top faculty. Higher standards, broader searches, and a new emphasis on research had "an extra dividend," recalled one such professor, sociologist Sanford Dornbusch: they left less room for bias or discrimination to influence faculty appointments. However, it is unclear whether the administration fully understood the religious or cultural experience of this more diverse faculty. Dornbusch, who considered himself an ethnic Jew, was surprised when asked to join Sterling's committee to review the role of Memorial Church; he was especially surprised since Professor Herb Solomon, a religiously observant Jew, already had been appointed. "Perhaps they wanted breadth of representation in appointing such different Jews?" Dornbusch asked his colleague. No, responded Solomon, "they probably don't know there's any difference."

Sterling and Terman leveraged talented Jewish faculty with highly respected research records into departments known to be antisemitic. These shifts were done, Dornbusch related, without overt acknowledgment of such bias. But reactions from older faculty, many of whom had been at Stanford since the Depression, could

be passionate, especially when new faculty openly commented, however well-meaningly, on Stanford's upward trajectory. "The university that they had chosen, and that had chosen them, was no longer the same unruffled place," Dornbusch later commented. In some cases, unhappiness unraveled into overt antisemitism. The outspoken Dornbusch ran afoul of political science Professor Thomas Barclay, since 1927 a noted teacher beloved by many alumni. Barclay had no patience with this new crop of "prima donnas and wonder-boys who have rescued Stanford from academic oblivion, or think they have. . . ." Dornbusch did not mind the nasty letter he received from Barclay after he had commented on Stanford's latest improvements and the shedding of its former country-club image, but he did mind being dismissed, he later recalled, as a "New York Jew."

As the civil rights and antiwar movements progressed during the 1960s, some Jewish faculty who also served as administrators, including Herb Packer and Robert Rosenzweig, struggled with the rise of overt distrust among Black nationalist student activists. Stereotypes of wealthy, powerful Jews with easy access to a Stanford-type education mixed with suspicion of Jewish participation in more traditional biracial civil rights efforts. This new layer of antisemitism complicated reform efforts at the end of Sterling's presidency, described in this chapter, to introduce more diversity to Stanford's student body and to reevaluate undergraduate life through the Study of Education at Stanford. So, too, did the impatience of Stanford's new elite faculty to work with minority students who did not come from the "competitive norm." As the Sterling era closed, how Stanford might become more inclusive while retaining its concept of an elite student body remained to be seen.

SOURCES: The task force's extensive report, "*A Matter Requiring the Utmost Discretion*": *A Report from the Advisory Task Force on the History of Jewish Admissions and Experience at Stanford University* (September 2022), available online; Antonucci (2014); Barclay (1980) 34–35, [71–75]; Dornbusch (2007) 7; Dornbusch (2016); Levison (1983) 24–26; Rosenzweig (1984) 16–17, 25, 49; Rosenzweig (2010) 25–26; Snyder (1983) 29; *Stanford Daily*; and "What It Was Like" (2017).

By 1967, at least 7 of Stanford's 24 fraternities had clashed with their nationals after pledging Jewish or Black members. Delta Tau Delta's 1963 pledging of Black scholar and athlete Morrison Warren resulted in censure, not removal of its charter, due to strong alumni cooperation. Members included Jim Plunkett, Gene Washington, and Al Harris, here in 1968, the year Stanford's Interfraternity Council reiterated its 1957 ban on discrimination.   *STANFORD QUAD* 1968

John Hanson (who worked with the fraternities). The IFC recognized that the number of freshmen pledges was declining, and they now worried about "the thinking that Harris provoked." Changes to hazing and academic requirements were soon made simply because fraternities had to compete with the new residential options in a changing student environment. A new rush policy was quickly put into place, and even the function of IFC (as an event organizer, rather than a means of communication and problem-solving) was questioned.[26]

In 1957, the IFC had resolved that Stanford fraternities would "neither endorse nor condone religious or racial restrictions," noting that 13 of the 24 fraternities still had restrictive clauses in their national membership charters. The IFC reiterated this stand in May 1968, when it formally banned membership discrimination at all member fraternities and urged Stanford chapters to influence changes in the charters of their national organizations.[27]

ESCALATION
ANTIWAR PROTESTS, WINTER-SPRING 1967

By early 1967, local reaction to national events became the driver behind campus confrontations. Stanford's antiwar protests and counter-protests, vigils, and sit-ins had escalated through 1966 but had been relatively small, localized, and nonviolent. As U.S. bombing of North Vietnam ramped up use of napalm and as draft quotas continued to grow (U.S. troop deployment reached 500,000 in 1967), local efforts more effectively joined national strategies.

At a January rally organized by the Students for a Democratic Society (SDS) in White Plaza, David Harris argued that students had two choices: be drafted and serve the purposes of the war, or "save America from violence" by refusing to be drafted. The war would end only when "we, the conscriptees, refuse to be cannon fodder anymore." Protests had changed little, he said. Personal example was the only alternative. "It may jolt America when a lot of middle-class sons choose jail rather than military service." Harris had turned in his II-S deferment and was already classified as I-A by his draft board, awaiting his graduation. He would rather go to jail, he stated, than accept military service. (True to his word, he later served 20 months in federal prison, 1969–70, for draft evasion.)[28]

Vice President Hubert H. Humphrey, who carried the load of public appearances for the Johnson administration, was accustomed to demonstrations. But his appearance at Stanford, on February 20, 1967, was among the first to show a potential for campus violence, and foreshadowed serious disruptions at the university as the American war effort intensified.[29]

Humphrey was the speaker at an open forum of students that morning in Memorial Auditorium, the third in a series of "Focus on the Great Society in America," sponsored by the Political Union. Nearly 2,000 filled the auditorium to capacity, with more than 1,000 listening on loudspeakers in adjacent plazas. Initially, roughly half of the audience stood in silent protest as Humphrey began speaking. Some 60 people conspicuously walked out at the end of his opening remarks, and an estimated 180 walked out later, but in general the vice president's remarks were politely received. He was given a standing ovation by

A volunteer attached a white armband to a student entering Memorial Auditorium for the February 1967 talk by U.S. Vice President Hubert Humphrey. A peaceful anti–Vietnam War protest called on Stanford community members to object to the Johnson administration's escalation of the war. The sign instructed: *If You Oppose the War, 1. Wear a white arm band, 2. Maintain silence— don't applaud, don't boo, 3. Join the walk-out.* STANFORD NEWS SERVICE

the other half of the crowd, amid more than 800 others who remained silent, wearing white armbands to show their support for peaceful withdrawal from Vietnam.[30]

Trouble arose as Humphrey left Memorial Auditorium to walk to his limousine, parked nearby on Galvez Street. Provost Richard Lyman, at the event, thought the Secret Service changed plans abruptly, trying to trick protesters by having Humphrey use a rear exit. The result was a rush to catch up with him, with a good deal of running and shouting by both sides, but the antiwar demonstrators' shouts of "shame, shame, shame" and "murderer" stood out. Several protesters tried to crash through the cordon of police; another threw himself under the front wheel of Humphrey's car but was dragged back by a policeman.[31]

Stanford's administrators later concluded that the Secret Service was a significant part of the problem. "We were not adequately prepared for . . . the possibility of mob reaction outside the building, with its ominous potential," Sterling wrote a former president of the Stanford Alumni Association. "In part this was because the Secret Service made it clear that it was their responsibility to get the Vice President into and away from the building; Stanford was in charge inside the building only. We may have relied too much on the Secret Service."[32]

National news coverage, particularly through United Press International wire service, exaggerated the disruption, suggesting that a riot had ensued.[33] Two days after the event, the *Washington Post* editorialized, "No group of critics has the right to send their roughnecks, rowdies and storm troopers into the streets or meeting rooms to intimidate those with whom they do not agree."

> The Stanford students deserve reproach because they were threatening the second-ranking constitutional officer of the Republic, and that is indefensible enough. But they deserve it, in addition, because their disorderly behavior is the typical anti-intellectual response to orderly discussion. It is the kind of violent intervention in disciplined debate that the world grew accustomed to in Germany during the rise of Nazism. The first resort of a sterile anti-intellectual fringe in a country is to rowdyism.[34]

Vice President Humphrey spoke at a forum in Memorial Auditorium. The crowd inside had been quiet (including a dramatic walk-out of some 240 people), but the Secret Service became anxious about the gathering out back, as Humphrey walked to his limousine on Galvez Street. An ensuing scuffle made headlines as "a riot."
STANFORD NEWS SERVICE

Sterling had already issued a public apology to Humphrey immediately after the incident. "Stanford regrets this incident," he said, "and offers its apology to the Vice-President for any inconvenience or embarrassment that it may have caused him." He downplayed the unsuccessful attempt of protesters to impede Humphrey's departure, noting that the convocation at which he spoke "was orderly and consistent with the tradition of free expression in a university community."

Still troubled, Sterling also wrote an open letter on March 3 to students, faculty, and staff, to clarify the events surrounding Humphrey's visit and to express "deep concern for the preservation of free and civilized debate on the Stanford campus." He asked: "If Stanford University cannot provide assurance, not only of courtesy but of basic physical safety, to visiting speakers, no matter how controversial their subject and opinions, can we in conscience continue to invite speakers to the campus?" Sterling felt strongly that "the basic purpose of the University would be in jeopardy if intimidation or obstruction were permitted to threaten fair discussion. I want to express my resolution to ensure that intimidation or obstruction will not be tolerated."[35]

While there was a lack of consensus about what really happened, Sterling said, there was agreement about the "threatening degree of anger among many in the crowd" that gathered on Galvez Street. He warned that "the ease with which a crowd, in the sway of strong emotion, can be transferred into an ugly and dangerous mob . . . has apparently been overlooked by a disturbingly large number of people."

Sterling's March 3 statement went largely unnoticed until Humphrey, on March 6, added to the media uproar by describing the demonstrators to *U.S. News & World Report* as "hooligans—just a group of ruffians who decided to exercise their protest in a violent and unsavory manner. . . . They rushed at us, threw urine, which they have saved up, on the police, called out dirty names." The magazine surmised that the incident had taken place because of Stanford's "recent relaxation of school rules" on student discipline, drinking, and dorm activities, adding that no disciplinary action against those involved in the Humphrey incident was planned.[36]

The *Stanford Daily* directly challenged Humphrey's *U.S. News* description. The editors sent Humphrey a March 7 telegram calling his comments "blatant factual errors," and insisting that he confirm or deny the statements attributed to him. Humphrey subsequently minimized Stanford's role. Rather than respond directly to the telegram, however, he sent the *Daily* a copy of his subsequent letter to the editor of *U.S. News & World Report*. "In fairness to the vast majority of students at Stanford and to the administration of that great University, it is important to know that the 'hooliganism' during my visit was not organized by Stanford students. There were no students among the ring-leaders," Humphrey stated, although this, too, was without clear evidence. "This is a developing pattern of off-campus militant irresponsibility stirring up legitimate student concerns," he said. The students in the audience were attentive, courteous, and "willing to listen," he added. "I was afforded every consideration by President Wallace Sterling and his administration who did everything possible to make my visit worthy of the best traditions of Stanford."[37]

A group of about 35 students (and at least one lecturer) described by the *Daily* simply as "long opposed to the war" marched to the President's Office with signs saying: "You Owe Us, Not Humphrey, An Apology," and "We Are Not Non-Students." They demanded that Sterling publicly repudiate Humphrey's allegations that the February 20 outside protesters were violent hooligans led by non-student ringleaders. Lyman met with several of them, stating that Sterling (who was sick at home) could not be blamed for Humphrey's description and that the Secret Service had not shared their report. He reiterated that any display of force or intimidation, including lying in front of a car, had no place on campus. Meanwhile, many other students asked the President's Office for copies of Sterling's March 3 letter to send home to parents.[38]

Humphrey also sent a belated response to Sterling's personal apology: "Men in public office get used to these little embarrassments. I am concerned, however, lest the incident in any way damaged the good and well-deserved reputation of Stanford." Humphrey concluded by saying he hoped someday to return to Stanford and invited Sterling to call on him if he visited Washington, D.C.[39]

Humphrey's reappraisal did little to stop letters, particularly from alumni, critical of Stanford's alleged soft handling of the event. A prominent San Jose lawyer warned, "The image of Stanford has changed to the point where not one but many of our clients have changed their Wills and removed Stanford as a partial or total beneficiary. For the same reasons I have ceased to contribute to either the University or the law department of which I am a graduate."[40] Another law alumnus, Judge Stanley R. Evans of the Santa Clara County Superior Court, told Sterling, "I have been disappointed that acts of impatience, selfishness, and intolerance, which result in a violation of law, have not been the subject of greater criticism and control, particularly by other university administrators and faculty members."[41]

On campus, a new source of Sterling administration critics—lecturers, research associates, and younger, non-tenured faculty members—also was growing. A lecturer in English wrote Sterling, "In truth, I find it deplorable that you can apologize in the name of the University when many of us feel we owe the Vice President no apology. Many of your faculty members are quite proud to have vigorously joined . . . in our

protests. It is this group of faculty which do your University most credit."[42]

Sterling remained consistent: "If any campus speaker, regardless of his subject or performance, can be physically intimidated in such a way by individuals claiming a higher morality or any other motivation," Sterling wrote a protesting Psychology Department research associate, "the way is then open for any other group to act as it pleases in the name of whatever cause it espouses. The role of a university is not to indict campus speakers who come as our guests, but to preserve an atmosphere of freedom and safety in which they can speak."[43]

HARRIS PRESIDENCY ABBREVIATED
THE TURN-OVER BEGINS

To the surprise of many, a week after release of the Housing Commission's report and the day after Humphrey's controversial visit, David Harris resigned his ASSU presidency. "All the motivation for me being student body president, all the things I had hoped to say, I've said," he stated. "I have done all I am capable of doing for the realization of education at Stanford."[44]

Harris intended to devote himself to organizing resistance to the draft. A month later, he and three colleagues (housemate Dennis Sweeney, and Lennie Heller and Steve Hamilton of Berkeley) co-founded the Resistance as part of the national draft-resistance movement.[45]

His stepping down, four months before the end of his term, was as controversial as his candidacy. "Apathetic acceptance seems to characterize many student reactions to Dave Harris's resignation," reported the sympathetic *Daily*. Was he wrong to give up on a job before finishing it, as some students complained, or was he justified since, as others said, student apathy and the administration's prejudices prevented him from reaching his goals? What were those goals, and were they the

Alumnus and former ASSU President David Harris, '67, joined a group burning draft cards at a White Plaza rally, November 14, 1968. Students had gathered, despite the cold, to listen to David Harris, among others, as they invited young men to cast their "votes" for humanity by burning their Selective Service cards. Eight men followed, casting their cards into a broken Army helmet.
STANFORD NEWS SERVICE

goals of the student body or of a small, organized in-group dubbed "the establishment"?[46]

"By calling him a prophet or saying that his mission was through, you're giving him more charisma than I think he deserved," commented an unconvinced undergraduate. "I don't think a great number of people really care," commented Stern Hall's faculty resident, Robert Freelen. "Harris's resignation came at a time when there's more hope for change than ever before with the promotions of Provost Lyman and Dean Smith and the initiation of the Packer Committee," noted Freelen. He did not think the progress of education would be impeded. "We've never had a time of greater discussion or opposing opinions, but still too few are involved."[47]

Harris left a response to the questions he believed he had raised "in the hands of the community," effectively, those of his vice president Michael Collins, '66, and the ASSU commissioners. Collins agreed that educational reform remained foremost, but he believed the student-power angle was anachronistic. *In loco parentis* was reaching its end, even among administrators, Collins, now ASSU president, argued. He added that the real possibility for change lay with the Study of Education at Stanford. Students must participate fully, laying the groundwork for a community-based model of what the university should be. In addition to ASSU commission work already underway, he sought to get more students involved through weekend seminars to augment SES.[48]

THE EXPERIMENT
"WE ACCUSE"

On April 13, 1967, six weeks after the Humphrey incident and Harris' departure, a crowd gathered in White Plaza for an antiwar rally organized by members of the Experiment, an ASSU-sponsored student organization, as part of a national week-long Spring Mobilization for Peace. Subsequently, an estimated 65 people, joined by some 75 high school students, marched to the Stanford Research Institute in Menlo Park to protest its alleged role in research on classified weapons and chemical warfare. Counter-protesters (among them, the Stanford Young Republicans, the Ad Hoc Group for Equal University Treatment, and the Concerned Students for Responsible Debate) gained little traction trying to speak at the April 13 rally, but

A 1967 nationwide Spring Mobilization for Peace included, at Stanford, an April 13 White Plaza rally and march by university and local high school students (here down El Camino Real) to the Stanford Research Institute in Menlo Park. Sterling and GSB Dean Ernie Arbuckle, then chair of the SRI board, were among six leaders that the students accused of being complicit in war crimes, including weapons development. (Insets in the posters are photos of the Vietnam War.)
STANFORD NEWS SERVICE

continued to snipe at the Experiment and the SDS along the protest route.[49]

The Experiment—literally an experimental creation of an anti–status quo community where students and faculty were to be equal—had been founded, with Barry Greenberg as coordinator, the previous fall quarter. It was initially an effort at educational reform, an unstructured and highly personalized alternative to what was described as Stanford's pragmatic, materialistic, corporate-liberal ideology based on usefulness. Endorsed by Harris and the ASSU, the Experiment's classes, and especially its digs in the former Western Civ Library, provided hundreds of students a chance to "find themselves" and enjoy temporary respite from "the pressure to get high grades."[50]

A significant majority of the Experiment's members were not politically engaged, but its premise that "everything is basically wrong" provided a welcome environment for campus New Left activists. Members had been involved in the outdoor protest of Humphrey's speech; the march to demand Sterling's apology had stemmed from a meeting there.

The April 13 antiwar White Plaza rally included a new motif: a "trial." A series of six "We Accuse" posters appeared at the rally and elsewhere on campus. The six—President Sterling, GSB Dean Ernie Arbuckle, and four individual trustees—were accused of complicity in war crimes.[51]

The Experiment soon found itself defending its ASSU funding, along with its moral authority. SDS and Stanford Anti-Draft Union spokesman Leonard Siegel, a freshman member of the Experiment who was involved in the posters' production, explained that it was not personal: "they are men in power, and their power supports the war." Other members of the Experiment, however, asserted that the posters did not truly represent their organization, but were the effort of a very small percentage of their group. Nev-

ertheless, the fragile organization was losing the support of formerly sympathetic, if less radical, students. "They conducted themselves," concluded one former supporter, "with all the educated political dexterity, articulation, and aplomb of an Alabama lynch-mob." In June, the Experiment, already strained by lack of cohesion and faculty support and about to lose its free space, merged with the Free University of Palo Alto.[52]

In spring 1967, David Harris and Michael Collins characterized contrasting approaches to student power. Was ASSU merely a "company union" and the administration a "mechanistic authority," as Harris argued, and student autonomy the ultimate goal? Or, as Collins held, were students part of a complex community ready and able to engage in broad educational questions?

Collins' successor as president for 1967–68 was Peter Lyman, a 27-year-old graduate student interested in political theory, not political battles. The soft-spoken Lyman (no relation to the provost) was idealistic, almost ethereal. He quickly concluded that ASSU was "a hollow bureaucratic process" incapable of representing the intellectual

ASSU Vice President Michael Collins (left), who filled out the remainder of Harris' term (February-June 1967) as president, preferred a more pragmatic, collaborative approach to move ahead on reforms. Peter Lyman, a graduate student in political theory, was elected ASSU president for 1967–68 but resigned in frustration in November 1967.   STANFORD NEWS SERVICE

ASSU Vice President Cesare Massarenti became the first foreign student to serve as president when he took over for Peter Lyman, November 1967. He enjoyed leading student-administration skirmishes and antiwar protests. He was perhaps the first student body president to be censured in a referendum.
STANFORD NEWS SERVICE

community. He was annoyed that SES did not favor his concept of community government (a joint faculty-student senate), although he also promoted the idea of student government legally and financially independent of the university. Struggling to gain student support and losing momentum with SES, he recalled Harris' advice: "When it gets too deep, you can always quit." He did so in November 1967. Unfortunately, a number of important university advisory committees had just opened up to student members, and recommendations for these and other advisory committees and SES committees were yet to be made. In Provost Richard Lyman's view, the lack of continuity made it difficult to work constructively with student government.[53]

Peter Lyman's vice president and successor, sociology graduate student Cesare Massarenti, 26, was a stark contrast. Massarenti had had considerable student government experience at his alma mater in his native Milan. The multilingual Italian activist and politician was likely the first foreign student to serve as student-body president. He was a talented musician and had been determined, as vice president, to bring more cultural opportunities to provincial Stanford. Unlike his predecessor, who avoided conflict, he

was more than willing to lead antiwar protests as well as ASSU-administration skirmishes. He was also considered abrupt, even flamboyant. With the purpose of ASSU in doubt among students, and the status of the judicial process still uncertain, even supporters worried that his greatest challenge was to build trust and to involve the student body broadly, formally and informally, in whatever university mechanisms were available.[54]

THE CIA PROTEST, NOVEMBER 1967

As the numbers of silent protesters in the Humphrey audience revealed, a broader spectrum of the Stanford community was deeply concerned about the draft and escalation of the war than was represented by SDS protesters.

Proposed revisions in the nation's 1967 Draft Act made it clear that both Congress and the Johnson administration aimed to drop II-S student deferments for registered graduate students by 1968. Provost Lyman protested the move on Walter Cronkite's prime-time *CBS Evening News*, which had reported that some 85 percent of Stanford's law students, for example, would be subject to the draft. In late April 1967, 169 students signed an ad in the *Stanford Daily* saying they would not fight in Vietnam if drafted. Three-quarters of the signatories also stated that they would not allow themselves to be drafted. This was followed, on May 24, with another *Daily* ad signed by more than 75 faculty and teaching staff supporting student draft resistance.[55]

Throughout October 1967, protests were staged around the country to shut down or slow the process of inducting U.S. Army draftees and to protest American involvement in Vietnam. "Stop the Draft Week" (October 16–20) resulted in demonstrations in places as diverse as Oakland and Wichita, Kansas. On the last day of the week, more than 100,000 protesters staged a

demonstration in Washington, D.C., organized by the National Mobilization Committee to End the War in Vietnam. An estimated 30,000 later marched to the Pentagon, staging an all-night vigil. Clashes with soldiers and police resulted in 647 arrests.

With Central Intelligence Agency job interviews set for November 1–2, Stanford officials, as a precaution, moved the interviews from the Placement Service to Encina Hall, now a major administration building housing the university's business, planning, and financial offices. (Two weeks before, at the University of Wisconsin, a protest against recruiters from Dow Chemical, a maker of napalm, turned violent when police used tear gas to disperse the crowd, with many injuries.) On the first day of Stanford's interviews, members of SDS and the Resistance blocked access to Encina's West Wing, where three of the first day's six interviews were held. (Dean Joel Smith subsequently locked the door, further limiting access.) About two dozen protesters had managed to get inside, including through the outside fire escape. From there, they stomped on the floor of the room above to disrupt the interviewer. But many of the approximately 100 protesters stayed on the front lawn, talking and singing. The second day's protest was called off when few demonstrators showed up. The recruiter had

Protests were staged around the country in October 1967 as part of "Stop the Draft Week" to shut down or slow the process of inducting U.S. Army draftees and to protest American involvement in Vietnam. At the Oakland Induction Center, Stanford students and faculty were among protesters blocking incoming buses of inductees. David Harris (lower photo) was among the protest leaders.   BOB FITCH PHOTO ARCHIVE / STANFORD UNIVERSITY ARCHIVES

an easier time with his 12 interviews, but on both days about half the interview slots had been reserved by SDS members.[56]

The short-lived occupation was not considered particularly successful by either side.

However, there had been verbal confrontations with the interviewer, minor physical damage to the building, and unlawful entry. Ten students, including two already on probation, were charged later that month by Dean Smith with violating the University Policy on Campus Demonstrations. Smith referred the case to the Student Judicial Council (SJC), asking it to act expeditiously, but did not press for any particular disciplinary action. The SJC initially refused to hear the cases. The council would not be forced, chairman John Raskin told Smith, to punish fellow students for actions it perceived not in violation of the Fundamental Standard.[57]

The SJC reconsidered when Smith appealed the decision to the all-faculty Interim Judicial Board (IJB), chaired by law Professor Howard Williams. A six-month crime-and-punishment tug-of-war was now underway.

Complicating matters was a recent action by the Associated Students' legislature (LASSU) that had ruled the IJB illegitimate, ending the 1965 temporary judicial formula worked out after the Morse case and Allen affair *(see Chapter 19)*. Smith, backed by the administration, refused to recognize LASSU's ruling as being retroactive, much less relevant. "The state of the student judicial system is a mess," concluded the *Daily* only a month into the crisis. "The root of the problem is mistrust on both sides. Students want the right to be heard by their peers. The administration, on the other hand, wants to make sure infractions of their rules are punished and are not sure students can be trusted to do it."[58]

The Committee of 15 (C-15), set up in 1965, had formulated an acceptable appeals process but despite widespread agreement that the proposed

On the first day of CIA job recruitment, November 1, 1967, members of SDS and the Resistance blocked access to Encina Hall West Wing, where interviews were to be held. About two dozen protesters managed to get inside, including English Professor H. Bruce Franklin, who later talked to some of the 100 who relaxed on Encina's front lawn. Over two days, the recruiter completed about 15 interviews, including some SDS members who had registered for slots. Proposed suspensions led to the May 1968 Old Union sit-in.   STANFORD NEWS SERVICE

joint student-faculty appeals board must be launched, C-15 had yet to negotiate a satisfactory means for its faculty- and student-member selection. How much longer would an "interim" board, with no student representation, be in place? C-15 was an unusual and widely respected joint faculty-student-administration advisory committee created, said its first chair, Professor Philip Rhinelander, to "put oil rather than sand in the gears." Its portfolio was to tackle thorny, even explosive issues. Now, it, too was being questioned.[59]

As 1968 opened, the IJB handed the CIA protest cases back to the SJC, hoping to encourage student participation in disciplinary matters. It would take more than three months for the cases to work their way, again, through both councils, igniting yet another major protest in May.[60]

In the meantime, another protest, years in the making, occurred in April 1968. Several Black students who had participated in antiwar protests turned to more immediate concerns, joining others among Stanford's small Black community to fight campus racism through the Black Student Union. The movement for student empowerment, Black activist Leo Bazile later recalled, had led to "self-awareness among African-American students, and a greater determination among students to apply the skills acquired at Stanford within their home communities."[61]

CATALYST FOR CHANGE
THE BLACK STUDENT UNION, 1968

While antiwar feeling ran high over the 1967–68 academic year, and as the cases of those involved in the November 1967 Encina CIA protest made their way through the university's judicial system, a major reform effort emerged that was equally influenced by external events: Stanford's approach to attracting and retaining minority students, faculty, and staff. Linked in the public mind to the antiwar and anti-university student protests, the efforts of the Black Student Union (BSU) to change Stanford's white, upper-middle-class persona were independent and highly focused. The reforms embodied in their

Dr. Martin Luther King Jr.'s second speech at Stanford, in April 1967, brought more media attention, drawn by his broadening critique of American poverty and the Vietnam War, and underscored the tense balance between his nonviolent approach and growing student interest in Black Nationalism.
STANFORD NEWS SERVICE

10 demands of April 1968 relied on the continued existence, not destruction, of the university to accomplish their goals.

On Thursday, April 4, 1968, Dr. Martin Luther King Jr. was assassinated in Memphis, Tennessee. That night, Provost Lyman condemned King's murder as a "vicious and deadly blow struck at the heart of mankind. . . . We at Stanford join a sickened and disheartened world in mourning his death." LASSU, condemning American society at large for the assassination, called on Sterling to cancel classes the next Monday, and the BSU called for a student boycott of classes by "all sympathizers and especially Black students as a show of our disgust and our resolve."[62]

On Friday, an overflow crowd of more than 2,400 attended a noon service in Memorial Church featuring a sermon by former Freedom Rider and religion Professor Robert McAfee Brown, "Grieve Not for Dr. King, Grieve for a Nation Torn." Paralleling the grief, frustration, and anger breaking out in cities across the country, about 400 attended a BSU rally at which an American flag was burned. Later that afternoon, more than 2,000 marched from downtown Palo Alto to the steps of the Quadrangle, where they heard B. Davie Napier, dean of the chapel, deliver a tribute.[63]

Campus reaction varied far more than these newsworthy events suggest, ranging from agony to a good deal of apathy, reported the *Daily*'s Philip Taubman (a future *New York Times* Washington bureau chief). In one freshman house, "some students cheered when they heard of King's death and followed up with a food fight at dinner," he wrote. Fraternities, wrapping up Rush Week, held their open houses without comment. "When asked whether his fraternity thought of cancelling its program, one member at Kappa Alpha remarked, 'I've heard of mourning, but you don't cancel open houses for it.'" A tutor at Wilbur Hall told Taubman, "There's

a cancer in our society and I was too ill after hearing to even eat dinner." However, he added, "members of the house didn't seem concerned about King." On the other hand, when the news of King's assassination came over the radio, one girl in Grove House ran from her room into the street "with tears running down her cheeks." Dinner discussion at Grove House was subdued "as most people quietly talked about King and possible repercussions this summer."[64]

Belying its pioneer years, when working-class students and those needing special admissions opportunities were welcome, Stanford was and had long been a white, middle- and upper-middle-class university. Its few Black students were isolated. In 1964, the incoming freshman class of about 1,200 included 10 Black students (up from 2 in 1960). A mid-1960s effort to attract applications from targeted high schools brought the numbers up somewhat, to 22 freshmen in 1965 and 37 in 1967. By fall 1967, 148 total Black undergraduate and graduate students were enrolled (just over one percent of the student body), along with an estimated 282 other minority students.[65]

Stanford, in 1968, was still trying to find the right path. Earlier, in 1964, a Committee on Educational Opportunities for Disadvantaged Minorities was created to study, quietly and without publicity, what role the university might play in fostering racial equality. But little was done beyond admitting more students from among the same recruiting pool as before—top students from top high schools, a pool of candidates also sought by Stanford's peers.[66]

As Richard Lyman later observed, "The university that had contributed the largest contingent of volunteers to 'Mississippi Summer' [in 1964] was certainly not leading the way at home."[67] While some faculty and administrators were clearly committed to civil rights and social justice, and many in Stanford's predominantly white student body at least sympathized, the

On April 5, 1968, the day following Dr. Martin Luther King Jr.'s assassination, more than 2,000 community members from Stanford, Palo Alto, and East Palo Alto (seen here at the Oval) joined hands for a silent walk from downtown Palo Alto to the Quad steps. Earlier, an overflow crowd, including Sterling, paid tribute to King at a noon service at Memorial Church.   STANFORD NEWS SERVICE

presence of Black and other students of color barely registered.[68] "You were supposed to almost blend in, to the point of disappearing," recalled Joyce King, '69, Ph.D. '74. "There were Black students ahead of me who did that. I was concerned about those I would leave behind."[69]

Jean McCarter Leonard, '57, a Cap and Gown member who would graduate Phi Beta Kappa, wasn't thinking of blending in when she tried out to be a pom-pom girl. Although she was an accomplished dancer and did well at her tryout, she was told by a dean that alumni were simply not ready for a Negro pom-pom girl, she later recalled; it was not fellow students but staff and faculty who made her feel different. (On arriving in fall 1953 as one of only two Black students, she was assigned a single room at Roble, despite requesting a roommate, because, she was told, parents might not appreciate their white daughter having a Negro roommate.) It would take decades for well-meaning administrators and faculty who did not think of themselves as racist to move beyond naively assuming that "if you just admitted students, the rest would take care of itself," recalled Ray Bacchetti, a young assistant dean of humanities and sciences, and later assistant provost, in the 1960s.[70]

The Study of Education at Stanford was the first formal effort to grapple with the university's understanding of what its student body might be and what kind of education was most relevant. One element was the place of minority students within that community. The April 2, 1968, Interim Report of its subcommittee on Minority-Group Students at Stanford (Clebsch Report) acknowledged that Stanford culture was not supportive of those who did not fit what was considered the "competitive norm." (The report said nothing about those Black students who had heretofore clearly fit in academically, but who had been isolated by their racial difference.)[71]

Committee discussion was heavily influenced

by the assumption that more robust minority admission would challenge, if not threaten, Stanford's reputation as a highly competitive academic environment that groomed the country's best students. With so much of Stanford devoted to graduate instruction and research, the report explained, many faculty members had little time or inclination to help undergraduates who might have academic or social problems. "To recruit to this community students who can be expected to have extreme problems of academic and social adjustment would be cruel, fruitless, and self-defeating," it added condescendingly.[72]

Although the report proposed financial aid priority for minority students at Stanford, its authors admitted that "for most of its history, Stanford's record in the education of students who are outside the mainstream of white, middle-class America leaves much to be desired. In the last three years, the record has improved to the point where it can now be characterized as merely bad." Stanford might be getting the best students, "but they are the best of only a partial universe. . . . We are convinced that the talent exists and that it can be found. . . . Moreover, the education of our white students requires that they have greater opportunity for contact with Black students." How those students would be made to feel an integral part of Stanford was not explored.[73]

The answer came from student initiative. While at an East Palo Alto event in late 1966, Gene Washington, then an up-and-coming sophomore Stanford football star, had been struck by the desire of Ravenswood High School students to talk with a Black collegiate athlete. Soon after, Washington and fellow varsity football player Ron Miller, '67, initiated the student group Interact to provide role models for East Palo Alto youth and to raise money for scholarships. They also hoped to bring Stanford's Black students together for mutual support and ease the tension

Anthropology Professor James L. Gibbs Jr., an expert on African law and society and Stanford's first Black tenured faculty member, was the Black Student Union's first faculty advisor. Gibbs, seen here in 1969, helped found African and Afro-American Studies, became the first dean of undergraduate studies, and later chaired the Anthropology Department.
STANFORD NEWS SERVICE

of adjusting for new students who, like Miller and Washington, had come from largely Black communities.[74]

In October 1967, Interact was succeeded by the Black Student Union, with anthropology Professor James Gibbs, Stanford's first Black tenured faculty member, as its faculty advisor.[75]

The BSU's goals were similarly multi-dimensional. While building unity among Black students on campus, the BSU worked closely with nearby East Palo Alto (then about 65 percent Black), particularly as mentors and tutors at Ravenswood High School.[76] As Ken (Keni) Washington, '68, later recounted: "We saw ourselves as well beyond Stanford, as a national and possibly global movement."[77]

As civil rights activities broadened in 1964, some students volunteered close to home by tutoring Ravenswood High School students. BSU members, particularly in the School of Education, lobbied as early as 1967 to take over in East Palo Alto, arguing they could better empathize with the students.
STANFORD NEWS SERVICE

Many, especially graduate student members studying in Stanford's School of Education, had experience working with the East Palo Alto community. The BSU pressed the administration to allow them to take over Stanford's tutoring program at Ravenswood, arguing that Black students had a personal understanding of social, cultural, and economic issues faced by East Palo Alto students, unlike the program's white volunteer tutors.[78]

The BSU was also determined to build cultural recognition and awareness within Stanford's distinctly white environment. They began a campus speaker series on a range of Black viewpoints, including Black power advocate Ron Karenga and a panel discussion, "Is White Education Relevant to Black People?" An array of programs was planned for an African American Arts week later in April.[79] Otherwise, the Black Student Union largely shunned publicity about its activities, keeping internal disagreements quiet and distrusting the *Stanford Daily* to accurately report its viewpoints.[80]

Ken Washington, Charles Countee, and others had developed connections with similar organizations at other Bay Area campuses, particularly at San Francisco State (the first Black Student Union organization), and with Black Panther Party leadership in Oakland. The tense balance between Black Nationalism and respect for Dr. King's nonviolent approach, particularly after his refocus on poverty and denunciation of the Vietnam War, reflected members' varying perspectives. Yet while King's second and last speech at Stanford, in April 1967, may have impressed white liberal and activist students more than some future BSU members, as Washington later recalled, Dr. King remained a respected figure of integrity and courage.[81]

In contrast to the university's ambivalent support of student and faculty interest in the 1964 Mississippi Freedom Summer, in spring 1968,

three academic departments supported a BSU effort to send 30 students as observers in Dr. Martin Luther King's "Poor People's Mobilization," scheduled for April 22. But that project came to a confused halt with King's April 4 murder.[82]

"I could not understand how the message that Dr. King brought could have ended up with his being assassinated," recalled Mary Montle Bacon, M.A. '71, Ph.D. '78. "But I think it was more of a question of a loss of hope that there was any possibility that we were going to make substantive change unless we as individuals decided that we [would] become actively involved in the level that we could." Bacon, who participated in the Poor People's Campaign organized by King and the Southern Christian Leadership Conference, would be among those who took the stage for the historic campus event later labeled "Taking the Mic."[83]

TAKING THE MIC, APRIL 1968

On Monday, April 8, a capacity audience of 1,700 filled Memorial Auditorium for a campus assembly, "Stanford's Response to Racism," to illuminate issues raised by King's assassination. Kenneth Prewitt, visiting assistant professor of political science, who had organized the program with his Student Involvement Team of Stanford University, expected to formulate an action plan that would address both local and broad goals: Black student admissions and employment policies, as well as university influence on public policy, land use policy, investment policy, and relations with the Black community.[84]

As Provost Richard Lyman began his remarks, BSU members, joined by East Palo Alto Day School students and members of Mothers for Equal Education, walked onto the Memorial Auditorium stage. (Some sort of group action was expected; the *Daily*'s front-page description of the day's planned events noted reports of a

Four days after King's murder, graduate student Frank Satterwhite, joined by BSU members and others, read demands for increased minority enrollment and other issues at a Memorial Auditorium discussion. Provost Richard Lyman and professors C. Kenneth Prewitt, Robert McAfee Brown, and Kenneth Arrow were on the stage for what has come to be known as "Taking the Mic."   STANFORD NEWS SERVICE

possible demonstration with demands.) BSU leader Ken Washington took the microphone from Lyman's hand. It was time, Washington declared, "to put your money and action where your mouth is."[85]

Ken Washington later noted that he did not doubt Lyman's sympathy, but King's death had galvanized them to take action. He turned the mic over to Omowale (Frank) Satterwhite, Ph.D. '77, a School of Education grad student, to read the list of 10 carefully composed demands, challenging the university to prove its sincerity. "We knew we had to do this carefully. We had to do it deliberately and effectively," said Washington. "We had one shot at that as far as we were concerned."[86]

Many of the issues covered by the demands were not new. BSU leadership had been negotiating with the administration throughout the pre-

vious year for reforms in admissions, treatment of staff, recruitment of faculty, housing issues, and financial aid, but little had changed. The SES subcommittee on Minority-Group Students at Stanford, which had been working throughout the school year, suggested important structural changes to recruit, admit, and support minority students. But the April 2 report's content was not generally known and there had been little, if any, interaction with the Black student community. The subcommittee did not expect to see immediate progress, assuming that its recommendations would be debated by multiple constituencies, inside and beyond the university. They could only hope their report would cause the debate "necessary to move the university forward," they said.[87]

What was somewhat better known to students was that LASSU had passed, in February, with few dissenting votes, a resolution that Stanford should "make every effort to increase the number of Black students at Stanford" for the next academic year. The resolution called for: 1) admission of Black applicants who met minimal standards and that they be given additional tutoring; 2) recruiting of minority groups through publicity and employment of Black recruiters; 3) a summer program to develop verbal and mathematical skills; 4) a full-time supervisor for minority tutoring and counseling programs; and 5) academic courses in Black culture. As usual, the resolution was little more than symbolic.[88]

Determined to push what appeared to be an unresponsive university, the BSU had mobilized to assemble into one concise document a new iteration of its goals. These included proportional representation not only for Black students but also for American minority groups generally in the freshman class of 1969–70. They insisted current Black students play a role in recruiting and admissions decisions. Knowing that the SES subcommittee was at work, they insisted that the university not act on any faculty recommendations without BSU approval. They claimed exclusive jurisdiction in recruitment and selection of five Black "marginal" students for the incoming year and insisted that admission of any minority student be the decision of a committee made up of representatives of each minority group on campus, the BSU faculty advisor, and a new full-time Black administrator responsible for minority group affairs. They also insisted that maximum consideration be given to appropriate job opportunities for incoming students.[89]

After Satterwhite finished reading the demands (including a 7 p.m. deadline the following night), the group walked out of the auditorium to a standing ovation. "Everyone sensed," writes BSU historian Steven Phillips, '86, "that for hope to survive and the community to stay intact, Stanford had to take swift action and make substantive changes."[90]

Well into a second year of antiwar protests, mass meetings, sit-ins, and student demands, Stanford administrators knew the prospect of campus violence was real. But the sense of vulnerability was mutual. If arrested, the Black students expected to be treated far more harshly than white students. Perhaps they, like King and others, would be shot down. They went to the Monday event, Washington recalled, "not for violence, but to make a point in whatever pointed significant way we could at the time."[91]

During the previous months of protest, administrators had adopted a widely accepted defensive stand: Never negotiate with a gun to your head.[92] Neither President Sterling nor Provost Lyman were inclined to jump at a threat, but, in the case of the BSU demands, "it was the matter, not the manner" that counted, as Sterling and Lyman stated in their formal response the following day. "In our community, they are among the prime witnesses to racial injustice, and it is important that all members of the community listen to these witnesses. Much of what they advocate constitutes the basis for a constructive program of action." They asked the BSU to send representatives to meet that night.[93]

The Tuesday night meeting, held outside at Tresidder Union due to an audience of nearly 1,000, got off to a rocky start, with an edgy interchange between Washington, who wanted a direct yes or no answer to each demand, and Vice Provost Herb Packer, who wanted first to describe what efforts the university had already made or planned to make. Washington "wisely called for a break so that everyone could collect themselves," remembered Willard (Bill) Wyman, associate dean of students and administrative advisor to the BSU. Wyman then pointed out to Packer that the university was already on its way to positively answering each demand but one, and that one could be worked out. "So, we made a commitment to meet their demands . . . and we did, a lot faster than we would have otherwise."[94]

They reconvened.

There was much agreement on many of the points. A concerted effort had already increased the number of Black freshmen in the incoming class, and they were given priority for financial aid. Sterling had established, some weeks before King's assassination, a Human Relations Commission of students and faculty, with Black representation, to investigate discriminatory and racially motivated incidents. And the administration had committed to providing adequate staff and funding to support Black student recruiting and counseling, and the hiring of Black staff.[95] Additional meetings were scheduled to work out the more difficult, pragmatic details.[96]

On Thursday, April 11, representatives of the BSU, administration, and faculty again met,

this time in an upstairs Tresidder conference room, where they formulated a plan of action that responded directly to the BSU demands.[97] On the back patio below, several hundred white and Black students held a vigil, called by a newly organized group of white students, the Students Against White Racism. Among them were white student groups with their own "demands" (one group insisted the university stop all new construction and donate the funds to Oakland's Black community), while others hoped to incorporate Black students into ongoing antiwar confrontations.

Despite the productive discussions regarding 9 of the 10 demands, a portion of one demand nearly brought negotiations to a standstill: the dismissal of Associate Provost Robert M. Rosenzweig (whose broad portfolio of duties included minority affairs) over his mishandling of an incident in March at Tresidder Union and his

Provost Lyman, here at the April 11 meeting, credited Charles Countee (middle) and Ken Washington for skillfully negotiating an effective outcome to the BSU demands. The students earned administrators' respect as they worked together on minority student recruitment, housing issues, and staff hiring. STANFORD NEWS SERVICE

At the conclusion of negotiations, Ken Washington, flanked by BSU colleagues, announced from the Tresidder Union balcony to the crowd waiting below that the administration had met all Black Student Union demands.   STANFORD NEWS SERVICE

perceived lack of interest in Black students. (During the meeting, he was assailed as racist, an attack the Jewish administrator thought antisemitic but not unexpected.) However, the BSU had unwittingly confronted the administration's firm commitment to never give in to external pressure to dismiss a faculty member or administrator without due process. With emotions high, the Thursday meeting was at an impasse and the students ready to break off negotiations when Robert McAfee Brown chimed in.[98]

Brown had firmly supported the other demands, but explained that he, too, had been a target for dismissal after writing a magazine article in which he admitted his willingness to advise a student to avoid the draft if he thought it best for that student. President Sterling was heavily pressured, including by some major donors, to dismiss Brown. Sterling had refused. "The University has stood up for me and has protected my right to say what I believe is right," Rosenzweig later remembered Brown saying. "And if we were to yield to your demands to get rid of Bob because you don't like what he's said or what he's done, then nobody else in the University would be safe

from any group that could muster a powerful enough threat."[99]

Ultimately, the 10th demand was met halfway, with a promise to hire a Black minority officer who would work more directly than Rosenzweig with students. (After a search in which the BSU participated, James E. Simmons, a Hampton and Harvard graduate, would be hired the following month as assistant provost for minority affairs with a special portfolio as liaison with Black students and the local community, particularly East Palo Alto. A year later, his title was changed to assistant to the president for Black Affairs.)[100]

After two hours of work, Washington shouted

Jim Simmons, a Hampton and Harvard graduate, was hired in May 1968 as assistant provost for minority affairs, with a special portfolio as liaison with Black students and the local community. The BSU participated in the search.

Popular Associate Dean of Students Bill Wyman was often sent into scenes of conflict. A month after helping resolve the April 1968 BSU demands, he was the only administrator left in the Old Union, talking informally with students occupying the building, May 6–8. STANFORD NEWS SERVICE

to the waiting crowd, "All our demands have been met. There has been no watering down." The BSU had carved out its own territory, Bill Wyman later recalled admiringly. "They knew what they wanted, they made it clear through a number of points, and they went after it in a very focused way."[101]

Some students and liberal critics assumed the administration's negotiating team had acted merely to save face, an excuse Lyman, among others, strongly discounted. "There was a sense of purpose in moving forward, an interesting political mix of reactivity and pro-activity," said Ray Bacchetti, "which I think had a lot to do with the momentum that the university had when it put these demands into operation." That

sense of purpose proved useful as the administration braced for backlash from trustees, alumni, and faculty who believed that Stanford had acted in haste, giving in to student pressure, to dilute its academic quality. Complaints from alumni and others poured into the President's Office after local newspapers stated—erroneously—that the university had fired Rosenzweig and given up its authority over academic affairs to the BSU.[102]

It was rumored that trustees William Hewlett and David Packard, both members of the board's Committee on Academic Affairs, disapproved of the speed of negotiations. But the board quickly accepted Sterling and Lyman's report on the matter. Board President W. Parmer Fuller III had remained in touch with Sterling and Lyman throughout the week. "The opportunity for meaningful discussion depended on prompt follow-through by the University," Fuller responded to one critic. "I believe if we had postponed meeting the issue firmly, promptly, and reasonably we would have done far more harm than good."[103]

Lyman credited Washington and Countee for skillfully negotiating a constructive outcome, but the entire student group earned the respect of many administrators who were soon working together with BSU students on specific efforts, such as the admission of special students, housing issues, and the hiring of minority affairs officers.[104] In 1969, the university provided the BSU with the small 1920s house at 418 Santa Teresa Street, next to Bowman Alumni House (now the Humanities Center), as a student meeting place and cultural headquarters (today's Black Community Services Center).[105]

For BSU members, the "Taking the Mic" effort and its resolution had a long-lasting meaning beyond the immediate goals. Their demands had pushed Stanford ahead not only for Black students but for minority students generally. Mary Montle Bacon, one of the BSU negotiators, recalled "an understanding that we had to have an impact on this university not just for us, but for all people who bring a different kind, perhaps, of preparation and experience to the teaching and learning process."[106]

THE OLD UNION SIT-IN
PROTESTING SUSPENSIONS, MAY 1968

Negotiations with the Black Student Union had shown results comparatively quickly. But the cases of the CIA demonstrators of the previous November were still unresolved.

In February, after animated public hearings, interviews, and a study of constitutional law, the Student Judicial Council found the students not guilty of infractions against both the university's policy on demonstrations and the Fundamental Standard. In their long, detailed opinion, published in the *Stanford Daily*, the SJC essentially declared the university's demonstrations policy

overbroad and too vague to be enforceable, but they did so, they said, on the expectation that it could be updated and improved for future use. As for the Fundamental Standard, they found that the defendants had not interfered with anyone else's rights enough to outweigh their First Amendment right to political expression. (Economics Professor Lorie Tarshis, SJC's faculty representative, joined the nine student members in the acquittal.)[107]

The administration later complained that little, if any, consideration had been given to evidence of allegedly damaged property or to disruption of university activities. The SJC did, in fact, consider that evidence but found it too minimal or inadvertent to warrant a precedent-setting punishment.[108]

Sterling later observed that, although he found the SJC decision legally objectionable, it was understandable. Council members were united

In 1969, the university gave the BSU use of a cottage on Santa Teresa Street, next to Bowman Alumni House, as its headquarters. The house, built in the mid-1920s, had been used most recently by a magazine publisher. A major annex, barely visible behind, was added in 2007 for BSU programs and cultural events. SUNNY SCOTT

in agreeing that the Vietnam War was immoral, he believed, and had come to their decision based on the question of morality rather than on what he considered to be their responsibility to act judicially. At the time, a *Daily* editorial noted that even the interpretation of morality was open to question. The Fundamental Standard no longer worked as a disciplinary code, the editorial noted. The Standard's "vague demand for 'respect for order, morality, personal honor, and the rights of others' breaks down when the generations sincerely disagree on moral imperatives," according to the *Daily*. Indeed, during the hearings, some defendants had argued that the Fundamental Standard itself dictated that Stanford students must object to the war.[109]

For the administration, the ultimate question remained: Did the university not have the right to discipline those who used physical force to prevent a legal university activity or those who sought to prevent protected free speech, even if some community members found that speech disagreeable?

Dean of Students Joel Smith, in turn, criticized the SJC's decision as political, and charged that it had assumed "law-making powers" by invalidating university policy and regulations. He asked the Interim Judicial Board for a new trial. On Friday, May 3, the IJB published its ruling, finding seven students guilty of violating the demonstrations policy. The board recommended to President Sterling one-quarter suspensions for five cases, and two-quarter suspensions for two men considered repeat offenders. "By its unanimous decision, the IJB heated up the coals of a controversy which has dragged on since the anti-CIA protest of November," reported the *Daily*.[110]

Such was the background leading to the nearly three-day occupation of the Old Union that began on Monday, May 6, 1968. As students, faculty, and administrators understood, the stakes were high for those who might be suspended or

expelled. With the draft now looming over the majority of 18- to 21-year-old male students, even a short-term suspension could mean loss of their student deferments and an unavoidable invitation from the U.S. Army.

ASSU President Cesare Massarenti, Michael Weinstein (speaker of the student legislature), and other student officers met with Sterling, Associate Provost Herb Packer, and Dean Smith on Friday, after the IJB ruling came out. Massarenti insisted, unsuccessfully, that Sterling ignore the IJB sentences. Shortly after, Massarenti led a brief gathering at White Plaza, then returned to the President's Office backed by about 100 demonstrators. Staging a sit-in in the arcade in front of Building 10, they presented demands: The Encina demonstrators' cases must be dismissed and the IJB disbanded in favor of an appeals board composed of a majority of students. The administration must surrender to the demand, in public, at high noon on Monday. It was hardly surprising that Sterling said no.[111]

Other weekend meetings ensued, including a Friday night gathering of faculty from the Academic Council's Executive Committee, the Committee on University Policy, four top ASSU officers, and two of the convicted Encina demonstrators. Little came of the meeting, according to law Professor William Baxter, one of the faculty participants. He acknowledged that he now had a better understanding of student frustration with the judicial system, but he hoped that students understood that good faith efforts had been made through the Committee of 15's long deliberations. But Baxter also suspected that the recent demands deliberately violated previous ASSU-administration agreements, and that they were intended to be rejected.[112]

In his response, published on Monday in the *Daily*, Sterling stated his ongoing commitment to significant student representation in both rule making and adjudication. Fully backing the work of C-15, he also agreed that even in an academic community, discussion and debate must stop and decisions be made. He expected C-15 to conclude its work by the end of spring quarter, and revised structures to be in place by fall quarter, thus solving the judicial ambiguity. Discussions were close to producing an agreement that should satisfy "all but a very few zealots of the far Left and far Right." As for the defendants, Sterling hoped to meet with each of them before accepting or rejecting the IJB recommendations. He also invited student leaders to attend the special Academic Council meeting he had called for Wednesday.

While extending his hand, Sterling made his position clear: "Issues this complex are not going to be resolved in White Memorial Plaza, this noon or any other noon. Issues this ambiguous are not going to be resolved in answer to an ultimatum."[113]

But protest strategies had already been formulated. "I think we have to construct a mass movement around this issue, a really big one," Massarenti reportedly said the day before. "Either Sterling answers on White Plaza tomorrow, or we don't want anyone to answer." A "mill-in" at the Old Union, Encina Hall, or the Inner Quad—each being a location of administrative offices—had been discussed. Steve Weissman, a former Berkeley Free Speech Movement veteran now a grad student at Stanford, chided his listeners "that the best thing Stanford students do is to 'be concerned.'" He wanted a demonstration "militant enough so that students have to choose sides." On the *Stanford Daily*'s editorial page was the warning: "Dear Wally: They that have sown the wind . . . shall reap the whirlwind . . . Hosea 8:7."[114]

Protesting proposed student suspensions over participation in the earlier anti-CIA fracas, more than 250 students began a nearly three-day occupation of the Old Union on the afternoon of May 6, 1968. The front doors had been locked in anticipation, but these protesters went in through a window. Graduate student Steve Weissman (at microphone), a UC Berkeley Free Speech Movement veteran, chided the crowd at the Old Union sit-in that what Stanford students did best was "be concerned." He argued that the demonstration should be "militant enough so that students have to choose sides."   STANFORD NEWS SERVICE

Early evening of the first day, May 6, some 1,500 gathered in the Old Union courtyard to debate strategy. In a straw vote, they largely favored amnesty over suspension in the CIA protest, but split 3 to 2 against continuing the sit-in. Petitions also began to circulate supporting Sterling and the administration. Many students went from the Old Union to Memorial Auditorium for a convocation, called by Provost Lyman, to discuss issues related to the Old Union sit-it. An animated student audience included many raising their hands with the victory sign.   STANFORD NEWS SERVICE

After the noon Monday, May 6, White Plaza rally grew to about a thousand, many students headed to the Old Union—site of the Registrar's Office, the Admissions Office, the Dean of Students Office, and other student services. Assuming the Old Union would be targeted, staff had locked the building before noon and many had left for lunch. Some students gained entry through unlocked windows, however. Others got in through the back door when a policeman opened it to let out a staff member. Once inside, demonstrators were able to open the front doors. More than 250 students entered the building.[115]

The protesters vowed to occupy the building until the suspensions were dropped. That evening, another 1,500 gathered in the Old Union courtyard. In a series of hand votes, the assembled crowd split roughly 3 to 2 against the sit-in as a tactic, but, by a large margin, supported amnesty for the students and the creation of a student-dominated review procedure. Later that evening, students filled Memorial Auditorium to capacity for a campus-wide meeting called by Provost Lyman, who explained the administration's support for the IJB and opposition to a student-only appellate judicial board. He also criticized Massarenti and his predecessor, Peter Lyman, for procrastinating in appointing student members to the Committee of 15 (still working on the faculty-student appellate court formula), and to SES advisory committees.[116]

In his report to the Board of Trustees, Sterling mentioned the slowness of judicial reform, but also commented on the apparent frustration of the original CIA protesters. Not only had they failed to stop the interviews, but only seven of several dozen identified had been tried. Sterling believed that this frustration, combined with ongoing SDS propaganda against the CIA and "the university's alleged complicity in war-making," had resulted in the Old Union gathering.[117]

Sterling reported minor damage to windows and doors of the Old Union but emphasized that the protesters made an effort not to destroy university property. (Richard Lyman described "an orderly peacefulness.") Staff in Admissions and Registrar's offices were given the rest of the day off. Campus police and firemen were put on alert but were not called on to act. Sanitary conditions deteriorated.[118]

On the second day, a 13-hour meeting of a committee consisting of six faculty members and five students finally reached a unanimous agreement on a new legislative and judicial structure covering student conduct, one that basically confirmed the original recommendation by the Committee of 15. The committee also urged Sterling to reach an independent decision on cases of the anti-CIA demonstrators, which he had intended to do anyway.[119]

Sterling endorsed the judicial procedures that required reform, but he upheld the IJB decision on the suspensions. But he was also prepared for further protest. In response to the Free Speech Movement's disruptions at Cal in 1965, the Sterling administration had developed procedures to handle just this sort of emergency. Aimed at avoiding an outbreak of violence, the procedures set up a path: engage peacefully with the students, have clear lines of negotiation, keep faculty involved in problem solving, and keep trustees engaged and informed. This approach had a proven track record, most obviously with the BSU negotiations. He now relied on the structures of faculty governance to back him in moving forward.[120]

CONTENTIOUS ACADEMIC COUNCIL MEETING, MAY 1968

Sterling and his staff had worked closely with the Advisory Board, the Academic Council's Executive Committee, and the Committee on University Policy to formulate and, they hoped, expedite formal approval of the judicial reforms. A team

On May 7, on their second try, arsonists destroyed the Naval ROTC building, located in the Arboretum near Campus Drive. Faculty men had built the wooden clubhouse in 1898, not far from early athletics fields. Provost Lyman later said that he doubted the arson had anything to do with the Old Union sit-in.
STANFORD NEWS SERVICE

of the 800 members, with many non-members, such as lecturers and research assistants, also attending. The meeting in Dinkelspiel Auditorium went on for nearly four volatile hours.[121]

Almost from the start, at the introduction of the Executive Committee's first of four resolutions, the assembled faculty abandoned the agenda and focused on a new resolution presented by medical Professor Halstead Holman. The Holman Resolution closely paralleled the narrowly focused demands of the Old Union sit-in protesters: amnesty for the Encina defendants and for all engaged in the current sit-in.[122]

"It became obvious that some groups among those remaining [throughout the meeting] had caucused before the meeting," Sterling later recalled. "Every sort of parliamentary jockeying and maneuvering took place. There were motions, amendments to motions, and amendments to amendments, as well as many a call for points of order." After two hours, a significant number of older, more moderate faculty members had left the meeting.[123]

At one point, Holman went up to the podium and attempted to shoulder Sterling away from the microphone while the president was speaking. "I simply took him by the lapels and asked him, while I was still on the microphone, whether he could sit down by himself or whether he needed a little help. That got a laugh and broke some of the tension," Sterling recalled.[124]

After the Holman Resolution passed by a vote of 284 to 241, the Academic Council voted down each of the recommendations submitted to them by their Executive Committee, the president, and the provost. Some who were not Academic

of trustees was on hand for advice and, ultimately, support. The next step was the Academic Council. Sterling expected this rather amorphous gathering of the whole faculty to endorse recommendations formulated by the faculty advisory bodies. He did not anticipate a faculty crisis.

On the third day of the Old Union sit-in, Wednesday, May 8, the Advisory Board and Academic Council Executive Committee resolutions were to be presented at the Academic Council meeting. The board and the committee had composed four resolutions that included confirmation of university policy permitting orderly demonstrations but prohibiting disruption of classes and activities, property damage, or individual endangerment. They suggested that the university act against those involved in disruption, including the recent IJB suspension rulings. They also recommended approval, in principle, of the proposed new judicial plan.

Academic Council meetings were usually sparsely attended, but this one drew nearly 600

Council members had attempted to vote in a voice vote. The final vote, at the suggestion of history Professor David Potter, required members to stand. Sterling later said that he had never felt such shame for his profession, as an unpredicted number of professors voted, with the recent violence at Columbia University in mind, in what he and others thought was an appeasement.[125]

Sterling found it ironic that after his position was rejected, "the professor who had been on his feet so often then rose once more and said he wanted to make a motion which he hoped would be adopted unanimously. It was a vote of complete confidence in the elected representatives of the faculty and in the President of the University. It was a weird vote of confidence!"[126]

After the Academic Council meeting, Sterling, Lyman, and their staff regrouped in the President's Office. They referred the council's decision to give amnesty to the defendants to the IJB, but the board that night bowed to the faculty vote in what they saw as the university's best interest. Thus ended what Sterling later called his "most exasperating and rather humiliating experience with 'student unrest.'"[127]

Provost Lyman was furious. "It seemed that the faculty was unwilling to draw any line," he later recounted. He and Vice Provost Herbert Packer each wrote letters of resignation that night, only to tear them up the next morning, not wanting to abandon President Sterling so near his retirement.[128]

Sterling ruefully commented a decade later, "I could understand, and indeed sympathize with the widespread national opposition to the war in Vietnam, and to the sense of outrage it invoked in many. But I could not understand," he told an interviewer, "the failure of a majority of distinguished faculty to authorize penalties for those who had disrupted [the] University and damaged University property—and, moreover, had done so under the banner of morality."[129]

FACULTY VOTE FALLOUT, MAY 1968

The protesters at the nearby Old Union cheered the faculty vote and, after celebrating, left the building later that evening. The following day, Sterling and Lyman issued a statement to the ASSU legislature, stating their serious misgivings about the wisdom of the Academic Council's resolutions, but stating "we nevertheless accept those recommendations and commit ourselves to their implementation." They urged speedy action to approve the C-15 judicial reform proposals.[130]

After nearly 57 hours occupying the Old Union, sit-in participants (seen here filling the hallway at the Registrar's and Bursar's counters and spilling out into the courtyard) voted to end their stay on the evening of May 8. This followed a vote at a special meeting of the faculty Academic Council that favored amnesty for the protesters. STANFORD NEWS SERVICE

The May 1968 ASSU presidential run-off election pitted activist Denis Hayes against self-described topless dancer Vicky Drake, running as a joke. Hayes won, but Drake drew nearly 40 percent of the student vote.
STANFORD NEWS SERVICE

A May 8 student petition with 1,600 student signatures, supporting President Sterling generally, called for a student referendum opposing sit-in tactics to be placed on the next student-body primary election ballot.[131]

Soon after, in the largest vote ever cast in a primary referendum, students voted by a margin of 6 to 1 in favor of the proposition that "all employers—not illegal in the eyes of the civil courts—be allowed equal access to recruiting facilities at Stanford." In the final election a week later, a resolution describing forcible occupation of university buildings as "unacceptable behavior" passed by a margin of 2 to 1.

Another measure censured Cesare Massarenti, outgoing ASSU president, for advocating and participating in the Old Union sit-in; it passed by

a 3 to 2 margin. "After two years of radical leadership, the inevitable reaction has set in," Massarenti complained, "the reaction of those who still see Stanford as a playground rather than as a place for serious intellectual work. Let's see what Stanford will look like in two or three years."[132]

Later that month, the ASSU presidential race pitted activist Denis Hayes in a run-off election against self-described topless dancer Vicky Drake. Hayes wanted student appointments to the trustee presidential search committee and ratification of the university's new president by student referendum; Drake, running as a joke, had no platform. Hayes won, but Drake attracted nearly 40 percent of the student vote.[133]

Later that fall, both the new Faculty Senate of the Academic Council and the student body adopted the final recommendations of the Committee of 15 that clarified rules of student conduct, stating that disruption of university activities or physical damage to university property would not be tolerated. The new system established the Stanford Judicial Council, with five faculty members and four students, to hear disciplinary cases of both students and faculty, and a Student Conduct Legislative Council, with six faculty members and five students to establish rules of conduct. Both were underway, as Sterling had predicted, in January 1969.[134]

In reporting to the Board of Trustees, Sterling took the high road. He made three points. First, many faculty members did not want a showdown with the students, believing the risks of "another Columbia" to be too great or the issues too unclear.[135]

Secondly, the verbal support given to Sterling's administration (the standing vote of confidence at the end of the meeting) provided "a basis, although it is at best a tenuous one, for reuniting the faculty and reaching consensus among the majority that a line must be drawn and reform-via-disorder meaningfully condemned in favor of orderly procedure and abiding by established rules of conduct." Finally, Sterling noted that some of the faculty who had voted for amnesty on Wednesday "were genuinely shocked by the revolutionary statements emanating from the hard-core sit-in leaders." (At the end of the Old Union sit-in, Steve Weissman, for example, called for "confrontation politics" to achieve two new goals: student control of faculty tenure and of presidential searches.)[136]

After hearing Sterling's report, the Board of Trustees, at its May 16 meeting, unanimously resolved that "sit-ins and other activities by any member of the university community that disrupt or attempt to disrupt the activities of the university must no longer be tolerated at Stanford." Trustees Richard Guggenhime, Robert Minge Brown, W. Parmer Fuller III, and Judge Ben Duniway had provided counsel by phone throughout the crisis, supporting Sterling's decision that to summon police intervention without faculty support would be a serious mistake. Their backing was also needed during the ensuing trustees meeting. "Those of us who have been bloodied by students and by faculty are in no mood to be bloodied by trustees," Herb Packer told Guggenhime. "If we have to assume the entire burden of our own defense, things may well get said that will fatally impair our continuing relationship with many members of the Board, a result I would greatly regret."[137]

"I should find it altogether agreeable if this 'mess' could have been avoided during my last year in office, but events have proved otherwise," Sterling had written a friend before the trustee meeting. "And this is not altogether surprising, given the malaise that exists in so many places around the world. I don't quote the great bard precisely, but I think there is a line to the effect that 'out of this nettle, danger, one may pluck' victory. We are going to try."[138]

Sterling was, again, in the midst of a deluge of alumni letters. The Old Union sit-in and particularly the outcome of the Academic Council meeting received widespread news coverage. "I would not regret seeing you go out in the eyes of history as the weakest of all Stanford Presidents. For God's sake take over and run the school—fire 7 or 107 if necessary," wrote one man from Borrego Springs, California. Wrote another, from Costa Mesa, "Is it so very difficult to act in the capacity for which you are paid? EXPEL THEM IMMEDIATELY & FINALLY and if they won't move stuff them in jail."[139]

Sterling received dozens of copies of newspaper articles citing, with approval, the actions of other presidents, such as the University of Denver's Chancellor Maurice Mitchell, who dismissed 40 students who seized the Registrar's Office and had them arrested for loitering and obstruction when they refused to move.[140]

Not all alumni were critical of Sterling and the administration, however. Some supported Sterling at the expense of the faculty. An alumnus, class of 1917, commented in the *Palo Alto Times*: "Perhaps it is too much to expect a faculty to support an administration. Professors, with the exception of some scientists, don't make decisions. They spend their lives avoiding them; whereas the administrative force must make decisions, or universities would grind to a halt."[141]

Others understood the complexity of the matter. "I do not believe this situation was a matter of giving in to tantrum-throwing children," wrote an alumna. "I believe that important, justified complaints were voiced by the students and supported by a majority of the faculty, and I am deeply grateful to you and Provost Lyman for *listening* to the arguments and committing yourself to the Academic Council's recommendations."[142]

Sympathetic trustees also lent their support, in their own way. "I agree that education and research are the fundamental purposes of

At the May 18 Alumni Association's annual Campus Conference, Sterling expressed frustration with the faculty amnesty vote for the CIA protesters and with alumni criticism of his administration's acceptance of that vote. He nevertheless confirmed his confidence in Stanford's future. The president's final speech to alumni took place in the oak grove between the Faculty Club (left) and Bowman Alumni House (out of view). Kingscote Gardens apartment house is in the background.   STANFORD NEWS SERVICE

a university, but I believe social reform is part of what must be researched and taught," the influential businessman Charles Ducommun replied to an alumnus in Texas (with a copy to Sterling):

> In other words, the university cannot be isolated from the real world and must play a part in seeking solutions to social problems. Therefore, an understanding of how these problems arose and . . . thinking about new ways to solve them, I believe, are an integral part of the responsibility of any first-rate institution. This does not mean that I believe that teaching assistants or professors have an inalienable right to preach nihilism, destruction of the university, or our country in order to have their beliefs prevail.[143]

The faculty seemed as divided as ever. A Medical School faculty member who had voted for the Holman Resolution wrote Sterling that he had voted in favor of the amnesty motion, "from a conviction that in times like these justice and legalism must be tempered with mercy. I do not believe the action in any way represented a repudiation of the administration. . . . It illustrates the important principle of obtaining faculty opinion before positions on an issue become rigid."[144]

An administrator of the Stanford Electronics Laboratory had the opposite view:

> The issue is rather whether the University is to be guided by experience and wisdom or by coercion, force, and the threat of force. The workings of the interdependent components of this complex university are woefully vulnerable to sabotage and malicious acts. The temptation to avoid trouble by acquiescing to militant threats is certainly great.[145]

Speaking at the May 18 alumni conference on campus, Sterling allowed himself to vent his frustration, with both the faculty vote and off-campus criticism, and to set the record straight—as he saw it—with doubting alumni. He referred to an important element of the Declaration of Principles enunciated in 1915 by the American Association of University Professors: Academic freedom comes with academic responsibility. Unless those who enjoy that freedom discipline colleagues who abuse it, others less qualified will do so. Sterling was unimpressed with criticism alleging he had capitulated to coercion or blackmail in accepting a faculty vote that recommended amnesty. Explaining his willingness to accept the Academic Council's recommendation, Sterling said:

> What was at stake in last week's crisis was, in my judgment, the opportunity for all members of this University more fully to inform themselves of what was really at issue if coercive tactics were to be employed and tolerated. What was at stake was the opportunity to avoid a polarized and bitterly divided house from which constructive recovery would have been difficult and long. What was at stake was the opportunity to complete and put into effect the work which had produced the proposal for the [new] Academic Senate and the proposals for University agencies which would codify rules of conduct and provide judicial procedures with appropriate sanctions.
>
> I did not favor total amnesty "to date" for the Old Union sit-inners. I could have disregarded the faculty vote and taken presidential action. But I did not do so because I had, and still have, confidence that the great majority of students and faculty on this campus disapprove of coercive tactics and will make that disapproval known—and because I believe that this University has more to gain from the maximum unified and cooperative effort which can be attained than from an extended and rancorous divisiveness. I made this judgment and I state this belief on the basis of my experience at Stanford during the past 19 years—an experience which has been only peripherally shared by those who charge capitulation.
>
> I have confidence that Stanford will emerge from last week's crisis with a clearer perception of what is required by way of order and discipline if she is to continue her progress. I have confidence that Stanford will contribute positively and greatly to the restoration of public confidence in higher education.[146]

At his conclusion, Sterling received a standing ovation.

"You will not be surprised to have me tell you that this past month has been one of the most taxing of my term of office," Sterling wrote to a Los Angeles attorney who had congratulated him on his handling of the sit-in crisis:

> I could say that we have survived it and let the matter rest there, but mere survival is inadequate. There is still much work to be done, and not the least of all on two fronts: one to develop a better understanding among the faculty of what is truly at stake; and two, to develop among the great majority of Stanford students the realization that their own educational opportunities are jeopardized when a minority of students is allowed to take over.[147]

ARSON AT PRESIDENT'S OFFICE
MARS FINAL MONTHS, JULY 1968

Early in the morning of July 5, less than two months after the Old Union sit-in and less than two months before the end of his presidency, a fire was reported at Building 10, the location of the President's Office. An arsonist had poured gasoline throughout Sterling's office, as well as in opened file cabinets in the office above his. Although the fire department was able to get to the scene fairly quickly, the damage was extensive. Some described the scene as "grim." The damage was estimated at $300,000, but the personal loss to Sterling was inestimable. The fire destroyed his personal papers (including the unfinished manuscripts of his books), rare books and documents destined as gifts to the University Library, antique furniture, and treasured memorabilia collected over his lifetime.[148]

His greatest losses, he later commented, were things of sentimental, not monetary value. In his office were the notes and files he had maintained over the years regarding Stanford's major developments and challenges. In lieu of annual reports, he had promised the trustees that he would write

Early in the pre-dawn morning of July 5, 1968, an arson fire gutted President Sterling's office in Building 10, consuming books, manuscripts, and memorabilia he had collected during his decades in higher education. Sterling, two months away from retirement, did not consider the arson a personal vendetta, later calling it a "fate of the times." (Sterling's office faced north, looking out on Building 170.)

JOHN POLICH / STANFORD UNIVERSITY ARCHIVES

his analysis of the past 19 years. His draft, and the files supporting it, were lost in the fire.[149]

Arson proved to be an effective way for some to express contempt. On the second day of the Old Union sit-in, fire destroyed the Naval ROTC building between Lasuen and Galvez streets, off Campus Drive, in the Arboretum, completing an attempt made two months earlier. Three other major fires occurred after the July fire in the President's Office. A 1970 fire at the Center for Advanced Study in the Behavioral Sciences destroyed the life work of a prominent scholar from India. The following year, the lounge of the Black-themed Junipero House in Wilbur Hall (site of frequent Black Student Union meetings) was set ablaze. In June 1972, the largest and most devastating fire was set: a million-dollar blaze that gutted the upper east floor and central attic of Encina Hall (many administrative records had been stored in the attic). Fortunately, what had once been a small paid fire department, backed by student firefighters, had been significantly expanded in the early 1960s after a rash of accidental fires.[150]

The President's Office fire was investigated by the FBI but no one was indicted, and the crime remains unsolved.[151] Although no one, however obliquely, claimed responsibility, some in the radical press considered it "an effective attack on state power," while others considered it a waste of time since it occurred during the summer. A satiric poem taking up the front page of the *Midpeninsula Observer* taunted Sterling, pictured walking in his shirtsleeves among the ashes, considering the demise of his "precious things, fit for a showcase in some dead museum."[152]

For Richard Lyman, the poem was a reminder, "if one is needed, of how sad it was for Sterling to have his final year in office so beclouded and himself so much reviled, Sterling, who in better days had been widely loved and admired, and who had done so much to convert Stanford into a university of national and growing international repute."[153]

Those who had been on the scene that day recalled Sterling walking through the debris, lending words of support and thanks to those who had contained the blaze to that portion of Building 10, preventing further damage. One firefighter later emotionally recalled Sterling's graciousness and his relief that no one had been hurt.[154]

Incoming ASSU President Denis Hayes wrote to Sterling that morning: "The student body wishes to express its profound regrets at the outrageous destruction of your office this morning. It is tragic that your years of service to Stanford should be scarred in their closing weeks by this act of nihilistic violence." Hayes added that "this heinous act is repudiated by every responsible student on the campus."[155]

Sterling did not view the destruction as a vendetta. He and his colleagues had concluded that the arsonist assumed, wrongly, that the president's suite of offices contained documents that would prove that Stanford Research Institute was complicit in classified research for the U.S. military or that files there held incriminating evidence about protesting faculty. "It was the fate of the times," Sterling told an interviewer 11 years later. "I don't think there was anything personal in it."[156]

21

CHANCELLOR STERLING

From his first day in office on April 1, 1949, to his stepping away on August 31, 1968, J. E. Wallace Sterling served Stanford for 19 years and 5 months.

"There is nothing sudden about this," Sterling had told the *Stanford Daily* in April 1967 about his impending retirement. "It's been on my mind for a long time." While the 60-year-old president's health clearly was a factor, Sterling also felt it was time for a change. "Every person and every institution needs a change periodically, about every 20 years, plus or minus," he added.[1]

Soon after, President Richard Guggenhime announced that Sterling would become chancellor for life when he retired. "It seems almost superfluous to observe," said Guggenhime, "that the contributions of Wallace Sterling to the growth, development and stature of Stanford University since becoming president in 1949 have been magnificent."[2]

In Stanford's first 125 years, only three individuals would hold the honored position of chancellor. The concept of a Stanford chancellorship had been devised for David Starr Jordan at the time of his retirement as president in 1913. The trustees chose not to extend his chancellorship in 1916, when he turned 65, then the normal retirement age for faculty members, and he was named chancellor emeritus. (His controversial pacifism and antiwar activities were the likely cause.) Ray Lyman Wilbur was named chancellor in January 1942, and served in that capacity until his death, in 1949. Unlike these two, Sterling's appointment was specified "chancellor for life." Subsequent Stanford presidents (except for Kenneth Pitzer) have been named president emeritus when they stepped away.[3]

Invited by officers of the class of 1968 to deliver their commencement address, Sterling used familiar themes of hard work and personal responsibility, framing them with his own memories and his recognition of those who came before. "Overarching all others is the memory of gratitude to my predecessors and their colleagues for having laid well and strong foundations of a university of high degree, and of gratitude to

< Wally and Ann Sterling, here in 1979, enjoyed the nearly 3 acres on Stockbridge Avenue, Woodside, where they lived after leaving the Lou Henry Hoover House. Mae Vrooman Forbes, daughter of an early Stanford trustee, donated the house and property to Stanford as a life tenancy for the Sterlings.

In his final commencement speech as president, June 16, 1968, Sterling cautioned patience. "The road to social improvement is likely not a racetrack." Back in the day, the president handed each graduate their diploma.   STANFORD NEWS SERVICE

the controversial move of the Medical School from San Francisco; the development of Stanford lands; changes to the university's curriculum and the decision to create overseas campuses; efforts to tackle a major fundraising campaign; and even "the ups and downs" of student governance and faculty and administrative reorganization.

It was up to the younger generation to produce new architects with better plans to improve the human condition, he said, but he warned that "in the tugging and hauling of a free society, the road to social improvement is not likely to be a racetrack." Patience should not be a dirty word:

> No generation had, or has, a monopoly on aspiration to improve the human condition. Each generation has had its builders, its own architects of change. And each generation learns in its own way and in its own time that constructive change is not as responsive to command as one could wish. Nothing tests more the fiber of a generation than does the test of sustaining its aspirations in the face of delays and disappointment. . . . Your chances of further improving the human condition are greater because of the freedoms and opportunities which you have inherited. Please do be builders, but don't let yourselves be burned out by impatience and by inflated hopes for instant Utopia.[5]

all who have for the past 19 years so generously shared the task of building on those foundations." He hoped that the graduating seniors would similarly "feel the deep appreciation which I feel for the university heritage which we have shared. The temper and thrust of the day is to deploy one's social conscience in the cause of reform . . . I suggest that a good way to begin such deployment is to count and remember one's blessings."[4]

Sterling spoke of "what goes into the building process," referring to the major debates and difficult decisions during his administration:

ACCOLADES OF 1968

Looking back a decade later at that final year of his presidency, Wallace Sterling did not dwell on the July 1968 arson attack on his office (see Chapter 20). Instead, he recalled the many letters and phone calls of support from faculty, students, alumni, and non-Stanford friends—even an unexpected laudatory editorial in the *Stanford Daily*—that he received in summer 1968. Nineteen years of happy memories, he said, outweighed the "slings and arrows" of sit-ins and other campus disruptions. That summer, as commendations flowed from national newspapers and organizations, he had been gratified that the evidence of Stanford's national standing and growing international reputation took precedence.[6]

"Someday there will be a sandstone red-tiled Wallace Sterling hall or quad or residence or library," the *Stanford Daily*'s Patrick McMahon speculated; a simple plaque stating "J. E. Wallace Sterling, Fifth President of Stanford University, 1949–1968," wouldn't be enough:

> President Sterling brought Stanford effective leadership for academic and institutional innovation. No one touted or joked about the "edge of greatness" before Wallace Sterling was president. And nineteen years later he leaves the Stanford presidency because "every person and every institution needs a change periodically."
>
> Change was Wally's thing: PACE and its $100 million, the Study of Education [at Stanford], the Medical Center, SLAC, the overseas campus program, the Committee of 15. And there were less tangible changes. The "country club" atmosphere has vanished and in its place are many of the brightest students and best faculty in the country. The University has firmly committed itself to public service, although too heavily in defense work.
>
> A university president wears many hats. John Gardner said last year of Sterling: "The press demand access to him, donors expect courtesies from him, the general public counts on him for pontifical statements. If he's not firm enough, the trustees will scold him; if he's too firm the faculty will go up in smoke, and that's bad for air pollution. If he's a father figure, all the students will love him, except those who hate him."
>
> Wallace Sterling has been many things to us, from an enlightened administrator to a stalwart reactionary, but we will remember him as the man who made Stanford worth worrying about. We only hope that his successor can do for the seventies what he did for the fifties and sixties.[7]

At his last Academic Council meeting, in June, only a month after the confrontational council meeting about student disciplinary recommenda-tions (*see Chapter 20*), President Sterling received a standing ovation. The council had just adopted, unanimously, a resolution commending the president for his "energy and dedication in the pursuit of excellence." Success had not bred complacency, the resolution stated. "Both the existence of the current ferment and its relatively peaceful manifestation here are tributes to your leadership, for the direction you have given the university has encouraged challenge to existing ways." Acknowledging the earlier conflict between some faculty members and the administration over the recent Old Union sit-in, the resolution added, "You have vigorously championed the autonomy of the university's values and fought repeatedly in the most difficult times for the preservation and extension of academic freedom."

The resolution also tried to calm the waters by acknowledging proactive changes the Sterling administration already had underway to recruit minority students and faculty: "The magnificent response to the racial crisis of conscience and the flexibility in adjustment shown more recently by you and your administration in accommodating to the desires of the faculty show anew that the vitality created in the university by your administration is a lasting accomplishment."[8]

Also that June, hundreds of students took a break from evening study, marching behind the Stanford Band to pay tribute to the president at the Lou Henry Hoover House. The Associated Students presented Sterling with a scroll reading, in part, that "his primary concern throughout his years as President has been the application of the educational processes to us," and expressing students' "high esteem and great affection." The students and band ended by serenading the Sterlings and their guests with the Stanford hymn, *Hail, Stanford, Hail*. The event, noted the following news coverage, "was reminiscent of earlier and calmer days on campus."[9]

Shortly before his retirement, the Board of

On Saturday evening June 1, 1968, three months before his final day in office, the Stanford Band led students to the lawn below the Lou Henry Hoover House to serenade and bid farewell to Wallace and Ann Sterling.   STANFORD NEWS SERVICE

Trustees created the J. E. Wallace Sterling Professorship in the Humanities. Eleven years earlier, Sterling had called Humanities and Sciences "the central pillar of our seven schools," and the trustees noted that, in an era of generous funding for the sciences, he had overseen greater balance of support among all disciplines. A second professorship was added later. The range of possible appointments to the professorships are noteworthy, encompassing not only his own field of history, but also anthropology, art, classics, drama, English, languages, music, and philosophy.[10]

Today, three other awards also honor Sterling:

• **The J. E. Wallace Sterling Award**, established by the Stanford Alumni Association in 1979, recognizes a graduating senior "whose leadership and volunteer activities have made the largest impact on the Stanford community."

• **The J. E. Wallace Sterling Award for Academic Achievement**, established by the School of Humanities and Sciences in 2006, annually honors the school's top 25 graduating seniors for overall academic performance.

- **The J. E. Wallace Sterling Lifetime Achievement Award in Medicine**, established by the Stanford Medicine Alumni Association in 1983 at the suggestion of retired faculty surgeon Gunther W. Nagel, M.D. '21. It recognizes Sterling's foresight in relocating the Medical School, despite intense opposition, from San Francisco to the campus to encourage interaction with other disciplines. One or more alumni are honored annually for "exceptional lifetime achievement in medicine."

Days after Sterling formally stepped down on August 31, the *San Francisco Chronicle* editorialized that "his commanding figure, his warm personality and his engaging style of speaking fortunately will continue as part of the Stanford scene and image. . . . There must be hundreds of thousands of Californians who count Wally Sterling as a friend, who value the integrity of the things he stands for and who admire without reserve his tremendous achievement at Stanford." Aside from the impressive statistics, the editorial noted, "he has given Stanford a new vision of its obligations to itself and to society."

Amid the praise, the newspaper also recognized the president's unenviable role in balancing the Stanford community's inner conflicts: "Above all, Wallace Sterling has fought to keep freedom for members of the university viable in the face of vicious challenges that have at times threatened the civility and order of the campus."[11]

WHEREAS J.E.WALLACE STERLING
has devoted himself to the betterment
of education throughout the world,
WHEREAS he has contributed greatly to the growth
and improvement of Stanford University
during his 19 years as President, and
WHEREAS his primary concern throughout his years
as President has been the application
of the educational processes to us, the Students,
THEREFORE BE IT RESOLVED
that we, the Students of Stanford University,
do hereby offer our Most Sincere Thanks
to President Sterling in appreciation
of all that he has done for us—
and that a copy of this resolution be
presented to President Sterling with
the high esteem and great affection of
the Associated Students.

Stanford University   28 May 1968

Law student Jeff Mason, senior econ student Tripp Snyder, and junior history major Dee Hermann (above) with a proclamation praising Sterling's 19 years of service to the university. The calligraphed scroll burned up a month later in the arson-caused destruction of Sterling's office.   STANFORD NEWS SERVICE

A male choral group—likely the Mendicants—entertained hundreds of guests attending an April retirement celebration honoring Wally Sterling at the Fairmont Hotel in San Francisco.
LEO HOLUB / STANFORD UNIVERSITY ARCHIVES

Sterling thanked sophomore Jennifer (Jenni) Bond, '70, moments after she delivered impromptu remarks at his retirement party. One of few students invited to the event, she recalls seeing on the printed program that no student had a speaking slot. As the program wound down, she walked up to the podium and thanked Sterling, on behalf of students, for his important contributions. "I am certain," she recalled in 2020, "that I also thanked him for supporting and increasing scholarships and for developing the overseas campus programs." She left three months later, on her scholarship, for Stanford-in-France.
STANFORD UNIVERSITY ARCHIVES

CHANCELLOR AS STANFORD TRUSTEE

By announcing his retirement plans in early spring 1967, Sterling gave the Board of Trustees nearly a year and a half to select a successor. He purposefully remained aloof from the process, believing that his role as chancellor would be to respond to requests for counsel, but never to initiate advice.

The 16-month presidential search was made more difficult by nationwide social unrest and violence, as well as confrontations taking place on campuses across the country. Eventually, the Board of Trustees chose Kenneth S. Pitzer as Stanford's sixth president.[12] Pitzer, a renowned physical and theoretical chemist, was then serving as president of Rice University, where he had earned a reputation for leadership, especially for his role in persuading the Texas university's Board of Trustees to finally admit African-American students.[13]

On schedule, by September 1, Sterling had moved his office from its interim quarters on the Quad to his Chancellor's Office on the fourth floor of the new Meyer Undergraduate Library. He had resolved not to interfere with, nor comment on, the next administration, beginning with the acting presidency of Robert J. Glaser, dean of the Medical School, who served until Pitzer's arrival in December 1968.[14]

The proactive Glaser, 49, vice president for medical affairs and dean of the School of Medicine since 1965, was applauded by students and faculty for his leadership during the transition. The *Stanford Daily*'s Philip Taubman praised Glaser's energy, frankness, and leadership. "In private and public he says exactly what he thinks, often in blunt language. Quite simply, Glaser doesn't mess around, and it increasingly seems a pity he can't remain as president."[15] (Glaser would leave the university, in 1970, to become vice president and trustee of the Com-

Robert Glaser, vice president for medical affairs and dean of medicine, served as Stanford's acting president from September until Kenneth Pitzer's arrival, in December 1968. Glaser was praised by both students and faculty for his proactive leadership and frankness.
STANFORD NEWS SERVICE

monwealth Fund of New York; he later headed the Henry J. Kaiser Family Foundation.)

Pitzer faced immediate criticism because of a lack of student involvement in the presidential search and his membership on the board of RAND Corporation, a government-financed think tank heavily engaged in military research and under attack from antiwar groups for its involvement in the Vietnam War. Pitzer also defended Stanford's controversial role in creating and maintaining the Stanford Research Institute, also associated with war-related research.

As campus controversies proliferated, the administrative staff and faculty leaders found Pitzer difficult to work with, due to his indecisiveness and poor communication skills.[16]

Sterling was troubled when Stanford trustees subsequently approached him, in 1969, proposing his election to the board; in keeping with his resolution, he initially turned them down. However, President Pitzer, enmeshed in student protests and campus discord, told Sterling that his refusal was being interpreted as a sign of Sterling's disapproval. Such an interpretation

The university's newly appointed sixth president, Kenneth Pitzer, at his first press conference, August 27, 1968. A renowned chemist, Pitzer was president of Rice University when he was tapped by Stanford. Earlier, he had served on the faculty at his alma mater, UC Berkeley, and had headed its Chemistry Department.   STANFORD NEWS SERVICE

finance side while he handled the development side.[18]

Sterling also played a vital role as national co-chairman with another friend—trustee Dick Guggenhime, the prominent San Francisco lawyer who had served as board president from 1964 to 1967—of the university's second innovative university-wide fund-raising campaign. The five-year, $300 million Campaign for Stanford was launched in April 1972. They worked closely with Stanford staff, led by Ken Cuthbertson and Daryl Pearson, and with more than 5,500 volunteers. Logging in more than $304 million a few days before its five-year deadline in 1977, it was then the largest single concentrated fundraising drive by any university in the United States. The campaign targeted $83 million for buildings (including a new Law School, a major addition to the Main Library, and the Terman Engineering Center), $93 million for operational expenses, and $125 million for endowments (including professorships, scholarships, and fellowships). Endowment support for faculty positions doubled.[19]

was "unmitigated poppycock," Sterling said later, but it appears that following Pitzer's visit to campus for interviews, Sterling had admitted privately to presidential assistant Fred Glover that he thought Pitzer a poor prospect. He soon regretted the comment, Glover said, and "never after that did I hear him say anything critical about Pitzer."[17]

Judging it unfair that Pitzer had to deal with such rumors, the chancellor relented and was elected to the Board of Trustees on October 14, 1969. To date, no other retired president has been so honored. (Sterling's presidential successors serve on the board as ex-officio members during their presidential tenure.)

Sterling served until June 1, 1976, when he reached mandatory retirement at age 70. During these years, he served as co-chair, with Fred H. Merrill, of the trustees' Committee on Finance and Development. Sterling considered Merrill, a good friend, to be conscientious and generous, and recalled that Merrill ably took on the

Serving on the board challenged Sterling's resolution not to interfere in the administrations of Kenneth Pitzer and Stanford's seventh president, Richard W. Lyman.[20] He refrained from speaking on academic policy issues or programs at trustee meetings. The only time Sterling spoke critically, Glover later said, was when Pitzer suggested that a study of undergraduate education be undertaken, seemingly unaware of studies conducted in the mid-1950s and as part of the 1967–69 Study of Education at Stanford, both during the Sterling administration and sources of considerable personal pride.[21]

LEADER OF AMERICAN REVOLUTION BICENTENNIAL COMMISSION, 1969–70

Less than a year after his retirement, Sterling received an unexpected call from the White House. Newly elected U.S. President Richard M. Nixon asked him to assume the chairmanship of the American Revolution Bicentennial Commission, the federal agency charged with planning the 1976 commemoration of the nation's 200th anniversary.[22]

Sterling was reluctant to accept the invitation. In addition to his Stanford activities, he wanted ample time to complete his study of British higher education, a project for the Ford Foundation. But Ann Sterling urged him to take it on. Before doing so, he asked President Nixon if he was sure he wanted a naturalized citizen as chair. Nixon reassured him, saying that he viewed the United States as a nation of immigrants. Sterling agreed to serve one year as chair—a year that turned out to be busy, enlightening, and at times frustrating, he later remembered.

Godfrey Harris, '59, who served as a consultant to the new chairman, recalled, "Wally told me he felt that the appointment was Nixon's way of apologizing for an incident at Stanford during Nixon's term as vice president." During the 1960 presidential campaign, Nixon had rushed a visit to Stanford after learning of a popular appearance by John F. Kennedy, but, unlike his competitor, had come unprepared. "Sterling had severely, but privately, criticized

Ann and Wallace Sterling, in June 1968, at their much-loved rustic cabin near La Honda. Sterling was determined not to interfere in the work of his successor, moving his office from the Quad to Meyer Library and taking up residence off campus. The following year, he reluctantly accepted appointment to the Board of Trustees, where he focused on fundraising. STANFORD NEWS SERVICE

the vice president for not preparing any specific remarks for a long-scheduled and well-publicized address to the student body. Sterling felt no one, no matter his position, had the right to treat students so disdainfully."[23]

Congress had established the commission on July 4, 1966, at the instigation of President Lyndon Johnson. Johnson was then deeply engaged in the war in Vietnam and stressed by growing antiwar feeling at home, as well as domestic economic and social issues. He was eager to fend off pressure by Pennsylvania's Senator Hugh Scott, who wanted a bicentennial celebration focused on Philadelphia. Boston was also vying to be the center of attention. The commission was created to recommend plans for the anniversary celebration. Representation on the 34-member commission was broad, and cumbersome: 17 public members, appointed by the president; four representatives from each house of Congress; four secretaries of federal departments; the U.S. attorney general; and four ex officio members (the librarian of Congress, the secretary of the Smithsonian Institution, the archivist of the United States, and the chairman of the Federal Council of Arts and Humanities). Congress initially appropriated no federal funds for the commission, however, intending that it be financed by private contributions.

From the time of its establishment until Sterling's appointment as chair, the commission had made little headway. Under its first chairman, Carl Humelsine, president of Colonial Williamsburg, the commission had met infrequently and had completed some preliminary planning, but at its meeting on the eve of the 1968 presidential election, the members had all resigned to give the newly elected president a clean slate. Some were reappointed, but one of Sterling's first tasks as the new chair would be to fill the now-vacant commission seats.

When Sterling went to Washington in July 1969, Nixon urged him to suggest candidates, emphasizing that appointments would be strictly nonpartisan, and handled through presidential assistant Harry Dent. Sterling's first liaison with the White House was, in fact, Charles (Bud) Wilkinson, the articulate former football coach of the University of Oklahoma, whom Sterling had tried to hire for Stanford in 1962.[24] Wilkinson escorted Sterling to Dent's office to discuss the vacancies. Sterling quickly found Dent to be "a political animal," disposed to fill all vacancies with Republicans. Sterling referenced Nixon's emphasis on nonpartisanship, adding that perhaps he had misunderstood the president. If so, Sterling suggested that Dent talk to Nixon before sunset; otherwise they would have Sterling's resignation the following morning. Ultimately, Nixon's appointees represented a reasonable political balance, although still tilted to the Republican side, due to the unrelenting Dent.

The former university president, accustomed to getting things done, found federal bureaucracy frustrating. The four departments were usually represented by silent junior members, without authorization to vote; only the representative of the attorney general was permitted to vote without waiting for clearance from above. As the commission wrestled with drafting recommendations later that year, Sterling informed the four cabinet secretaries that if they did not personally attend the meetings, they must endow their representatives with authority to vote. Decisions would be made, if necessary, without their vote. The representatives were so authorized.

Sterling found Hobart (Hobe) Lewis, managing editor of *Reader's Digest*, a valuable vice chairman. Lewis was especially helpful in getting access to Nixon. As Sterling later learned, *Reader's Digest* had financed many of Nixon's travels abroad when he had been out of political office, and Lewis had become a close friend of Nixon.[25]

President Nixon, too, was helpful, Sterling

later recalled. When Sterling tried without success to get on the agenda of the Governors' Conference in August 1969 in Colorado Springs, he turned to Nixon. After a presidential phone call, he was on the agenda—a six-minute pitch during which he urged the governors to establish bicentennial commissions in their respective states. Nixon also hosted an initial reception for the members and staff of the new commission, asking Sterling to introduce each member to him. Sterling thought Nixon's brief remarks were well spoken and enthusiastic about the potential contributions of the Bicentennial celebration.

Given the lack of progress of the previous three years, the new commission was charged with preparing a report for Nixon, with specific recommendations, by July 1, 1970. Sterling initially scheduled meetings every other month, and later in the year, every month (eight meetings in the course of the year).

The commission was allocated an annual budget of $75,000, to include a very small staff and all commission travel and meeting expenses. Sterling found this ludicrous, and in sharp contrast to Canada's financing of her centennial in 1967, where the federal government had appropriated substantial resources, matched on a one-for-one basis by provinces, cities, towns, and hamlets.

In 1969, President Richard Nixon and his Bicentennial Commission chair, Wallace Sterling, presided at a White House Blue Room reception. The elegant room, with its Empire-style furniture and striking blue drapes, had been famously redecorated by Jackie Kennedy. Sterling chaired the commission in 1969–70 and remained a member for another two years.
STANFORD UNIVERSITY ARCHIVES

Sterling was frequently on Capitol Hill, often accompanied by the commission's executive director, Melbourne L. (Mel) Spector, on courtesy calls to key legislators.[26] At one such visit, the speaker of the House of Representatives, John McCormack, expressed hope that the commission's recommendations for the celebration would not require any public funding. Sterling, already irritated by the commission's minuscule budget, replied that the commission could make such recommendations but that some might tax the public purse.[27]

Godfrey Harris recalled an amusing incident he and Sterling had enjoyed. In 1970, the Ladies of Mount Vernon invited Chairman Sterling to dinner. "Wally asked me to go along as the Bicentennial Commission's executive consultant,"

Harris later recalled. "We were greatly amused by the tenor of the questions we had fielded. Both of us felt that there had been an undercurrent of suspicion that Wally—Canadian by birth—and I—born in England—were somehow envisioning a commemoration that would culminate in the former colonies rejoining the British Empire."[28]

Midway through the year, a draft outline of the commission's report to Nixon advanced three concepts: 1) that the dramatic events of the American Revolution, the writing and signing of the Constitution, and "the winning of the West" all be memorialized; 2) that grassroots participation be encouraged and be as broadly based as possible, with states, counties, cities, and hamlets organizing their own celebrations; and 3) while the original legislation had emphasized the nation's early history, both the commission and the president suggested a forward look, with a special nod to the nation's young people. Sterling found this notable, since this viewpoint was offered when student unrest was at its peak and several universities were shut down for weeks at a time.

The commission approved the draft Report to the President a few days before the July 1, 1970, deadline. After a final proofreading, Sterling personally provided food and drink as a hearty thank-you to the staff for their hard work of proofreading.

The commission advised Nixon that, as constituted and funded, it was not suited to coordinate and implement the recommended programs. In his September 11, 1970, communication to Congress, Nixon complimented the report but would not commit to any particular item or reorganization until timing and cost data were submitted and studied. The commission was back in limbo.

As his year came to a close, Sterling breakfasted with David Mahoney, a highly paid executive in the Norton Simon manufacturing empire, who was being considered as his successor. Sterling and Mahoney spent more than two hours discussing the commission and the potential of the Bicentennial. Asked his opinion of Mahoney later that day, the dubious Sterling noted that it appeared that Mahoney needed the commission more than the commission needed him. Mahoney, he was then told, had already been offered and accepted the position. "Such are the devious ways of Washington," Sterling recalled.[29]

Sterling remained a member of the commission for two more years. Mahoney may have been a corporate "whiz kid" in the boardroom or a shareholders meeting, Sterling concluded, but he never seemed to have a feel for working with the diverse and independent-minded membership of a public commission. In 1973, the commission was replaced by the American Revolution Bicentennial Administration, with John Warner, later a senator from Virginia, in charge.

In retrospect, Sterling felt his service on the commission, although time-consuming and often frustrating, had been worth the effort. He once estimated that he had spent the equivalent of three weeks just sitting in airplanes.

KNIGHT COMMANDER AND UNCOMMON MAN

Sterling received many honors during his presidency and chancellorship, but two were especially meaningful to him: an honorary knighthood, conferred by Queen Elizabeth, and Stanford University's highest honor, the Degree of Uncommon Man.

Sterling was awarded an honorary Knight Commander of the Grand Order of the British Empire (KBE) in 1976. (In 1957, he had been awarded the third class of the order, as Commander of the Order, or CBE).[30] He was recognized as an academic figure of international status, as well as a scholar of British history and a devoted friend of Britain. He had just completed his third term as chairman of the Pacific Region Committee of the Marshall Scholarships, given by the British people each year to 30 outstanding American students to study at any British university. His long-standing interest in British-American, and especially Canadian-American, political, economic, and cultural relations had led to his work on many joint committees to promote educational and economic cooperation.[31]

The presentation ceremony took place at the British Embassy in Washington, D.C., on July 1, 1976, with Britain's ambassador to the United States, Sir Peter Ramsbotham, presenting the awards. In addition to Sterling, the recipients of the KBE were Walter Annenberg, publisher, philanthropist, and diplomat, who had served as U.S. ambassador to the United Kingdom; Eugene Ormandy, internationally known violinist and director of the Philadelphia Symphony Orchestra; and Dean Rusk, former U.S. secretary of state and past president of the Rockefeller Foundation. Three others received the CBE: Hoyt Ammidon, highly successful businessman and influential philanthropist who was president of the American Friends of Canada; Angier Biddle Duke, diplomat, ambassador, and chief of protocol for the U.S. Department of State; and the London-born Leslie Townes (Bob) Hope,

world-renowned comedian, actor, and singer. In reminiscing about the award, Sterling noted that, of course, Bob Hope was the one who grabbed the attention of the press.[32]

The other honor that gave Sterling special pleasure was Stanford's Degree of Uncommon Man, the university's highest tribute. Stanford grants no honorary degrees, believing only substantive academic efforts merit an academic degree. The Degree of Uncommon Man had been established in 1953 to honor those who render unique and outstanding service to the university. The name is inspired by a comment by Herbert Hoover: "We believe in equal opportunity for all but we know that this includes the opportunity to rise to leadership—in other words, to be uncommon." In times of need, said Hoover, people want to be served by men and women of uncommon abilities.[33]

On March 9, 1978, Sterling received the award, bestowed with great ceremony by the Stanford Associates. He was honored for leading the university's dramatic rise in academic stature, as well as for his contributions as chancellor. "As chancellor he not only personifies the development of a truly world class independent

Ann and Wally Sterling, with Jing and Richard Lyman, at the Uncommon Man Award dinner, March 10, 1978. In presenting Chancellor Sterling with the award, President Lyman honored him for his leadership and "unflagging efforts" as both president and chancellor in Stanford's dramatic rise.
STANFORD NEWS SERVICE

In 1950, Sterling received an honorary degree from his undergraduate alma mater, the University of Toronto, with Chancellor Vincent Massey doing the honors. The last in Sterling's string of 21 was from another alma mater, the University of Alberta, in 1970.
KEN BELL / STANFORD UNIVERSITY ARCHIVES

university on the Pacific rim of this continent," said President Richard Lyman. "He also contributes mightily to its continued good health, by travel and effort on its behalf that I cannot in good conscience call 'untiring'—it's exhausting—but I can and do call unflagging."[34]

During his presidency and chancellorship, Sterling also received 21 honorary degrees from universities across the United States (including UC Berkeley and Harvard) and Canada, as well as England (Durham) and France (Caen). Among the first was an honorary LL.D. from his alma mater, the University of Toronto, in 1950, and the last was from another alma mater, the University of Alberta, in 1970.

In 1964, Sterling had been the second (after Herbert Hoover, in 1963) to be honored with the Herbert Hoover Medal, awarded by the Stanford Alumni Association for distinguished service by a Stanford alumnus. This special tribute to Sterling came on the 15th anniversary of his presidency.[35]

The year following his retirement, Sterling received the Clark Kerr Award, bestowed by the faculty of UC Berkeley, and given in recognition of "extraordinarily distinguished contributions to the advancement of higher education." During his presidency, the award noted, Sterling provided leadership for Stanford's greatest period of growth but "more important was the steady advance in the quality of undergraduate and graduate instruction and in scholarly, scientific, and professional recognition." (Sterling was the second recipient, following Clark Kerr, former UC president and Berkeley chancellor.)

SERVICE ON CORPORATE BOARDS

Sterling participated in many professional, philanthropic, and governmental organizations during his career, and he continued a number of those activities on retiring as president. Unlike many of his Stanford successors, however, his participation on corporate boards was relatively small, largely after retirement from the presidency, and usually at the behest of a personal friend. Corporate board service was also financially helpful.

At Caltech and later at Stanford, Sterling found himself at close quarters with the business world. His Caltech mentor, William Munro, had introduced him to key Southern California business leaders, who were also involved with major Southern California philanthropies, including Caltech. Sterling, like Munro, became a member of the Century Club of Los Angeles, just as he would later become a member of Northern California's influential Bohemian Club.

While at Caltech, Sterling met William Freeman, a salesman and editor with Macmillan Publishing. In 1946, Freeman established the W. H. Freeman Publishing Company (his first book was a general chemistry text by Sterling's Caltech colleague Linus Pauling), and he asked Sterling to serve on his board. The company prospered, thanks to successful sales of high-quality textbooks written by distinguished academics.

Sterling's longest corporate board commitment, 1952–79, was with Fireman's Fund Insurance Company of San Francisco. During his board years, the company, already a venerable San Francisco institution, grew into one of the largest insurance companies in the United States (it was acquired by American Express in 1968). Sterling knew two of the company's presidents as members of Stanford's Board of Trustees, James Crafts and Fred Merrill.[36]

Sterling served on other corporate boards, of which four were particularly memorable: Kaiser Aluminum and Chemical Company, 1967–76; Shell Oil Company, 1968–77; Tridair, 1972–76; and Dean Witter, 1972–78.

Shell Oil was the largest board, and, in many ways, the most interesting to him, giving him insight into international energy issues, particularly during the 1973 oil crisis. He served on its compensation committee, and was impressed with the level of detail provided about all levels of management in every division. At Kaiser Aluminum and Chemical Company, headquartered across the Bay in Oakland, Sterling served on three board committees, including compensation.

Tridair was a small corporation of $20 to $25 million in annual sales, mostly serving the airline industry, for which it made highly specialized small parts. It was in financial difficulty when Sterling joined the board, in 1972. (A year after he left the board, in 1977, the company was sold to Rexnord.)

Sterling was the first, and for three years the only, outside director of the financial firm Dean Witter. He had been appointed by Marco (Mickey) F. Hellman, a longtime good friend. Hellman, a grandson of the great San Francisco financier Isaias W. Hellman, had been president of Barth and Co. when the company was sold to Dean Witter. As the only outside director, Sterling considered himself something of a token and encouraged the election of two more outside directors. He also urged the Dean Witter board, which had no retirement age for directors, to set retirement age at 72, and demonstrated his belief in this policy by retiring from the board when he reached that age, in 1978.

The front entrance of the mansion at Filoli, a year before the Woodside estate was donated, in 1975, to the National Trust for Historic Preservation. Sterling served as inaugural president of the Filoli Center of Woodside's Board of Directors, 1975–79.
HISTORIC AMERICAN BUILDINGS SURVEY / LIBRARY OF CONGRESS

NURTURING FILOLI CENTER

Sterling's last directorship, and one of his favorites, was serving from 1975 to 1979 as founding president of the board of the Filoli Center of Woodside.

Sterling had a long-standing interest in gardening and landscaping, and although he described himself as an amateur, he was, in fact, an accomplished horticulturist. In addition to helping tend the large garden surrounding the Lou Henry Hoover House, he grew flowers, as well as tree and shrub seedlings, in a small greenhouse next to the house, and often gave plants and fertilizer to faculty members moving into new homes.

On retirement, the Sterlings moved to a large 1913 Mediterranean house on Stockbridge Avenue in Woodside. One of the home's attractions was the nearly 3 acres of grounds, where he could pursue his gardening avocation. The property

had been donated to Stanford by Mae Vrooman Forbes, daughter of early Stanford trustee Henry Vrooman, as a life tenancy for the Sterlings.[37]

The Sterlings, with their combined interest in horticulture and English antique furniture, could not help but be interested in the preservation of the nearby Filoli estate, on Cañada Road, in Woodside. The 654-acre estate had 16 acres of extensive gardens that Sterling described as "one of the most varied and beautiful gardens west of the Mississippi."[38]

William B. Bourn II, president of the Spring Valley Water Company, had purchased the rural property near Crystal Springs Lake, and began construction in 1915 on a large Georgian mansion designed by Willis Polk. The house and surrounding English gardens, designed by Bruce Porter, were completed two years later. William and Agnes Moody Bourn lived there until their deaths, both in 1936.

A year later, the property was purchased by William P. and Lurline Matson Roth as their family home. William Roth had worked his way up in the Matson Navigation Company, becoming company president in 1927. His wife, the daughter of shipping magnate Captain William Matson, was an avid horsewoman and knowledgeable horticulturist. Lurline Roth took special interest in the Filoli gardens, working closely with Isabella Worn, who had supervised the original planting of the grounds, until Worn's death, in 1950. The gardens earned an international reputation, and Mrs. Roth hosted many distinguished visitors from botanical and horticultural societies and garden clubs from around the world.[39]

In the early 1970s, Mrs. Roth decided to move to a smaller house in Hillsborough (her husband had died in 1963), but she continued to support the maintenance of the house and gardens. Potential buyers had little interest in the garden, however, and it was rumored that the property would be converted into a private golf course. In 1975, with strong encouragement of prominent horticulturists, she donated 125 acres, including the house and the surrounding formal gardens, to the National Trust for Historic Preservation, along with a trust of $2.4 million. An additional 528 acres were later added to the Filoli Center.[40]

Lurline Roth stipulated that the Filoli property be managed and promoted by a local board of trustees. In early 1975, with Filoli's future still uncertain, her son, William Matson Roth, asked Chancellor Sterling to be a trustee and to oversee the transition, including an effort by prominent local citizens to build up the endowment. Thus, Sterling became founding president and chair of the Filoli Center. After working out two oper-

ating agreements with the National Trust, the Filoli Center was established as a historic site and nonprofit corporation in February 1976.

The Filoli board started from scratch with five trustees and no funding except income from the endowment, which the National Trust charged a fee to administer. The first executive director, Warren Lemmon, had had a long association with the Roth properties. Fortunately, Sterling later recalled, Lemmon had the patience to deal with the National Trust staff, which initially insisted on reviewing and approving every physical change they suggested.

Lemmon negotiated the first of many movie and television company contracts with the on-site filming of Warren Beatty's 1978 film, *Heaven Can Wait*. In addition to a stiff fee for use of the property, the film company paid for a major restoration of the floors and other parts of the house.

With Lemmon's early retirement, a nationwide search resulted in the 1978 appointment of

Inside Filoli's walled garden, looking north toward the garden house, 1974. The 654-acre estate included 16 acres of extensive gardens surrounding the house. Filoli's research library is named in Sterling's honor.
HISTORIC AMERICAN BUILDINGS SURVEY / LIBRARY OF CONGRESS

Hadley Osborn, a distinguished horticulturist and president of the Strybing Arboretum Society in San Francisco's Golden Gate Park. Sterling remembered Osborn as very competent and well liked by the Roth family. Osborn appointed Lucy Erickson, then a Filoli gardener, as garden superintendent; she became a widely acclaimed horticulturist.[41]

By 1978, the Filoli board had grown to 24, and a nonprofit volunteer group, Friends of Filoli, had been established to lead tours, raise funds, and provide other support. Sterling observed that Filoli might not have survived without the Friends, who even labored in the gardens when necessary. A major fundraising drive got underway in August 1978. Soon after, Sterling's doctors insisted that he resign from his Filoli responsibilities, as he had already done with other board memberships. He did so with regret in January 1979. The J. E. Wallace Sterling Library, a research library focusing on horticulture, garden design, and decorative arts, opened in his honor at the mansion in 1988.

HE NEVER STOPPED WORKING FOR STANFORD

Throughout his retirement, Sterling continued to work on Stanford's behalf, but he preferred to do so behind the scenes. Although often prodded for his opinion, and even his intercession, he took care to avoid expressing opinions publicly about university affairs. "I made a vow when I retired

Chancellor Sterling served as master of ceremonies at the 1980 inauguration of Stanford's eighth president, Donald Kennedy (center). Richard Lyman (left), Stanford's seventh president, and provost under Sterling, had become president of the Rockefeller Foundation. STANFORD NEWS SERVICE

Nini and Fred Glover joined Wally and Ann Sterling at the October 1981 groundbreaking ceremony for the Sterling Quadrangle dormitory complex. The Glovers had occasionally served as hosts at Hoover House social events when President Sterling was ill or out of town.
STANFORD NEWS SERVICE

never to comment, never to interfere with the administration after I left," he explained to local journalist Mary Madison in 1980. "I keep myself ignorant in self-defense," he told her, although he enjoyed staying in touch with old friends on and off campus, and he visited and corresponded with Stanford alumni across the country.[42]

When he was interviewed by Donald Stokes for two articles in the *Stanford Observer* in 1979, he was asked how he visualized Stanford's next decade. "These are worrisome times for those in higher education," he told Stokes. The image of universities had been tarnished, as had that of government and corporations. Yet, he did not accept the "gloomy prospect that universities have fallen from grace," and offered as evidence Stanford's successful fundraising in the Campaign for Stanford, which had exceeded its goals two years before. Universities "have survived wars, depressions, revolutions and student riots. Surely they can survive current financial stress and the arrogant intervention of federal bureaucracy."[43]

Sterling continued, as his health permitted,

to be a popular guest at Stanford functions. He "never stopped working for Stanford," Mary Madison wrote in her feature on Sterling, as he was about to preside over the inauguration of Donald Kennedy (he had earlier acted as master of ceremonies for Richard W. Lyman's inaugural dinner). Sterling also participated in events across campus, from dedications and award ceremonies to special events. Although slowed by arthritis, he still enjoyed attending the Alumni Association's annual presentation of the J. E. Wallace Sterling Award to a graduating senior, given for outstanding scholarship and leadership.

In 1981, the Sterlings took part in the groundbreaking of the Ann and J. E. Wallace Sterling Quadrangle at Governor's Corner, a new residential housing complex for undergraduates. Wallace Sterling's last major public appearance was at the dedication of the new 800-bed complex (360 beds in Sterling Quadrangle) in October 1983. At that time, President Kennedy said of Sterling, "In all of academic history in this country, no university has ever advanced so far under the leadership of a single man."[44]

22

DEATH AND REMEMBRANCES

Wallace Sterling died of cancer on July 1, 1985, at his home in Woodside. He was 78. Long obituaries appeared across the country lauding Sterling's role in Stanford's rise to international recognition: the "gold rush" of faculty appointments; innovative curriculum changes; the increasing selectivity of admissions; pathbreaking fundraising success; and landmarks like the new Medical Center, SLAC, overseas campuses, and the Stanford Industrial Park.

Sterling's biography, summarized in the program printed for his service at Stanford's Memorial Church, began succinctly, and evocatively:

> J. E. Wallace Sterling, Canadian by birth, American citizen by choice, British in spirit, gardener at heart, Stanford University's chancellor from 1968 until his death, its President from 1949 to 1968, brought this institution up from a well-respected university on the west coast of the United States to stand among the world's finest.

< Chancellor Wallace Sterling, in the garden at his Woodside home, sat for a series of formal portraits for San Francisco / Stanford photographer Leo Holub in 1979.
LEO HOLUB / STANFORD UNIVERSITY ARCHIVES

LONGTIME MEDICAL CHALLENGES

Health issues had plagued Sterling for years, leading to his early retirement from Stanford's presidency in 1968, at age 62. In addition to back problems from collegiate football injuries, Sterling's "trouble with my pipes," as he called them, had begun during the war, he told a friend in 1964. Recurring from time to time, they had resurfaced early in his presidency. In an October 1949 letter to another friend, he noted that his "'insides' have been on another rampage and once more I have gone through a barium diet and they finally decided that I may have a low grade infection stemming from an appendix. So after I get inaugurated I go to the hospital for awhile." It was more than a year later, in early December 1950, that he had an appendectomy at Palo Alto Hospital.[1]

Sterling's stomach problems (chronic intestinal inflammation) flared up again in 1963, just as he finished two years as president of the Association of American Universities. He was in the midst of Stanford's PACE fundraising campaign and of major recruiting efforts for deans and faculty. He was admitted to the new Palo Alto–Stanford

539

Hospital in October for several days of observation and testing of an abdominal inflammation that had been bothering him for months.[2] Sterling wrote Donald Russell, a trustee, on October 16:

> It was a recurrence of diverticulitis, with which I've had some chronic troubles. The docs were good to me, so the pain went away. They seem to have been delighted to have found something a little unusual in part of my insides, so that I guess both the cause of the patient and the cause of science were thus served. Except for feeling a little wobbly—because they fed me intravenously for three days—I feel fine.[3]

In February 1964, Sterling again became seriously ill with an abdominal inflammation. This time, the diverticulitis was complicated by a ruptured diverticulum, which, on the night of February 12, led to acute peritonitis. On his doctors' advice, he canceled his upcoming speaking engagements in Southern California, and rested at home, where his doctors initially believed he responded well to treatment. But he was admitted to the hospital and underwent surgery on March 30.[4]

After Sterling's 1964 surgery, Fred Glover later recalled, "We were told by the doctors that he would never have the same energy he had before."[5]

Don Carlson also remembered that he and other staff members were aware of Sterling's declining stamina after the operation. Carlson quoted Dr. Russel V. Lee as saying that Sterling "will only be half of what he was before." It was "almost true," Carlson said. "You could tell from that point on . . . the way he conducted meetings was very different. They were much more casual, and he liked to have lots of people" around. Before the surgery, meetings had been "rather limited to just people who had something he wanted to know."[6]

While recovering in the hospital, Sterling was serenaded from outside his ground-floor room one afternoon by the Mendicants, a student group of male *a cappella* singers frequently invited to sing at alumni functions. They began with some Stanford songs and a few old '20s tunes like "Coney Island Baby," then did the 1960s spiritual "Glory Road to Heaven." Sterling later recalled that he was a bit miffed because he had no plans for an early departure from life.[7]

Trustee President Morris Doyle visited soon after Sterling returned home. The trustees, Doyle told him, insisted that Sterling take a vacation long enough to get well and recover his strength. After convalescing that spring, Wally left with Ann in mid-May for Europe. Following a brief visit to Britain, they vacationed in southern Germany. In late June 1964, he was among a select group of presidents, representing the Association of American Universities, who joined the heads of Germany's major universities for the German Rectors Conference in Bad Godesberg (part of Bonn) for several days of discussions. Sterling and the other Americans then visited various West German universities. He was back in California in July, and ready to resume his duties that September.[8]

While Sterling was absent, Fred Terman, vice president and provost, served as acting president. The transition was a smooth one. "Of course, we do tend to lose some momentum," News Service Director Bob Beyers commented while Sterling was recuperating, "but the University doesn't disintegrate while he's out." Fred Glover also noted that Sterling was always available by phone, although they tried not to bother him. The president had left for lengthy trips before, including long trips to Europe, when he was capably backed by his staff. "Nobody is saying: 'My God, Wally's not here,' " reported the *Daily* in April. "The key thing is that people who worked around him knew what he wanted done. And they're doing it in his absence." The president's absence provoked rumors of impending retirement, which university officials denied.[9]

Back on active duty in the fall, Sterling told the *Daily*'s associate editor, Nancy Steffen, that his time off had "recharged his batteries." Steffen concluded that, "barring catastrophe," Sterling likely would remain president for many years to come.[10]

In March 1967, however, in announcing Sterling's intention to retire, board President Richard Guggenhime admitted the trustees had known for several years that Sterling was considering early retirement. "Dr. Sterling's wish to retire early is understandable," he commented, "and the academic community can rejoice that he will become lifetime chancellor, thereby enabling him to give counsel born of rich experience."[11]

A FITTING TRIBUTE

Sterling's memorial service was held at Stanford Memorial Church on July 9, 1985. Many of those attending had joined the ranks of Stanford's faculty and staff during Sterling's administra-tion. Thirty special places were reserved for the plumbers, gardeners, and other workers of the university's building and grounds office.[12]

Continuing his devotion to the man he served for many years, Fred Glover was principal organizer of the service.[13] The Rev. Robert Hamerton-Kelly, dean of the chapel at Stanford, and the Rev. C. Julian Bartlett, dean emeritus of Grace Cathedral and archdeacon of San Francisco, officiated. Scriptural readings were delivered by Peter S. Bing, student body president, 1954–55, and Board of Trustees president, 1976–81, and Robert Minge Brown, student body president, 1931–32, and trustee president, 1971–76. Delivering formal tributes were Morris M. Doyle, trustee president, 1962–64, and university President Donald Kennedy.

Grace and friendship were themes of many of the eulogies at death and during the service eight days later.

Peter Bing noted that "Wally found in each

The service for Chancellor Sterling was held in Memorial Church on July 9, 1985. He had died on July 1, at age 78. STANFORD NEWS SERVICE

of us the qualities that made us worthy, and then, with infinite civility, he guided and encouraged us to develop them." He continued:

> His formidable knowledge of human experience, and his personal fairness and dignity, made us instinctively turn to him, whether as a teacher, a colleague or a steadfast and sensitive friend. The Stanford he built, with its exuberant and changing existence and its abiding commitment to pass his values from generation to generation, are truly the most permanent memorials to Dr. Sterling.

Former trustee Brown, who worked closely with Sterling as general counsel for the university, said, "Wally Sterling was greatness with grace—a friend who enriched our lives with fond memories which we shall always treasure." He also told those assembled:

> Wally Sterling molded the character of modern Stanford into an institution of exceptional intellectual quality operating in an atmosphere of pervasive friendship. His personal charisma attracted the outstanding faculty essential to the academic eminence Stanford achieved under his guidance, and his genuine love of people created friends for Stanford in all walks of life.

On learning of Sterling's death, former trustee President Morrie Doyle said, "I think Wally Sterling was Stanford's greatest president. [David Starr] Jordan was tenacious and defended the new venture against imminent collapse, but Sterling led a renaissance that moved Stanford into the front rank—the veritable blooming of the aspirations of the Founders."

In his memorial service remarks Doyle added, "It is impossible to overstate Wally's contribution to the stature of Stanford. . . . [H]is dedication was to the whole cause, and in rapid succession department after department and school after school gained strength and prominence." Doyle continued: "Whether presiding at commencement, tending to his lovely garden, chatting with his friends

and family, cutting wood for the winter fireplace, or siring the Sons of Preachers Night at the Bohemian Grove, he was an extraordinary man."

Sterling "understood that leadership requires the radiation of belief, of confidence, and of good cheer," said Donald Kennedy, who had come to Stanford as a biology professor and was now Stanford's president. "There were struggles, but he made them contests of principles and not of people. . . . There were discouragements; he came through each one smiling and never looked for a place to put blame. There were discomforts, and he danced gallantly around them, refusing to let them dampen an occasion for others."

Kennedy recalled a recent phone conversation in which Sterling announced that after six weeks of radiation therapy, he had experienced a set-

Robert A. Laurie of the Stuart Highlanders piping "Amazing Grace" at the end of the service. STANFORD NEWS SERVICE

back: "An injury sustained, he reported, because he tripped carrying a sack of bone meal out of the potting shed," Kennedy said. "He said this, I might add, with some asperity."

After paying tribute to Ann Sterling "for being there for him and for the rest of us as well," and, with her late husband, serving as "examples of what partnership means," Kennedy spoke on behalf of the institution, "venturing to represent the legatees of Wally's work as a builder and a leader":

> There is scarcely a single aspect of Stanford's contemporary quality as a university that does not trace to Wally Sterling's creative and devoted management of its great postwar transformation. His success was based on simple strengths. He was able to collect and motivate talented colleagues, and then give them room to work. He had strong principles and said firmly what they were. He had the stomach for daring decisions, and they generally paid off.
>
> Most of all, he came somehow into a close and abiding resonance with the aspirations and qualities of Stanford, so that one scarcely knew which were the institution's and which were the man's. He came to epitomize our sense of spiritual growth and, at the same time, our concern for students and Stanford's humane qualities. By reflecting our own values and ambitions back to us, he reminded us constantly of where we were headed and how far we could go.

Stanford President Emeritus Richard W. Lyman, in 1985 serving as president of the Rockefeller Foundation, wrote in tribute, "When I came to Stanford to teach history in 1958, Wally Sterling was almost exactly halfway through his 19-year presidency, and operating at the top of his form":

> Perhaps the key to his phenomenal success at Stanford was his ability to bring together diverse elements in the University and its outside constituencies, to appeal to old supporters and new with equal effectiveness. To old Stanford stalwarts he brought assurance that the institution as conceived by the Founders was intact and would remain so, even through enormous changes in funding and overall quality. To new and potential friends he brought a vision of unlimited possibilities for this thriving campus on the rim of the Pacific. This was not done by deception or by concealing his ambitions for the place. Rather it was a triumph of personal style and sensitivity to the hopes and fears of others.
>
> Later on, developments at Stanford as at other universities put this success seriously at risk; institutional loyalties were strained by the unprecedented waves of dissension and rebellion on campus. Consensus as to the nature and purposes of a university were simply impossible for a time, and I have always thought it particularly poignant that towards the close of "the Sterling years" Wally had to face so much damage to the climate in which the University had flourished. Fortunately, he lived to see all that change, too, and to find himself reestablished in the overwhelming majority of Stanford hearts and minds as the heroic figure who had led the University to and then over that famous "edge of greatness."
>
> For Wally Sterling of Stanford it is impossible not to think of Sir Christopher Wren's epitaph in the great Cathedral of St. Paul's: *Si monumentum requiris, circumspice*—If you seek his monument, look about you!
>
> He will need no other, he deserves no less.

HIS SON'S REMEMBRANCE

In a voice uncannily like his father's, William Sterling shared a memorable story of his father the gardener:

> You know he loved to garden. When we resided on campus at the Hoover House, he would often find a moment to relax outside, tending flowers and lawn and shrubs. He would don old khaki working clothes, a long-sleeved shirt, and pants cinched up by a questionable and ancient belt, a pair of disreputable but infinitely comfortable old shoes, and a tattered straw hat.

In a voice remarkably like his father's, Sterling's son, William, paid tribute to him. Also participating (from left): former Board of Trustee presidents Peter Bing, Robert Minge Brown, and Morris Doyle, as well as President Donald Kennedy. Emeritus Professor Eric Hutchinson is partly obscured behind Sterling. Bill Sterling compared the university to a large garden, saying his father "was ever pleased and grateful for the privilege he felt in being permitted to tend it for a while." STANFORD NEWS SERVICE

On the particular afternoon in question, he was watering shrubbery by the front door. He was standing on the driveway, clad as described, when a car of curious tourists turned in and stopped beside him.

"Is this the Hoover House?" they asked.

"Yes, it is," he said.

"Do you work here?"

"Yes, I do," Dad said.

"Who lives here now?" they wanted to know.

"The president of Stanford University and his family."

"Is the president inside right now?"

"No, he is not," was the accurate reply.

"Do you think," they wondered, "we could have a peek inside the house?"

And the result was that Dad showed them through the front hall, out onto the terrace which looks over the garden and beyond to the campus. They were quite pleased. So was he. They thanked him as they left, and he thanked them ever after by relating how delighted he was to have been accepted for what he appeared to be, and for what, in fact, he truly was, a friendly gardener.

"This University, in a sense," William Sterling concluded, "was a larger garden, and he was ever pleased and grateful for the privilege he felt in being permitted to tend it for a while."[14]

STANFORD ACREAGE
FROM THE BEGINNING

Stanford's total acreage has changed often since creation of the Founding Grant of Leland Stanford Junior University. Purchases, like that of Searsville Dam, its reservoir, and environs, added acreage. During the 1950s and 1960s, acreage was lost to government-agency condemnations (among them Interstate 280 and the Veterans Hospital). This does not include lands annexed to neighboring municipalities but still owned by the university, such as the Stanford Shopping Center. Lands condemned by school districts have carried reversion clauses. The following list illustrates the difficulty of pinning down a single total acreage number during the Sterling administration. (Sources listed below.)

1885	6,967 acres	John Coombe 1883 survey of Palo Alto Farm at time of Founding Grant (SUA M[ap]7)
1893	8,448 acres	Estimated total purchased by Senator Stanford between 1876 and his death in 1893 (Tutorow)
1908	8,248 acres	Herrmann Brothers survey made for trustees, after boundary adjustments (SUA M700)
1930	8,642 acres	Albert J. Krutmeyer survey, including purchase of Searsville Reservoir and environs (Tutorow)
1950s	8,800 acres	Estimated acreage often used in master plan documents and news reports, including by Skidmore, Owings & Merrill
1951–52	8,660 acres	LSJU lot survey (unsigned but likely requested by the Planning Office, ca. 1951). Acreage calculated from this survey's listing of individual lot sizes (SUA M701)
1955	8,486 acres	C. H. Maier survey, Stanford Planning Office (SUA M704.1)
1964	8,762.9 acres	Land Development Office, Annual Reports to Trustees, August 31, 1963, and August 31, 1964 (Trustee minutes)
1970	8,800 acres	Livingston and Blayney Planners, "Presentation to the Board of Trustees," November 9, 1970 (Trustee minutes)
1979–2022	8,180 acres	University lands official acreage as used in *Stanford Facts* and in *General Use Permit* negotiations with the County of Santa Clara

IMPORTANT CONDEMNATIONS 1949–68

Not including land for easements, road widenings (such as El Camino, Page Mill, and Sand Hill), border adjustments, utilities, and other minor matters.

1950	8 acres	Oak Knoll Elementary School, Menlo Park School District
1955	93 acres	Veterans Administration Hospital
1956	53 acres	Gunn High School (completed 1964)
1961	40 acres	Proposed school for Sequoia Union High School District (Stanford repurchased the land, 1980)
1959 & 1964	8 acres	Escondido Elementary School
1966	9.4 acres	Lucille M. Nixon Elementary School
1966	215 acres	Interstate 280 freeway (approximation)
1961–71	[542 acres]	Failed attempt by Army Corps of Engineers to build Ladera Dam
1966	[30 acres]	Failed attempt by Palo Alto to create a park along Old Page Mill Road

Sources for total acreage: Tutorow (2004) 427, 429, 431, 941; Stanford University Map Collection, SC1049, Stanford University Archives (SUA); Ray Faulkner, "To Members of the Faculty and Staff" and "Statement by David Packard, President, Stanford Board of Trustees," *Faculty-Staff Newsletter*, Special Edition, March 28, 1960; "Stanford Plans Use of Lands," *San Mateo Times*, October 13, 1950; "Stanford Leases Site for Homes and School," *San Mateo Times*, April 6, 1951; "The Shrinking Stanford Lands," *Stanford Review* (May 1960) 10, 13; *Stanford Today* (May 1960) 4; Land Development Annual Report (1962–63) in Trustee minutes, December 19, 1963, and (1963–64) in Trustee minutes, February 18, 1965; Livingston and Blayney City and Regional Planners, Report to Trustees Committee on Land Development, November 9, 1970, p. 15, in Trustee minutes, November 10, 1970; *Stanford Facts* (1979–2022); Stanford University General Use Permit 2000, Annual Report No. 20 (Santa Clara County Planning Office, 2000) 1.

Sources for condemnations: Minutes of the Board of Trustees, various years.

NOTABLE BUILDING PROJECTS DURING THE STERLING ERA

Building construction, 1887 to 1949 = ca. 2.5 million square feet
Building construction, 1950 to 1969 = ca. 4.1 million square feet*

MAJOR PROJECTS

1959–68	Stanford Medical Center, including Palo Alto–Stanford Hospital and ongoing additions and remodels
1966	Stanford Linear Accelerator Center (dedicated 1967)

ACADEMIC BUILDINGS

1949	Original Microwave Lab, W.W. Hansen Laboratories of Physics/High Energy Physics Lab (expanded 1953, 1959, 1963)
1950	Organic Chemistry Lab
1951	Electronics Research Lab (expanded 1952, 1956, 1959, 1964)
1952	Sequoia Hall (1891 Roble Hall reduced from three to one story for Statistics)
1954	Second Microwave Lab, W. W. Hansen Laboratories of Physics/Microwave Lab (expanded 1957, 1959; renamed Ginzton Lab in 1976)
1954	Henry Salvatori Geophysics Laboratory
1957	Lloyd Noble Petroleum Engineering Lab
1957	Physics Lecture Hall (Physics Tank)
1958	Applied Electronics Lab (expanded 1959)
1958	Biophysics Laboratory
1960	John Stauffer Sr. #1 Organic Chemistry Building (dedicated 1961)
1961–64	Jordan Quad (Redwood, Pine, Cedar, Spruce, Cypress) "temporary" academic/office buildings

ACADEMIC BUILDINGS *(continued)*

1963	George Polya Hall computation center (in Jordan Quad)
1962	Russell Varian Physics Laboratory
1964	John Stauffer #2 Physical Chemistry Building
1965	Old Chemistry (largely empty, but part of 1902 structure remodeled for continued use; decommissioned 1980s, dramatically repurposed 2016)
1965	Jack A. McCullough Building
1966	John Stauffer #3 Chemical Engineering Research Laboratory
1966	Graduate School of Business
1967	Herrin Biology Hall and Herrin Research Labs

Started during Sterling's presidency but completed later

1969	Durand Building for Space Engineering and Science
1969	Skilling Building (classrooms and TV teaching facilities)
1969	Nathan Cummings Art Building
1969	Roscoe Maples Pavilion

MAIN QUADRANGLE BUILDINGS

Outer Quad

1950	Building 160 (Thomas Welton Stanford Library, 1900, later Administration Building). Remodeled and double-decked for the Law School (project started before Sterling's 1949 arrival).
1964	Building 380 (Physics Corner, 1903) remodeled and double-decked as the Alfred P. Sloan Mathematics Corner. History Corner, Engineering Corner, and Geology Corner were remodeled more recently.
1970	Building 420 (Jordan Hall, 1903) interior and fancy roof skylight demolished, 1968. Remodeled and double-decked for Psychology Department. (Jordan Hall, originally home to zoology, was considered the least efficient building on campus, with a large atrium where animal skeletons and other exhibits were displayed in the second-floor gallery.)

As late as 1967, when this photo was taken, Jordan Hall (Building 420 on the Outer Quad) retained some of its 1903 Victorian touches. It originally housed zoology, with several animal skeletons still occupying the second floor of the large, but inefficient atrium, after the biologists had moved to the new Herrin Hall and Labs. This interior was gutted starting in 1968 and reopened, minus a skylight, in 1970 for psychology.   LEO HOLUB / STANFORD UNIVERSITY ARCHIVES

Inner Quad

Between 1949 and 1968, all Inner Quad buildings—except Building 30—and two of the low Outer Quad structures were "double-decked" from one interior above-ground floor to two. Building 30 remains the only Quad structure kept largely as it was in 1891. (Double-decking accounts for the odd alignment of windows and floors in these buildings. Years ago, trustees decided to maintain the exterior appearance of the Quad, with the original sandstone fenestration. Quad structures are updated by constructing new flexible "buildings" within the sandstone walls.)

Original Engineering Row (behind Quad)

1949	Building 550, Metallurgical Engineering (later Materials Science), courtyard covering for more space in ca. 1900 structure. Renovation and expansion, 1963, and named Peterson Engineering Lab.
1962	Building 500, Electrical Engineering laboratory, renovation of the 1903 building it shared with Mechanical Engineering. Dedicated 1965 as Frederick E. Terman Laboratory.
1962	Building 520, Engineering Mechanics laboratory (1891 powerhouse and boiler room). Double-decked, remodeled, and renamed George Havas Engineering Building.

COMMUNITY & ADMINISTRATIVE BUILDINGS & SPACES

1951	Eating Clubs
1952	Bowman Alumni House (expanded 1955)
1954	University Press expansion (also 1962)
1954	Stanford Museum (renovation of 1891 building closed after 1906 earthquake; reopened 1909; ichthyology, other zoology collections added to basement and main floor of south wing, 1924; Dudley Herbarium installed in south wing's second floor, 1925; art collections closed 1945, some art sold off 1951–52; remodeled and reopened 1954; art component dramatically boosted, 1960s, under Art Department direction, with further renovations; natural history collections transferred on indefinite loan to California Academy of Sciences, with fish and other zoological collections going in early 1970s, the herbarium in 1976).
1957	Florence Hellman Dinkelspiel Auditorium
1960	Encina Hall (center section renovated; east wing and basement, 1963; west wing, 1969)

In the 1950s, biology students moved 500,000 fish in 150,000 bottles to temporary storage while new shelving was built for the famous ichthyology collection started by Stanford's first president, David Starr Jordan. Here graduate student Jay Savage poses with a stuffed sturgeon, three classmates, and some of the bottled fish (they dropped only one) on the Stanford Museum's grand staircase. The fish were part of the Natural History Museum, housed in the south wing of the 1891 museum from the mid-1920s to the early 1970s. During Sterling's tenure, the museum's art collections rebounded and expanded under the Art Department and the new Committee for Art at Stanford.   STANFORD NEWS SERVICE

1960	Post Office
1960	Stanford Bookstore
1962	Tresidder Memorial Union, honoring President Donald B. Tresidder
1963	White Memorial Plaza (dedicated 1964 in memory of brothers John Barber White and William Nicholas White)
1963	Bechtel International Center (remodel of 1917 Zeta Psi fraternity house)
1964	Storke Student Publications Building
1965	Faculty Club
1966	Bing Nursery School
1966	J. Henry Meyer Memorial Library (Meyer Undergraduate Library)
1966	Plant Services (Physical Plant/Corporation Yard) relocated to Bonair Siding
1966	Old Corporation Yard structures taken over by School of Engineering (Panama/Duena/Santa Teresa streets)
1966	Cowell Student Health Center
1967	Lou Henry Hoover Building (Hoover Institution)
1967	Old Union (remodel of 1922 Stanford Union)
1967	Placement Service (remodel of 1913 Bookstore)
1968	Fire and Police Station

STUDENT RESIDENCES

1949	Lucie Stern Hall (additions 1956, 1958)
1951	George Edward Crothers Hall (addition to 1948 dorm)
1955	Margaret Jane Crothers Memorial Hall
1955	Ray Lyman Wilbur Hall (dedicated 1956)
1956	Florence Moore Hall
1959	Escondido Village I: married and single graduate student housing, 250 apartments in 23 two-story buildings and 31 one-story buildings
1964	Escondido Village II: 459 apartments in 3 eight-story buildings and 41 two-story buildings
1966	Escondido Village III: 228 apartments in 2 eight-story buildings and 15 two-story buildings
1962	Fraternity cluster #1: built between the Knoll and Campus Drive East for Phi Delta Theta, Kappa Sigma, Sigma Alpha Epsilon, and Theta Delta Chi
1963	Fraternity cluster #2: built near the Knoll, adjacent to the campus lake, Lagunita, for Kappa Alpha, Zeta Psi, Alpha Delta Phi, and Alpha Kappa Lambda (Lambda Nu)
1968	Fraternity cluster #3: Cowell, built at the conjunction of Bowdoin Street and Campus Drive for Alpha Sigma Phi, Alpha Tau Omicron, Chi Psi, Delta Kappa Epsilon, and Phi Gamma Delta

FACULTY SUBDIVISIONS

1958	Pine Hill #1 neighborhood: Bounded by Bowdoin Street, Stanford Avenue, and, roughly, Mayfield Avenue, also extension of Alvarado Row, with 166 homesites on 40 acres.
1961	Pine Hill #2 neighborhood: Bounded by Pine Hill #1, Stanford Avenue, Junipero Serra Boulevard, and Frenchman's Road, with 120 homesites on 75 acres, including the 3-acre Lathrop Park atop Pine Hill.
1968	Frenchman's Hill neighborhood: Bounded by Stanford Avenue, Junipero Serra Boulevard, Page Mill Road, and Peter Coutts Road, with 190 homesites on 55.75 acres.

* **Sources:** Square footage for 1950–69 does not include SLAC, the shopping center, and the industrial park. Calculated by K. Bartholomew, March 2022, from Stanford University Planning Office, "Stanford University Chronological Summary of Construction," both 1966 and 1972 revisions, editor's collection and SUA, and Stanford University Maps and Records Office, spreadsheet provided by Dobie Howard, manager of Facilities Information Services.

TRUSTEES SERVING DURING STERLING'S PRESIDENCY
(*In chronological order of appointment*)

HERBERT CLARK HOOVER (1875–1964)

Stanford, B.A., geology (1895). On board 1912–61, emeritus 1961–64.

Mining management and investment; chairman, Committee for Relief of Belgium, 1914–19, U.S. Food Administration, 1917–19, and the American Relief Commission, 1919–23; U.S. Secretary of Commerce, 1921–28; 31st President of the United States, 1929–33.

Served as junior class secretary and Associated Students' treasurer, helping reorganize fund management for the student body just as he later improved the Board of Trustees' investment portfolio. Founder of the Hoover War Library (later Hoover Institution on War, Revolution and Peace). He posthumously received Stanford's Degree of Uncommon Man in 1965.

LELAND WHITMAN CUTLER (1885–1959)

Stanford, B.A., English (1906). On board 1920–59, president 1931–42.

Finance executive (bonds, insurance); chairman, San Francisco World Trade Center Authority, San Francisco Chamber of Commerce; participated in organizing the Panama-Pacific International Exposition, 1915, and Golden Gate International Exposition, 1939.

Cutler, a member of the English, Euphonia, Mandolin, and Quadrangle clubs, and leader of the Stanford Band, also was junior class president and on the varsity baseball team.

He later served as president of the Alumni Association and was a founding member of the Board of Athletic Control, 1917–26.

M.C. [MARCUS CAUFFMAN] SLOSS (1869–1958)

Harvard, B.A. (1890), LL.B, A.M. (1893). On board 1920–50, emeritus 1950–58.

Lawyer: Sloss & Elliot, San Francisco; judge, San Francisco Superior Court, 1900–06; associate justice, California State Supreme Court, 1906–19; arbiter, San Francisco Longshoremen's Board, 1934–36.

Sloss replaced his brother Leon (1858–1920), who had been selected by Senator Stanford as a trustee in 1891. Judge Sloss remained active on trustee committees until his death at 89; his trustee colleagues remembered him for his "good and patient counsel in time of stress."

IRA SHELL LILLICK (1876–1967)

Stanford, B.A., law (1897). On board 1923–61, emeritus 1961–67.

Lawyer: Founded Lillick and Charles law firm in San Francisco, 1906; later, Lillick, Treat, Adams & Charles, San Francisco (admiralty, corporate, and insurance law). Trustee and treasurer of California College in China, founded in 1929.

Lillick, a Santa Clara County native, became active in alumni affairs soon after graduating, and raised funds for scholarships and for the Stanford Children's Convalescent Home; he also served Con Home as president of its Board of Directors. He was the Board of Trustees' secretary-treasurer for many years.

CHRISTIAN OTTO GERBERDING MILLER (1865–1952)

UC Berkeley (U1885). On board 1923–50, emeritus 1951–52.

Utilities executive: President, Pacific Lighting Corp., Pacific Gas & Electric Co., director of many California gas companies. Regent, University of California, 1897–1900.

W[ILLIAM] PARMER FULLER JR. (1888–1970)

Stanford, B.A., pre-legal (1910). On board 1933–58, president 1943–48, emeritus 1958–70.

Business executive: President, W. P. Fuller & Co. Director, American Relief Commission in Poland, 1919.

Fuller, who served as editor of the Stanford Daily*, 1909, was a member of Sigma Alpha Epsilon and was briefly suspended for his role organizing a "Plug Ugly" mêlée but graduated with his class. He served in the Navy during World War I. An avid Stanford athletics booster throughout his life, he served on the Board of Athletic Control, 1929–34.*

CHARLES R. BLYTH (1883–1959)

Amherst, B.A. (1905). On board 1941–59.

Investment banker: Co-founder and president, Blyth-Witter & Co., was considered one of the most skilled investment experts in the U.S. when appointed. He raised money for Republican Earl Warren's gubernatorial and presidential campaigns, and he served as a trustee of Mills College.

GEORGE ARMAND DITZ (1889–1971)

Stanford, B.A., pre-law (1911), J.D. (1913). On board 1942–62, emeritus 1962–71.

Lawyer: Neumiller, Ditz, Beardslee & Sheppard, Stockton.

Ditz, a varsity rugby player, served as president of the Associated Students, 1910–11. Active in alumni affairs,

he was president of the Alumni Association, 1935–36. Ditz was a founding member of the Stanford Associates and its president, 1937–41, and recipient of its Degree of Uncommon Man in 1965.

MAY CHANDLER GOODAN (MRS. ROGER GOODAN) (1892–1984)

Stanford, B.A., German (1914). On board 1942–62, emeritus 1962–84.

Los Angeles civic and cultural philanthropist, and a director of the *L.A. Times*. She took the place of her father, Harry Chandler, as trustee (1923–42), and was the first woman to join the board since Jane Stanford.

Goodan, a member of Alpha Omicron Pi sorority, was active in the Women's Athletic Association, playing tennis and basketball. She participated in campus musical events and was a member of the Schubert Club. She was later active with the Alumni Association (alumni conference organizer) and with the Stanford Fund. Goodan was among the first women chosen, in 1954, as members of the Stanford Associates, and in 1975 was the first woman to receive its Degree of Uncommon Man.

PAUL CARROLL EDWARDS (1882–1962)

Stanford, B.A., English (1906). On board 1943–53, president 1948–53, emeritus 1953–62.

Scripps-Howard Publishing: Founding editor, *Dallas Dispatch*, 1910, and *Houston Press*, 1911; editor, *San Diego Sun*, 1925–32; and associate editor, *San Francisco News*, 1932–52. Trustee, Rosenberg Foundation, and president of the Commonwealth Club.

Prize-winning writer and editor of the Sequoia *who covered the 1906 earthquake and a member of the English Club, Edwards also was involved in campus dramatics. He was active in the Alumni Association, chaired the Stanford Fund, and was a founding member of Stanford Associates and its president, 1941–44. In 1953, he received the Degree of Uncommon Man.*

GEORGE FOWLER MORELL (1886–1978)

Stanford, pre-law (U1909); granted an "at large" degree, 1930. On board 1944–56, emeritus 1956–78.

Publisher and chairman, Peninsula Newspapers Inc. (*Palo Alto Times*, 1919–79; *Redwood City Tribune*,

1923–79); *Burlingame Advance*, 1936–54?); president, California Newspaper Publishers Association, 1937–38. President, San Mateo County Cattlemen's Association, 1943–44. Active with Chamber of Commerce, Rotary Club, and Boy Scouts.

Morell, a member of Delta Kappa Epsilon fraternity, belonged to the Hammer and Coffin Society and was business manager of the Chaparral, *1908–09. He entered Stanford in 1904 and dropped out more than once to pursue business opportunities in land development and, later, newspaper publishing. His "at large" degree was unique, granted after Morell played an active role in fundraising efforts during the 1920s as a leader of local alumni. He served as a U.S. Army infantry captain in World War I, and established the Fremont American Legion Post, No. 52, on his return to Palo Alto in 1919.*

HERMAN PHLEGER (1890–1984)

UC Berkeley, B.A. (1912); Harvard, J.D. (1914). On board 1944–64, emeritus 1964–84.

Lawyer: Brobeck, Phleger and Harrison, San Francisco (international, maritime law). Associate director, Legal Division, U.S. Military Government for Germany, 1945; legal adviser, Dept. of State, 1953–57; U.S. representative to 13th General Assembly of the United Nations, 1958; U.S. member, Permanent Court of Arbitration under the Hague Treaty, 1957–63 and 1969–75; chairman, U.S. delegation to the Antarctica Conference, 1959.

JOHN ELDRIDGE CUSHING (1887–1956)

Stanford, B.A., history (1909). On board 1945–56.

Maritime executive: President, American-Hawaiian Steamship Co., Oceanic Steamship, Matson Navigation companies. President, San Francisco Marine Exchange.

Cushing, on the staff of Sequoia *and 1907* Daily *editor, was elected to the Quadrangle Club and was a member of Chi Psi fraternity. He served on U.S. Army transport vessels during World War I; during World War II, he was deputy administrator of the War Shipping Administration. Cushing later was a founding director of the Stanford Research Institute.*

SEELEY GREENLEAF MUDD (1895–1968)

Stanford, chemistry (U1917); Columbia, B.S., mining engineering (1917); Harvard, M.D. (1924). On board 1946–54.

Physician (cardiologist), professor, and university administrator: Caltech professor, USC Dean of Medicine. Also on boards of Caltech, Carnegie Tech, Pomona, and USC.

During his two years at Stanford, Mudd participated in track and field, and rugby.

LLOYD WILLIAM DINKELSPIEL (1899–1959)

Stanford, B.A., pre-law (1920); Harvard, J.D. (1922). On board 1947–59, president 1953–58.

Lawyer: Heller, Ehrman, White & McAuliffe, San Francisco. President of Jewish National Welfare Fund, the San Francisco Jewish Welfare Board, and the Jewish Community Center. President of the San Francisco Bar Association.

Dinkelspiel served as Stanford Daily *editor,* Quad *co-editor, and* Chaparral *associate editor. He ran varsity track with Fred Terman and was a member of the Breakers Eating Club. During World War II, he was in the U.S. Army Air Force. He was posthumously awarded Stanford's Degree of Uncommon Man in 1959. Stanford's Lloyd W. Dinkelspiel Award for Outstanding Service to Undergraduate Education was created in his honor.*

JAMES BYERS BLACK (1890–1965)

UC Berkeley, B.A., mechanical engineering (1912). On board 1950–60, emeritus 1961–65.

Utilities executive: Pacific Gas & Electric Co. president, 1935–55, and chairman, 1955–65.

HOMER ROBERTS SPENCE (1891–1973)

Stanford, B.A., pre-law (1913), LL.B. (1915). On board 1950–61, emeritus 1961–73.

Lawyer: California state assemblyman, 1920–26; justice of 1st District Court of Appeals, 1930–45, associate justice, California Supreme Court, 1945–60.

Spence was a Daily *editor and member of Ram's Head. He played first violin in the Stanford orchestra, played rugby, and ran track. During the 1912 presidential campaign, he was a member of Stanford's Bull Moose Committee, supporting Teddy Roosevelt. He served as an artillery officer during World War I.*

ERNEST CUMINGS ARBUCKLE (1912–86)

Stanford, B.A., history (1933), MBA (1936). On board 1954–58, 1968–76.

Business executive, university administrator: After positions at Standard Oil, Golden State Co., and W.R. Grace, became dean of Stanford Graduate School of Business, 1958–68; chairman, Wells Fargo Bank, 1968–77; chairman, Saga Corporation, 1978–81. Trustee, David and Lucile Packard Foundation.

Arbuckle, a member of Alpha Tau Omega fraternity, also was chairman of the Men's Council and senior sponsor at Encina Hall. He was manager of the track team and earned a Block S as a javelin thrower. He worked his way through Stanford at many jobs, including pumping gas at the campus Shell station. He was elected to Phi Phi, national senior honor society. He earned a Silver Star and a Purple Heart during World War II while commanding a PT boat squadron off the coast of Italy; he later served in occupied Germany.

CAROLINE MOORE CHARLES
(MRS. ROBERT CHARLES) (1905–81)

Stanford, B.A., math (1927), B.A., education (1927). On board 1954–75.

Civic leader: president, League of Women Voters of San Francisco, 1948–50; lecturer, Mills College (1949–59); director, Rosenberg Foundation, 1948–74, president 1971–74; chairman, Bay Area Educational TV (KQED).

Charles, a member of Chi Omega sorority (president, 1927), was active on many committees of the Women's Athletic Association and the Associated Women Students. She played field hockey and basketball, and she performed in campus dramatics and light opera. She was elected to Cap and Gown in 1926 and was among the first women, in 1954, elected to the Stanford Associates.

JAMES FRANKLIN CRAFTS (1899–1980)

On board 1954–1968.

Business executive: president (1946–62) and chairman (1962–68), Fireman's Fund Insurance. Crafts began work in insurance out of high school, joining the Fireman's Fund in 1930.

Crafts was an early member of the Stanford Research Institute's Executive Committee.

RUTH FESLER LIPMAN
(MRS. ROBERT LIPMAN) (1896–1982)

Stanford, B.A., history (1918). On board 1954–59.

Social secretary to first lady Lou Henry Hoover, 1927–31. Alumni Association leader.

Lipman, the daughter of Encina Hall's first manager, Bert Fesler, was a member of Delta Gamma sorority. She studied international law in Washington, D.C., before joining Lou Henry Hoover's staff (Mr. Hoover was then secretary of commerce). Active in alumni affairs after her return to California, she was among the first women, in 1954, elected to the Stanford Associates.

TEX [JOEL DUGGAR] MIDDLETON (1902–76)

Stanford, B.A., history (1926). On board 1954–59.

Finance executive: Mitchum, Tully & Co., Los Angeles (started with the firm of Charles Blyth).

Middleton, a member of Kappa Sigma fraternity, was Stanford Daily editor (1925–26). He also played varsity football for Coach Pop Warner and was a high-scoring intramural basketball player. He served as a student member of the Board of Athletic Control. Active in alumni fundraising in Southern California, he later received the Stanford Associates' Gold Spike Award for exceptional volunteer service.

DAVID PACKARD (1912–96)

Stanford, B.A., engineering (1934), Engr., electrical engineering (1939). On board 1954–69, president 1958–60.

Business executive: Hewlett-Packard Co. co-founder, 1939, president, 1947–64, CEO, 1964–68, and chairman of the board, 1964–68, 1972–93. U.S. deputy secretary of defense, 1969–71. Established the David and Lucile Packard Foundation in 1968 (for education, health care, conservation, and the arts). Trustee, Herbert Hoover Foundation and of American Enterprise Institute.

Packard, a member of Alpha Delta Phi fraternity, played varsity football (as a "Vow Boy") and varsity basketball. He later headed the major gifts section of the PACE Campaign. In 1986, he and his wife, Lucile, pledged $40 million toward construction of the Lucile Salter Packard Children's Hospital. Other gifts totaling $55 million followed for pediatric-related projects and services. The Packards funded three Stanford professorships and endowed, with William Hewlett, the Terman Fellows program. He and his family also created the Monterey Bay Aquarium and Monterey Bay Research Institute. Packard was a longtime member of the Hoover Institution Board of Overseers. In 1987, he and Lucile each received Stanford's Degree of Uncommon Man.

NEIL PETREE (1898–1991)

Stanford, B.A., economics (1919). On board 1954–57.

Business executive: president, 1938–60, and chairman, 1960–68, of Barker Bros. furniture company; Southern California civic leader, president of Southern California Automobile Association.

Petree was a busy student journalist with the Daily, *the* Quad, *and* Sequoia, *before leaving for France with Stanford's First Ambulance Corps, 1916–17. With U.S. entry into the war, he served with the American Air Service. Returning for his senior year, he became editor of the* Daily *and a member of the English Club and Press Club. In New York, and later Los Angeles, Petree was active in alumni affairs, including serving as president of the Alumni Association.*

DONALD JOSEPH RUSSELL (1900–85)

Stanford, civil engineering (U1921). On board 1954–64.

Business executive: President, 1952–64, and chairman, 1964–72, Southern Pacific Railroad.

Russell, a member of Delta Tau Delta fraternity, left Stanford to serve in the Canadian Air Corps during World War I. He returned to campus but left in 1920 to work at Southern Pacific as a timekeeper. He was on the Stanford Research Institute Board of Directors.

MONROE EDWARD SPAGHT (1909–93)

Stanford, B.A. (1929), M.A. (1931), and Ph.D. (1933), chemistry. On board 1956–65.

Research chemist 1933–53, vice president, 1953–60, president, 1961–65, and chairman, 1965, of Shell Oil Co., New York; managing director, Royal Dutch Shell, 1965–80.

Spaght played with local dance bands as well as with the Stanford Band. He earned membership in the Sigma Xi science honor society. As a member of Stanford Associates, Spaght played an influential role in the PACE Campaign.

ARTHUR CHICESTER STEWART (1905–98)

Stanford, B.A., mechanical engineering (1927). On board 1954–74.

Oil executive: Vice president of marketing, 1940–65, and director, 1941–77, Union Oil Co.; head, Union Oil Foundation; Southern California civic leader.

Stewart, a member of Beta Theta Pi fraternity, graduated with distinction. A grandson of Union Oil founder Lyman Stewart, he joined the company as an oil field roustabout and a wiper on an oil tanker. During World War II, he was a member of the Petroleum Administration for War. Stewart later became active in Stanford fundraising.

EDMUND WATTIS LITTLEFIELD (1914–2001)

Stanford, B.A., social science (1936), MBA (1938). On board 1956–69.

Business executive: Vice president, 1951–58, and principal officer, 1958–79, Utah Construction & Mining Co./Utah International.

A member of Chi Psi fraternity, Littlefield was president of the Interfraternity Council. He played varsity golf (and was the team's senior manager) and graduated with great distinction. He was widely praised as an outstanding business leader. A grandson of Utah Construction's founder, he started with the company as a water boy. He served in the U.S. Navy during World War II. He donated the Littlefield Building on campus, as well as an endowed GSB professorship, and supported the Hoover Institution, Stanford Medical Center, and the Stanford School of Earth Sciences, among many other campus entities.

THOMAS POTTER PIKE (1909–93)

Stanford, B.A., economics (1931). On board 1959–79, president 1960–62.

Business executive: Founder and president, T.P. Pike Co., 1938–56; president, Republic Supply Co., 1961–65; chairman, Pike Corporation of America, 1965–69; honorary vice chairman, Fluor Corporation, 1970. An assistant secretary of defense, 1953–54, and special assistant, 1956–58, to President D. Eisenhower. Chaired Richard Nixon's California campaign for president, 1960. Trustee, Loyola-Marymount University. A vocal advocate for alcoholism programs and legislation, he founded the Alcoholism Council of Greater Los Angeles and endowed the Pike Professorship in Alcohol Studies at UCLA.

Pike, a member of Alpha Delta Phi, was Associated Students president, 1930–31, and a member of the Men's Council. He enjoyed performing in student musicals and had his own dance band. As a freshman, he chaired the Frosh Rally Committee, taking charge of the Big Game Bonfire, and was president of the Encina Club. He was the son of the founder of Pike Drilling Co. and Republic Supply Co., and a first cousin of trustee W. Parmer Fuller Jr. Pike was a member of the Hoover Institution Board of Overseers for nearly 30 years.

PAUL PIGOTT (1900–61)

Stanford, B.A., metallurgy (1923). On board 1957–61.

Business executive: President, Pacific Car and Foundry Co., Seattle. Stanford Associate. Regent, Seattle University.

Pigott, a member of Phi Delta Theta fraternity, played varsity basketball, golf, and baseball. He later was a Stanford Associate and served on the Board of SRI.

RICHARD ELIAS GUGGENHIME (1909–88)

Stanford, B.A., political science (1929); Harvard, J.D. (1932). On board 1958–78, president 1964–67.

Lawyer: Heller, Ehrman, White & McAuliffe, San Francisco. Director, Rosenberg Foundation, 1954–69 (president, 1954–58).

Guggenhime, a member of Hammer and Coffin, was business manager of the Chaparral *and co-edited the* Quad. *(He later was an editor of the* Harvard Law Review.*) He was also a member of the Scabbard and Blade military honor society. A member of Stanford Associates, he later received its Gold Spike Award for exceptional volunteer service.*

W[ILLIAM] PARMER FULLER III (1913–93)

Stanford, B.A., economics (1934); Harvard, J.D. (1937). On board 1959–83, president 1967–71.

Business executive: Vice president and director, W. P. Fuller & Co., and Pittsburg Plate and Glass.

Fuller, a member of Alpha Delta Phi fraternity, was on the varsity basketball and swimming teams. He and his two brothers attended Stanford while their father was a trustee. He was among several Stanford alumni to serve on the Rosenberg Foundation board. Active in the Stanford Associates, he served on its board and chaired the Stanford Medical Fund drive. He received the Associates' Gold Spike Award for exceptional volunteer service.

STEPHEN DAVISON BECHTEL SR. (1900–89)

UC Berkeley (U1923). On board 1959–64.

Business executive: Bechtel Corp. vice president, 1925–33, president, 1933–60, and chairman, 1960–69.

Bechtel left Cal to serve with the 20th Engineers (American Expeditionary Force) during World War I. On his return, in 1919, he attended only one more year, leaving to work for his father's company full-time.

ALFRIDA POCO TEAGUE
(MRS. MILTON M. TEAGUE) (1905–99)

Stanford, French (U1926). On board 1959–64.

Art patron, Santa Paula rancher, Camarillo State Hospital board member, and community activist.

Teague, a member of Kappa Alpha Theta sorority, was also in the Wranglers women's debating club and Cercle Français. She also participated in campus dramatics. Later active in the Alumni Association, she was elected as an alumni trustee. (Her husband was then president of the Alumni Association.)

MORRIS MACKNIGHT DOYLE (1909–97)

Stanford, B.A., philosophy (1929); Harvard, J.D. (1932). On board 1959–79, president 1962–64.

Lawyer (anti-trust and environmental protection law): McCutchen, Doyle, Brown & Enersen, San Francisco; James Irvine Foundation director, 1965–89, and chairman, 1976–89.

Doyle, who entered Stanford at 16, joined Phi Kappa Sigma fraternity and played varsity football for Coach Pop Warner. He also enjoyed being in campus dramatics, playing the Ghost in a 1926 campus production of Hamlet. At Harvard, he roomed with Stanford friend and future trustee President Richard Guggenhime. Doyle later was active in alumni affairs, serving on the executive board of the Alumni Association. He was also a leader in Stanford fundraising, serving as president of Stanford Associates and playing an important role in the PACE Campaign. In 1997, he received Stanford's Degree of Uncommon Man.

[HENRY] GARDINER SYMONDS (1903–71)

Stanford, B.A., geology (1924); Harvard, MBA (1927). On board 1960–70.

Business executive: Chicago Corp., 1930–43; CEO, later president and chairman, Tennessee Gas Transmission Co. (renamed Tenneco Oil Co. in 1966), 1943–71. Also, a trustee of Rice University and Texas A&M.

Symonds, a member of Kappa Sigma fraternity, managed Pop Warner's varsity football team when his fraternity brothers William "Lefty" Rogers and Tex Middleton were on the team. He also served as Associated Students' financial manager and senior class president. He later served as Kappa Sigma national president and was the major donor to Kappa Sig's new chapter house on campus. Symonds was elected to the Stanford Associates, and also served on the Alumni Association Executive Board, the GSB Advisory Council, and the Stanford Research Institute Board of Directors.

EDWARD ROBINSON VALENTINE (1908–1968)

Stanford, B.A., economics (1930). On board 1960–61.

Business executive: President, J. W. Robinson Co., and president, Robinson Building Co., Los Angeles; president of the Automobile Association of Southern California and of the California Chamber of Commerce. Trustee, California Institute of Technology, and Board of Councilors of USC Medical School.

Valentine, a member of Alpha Delta Phi fraternity, was captain of the freshmen responsible for guarding the 1926 Big Game Bonfire and was secretary of the Encina Club.

CHARLES EMIL DUCOMMUN (1913–91)

Stanford, B.A., economics (1935); Harvard, MBA (1942). On board 1961–71.

Business executive: President, Ducommun Metals & Supply Co. (founded by his grandfather), 1950–73, chairman, 1973–78; director and vice president, Ducommun Realty Co. Trustee of Claremont Men's College (today's Claremont McKenna). Chairman, California Republican Party Finance Committee, Los Angeles County chairman of the 1952 Eisenhower-Nixon campaign, and vice chairman of Nixon's California campaign for president, 1960. Los Angeles civic and cultural leader.

Ducommun was a team captain of freshmen constructing the 1931 Big Game Bonfire. He joined Delta Kappa Epsilon fraternity, was elected to Scabbard and Blade honorary military fraternity, and served as Class of 1935 secretary. Ducommun served in the Navy during World War II, including as aide to the chief of staff, U.S. Fleet, 1944–46. He was a major PACE fundraiser, and later received the Stanford Associates' Gold Spike Award for exceptional volunteer service.

OTIS CHANDLER (1927–2006)

Stanford, B.A., history (1950). On board 1961–65.

Newspaper executive: Publisher, *Los Angeles Times*, 1960–80; chairman, Times-Mirror Co., 1980–86.

Chandler, a member of Delta Kappa Epsilon fraternity, was captain of the varsity track and field team. He later served as a member of the Alumni Association Board of Directors, was elected to Stanford Associates, and served on the Southern California Stanford Fund. He was the third Chandler to serve as a Stanford trustee.

LAWRENCE ALPHEUS KIMPTON (1910–77)

Stanford, B.A., philosophy (1931), M.A. (1932); Cornell, Ph.D. (1935). On board 1961–70.

Professor and university administrator: Dean of students, University of Chicago, 1944–47; dean of students, Stanford, 1947–50; vice president of development, 1951, and chancellor, 1951–60, University of Chicago; Standard Oil of Indiana executive, 1960–71.

Kimpton, a member of the varsity debate team, was elected to the Delta Sigma Rho national debating society. He graduated with distinction.

THEODORE (TED) SCARBROUGH PETERSEN (1896–1966)

On board 1961–65.

Oil industry executive: President, Standard Oil of California, 1948–61. Trustee, California Academy of Sciences, as well as the Asia Foundation.

Petersen did not attend college, beginning his career at Standard Oil as a Portland, Oregon, service station attendant. He was a director of SRI and chairman of national major gifts for the PACE Campaign.

GENE KIMBALL WALKER (1903–97)

Stanford, B.A., history (1929). On board 1961–67.

Film producer (Gene K. Walker Productions) and San Francisco public relations and advertising businessman.

Walker, a member of Sigma Chi fraternity, served on the Men's Council and graduated with distinction. He later served as Stanford Alumni Association president and chaired many alumni fundraising and service activities. He also served as a president of Stanford Associates.

BENJAMIN CUSHING DUNIWAY (1907–86)

Carleton, B.A. (1928); Stanford, LL.B. (1931); Oxford (Rhodes scholar), B.A. (1933), M.A. (1934). On board 1962–72.

Lawyer, private practice, 1933–42, 1947–59; Federal Office of Price Administration, 1942–47; judge, First District Court of Appeal, 1959–61, and Ninth U.S. Circuit Court of Appeals, 1961–76. Director, Rosenberg Foundation, 1960–75 (president 1964–65, 1968–71). Trustee, Carleton College.

Duniway, the son of Stanford history professor Clyde Duniway, grew up on campus. One of the few Democrats on the board, he was San Francisco campaign chairman for President Harry Truman in 1948.

LILIAN FORCE FLETCHER NICHOLS (MRS. LAWRENCE S. FLETCHER; after 1966, MRS. JESSE E. NICHOLS) (1906–85)

Stanford, B.A., English (1928). On board 1963–76.

Arts patron: Trustee, California College of Arts & Crafts.

Nichols had attended Cal and Mills before transferring to Stanford, where she joined the staff of the literary magazine, Sequoia, *and competed in archery. She was a member of the senior class executive committee and served as president of Pan-Hellenic and was elected to Cap and Gown. She became active in alumni affairs and was elected to Stanford Associates.*

WILLIAM REDINGTON HEWLETT (1913–2001)

Stanford, B.A., engineering (1934); M.I.T, M.S. (1936); Stanford Engr., electrical engineering (1939). On board 1963–74.

Business executive: Hewlett-Packard Co. co-founder, 1939, president, 1964–77, CEO, 1968–78, and executive committee chairman 1978–83. Member, President Lyndon Johnson's Science Advisory Committee. Trustee, Mills College, California Academy of Sciences, and Carnegie Institution of Washington.

Hewlett was already an accomplished climber and outdoorsman when he and fellow students were the first amateurs to climb Yosemite's "Ice-Cone." He was a member of Kappa Sigma fraternity and ROTC, later serving as an Army Signal Corps officer during World War II. He received many awards and honorary degrees and, in 1987, was awarded Stanford's Degree of Uncommon Man.

EMILIE DOHRMAN COSGROVE
(MRS. JOHN C. COSGROVE) (1912–69)

Stanford, B.A., economics (1933). On board 1964–67.

Los Angeles civic leader.

Cosgrove, a member of Kappa Kappa Gamma, was president of Pan Hellenic, 1932–33, and president of the Associated Women Students in 1932. Graduating with distinction, she was elected to Cap and Gown, 1933, and pursued graduate study at Bryn Mawr. Considered one of Stanford's best-known Southern California alumnae, she was very active in fundraising programs in Los Angeles and at Stanford.

[JOHN] ROGER LEWIS (1912–87)

Stanford, B.A., economics (1934). On board 1964–82.

Aerospace industry: Lockheed, 1934–47; Canadair and Pan American executive; assistant secretary, U.S. Air Force, 1953–55; president, chairman, and CEO, General Dynamics (1962–71); founding president, National Railroad Passenger Corp. (AMTRAK), 1971–75.

Lewis, a member of Sigma Nu fraternity, played varsity rugby and soccer. He started out in Lockheed's machine shop in 1934. He later was elected to the Stanford Associates and served on the national executive board of the PACE Campaign and the GSB Advisory Board. He received the Stanford Associates' Gold Spike Award for exceptional volunteer service.

FRED HOMER MERRILL (1907–81)

Stanford, B.A., economics (1929). On board 1964–77.

Business executive: President, Fireman's Fund American Insurance of San Francisco, 1962–72. President, Board of Governors, San Francisco Hospital, and director, Rosenberg Foundation.

Merrill was a member of Phi Alpha Theta fraternity. He later served on the Graduate School of Business Advisory Board and as a director of SRI. He was on the Executive Board of the Stanford Associates and played an active role in the PACE Campaign.

ROBERT MINGE BROWN (1911–94)

Stanford, B.A., history (1931); Oxford (Rhodes scholar) bachelor of civil law, with highest honors (1934). On board 1965–81, president 1971–76.

Lawyer: finance and public utility law, McCutchen, Doyle, Brown & Enersen, San Francisco, 1934–80 (corporate finance and public utility regulation). Trustee of Mills College and service on numerous other boards.

Brown started at Stanford at age 15, joining Breakers Eating Club and the track team (he won the Jake Gimbel Award for "best competitive attitude"). He was president of his ROTC class and graduated with great distinction. While a first-year law student, he was elected ASSU president, 1931–32. At Oxford, he also earned letters in track, tennis, and rugby. He later served in Naval Intelligence during World War II. Brown was elected a Stanford Associate, winning its Gold Spike Award for exceptional volunteer service. He was active in the PACE Campaign.

RICHARD CLARK MCCURDY (1909–97)

Stanford, B.A., engineering (1931), Engr., mining engineering (1933). On board 1965–70.

Business executive: President, Shell Oil Co., 1965–74. Consultant to National Aeronautics and Space Administration, 1974–82.

McCurdy was an accomplished banjo player and water polo player, and graduated with distinction, earning membership in Sigma Xi honor society. He joined Shell Oil Co. in 1934 as a California oil-field laborer. As a Stanford Associate, he was active in the PACE fundraising campaign.

WILLIAM LISTER ROGERS (1902–87)

Stanford, B.A, physiology (1923), M.D. (1926). On board 1966–70.

Physician: Professor of clinical surgery, Stanford School of Medicine.

A star basketball and rugby player, Rogers earned an Olympic gold medal in 1924 with the U.S. Rugby Team. He later served as president of the Alumni Association.

DEAN ALLEN WATKINS (1922–2014)

Iowa State, B.A., electrical engineering (1944); Caltech, M.A. (1947); Stanford, Ph.D. (1951). On board 1967–69.

Stanford associate professor of electrical engineering, 1953–63, and lecturer, 1964–70; director, Stanford Electron Tube Laboratory; co-founder, president, CEO, director, 1957–2000, of Watkins-Johnson Microwave Co. Consultant to the Defense Department, 1956–66, and member of White House Science Council, 1988–89. Regent, University of California, 1969–96, chairman, 1972–74.

Watkins served in the U.S. Army Corps of Engineers in Europe and the Pacific during World War II before completing his graduate work. While on Stanford's faculty, he became a director of the Applied Electronics Laboratory, and later served on the Hoover Board of Overseers.

THOMAS VICTOR JONES (1920–2014)

Stanford, B.A., aeronautical engineering, with great distinction (1942). On board 1968–74.

Business executive: Joined Northrup Corporation in 1953, president, 1959–60, CEO, 1960–89, chairman, 1963–90.

Jones transferred from Pomona Junior College as a junior, working his way through Stanford by hashing at sororities. He resigned from the board in 1974 when he was indicted on charges of making illegal corporate donations to the Committee to Reelect the President [Nixon]. (Jones pleaded guilty.)

JOHN WILLIAM GARDNER (1912–2002)

Stanford, B.A., psychology (1935), M.A. (1936); UC Berkeley, Ph.D. (1938). On board 1968–82.

President, Carnegie Corp., 1955–65; U.S. Secretary of Health, Education, and Welfare, 1965–68; chairman and CEO, National Urban Coalition, 1968; founder and chairman, Common Cause, 1970–78; co-founder, Independent Sector, 1980–89. Stanford professor of public service, 1989–2002.

Gardner, captain of the 1932 varsity swim team, set Pacific Coast Conference freestyle records. (In 1976, he received the Stanford Athletic Board's Distinguished Achievement medal.) He graduated with great distinction. During World War II, he headed the Latin American section of the Foreign Broadcast Intelligence Service, then joined the Marine Corps in 1943. In 1984, he was awarded Stanford's Degree of Uncommon Man. He was the first Miriam and Peter Haas Centennial Professor of Public Service, 1989–96, and helped steer development of Stanford's Haas Center for Public Service as co-founder and national advisory board member. The John W. Gardner Center for Youth and Their Communities was established at Stanford in his honor in 2000.

STATISTICAL HIGHLIGHTS

(Years ending August 31)

(Dollars in thousands, except tuition)		1949	1959	1968
OPERATING EXPENDITURES	Total operations	$13,066	$33,249	$115,291
	Instruction	3,950	9,250	32,219
	Research	1,950	10,530	39,398
	Libraries	444	1,133	5,699
	Plant operations	678	1,437	4,615
SOURCES OF FUNDS FOR OPERATIONS	Student tuition and fees	1,886	8,118	20,613
	Gifts and grants	1,211	4,316	11,054
	Endowment income	1,772	3,525	9,436
	Sponsored projects— contracts	1,308	8,363	24,204
	Sponsored projects— grants	127	2,868	32,901
PLANT EXPENDITURES		1,981	13,728	17,734
GIFTS	Total gifts received	2,286	16,962	29,720
	To endowment funds	574	9,400	13,277
	To physical plant	414	2,186	2,604

(Dollars in thousands, except tuition)		1949	1959	1968
STUDENT AID	Scholarships and fellowships	327	1,742	7,970
	Loans to students	108	302	2,427
ENDOWMENT	Estimated market value	41,172	126,064	268,242
STUDENTS	Enrollment—undergraduate	5,347	5,264	5,917
	Enrollment—graduate	2,970	3,157	5,562
	Degrees awarded—bachelor	1,555	1,265	1,515
	Degrees awarded—advanced	1,210	1,248	2,398
TUITION	Full time	$600/yr	$1,005/yr	$1,770/yr
FACULTY	Academic Council members	332	528	983

Sources: *Stanford University Financial Report*, 1968 and 1969.

News and Publications staff members Sue Hoover and Bob McCann bicycle along eucalyptus-lined Governor's Avenue in 1962. Many of the 700 Tasmanian blue gums, planted in the late 1870s to mark the carriage road from Senator and Mrs. Stanford's residence to the trotting farm, did not survive the early 1970s drought and a severe freeze in 1978. Little remains of this mile-long 19th- and 20th-century Stanford landmark.   STANFORD NEWS SERVICE

PREFACE

1   Jack Fraser, "Stanford's Sterling in 15th Year on 'Farm,'" *San Jose News,* January 18, 1964.

2   Fred Glover, in "A Session on Wally: Transcription of an Oral History about J. E. Wallace Sterling, Recorded for the Stanford University Archives" (1985) 55, Stanford University Archives.

3   J. E. Wallace Sterling, "The Stanford Presidency, 1949–1968: Part II, A Noble Purpose Shared," 94–95, in J. E. Wallace Sterling Personal Papers and Memorabilia, SC0415 (arch 1993-061), SUA.

4   Sterling at his Stanford Today and Tomorrow presentation, January 8, 1960, in J. E. Wallace Sterling Speeches, Stanford News Service. J. E. Wallace Sterling, "The Stanford Presidency, 1949–1968: Part II, A Noble Purpose Shared," 96, SUA.

5   Gardner quoted in *Stanford Daily* (editorial), April 3, 1967.

INTRODUCTION

1   Donald Stokes, "The Sterling Touch: How Stanford Became a World Class University," *Stanford Observer* (October 1979). Much of Stokes' article is based on the recollections of Sterling and numerous faculty and staff.

2   Donald T. Carlson, director of university relations, "Complex history," letter to the editor, *Stanford Observer*, November 1979. Carlson, '47, began his 35-year Stanford career as Sterling's presidential aide in 1951.

3   "Statement of William W. Hansen," n.d., in William Webster Hansen Papers, SC0126, box 4, folder 35, Stanford University Archives (hereafter SUA). See also C. Stewart Gillmor, *Fred Terman at Stanford: Building a Discipline, a University, and Silicon Valley* (Stanford: Stanford University Press, 2004) 161.

4   Richard W. Lyman, "Sterling Personifies Stanford's Development as a World Class University," *Campus Report*, March 15, 1978, 3. In 1957 Stanford ranked 15th by the American Council on Education in overall excellence; by 1966, it had risen to third, a feat unmatched by any other American institution. On Stanford's rankings during the Sterling era, see also Gillmor (2004) Appendix D, 513–17.

5   Frank Taylor, "Stanford's Man with the Midas Touch," *The Saturday Evening Post* (December 3, 1960) 36ff.

6   Contemporary statistics from *Stanford University Financial Report 1968* (November 1968) 15, and *Stanford University Financial Report 1969* (November 1969) 24 (Stanford University Controller's Office); *Alumni Almanac*, June 1968; *San Francisco Chronicle*, June 8, 1968; and J. E. Wallace Sterling, "The Stanford Presidency 1949–1968: Part II, A Noble Purpose Shared," in SC0415 (arch 1993-061) 15–16, SUA. These comparisons used the period 1905–1949 because it came after the era defined by the gifts of founders Leland and Jane Stanford, 1885–1905.

7   John Walsh, "Stanford's Search for Solutions," in *Academic Transformations: Seventeen Institutions Under Pressure*, edited by David Riesman and Verne A. Stadtman (Carnegie Commission on Higher Education, 1973).

8   "Wally Recalls the Early Sterling Years as President, 25 Years Ago," *Campus Report*, April 24, 1974, 10–12.

9   As Ken Cuthbertson, one of Sterling's presidential assistants and later vice president for development and finance, said: "History is made with the right people in the right place at the right time, and Wally was the epitome of that." "A Session on Wally: Transcription of an Oral History about J. E. Wallace Sterling, Recorded for the Stanford University Archives" (1985) 74. *Time* magazine, November 9, 1962, in an article about Stanford's successful raiding of Ivy-League faculty, described Sterling as "a Canadian-born historian who looks like a heavy-weight Jimmy Durante, sounds like Edward R. Murrow and thinks like Tycoon Stanford."

10 Jack Fraser, "Stanford's Sterling in 15th Year on 'Farm,'" *San Jose News*, January 18, 1964. Chet Huntley speech delivered before the Pasadena Junior Chamber of Commerce in honor of Dr. Wallace Sterling, March 14, 1949, in J. E. Wallace Sterling file: Miscellaneous, Stanford News Service.

11 Bruce Bliven, comments on Sterling retiring as president and becoming chancellor, March 1968, in J. E. Wallace Sterling file: Miscellaneous, Stanford News Service.

12 J. Kapp [profile of President Wallace Sterling], November 20, 1964, in J. E. Wallace Sterling file: Miscellaneous, Stanford News Service.

13 Ray Lyman Wilbur, *The Memoirs of Ray Lyman Wilbur, 1875–1949* (Stanford: Stanford University Press, 1960) 670.

14 "Address of Herman Phleger at Trustees and Stanford Associates Dinner Honoring President and Mrs. Sterling," San Francisco, April 18, 1968 (in SC0843 box 1, folder 1). Staff member quoted in Fraser, *San Jose News*, January 18, 1964.

15 Nancy Steffen, "Who is Wallace Sterling?—A Profile," *Stanford Daily*, January 12, 1966.

16 "'Gradualism' plus guts, has been profitable, in both material and human terms," added Steffen. "And profit is not to be ignored. Thus it does not seem unreasonable to suggest that Stanford will continue pursuing such goals, in such manner, as she has for the past 15 years." Steffen (1966).

17 See, for example, comments by Philip Rhinelander in Jim Wascher, "Wallace Sterling—Giant of Two Stanford Decades," *Stanford Daily*, March 14, 1974, and Steffen (1966).

18 "Six Radicals Spurn Offer by Sterling," *San Francisco Examiner*, May 9, 1968. See also Sterling, "The Stanford Presidency: Part II, A Noble Purpose Shared," 88, and staff comments in "A Session on Wally" (1985) 74–76.

19 See, for example, his last convocation speech, January 1968; "'Tough' Problems Will Stay, Outgoing President Predicts," *Stanford Daily*, January 17, 1968.

20 September 4, 1968, in J. E. Wallace Sterling file: Miscellaneous, Stanford News Service.

21 Wallace Sterling, L.A. Conference, February 1968, 9–10, in J. E. Wallace Sterling file: Speeches, 1965 to Present, Stanford News Service.

22 Richard W. Lyman, tribute to the late J. E. Wallace Sterling, *Sandstone & Tile* 9:4 (Summer 1985) 20, also in *Stanford Observer* (July 1985) 3.

CHAPTER 1: FINDING STERLING

1 Edwin Kiester Jr., *Donald B. Tresidder: Stanford's Overlooked Treasure* (Stanford: Stanford Historical Society, 1992) 109–23; *Stanford Alumni Review* (March 1948); "Address of W. P. Fuller, Jr.," *Report of the President* (Stanford University, 1948), 53–58. Tresidder's 1947 speech to the Academic Council quoted in Kiester (1992) 104. In 1943, following a difficult wartime search for President Ray Lyman Wilbur's successor, the trustees recruited their own board president, Donald B. Tresidder, to serve as Stanford's fourth president.

2 "Committee of Trustees Will Conduct Search for New President," *Stanford Alumni Review* (March 1948) 5. Deliberations of the trustee search committee can be followed in the Herman Phleger Papers, SC0843; Phleger (1968); the Paul C. Edwards Papers, SC0170, SUA. See Chapter 12 and Appendix C for trustee bio information.

3 On Paul C. Edwards (1882–1962), '06, see Templeton Peck, "Paul C. Edwards: From Newsman to Trustees' President," *Sandstone & Tile* 11:1 (Fall 1986) 2–11. The Paul C. Edwards Papers, SC0170, include papers relating to Edwards' tenure on the Board of Trustees as well as his memoir, *An Uncommon Man: Paul C. Edwards, His Story and Writings*, edited by Carroll Edwards Beckett (privately printed, 1991).

4 On the troubled but productive acting presidency of Alvin C. Eurich, see Chapter 3. See also "Alvin Eurich: An Interview Conducted by Frederic O. Glover" (1980), Stanford Oral History Project, SUA; and "Frederic O. Glover, An Oral History Interview Conducted by Harry Press, Don Carlson, and Roxanne Nilan" (1993), Stanford Oral History Project.

5 An overview of the search process from the faculty perspective can be found in C. Stewart Gillmor, *Fred Terman and Stanford University: Building a Discipline, a University, and Silicon Valley* (Stanford: Stanford University Press, 2004) 292–99. See also the Frederick E. Terman Papers, SC0160, series III, box 78, and the Paul C. Edwards Papers, SC0170. In 1948, Dodds (1902–89) founded Special Studies in the Humanities, a graduate studies program that later became Humanities Special Programs. A trustee of Mills College at this time, he later served on the Board of Trustees of Pomona College.

6 Walker to Lillick, July 28, 1949, SC0843, box 1, folder 9. Stanford Alumni Association President William S. Kellogg, '19, appointed the Alumni Committee, with Walker, '18, as chair; William C. Corbus, '33; Martha Alexander Gerbode, '32; J. Pearce Mitchell, '03; Alonzo W. Peake, '12; Neil Petree, '20; and Justice Homer Spence, '13. Walker (1896–1978) had served as financial vice president (1940–45), a member of the Board of Trustees (1939–40), and for many years as a member of the Alumni Association's Executive Committee.

7 List in SC0843 box 1, folder 2; see also Peck (1986) 9, and Phleger (1968). Caltech chemist and Nobel Laureate Linus Pauling was among the nominees.

8 Sterling turned down the Scripps offer in 1943 and withdrew his name from final consideration by USC in 1946. (J. E. Wallace Sterling Presidential Papers, SC0216 box D2, folders 39 and 14). Seeley Mudd noted that the University of Michigan also was considering Sterling in 1948 (SC0843 box 1, folder 7).

9 Farrand, an authority on the American constitutional period, had had a long and successful career at Stanford, Cornell, and Yale before he was hired, in 1927, to transform the Huntington from a private collection to a research library. Wright, an early colonial expert, succeeded Farrand in 1941 and further developed the collections, but took charge of the Folger Shakespeare Library, Washington, D.C., in 1948.

10 Sterling's correspondence with Harold Fisher and

Alvin C. Eurich regarding the Hoover position is in SC0216 box D2, folder 14.

11 Dr. Seeley G. Mudd (1895–1968) had studied mining engineering at Stanford for two years before transferring to Columbia. He was an eminent Harvard-trained cardiologist and Caltech (and later USC) professor, and a Stanford trustee (1946–54). His brother, mining engineer Harvey S. Mudd (1888–1955) also had attended Stanford for two years before transferring to Columbia. Seeley Mudd had joined Caltech's Board of Trustees in 1929 and was a member of the advisory committee of the Huntington Library and Art Gallery, as was their good friend, Herbert Hoover. The brothers were generous donors to American private universities.

12 "Herman Phleger: Sixty Years in Law, Public Service and International Affairs," with an introduction by J. E. Wallace Sterling, an interview conducted by Miriam Feingold Stein in 1977 (Berkeley: Regional Oral History Office, The Bancroft Library, University of California, Berkeley, 1979) i; Mudd correspondence with Hoover, SC0843 box 1, folder 7; and Donald Stokes, "The Sterling Touch: How Stanford Became a World Class University," *Stanford Observer* (October 1979).

13 George Nash, *Herbert Hoover and Stanford University* (Stanford: Hoover Institution Press, 1988) 124. Nash quotes from correspondence in the Herbert Hoover Post-Presidential subject files at the Hoover Presidential Library, West Branch, Iowa. On the meeting, and on Hoover's influence on Sterling's candidacy, see also Mudd's correspondence with Hoover in SC0843, SUA, and Peck (1986) 9.

14 Stokes (October 1979). A Stanford trustee from 1944 to 1964, Phleger (1890–1984) was one of several Cal graduates to serve on the Stanford board. On Phleger's impressions of the process, see Phleger speech (1968), and "Herman Phleger: Sixty Years in Law, Public Service and International Affairs" (1979).

15 Fisher to Sterling, October 15, 1948, in SC0216 box 26. V. I. Gurko, *Features and Figures of the Past: Government Opinion in the Reign of Nicholas II* (Stanford: Stanford University Press, 1939). Xenia Joukoff Eudin (d. 1983) was a research associate at the Hoover War Library (later Hoover Institution) from 1932 to 1968, and the co-author or co-editor of numerous academic volumes. Eudin had become a U.S. citizen in 1936.

16 Stokes (October 1979). The injury also is mentioned in some accounts of his appointment, such as *San Francisco News*, November 19, 1948. Edwards to Lillick, telephone note, SC0843 box 1, L-65-E, pg. 9. The U.S. citizenship process took roughly seven years.

17 Edwards to Mudd, October 4, 1948, SC0170 box 1, folder 6; Paul C. Edwards, *Stanford Alumni Review* (April 1949) 14.

18 Edwards in *Stanford Alumni Review* (April 1949) 14.

19 SC0216 box 26.

20 After two years at SUNY (1949–50), Eurich became vice president of the Fund for the Advancement of Education, 1951–63, and later served as president of the Academy for Educational Development, 1963–87. Eurich (1902–87) had earned his Ph.D. in educational psychology at the University of Minnesota, and taught at Minnesota and Northwestern before joining Stanford's faculty in 1938.

21 Sterling to A. E. Wilson, February 23, 1949, in SC0216 box D1, folder 35; Phleger speech (1968); Stokes (October 1979). *Stanford Alumni Review*s of December 1948 and May 1949 provide snippets of the Sterlings' reintroduction to the campus community.

22 SC0216 box 47. Edwards comments and Sterling's itinerary are in *Stanford Alumni Review* (December 1948).

23 Peter C. Allen quoted in "A Session on Wally: Transcription of an Oral History about J. E. Wallace Sterling, Recorded for the Stanford University Archives" (1985) 4. The Lark was the Southern Pacific Railroad's overnight passenger train from Los Angeles to San Francisco.

24 "Cal Wins Another Close Game," *Stanford Daily*, November 22, 1948, and *Stanford Alumni Review* (December 1948) 14–15. Edwards describes the locker room visit in *Stanford Alumni Review* (April 1949) 14. Al Masters quoted in Peck, "Paul C. Edwards" (1986) 10.

25 *Stanford Alumni Review* (December 1948) 7. The invitation was the idea of Alumni Association President William Kellogg, "who felt that the Sterlings shouldn't miss all the Big Game fun." EVC [Elinor Valoy Cogswell], "Editor at Bat," *Palo Alto Times*, November 27, 1948.

26 Letter December 8, 1948, in SC0216 box D2.

27 Mary Tresidder to Sterling, November 29, 1948, in SC0216 box D2; Mary Tresidder to Paul Edwards, May 17, 1949, in SC0170 box 2, folder 3.

28 November 23, 1948, in SC0216 box D2. Preston Hotchkis (1894–1989) of San Marino was a prominent Southern California lawyer and businessman. A Cal graduate, '16, he subsequently served as a University of California regent and president of the UC Alumni Association.

29 November 30, 1948, in SC0216 box 47. Lee DuBridge (1901–94), president of Caltech from 1946 to 1969, was presidential science advisor to Truman and Eisenhower.

30 November 19, 1948, in SC0216 box D2. Medievalist William C. Bark (1909–96), '31, had returned to Stanford after earning his Ph.D. at Cornell to teach Western Civilization (1936–40). He went on to teach at Lawrence College and University of Chicago before again returning to Stanford's History Department in 1947. He directed the History of Western Civilization Program until 1960.

31 December 7, 1948, in SC0216 box D2.

32 December 7, 1948, in SC0216 box D2. Three of Sterling's predecessors had medical degrees (David Starr Jordan, Ray Lyman Wilbur, and Donald Tresidder), but only Wilbur was a practicing physician, as well as medical

school professor and dean. Faculty objections to Tresidder were more often based on his background as a business-man whose experience with Stanford was not as an academic, but rather as an alumnus and former trustee. On faculty opposition to Tresidder, see Kiester (1992).

33 December 8, 1948, in SC0216 box D2.

34 The *Los Angeles Mirror*, December 6, 1948, jokingly noted that while *Time* called him "cob-nosed," an advertisement in the *The New Yorker* that same week stated: "Only Wallace Sterling [a brand of sterling silver flatware] is like the full-formed sculpture . . . lovely from every angle." Sterling, the *Mirror* said, "obviously cannot be sized up in one sentence."

35 Wilson was president of Princeton University from 1902 to 1910.

36 Edwards to Sterling, January 24, 1949, SC0170, box 1.

37 Sterling reported Hoover's comments in his letter to Paul C. Edwards, January 13, 1949, in SC0170, box 2, folder 3. President and Mrs. Tresidder lived in Hoover House for more than a year before it was officially donated.

38 Don Tresidder, as president of Yosemite Park and Curry Company, and Mary Curry Tresidder, both retained family as well as professional ties to Yosemite Park and to the Ahwahnee, an architectural gem built in 1927 and now a National Historic Landmark.

39 Mary Tresidder to Edwards, May 17, 1949, SC0170, box 2, folder 3.

40 Gillmor (2004) 298. After Sterling's arrival in April, Faust continued as dean until 1951, when he left Stanford to become president of the Fund for the Advancement of Education and later vice president of the Ford Foundation. He died in 1975.

41 On the transition, see Paul Edwards' correspondence with Sterling in SC0170 box 2, and with Robert Millikan, head of the Huntington board, SC0170 box 1.

CHAPTER 2: EARLY LIFE

1 *Stanford Alumni Review* (December 1948) 3–4. His birth is recorded in the Ontario, Canada, birth records, 1869–1909, and Canada's 1911 census, when the family was living in the village of Appin, Ekford Township, Ontario. The village of Linwood was one of a dozen communities making up the township of Wellesley, in the regional municipality of Waterloo. The Canadian censuses for 1911 and 1921 record their arrival from England as 1905.

2 William Sterling (1876–1950) and Annie Wallace (1877–1931) were married at New Seaham, County Durham, in 1897. United Kingdom census records, 1841–1901, document the moves of the Sterling and Wallace families from mining district to district over the decades, and their various occupations in the mines.

3 *Stanford Alumni Review* (December 1948) 4. According to census records and articles in the *Windsor Star* (Ontario), these villages included Linwood, Appin, Cottam, Sparta, Elma, Cedar Springs, Thorndale, and Colborne.

4 "Fathers and Sons: An Address by Dr. J. E. Wallace Sterling, President of Stanford University, at the Commencement Exercises of Menlo School and Menlo College, June 8, 1956," in J. E. Wallace Sterling Chancellorship Papers, SC0333, box 38, folder 40. This recollection of his boyhood was later repeated in part for the *Edgewood Homes* supplement of the *San Francisco Examiner*, March 21, 1960.

5 Frank J. Taylor, "Stanford's Man with the Midas Touch," *The Saturday Evening Post* (December 3, 1960) 36ff. Unfortunately, Taylor includes some factual errors relating to this chapter. "Pastor's Son Gets Praise for Work," *Windsor Star*, February 23, 1925, regarding his work in Alberta the previous summer.

6 "Fathers and Sons" (1956). Unless otherwise noted, all boyhood recollections in this section are from this text.

7 On Annie Wallace, see Elizabeth Haynes, "A Granddaughter's Tribute: A Biographical Profile of Elizabeth Sterling Haynes," Edmonton Public Library (Edmonton, Alberta: 2008).

8 J. E. Wallace Sterling Presidential Papers, SC0216, box D2, SUA. Regarding death of Annie Wallace Sterling, see *Edmonton Journal*, October 2, 1931.

9 "Fathers and Sons" (1956).

10 *Torontoensis: The Yearbook of the University of Toronto, 1925* (p. 93) notes that when Sterling was elected class (2T7) president for spring term 1924, "he went into office with the whole class behind him." Haynes (2008).

11 Taylor (1960). It has been written that Sterling was student body president, but his yearbook reveals that while Sterling was president of the Athletic Union, F. S. Daly served as president of the Students' Parliament (in group photo page 218, Daly is third from left, front row). *Torontoensis: The Yearbook of the University of Toronto, 1926* and *1927*.

12 Donald Stokes, "The Sterling Touch: How Stanford Became a World Class University," *Stanford Observer* (October 1979). See also "Ann Sterling, Widow of Stanford's Fifth President, Dies at 85," *Campus Report*, August 14, 1991. The extended Shaver (Shaeffer) family still has a strong presence in Ancaster, Ontario. Anna Marie (1905–91) was the daughter of Albert Morley Shaver (1875–1967), a rancher, and Mary Isabella Robinson. On Ann Shaver at Victoria College, see *Torontoensis: The Yearbook of the University of Toronto, 1927*. Ann had been educated at Havergal, one of Toronto's leading girls' schools.

13 Toronto won the inaugural Grey Cup, in 1909, when both amateur (university) and professional (town) teams competed. The Canadian game, derived from English rugby, was introduced into the U.S. in 1874 with a

McGill-Harvard game. Canadian rules continued to evolve during Sterling's years on the field, including refinement of a "forward" pass, a "conference" of team players in a huddle on the field, the center's snap of the ball to start play, and fewer players on the field.

14 "Wallace Sterling, Ph.D. '38, Scholar, Administrator, and Former Athlete, Takes Stanford University Helm," *Stanford Illustrated Review* (December 1948) 4; Frank Huntress, "J. E. Wallace Sterling: Stanford's Fifth President," *Stanford Daily*, March 1, 1956, 4.

15 Elizabeth Sterling Haynes (1897–1957) played a key role in developing provincial and later Canadian theatre. She founded the Alberta Drama League and, in 1929, Edmonton's Little Theatre. In 1932, she was named director of drama at the University of Alberta, and a year later she helped found the Banff School of Fine Arts, now the Banff Center for Continuing Studies. See Moira Day and Marilyn Potts, "Elizabeth Sterling Haynes: Initiator of Alberta Theatre," *Theatre Research in Canada* 8:1 (Spring 1987); Moira Day, "Elizabeth Sterling Haynes and the Development of Alberta Theatre," unpublished dissertation, University of Toronto, 1990; and Haynes (2008).

16 Burt did not, as Taylor (1960) assumes, teach at Toronto but at the University of Alberta (1913–30) and later at the University of Minnesota (1930–57).

17 Walter Hugh Johns, *A History of the University of Alberta, 1908–1969* (Edmonton: University of Alberta, 1981) 103; *University of Alberta Folio*, October 31, 1970. Ellen Schoeck, *I Was There: A Century of Alumni Stories About the University of Alberta, 1906–2006* (Edmonton: University of Alberta, 2006) 204–05, calls Sterling "the substitute coach who, as a history student, led a Cinderella team to victory."

18 Taylor (1960). The Calgary rugby football team soon reorganized with a new name (the Altomah-Tigers) but struggled through the 1930s until settling down as the Calgary Stampeders in 1945. This earlier Tigers Team should not to be confused with the Calgary Tigers Hockey Team, which folded in 1927 and was revived in 1932.

19 On Stanford and its environs at this time, see Margo Davis and Roxanne Nilan, *The Stanford Album: A Photographic History, 1885–1945* (Stanford: Stanford University Press, 1989) 217–26; J. Pearce Mitchell, *Stanford University, 1916–1941* (Stanford: Stanford University Press, 1958); and issues of the *Stanford Daily* and the *Stanford Alumni Review*.

20 Taylor (1960).

21 *Annual Register* (Stanford University) 1930 through 1937.

22 Ibid., street numbers on Madroño have since changed; "The Other Half: Mrs. J. E. Wallace Sterling's Schedule is a Busy One," *Palo Alto Times*, February 23, 1954.

23 On the evolution of the Hoover Library, now known as the Hoover Institution, at this time, see George Nash, *Herbert Hoover and Stanford University* (Stanford: Hoover Institution Press, 1988); Charles Burdick, *Ralph Lutz and the Hoover Institution* (Stanford: Hoover Institution Press, 1974); Peter Duignan, *The Hoover Institution on War, Revolution and Peace: Seventy-five Years of its History* (Stanford: Hoover Institution Press, 1989); and Gary Norman Paul, "The Development of the Hoover Institution on War, Revolution and Peace Library, 1919–1944," unpublished Ph.D. dissertation, University of California, Berkeley, 1974.

24 Stokes (October 1979).

25 J. E. Wallace Sterling, "Austrian-Hungarian Diplomacy and the Austro-Hungarian Press," unpublished dissertation, Stanford University (January 1938). SC0216 box D2 includes class and lecture notes and some committee files.

26 On the Western Civilization program, see George Knoles, "History of Western Civilization," *The Stanford Historian* (April 1980), abridged in "The New/Old History Corner: 40,000 Students Took It: The History of History of Western Civilization," *Stanford Observer* (April 1980).

27 Don Carlson, "In Memory of Wallace Sterling," *Palo Alto Weekly*, September 4, 1985. See also Don Carlson, "The Lighter Side of Wally Sterling at Stanford," *Sandstone & Tile* 9:4 (Summer 1985) 22. On Robinson's many contributions, see *Memorial Resolution: Edgar Eugene Robinson (1887–1977)* Stanford University. Robinson's papers, along with the department's records of his era are in SC0029, SUA. See also the George H. Knoles Papers, SC0328.

28 Bunn to Sterling, January 4, 1949, SC0216 box D1, folder 35.

29 Sterling's 1937 correspondence with Munro in SC0216 box D2. See also Harvey Eagleson, "William Bennett Munro: A Memoir by Harvey Eagleson," *Caltech Engineering and Science* (January 1960) 31–32, 36.

30 January 22, 1945, in SC0216 box D2.

31 SC0216 box D2. An excellent history of this period at Caltech is Judith R. Goodstein, "The Rocket's Red Glare" (chapter 13) in her *Millikan's School: A History of the California Institute of Technology* (New York: Norton, 2007) 239–60.

32 SC0216 box D2 contains files on Sterling's activities with the Research Council.

33 Sterling's CBS correspondence is in SC0216 boxes D1 and D3. Elevator story told in Stokes (October 1979).

34 Evelyn Bigsby, *Radio Life* 15:22 (August 3, 1947) in SC0216 box D3.

35 Stokes (October 1979); SC0216 box D3.

36 Gayb Little letter, July 13, 1943, and other correspondence with Sterling in SC0216 box D3.

37 SC0216 box D3. CBS, "Thousands of War News Broadcasts, but Only One 'Question of the Week'" [flyer] (1943) in SC0216 box D3, folder 24. See also "On Signal Round Table," *Engineering and Science* (November 1943) 20.

38 March 4, 1944, in SC0216 box D3.

39 July 21, 1945, in SC0216 box D3.

40 SC0216 boxes D1 and D3; the latter includes transcripts of Sterling's broadcasts. Henry Wallace had called for: 1) World economic reconstruction through the United Nations; 2) Enforceable control of atomic energy through the United Nations; 3) Disarmament and international-ization of strategic areas under the United Nations; and 4) All-out support by all countries of the United Nations.

41 Ibid., box D1.

42 Ibid., box D3.

43 Ibid., box D1.

44 Letters about his broadcasting are in SC0216 boxes D1, D2, and D3.

45 Arbuckle in "A Session on Wally: Transcription of an Oral History about J. E. Wallace Sterling, Recorded for the Stanford University Archives" (1985) 6, SUA.

46 *New York Times*, December 18, 1946, and other papers regarding the National War College, are in SC0216 box D2. Vice Admiral Harry W. Hill had a long, distin-guished career in WWI and WWII. General Alfred M. Gruenther was a principal American planner of the inva-sions of North Africa (1942) and Italy (1943) and served as Supreme Allied Commander in Europe from 1953 to 1956. Lt. General Leslie R. Groves Jr., U.S. Army Corps of Engineers, also oversaw construction of the Pentagon.

47 Taylor (1960).

48 Materials from the following paragraphs are from SC0216 box D2. During the Sterling administration, Brandt (1899–1975) served as associate director (1952–62) and director of the Food Research Institute (1962–64).

49 Field Marshall Sir Harold Alexander (1891–1969) was a popular governor general of Canada from 1946 to 1952.

50 Sterling, "The Stanford Presidency: Part III[a], Bits and Pieces," 56–57, in SC0415 (arch 1993-061), SUA.

51 Sterling, "The Stanford Presidency: Part III[a], Bits and Pieces," 57.

52 SC0216 box D2.

53 Ibid.

54 Sterling to Fisher, September 16, 1946, in SC0216, box D2, folder 14.

55 SC0216 box D2.

56 Ibid., this includes Sterling's Huntington Library files.

57 Ham Stewart, "Jaycee Interviews Dr. Wallace Sterling," *Jaycee Commentator* [Pasadena Junior Chamber of Com-merce], March 1949, in J. E. Wallace Sterling Personal Papers and Memorabilia, SC0415, series 1, box 1, folder 17, SUA.

58 "Stanford's New President Feted by Friends, Associates," *Pasadena Star-News*, March 15, 1949.

59 Chet Huntley speech delivered before the Pasadena Junior Chamber of Commerce in honor of Wallace Ster-ling, Pasadena, March 14, 1949, in J. E. Wallace Sterling file: Miscellaneous, Stanford News Service.

CHAPTER 3: LAUNCHING PRESIDENCY

1 "Dr. Sterling 'Comes Home' to Stanford and Plunges into a Rigorous Schedule of Public Appearances," *Stan-ford Alumni Review* (May 1949) 8.

2 *Stanford Alumni Review* (May 1949) 7–10; *Stanford Daily*, April 8, 1949.

3 *Stanford Alumni Review* (May 1949) 8; Sterling to McKay, September 13, 1949, in J. E. Wallace Sterling Presidential Papers, SC0216 box 23, SUA.

4 "The Sterling Years at Stanford," *Sandstone & Tile* 9:4 (Summer 1985) 3–11. Donald Stokes, "The Sterling Touch: How Stanford Became a World Class University," *Stanford Observer* (October 1979). Stokes overdramatizes campus conditions in 1968 as "almost rudderless" and without "enough money to keep the place running prop-erly." For a more balanced view, see "Address of W. P. Fuller, Jr., Delivered at Stanford Alumni Conferences," (1948) *President's Report*, 1947–48, 53–58; Edwin Kiester Jr., *Donald B. Tresidder: Stanford's Overlooked Treasure* (Stanford Historical Society, 1992); and "Alvin Eurich, Interview Conducted 1980 by Frederic O. Glover" (1983), Stanford Oral History Project, SUA.

5 This theme is illuminated by Frank Medeiros, "The Sterling Years at Stanford: A Study in the Dynamics of Institutional Change," unpublished Ph.D. dissertation, Stanford University (1979) 249–50. See also his "The Sterling Years at Stanford," *Sandstone & Tile* 9:4 (Summer 1985) 3–11.

6 Allen, in "A Session on Wally: Transcription of an Oral History about J. E. Wallace Sterling, Recorded for the Stanford University Archives" (1985) 22. *San Jose Mercury News*, July 3, 1985.

7 "Frederic O. Glover, An Oral History Interview Con-ducted by Harry Press, Don Carlson, and Roxanne Nilan" (1993), Stanford Oral History Project, SUA, session two.

8 Frederic O. Glover to former Princeton president Harold Dodds, October 1, 1960, letter quoted in Medeiros (1979) 87–88. Dodds, the brother of Stanford Professor John Dodds, had retired as president of Princeton University in 1957. Paul Edwards also praised the Tresidder admin-istration in his "Stanford Today and Tomorrow" speech to alumni conferences, *Stanford Alumni Review* (April 1949) 9–15.

9 "Alvin C. Eurich, Interview by Frederic O. Glover, 1980," Stanford Oral History Project (1983), 48, 50. "Thomas A. Bailey, Interview by Frederic O. Glover," Stanford Oral History Project (1978) 23.

10 Sterling to Board of Trustees, November 17, 1948, in SC0216 box 26, folder 7.

11 Medeiros (1985) 7; Sterling to Herbert Hoover (February 6, 1958) quoted on same page.

12 Ken Cuthbertson and Fred Glover quoted in "A Session on Wally" (1985) 9–10, and Howard Brooks, in "A Ses-sion on Wally" (1985) 56.

13 Owen ran Stanford Men's and Women's Rest Home, a campus convalescent health center operated by the Stanford Mothers' Club from its establishment in 1928 to 1937, while also working in the Graduate School of Business. She retired as executive secretary emerita, in 1966. "Miss Owen Celebrates 30 Years Work on Farm," *Stanford Daily*, April 1, 1952.

14 Kiester (1992) 70–74. Glover (1993) session two. Spragens (1917–2006) returned to Kentucky to serve as president of Centre College from 1957 to 1981, where he is credited with increasing the college's endowment nine-fold, revising the curriculum, doubling the faculty, integrating the student body, and improving student scholarship. He also was active in the Danville, Kentucky, community, with a strong interest in civil rights issues. Sterling spoke at Spragen's 1957 inauguration. "Thomas A. Spragens, Centre College President, 1957–1981," Special Collections, Grace Doherty Library, Centre College, Danville, Kentucky. See also Thomas A. Spragens, interview by Frederic O. Glover and Edwin Kiester (1991) in *Donald B. Tresidder, Stanford's Overlooked Treasure* Research Materials 1912–1991, SC0438, SUA.

15 "Assistant to President Joins Ford Foundation," *Stanford Daily*, June 1, 1951, and *Stanford Daily*, July 3, 1951. The new president of the Fund was Clarence H. Faust, Stanford's former dean of Humanities and Sciences and interim president.

16 Wert (1922–91) helped organize the first undergraduate special courses, the freshman seminar program, and developed a field study program in areas of social concern. He also worked closely with students, faculty, and administrators to revise the student judicial system, 1966–67. He was a member of the California Master Plan for Higher Education team, 1959–60. When named president of Mills College in 1967, he succeeded Sterling's friend and fellow Stanford graduate student, Easton Rothwell. He retired in 1976. Wert was nationally recognized as an advocate of liberal education. "Wert Appointed President of Mills," *Stanford Daily*, April 27, 1967; *New York Times* obituary, January 24, 1991.

17 Glover (1993) session two. From 1937 to 1941, Peck was Stanford's first and only full-time publicity man working on non-athletic news of the university. Templeton Peck, "Recollections of a Lifetime: 1908–1988," privately printed (1988) (copy in editor's collection). On Stephens, see *Stanford Daily*, September 23, 1946.

18 Glover (1993) session two. Glover added that Tresidder initially was reluctant because he had had some unfortunate experiences with the press while president of Yosemite Park and Curry Co.

19 Allen (1915–2001) became the first director of News and Publications Service, 1952. He was university editor when he retired in 1977, then university editor emeritus until his death. [Roxanne Nilan,] "The Incomparable Peter C. Allen," *Sandstone & Tile* 25:1 (Winter 2001) 14–26.

20 "Carlson Looks Back on 35 Years at Stanford," Stanford News Service press release, January 23, 1986 (reproduced as "Don Carlson, Trouble-shooter, Looks Back With a Smile," *Campus Report*, January 22, 1986). Donald T. Carlson, CV, 1986, Carlson biographical file, Stanford News Service.

21 Glover (1993) session two.

22 November 30, 1948, in SC0216 box 26.

23 Glover (1993) session two. Cogswell to Sterling, March 28, 1952, in SC0216 box 17.

24 Glover (1993) session two.

25 Glover (1993) session two. "Don Carlson" (1986).

26 "Don Carlson" (1986). Cuthbertson in "A Session on Wally" (1985) 56.

27 *San Francisco Chronicle*, April 6, 1949, editorial.

28 *Stanford Alumni Review* (December 1948) 3.

29 On the impact of McCarthyism on academia, see Ellen W. Schrecker, *No Ivory Tower: McCarthyism and the Universities* (New York: Oxford University Press, 1986).

30 The complex events are included in an AAUP report on developments concerning academic freedom and tenure published in the *Bulletin of the American Association of University Professors*, 42:1 (Spring 1956), Appendix A, 100–07. The California loyalty oath crisis has been much studied. See for example: David Gardner, *The California Oath Controversy* (Berkeley: UC Press, 1967), and Bob Blauner, *Resisting McCarthyism: To Sign or Not to Sign California's Loyalty Oath* (Stanford University Press, 2009). See also the papers, contemporary documents, and a detailed chronology included in the proceedings of the 1999 Berkeley symposium, "The University Loyalty Oath: A Fiftieth Anniversary Retrospective," available online.

31 "Kimpton says 'No Speech,'" *Stanford Daily*, February 25, 1949.

32 *Stanford Alumni Review* (May 1949) 8. See also *Stanford Daily*, April 6, 1949.

33 "Sterling Takes Stanford Post, Assails Reds," *San Francisco Examiner*, April 6, 1949. See also Thelma Miller, "Sterling discusses Communist Menace," *San Jose Mercury Herald*, April 6, 1949; Jeanette Defame, "New Stanford President Takes Over Job, Sees Education as Answer to Menace of Communism," *San Jose News*, April 5, 1949; "Sterling Discusses Reds, Curriculum and Athletics," *Stanford Daily*, April 6, 1949; "New Stanford Chief Tells Theories: Communism Study Urged," *San Francisco Call Bulletin*, April 5, 1949; Alvin D. Hyman, "Stanford's Chief: Knowledge of Communism Needed, Says Dr. Sterling as He Assumes Job," *San Francisco Chronicle*, April 7, 1949; "New Stanford Head Hits Red Teachers," *New York Times*, April 6, 1949; "Teaching of Red Principles Urged," *Arizona Republic*, April 6, 1949.

All are available at Stanford News and Publications Service, Sterling News Clippings, 1949.

34 *Stanford Alumni Review* (May 1949) 9–10; *Stanford Daily*, January 31, 1949, editorial. See also subsequent articles through April.

35 Rosebery to Edwards, May 21, 1948, and Edwards to Roseberry, August 27, 1948, in Paul C. Edwards Papers, SC0170 box 2, "R," SUA.

36 Weinmann to Edwards, April 20, 1950, SC0216, box B1, folder 20.

37 Edwards to Weinmann, April 28, 1950, and Weinmann to Edwards, May 10, 1950, SC0216 box B1, folder 20.

38 Edwards to Roy E. Nafzger, May 3, 1950, in SC0216 box B1, folder 20.

39 Sterling to Paul Smith (editor, *San Francisco Chronicle*) March 7, 1950, "rough draft" (1952) in Sterling biographical file, Stanford News Service. In Sterling's hand: "This was drafted during the general discussion re: UC loyalty oath. It is simply to place on record my thoughts on the controversy at the time, and in light of circumstances then existing. WS 9–22–52."

40 Sterling, speech to Alumni Conference, May 1950, in Sterling speeches, Stanford News Service. Faculty loyalty continued to be a concern for off-campus letter writers throughout the decade.

41 Don Winbigler, "From the Inner Quad [column]," *Stanford Alumni Review* (December 1950) 13–14.

42 Sterling, "From the Inner Quad [column]," *Stanford Alumni Review* (May 1951) 15.

43 "Stanford President Flays US Draft Policy: Morale of Young Men Affected," *Salinas Californian*, April 28, 1951; *San Francisco Chronicle*, April 29, 1951.

CHAPTER 4: WALLY'S FOLLY (MED SCHOOL)

1 Donald Stokes, "The Sterling Touch: How Stanford Became a World Class University," *Stanford Observer* (October 1979).

2 Frank J. Taylor, "Stanford's Man with the Midas Touch," the *Saturday Evening Post* (December 3, 1960) 36ff.

3 On the Medical School's history into the 1950s, see John Wilson, *Stanford University School of Medicine and the Predecessor Schools: An Historical Perspective* (1998) (available only as an electronic book online). See also Ray Lyman Wilbur, *The Memoirs of Ray Lyman Wilbur, 1875–1949* (Stanford: Stanford University Press, 1960); David A. Rytand, *Medicine and the Stanford University School of Medicine: Circa 1932, The Way It Was* (Stanford: Stanford Dept. of Medicine and Alumni Association, 1984); Wilmer C. Allen, *Stanford University School of Medicine: The First Hundred Years* (Stanford School of Medicine, 1959); Sydney Raffel, "Stanford Medical School: An Anecdotal History," *Sandstone & Tile* 16:1 (Winter 1992) 1–7; "Interview of Robert Alway by Frederic O. Glover"

(1980), Stanford Oral History Project; and "Loren Roscoe Chandler, Interview with Frederic O. Glover" (1979), Stanford Oral History Project. Institutional records, oral histories, and faculty personal papers relating to Cooper Medical College and Stanford Medical School are preserved in the Stanford Medical History Center, Lane Medical Library, Stanford School of Medicine.

4 On this first of several reconsiderations of the Medical School's relationship with the university, see George Nash, *Herbert Hoover and Stanford University* (Stanford: Hoover Institution Press, 1988) 40–46.

5 Wilbur (1960) 179.

6 Ibid., 161, 179; Sterling, Report to Trustees, June 22, 1953, in J. E. Wallace Sterling Presidential Papers, SC0216, box 48, SUA.

7 Sterling, Report to Trustees, June 22, 1953, in SC0216 box 48; Loren Chandler and Lowell Rantz, "The Development of Stanford's School of Medicine," Committee on Future Plans, 1952–53, Stanford School of Medicine, in Stanford Medical School Committee on Future Plans, SCM092, SUA. Concerning President Tresidder's plans for the Medical School, see Edwin Kiester Jr., *Donald B. Tresidder: Stanford's Hidden Treasure* (Stanford: Stanford Historical Society, 1992) 93–95, and Wilson (1998), Chapter 36.

8 Spyros Andreopoulos, "Reinventing the Medical School: A Conversation with Henry S. Kaplan," *Sandstone & Tile*, 32:3 (Fall 2008) 13.

9 Frank Medeiros, "The Sterling Years at Stanford: A Study in the Dynamics of Institutional Change," unpublished Ph.D. dissertation, Stanford University (1979) 146–56; Sterling, Report to the Trustees, June 22, 1953, in SC0216 box 48. See also Wilson, Chapter 36; Chandler and Rantz Report (1953) in SCM092.

10 Replies to Sterling's survey are in SC0216 box 64.

11 Kaplan (1918–84) had earned his M.D. by age 22 from Rush Medical College, in Chicago, and in 1948 was recruited to head Stanford's Radiology Department. He was highly respected as a physician, a radiation therapist, cancer researcher, and mentor. *Memorial Resolution: Henry S. Kaplan (1918–1984)*, Stanford University. See also Charlotte Jacobs, *Henry Kaplan and the Story of Hodgkin's Disease* (Stanford: Stanford University Press, 2010); Spyros Andreopoulos, "A Conversation with Henry S. Kaplan, 1984," Stanford Medical History Center. Excerpts are provided in Andreopoulos (2008). The Henry S. Kaplan Papers, SC0317, are in SUA. On Gordon Isaacs' pathbreaking retinoblastoma treatment, see Ellen Isaacs, "An Atomic Cannon Saved My Baby's Sight," *American Weekly* [syndicated Sunday newspaper supplement], June 16, 1957, published 18 months after initial treatment.

12 Stokes (October 1979). On Sterling's direct involvement and "The Lessons of Relocating Stanford's Medical

School" by Stanford's administration, see C. Stewart Gillmor, *Fred Terman at Stanford: Building a Discipline, a University, and Silicon Valley* (Stanford: Stanford University Press, 2004) 349–56.

13 Coggeshall (1901–87), physician and professor of epidemiology, was an authority on tropical diseases. He served as special assistant for health and medical affairs to the secretary of the Department of Health, Education, and Welfare (1956–57), a member of the U.S. delegation to the World Health Organization, and, in 1959, of the International Development and Advisory Board. Gregg (1890–1957), had joined the Rockefeller Foundation in 1919 as a field officer and finished his long career there as the foundation's vice president. Gregg oversaw foundation expenditures of millions of dollars to physicians, scientists, universities, and institutes engaged in medical training and research, and helped create today's model of medical research funding.

14 J. E. Wallace Sterling, "The Stanford Presidency, 1949–1968: Part II, A Noble Purpose Shared," 22, in J. E. Wallace Sterling Personal Papers and Memorabilia, SC0415 (arch 1993-061), SUA.

15 Sterling's Report to the Trustees, June 22, 1953, in SC0216 box 48.

16 Kaplan in Andreopoulos (2008) 14.

17 Sterling's Report to the Trustees, June 22, 1953, in SC0216 box 48.

18 Stanford Office of Information [News Service] press release, July 16, 1953.

19 "Loren Roscoe Chandler, Interview with Frederic O. Glover" (1979), Stanford Oral History Project, SUA. *Memorial Resolution: Loren R. ("Yank") Chandler (1895–1982)* Stanford University.

20 See Wilson, Chapter 36, and Chandler (1979).

21 "Frederic O. Glover, An Oral History Interview Conducted by Harry Press, Don Carlson, and Roxanne Nilan" (1993) session two, Stanford Oral History Project, SUA.

22 Alway (1980) 7–9.

23 Glover (1993) session two.

24 Alway (1980) 31; Kaplan in Andreopoulos (2008) 14.

25 Sterling, "The Stanford Presidency: Part II, A Noble Purpose Shared," 24. Rogers (1902–87) also later served as president of Stanford Alumni Association and was elected to the Board of Trustees in 1966.

26 Stanford News Service press release, August 4, 1956, and *Stanford Review* (June-July 1958). See also "Notes for a Talk by Kenneth M. Cuthbertson to the Stanford Historical Society, May 27, 1990," 13, in Cuthbertson biographical file, Stanford News Service. On Parmer Fuller III, Black, and Blyth, see Chapter 12. On Arbuckle, see Chapter 11.

27 Stokes (October 1979).

28 SC0216 box 48.

29 Andreopoulos (2008), 15–16. Laura Jones provides an

excellent description and evaluation of the plan, the design process and aftermath in "'A Little Versailles for the Sick,' Edward Durrell Stone and the Stanford Medical Center," *Sandstone & Tile* 32:3 (Fall 2008) 3–12.

30 Andreopoulos (2008) 17.

31 *Palo Alto Times* (September 15, 1959) quoted in Jones, "A Little Versailles" (2008) 11.

32 Stokes (October 1979).

33 Ibid.

34 Glover (1993) session two. See also Alway (1980) 19.

35 SC0216 box A26.

36 Stanford News Service press release, January 25, 1956, in SC0216 box A23.

37 Jones, "A Little Versailles for the Sick" (2008) 6.

38 Stokes (October 1979).

39 The symposium's six speeches were published as *Medical Care, the University, and Society* (Stanford: 1959), with a foreword by President Sterling. Dr. Frank Stanton (1908–2006), founding chairman of the Center for Advanced Study in the Behavioral Sciences, served in that role until 1960. After graduating from Ohio Wesleyan, he earned a doctorate in psychology at Ohio State. He was president of CBS from 1946 to 1971; he served as chair of the Rand Corporation, 1961–67. He also served on the boards of the Rockefeller Foundation, Carnegie Institution, and Stanford Research Institute.

40 Stanford News Service press release [1959], in SC0216 box A23.

41 Taylor (1960). On Alway as dean, see also Chapter 11.

42 Taylor (1960); Andreopoulos (2008) 17–19. On the relationship of these "raids" to Stanford faculty recruiting, see Gillmor (2004) 372–79.

43 May 8, 1957, in SC0216 box A39.

44 SC0216 box 23.

45 Stanford News Service press release, August 4, 1956.

46 Alway (1980) 15.

47 Arbuckle in "A Session on Wally: Transcription of an Oral History about J. E. Wallace Sterling, Recorded for the Stanford University Archives" (1985) 42–43; Kaplan in Andreopoulos (2008) 14.

48 SC0216 box 23. Wilson, Chapter 37.

49 SC0216 box C5. An excerpt from Glaser's comprehensive Plan for the Next Decade (1966), which noted not only the "unwieldy" nature of the joint hospital's administration but its inadequacy for both university and community needs, is included in Wilson, Chapter 38.

50 SC0216 box C5.

51 Co-author Cassius Kirk Jr., as staff counsel for Stanford Business Affairs, along with Dean Robert Glaser, Lawrence Kleiner, assistant dean for medical affairs, and Courtney Jones, director of business and fiscal affairs for the Medical Center, were appointed as the university's representatives in the negotiations with the City of Palo Alto.

52 A joint city-university committee, lead by key members Dean Glaser and city manager Jerome Keithley, worked on the complicated language of the document. Glaser presented it to the City Council, which approved the document in an 8 to 1 vote. Wilson, Chapter 38.

53 "Hospital is Taken Over by Stanford," *Stanford Observer,* June 1968.

54 SC0216 box C9.

CHAPTER 5: DEVELOPING LAND

1 Frank Taylor, "Stanford's Man with the Midas Touch," *Saturday Evening Post* (December 3, 1960) 60; Donald Stokes, "The Sterling Touch: How Stanford Became a World Class University," *Stanford Observer* (October 1979). Sterling's conversation with Rusk likely took place in 1951–52. Rusk earned his LL.B. from UC Berkeley in 1940, while teaching at nearby Mills College, 1934–49. He became a Rockefeller Foundation trustee in 1950 and president in 1952. (He later served as secretary of state under Presidents John F. Kennedy and Lyndon Johnson.)

2 For a definitive study of the early land holdings of Leland and Jane Stanford, see Norman E. Tutorow, *The Governor: The Life and Legacy of Leland Stanford, A California Colossus* (Spokane: The Arthur H. Clark Co., 2004) volume I: 401–36, II: 712–14, 936–41. Tutorow scoured property records to document and enumerate Leland Stanford's many land purchases throughout the state, providing an extensive description of the Stanford Estate's land holdings. See also Stanford Ranches and Lands Records, SC0003, SUA.

3 Stanford's 1885 speech is excerpted in George T. Clark, *Leland Stanford*, *War Governor of California, Railroad Builder, and Founder of Stanford University* (Stanford: Stanford University Press, 1931) 389–92.

4 Ibid. The Founding Grant states that the Board of Trustees shall hold the property intact and "that the rents, issues, and profits thereof shall be devoted to the foundation and maintenance of the University hereby founded and endowed." *Stanford University: The Founding Grant with Amendments, Legislation, and Court Decrees* (Stanford: Stanford University, 1987) 6.

5 Mrs. Stanford's Address, October 3, 1902, in *The Founding Grant* (1987) 18. A federal lawsuit against her husband's estate, brought during the crippling national economic depression of the mid-1890s, forced the widowed Jane Stanford, as Stanford Estate executor, to review the estate's entire property portfolio. Many marginally productive ranches, not a part of the university trust, were sold during the 1890s. Vina's historic vineyard remained in operation, though cut back from its original 4,000 acres of vines, until 1916 when it was transitioned to alfalfa and dairy, like surrounding ranches. Most of that land was sold off in 1919 and the 1920s. A group of Trap-

pist monks in 1955 bought 580 acres that had been central to the old ranch. Tutorow (2004) II 936–41, 948–53. Total Palo Alto Farm acreage was recorded in the 1885 (John Coombe) and 1908 (Herrmann Brothers) land surveys. Tutorow (2004) 427, 429, includes further calculations.

6 The tax-exempt acreage, limited to 100 acres until 1959, was only a portion of the campus, as defined by the trustees in 1918. *Stanford Annual President's Report (1918–1919)* 8. In 1934, the trustees substituted a new description based on careful surveys of their 1918 main campus definition. *Stanford Annual President's Report* (1933–1934) 11. On the 1898–1900 tax legislation and amendment campaign, see Orrin Leslie Elliott, *Stanford University: The First Twenty-Five Years* (Stanford: Stanford University Press, 1937) 310–24 and George E. Crothers, *Founding of the Leland Stanford Junior University* (Stanford: Stanford University Press, 1932). The 1901 legislation (Stats 1901 Ch.9) was amended in 1993 (Stats 1993, Ch.8, Sec 50): "The exemption from taxation of the Leland Stanford Junior University is as provided in Section 3 of Article XIII of the California Constitution. However, the university shall hold exempt from taxation all real property used by it exclusively for educational purposes."

7 Lot 40, bounded by El Camino, Alma, Churchill, and Evergreen Park, was sold to A. E. Edwards to be developed for residences as "College View Terrace," today's Southgate. "'Stanford Field' in Palo Alto Will Be Developed," *Stanford Daily*, August 4, 1922; J. Pearce Mitchell, *Stanford University, 1916–1941* (Stanford: Stanford University Press, 1958) 15. On the Palo Alto Stock Farm operation and its demise, see Roxanne Nilan and Karen Bartholomew, "The Palo Alto Stock Farm: Stanford's First Experimental Biological Laboratory," *Historic Houses VII: South San Juan Neighborhood and Stock Farm* (Stanford: Stanford Historical Society, 2015) 30–40.

8 Mitchell (1958) 10, 15–17, 26. "Plans Call for Construction of Hotel on Campus," *Stanford Daily*, April 30, 1925.

9 In 1950, board President Paul C. Edwards calculated that of Stanford's estimated $8 million budget, some $5 million came from tuition. *Stanford Alumni Review* (June 1950) 15. A 1946 report to the president noted that current tenants cost more than they paid in rent. Edwin Kiester Jr., *Donald B. Tresidder: Stanford's Overlooked Treasure* (Stanford: Stanford Historical Society, 1992) 90.

10 J. E. Wallace Sterling Presidential Papers, SC0216 boxes 30 and 48, SUA. University Legal Counsel Morris Doyle confirmed, in October 1945, the trustees' legal right to lease those inalienable "surplus" lands, noting that the Founding Grant clearly had intended the trustees to have power to lease portions of the Palo Alto Farm for income purposes. Doyle also concluded that the board could negotiate leases for periods as long as 99 years (or 15 years for agricultural leases).

11 Spencer to Tresidder, August 10, 1944, SC0216 box 57,

folder 1. On Spencer and Tresidder, see also Kiester (1992) 26, 75–76.

12 Tresidder to Spencer, November 27, 1944, in SC0216 box 57, folder 1; *Palo Alto Times,* November 12, 1944. See also SC0216 box 57, folder 1 for origin of the Planning Department, including correspondence between Spencer and Tresidder, Spencer's Memorandum on Planning for Stanford University (1944), and notes of Tresidder-Spencer discussions (July 1947). On Planning Office activities during Spencer's years, 1944–59, see also President Donald B. Tresidder Papers, SC0151 box 15, and Stanford Planning Office Records, SC0486.

13 Spencer to Tresidder, August 10, 1944, includes Spencer's résumé, in SC0216 box 57. On Spencer's influence on postwar Stanford architecture, see Andrew Pearson, "Beyond Sandstone and Tile: Defining Stanford's Architectural Style," *Sandstone & Tile* 14:2 (Spring 1990) 1–11. Eldridge Theodore (Ted) Spencer (1892–1978) had received his B.A. in architecture in 1917 from UC Berkeley and graduated from L'École des Beaux-Arts of Paris in 1925. In 1927, he became park architect and his wife, Jeannette Dyer Spencer, artist consultant for Yosemite Park and Curry Company. Spencer Associates continues as a major firm in educational, civic, institutional, and recreational design. See also "They Left Their Mark: Eldridge 'Ted' Spencer," *Continuity* [Preservation Action Council of San Jose] (Spring 2002) 13–14, and "Eldridge T. Spencer" (obituary) *Berkeley Gazette,* September 25, 1978.

14 Planning Office Records, SC0486 (accession 99-093) box 1, includes Spencer's early planning reports, 1945–1950, while SC0486 (accession 2000-104) (originally #9150/949), includes Spencer's 1949 report. (The report also describes establishment of the Planning Office and its goals and mission.)

15 Kiester (1992) 81–82. Lewis Mumford, Memorandum on Planning, March 6, 1947, in SC0486 (accession 2005-041) box 1, folder 14 (includes correspondence). (Another copy is in Donald Bertrand Tresidder Records, SC0151 box 15, folder 8.) Lewis Mumford (1895–1990), architectural critic, philosopher of technology, and advocate for planning, had served briefly as a professor of humanities at Stanford during the war.

16 Lewis Mumford, Memorandum on Planning, March 6, 1947, op. cit. Encina Hall, the original men's dormitory, opened in 1891.

17 Ibid.

18 Spencer to President's Office, March 15, 1949, in SC0216 box 57, folder 2, including his 1946 map. Spencer was now clearly operating with acting President Al Eurich's encouragement. After Tresidder's death, Eurich carefully reviewed with the trustees the planning progress since 1944, including Ted Spencer's "general premises" for future development of campus lands and Mumford's 1947 report. Spencer's 1949 report, op. cit.

19 Alf Brandin's influence is highlighted in Rosemary McAndrews, "The Birthplace of Silicon Valley: A History of Land Development at Stanford University," *Sandstone and Tile* (Stanford Historical Society) 19:1/2 (Spring 1995) 3–11, and Alf E. Brandin, oral history interview conducted by Robert de Roos (1987) SOHP, SUA. Bob de Roos notes Brandin's wide-ranging responsibilities in his introduction.

20 Alf E. Brandin, oral history interview conducted by Fred Glover (1990) 13, SOHP, SUA. "Ball carrier," in Falcon O. Baker, "City on the Campus," *Saturday Evening Post*, December 31, 1955. Brandin memo to presidential assistant Thomas Spragens, November 1, 1950, in SC0216 box 48, folder 8.

21 Frank Fish Walker, as Stanford's financial vice president and a member of the Board of Trustees, first asked the board to officially appoint Coldwell. Board Finance Committee minutes, March 15, 1941. Coldwell's formal appointment as real estate advisor was made at the recommendation of the Special Committee on Land Development. Board of Trustees Minutes, December 16, 1950. Spragens to Brandin, December 27, 1950, SC0216 box 48, folder 8. Brandin/Glover interview (1990) 11. George Morell, chair of the Trustee Committee on Buildings and Grounds, put up $25,000 for the Cormac-McConnell survey.

22 Brandin/Glover interview (1990) 13–14. On lot 76, see Sterling notes, November 1, 1950, in SC0216 box 47, and Brandin to Tom Spragens, November 1, 1950, SC0216 box 48, folder 8. On Tresidder's difficult relationship with Palo Alto, see Kiester (1992) 93–95, and SC0216 box 25, folder 39 "Palo Alto Hospital Expansion, 1946–47."

23 Spencer to President's Office, March 15, 1949, SC0216, box 57, folder 2. Spencer's idea was ignored for 60 years, but today part of the area is used for faculty housing.

24 Taylor (1960) 60. With veterans enrolling in waves, boosted by the GI Bill of Rights, student body totals became unpredictable. Gifts were expected to pay for construction of the long-planned new student union, to be named for Dr. Tresidder, and the alumni building, beginning with a major gift from Guy C. Bowman, '02.

25 Tom Spragens to Alf Brandin, October 2, 1950, Brandin to Spragens, November 1, 1950, and November 2, 1950, SC0216 box 48, folder 8. Spragens and Brandin raise important issues that they will take to the board, including precedents and the legal and pragmatic ramifications of incorporation, annexation, and condemnation, especially in regard to neighboring Palo Alto.

26 Cuthbertson and Brooks in "A Session on Wally: Transcription of an Oral History about J. E. Wallace Sterling, Recorded for the Stanford University Archives" (1985) 33.

27 Board meeting, April 20, 1950. SC0216 box 30 includes a summary of board actions on land planning.

28 "Farm May Be Subdivided Into Exclusi[v]e Home Sites,"

Stanford Daily, October 5, 1923. Roth, an avid golfer, did succeed with a portion of his plan: In 1929, he persuaded the Board of Trustees to set aside land for construction of the Stanford Golf Course and enlargement of Felt Lake to provide water to the course. See stories on opening of the Stanford Golf Course in January and February 1930 issues of *Stanford Illustrated Review.*

29 Sterling also called Lot 79 "a sort of appendage of the heartland." Stokes (October 1979). The Trustee Investment Committee, March 21, 1949, first discussed a staff suggestion to lease acreage on the west side of San Francisquito Creek for housing. No objection was recorded, as long as it was approved by the Buildings and Grounds Committee and the incoming university president. Trustee Investment Committee Minutes (1948–49) in SC0216 box 47. Leasing Lot 79 was formally approved March 15, 1951. "Stanford Leases Site for Home and School," *San Mateo Times,* April 6, 1951, describes the site.

30 "Stanford Leases Site for Homes and School," *San Mateo Times,* April 6, 1951; "7000 Acres of Stanford's Land Studied for Future Development," *Stanford Alumni Review* (November 1950) 9–10; "First of Stanford Lands Leased to Subdivider," *Stanford Alumni Review* (May 1951) 10–11. House prices were initially in the $15,000 range, but with quickly rising home prices, they went on sale for $25,000 and up. *Palo Alto Times,* August 1, 1952. "Campus Subdivision," *Stanford Review* (April 1952) 13. The Peninsula Pacific Construction Company was incorporated in Menlo Park, in 1949, not Redwood City, as some have said.

31 "Stanford Leases Site for Homes and School," *San Mateo Times,* April 6, 1951. Non-faculty residential leases of Stanford land had been restricted by the trustees in 1921. Mitchell (1958) 14.

32 "Stanford Plans for Use of Lands," *San Mateo Times,* October 13, 1950; "First of Stanford Lands Leased to Subdivider," *Stanford Review* (May 1951) 10; "Stanford Leases Site for Homes and School," *San Mateo Times,* April 6, 1951.

33 The original 99-year ground leases, due to expire in 2051 and 2058, had no provision for extension. In 2013, the 123 leaseholders at Stanford Creek (Oaks) and Stanford Hills were offered 51-year extensions beyond their existing expiration dates. In exchange, the university has the first option to buy at market rates should an owner decide to sell. The change provided leaseholders an extended time to remain in their properties, while giving Stanford an opportunity to gradually transition the houses into the university faculty housing program. "Stanford Lease Holders in Menlo Park Offered Lease Extension Program," *Stanford News,* April 25, 2013.

34 Tom Spragens to Alf Brandin, October 25, 1950, Brandin to Spragens, November 1 and 2, 1950; memos about these issues, historical precedent, and possible solutions,

including discussions with Coldwell and Comptroller Al Manspeaker, SC0216 box 57.

35 The board approved the Punnett, Parez & Hutchison contract September 21, 1950, but had selected the firm in July. Trustee minutes, September 21, 1950. The announcement of the Punnett, Parez & Hutchison hire was made at the same time as both the Stanford Oaks project and industrial development of the 40-acre Lot 41. "7000 Acres of Stanford's Land Studied for Future Development," *Stanford Alumni Review* (November 1950) 9–10. "A Session on Wally" (1985) 27. The Newhall Company's president was Stanford alumnus Atholl McBean, who also played a role in the establishment of the Stanford Research Institute.

36 *San Francisco Chronicle,* October 13, 1950; "Stanford Plans Use of Lands," *San Mateo Times,* October 13, 1950. (Similar articles appeared in the *San Francisco Examiner* and *Oakland Tribune.*) *Stanford Review,* November 1950. Correspondence in Sterling's files reveals that many real estate developers were interested in doing the job for Stanford. In 1950, Benjamin Swig, then owner of the Fairmont Hotel in San Francisco and a major developer, spoke to Brandin about developing a small commercial center along El Camino Real.

37 Spencer to Spragens, September 19, 1950, SC0216 box 57, folder 3.

38 "7000 Acres of Stanford's Land Studied for Future Development," *Stanford Alumni Review* (November 1950) 9–10. E. Elmore Hutchison, "Report on Land Use Survey of Stanford University Properties, San Mateo and Santa Clara Counties, California, June 5, 1951," in SC0486 (accession 2000-104) box 1, folder 2, and in SC0216 box 48, folder 8. Hutchison provided an aerial topographic survey, sewage report, drainage system plan, and water and other utilities plan, as well as a recommended master plan with estimates of costs. Hutchison's recommendations for a shopping center had prompted the board to ask him for a detailed engineering study of Lot 41 (light industry) and recommendations on a proposed extension of Willow Road from Middlefield to Sand Hill Road. Trustee minutes, October 19, 1950.

39 The board's Special Committee first met October 16, 1950. Initial appointments to the Special Committee were Paul C. Edwards, Charles Blyth, John Cushing, George Ditz, W. Parmer Fuller Jr., Ira Lillick, George Morell, and Herman Phleger, with Wallace Sterling and Tom Spragens. SC0216 box 48, folder 8.

40 "A Session on Wally" (1985) 33. See also University Committee on Land and Building Development Records, SC0813, SUA.

41 *Faculty Staff Newsletter,* special edition, March 28, 1960. Ray Faulkner refused to be full-fledged dean of Humanities and Sciences, insisting year after year that a replacement be found.

42 John Cushing to Tom Spragens, December 19, 1950, SC0216 box 48, folder 8. Trustee minutes, May 17, 1951, and Spencer memorandum on conference with Harry Arnold, August 3, 1951, SC0216 box 57, folder 3.

43 Ibid. (Spencer memorandum)

44 At the trustees' June 16, 1949, meeting, Sterling asked the board to authorize development of eight parcels on either side of Foothill Road, and four parcels fronting Mayfield, east of Coronado, but utilities remained an issue. The Arnold proposal was approved at its March 15, 1951, meeting. "Ten new ranch style homes," Stanford Office of Information [News Service] press release, May 8, 1951, and "Announcement to Faculty," June 8, 1951; "New Campus Homes," *Stanford Alumni Review* (June 1951) 21. Alturas Drive was later absorbed as the end of Gerona Road, Mayfield Avenue became Campus Drive, and Foothill Road became Junipero Serra Boulevard.

45 Spencer to Sterling (with copies to Brandin and Faulkner), July 18, 1951, SC0216 box 57, folder 3.

46 Ibid.

47 "Searsville Block," *Historic Houses VII: South San Juan Neighborhood and Stock Farm* (Stanford: Stanford Historical Society, 2015) 236–59. This volume also includes most of the faculty houses along Junipero Serra Boulevard.

48 "A Session on Wally" (1985) 58. At the time, Cuthbertson was one of four presidential assistants, each with his own portfolio. (Cuthbertson's was finance and planning).

49 Stanford Office of Information [News Service] press release, April 6, 1959, regarding Spencer's resignation, in Stanford News & Publications Service, SC0122 (possibly accession 1993-005) box 12, folder 61.

50 Glover, introduction to Brandin/Glover (1990). Trustee minutes, September 18, 1952. Brandin/de Roos (1987) 25.

51 Brandin/de Roos (1987). McAndrews (1995) 5.

52 Lot 1 was Coldwell's "number one spot on Stanford lands." Brandin to Spragens, November 1, 1950, SC0216 box 48, folder 8. Stonestown, constructed between 1949 and 1951, was officially opened November 1952 with the Emporium as its first and keystone tenant. Considered, at the time, the fourth largest shopping center in the United States, the complex included department stores, restaurants, Woolworth's and Walgreens, along with a grocery store, bakery, and movie theater. The $23 million project of brothers Ellis and Henry Stoneson was designed by architect Welton Becket. *Architect and Engineer* (July 1950); "California Architecture Wins World-Wide Fame," *Los Angeles Times*, July 6, 1952.

53 Coldwell to Sterling, May 2, 1952, in SC0216 box 48. On Lot 76, see SC0216 box 47. Teresa Grimes, "Welton Becket and Associates," Historic American Building Survey. Becket's award-winning firm prospered in postwar Southern California, working on a range of ventures from major defense projects, public housing, and commercial projects to Hollywood film star residential commissions. Iconic LA Modernist designs included the Capitol Records Building (1954–56) and the Cinerama Dome, the world's first concrete geodesic dome (1963–1964), the Beverly Hilton Hotel (1955), Memorial Sports Arena (1959), Los Angeles International Airport Theme Building (1962, with Pereira & Luckman and Paul R. Williams), and the Federal Office Building in Los Angeles (1966, with Paul R. Williams and A.C. Martin & Associates).

54 June 4, 1952, in SC0216 box 30.

55 "Stanford Plans Retail Center," *Oakland Tribune*, July 6, 1952; "Stanford Maps Store Center," *San Francisco Examiner*, July 2, 1952; Stanford Office of Information [News Service] press release, August 1, 1952, SC0122 box 57, folder 4.

56 Brandin to Sterling, August 13, 1952, SC0216 box 30, folder 24; news release by R. M. Williams and *Palo Alto Times*, May 23, 1952, on Shoppers World, in SC0216 box 57, folder 4; and *Palo Alto Times,* April 9, 1953, and *San Jose News*, April 9, 1953, in SC0122 box 34.

57 Brandin to Sterling, August 27, 1952, SC0216 box 30 folder 24.

58 Fred Glover to Sterling, January 8, 1950, SC0122 box 33. "Officials deny Emporium-Stanford deal," *Palo Alto Times*, February 6, 1953, SC0122 box 34.

59 "New Stanford Developments are Denied Palo Alto Sewer Service," *Palo Alto Times*, August 12, 1952; "Stanford Annexation Hits Snag," *Palo Alto Times*, August 30, 1952.

60 Jerome Keithley to Brandin, March 6, 1953, SC0216 box 30, folder 24, mentioning his reading a February 26, 1953, article in the *Palo Alto Times* regarding Stanford's intentions for Lot 1; Brandin to Keithley, March 19, 1953, SC0216 box 30, folder 24.

61 SC0216 boxes 30 and 48.

62 "Frederic O. Glover, An Oral History Interview Conducted by Harry Press, Don Carlson, and Roxanne Nilan" (1993) session four, SOHP, SUA.

63 Cuthbertson to Sterling, June 15, 1955, SC0216 box 30, folder 35. See also Committee on Land and Building Development Records, SC0813.

64 [Matt Bowling] "The Stanford Shopping Center: Puttin' on the Ritz," the Palo Alto History Project, available online. A September 1955 Roos Brothers postcard reads, "All roads lead to the new Roos store." In a September 26, 1955, press release, J. Magnin called its new location the "store of the future." Both are in SC0122 box 33, folder 1.

65 Allen to Richard Johnston (business office), July 11, 1955, SC0216 box 30, folder 35. Sterling was accompanied at the May 6, 1956, ceremony by Provost Fred Terman, trustee W. Parmer Fuller Jr., staff members Fred Glover and Alf Brandin, Palo Alto Mayor Noel Porter, and Benjamin Banker of Coldwell-Banker.

66 Brandin/de Roos (1989) 35.

67 *Stanford Review* (January 1953) 11.

68 The Skidmore, Owings & Merrill partnership, established in Chicago in 1936, had grown into a large company by 1952, with 14 partners, more than 1,000 employees, and offices in Chicago, New York, San Francisco, and Portland. The firm was well known for high-end commercial buildings emphasizing clean lines and functional designs, such as Mount Zion Hospital in San Francisco, and Manhattan House (1950) and Lever House (1952) in New York City. The 1955 Istanbul Hilton was hailed as one of the firm's great architectural and interior design achievements.

69 Agreement dated April 9, 1953, between Stanford and Skidmore, Owings & Merrill; SOM file memo, June 30, 1953, in SC0216 box 23. See also SC0216 boxes 30 and 37.

70 Skidmore, Owings & Merrill, "Interim Report: Stanford Master Plan—Stanford Shopping Center, Industrial Area, Proposed Residential Development," August 15, 1953, in SC0216 box 23, folder 21; SOM, Land Use Study Stage I, September 10, 1953, SC0486 (accession 2000-104) box 1, folder 56 [folder 56 in collection guide probably means folders 5 and 6]; SOM Supplement 1: Economic Factors of the Master Plan," SC0486 (2000-104) box 1, folder 4.

71 Skidmore, Owings & Merrill interim report, August 15, 1953, in SC0216 box 23, folder 21. Arnold was interested in Lots 44, 45, 46 and portions of 47, 49, and 50.

72 Stokes (October 1979).

73 Lyle E. Cook to Spencer, February 1, 1951, SC0122 box 33, folder "Land Development 1950–55," reports his and Fred Glover's impressions; Wert to Spencer, January 12, 1954, SC0216 box 57, folder 6; David S. Jacobson to Sterling, May 18, 1953, SC0122 box 33, folder "Land Development 1950–55." Faulkner expressed his frustration to Provost Douglas Whitaker that the committee was mired in "misinterpretations of signals." Faulkner to Whitaker, May 1953, SC2016 box 30, folder 24; Spencer to the Advisory Committee on Land and Building Development, July 7, 1954, SC0216 box 30, folder 24.

74 Report of the President's Advisory Committee on Land and Building Development, June 1, 1954, in SC0216 box 23. On Terman's influential role, see C. Stewart Gillmor, *Fred Terman at Stanford: Building a Discipline, a University and Silicon Valley* (Stanford: Stanford University Press, 2004) 325–26.

75 "Land Use Study: Stage I," September 10, 1954, was approved at the September 16, 1954, trustee meeting. Frank Medeiros, "The Sterling Years at Stanford: A Study in the Dynamics of Institutional Change," unpublished Ph.D. dissertation, Stanford University (1979) 111.

76 Expansion of the campus boundary was recommended in February, approved in July, and amended in September 1955. Trustee minutes, February 17, July 21, and

September 15, 1955. The amended official description of the campus boundaries is in the September 15, 1955, trustee minutes, p. 477. [James F.] Crafts, "A Summary of the Statement made to the joint meeting of the Land Development Committee and the Special Committee appointed to review certain phases of the land development program," trustee minutes, November 18, 1959, documents the 4,800 figure.

77 Trustee minutes, June 16, 1955, p. 341. The trustees later noted that they were making an exception when, in 1958, they approved a hilltop site for the highly visible 150-foot "Dish" antenna, completed in 1962 to detect nuclear bomb blasts, at the time a classified government-sponsored project. (It has since been used for many other scientific purposes.)

78 The meeting, held July 3, 1953, is documented in SC0216 box 30. The discussion appears in the Skidmore, Owings & Merrill interim report, August 15, 1953, in SC0216 box 23, folder 21.

79 SOM job memo July 3, 1953, SC0216 box 30, folder 24.

80 The historiography of Silicon Valley is voluminous, but few have studied early staff efforts at developing this area for commercial, industrial, and residential use. An essential starting point is Henry Lowood, *From Steeples of Excellence to Silicon Valley: The Story of Varian Associates and Stanford Industrial Park* (Varian Associates, 1988). As Lowood emphasizes, the industrial park owed its birth not to visionary planning, but to a mix of genial opportunism and informal personal contacts. He also distinguishes the evolution of the industrial park from that of Silicon Valley, where Stanford was but one element, "diffuse rather than concentrated in time and space," along with unprecedented government funding on grants and contracts, especially in aerospace and defense. Henry Lowood, "Steeples of Excellence and Valley of Silicon: Origins of the Industry-University Connection at Stanford" (History of Science Society, 30 October 1987; an edited version first appeared in *Stanford Campus Report,* March 9, 1988, and later as the Varian Associates 1988 publication above).

81 Peter C. Allen to M. J. Lightbown, *Architectural Forum*, March 6, 1954, SC0122 box 33, folder "Land Development, 1950–55."

82 March 15, 1949, Eldridge T. Spencer to President's Office (Acting President Clarence Faust), SC0216 box 52, folder 2. This report includes his 1946 maps showing these sites and reflected "considerable study" from previous reports. Similarly, Spencer's "A Coordinated Plan for the University: Report of the Planning Department, February 1, 1947" focuses on the east side of the campus along El Camino, including the green corridor, and the section from Lot 41 up to Foothill Road; his "Master Plan Land Use, showing existing leases of proposed zoning, Stanford University, September 18, 1950" again outlines the same

commercial development at Lot 1 and the industrial site at Lot 41, backed by campus housing in the southeast corner, with 100- to 300-foot-wide greenbelt planting extending along El Camino from Menlo Park to South Palo Alto. SC0486 (accession 1999-093) box 1, folder 3.

83 Brandin to Sterling, April 24, 1951, SC0216 box 30, folder 24. Brandin was authorized to negotiate with Varian and move ahead on infrastructure at the board's April 19, 1951, meeting. Lowood also notes that Dean of Engineering Frederick E. Terman, who was a Varian board director, helped with these discussions. *San Francisco Chronicle*, October 13, 1950. See also "Stanford Plans Use of Lands," *San Francisco Examiner*, October 13, 1950; *San Francisco Chronicle*, October 13, 1950.

84 Brandin to Sterling, September 11 and December 5, 1950, SC0216 box 30, folder 24 "Land Development 1952–53."

85 According to Lowood, this "financial move was made possible by recently enacted tax laws which benefited rapidly expanding technology-based companies in areas deemed vital to national defense." Lowood (1988) 9.

86 Mel Wax, Business and Finance (column), "How University 'Wooed' Industry: Stanford Park—Weird Success," *San Francisco Chronicle,* November 16, 1958, SC0122 box 35, folder "Land Development Clippings 1958–60." On the evolution of the industrial park from Stanford's perspective, see Lowood (1988) and Margaret Pugh O'Mara, *Cities of Knowledge: Cold War Science and the Search for the Next Silicon Valley* (Princeton: Princeton University Press, 2005). See also her "Campus and City Plans: The Design and Influence of Stanford's Land Developments," lecture to the Stanford Historical Society, January 22, 2004. Audio tape available in Stanford Historical Society Program Recordings, SC0683 box 1, SUA.

87 SC0216 boxes 30 and 37.

88 Brandin, having been authorized to negotiate with Varian Associates, was moving ahead as early as April 1951 to figure out the utilities and leasing issues. Brandin to Sterling, April 24, 1951, SC0216 box 30, folder 24. Sterling reported the first meeting of a "joint committee" of Stanford and Palo Alto officials regarding a variety of issues, including water supply, civil defense, the Palo Alto Hospital, and "general planning of mutual concern," at the October 19, 1950, Board of Trustees meeting. Brandin to Keithley, March 19, 1953, SC0216 box 30, folder 24 op. cit., regarding help with Eastman Kodak.

89 Keithley to Brandin, March 6, 1953, SC0216 box 30, folder 24 op. cit. "New Stanford Developments Denied Palo Alto Sewer Service," *Palo Alto Times,* August 8, 1952; "Stanford Annexation Strikes Snag," *Palo Alto Times*, October 30, 1952, regarding Lot 41.

90 "Planning Began in 1950; Financing Set in 1951," *Varian Associates News-Letter* (May 1953); Mendelsohn's plans, dated September 7, 1951, as well as Sigurd Varian's copy of "Varian Associates Schedule for R&D Plant, Palo Alto,

October 15, 1951," are in the Russell and Sigurd Varian Papers, SC0345, SUA. Lowood (March 1988) 8.

91 Brandin/de Roos (1987) says this came later, with second building; *Palo Alto Times* quoted in Lowood (1988) 8.

92 McAndrews (1995) 11; see Spencer's 1950 Planning Office report, September 18, 1950, SC0486 (accession 1999-093) box 1, folder 3.

93 Kelley to Sterling, June 3 and August 4, 1955, Sterling to Kelley, July 11, 1955, William Kelley Jr. and Ryland Kelley letter, March 23, 1956, and Brandin memo to file, June 5, 1956, SC0216 box 30, folder 27.

94 Allan Temko, *Architectural Forum* (January 1961).

95 Mel Wax, op. cit.

96 Cuthbertson to Brandin, December 20, 1954, regarding December 16, 1954, trustee approval for Houghton-Mifflin and Scott-Foresman, SC0216 box 30, folder "Land Development 1941–56." Brandin quoted in Mel Wax, op. cit.

97 Mel Wax, op. cit.

98 Brandin quoted in Mel Wax, op. cit.

99 "Session on Wally" (1985) 12–13.

100 "Session on Wally" (1985) 13.

101 "Frederick E. Terman, interviews by Arthur L. Norberg, Charles Susskind, and Roger Hahn," 1971, 1974, 1978 (transcript 1984), Bancroft Oral History Project on the History of Science and Technology and Stanford Oral History Project, SUA, 127.

102 Gillmor (2004) 305–06, 322–27.

103 Phleger to Cushing, February 23, 1956, in SC0216 boxes 48 and A29.

104 *Report of the Special Committee to Review the Land Development Program*, November 17, 1959, with trustee minutes, December 17, 1959 (also in SC0216 box A33). Both include a copy of Phleger's 1956 letter. Members of the 1959 special committee were trustees Arthur Stewart (chairman), Herman Phleger, Paul Pigott, Thomas Pike, and Monroe Spaght.

105 Crafts, "A Summary of the Statement," November 18, 1959, op. cit. Crafts, a trustee since 1954, was president of Fireman's Fund Insurance.

106 Trustee minutes, January 21, 1960, 17–18, 44–45.

107 Falcon O. Baker, "City on the Campus," *Saturday Evening Post*, December 31, 1955.

CHAPTER 6: REAPPRAISING DEVELOPMENT

1 Falcon O. Baker, "City on the Campus," *Saturday Evening Post,* December 31, 1955. According to Baker, who interviewed Alf Brandin, homes in the Stanford Oaks area were going for $20,000 to $45,000.

2 The agency had expressed interest as early as 1952 in this acreage, as documented by Brandin, memo to file, August 11, 1952, SC0216 box 30. "Stanford Site Still Sought for Hospital," *Stanford Daily*, December 3, 1954.

3 "Stanford Site Still Sought for Hospital," *Stanford Daily*,

December 3, 1954. Letter, May 5, 1954, in SC0216 box 33. The campus protest, led by Professor Virgil A. Anderson, died down with the change in siting. "VA, Farm Agree to Build Hospital on Stanford Site," *Stanford Daily*, January 3, 1955.

4   This section of Junipero Serra Boulevard, also labeled as Foothill Road on some early maps, was renamed Foothill Expressway in 1964 when it was extended into Los Altos on an old railbed.

5   December 21, 1954, in SC0216 box 33.

6   SC0216 box 30. On the Veterans Hospital, see also SC0216 boxes 33 and A36.

7   The state also refused to fund access roads from towns to the western route.

8   SC0216 box 57. "Cities Begin Battle on Serra Freeway Routing," *San Mateo Times*, April 6, 1957; "Fighting Front Against Serra Route Shown Here," *San Mateo Times*, April 24, 1957; "Most Cities Support Western Serra Route," *Palo Alto Times*, April 5, 1957; "Planners Agree on Serra Route," *Palo Alto Times*, March 21, 1957. On the other hand, Los Altos was "disgusted" with both routes, which, Mayor Irving L. Atkinson said, were "an insult to the intelligence of a municipality to think that they [highway engineers] can put an eight-lane divided highway through a municipality without a fight on their hands," in "Most Cities Support Western Serra Route," *Palo Alto Times*, April 5, 1957.

9   "Solid Support for C Route Is Anticipated," *San Mateo Times*, September 25, 1957. The Highway Division initially avoided the western-most route, claiming potential damage to Hetch Hetchy water supply in Crystal Springs Reservoir. Citizens groups called on hydrology experts, including Stanford Professor Ray Linsley, to testify that such fears were unwarranted.

10   "Serra Route: Campus Land Division Not Favored," *Palo Alto Times*, March 12, 1957. See also Sterling files on the freeway controversy, SC0216 box 57.

11   SC0216 box 57.

12   "Witnesses Split Over Freeway," *Oakland Tribune*, August 16, 1957; "Serra Freeway Route," *San Mateo Times*, October 26, 1957; "Freeway Facts" [Citizens Committee for Peninsula Highways], *San Mateo Times*, September 19, 1957.

13   Stanford received more than $5.6 million for the land. Trustee minutes, December 15, 1966.

14   SC0216 box 37.

15   "JC Considers Stanford Sites," *Stanford Daily*, November 10, 1961.

16   Trustee minutes, February 17, March 17, July 21, and September 15, 1955. "Toward Financial Security: Stanford is Developing Land for Added income," *Stanford Daily*, August 11, 1955. Campus officials and the *Daily* used the figure of 3,820, but the final legal description of the area deleted the Weekend Acres acreage.

17   *Stanford Daily*, ibid. "The Campus Scene," *Stanford Review* 57:1 (October 1955) 14. Manuel Piers' lease in trustee minutes, September 15, 1955. Other leases that year included more than 1,000 acres in crop production, such as hay, vetch, asters, chrysanthemums, gladiolus, and iris.

18   Ibid.; Baker (1955).

19   Ferris Miles to Brandin, April 1, 1955, and Brandin to Miles, January 4, 1955, SC0216 box 30, folder 28. Trustee minutes, September 21, 1961, and April 8, 1980.

20   Trustee minutes, June 16, 1955, p. 341. "Toward Financial Security: Stanford is Developing Land for Added income," *Stanford Daily*, August 11, 1955. *Palo Alto Times*, August 11, 1955.

21   "New Research Center Leases Eleven Acres of Farm Property: Old Lathrop Home is Site," *Stanford Daily*, April 1, 1954. The Lathrop estate was razed and the center's new buildings (an award-winning design by Wurster, Bernardi and Emmons) were tucked into the site, not visible from Junipero Serra (Foothill) below. CASBS opened September 1954. On the history of the Alta Vista site, see Mary Montella and Roxanne Nilan, "Alta Vista: The House on the Hill" in *Historic Houses VII: South San Juan Neighborhood and Stock Farm, Stanford University* (Stanford: Stanford Historical Society 2016) 50–58 and "William Wilson Wurster," 9–10.

22   Peter C. Allen to Christopher Arnold, March 11 and 17, 1957, exchange of letters, *Palo Alto Times,* in SC0122 box 33. Christopher Arnold (no direct relation to contractor Harry L. Arnold) had received his master's degree in architecture from Stanford in 1953.

23   Harry Arnold to Brandin, April 19, 1954, SC0216 box 30, folder 26. Brandin to files, May 28, 1952, SC0216 box 30, folder 24, and April 1953, SC0216 box 30, folder 8, regarding Arnold's interest and Coldwell's enthusiasm for housing in area, and March 8, 1955, SC0216 box 30, folder 26.

24   Regarding Webb, Glover to Brandin, May 4, 1955, SC0216 box 30, folder 26. An undated copy of a letter from Jerry S. Engle, for Joseph L. Eichler, regarding 700 acres near College Terrace may date from Spencer's 1950 recommendations for the area. SC0216 box 30, folder 26. Utah Construction Company proposal to Brandin, April 11, 1955, SC0216 box 30, folder 26.

25   Brandin was authorized to put five lots of 3–5 acres in this 17.5-acre area near Searsville as a test of market interest, trustee minutes, September 16, 1954. At the November 18, 1954, meeting, Brandin reported limited interest. See also Brandin note to file, February 1955, in SC0216 box 30, folder 25.

26   May 25, 1956, SC0216 box 30, folder 27.

27   SC0216 box 30, folder 26. "Stanford Tract Under Study for Major Housing Project," *San Francisco Examiner*, May 24, 1955. "Board Approves Development," *Stanford Daily*, October 21, 1955, notes that Webb undertook the

study "in the interests of Stanford," but gives away little about choice of developer; "Stanford to Begin Big Home Project," *San Francisco Examiner*, October 21, 1955. The trustees asked SOM to draw up plans for development portions of 50 to 100 acres; Webb and other builders remained interested. In 1956, Brandin was still discussing a possible new golf course residential project. June 27, 1956, SC0216 box 30, folder 26. Del E. Webb (1899–1974) had built his Phoenix contracting business into a multi-million-dollar construction business throughout the Southwest. The first Del Webb retirement community, Sun City, opened in 1960. Webb also was co-owner of New York Yankees, 1945–65. Margaret Finnerty, *Del Webb: A Man, A Company* (Heritage Publishers, 1991).

28   Stanford press release, March 4, 1957, in SC0122 box 173, folder "Land Development 1956–69." "Menlo Park Approves Construction of 30-acre Rural-Residential Area on Stanford Property," *Stanford Daily*, March 5, 1957. Stanford press release, March 4, 1957, in SC0122 box 173, folder "Land Development 1956–69." Arnold had expected to start by August 1957. But according to the "Plans Determined for Construction on Stanford Land," *Palo Alto Times*, August 8, 1958, the PPCC's plans were delayed until selection of the Junipero Freeway route, then were rescheduled for early 1959. Today, many residents are current or retired faculty, staff, or alumni of the university.

29   *Palo Alto Times*, April 16, 1958.

30   Peninsula Pacific Construction Company proposal to the Faculty Advisory Committee, June 6, 1955, SC0216 box 30. John Cushing, chair of the Special Land Development Committee, urged that Stanford should "get the cash" Arnold's proposal represented "unless there are more compelling reasons against doing it than those already advanced." Cushing to Wallace Sterling, October 6, 1955, SC0216 box 30, folder 27. Willow Road was constructed in 1955 and connected to Alpine and Sand Hill roads via a two-lane bridge. In 1984, Palo Alto approved its connection to El Camino Real and renamed it Sand Hill.

31   Faulkner to Sterling, October 14, 1955, SC0216 box 30, folder 27 (Faulkner stated that the committee's conclusion was "remarkably consistent on this question"); see also May 26 and September 22, 1955, in SC0216 op. cit. for a summary of committee discussion.

32   Trustee minutes, April 16 and May 21, 1959. "Stanford Approves Luxury Apartments up to 12 Stories High," *Palo Alto Times*, April 17, 1959, SC0122 box 35; "Menlo Park to Fight Towering Apartments," *Menlo Park Recorder* (editorial) October 8, 1959; "Tower Apartments Stir Family Quarrel" (alumni protest), *Palo Alto Times*, October 21, 1959; "Menlo Park Residents Unhappy," *Palo Alto Times*, October 28, 1959. "Apartment Size to be Discussed," *Palo Alto Times*, November 3, 1959; trustee minutes, November 19, 1959.

33   "P.A. Negroes Ask No-Bias in Contracts: Request Stan-

ford Reconsider Stand Against Clauses" and "Stanford and Discrimination" (editorial), *Stanford Daily*, April 5, 1957. The Santa Clara County branch, founded in 1942, had spilt into Palo Alto and San Jose branches in 1952.

34   Herbert G. Ruffin II, *Uninvited Neighbors: African Americans in Silicon Valley, 1769–1990*, in Race and Culture in the American West Series #7 (Norman, OK: University of Oklahoma Press, 2014) 75–78.

35   Paul Adamson and Marty Arbunich, *Eichler: Modernism Rebuilding the American Dream* (Gibbs Smith, 2002) 198; "Robert H. Bragg: African American Faculty and Senior Staff Oral History Series," interview conducted by Nadine Wilmot in 2002 (Berkeley: Regional Oral History Office, The Bancroft Library, University of California, Berkeley, 2005) 229–30.

36   Adamson and Arbunich (2002) 197–205; Ruffin (2014) 104–07. See also Ocean Howell, "The Merchant Crusaders: Eichler Homes and Fair Housing, 1949–1974," *Pacific Historical Review* 85:3 (August 2016) 379–407, and *Race and Housing: An Interview with Edward P. Eichler, President, Eichler Homes, Inc.* (Center for the Study of Democratic Institutions, The Fund for the Republic, 1964). Eichler's sales policy put him at odds with the National Association of Home Builders, from which he resigned in protest in 1958, and with the California Association of Realtors, the prime mover against state fair housing legislation. That same year, newly arrived San Francisco Giant's star outfielder Willie Mays found it difficult to buy and, once bought, reside in a home where he wished to live.

37   Ladera Community Association history by Hallis Friend and Nancy Lund available online at the association's website.

38   "Stanford Rejects NAACP Bid for Anti-Discrimination Clause," *Palo Alto Times*, March 11, 1957; "NAACP Seeks Unrestricted Stanford Leases," *San Francisco Examiner*, March 12, 1957; "NAACP Unit Seeks Stanford Ban Against Housing Discrimination," *Fresno Bee*, March 13, 1957.

39   "FEPC [Fair Employment Practices Commission] Talk Slated Here," *San Mateo Times*, April 16, 1957. "Fraternal Discrimination" (editorial), "No Colored Brothers" Allowed (Letter to editor), *Stanford Daily*, January 8, 1957. "Stanford and Discrimination" (editorial), April 5, 1957.

40   "NAACP Seeks Unrestricted Stanford Leases," *San Francisco Examiner*, March 12, 1957.

41   Elinor V. Cogswell, "EVC at Bat: Stanford in a Hot-Spot," *Palo Alto Times*, March 12, 1957; "Racial Problem at Stanford," *San Francisco Chronicle*, March 12, 1957; "NAACP Seeks Unrestricted Stanford Leases," *San Francisco Examiner*, March 13, 1957; "NAACP Unit Seeks Stanford Ban Against Housing Discrimination," *Fresno Bee*, March 13, 1957. Glover to Sterling, March 15, 1957, SC0216 box A21, folder 6.

42 Petition, March 18, 1957, to the Board of Trustees from the West Coast Region and the Palo Alto–Stanford Branch of the NAACP (Norman Howard and Lester Bailey), SC0216 box A21; "P.A. Negroes Ask No-Bias in Contracts," *Stanford Daily*, April 5, 1957.

43 Glover to Sterling, January 25, 1957, on Brown's views, SC0216 box A21.

44 "Stanford: No Racial Bans," *San Francisco Examiner*, March 22, 1957; "NAACP Petition to Board of Trustees," *Stanford Daily*, April 5, 1957. "Stanford and Discrimination" (editorial), *Stanford Daily*, April 5, 1957. Glover to Bailey, March 26, 1957, SC0216 box A21.

45 "Stanford Rejects NAACP Bid for Anti-Discrimination Clause," *Palo Alto Times*, March 22, 1957; "P.A. Negroes Ask No-Bias in Contracts: Request Stanford Reconsider Stand Against Clauses," *Stanford Daily*, April 5, 1957.

46 Letters in March 1957 in SC0216 box A21.

47 "NAACP Meeting Tonight on Stanford Race Stand," *Palo Alto Times*, April 8, 1957.

48 SC0216 box A21.

49 Merryman to Sterling on March 29, 1957, SC0216 box A21.

50 Sterling to Merryman on April 4, 1957, SC0216 box A21.

51 "NAACP Meeting Tonight on Stanford Race Stand," *Palo Alto Times*, April 8, 1957; Lloyd Dinkelspiel to Lester Bailey, April 3, 1957. SC0216 box A21.

52 Brown to Dinkelspiel, May 1, 1957, SC0216 box A21.

53 Packer to Bailey, April 8, 1957, and Sterling to Packer, April 10, 1957, SC0216 box A21. Sterling appreciated Packer's support, agreeing with his logic.

54 Glover to Sterling, May 29, 1957, SC0216 box A21.

55 Wallace Sterling, press statement, October 13, 1958, SC0216 box A21.

56 Ruffin notes that the two branches were losing membership as most members could not commit consistently to the heavy task of fighting for fair employment and fair housing, but membership revived with civil rights activism of the 1960s. Ruffin (2014) 87, 89.

57 Sally Hornig, "Discrimination 'tendency' seen" (letter to editor), *Palo Alto Times*, March 30, 1955. "IFC Passes Unanimous Resolution Condemning Racial Restrictions on Fraternity Membership," *Stanford Daily*, April 10, 1957.

58 Ruffin (2014) 93, 105, 109–19. California's Unruh Act forbid discrimination in all business transactions, including real estate renting, leasing, and sale, but left it to courts to enforce on a case-by-case basis. In 1963, California's legislature passed the Rumford Fair Housing Act after numerous suits worked their way through California courts and many years of legislative debate. The Act was immediately challenged by the California Real Estate Association, and in a state referendum, their Proposition 14 briefly put the Rumford Act out of commission. Prop. 14 was ruled unconstitutional by the California

59 May 13, 1958, in SC0216 box 57.

60 *Report of the Special Committee to Review the Land Development Program*, November 17, 1959, in trustee minutes, December 17, 1959 (also in SC0216 box A33). Trustee minutes, January 21, 1960, 17–18, 44–45. Lands unsuited for any other kind of development, such as the Stanford Oaks residential development across San Francisquito Creek, were exempted.

61 The university presented its reasoning behind development of the 254 acres in its alumni magazine, the *Stanford Review* (May 1960) 9–13.

62 Trustees minutes, March 17, 1960.

63 "The Shrinking Stanford Lands," *Stanford Review* (May 1960) 9–13. The *Review* also notes that despite critical letters to newspaper editors and a local petition, fewer than 300 took up the open invitation to gather at Bowman Alumni House. The *Stanford Daily*, April 4, 1960, reported attendance at around 150.

64 California Assembly Bill 2719, introduced May 1, 1959, by assemblymen Clark L. Bradley (28th district) and Bruce F. Allen (29th district) to amend Section 30031 of the California Education Code, was passed in July 1959. It allowed Stanford to "hold exempt from taxation all land used by it exclusively for educational purposes." The code was again amended in 1976 as Section 94020 of the Education Code.

65 [Sterling speech, Land Development Open House, April 2, 1960] 8 pp. in SC0122 box 33, folder "Land Development 1960." University officials at the time were using conflicting figures—4,700 and 4,800 acres—as the size of academic lands, for example: *Stanford Review* (May 1960) and *Faculty-Staff Newsletter*, March 28, 1960, use 4,700; *Stanford Today* (May 1960) uses 4,800.

66 Clark to Sterling, May 28, 1960, in SC0216 box A29.

67 SC0216 box A29. *Palo Alto Times*, September 14, 1960.

68 Dan Endsley, "Oasis in the Asphalt," *Stanford Review* (January 1960) 1, and "Drainage Problem," *Stanford Review* (May 1960) 1.

69 *Stanford Review* (June-July 1960) following p. 16.

70 Sterling letter, June 22, 1960, in SC0216 box A29.

71 William Roberts to Sterling, November 30, 1961, in SC0216 box A29. In a turn of fate, Stanford University offices now occupy 35 acres of the former Ampex site in Redwood City.

72 Ward Winslow, *Palo Alto: A Centennial History* (Palo Alto: Palo Alto Historical Association, 1993) 53–54.

73 Winslow (1993) 54–55, 159.

74 Winslow (1993) 55. Preliminary vote figures in *San Mateo Times*, June 6, 1962. Andy Doty, "Stanford and Palo Alto After World War II," *Sandstone & Tile* 18:2 (Spring 1994)

14. See also "The Oregon Expressway: Residentialists Unite," Palo Alto History. org. The battle was covered in the *Palo Alto Times*.

75 Winslow (1993) 55–56; Doty (1994) 13–14.

76 U.S. Army Corps of Engineers, South Pacific Division, San Francisco, *Notice of Survey Report for Flood Control and Allied Purposes, San Francisquito Creek, Santa Clara and San Mateo Counties*, 25 September 1961. In Lyle M. Nelson Papers, SC0989 box 1, folder 10; Stanford News Service press release, October 18, 1961, in Stanford News and Publications Service, SC0122 box 70, folder "Ladera Dam"; Donald T. Carlson to Board of Trustees, "Status of San Francisquito Creek Project [Ladera Dam]," February 3, 1962, and "Data Sheet: Proposed Ladera Dam Project," February 10, 1962, in SC0216 box C5, folder 6. By comparison, Lexington Reservoir in nearby Los Gatos has a surface area of 412 acres, but is deeper, for a total of 19,044-acre-feet of water, according to the Santa Clara Valley Water District.

77 In 1919, university trustees agreed to purchase the 1891 dam from the Spring Valley Water Company. Dorothy F. Regnery, *The History of Jasper Ridge: From Searsville Pioneers to Stanford Scientists* (Stanford: Stanford Historical Society, 1991) 125. By 2015, sedimentation had reduced the reservoir to 10 percent of its original water capacity, Kate Chesley, "Stanford Identifies Its Preferred Approach for the Future of Searsville Dam and Reservoir," News Service online, May 1, 2015. The drought thereafter left parts of the lake dry, whereas it previously held standing water year-round. *Jasper Ridge Biological Preserve Annual Report 2020–2021*, p. 19.

78 Winslow (1993) 97. Report to Board of Engineers, February 7, 1956, in Stanford Public Affairs Office Records, SC0105 box 2, folder 1; "Army Engineers Select Location for Dam on San Francisquito Creek," *Palo Alto Times*, January 31, 1958; *Palo Alto Times*, April 10, 11, and 14, 1958; "Col. John S. Harnett Reveals Details of U.S. Corp's Plan for a 13,100-acre-foot Reservoir to 40 City, County, and State Officials and Others at PA City Hall," *Palo Alto Times*, April 15, 1958.

79 Professor Ira L. Wiggins, biology, to Seraphim F. Post, assistant business manager, October 2, 1961, and Professor Paul R. Ehrlich, biology, to Post, October 5, 1961, in SC0122 box 70, folder "Buildings & Grounds: Ladera Dam." Professor Winslow R. Briggs to Col. Clark Bronn, Board of Engineers for Rivers and Harbors, October 10, 1961, in SC0216 box C5, folder 6.

80 Wallace Sterling to the Board of Engineers for Rivers and Harbors, Washington, D.C., "Regarding the U.S. Corps of Engineers Flood Control and Allied Purposes Project, San Francisquito Creek," October 18, 1961, in SC0105 box 2, folder 1. "Farm Board Lists Ladera Dam Faults," *Stanford Daily*, September 25, 1961; "Stanford Fighting Army Dam," *Stanford Daily*, October 4, 1961.

81 In January 1962, the Board of Engineers' reversed its negative November 21, 1961, decision; instead it approved the Ladera Dam project and submitted the Corps' report to relevant federal agencies. Thomas H. Kuchel to Tom Pike, February 2, 1962, Sterling to Kuchel, February 9, 1962, in SC0989 box 1, folder 10. Madison quoted in "Politician Raps SU Influence," *Stanford Daily*, April 23, 1962.

82 Don Carlson to Lyle Nelson, February 21, 1962, in SC0989 box 1, folder 10; *Stanford Daily*, October 11, 1961.

83 Nelson to Sterling, February 21, 1962, SC0989 box 1, folder 10. Some letter writers blamed Stanford land development for Palo Alto's drainage problems. "I, for one, would prefer a lake to more scarred hills, factories and houses," wrote Gerald A. Peterson, *Stanford Daily*, October 6, 1961.

84 Nelson to Sterling, Alf Brandin, and Fred Glover, February 21, 1962, SC0989 box 1, folder 10. One senator told Don Carlson that the Corps of Engineers was "more powerful, oftentimes, than the Congress itself," and another federal official added, "you have taken on the best organized lobby in the federal government," in "Report to Trustees: Status, Ladera Dam Project," February 27, 1962, SC0105 box 2, folder 3. University Relations office files include an insightful article by Stanford alumnus Robert de Roos, '33, and Harvard political scientist Arthur A. Maass, "The Lobby That Can't Be Licked: Congress and the Army Engineers," *Harpers Magazine* (August 1949), 21–30. On Lyle Nelson, see Chapter 14 sidebar.

85 Strategy memos can be found in SC0989, such as "Schedule of immediate assignments, 2/23/61" for Sterling and 10 staff members, and "For President Sterling: Briefing Notes on Appts, Monday, March 26, 1962." Kuchel to Sterling, Feburary 23, 1962, SC0989 box 1, folder 10.

86 Nelson in "A Session on Wally: Transcription of an Oral History about J. E. Wallace Sterling, Recorded for the Stanford University Archives" (1985) 34.

87 Carlson to Pike, November 10, 1961, SC0216 box C5, folder 6; Nelson to Robert Wert, March 12, 1962, in SC0216 box C5, folder 6. *Palo Alto Times*, February 2, 1962, and April 13, 1959; "Why So Big a Dam, Asks Menlo Park," *San Francisco Chronicle*, May 25, 1958; "Menlo Park Aide Objects to Proposed Ladera Dam," *Palo Alto Times*, May 21, 1958.

88 Nelson to Sterling, February 21, 1962, SC0989 box 1, folder 10; Carlson to trustees, "Status of San Francisquito Creek Project (Ladera Dam)," March 3, 1962, SC0216 box C5, folder 6.

89 Joseph Eichler to Governor Edmund G. Brown, March 27, 1962, SC0989 box 1, folder 9.

90 Ray Linsley, head, Department of Civil Engineering, to Sterling, December 7, 1961, SC0216 box C5, folder 6. Ray K. Linsley and Robert E. Lee, "The Proposed

Ladera Dam: A Preliminary Economic Review," Project on Engineering-Economic Planning, Stanford University, Pub. No. 2, April 1962, SC0122 box 70, folder "Buildings & Grounds: Ladera Dam." *Stanford Daily*, April 12 and 18, 1962. During his 25 years at Stanford, Linsley also served as associate dean of engineering and co-founded the Program in Engineering-Economic Planning.

91 Wolfgang K. Panofsky to Maj. Gen. Walter K. Wilson, March 14, 1962, SC0989 box 1, folder 9.

92 Carlson to Nelson, March 22, 1962, SC0989 box 1, folder 10; Carlson to trustees, February 2, 1962, SC0216 box C5, folder 6; Carlson to Nelson, June 11–12, 1962, SC0989 box 1, folder 9.

93 Carlson to trustees, February 2, 1962, SC0216 box C5, folder 6.

94 David Packard to Charles S. Gubser, March 8, 1962, SC0989 box 1, folder 9.

95 Carlson to Nelson, March 20, 1962, SC0989 box 1, folder 9, regarding a discussion with E. Robert Stallings, San Mateo County manager.

96 "Army Engineer Issues Rebuttal Against Ladera Dam Protests," *Menlo Park Recorder*, April 12, 1962.

97 "Ladera Flood Project Shelved," *Palo Alto Times*, May 24, 1962, in SC0105 box 2.

98 John A. Morrison, district engineer, Corps of Engineers, to Board of Supervisors, San Mateo County, June 1, 1962, SC0989 box 1, folder 9.

99 Sterling to Kuchel, April 17, 1962, SC0216 box C5, folder 6.

100 John Johnson, Menlo Park city manager, to Stallings, June 18, 1962, SC0989 box 1, folder 9, and Bob Miller to Nelson and Glover, July 10, 1962, SC0216 box C5, folder 6; Sterling to James V. Fitzgerald, March 2, 1962, SC0216 box C5, folder 6. Stanford augmented earlier independent studies on water conservation and flood control by Carroll E. Bradberry (*Water Conservation and Flood Control, San Francisquito Creek*, Los Altos, 1961) and Clyde C. Kennedy (*Report on Water Sources for Stanford University*, San Francisco, 1960) with engineering analysis and cost studies by an expert in the field, its own Professor Linsley.

101 Governor Pat Brown to Sterling, May 29, 1962, SC0989 box 1, folder 9.

102 *Palo Alto Times*, April 29, 1963. Wilsey, Ham and Blair Report, described in *Palo Alto Times*, April 28, 1963, showed downstream improvements to be $4 million less costly than the modified dam project. James R. Vincent, Water Pollution Control Agency, December 1968 report, SC0122 box 70, folder "Buildings & Grounds: Ladera Dam."

103 "San Francisquito Project Ruled Out," *San Jose Mercury News*, January 30, 1971, SC0122 box 70, folder "Buildings & Grounds: Ladera Dam." "Army Rejects Flood Work for Creek," *Palo Alto Times*, January 30, 1971; "New Look at Flood Control," *Palo Alto Times*, March 9, 1971.

104 Carlson to John Walsh of *Science Magazine*, January 3, 1966, SC0122 box 70, folder "Buildings & Grounds: Ladera Dam." The municipalities are Palo Alto, Menlo Park, Woodside, Portola Valley, and Los Altos Hills. Ladera, an unincorporated neighbor within the Portola Valley sphere of influence, also touches Stanford land. As of 2022, of Stanford's 8,180 acres, 4,017 acres are located in unincorporated Santa Clara County and 2,700 acres in San Mateo County. Palo Alto has annexed 1,161 acres, Menlo Park 111 acres, Woodside 114 acres, Portola Valley 76 acres, and 1 acre in Los Altos Hills.

105 David Casto quoted in *Stanford Faculty-Staff Newsletter*, January 4, 1966.

106 "Stanford Sees Red on Land Grabs," *San Jose Mercury News*, May 14, 1966. Vigorous opposition to condemnations of Stanford lands by public agencies was one of numerous policies reiterated in a major review of Stanford land use policies conducted in early 1974. See "Stanford Land Use—An Overview of Policy Determinants," trustee minutes, January 8, 1974, pp. 77–84, and "Stanford Land Use Policies," Committee on Land and Buildings, March 12, 1974, pp. 247–49.

107 *Stanford Faculty-Staff Newsletter*, January 4, 1966.

108 Carlson to Walsh, January 3, 1966, op. cit.; Tom Ford to Nevin K. Hiester, April 1963, SC0989 box 1, folder 9.

109 *Stanford Daily*, April 21, 1967. As late as 1967, Ladera Dam was still considered one of the more difficult of disagreements between the university and Palo Alto. "Two Communities in Conflict: Stanford Vies with Palo Alto," *Stanford Daily*, April 17, 1967.

110 As early as 1964, leased lands annually yielded about $5.4 million for local schools and governments, with the Palo Alto Unified School District ($2.4 million), the City of Palo Alto ($1.5 million), and Santa Clara County ($960,000) the main beneficiaries. Nearly half of the university's tax bill on idle, non-academic lands also went to the Palo Alto School District. *Stanford Faculty-Staff Newsletter*, January 7, 1964. Kenneth M. Cuthbertson, "Comments at Earth Day Panel Discussion on Stanford Land Use," April 22, 1970, in Kenneth Cuthbertson biographical file, Stanford News Service.

111 "New Architectural Plan for Campus Depicted in 'Stanford Builds' Exhibit," *Stanford Alumni Review* (July 1948) 5–7; "New Laboratory and Stern Hall and Expansion Push Construction Program Above $3 Million Mark," *Stanford Alumni Review* (September 1948) 11–12.

112 "Stanford Architecture" letters published in *Stanford Alumni Review*, September, November 1948, and February, March, April, and June 1949; "Written and Verbal Protests of Alumni to Plans for Stanford Architecture Continue to Pile Up" (November 1948) 3–6, includes Kellogg's October 18, 1948, letter to trustees; Paul C.

Edwards' response, "Stanford Architecture: Too Late to Eliminate Flat Roofs, Trustee Head Writes" (December 1948) 11. The controversy was also covered in the *Stanford Daily*.

113 Trustee minutes, October 21, 1948, and March 21, 1949; "Chairman Says Board of Trustees' Buildings Committee Not to Recommend Modification of Stern Hall Roof," *Stanford Alumni Review* (March 1949) 3–5.

114 John Carl Warnecke, "Stanford's Architecture at the Crossroads," n.d. [Report to Board of Trustees, April 1949], SCM0129, SUA. Warnecke was asked to respond by, among others, his father-in-law, John Cushing, '09, an unhappy member of the trustees' Buildings and Grounds Committee. See also Andrew Pearson, "Beyond Sandstone and Tile: Defining Stanford's Architectural Style," *Sandstone & Tile* 14:2 (Spring 1990) 1–11, with introduction by Paul V. Turner.

115 As calculated by Karen Bartholomew, March 2022, from Stanford University Planning Office, "Stanford University Chronological Summary of Construction," both 1966 and 1972 revisions (photocopies from SUA, in the editor's collection), and Stanford University Maps and Records Office, [Building List Construction Dates and Square Footage], spreadsheet provided by Dobie Howard, manager of Facilities Information Services, March 21, 2022.

116 Stanford News Service press release, April 6, 1959; Constance W. Glen, "Ansel Adams," *Architectural Digest* (November 3, 2002).

117 "Planning Head Resigns Post," *Stanford Daily*, April 7, 1959; "First Full-Time Campus Planner Oversaw Major Building Boom Under President Wallace Sterling," Stanford News Service, April 28, 2004, and "Harry Sanders: A Stanford Planner Charts the History of Campus Planning, and Church's Contribution," interview by Suzanne Reiss (Berkeley: Regional Oral History Office, The Bancroft Library, UC Berkeley, 1978) 649. A copy is available in SCM0131, SUA.

118 Richard Joncas, David J. Neuman, and Paul V. Turner, *Stanford University: The Campus Guide* (New York: Princeton Architectural Press, 2004, 2nd edition) 84, 104.

119 Ford (1921–98), Yale '42, Michigan (law) '49, is considered the driving force behind making Sand Hill Road a venture capital hub. He became a commercial developer, philanthropist, and member of the Stanford Board of Trustees (1980–90). "Remembering Tom Ford, 1921–1998: A Developer Who Made a Difference," *Stanford* [magazine] (March–April 1999).

120 Gene Kershner to Karen Bartholomew, March 14, 2022, email.

121 Brandin, "A Session on Wally" (1985) 29, and Brandin as quoted in "Remembering Wally," *Stanford* [magazine] (Winter 1985) 61. This wording, as edited by Don Carlson, does not appear in the original transcript, "A Session on Wally" (1985), on which the article was based.

CHAPTER 7: MIDAS TOUCH

1 Frank Medeiros, "The Sterling Years at Stanford: A Study in the Dynamics of Institutional Change," unpublished Ph.D. dissertation, Stanford University (1979) 96–99, 102. Medeiros concludes that Sterling's understanding of, and personal participation in, fundraising activities was one of the most striking and effective features of his presidency. On the history of Stanford fundraising, see also "Notes for a Talk by Kenneth M. Cuthbertson to the Stanford Historical Society, May 27, 1990," in Cuthbertson biographical file, Stanford News Service; Kenneth M. Cuthbertson, "Fundraising at Stanford: The First Half Century," *Sandstone & Tile* 14:4 (Fall 1990) 3–6; Bob Beyers, "Ken Cuthbertson: Stanford's Financial Architect," *Sandstone & Tile* 24:2/3 (Spring-Summer 2000) 14–21; Kenneth M. Cuthbertson Papers, SC0582, SUA; *Annual Report of the President of Stanford University;* Records of the Office of Development, SC0319, SUA; and Sterling's Speeches files, Stanford News Service.

2 Frank J. Taylor, "Stanford's Man with the Midas Touch," *The Saturday Evening Post* (December 3, 1960) 36; *Time* magazine, September 27, 1961. In a November 9, 1962, article about Stanford's raids on Ivy-League faculties, *Time* offered a more grudging compliment: Sterling "looks like a heavy weight Jimmy Durante, sounds like Edward R. Murrow, and thinks like tycoon Stanford." Statistics from *Stanford University Financial Report 1968* (November 1968) 15, and *Stanford University Financial Report 1969* (November 1969) 24 (Stanford: Stanford University Controller's Office).

3 Sterling to trustees, November 17, 1948, in J. E. Wallace Sterling Presidential Papers, SC0216 box 26, SUA.

4 Jim Wascher, "Wallace Sterling—Giant of Two Stanford Decades," *Stanford Daily,* March 14, 1974.

5 Taylor (1960) 36. Wascher (1974). Cuthbertson (May 1990) 11, states that Sterling's "enthusiasm was infectious among alumni and other existing and potential friends of the university."

6 J. E. Wallace Sterling, speech to San Francisco PACE dinner, October 18, 1962, and J. E. Wallace Sterling, speech to the Stanford Today and Tomorrow convocation, January 10, 1961. Transcripts in Sterling Speeches files, Stanford News Service.

7 A contemporary review of Stanford's condition, highlighting the many improvements and accomplishments of President Donald B. Tresidder is in "Address of W. P. Fuller, Jr., Delivered at the Stanford Alumni Conferences," *President's Report* (1947–48) 53–58, and in memorial articles in *Stanford Alumni Review* (March 1948) 6–12. See also Edwin Kiester Jr., *Donald B. Tresidder: Stanford's Overlooked Treasure* (Stanford: Stanford Historical Society, 1992).

8 Sterling to Academic Council, April 4, 1958. Taylor

(1960); Medeiros (1979) 123–24. Stanford's faculty numbered 309 in 1940, with total student enrollment of 4,464. In 1950, enrollment was up to 7,540, with a faculty of 372.

9 Taylor (1960) 55.

10 Glover in "A Session on Wally: Transcription of an Oral History about J. E. Wallace Sterling, Recorded for the Stanford University Archives" (1985) 9. J. E. Wallace Sterling, San Francisco PACE Dinner, October 18, 1962, pg. 4, in Sterling Speeches files, 1961–62, Stanford News Service.

11 "Fast PACE at Palo Alto," *Time* magazine, November 9, 1962. Beyers (2000) 14. During the 1920s, "too many of our alumni and friends had responded apathetically to our appeals for help, under the false impression that the University was rich and could get along without them." Ray Lyman Wilbur, *The Memoirs of Ray Lyman Wilbur, 1875–1949* (Stanford: Stanford University Press, 1960) 573.

12 Orrin Leslie Elliott, *Stanford University: The First Twenty-Five Years* (Stanford: Stanford University Press, 1937) 251–52. The actual value of the endowment is difficult to determine. See Norman E. Tutorow, *The Governor: The Life and Legacy of Leland Stanford* (Spokane: Arthur H. Clark, 2004) vol. II 932–33, 970, and George E. Crothers, Founding of the Leland Stanford Junior University (San Francisco: A.M. Robertson, 1932). An abridged version appeared in *Stanford Illustrated Review* (October 1931). The first report of the value of the founders' endowment by the university was published in the *President's Report* (1913–14) 24, where it is listed at $20,864,835.

13 Elliott (1937) 571; Roxanne Nilan, "The Tenacious Jane Lathrop Stanford," *Sandstone & Tile* 9:2 (Winter 1985) 3–13. On financial and legal implications of the original founding grant, see Crothers (1932).

14 Elliott (1937) 571; Cuthbertson (Fall 1990) 3.

15 Wilbur (1960) 300.

16 George H. Nash, *Herbert Hoover and Stanford University* (Stanford: Hoover Institution Press, 1988) 63.

17 Cuthbertson (Fall 1990) 4. *President's Report* (1920–21) 20, notes the board's forecast of $4 million needed to improve faculty salaries and pensions, and build student housing.

18 *President's Reports* (1920–21) to (1928–29); Nash (1988) 62–70; and First Million for Stanford Collection, SC0452, SUA, which includes correspondence and records regarding the first three campaigns, 1921–1927. A fourth million target was added soon after. The "liberty bond" style of promoting small donations through local fundraising efforts and bulk letters written by Hoover and Wilbur was already out of style at major universities by the mid-1920s. Cuthbertson (May 1990) 5. Initial organization was led by Lyman L. Pierce, of Ward, Pierce, Wells and Co., a fundraising consultant and Palo Alto resident with two children attending Stanford. After a flurry of student and local alumni interest, the effort stalled. By 1924, it was in

the hands of John A. Sellards, M.A. '16, an instructor of Romance Languages who had participated in Herbert Hoover's Belgian and Russian relief efforts (1920–21). As endowment secretary, 1924–30, Sellards was to "take care of the endowment problem in all of its phases and to be available to give information whenever opportunity arises." He simultaneously served as director (later dean) of Summer Quarter (1925–31). After two years in France completing his doctorate at the University of Paris, he returned to Stanford to teach French in 1934. *Annual Register 1935–36*; *President's Report* (1923–24) 6.

19 On Wilbur's discomfort with approaching individual donors, see "David S. Jacobson: An interview conducted by Frederic O. Glover and George H. Knoles, Stanford Oral History Project" (1988) 31; "Robert Mark Levison, Interview by Frederic O. Glover," Stanford Oral History Project (1983) 3; "Thomas S. Barclay, interview by Frederic O. Glover," Stanford Oral History Project (1980) 6, 14. Trustee Paul Edwards and Professor Edgar Robinson, however, note that, unlike many of his presidential colleagues, Wilbur never complained about having to seek out funding, but "welcomed every chance to encourage wealthy individuals or the foundations to give financial support to scholarships or fellowships, to the promotion of new or wider fields of study, and to University research projects of benefit to all mankind." Wilbur (1960) 300, editors' note.

20 Editorial, *Stanford Daily*, April 15, 1929; "'First Million' Mark Passed in Stanford Endowment Drive," *Stanford Daily*, May 3, 1929; *President's Report* (1928–29) 7–8.

21 On Branner Hall, see "Branner Hall, New Men's Dormitory, is Open for Occupation," *Stanford Daily,* January 2, 1924; *President's Report* (1921–22) 2 and *President's Report* (1923–24) 1. On Roble Gym, *President's Report* (1930–31) 43–44. Additional fundraising by women's groups was needed to equip the new gymnasium. The BAC also funded professional coaches and physical education faculty salaries, and built major new facilities for football, basketball, and baseball. J. Pearce Mitchell, *Stanford University, 1916–1941* (Stanford University Press, 1958) 123–135.

22 Cuthbertson (May 1990) 4–5.

23 *President's Report* (1932–33) 32.

24 Margo Davis and Roxanne Nilan, *The Stanford Album: A Photographic History, 1885–1945* (Stanford: Stanford University Press, 1989) 218.

25 Mitchell (1958) 48. See also Roxanne Nilan, "A Longer View of Women's Enrollment at Stanford: 1891–2013," *Stanford & Tile* 38:3 (Fall 2014) 15–17, and Sam Scott, "Why Jane Stanford Limited Women's Enrollment to 500," *Stanford* magazine (August 2018).

26 On the Associates' important role in stabilizing fundraising, see Jean G. Coblentz, "Supporting Service to Stanford: Who, What, and Why are the Stanford Associates,"

speech to the Stanford Historical Society, February 4, 2003, transcript, Stanford Associates file, Stanford News Service; "Paul Herbert Davis: An Interview conducted by Frederic O. Glover and Paul R. Hanna, Stanford Oral History Project" (1983); Jacobson (1988); and Levison (1983). The records of the Stanford Associates, 1934–2005, SC0833, are in SUA. *Stanford Associates Handbook* includes a list of founding members and presidents. Early activities and accomplishments are recorded in the *President's Reports* (1935–36) to (1947–48).

27 Wilbur (1960) 574. Cuthbertson (Fall 1990) 5.

28 Davis had an advantage; he knew Wilbur and others in the president's circle from his days as student athletics manager and member of the BAC, sharing with them a love of fishing. Comptroller Almon Roth, a good friend of Wilbur's and a charter member of the Associates, was a mentor. Davis (1983) 20, 25–29, 54–55.

29 Cuthbertson (May 1990) 8–9; Jacobson (1988) 40–41; Levison (1983) 18. Lou Roseberry (1880–1956) was a prominent Los Angeles trust lawyer and former Security-Pacific Bank vice president. He had served as a California state senator, 1908–12. Dave Jacobson, a two-sport athlete at Stanford and chair of the Rally Committee, had served as assistant to Dean of Men George B. Culver from 1930 to 1934, when he completed his law degree. He joined the Associates after working three years for Loeb, Walker and Loeb of Los Angeles. Jacobson worked closely on R-Plan visits with the esteemed Stanford law Professor George E. Osborne (a Cal and Harvard alumnus).

30 Morgan Arthur Gunst (1887–1958), a noted bibliophile, had served as president of the Federation of Jewish Charities and a director of the Jewish Welfare Fund and on many charitable foundation boards. A member of the class of 1908, Gunst had to leave Stanford after his first year to help his father, Moses Gunst, recover from business losses due to the 1906 earthquake and fire. "In Memoriam: Morgan A. Gunst," *California Historical Society Quarterly* 1 (March 1958) 277–78. On December 4, 1954, Sterling presented the Degree of Uncommon Man, the Associate's highest honor, to Roseberry and Gunst, in gratitude for their innovative contributions. Stanford Office of Information (later Stanford News Service) press release, December 2, 1954; "Uncommon Men," *Stanford Review* (January 1955) 9.

31 Davis (1983) 31–34, 44–47, 52; Cuthbertson (Fall 1990) 6.

32 *Stanford Daily*, January 18, 1946; *President's Report* (1944–45) 9; Cuthbertson (Fall 1990) 6. Wallace Alexander had joined Paul Shoup and C.O.G. Miller on the trustees' revamped Endowment Fund Committee during the 1920s.

33 *President's Report* (1941–42) 8–9.

34 Davis notes the tension at Stanford during this period, and the lack of unity within the President's Office. Davis (1983) 34–36. (Tresidder had appropriated David Jacob-

son, Davis' assistant, to his own staff as presidential assistant.) Al Eurich, who thought Wilbur's administration "rather casual," believed Davis "promised anything to anybody if he could get money, whether it was consistent with Stanford policy or not." Eurich (1983) 31.

35 Eurich (1983) 31. Carpenter, A.B., Dartmouth, 1925, A.M, University of Chicago, 1926, had been president of Oak Park (Illinois) Junior College, 1929–38, and subsequently dean of freshmen and professor of sociology at Knox College (Illinois). *Annual Register*, *1945–46, 27*; *Stanford Daily*, January 18, 1946.

36 Medeiros (1979) 54–55.

37 *President's Report* (1947–48) 15. Lundborg spent the remainder of his career at the Bank of America, retiring as chairman of the board. While Eurich considered Lundborg "one of the best appointments I made" [Eurich (1983) 45], Jacobson thought Lundborg, as someone new to fundraising and to Stanford, accomplished little in the position, but nearly 40 years later he may have confused Lundborg with Carpenter. [Jacobson (1988) 110, 112]. Lundborg, an active Stanford Associate (chairing the Annual Fund), was a successful businessman and respected Stanford alumnus. He had been a class officer, track athlete, and member of the *Stanford Daily* staff, and was admired for accomplishing much while working various jobs, 1923–26. *Stanford Daily*, May 26, 1948, May 27, 1949, and September 23, 1949; "New Vice-President: Louis B. Lundborg to Head Public Relations," *Stanford Alumni Review* (June 1948) 6.

38 Jacobson thought Carpenter would have been happier as a dean of students. Jacobson (1988) 103–04.

39 September 6, 1949, in SC0216 box 17.

40 Donald Stokes, "The Sterling Touch: How Stanford Became a World Class University," *Stanford Observer* (October 1979). Sterling's presidential records (SC0216) contain voluminous files of memorandums and correspondence with the General Secretary's Office. "New General Secretary Announced," *Stanford Daily*, November 27, 1951. Cuthbertson (Fall 1990) 12, 30.

41 Jacobson (1988) 97. Jacobson subsequently served as secretary of the university, 1965–69, a new post to oversee regulatory activities affecting gifts to Stanford and higher education generally. Stanford News Service press release, April 16, 1965.

42 J. E. Wallace Sterling speech to San Francisco PACE dinner, October 18, 1962, p. 4, in Sterling Speeches files, Stanford News Service.

43 J. E. Wallace Sterling, "Stanford Today and Tomorrow: Address of J. E. Wallace Sterling, Student Assembly, 8 January 1960," p. 4, in Sterling Speeches files, Stanford News Service.

44 June 2, 1950, in SC0216 box 23.

45 The Alumni Association, independent since its founding in 1892, became a division of the university in 1997.

On Jack W. Shoup, younger son of Paul Shoup, see "Ex-Alumni Head Killed in Accident," *Stanford Daily*, November 9, 1961.

46 Cuthbertson in "A Session on Wally" (1985) 5, and comment by Pierce (director 1959–67), as recalled by Lyle Nelson in "A Session on Wally" (1985) 6.

47 Jacobson (1988) 114–16. As late as 1961, Southern California accounted for 26 percent of some 43,000 alumni and 35 percent of students, but only 11 percent of individual gifts. *Los Angeles Times*, January 20, 1961.

48 SC0216 box 17. Carlson in "A Session on Wally" (1985) 8. Jacobson (1988) 114–17. The office's first officer was Kenneth Setterdahl (1953–54), followed by Don Carlson (1954–59), Joe Ruetz (1959–60), Ed Raleigh (1960–61), and Hulbert Hale (Hap) Everett (1961–70s) with the title of regional director of university relations.

49 Stokes (October 1979).

50 Stokes (October 1979). John Walsh, "Stanford's Search for Solutions," in *Academic Transformations: Seventeen Institutions Under Pressure*, edited by David Riesman and Verne A. Stadtman (New York: McGraw Hill, 1973) 303–09.

51 Walsh (1973) 309. Rebecca S. Lowen, *Creating the Cold War University: The Transformation of Stanford* (Berkeley: University of California Press, 1997), and C. Stewart Gillmor, *Fred Terman at Stanford: Building a Discipline, a University, and Silicon Valley* (Stanford: Stanford University Press, 2004) are particularly insightful about the implications of Stanford's reliance on federal funding.

52 Medeiros (1979), 64–66.

53 Jim Palmer. "Sterling Dons Traveling Shoes: Farm's Genial Chief Executive Spends Ten Weeks 'On the Road' During Year," *Stanford Daily,* January 24, 1956.

54 The Ford Foundation was created by Henry Ford's youngest son, Edsel, in 1936, and reformulated by Henry Ford III in 1947 as a worldwide philanthropy dedicated to advancing human welfare. It awarded major grants to Stanford throughout the 1950s, including significant grants to the new Medical School, the Center for Advanced Study in the Behavioral Sciences, and for faculty development.

55 Taylor (1960) 55.

56 SC0216 box 14.

57 Taylor (1960) 56.

58 Medeiros (1959), 74, 78.

59 See Gillmor (2004).

60 Walsh (1973) 303–04.

61 Donald Kennedy quoted in "Kenneth Cuthbertson, Fund-raising Strategist, Dies at 81," *Stanford Report,* May 3, 2000, 2.

62 Beyers (2000) 14. See also "Cuthbertson Energized Stanford Fundraising: A Man of Integrity and Conviction," *Stanford Daily*, May 29, 1980, 5, 18.

63 "Frederic O. Glover, An Oral History Interview conducted by Harry Press, Don Carlson, and Roxanne Nilan" (1993) session two, Stanford Oral History Project, SUA. "Cuthbertson Energized Stanford Fundraising," *Stanford Daily*, May 29, 1980, 5.

64 September 19, 1954, in SC0216 box 14.

65 December 21, 1954, in SC0216 box 14. Robert H. Moulton Jr. (1918–2008), '40, was chairman of the student council while Cuthbertson was student body president. He returned to Stanford in 1957 as assistant to the president, serving as Cuthbertson's aide for financial forecasting. Moulton became Stanford's point man to convince Congress to appropriate millions for construction of what became the Stanford Linear Accelerator Center (SLAC). Like Glover, he had been a naval intelligence officer during the war. He served briefly with the CIA (see also Chapter 8).

66 Cuthbertson (May 1990) 13.

67 Campaign Vice Chairs James B. Black (UC) and Charles R. Blyth (Amherst) represented the trustees. Stanford Associates filled key organizational roles: W. Parmer Fuller III, general chair; Richard E. Guggenhime, personal gifts chair; Ed Littlefield, corporations and public phase chairman; Jack K. Horton, corporations vice chair; Morris Doyle, special gifts chair. The Medical Alumni Fund, chaired by Paul I. Hoagland, M.D., undertook to raise $1 million of the total. Cuthbertson (May 1990) 14. On Arbuckle, see *Stanford Review* (June-July 1958).

68 "Stanford President Urges Strong Faculty," *Los Angeles Examiner*, October 8, 1957.

69 Cuthbertson (May 1990) 14.

70 "College Presidents: Huntley Program Discusses Problem of Administration in Education Field," *New York Times*, July 13, 1959; "Sterling Likes Job, Finds Fundraising 'Inescapable' Task," *Palo Alto Times*, July 20, 1959.

71 Beyers (2000) 16. Cuthbertson (May 1990) 15–16. Robert Duncan of the academic fundraising consulting firm of Kersting, Brown and Co., the consultants hired to help Sterling and his staff prepare for a major campaign, worried that the chief officer for development would be overloaded with financial responsibilities as well.

72 Cuthbertson (May 1990) 13–16. Robert Duncan's 1958 study of the Medical Fund campaign noted that Stanford still needed to build a core of volunteer leaders willing to go after the large gifts essential to a major campaign. Duncan concluded that the president and his staff were ahead of the trustees, who needed to take a more active role.

73 *Stanford Illustrated Review* (May 1958) 8. Beyers (2000) 16. Kenneth M. Cuthbertson, "Long Range Financial Planning for Institutions of Higher Education," in *Long Range Planning in Higher Education*, ed. Owen A. Knorr (Boulder: Western Interstate Commission for Higher Education, 1965) 66.

74 Kenneth Cuthbertson, introductory remarks for

74 "Annual Fund Leadership Conference," September 16, 1967, p. 2, in Cuthbertson Text [speech] file, Stanford News Service.

75 Wascher (1974) 2.

76 SC0216 box A33; Medeiros (1979) 181–82.

77 Beyers (2000) 16. Cuthbertson later explained the process in "Long Range Financial Planning" (1965).

78 Stokes (October 1979). Cuthbertson (May 1990) 16. Cuthbertson quoted in Beyers (2000) 17.

79 Cuthbertson (May 1990) 16–17; Glover (1993) session three; and Beyers (2000) 17. The Armsey visit is a fondly remembered story, often told. See also Cuthbertson (1965) 8.

80 Beyers (2000) 17; Cuthbertson (1965) 67–68.

81 Wascher (1974); Cuthbertson (May 1990) 9. Stanford received $25 million as a 3-for-1 match, and Notre Dame ($6 million), Johns Hopkins ($6 million), University of Denver ($5 million), and Vanderbilt ($4 million) on a 2-to-1 matching basis. Beyers (2000) 17–18.

82 Wascher (1974).

83 Stanford Daily, September 28, 1960. Medeiros (1979) 184. Wascher (1974). For details on the PACE Campaign, see Cuthbertson (May 1990) 17–29.

84 Cuthbertson (May 1990) 19. Outgoing board president Tom Pike took Valentine's place as co-chair.

85 Beyers (2000) 16; Sterling speech, January 1961, to "Stanford Today and Tomorrow," 15, Sterling Speeches files, Stanford News Service.

86 Lyman quoted in Beyers (2000) 18.

87 Beyers (2000) 18; Sterling speech text in Stanford News Service press release, April 18, 1961.

88 Sterling speech, "Trustees Dinner," February 15, 1962, 12, in Sterling Speeches files, Stanford News Service; see also Sterling's account in Campus Report (April 24, 1974) 11.

89 The Case for Stanford (Stanford Pace Program, 1961). Cuthbertson (May 1990) 22–23. See also "A Session on Wally" (1985) 54–55.

90 Beyers (2000) 18. Glover (1993) session four.

91 J. E. Wallace Sterling, "The Stanford Presidency 1949–1968: Part II, A Noble Purpose Shared," 52, in J. E. Wallace Sterling Personal Papers and Memorabilia, SC0415 (arch 1993-061) box 1. Sterling estimated 6,000, while "over 5,000" is the figure given by Beyers (2000) 18.

92 Stanford News Service press release September 22, 1962, and Stanford Daily, September 24, 1962. "PACE Program Contributions Pass Halfway Point—$52 Million," Stanford News Service press release January 16, 1964; "PACE Sets New Record—Nets Over $109 Million," Stanford Daily, January 17, 1964.

93 Medeiros (1979) 198–200.

94 Cuthbertson (May 1990) 17. For news purposes, the final figure was rounded up to $114 million. Beyers (2000) 18. The expense rate of 4 cents per dollar raised was much lower than most appeals then or since. Stokes (October 1979).

95 Beyers (2000) 18–19; Cuthbertson (May 1990) 29.

96 Wascher (1974); Beyers (2000) 19.

97 Cuthbertson (1968) 1.

98 J. E. Wallace Sterling, "Stanford in Review and Prospect," to the Stanford Today and Tomorrow convocation, January 8, 1960, in Sterling Speeches files, Stanford News Service.

CHAPTER 8: SLAC

1 J. E. Wallace Sterling, "The Stanford Presidency 1949–1968: Part II, A Noble Purpose Shared," 71–73, in J. E. Wallace Sterling Personal Papers and Memorabilia, SC0415 (arch 1993-061), SUA. For an excellent overview of the evolution of the Project M/SLAC facility; of the questions it raised about federal funding and research agendas, individual faculty research, and "big science"; and the five-year political battle to gain funding, see C. Stewart Gillmor, Fred Terman at Stanford: Building a Discipline, a University, and Silicon Valley (Stanford: Stanford University Press, 2004) 361–66. See also Edward L. Ginzton, "An Informal History of SLAC, Part One: Early Accelerator Work at Stanford," SLAC Beam Line, special issue number 2 (April 1983); Stuart W. Leslie, Cold War and American Science (New York: Columbia University Press, 1993) ch. 6; Richard B. Neal, ed., The Stanford Two-Mile Accelerator (New York: W. A. Benjamin, 1968); Douglas W. Dupen, The Story of Stanford's 2-Mile Long Accelerator, SLAC-R-62 (1966); Wolfgang K. H. Panofsky, "An Informal History of SLAC, Part Two: The Evolution of SLAC and its Program," SLAC Beam Line, special issue number 3 (May 1983); and Bernard Butcher, "The Making of Project M," Stanford [magazine] (May/June 1997). Institutional records and other historical materials are at the SLAC Archives, History and Records Office.

2 Based on a 1932 proposal of Professor D. A. Rozhansky of the Leningrad Polytechnic Institute, Agnessa Arsenjev Heil and Oskar Heil (Göttingen) had designed and patented a device that was probably the first klystron. George Caryotakis, High Power Klystrons: Theory and Practice at the Stanford Linear Accelerator Center, Part I (SLAC-PUB-10620, August 2004).

3 On the early development of Stanford's klystron and accelerator, see Ginzton (1983); Dupen (1966); and Dorothy Varian, The Inventor and the Pilot (Palo Alto: Pacific Books, Publishers, 1983). Professor William W. Hansen, B.A. '29, Ph.D. '33, joined Stanford's physics faculty in 1935 and died in 1949, at age 39. The culmination of his work, a separate microwave laboratory, was expanded and renamed Hansen Laboratories in his memory. "William Webster Hansen, 1909–1949: A Biographical Memoir," by Felix Bloch, Biographical Memoirs, vol. 27, National Academy of Sciences (1952) 120–37. See also the

Hansen Papers, SC0126, SC0004, and SC1140, and the Russell and Sigurd Varian Papers, SC0345, SUA. John R. Woodyard, Ph.D. '40, worked with the rest of Hansen's Stanford team at Sperry Gyroscope during the war.

4   October 8, 1954, in J. E. Wallace Sterling Presidential Papers, SC0216, box 30, SUA.

5   Ginzton (1983) 10. See also Wolfgang K. H. Panofsky, *Panofsky on Physics, Politics and Peace: Pief Remembers* (New York: Springer, 2007) and W. K. H. Panofsky Papers, SLAC Archives, History and Records Office. Edward L. Ginzton, UC Berkeley B.S. '36 and M.S. '37, Stanford Ph.D. '41, trained as an electrical engineer with Fred Terman, who recommended him to Hansen. "Edward Leonard Ginzton, 1915–1998: A Biographical Memoir," by Anthony E. Siegman, *Biographical Memoirs*, vol. 88, National Academy of Sciences (2006) 110–43, and Edward L. Ginzton Papers, SC0330, SUA.

6   October 26, 1954, in SC0216 box 30.

7   On the "Clinac," see Charlotte DeCroes Jacobs, *Henry Kaplan and the Story of Hodgkin's Disease* (Stanford University Press, 2010).

8   Minutes quoted by Ginzton (1983) 11–12. See also Gillmor (2004) 367 and Panofsky (2007) 74.

9   Robert Moulton, "Physics, Power, and Politics: Fear and Loathing on the Electron Trail," *Sandstone & Tile* 25:1 (Winter 2001) 4.

10 Dwight D. Eisenhower, "Science: Handmaiden of Freedom," speech given at a symposium on basic research sponsored by the National Academy of Sciences, the American Association for the Advancement of Science, and the Alfred P. Sloan Foundation, Waldorf-Astoria Hotel, New York City, May 14, 1959. An excellent eyewitness account of the two-year campaign to gain congressional approval is Moulton (2001) 3–13. On Stanford as political hostage, see also Ginzton (1983) 13–15. On the objections of Democratic senators and congressmen to a proposal from a "Republican Country Club," see Gillmor (2004) 364–65. Full text of Eisenhower's speech available online.

11 Panofsky (2007) 81–82; Neal (1968) 32; Edward L. Ginzton, *Times to Remember: The Life of Edward L. Ginzton* (edited by Anne Kinston Cottrell and Leonard Cottrell) (Berkeley: Blackberry Creek Press, 1995) 141.

12 Ginzton (1983) 12–14, including an illustration of the first site along Foothill Road; Neal (1968) 34. See also Stanford University Map Collection, SC1049, box Na3, Map 720.

13 SC0216 box A19. Original acreage leased to the U.S. government has been reduced to 426 acres as the university has reclaimed property for a guest house, a staff athletic and recreation center, and a joint university-laboratory computing center.

14 Moulton (2001) 9. John McCone (1902–91) received his B.S. in mechanical engineering in 1922 from UC

Berkeley, where he met future business partner Stephen Bechtel. He served as chair of the AEC, 1958–61, and director of the CIA, 1961–66, and held many other federal posts. (On Packard and Pike, see Chapter 12.)

15 Moulton (2001) 8. Presidential assistant Bob Moulton, '40, worked closely with Panofsky, Ginzton, Frederic Pindar, the project's administrative director, and Richard Neal, its technical director. In 1968, Moulton was named SLAC associate director of administrative services (including community relations), serving until his retirement, in 1974.

16 SC0216 box A19 records McCone's tour. Moulton (2001) 9.

17 SC0216 box A19. Panofsky (2007) 82–83.

18 SC0216 box A19.

19 Ibid. Moulton (2001) 8.

20 October 5, 1959, in SC0216 box A19.

21 SC0216 box A19.

22 Donald Stokes, "The Sterling Touch: How Stanford Became a World Class University," *Stanford Observer* (October 1979).

23 SC0216 box A34. Bechtel served as a trustee from 1959 to 1964. The Bechtel Corporation was not involved in construction of the accelerator; Bechtel briefly withdrew from his position on the board to avoid conflicts of interest. Stephen Bechtel Sr. (1900–89), son of founder Warren Bechtel, was vice president (1925–33) and president (1933–60) of Bechtel Corporation. Paul Pigott (1900–61), '23, president of the Pacific Car and Foundry Company from 1934 until his death, had built the failing company into one of the top 300 industrial companies in the United States. He served on the Stanford board, 1957–61. After Pigott's death, his widow, Theilene, married John McCone. Ed Littlefield (1914–2001), '36, MBA '38, had retired in 1958 after 21 years as principal officer of Utah Construction, a worldwide natural resources and shipping company (later Utah International). He served as a trustee from 1956 to 1969, as well as on the boards of Stanford Research Institute, Stanford's Graduate School of Business, the Hoover Institution, and the Center for Advanced Studies in the Behavioral Sciences.

24 SC0216 box A19. Luedecke had trained as a chemical engineer, served in World War II, and then was executive secretary to the military liaison Committee of the U.S. Atomic Energy Commission. On retiring from the Air Force, he was appointed general manager of the AEC. In 1964, he became deputy director of the Jet Propulsion Lab at Caltech, working on various unmanned space explorations, and later was associate engineering dean and executive vice president (and briefly acting president in 1970) of Texas A&M University.

25 SC0216 box A19. Panofsky (2007) 81.

26 SC0216 box A19. See Moulton memo to file, March 5, 1960. In his biographical sketch of Panofsky, Butcher

(1997) notes that Panofsky recruited Sterling and Packard to join the final meetings with McCone, and that McCone was particularly impressed with Packard's testimony.

27 Moulton (2001) 8. Moulton also quotes Eisenhower's science advisor, George Kistiakowsky, who wrote in his diary in 1959 that McCone "objects to materials program as just a scientist's trick . . . predicts no money from congress . . . rather evident McCone does not think much of 'scientists'. . . ."

28 SC0216 box A19. The complete story of SLAC's planning and five years of construction are documented in Neal (1968).

29 SC0216 box A34.

30 SC0216 box A19. Negotiations in 2012 and in 2017 each extended the contract with the Department of Energy for five years (the latter through 2022).

31 The name had been changed among project staff in 1960. According to Bob Moulton, the project staff held a contest to name the newly created organization; the winning entry, the Stanford Linear Accelerator Center, was formally approved by the board at its December 21, 1961, meeting. Robert Moulton Papers, 1991-012 box 3, folder 115 "Project Name," SLAC Archives, History and Records Office. In October 2008, the name of the laboratory was changed to SLAC National Accelerator Laboratory ("SLAC" becoming a word rather than an acronym), signaling a major change in the laboratory's mission and function from a single-purpose high-energy physics laboratory funded through the Department of Energy's (DOE) Office of Science High-Energy Physics program to a multipurpose laboratory pursuing multiple areas of research and funded through the DOE's Basic Energy Sciences program office. The original 2-mile linear electron accelerator remains in use, repurposed to support the laboratory's expanded scientific research programs.

32 Panofsky (1983) 3.

33 "Robert Hofstadter, 1915–1990: A Biographical Memoir," by Jerome I. Friedman and William A. Little, *Biographical Memoirs,* vol. 79, National Academy of Sciences (2001) and the Robert Hofstadter Papers, SC0426, SUA.

34 On the power-line controversy, see Robert Moulton, "David and Goliath," *Sandstone & Tile,* 25:1 (Winter 2001) 10–11 for an eyewitness account, and extensive files in Public Affairs Office Records, SC0105, box 1, SUA.

35 SC0216 box A23.

36 Ibid. Regarding fear of delays, see also box A19.

37 Paul Norton (Pete) McCloskey Jr. (1927–) '50, J.D. '53, a decorated Marine Corps veteran of the Korean War who practiced law in Palo Alto, 1955–67. He served as U.S. Representative (R) from 1967–83. In 1972, he ran on an antiwar platform for the Republican presidential nomination.

38 SC0216 box A23.

39 August 14, 1963, in SC0216 box A23.

40 SC0216 box A23.

41 Ibid.

42 SC0216 box A23.

43 Ibid. Moulton (2001) 11. See also "Electric Lines Generate Feud," *Stanford Daily,* May 27, 1965.

44 William Kirk, *An Informal History of SLAC* (Stanford: SLAC, 1967–68). Rockefeller's surprise visit to SLAC and Woodside is described in a memo, Doug Dupen to Panofsky, March 19, 1993, in SLAC Archives, History and Records Office, quoted in Moulton (2001) 11. News clippings regarding Woodside's perspective are in Scrapbook 1991-046, SLAC Archives, History and Records Office.

45 Kirk (1967–68); *San Mateo Times,* September 25, 1965.

46 Sterling, "The Stanford Presidency: Part II, A Noble Purpose Shared," 73.

47 Donald Stokes, "The Sterling Touch: How Stanford Became a World Class University," *Stanford Observer* (November 1979).

48 Panofsky (1983) 3.

49 Thoughtful analysis of this conflict and its implications is provided by Gillmor (2004) "Bushfires and Sniping: Taking the SLAC out of Physics," 366–71; and Peter Galison, Bruce Hevly, and Rebecca Lowen, "Controlling the Monster: Stanford and the Growth of Physics Research, 1935–1962," in Peter Galison and Bruce Hevly, eds., *Big Science: The Growth of Large-Scale Research* (Stanford University Press, 1992) 46–77.

50 Ginzton (1983) 11.

51 Galison, Hevly, and Lowen (1992) 73–74.

52 Gillmor (2004) 367.

53 SC0216 box B3. Leonard I. Schiff (1915–71), MIT Ph.D. '37, joined Stanford's faculty in 1947, and served as department chair, 1948–66. He was highly respected as a scientist, teacher, and university citizen. "Leonard Isaac Schiff, 1915–1971: A Biographical Memoir" by Felix Bloch, *Biographical Memoirs,* v. 54, National Academy of Sciences (1983) 300–23, and Leonard I. Schiff Papers, SC0220, SUA.

54 March 13, 1963, in SC0216 box B3.

55 John Walsh, "SLAC: Stanford–AEC Accelerator is Coming Along on Schedule, but Creating Some High Tension," *Science* 143 (March 27, 1964) 1419–21. SC0216 box B3. Gillmor (2004) 371.

56 Frank Medeiros, "The Sterling Years at Stanford: A Study in the Dynamics of Institutional Change," unpublished Ph.D. dissertation, Stanford University (1979) 206. Gillmor (2004) 368–69 explains some of the inconsistencies in their arguments, and the particular clash between Panofsky and Bloch, "Big Science" and "Small Science." See also Panofsky, "SLAC and Big Science: Stanford University," in Galison and Hevly (1992).

57 Sterling, "The Stanford Presidency: Part II, A Noble Purpose Shared," 71–72. Gillmor (2004) 367–68, also quotes Bowker remembering that when Bloch and Hof-

stadter threatened to resign, he and Terman wanted to call their bluff.

58 May 19, 1964, in SC0216 box B3.

59 March 18, 1964, in SC0216 box B3. "Just as SLAC's directors hoped to attract top talent to the facility, it became increasingly clear that few of SLAC's physicists, regardless of the value of their research, could expect to become tenured or adjunct members of the Physics Department." Gillmor (2004) 370.

60 April 15, 1965, in SC0216 box B3.

61 April 20, 1965, in SC0216 box B3.

62 April 6, 1965, in SC0216 box B3. Gillmor (2004) 371.

63 December 11, 1964, "private" memorandum, in SC0216 box B3.

64 January 12, 1965, in SC0216 box B3.

65 August 7, 1965, in SC0216 box B3.

66 September 28, 1965, in SC0216 box B3.

67 October 13, 1965, in SC0216 box B3.

68 Schiff to Sterling, January 10, 1966, in SC0215 box B3. See also Galison, Hevly and Lowen (1992) 73–74. In 2020, SLAC had 69 faculty, 22 of whom held joint appointments with campus departments, including Physics. Of the 22, SLAC was the primary department for 8 faculty members.

69 SC0216 box B3. SC0216 box B3 folder 9.

CHAPTER 9: OVERSEAS CAMPUSES

1 On the early history of the Overseas Studies Program, see G. Robert Hamrdla, "Four Decades of Stanford Overseas Studies," *Sandstone & Tile* 24:2–3 (Spring-Summer 2000) 8–13; Norman Naimark, "Stanford Overseas Studies: Then and Now" (Stanford: Bing Overseas Studies Program, second revised edition 2013); Frederic O. Glover's series of first-hand accounts of visits to Stanford's overseas campuses: "The Overseas Studies Centers," *Stanford Observer* (February [Berlin], March [Florence], April [Vienna], May [Tours, Paris], and June [Cliveden] 1978); "Bob Walker Counted 8,000 Students in 15 Years Who Studied Overseas," *Stanford Historical Society Newsletter* 7:4 (Summer 1983) 2–3; and "*Stanford Daily* Supplement on the Overseas Campuses" (eight-page supplement), *Stanford Daily,* September 20, 1963. See also Robert A. Walker Papers, SC0546; the extensive records of the Bing Overseas Studies Program, SC0117; and J. E. Wallace Sterling Presidential Papers, SC0216, boxes 17 (folders 10–14), A29 (folders 1–7), and B8 (folders 2–12), SUA.

2 Austrian-born Kurt Steiner also helped open the Stanford-in-Austria campus, in 1965. "Kurt Steiner, Political Science Professor Emeritus, Dead at 91," Stanford News Service press release (January 14, 2004); *Memorial Resolution: Kurt Steiner (1912–2003)* Stanford University.

3 J. E. Wallace Sterling, "The Stanford Presidency, 1949– 1968: Part II, A Noble Purpose Shared," in J. E. Wallace Sterling Personal Papers and Memorabilia, SC0415 (arch 1993-061) 33, SUA.

4 Strothmann also founded Stanford's interdisciplinary Graduate Program in the Humanities. *Memorial Resolution: Friedrich W. Strothmann (1904–1982)* Stanford University.

5 "Robert Walker, Founder of Overseas Studies, Dies at 84," Stanford News Service press release (February 9, 1998); *Memorial Resolution: Robert Averill Walker (1914–1998)* Stanford University.

6 Sterling, "The Stanford Presidency: Part II, A Noble Purpose Shared," 33.

7 "A Session on Wally: Transcription of an Oral History about J. E. Wallace Sterling, Recorded for the Stanford University Archives" (1985) 80–81, SUA.

8 Cuthbertson, Long-Range Financial Planning for Institutions of Higher Education (June 8, 1964).

9 Naimark (2013) 5.

10 Bob Hamrdla email to contributing editor Karen Bartholomew, October 30, 2018.

11 Naimark (2013) 5–6; Sterling, "The Stanford Presidency: Part II, A Noble Purpose Shared," 34.

12 Naimark (2013) 8.

13 Ibid.

14 "Frederic O. Glover, An Oral History Interview Conducted by Harry Press, Don Carlson, and Roxanne Nilan" (1993) session five, Stanford Oral History Project, SUA.

15 Glover (1993) session five; Hamrdla (2000) 8; Sterling, "The Stanford Presidency: Part II, A Noble Purpose Shared," 34. Note that at the time, a large portion of undergraduates were from California.

16 Glover (1993) session five. Sterling, "The Stanford Presidency: Part III[c], Travelling à Deux and Otherwise," clarifies that Sterling was not with the students on the flight to Germany in June 1958. He had not planned to attend but changed his mind after learning that high-level German officials would be there.

17 "New Overseas Branches: Italy, France Welcome Undergrad Pioneers," *Stanford Daily,* September 23, 1960, and Hamrdla email exchanges with Karen Bartholomew, February 2021. Hamrdla, in 2021 a veteran of many cruises, was on the ship en route to Beutelsbach as an administrator. He says "it wasn't a gorgeous crossing" and "October in the North Atlantic is not renowned for sun." Although it was a Cunard ship, it was not of the luxury class. "The logistics in New York and Le Havre were extra burdens and not simple to overcome."

18 Glover (1993) session five.

19 Ibid.

20 Ibid.

21 Ibid. U.S. Ambassador to Italy David Zellerbach was among those present. Note that all campus names initially

were rendered with hyphens, emphasizing the notion that each was a physical representation of the university.

22 SC0216 box A29.

23 Ibid.

24 SC0216 box A29. Benjamin Cushing Duniway (1907–86), the son of Stanford history Professor Clyde A. Duniway, had received his law degree from Stanford in 1931, and was a Rhodes Scholar.

25 SC0216 box A16. Otis served as first director and professor at the center, which has hosted more than 3,300 students in nearly 50 years. In 1996, Stanford turned over administrative responsibility to Duke University, to manage academic and student-related aspects of the program, but the center is now organized as a separate nonprofit legal entity with its own endowment (about $8 million in 2014). See the center's website. Also, a history of the center, published in 2015, was prepared by several former center faculty coordinated by Professor Mary T. Boatwright of Duke, Professor Michael R. Maas of Rice, and S. Corbin Smith, formerly of Stanford Overseas Studies.

26 SC0216 box A32. Also, Stanford News Service press release March 7, 1961. Strong outside support for the center was supplied by the Carnegie Corporation of New York, which made a $134,000 grant. See Records of Center for Japanese Studies, SC0265, SUA. "Sterling Will Open Tokyo Center Today," *Stanford Daily,* April 12, 1961. "First Nine Months of Stanford-in-Japan Reviewed: Favorable," *Stanford Daily,* February 15, 1962.

27 "Taipei vs. Florence" (letter to the editor by student Charles B. Ridley describing the starkly different living arrangements), *Stanford Daily,* October 19, 1964. Ridley concluded, ". . . for the experiences and insights derived from living in Taipei, rather than what is learned in the classroom, are what justify the existence of the Center."

28 *Courses and Degrees,* various years. "Chinese Stanford Opens on Taiwan," *Stanford Daily,* September 21, 1962. "Peking Condemns Taiwan Campus," *Stanford Daily,* January 10, 1963. In April 1964, with a grant of $338,000 from the Ford Foundation, the programs expanded with Stanford administering on behalf of 10 other universities that participated in either one or both: Columbia, Cornell, Harvard, Princeton, Yale, and the universities of California (Berkeley), British Columbia, Oregon, Washington, and Michigan. "Ford Gives Grant to Asian Centers," *Stanford Daily,* April 30, 1964. "SU to Get Ford Cash," *Stanford Daily,* May 3, 1966.

29 "Campuses Approved in Austria, England," *Stanford Daily,* November 20, 1964.

30 "Stanford to Establish Branch in Germany," *Stanford Daily,* September 25, 1957; "Committee Selects 63 Students for New Stanford in Stuttgart," *Stanford Daily,* January 22, 1958; "Die Luft der Freiheit Weht," *Stanford Daily,* February 6, 1958.

31 "Study Center in Germany" (editorial), *Stanford Daily,* September 25, 1957.

32 George D. Green, April 28, 1960, in Alison Carpenter Davis (ed.), *Letters Home from Stanford: 125 Years of Correspondence from Students of Stanford University* (St. Louis, Missouri: Reedy Press, 2017) 212–13. See also "East German Refugee Flight Subject of Student Research" and "Berlin Sights Remain Vivid Impressions," *Stanford Daily,* September 20, 1963.

33 "Over 200 Chosen to Study Across Ocean Next Year," *Stanford Daily,* March 29, 1960; Keith F. Chrisman letter to the editor, *Stanford Daily,* May 1, 1960; "Overseas Forms Available on Quad," *Stanford Daily,* February 2, 1966. *Courses and Degrees 1964–1965* is the first to specify that attendance at an overseas campus automatically fulfills the humanities and social sciences portion of the General Studies requirement.

34 Naimark (2013) 9. Naimark provides a good summary of the campus debate about relevancy and the program's changes. See also "Critics Abroad: Centers Described as 'Isolated, Arbitrary, Pointless,'" *Stanford Daily,* September 20, 1963.

35 Hamrdla (2000) 11. Hamrdla was also director of programs in Berlin and Kraków; his later positions included assistant to the university president and secretary to the Board of Trustees. He taught for many years in Continuing Studies and led numerous Alumni Association Travel/Study trips to Central and Eastern Europe.

36 *The Study of Education at Stanford: Report to the University* (Stanford: Stanford University, 1968) vol. IX, "Study Abroad," 5–11. (See also Chapter 13 of this volume.)

37 Hamrdla (2000) 11; the "excessively bucolic qualities of the Semmering campus prompted its closing in favor of Vienna in 1967," Naimark (2013) 9.

38 Hamrdla (2000) 10, 13.

CHAPTER 10: BUILDING PARTNERSHIPS

1 On Sterling's reluctance to appoint an academic vice president, see C. Stewart Gillmor, *Fred Terman at Stanford: Building a Discipline, a University, and Silicon Valley* (Stanford: Stanford University Press, 2004) 332, and "A Session on Wally: Transcription of an Oral History about J. E. Wallace Sterling, Recorded for the Stanford University Archives" (1985) 58, SUA.

2 *Stanford Daily,* March 5, 1952; *Stanford Review* (March 1952).

3 The Douglas Merritt Whitaker Papers, SC0176, are in SUA.

4 March 11, 1952, in J. E. Wallace Sterling Presidential Papers, SC0216, box 31, SUA. See also J. E. Wallace Sterling, "The Stanford Presidency 1949–1968: Part II, A Noble Purpose Shared," 14, in J. E. Wallace Sterling

Personal Papers and Memorabilia, SC0415 (arch 1993-061), SUA. Sterling does not specifically name Whitaker.

5   Gillmor (2004) 332, 354.

6   Ibid., 331–34.

7   Ibid., 354; Sterling, "The Stanford Presidency: Part II, A Noble Purpose Shared," 14. Whitaker retired from the Rockefeller Institute in 1964.

8   Donald Stokes, "The Sterling Touch: How Stanford Became a World Class University," *Stanford Observer* (November 1979); Gillmor (2004) 331. The definitive biography of Terman is Gillmor (2004). The voluminous Frederick E. Terman Papers, SC0160, are in SUA. See also Sanford M. Dornbusch, "Termanalia: Anecdotes and Reflections about Fred Terman," *Sandstone & Tile* 31:3 (Fall 2007) 2–20; O. G. Villard Jr., "Frederick Emmons Terman, 1900–1982, a Biographical Memoir," *National Academy of Sciences* vol. 74 (Washington, D.C.: National Academies Press, 1998) 309–30; Rebecca Lowen, *Creating the Cold-War University* (Berkeley: University of California Press, 1997); and James C. Williams, "Frederick E. Terman and the Rise of Silicon Valley," in *Technology in America: A History of Individuals and Ideas*, 2nd ed., ed. Carroll W. Pursell Jr. (Cambridge: MIT Press, 1990) 276–91.

9   "Wally Recalls the Early Sterling Years as President, 25 Years Ago," *Campus Report,* April 24, 1974. See also "Terman 10th Recipient of Alumni 'Uncommon Man' Award," *Campus Report*, December 13, 1978.

10 Frank Medeiros, "The Sterling Years at Stanford: A Study in the Dynamics of Institutional Change," unpublished Ph.D. dissertation, Stanford University (1979) 263; Arbuckle in "A Session on Wally" (1985) 46.

11 Sterling quoted in Gillmor (2004) 335. Gillmor adds that when Sterling asked Terman why he agreed to take the post, Terman said that he had enjoyed helping build a stronger School of Engineering and thought it would be fun to help build a stronger university. Gillmor (2004) 335.

12 Lewis Madison Terman (1877–1956) developed the Stanford Achievement Tests (forerunner of the SAT college entrance tests) and conducted fundamental tests of gifted children and adults. See Henry L. Minton, *Lewis M. Terman: Pioneer in Psychological Testing* (New York: New York University Press, 1988). In recent years, Lewis Terman's reputation has been tarnished by his role in the now-discredited eugenics movement.

13 Terman began as a mechanical engineering major, since electrical engineering was a graduate program at that time. He changed to chemistry with the intention of perhaps becoming a chemical engineer, but also continued to take classes in electricity and applied mathematics. On his education and Stanford's engineering curricula of the era, see Gillmor (2004) 40–41.

14 *San Jose Mercury News*, February 21, 1965. The usual path for electrical engineers was to enter industry after acquiring, at most, a master's degree. Companies led universities in developing new technologies such as radio transmission and vacuum tubes. On Terman at MIT, see Gillmor (2004) 51–64.

15 Stokes (November 1979).

16 "Frederic O. Glover, An Oral History Interview Conducted by Harry Press, Don Carlson, and Roxanne Nilan" (1993) session two, Stanford Oral History Project, SUA. See also Gillmor (2004) 424–27.

17 "Frederick E. Terman, interviews by Arthur L. Norberg, Charles Susskind, and Roger Hahn," 1971, 1974, 1978 (transcript 1984), Bancroft Oral History Project on the History of Science and Technology and Stanford Oral History Project, SUA, hereafter Terman (1984) 1–26, and Gillmor (2004) 70–185.

18 Terman (1984) 50–107. See Gillmor (2004) 186–252 and Villard (1998) 315–23 on challenges and lessons learned from his RRL experience. The RRL, a spinoff of MIT's Radiation Laboratory, engaged in analysis and hardware development, and made significant contributions to the understanding of very-high and ultra-high radio frequencies. RRL staff developed aluminum strips, or "chaff," to be dropped by Allied airplanes to confuse radar beams, and jammers installed on all B-17 four-engine bombers to jam the German anti-aircraft radar. The jammers were used in the Normandy invasion.

19 Appointed by Tresidder in December 1944, Terman remained in Boston to wind down RRL business, including finding jobs for nearly 95 percent of his staff. His friend Hugh Skilling served as acting dean until January 1946.

20 Terman (1984). On Terman and the presidential searches, and his father's role, see Gillmor (2004) 178–82.

21 Associate Dean Joseph M. Pettit (1916–86), '38, Ph.D. '42, was appointed dean of engineering in 1958 (he left to serve as president of Georgia Tech 1972–86). On the 1959 reorganization, see Chapter 14.

22 For a description and analysis of Terman's approach to building many of these departments in the humanities and social sciences, as well as engineering, see Gillmor (2004).

23 Frederick E. Terman, "The Development of an Engineering College Program," *Journal of Engineering Education* 58:9 (May 1968) 84–85.

24 Terman (1984) 123.

25 Ibid., 124.

26 Nelson in "A Session on Wally" (1985) 68.

27 Terman (1984) 186–209.

28 On Terman's interest in the Microwave Laboratory, see Terman (1984) 134–38, and Henry Lowood, "From Steeples of Excellence to Silicon Valley: The Story of Varian Associates and the Stanford Industrial Park," *Campus Report,* March 9, 1988, 11–13. Klystron is the brand name for a vacuum tube containing an electron gun and a

resonator that changes the velocity of the electron beam in accordance with a signal.

29 Terman, introduction to "Stanford's Minimum Financial Needs in the Years Ahead," SC0216 box A33. On Terman's strategy for a successful university, see Gillmor (2004) 438–41.

30 Stokes (November 1979).

31 Ibid., and Sterling, "The Stanford Presidency: Part II, A Noble Purpose Shared," 37.

32 *Stanford Daily,* June 29, 1960, and March 1, 1961. Stokes (November 1979). On rebuilding the Chemistry Department, and particularly the recruiting of Johnson and Djerassi, see Gillmor (2004) 388–96.

33 "Deck the Halls with Ivy," *Newsweek* (February 20, 1961) 59.

34 *Time* (September 22, 1961).

35 Frank J. Taylor, "Stanford's Man with the Midas Touch," *The Saturday Evening Post* (December 3, 1960) 36ff. This was the first article to talk about what would come to be known as "The Big Raid." Taylor also called it a "safari." Medeiros (1979) 129–30; Gillmor (2004) 397.

36 Terman to Glaser, August 12, 1965, in SC0216 box A32. An informal agreement actually was in place as early as 1962. See Robert Wert to Strong, September 21, 1962, in SC0216 box A35. Strong was Berkeley's chancellor from 1961 to 1965.

37 April 25, 1963, in SC0216 box A35.

38 May 3, 1965, in SC0216 box A35. Arrow (1921–2017) received the Nobel Prize in Economics in 1972.

39 On criticisms of Terman, and of changes at Stanford through the 1950s and 1960s, see Lowen (1997) and "A Session on Wally" (1985). As Gillmor (2004) pointed out, renegotiation of power between faculty and administration is always fraught with difficulty.

40 Terman quoted in Medeiros (1979) 207, 209.

41 Glover (1993) session two.

42 [July] 11, 1964, in SC0216 box A32.

43 Terman's statement is in Sterling's Commemorative photo album, SC0415 [unindexed box Ster-Arch-personal, commemorative photo album].

44 The Sterling-Terman team, with Sterling's charming "good cop" playing well to Terman's single-minded "bad cop," is well described in Gillmor (2004) 8–9, 427–32, and by Arbuckle in "A Session on Wally" (1985) 46.

45 Gillmor (2004) 433.

46 SC0216 box A39. Almond (1911–2002) came to Stanford in 1963 after a career at Princeton and Yale, and is credited with rejuvenating the Political Science Department while serving as its executive head, 1964–69; Vennard (1909–69), a professor of fluid mechanics in the Civil Engineering Department, had joined the faculty in 1946, was a consultant to many industrial and engineering firms, and had served on many university committees, with a strong interest in undergraduate education.

47 SC0216 box A39.

48 Sterling to trustee President Richard Guggenhime, August 23, 1966, in SC0216 box A39. Hornig (1920–2013), who had earned his chemistry Ph.D. at Harvard, had joined the chemistry faculty at Brown University in 1946, after working on the Manhattan Project, moving on to Princeton in 1957. On stepping down as Brown's president, he joined the Harvard faculty, retiring in 1990. "Donald Hornig, Last to See First A-Bomb, Dies at 92," *New York Times,* January 26, 2013.

49 September 1, 1966, and November 3, 1966, in SC0216 box A39.

50 November 8, 1966, in SC0216 box A39. Considered a strong administrator, Truman (1913–2003) credited faculty, students, and staff with improvements at the college, and was remembered as a warm and caring leader. "In Memoriam: President David Truman, 1913–2003," *College Street Journal* (Mount Holyoke College), September 5, 2003.

51 Sterling, "The Stanford Presidency: Part II, A Noble Purpose Shared," 48.

52 Ibid., 49.

53 April 20, 1966, in SC0216 box A39.

54 *Memorial Resolution: Richard Wall Lyman (1923–2012)* Stanford University. Sterling, "The Stanford Presidency: Part II, A Noble Purpose Shared," 49. Lyman documented his perspective of events of his provostial years and early years of his presidency in his *Stanford in Turmoil: Campus Unrest, 1966–1972* (Stanford: Stanford University Press, 2009). See also "Richard W. Lyman Reflects on His Life and the Turbulent '60s and '70s," *Sandstone & Tile* 28:2 (Spring-Summer 2004) 3–5, and Richard W. Lyman Personal Papers, SC0562, SUA.

55 Lyman (2009) 53–55; Stokes (November 1979). Packer, Yale '44 and LL.B. '49, had been named a full professor in 1959. On his many contributions, see *Memorial Resolution: Herbert L. Packer (1925–1972)* Stanford University. See also Herbert L. Packer Papers, SC0819, SUA. In addition, "Packer Warns Faculty on 'Politics by Confrontation,'" *Sandstone & Tile* 28:2 (Spring-Summer 2004) 10–11.

56 Glover (1993) session three. *Memorial Resolution: Herbert L. Packer (1925–1972).* See also *Blood of the Liberals* (New York: Farrar, Straus and Giroux, 2000), by Packer's son, George Packer.

57 Lyman (2004) 5–6.

58 Glover (1993) session three. Sterling, "The Stanford Presidency: Part II, A Noble Purpose Shared," 49. Lyman (2009) 55, differs from George Packer's description of the trustees' reversal. (George Packer did not know of the deans' protest.) In fact, the trustees' meeting minutes do not document their change of mind; they simply "correct" the previous minutes as if both promotions had been made at the earlier meeting.

59 *Memorial Resolution: Herbert L. Packer (1925–1972)*.

60 On Lyman's reaction to his 19 months working with President Kenneth Pitzer and his selection as Pitzer's successor, see Lyman (2009) 169–78. See also "Robert M. Rosenzweig: An Interview Conducted by Don Carlson, Karen Bartholomew, and Roxanne Nilan" (1984) Stanford Oral History Project, SUA.

61 Donald Kennedy quoted in "Richard W. Lyman, Stanford's Seventh President, Dead at 88," *Stanford Report,* May 27, 2012.

CHAPTER 11: DEANS

1   Sterling, at a Business School Affiliates luncheon at the Bohemian Club March 24, 1960, in J. E. Wallace Sterling Presidential Papers, SC0216, box A6, SUA.

2   Attracting enough faculty to open predated by several years assembling a complete, planned list of departments. Throughout Jordan's administration, the university's idealistic "major-professor" or "major-subject" system held sway. Orrin Leslie Elliott, *Stanford University: The First Twenty-Five Years* (Stanford: Stanford University Press, 1937) 50–74.

3   Although Wilbur, in his memoir, said he used the title of dean from 1911 to 1916, he was in fact given the title in 1913. *President's Report* (1914–15) 5; Ray Lyman Wilbur, *The Memoirs of Ray Lyman Wilbur, 1875–1949* (Stanford: Stanford University Press, 1960) 172.

4   On the organization and subsequent reorganizations of Stanford's schools, see J. Pearce Mitchell, *Stanford University, 1916–41* (Stanford: Stanford University Press, 1958) 77–94, and Wilbur (1960) 290–97, 579–81, 585–86.)

5   J. E. Wallace Sterling, "The Stanford Presidency 1949–1968: Part II, A Noble Purpose Shared," in J. E. Wallace Sterling Personal Papers and Memorabilia, 40–41, SC0415 (arch 1993-061) SUA.

6   Sterling, "The Stanford Presidency: Part II, A Noble Purpose Shared," 41–42. *Memorial Resolution: J. Hugh Jackson (1891–1962)* Stanford University. The Graduate School of Business was launched when U.S. Secretary of Commerce Herbert Hoover gathered with West Coast business leaders (and fellow members of the Bohemian Club) to find a way to stem the tide of students going east to Harvard, the University of Chicago, and the Wharton School of Business (University of Pennsylvania). The University of California had established its College of Commerce (today's Haas School of Business) in 1898, but it offered only undergraduate study until later in 1925.

7   Sterling, "The Stanford Presidency: Part II, A Noble Purpose Shared," 42–43.

8   Herbert Edward Dougall (1903–96) received his B.A. from the University of Toronto (1925), and his MBA (1926) and Ph.D. (1930) from Northwestern. "GSB Pro-

fessor Emeritus Herbert Dougall Dies," Stanford News Service press release, August 27, 1986.

9   SC0216 box A39.

10 Ibid. Carleton A. Pederson (1910–78) served as associate dean, 1958–65. He directed the Sloan Program from 1960 to 1970 and taught in several of the school's executive programs. He had received his MBA from USC (1937) and his Ph.D. from Stanford (1946). *Memorial Resolution: Carleton A. Pederson (1910–1978)* Stanford University.

11 March 8, 1957, in SC0216 box A39.

12 April 8, 1957, in SC0216 box A39.

13 SC0216 box A39. Petersen would serve as Sterling's volunteer national campaign chair for Stanford's PACE fundraising campaign, 1961–63.

14 SC0216 box A39.

15 March 28, 1958, in SC0216 box A39.

16 Sterling, "The Stanford Presidency: Part II, A Noble Purpose Shared," 43. Edmund Wattis Littlefield (1914–2001), grandson of the founder of Utah Construction Company, was a prominent businessman and philanthropist who served on the Board of Trustees from 1956 to 1969 and the GSB Advisory Board from 1959 to 1984. Littlefield endowed a GSB professorship, and was a benefactor to the Stanford Medical Center, the School of Earth Sciences, and the Hoover Institution. He partially funded the Edmund W. Littlefield Center, built to house some Business School functions, but now used for other offices.

17 Arbuckle in "A Session on Wally: Transcription of an Oral History about J. E. Wallace Sterling, Recorded for the Stanford University Archives" (1985) 19–20.

18 Sterling, "The Stanford Presidency: Part II, A Noble Purpose Shared," 43.

19 "A Session on Wally" (1985) 19, 21.

20 Ibid. 40.

21 March 24, 1960, in SC0216 box A6.

22 On Arbuckle's accomplishments as dean, see "Dean Ernest Arbuckle" and "Ernie and Kitty Arbuckle: A Remembrance," in *Stanford Business* [magazine] (Spring 1968); *Memorial Resolution: Ernest C. Arbuckle (1912–1986)* Stanford University.

23 Gardner and Jaedicke quoted in "Ernie and Kitty Arbuckle: A Remembrance" (1986).

24 Cutting (1907–72), professor and chairman of the Department of Pharmacology, served as acting dean from September to November 1953, and as dean from December 1953 to March 1957. Cutting became the founding dean of the University of Hawaii Medical School in 1967. See Spyros Andreopoulos, "Reinventing the Stanford Medical School: A Conversation with Henry S. Kaplan," *Sandstone & Tile* 32:3 (Fall 2008) 15, and John Wilson, *Stanford University School of Medicine and the Predecessor Schools: An Historical Perspective* (1998) ch. 37 (available only online at the Stanford Medical History Center).

25 "Interview of Robert Alway by Frederic O. Glover, 1980," 11, Stanford Oral History Project, SUA.

26 SC0216 box A39. Alway (1980). On Robert Alway (1912–90), see also *The Alway Years, 1957–1964* (Stanford University: School of Medicine, 1964), and *Memorial Resolution: Robert Hamilton Alway (1912–1990)* Stanford University.

27 "Henry can be fairly brutal, and Avram certainly had barbs on his knives." Alway (1980) 10, 38.

28 SC0216 box A39. Dwight Locke Wilbur (1903–97), '23, M.D. University of Pennsylvania '26, was an esteemed gastroenterologist. He had served as president of the American Medical Association (as had his father, Dr. Ray Lyman Wilbur), the American Gastroenterological Association, the American College of Physicians, and many other organizations.

29 November 4, 1957, in SC0216 box A39.

30 February 6, 1958, in SC0216 box A39.

31 February 13, 1958, in SC0216 box A39.

32 April 11, 1958, in SC0216 box A39.

33 SC0216 box A39.

34 March 1958, in SC0216 box A39.

35 May 7, 1958, in SC0216 box A39.

36 May 12, 1958, in SC0216 box A39; Wilson (1998) chapter 37; Andreopoulos (2008) 15; and Alway (1980) 7–9, 11–12.

37 C. Stewart Gillmor, *Fred Terman at Stanford: Building a Discipline, a University, and Silicon Valley* (Stanford: Stanford University Press, 2004) 354.

38 *Memorial Resolution: Robert Hamilton Alway, M.D. (1912–1990)* Stanford University. The Dean Robert Alway Collection is in the Stanford Medical History Center, Lane Medical Library.

39 "Dr. Robert J. Glaser, New Dean of Medical School," *Stanford Daily*, February 19, 1965. Dr. Sidney Raffel, professor and executive head of the Department of Medical Microbiology, served as acting dean in the interim.

40 See *Memorial Resolution: Carl Bernhardt Spaeth (1907–1991)* Stanford University.

41 John R. McDonough Jr. (1919–2005) came to Stanford in 1946, where he was a professor of law for 22 years, after receiving his LL.D. at Columbia. He was active in the California Law Revision Commission (1954–59), and later served as associate deputy attorney general for President Lyndon Johnson. At the time of his retirement, he was a senior partner with Ball, Hunt, Hart, Brown and Baerwitz.

42 SC0216 box A39.

43 Ibid.

44 May 27, 1963, in SC0216 box A39.

45 May 20, 1963, in SC0216 box A39.

46 May 29, 1963, in SC0216 box A39.

47 June 3, and July 3, 1963, in SC0216 box A39.

48 October 30 and December 1, 1963, in SC0216 box A39.

49 December 1, 1963, in SC0216 box A39.

50 Ibid.

51 Ibid.

52 Ibid.

53 December 9, 1963, in SC0216 box A39.

54 December 31, 1963, in SC0216 box A39.

55 January 24, 1964, in SC0216 box A39.

56 June 3, 1964, in SC0216 box A39.

57 *Time* magazine, October 30, 1964.

58 Stanford News Service press release, April 20, 1971; "Stanford Law School Mourns the Loss of Bayless Manning, Former Dean and Corporate Law Scholar," Stanford Law School, September 23, 2011.

CHAPTER 12: TRUSTEES

1 Ernest Arbuckle in "A Session on Wally: Transcription of an Oral History about J. E. Wallace Sterling, Recorded for the Stanford University Archives" (1985) 16.

2 J. Pearce Mitchell, *Stanford University 1916–1941* (Stanford: Stanford University Press, 1958) 27. Richard E. Guggenhime, quoted in "President Discusses Board," *Stanford Daily*, April 5, 1965.

3 Orrin Leslie Elliott, *Stanford University: The First Twenty-Five Years* (Stanford: Stanford University Press, 1937) 466–67.

4 On the evolution of the Board of Trustees, see Elliott (1937) 466–67; J. P. Mitchell (1958) 27–40; and *Stanford University: The Founding Grant with Amendments, Legislation, and Court Decrees* (Stanford University, 1987). The minutes and records of the Board of Trustees are available in the Stanford University Archives. See also Isaac Stein, "What is Past is Prologue: The First Twenty-Five Years of the Board of Trustees," *Sandstone & Tile* 25:2 (Spring–Summer 2001) 18–23. Mrs. Stanford forced the resignations of Irving Scott, Dr. Edward R. Taylor, and Josiah Winslow Stanford for personal reasons unrelated to their work as trustees. Norman E. Tutorow, *The Governor: The Life and Legacy of Leland Stanford, a California Colossus* (Spokane: Arthur C. Clark Co., 2004) vol. 2: 975–79.

5 Duncan I. McFadden, "Gifts and University Income Have Increased . . . ," *Stanford Alumni Review* (February 1949) 9. A view of changes to the board's financial approach from Herbert Hoover's perspective is detailed in George H. Nash, *Herbert Hoover and Stanford University* (Stanford: Hoover Institution Press, 1988) 33–45.

6 In May 1933, the Board of Trustees voted to reinterpret Jane Stanford's limitation of 500 women to mean the proportion of women students enrolled in 1899, which had been approximately 40 percent. With the cap in place, enrollment of 500 had fallen to 14 percent of the student body. By 1937–38, some 1,455 women enrolled. In 1973, Santa Clara County Superior Court granted the university's request to invalidate Jane Stanford's 1899

amendment, thus reinstating the original language of the Founding Grant: ". . . to afford equal facilities and give equal advantages in the university to both sexes."

7   Ray Lyman Wilbur, *The Autobiography of Ray Lyman Wilbur, 1875–1949* (Stanford: Stanford University Press, 1960) 201–02.

8   *Stanford Daily,* October 13, 15, 17, and 24, 1930, and April 7, 1931. Wilbur agreed to no longer accept his usual presidential salary when his "leave of absence" was renewed by the board in 1930. While the board also stated that year that acting President Robert E. Swain would now "assume and exercise all the functions and responsibilities of the presidency," Stanford's administration continued to operate by long distance telephone, as the *Daily* had complained. Wilbur continued to influence major decisions until his return in March 1932.

9   Nash (1988) 50–53.

10   Edwin Kiester Jr., *Donald B. Tresidder: Stanford's Overlooked Treasure* (Stanford Historical Society, 1992) 32–33.

11   The Founding Grant, fourth section, number 9, in *The Founding Grant* (1987) 5. (The university president did not become a member of the board, ex-officio, until 1970.)

12   "Frederic O. Glover, An Oral History Interview Conducted by Harry Press, Don Carlson, and Roxanne Nilan" (1993) session four, Stanford Oral History Project, SUA.

13   Cuthbertson in "A Session on Wally" (1985) 15.

14   Leland W. Cutler, *America is Good to A Country Boy: Leland W. Cutler* (Stanford: Stanford University Press, 1954); "Trustee's Vacancies Filled," *Stanford Daily*, July 23, 1920. Cutler was a busy man on campus, as a student and young alumnus, and appeared often in the *Stanford Daily*. At 35, he was one of the youngest to be elected to the board: Timothy Hopkins had been appointed, in 1885, to the first board by Leland Stanford when he was 26. In 1902, 32-year-old Judge George Crothers was the first alumnus elected to the board. Herbert Hoover had been 36 when he joined the board in 1912. In 1961, Otis Chandler took the baton as the second youngest (after Hopkins) at age 34.

15   May Chandler Goodan [obit], *New York Times*, May 29, 1984. The other women asked to join the Stanford Associates that year were Caroline Moore Charles, '27; Elinor Cogswell, '16; Martha Gerbode, '32; Ruth Fesler Lipman, '18; Mildred Roth, '11; and Mary Curry Tresidder, '15.

16   The board's support of Tresidder and Eurich is summarized in Edwards' comments in "Stanford Today and Tomorrow," *Stanford Alumni Review* (April 1949) 9–10, 12.

17   "Trustee Election: Edwards Succeeds Fuller as President of the Board," *Stanford Alumni Review* (June 1948) 6. On Edwards's experiences with politicians, boosters, Ku Klux Klan threats, and others with an ax to grind, as well as the many people he worked with inside and

beyond the Scripps newspaper empire and at Stanford, see *An Uncommon Man: Paul C. Edwards, 1882–1962, His Story and Writings*, edited by Carroll Edwards Beckett (privately printed, 1991), and Templeton Peck, "Paul C. Edwards: From Newsman to Trustees' President," *Sandstone & Tile* 11:1 (Fall 1986) 2–11.

18   "Stanford Today and Tomorrow," *Stanford Alumni Review* (April 1949) 9–15.

19   Edwards, 1961, is quoted in the citation for the California Press Hall of Fame (1975) and the Media Museum of Northern California (2009).

20   August 28, 1962, in J. E. Wallace Sterling Presidential Papers, SC0216, box A11, SUA. Memorial service also in SC0216 box A11. See also Paul C. Edwards Papers, SC0170, SUA.

21   C. Stewart Gillmor, *Fred Terman and Stanford University* (Stanford: Stanford University Press, 2004) 37.

22   "National Jewish Organizations Mourn Death of Lloyd Dinkelspiel," Jewish Telegraphic Agency, May 18, 1959. See Fred Rosenbaum, *Visions of Reform: Congregation Emanu-El and the Jews of San Francisco 1849–1999* (Judah L. Magnes Museum, 2000). Frances Dinkelspiel Green speaks of her father and mother in her 1974 oral history, *Frances D. Green: President, Jewish Community Federation of San Francisco, the Peninsula, Marin and Sonoma Counties, 1975–1976,* Jewish Community Federation Leadership Oral History Project (Berkeley: Regional Oral History Office, The Bancroft Library, UC Berkeley, 1996).

23   Cuthbertson in "A Session on Wally" (1985) 44.

24   December 8, 1953, in SC0216 box A10.

25   Glover (1993) session two.

26   "'Ballad of Baby Doe' Premieres Tonight at Music Hall Opening," *Stanford Daily*, May 23, 1957.

27   "Rare Disease: Former Board of Trustees President, Lloyd W. Dinkelspiel, Dies Friday," *Stanford Daily,* May 18, 1959.

28   May 17, 1959, in SC0216 box A10.

29   May 18, 1959, in SC0216 box A10.

30   May 21, 1959, in SC0216 box A10.

31   "Dinkelspiel Given Degree Posthumously," *Stanford Daily,* November 2, 1959. Dinkelspiel was the fifth Uncommon Man award recipient; previous honorees were Paul Edwards (1953), Morgan Gunst and Lou Roseberry (1954), and Harry B. Reynolds (1957). Herbert Hoover was posthumously named sixth recipient in 1965. As of 2022, only 33 individuals have received the award.

32   One trustee wrote President Jordan in 1895, "One of the embarrassments of the Trustees is that they know so little." Elliott (1937) 466.

33   *Stanford University: The Founding Grant* (1987) 79–81.

34   Frank Medeiros, "The Sterling Years at Stanford," *Sandstone & Tile* 9:4 (Summer 1985) 8. Glover (1993) session four.

35 Stanford News Service press release June 1, 1954.

36 Glover (1993) session four.

37 Glover (1993) sessions two and five. Robert Minge Brown, Richard Guggenhime, and W. Parmer Fuller III were friends of Glover, who also was godfather to Brown's son.

38 Glover (1993) session four. See Caroline Moore Charles, *The Action and Passion of Our Times: Oral History Transcript* (Berkeley: Regional Oral History Office, The Bancroft Library, UC Berkeley, 1979).

39 Morris M. Doyle, *The Spirit and Morale of Private Philanthropy: Stanford University and the James Irvine Foundation: An Interview with Morris M. Doyle* (Berkeley: Regional Oral History Office, The Bancroft Library, UC Berkeley, 1990) 64–65.

40 "Death Take George Morell, PNI Founder," *Palo Alto Times,* April 13, 1978.

41 George Morell, "History of Black Mountain and Monte Bello Ridge," unpublished essay, September 15, 1959. Morell intended that Stanford use the land for educational purposes, but because Jasper Ridge Biological Preserve is closer to campus, university officials decided Black Mountain Ranch was not needed. Regarding Morell's donation and its subsequent controversial sale, see 1978 *Stanford Dailies* of February 27, March 16, May 26, June 27, and September 25.

42 Glover (1993) session four.

43 December 13, 1954, in SC0216 box 47.

44 Glover (1993) session four.

45 Ibid.

46 October 1, 1963, in SC0216 box A18.

47 February 24, 1964, in SC0216 box A26.

48 May 5, 1964, in SC0216 box A26.

49 May 12, 1964, in SC0216 box A32.

50 Cuthbertson in "A Session on Wally" (1985) 16.

51 Ibid., 18.

52 "Trustees Elect New Chieftain," *Stanford Daily*, May 19, 1958.

53 Thomas P. Pike (1909–93). In 1938, Tom Pike established the T. P. Pike Drilling Company; in 1961 he took over from his brother management of Republic Supply Co., the oil-well supply company established by their father. Thomas P. Pike, *Memoirs of Thomas P. Pike* (San Marino, Ca., privately printed, 1979).

54 Pike (1979) 165. Pike states that Lloyd Dinkelspiel, as board president, asked him to join, but Pike joined in spring 1959, after Packard had been president since early 1958. (Dinkelspiel died in 1959.)

55 SC0216 box A23.

56 Ibid. On Pike's political career and interests, see Pike (1979) 109–58.

57 See for example, *Los Angeles Times*, February 23 and 24, 1961; *San Francisco Examiner*, February 23, 1961; and *Stanford Daily*, February 24, 1961.

58 October 23, 1961, in SC0216 box A22.

59 April 26, 1949, in SC0216 box 28.

60 SC0216 box 28.

61 SC0216 box A26.

62 Fred Glover to Harold W. Dodds, October 21, 1960, in SC0216 box 14. Dodds, retired Princeton president, was the author of "The Study of the College and University Presidency at Princeton" and brother of John W. Dodds, Stanford professor and director of Humanities Special Programs.

63 October 31, 1961, in SC0216 box A39. Pike (1979) 174. Kimpton (1910–77), '31, and Stanford trustee (1961–70), had been dean of students (1947–50) and professor of philosophy when Sterling became president. Earlier, at the University of Chicago, Kimpton had risen through the faculty ranks and served as dean of students and later vice president and dean of faculties, during and after World War II. He returned to Chicago in 1950 as vice president for development and succeeded Robert Hutchins as chancellor, 1951–60.

64 Pike also became an advocate for those suffering from alcohol and drug addiction, and was founder and director of the Alcoholism Council of Greater Los Angeles. "Thomas P. Pike; Industrialist Led Fight Against Alcoholism [obit]," *Los Angeles Times,* August 3, 1993.

65 Doyle became legal advisor to the Irvine Foundation in 1962, joined its Board of Directors in 1965, and served as board chair from 1976 to 1989. See Doyle (1990).

66 "Doyle, Former President of Board of Trustees, Dies," *Stanford Report,* January 7, 1998.

67 Kenneth Cuthbertson, introduction to Doyle (1990) vii.

68 "Trustees Are Successful in Many Fields: Board Members Have Risen to High Posts in Business and Industry," *Stanford Daily*, April 6, 1956; "Trustees Fall Short of Ideal Standards," *Stanford Daily*, October 20, 1966. In May 1969, ASSU President Denis Hayes would tell a stunned Alumni Conference audience that he thought "a large number of Trustees are pompous, silly, or rather dull elderly people, the sort of intellectual lightweights which must be expected in any system of 'government by crony.'"

69 Bruce Campbell, "Trustees Fall Short of Ideal Standards," *Stanford Daily,* October 20, 1966.

70 Glover (1993) session two.

CHAPTER 13: HERBERT HOOVER

1 The definitive biography of Herbert Hoover as a Stanford man remains George H. Nash, *Herbert Hoover and Stanford University* (Stanford: Hoover Institution Press, 1988). Nash completed this while writing the first three volumes of the now six-volume series *The Life of Herbert Hoover* (Herbert Hoover Presidential Library Association).

2   Don Carlson, "The Lighter Side of Wallace Sterling," *Sandstone & Tile* 9:4 (Summer 1985) 22.

3   "Wally Recalls the Early Sterling Years as President, 25 Years Ago," *Campus Report,* April 24, 1974, 10.

4   J. E. Wallace Sterling, "The Stanford Presidency, 1949–1968: Part II, A Noble Purpose Shared," 74, in J. E. Wallace Sterling Personal Papers and Memorabilia, SC0415 (arch 1993-061), SUA.

5   Lou Henry (1874–1944), daughter of Monterey newspaper publisher and banker George Henry, was the first woman to graduate with a geology degree from Stanford. She was an avid outdoorswoman and athlete. Two recent biographies are Nancy Beck Young, *Lou Henry Hoover: Activist First Lady* (Lawrence, Kansas: University Press of Kansas, 2005) and Anne Beiser Allen and Jon L. Wakelyn, *An Independent Woman: The Life of Lou Henry Hoover* (Westport, Conn.: Greenwood Press, 2000).

6   See Ray Lyman Wilbur, *The Memoirs of Ray Lyman Wilbur, 1875–1949* (Stanford: Stanford University Press, 1960) 40.

7   Wilbur (1960) 74; Nash (1988) 21–23, and Nash, *The Life of Herbert Hoover: The Engineer, 1894–1914* (1983), 392. See also Herbert Hoover, *Memoirs of Herbert Hoover: Years of Adventure, 1874–1920* (New York: Macmillan, 1951) 99.

8   On the Commission for Relief in Belgium, see Nash, *The Life of Herbert Hoover: The Humanitarian* (1988), his *The Life of Herbert Hoover: Master of Emergencies, 1917–1918* (1996), and his "An American Epic: Herbert Hoover and Belgian Relief in World War I," *Prologue* 21:1 (1989) 75–86. See also *Public Relations of the Commission for Relief in Belgium: Documents*, by George I. Gay and H. H. Fisher (Stanford: Stanford University Press, 1929), 2 volumes.

9   See Bertrand Patenaude, *The Big Show in Bololand: The American Relief Expedition in Soviet Russia in the Famine of 1921* (Stanford: Stanford University Press, 2002).

10   Hoover to Harriette Miles, August 5, 1897, quoted in Nash (1988) 21. Wilbur (1960) 74. While in Medical School and for many years thereafter, Wilbur had not realized that Hoover had helped with his school expenses.

11   Nash (1988) 36. In 1912, the trustees decided that it was inadvisable to re-elect 10-year members at the expiration of their terms. George Crothers, '95, reluctantly stepped down that year, after one term. Hoover was later re-elected four times, serving from 1912 to 1961. *Stanford Alumnus* (1912) 125.

12   Nash (1988) 50–53. Wilbur, who received his medical degree in 1899, had worked his way through Stanford's professorial ranks while also serving as a local physician in Palo Alto. There was strong opposition to Wilbur, however, because of his forceful advocacy for the Medical School, seen as an expensive luxury by influential trustees, faculty, and President Branner.

13   Hoover secured initial financing from the Carnegie Corporation to establish the Food Research Institute (FRI), the first interdisciplinary research unit outside Stanford's departmental framework. The Board of Trustees approved closure of FRI in February 1996.

14   Donald Nielson, *A Heritage of Innovation: SRI's First Half Century* (Menlo Park: SRI International, 2006), and Rebecca Lowen, "Exploiting a Wonderful Opportunity," *Stanford* [magazine] (July–August 1997).

15   On the salary question, see Nash (1988) 32–34, 39.

16   Wilbur (1960) 386–87. The August 1928 *Illustrated Review,* justifying Stanford's departure "from the tradition of avoiding politics," stated that the Hoover campaign "is a sufficiently momentous event" for Stanford that it was the exception to the rule.

17   *Stanford Illustrated Review,* December 1928; Wilbur (1960) 401–02. The Stanford University Press published *The New Day,* a volume of Hoover's major campaign speeches, with an introduction by Wilbur, in December 1928.

18   *Stanford Daily,* October 13, 1930, and Hoover's response and editorial, October 14, 1930. [Stanford] *Chaparral* (October 1930) dubbed Wilbur "president-by-mail."

19   Wilbur (1960) 568–70. An excellent overview of Hoover's challenges as president is David M. Kennedy, "Don't Blame Hoover," *Stanford* [magazine] (January–February 1999) 44–51 (an edited excerpt from Kennedy's *Freedom from Fear: The American People in Depression and War* [Oxford University Press, 1999] 47–103).

20   Wilbur (1960) 570. See also Wilbur's 1928 radio talk, "Hoover—The Beloved Chief," in Ray Lyman Wilbur Papers, XX392, Hoover Institution Archives.

21   Edwin Kiester Jr., *Donald Tresidder: Stanford's Overlooked Treasure* (Stanford Historical Society, 1992) 31. The trustees had offered the position to Vannevar Bush, head of the Carnegie Institution of Washington, on December 5, 1941, but with the attack on Pearl Harbor on December 7, Bush decided to remain in Washington. Although a medical doctor, Tresidder never practiced, instead becoming a successful businessman and head of the Yosemite Park and Curry Company.

22   See also Chapter 1.

23   *Stanford Daily*, July 18, 1949. Sterling to Paul Edwards, January 13, 1949, in SC0170 box 2, folder 3.

24   "Wally Recalls," *Campus Report*, April 24, 1974. Other Stanford trustees and numerous faculty members also were Bohemian Club members. See Gillmor (2004) 428–32.

25   Hoover's last major address on campus had been in 1941, for the opening of Hoover Tower; his last speech in California had been in 1945, when he delivered an address in San Francisco on the occasion of the United Nations Charter. He gave the 1925 and 1935 commencement addresses, and later spoke at the 1956 and 1957 commencements, the only alumnus or trustee to have such a presence. Lou Henry Hoover gave the 1941 commencement address.

26 "Wally Recalls," *Campus Report,* April 24, 1974, 10, regarding Encina banner. See also *Stanford Daily*, August 10, 1949. Leonard W. Ely, ASSU president and a grandson of Ray Lyman Wilbur, presented the ASSU award.

27 Hoover's speech, "Think of the Next Generation," is quoted in "Complete Text of Address of Herbert Hoover, '95," *Stanford Alumni Review* (September 1949) 5–8.

28 *Stanford Daily*, letter, August 19, and editorial, August 24, 1949. Bunche had been involved in the creation of the U.N. and in recent Arab-Israeli peace negotiations; Pandit, Indian ambassador to the United States, was head of the Indian delegation to the U.N.

29 Carlson (1985) 22.

30 "Wally Recalls," *Campus Report,* April 24, 1974; Glover (1993) session four.

31 Glover (1993) session four.

32 Nash (1988) 127.

33 Hoover's letter, August 30, 1957, is quoted in "Herman Phleger: Sixty Years in Law, Public Service and International Affairs," with an introduction by J. E. Wallace Sterling, an interview conducted by Miriam Feingold Stein in 1977 (Berkeley: Regional Oral History Office, The Bancroft Library, UC Berkeley, 1979) 136–37.

34 George Nash documents the increasing campus discord from Hoover's perspective; Rebecca Lowen offers a counterpoint in *Creating the Cold War University: The Transformation of Stanford* (Berkeley: University of California Press, 1997). The *Stanford Daily* also makes for informative reading.

35 For an early description of creation of the Hoover Library and the role of Stanford professors, see J. Pearce Mitchell, *Stanford University, 1916–1941* (Stanford: Stanford University Press, 1958) 19–22. See also Peter Duignan, *The Hoover Institution on War, Revolution and Peace: Seventy-Five Years of its History* (Stanford: Hoover Institution Press, 1989). Adams (1865–1930), an expert on British-American relations, joined the Stanford faculty in 1902, heading the History Department from 1908–22.

36 Nash (1988) 83. Mitchell (1941) 19.

37 The tower, dedicated on June 20, 1941, was designed by the firm of Bakewell & Brown, which had designed several other university buildings, including the Main Library. Its inspiration was Spain's cathedral of Salamanca.

38 Hoover saw no benefit to building cooperative interest among other Stanford faculty, while suspecting possible constraint and faculty disagreement with his wishes and intentions. Equally important, the nature of tenure—which Hoover felt was overrated—and the protection of the university's Advisory Board would prevent him or his assigns from being able to hire and fire as they determined.

39 Nash (1988) 129, adds: "In quieter times, Fisher's political vision and optimistic assessment of Soviet behavior might have gone unnoticed," but this was not a time of tran-quility. "An international ideological and even military struggle was underway, in which scholarship itself was a weapon."

40 Nash (1988) 120–21.

41 Ibid., 121.

42 Fisher's colleagues noted that during the Red Scare, Fisher "maintained his intellectual balance and never wavered in his trust and confidence in America. . . . While he painstakingly investigated Soviet Communism and argued that Americans were wrong to react to it emotionally, he warned that the Communists could make great headway if Americans were made to lose faith in their own freedoms so that their country would take on the earmarks of a police state." *Memorial Resolution: Harold Henry Fisher (1890–1975)* Stanford University.

43 Fisher had appointed Charles Easton Rothwell (1902–87) his vice chair in April 1947. Wright had experienced the war in China. She, like Fisher and North, favored a U.N. settlement of China's revolution and spoke against the leadership of Chang Kai-shek. North, in his *Moscow and Chinese Communists* (Stanford: 1953), blamed American errors and the Chinese Nationalists for the loss of China, rather than the alleged infiltration of Communists into the U.S. State Department.

44 Fisher-Sterling correspondence in J. E. Wallace Sterling Presidential Papers, SC0216, box 43, SUA; Nash 134–35. Fisher was determined to resign after it was announced at the August 1951 Hoover Advisory Board meeting that a Chicago friend of Hoover refused to make a major contribution because of a public statement by a member of the staff, clearly referring to a statement signed by Fisher and many others in defense of Truman's U.S. Secretary of State Dean Acheson, then under attack as the head of a den of Communists.

45 Rothwell to Fisher, November 4, 1951, in SC0216 box 43.

46 Sterling to John Gardner, November 9, 1951, in SC0216 box 43.

47 April 7, 1954, in SC0216 box 14.

48 Nash (1988) 137.

49 See "Preliminary Report to President Sterling: Study on the Hoover Institution" (June 1952) and cover letter by Paul Farnsworth to Sterling, June 11, 1952, in SC0216, series II, box 1. Farnsworth had joined the Stanford faculty in 1925 and had served on many university, as well as national, committees; his wife, Professor Helen Farnsworth, worked at the Food Research Institute.

50 This was one of many special committees the postwar trustees formed to facilitate their work. Black, president and later chairman of PG&E, worked with Sterling on university fundraising as well as chairing the Special Committee on the Hoover Institution, 1958–60.

51 Rothwell, "Some proposals Concerning the Hoover Institution, Its National Position, and Its Relation to Stanford University," Hoover Institution Records, Series T-16,

Box 234C, Hoover Institution Archives, quoted in Nash (1988) 146.

52 Nash, 147–48. August 30, 1957, in SC0216 box A39.

53 Sterling, "The Stanford Presidency: Part II, A Noble Purpose Shared," 74; Nash (1988) 149. Robert Eccles Swain (1875–1961), Stanford '99, Ph.D. Yale '04, had served on Stanford's faculty since 1902, including as head of the Chemistry Department from 1917 to his retirement, in 1940. A close friend of Hoover and Wilbur, he was acting president of Stanford, 1929–33. He was active in Palo Alto politics, serving three terms as mayor, 1914–16, and on the city council, 1912–1921. J. Pearce Mitchell (1880–1973), who had received his bachelor's and Ph.D. at Stanford, was Wilbur's right-hand man as well as close friend. He devoted his life to Stanford as a professor of inorganic chemistry, registrar (1925–45), and community diplomat. Mitchell had been administratively responsible for undergraduate studies, admissions, financial aid, academic advising, and career counseling and placement services, as well as registration. He served on the Board of Athletic Control, the Executive Committee of the Academic Council, and on the committees on Athletics, Scholarship, Vocational Guidance, Graduation, and Schedule and Examinations. In addition, he was the university's faculty athletic representative, and the financial director of the Students' Organizations Fund. He also served 31 years on the Palo Alto City Council, including two terms as mayor.

54 Sterling, "The Stanford Presidency: Part II, A Noble Purpose Shared," 74–75. Nash (154) notes that the board asked Herbert Hoover to produce the statement of purpose, but in his memoir, Sterling says it originally was his idea.

55 Nash (1988) 154.

56 Ibid., 153–54.

57 May 21, 1959, Board of Trustee meeting, in Board of Trustees Meeting Records, SC1010, SUA.

58 May 27, 1959, in SC0216 box B3.

59 Hoover to Arnold G. Stifel, June 11, 1959, in Nash (1988) 155.

60 *Stanford Daily*, January 6, 1959, announced his impending resignation; Rothwell formally resigned March 19, 1959. Rothwell to Sterling, October 10, 1958, quoted in Nash (1988) 148. As Mills College president (June 1959–67), Rothwell followed Lynn T. White Jr. (at Mills 1943–59), another Stanford-trained historian and outspoken opponent of McCarthyism. Remembered as a mediator, buffer, and effective fundraiser, Rothwell brought greater diversity to the Mills student body through improved scholarship funding and recruited talented faculty against tough competition with increased salaries. *Oakland Tribune*, July 2, 1967.

61 Mary Wright became Yale's first tenured female that year, and later its first female full professor.

62 Hoover to Sterling, January 3, 1959, in SC0216 box A39; Nash (1988) 150. "A Session on Wally" (1985) 39–41; Jim Wascher, "Wallace Sterling—Giant of Two Stanford Decades," *Stanford Daily*, March 14, 1974, 7.

63 Sterling to Hoover, April 11, 1959, in SC0216 box 43. The *Daily* announced Rhinelander's appointment April 7, 1959. It was well known that Sworakowski, who disliked Sterling almost as much as he disliked Rothwell, was Hoover's confidante and mole. Sworakowski considered Sterling a "chameleon," according to Nash (1988) 162.

64 Nash (1988) 152–53, suggests that it was a leak, stating that Hoover welcomed the ensuing turmoil as a way to put Sterling and the trustees "on notice" that Stanford was not the only suitor for his affections.

65 November 1, 1958, in SC0216 box A39.

66 May 1, 1959, in SC0216 box A39.

67 March 31, 1959, in SC0216 box A39.

68 March 31, 1959, in SC0216 box A39.

69 August 21, 1959, in SC0216 box A39.

70 August 26, 1959, in SC0216 box A39.

71 September 3, 1959, in SC0216 box A39.

72 June 29, 1959, in SC0216 box A39. Moley (1886–1975), Ph.D. Columbia 1918, was professor of politics at Western Reserve and Barnard College, and a law professor at Columbia, 1938–54. A major figure among the Columbia professors of Roosevelt's 1932 "Brain Trust," as the decade progressed he became increasingly critical of Roosevelt and the New Deal, eventually becoming a conservative Republican. He became a columnist for *Newsweek*, and contributed often to the *National Review*, where he became a nationally known critic of the New Deal in particular and liberalism in general.

73 September 9, 1959, and September 18, 1959, in SC0216 box A39. Chester, a former president of the National Association of Manufacturers, was among the New York executives who in 1938 founded the American Enterprise Association (renamed the American Enterprise Institute in 1962) to promote free enterprise and limited government. Chester was an early chairman of the AEA board. It moved to Washington, D.C., in 1943, becoming the prototypical "think tank." Moley was also associated with the AEA.

74 October 3, 1959, in SC0216 box A39.

75 Hoover to Sterling, telegrams, October 14 and 16, 1959, in SC2016 box A39.

76 Special Committee Meeting, October 15, 1959, quoted in Nash (1988) 156. Packard later joined the board of the American Enterprise Institute, to which he was a major donor. He also was a major donor to the Nixon, Reagan, and Bush presidential campaigns. Packard was followed as board president in 1960 by Tom Pike, another strong Campbell supporter, who took over the position while also serving as chair of Richard Nixon's California presidential campaign.

77 Sterling, "The Stanford Presidency: Part II A Noble Purpose Shared," 75.

78 November 17, 1959, in SC0216 box A39.

79 Sterling, "The Stanford Presidency: Part II A Noble Purpose Shared," 75. Beyers letter to the editor, "Hoover's Central Role," *Peninsula Times Tribune,* March 13, 1984.

80 Sterling, "The Stanford Presidency: Part II, A Noble Purpose Shared," 76. "Sterling was embarrassed," recalled Professor Charles Drekmeier. "I think it was one of the first times that he felt beleaguered." Quoted in Wascher, *Stanford Daily*, March 14, 1974.

81 University officers were expected to retire at the age of 65, as Terman did in 1965. In 1988, facing impending retirement age, Campbell threatened to sue the university to retain his directorship, claiming that University President Donald Kennedy and biased faculty simply wished to be rid of him. The trustees reconfirmed his retirement at 65, as per Campbell's 1959 appointment as a non-tenured university officer. See *Campus Report* and *Stanford Daily* articles, March–July 1988.

82 Wascher, *Stanford Daily,* March 14, 1974. "This had nothing to do with Campbell as a person," the *Daily* quoted Rhinelander saying. "This had to do with University independence." In a memo to Sterling, Rhinelander predicted friction points "all up and down the line," regarding Campbell's participation on university committees and in considering university-wide financial priorities. Rhinelander to Sterling, October 10, 1959, in SC0216 box A39.

83 Sterling, "The Stanford Presidency: Part II, A Noble Purpose Shared," 77; Arbuckle in "A Session on Wally" (1985) 40.

84 Campbell's contempt for the university is clear in his autobiography, *The Competition of Ideas: How My Colleagues and I Built the Hoover Institution* (Ottawa, Illinois: Jameson Books, 2001). A longtime confidant of Ronald Reagan, who had more than two dozen Hoover analysts in his presidential administration, Campbell is remembered as the "Reagan administration official who built the Hoover Institution into one of the nation's most influential conservative think-tanks." *Washington Times*, November 28, 2001.

85 Nash (1988) 156–62; Sterling, "The Stanford Presidency: Part II, A Noble Purpose Shared," 75–76.

86 Glover (1993) session four.

87 Sterling statement to Academic Council, April 1, 1960, and minutes of the Academic Council, April 1, 1960, in Faculty Senate Records, SC0193, and Board of Trustees meeting, May 19, 1960, SC1010, both SUA.

88 The committee, chaired by Gordon Wright, was unsuccessful in persuading the trustees to accept its statement as the official one and to distribute a brochure that would counteract the one printed by Hoover. It had also advocated changes in the structural relationship of the institution to the university at "some appropriate time." Gordon Wright, et al., to Professor E.R. Hilgard, Advisory Board, May 6, 1960; Report to Academic Council, July 5, 1960, and Academic Council minutes, January 6, 1961.

89 Nash (1988) 160. Hoover to Lutz, June 2, 1960, quoted in Nash (1988) 161.

90 Sterling, "The Stanford Presidency: Part II, A Noble Purpose Shared," 76; Stanford Board of Trustees meeting, June 16, 1960, SC1010. Sterling's statement was not printed in the board minutes, but was filed in the President's Office.

91 Academic Council minutes, January 6, 1961, in SC0193; Sterling, "The Stanford Presidency: Part II, A Noble Purpose Shared," 76.

92 Nash (1988) 163. Stanford Board of Trustees minutes, March 24, 1961.

93 Nash (1988) 164–65.

94 Ibid., 165–66.

95 Sterling, "The Stanford Presidency: Part II, A Noble Purpose Shared," 77; "Wally Recalls," *Campus Report*, April 24, 1974. Howard Brooks, apparently the last of Sterling's staff to visit Hoover before his death, had been pleased to find Hoover very complimentary of Sterling, remembering particularly the Chief's praise of President Sterling's wisdom. "A Session on Wally" (1985) 39.

96 That week, for example, Aaron Henry, leader of the Mississippi Freedom Democrats, spoke on "Civil Rights Mississippi Style"; a visiting professor gave a talk on "Christianity and the Radical Right"; and KZSU presented a live radio broadcast of a debate on California's Proposition 14 (which would allow racial discrimination in housing) among Professor Robert McAfee Brown, Professor Charles Meyers, and Palo Alto attorney Richard Rowden. Robert Beyers and Margaret Rose spoke on their experiences in Mississippi during the recent Freedom Summer voter registration drive. *Stanford Daily*, October 21, 1964.

97 *Stanford Daily,* October 21, 1964.

98 Ibid.; *New York Times,* "Hoover's Talk on Name-Calling Recalled in Service at Stanford," October 24, 1964.

99 Sterling, "The Stanford Presidency: Part II, A Noble Purpose Shared," 77–78, and Glover (1993) session four.

100 Cuthbertson in "A Session on Wally" (1985) 39–40.

CHAPTER 14: REVIEWS, REORGANIZATION

1. J.E. Wallace Sterling, "The Stanford Presidency, 1949–1968: Part II, A Noble Purpose Shared," 32, in J.E. Wallace Sterling Personal Papers and Memorabilia, SC0415 (arch 1993-061), SUA; Donald Stokes, "The Sterling Touch: How Stanford Became a World Class University," *Stanford Observer* (October 1979).

2 Stanford Office of Information [News Service] press releases October 6, 1954, and July 14, 1955. Robert

Hoopes and Hubert Marshall, eds. *The Undergraduate in the University: A Report to the Faculty by the Executive Committee of the Stanford Study of Undergraduate Education, 1954–1956* (Stanford: Stanford University, 1957). On this study, see also the Stanford University Study of Undergraduate Education Records, SC0425; the Robert Averill Walker Papers, SC0546; and the Stanford University Office of General Studies Records, SC0077, SUA.

3   Walker (1914–98) also was an early and influential member (1952–69) of the University Committee on Land and Building Development, and he chaired the Committee on Faculty-Staff housing. He directed both the General Studies Program (1956–69) and the Overseas Campuses Program (1958–73) (see Chapter 9). He became professor emeritus in 1976. *Memorial Resolution: Robert Averill Walker (1914–1998)* Stanford University, and "Robert Walker, Founder of Overseas Studies, Dies at 84," Stanford News Service press release, February 9, 1998.

4   Hoopes-Marshall (1957) 1–2. "Sterling Heads Committee" and editorial, *Stanford Daily,* October 6, 1954.

5   Members of the Executive Committee, in addition to Sterling and the provost, were: Graham P. DuShane (replaced by Robert R. Sears), Robert Hoopes, Hugh H. Skilling, Friedrich W. Strothmann, Raynard C. Swank, and Donald W. Taylor (replaced by Robert A. Walker). Members of the Advisory Committee and the All-University Curriculum Subcommittee and the A.B. Curriculum Subcommittee are listed in Hoopes-Marshall (1957) page vii.

6   Stanford News Service press release, July 14, 1955. Donald Wayne Taylor (1919–75), professor of psychology, left Stanford in 1955 for Yale, where he later held a variety of administrative posts, eventually serving from 1969 until his death as dean of the Graduate School (now the Graduate School of Arts and Sciences). Robert Griffiths Hoopes (1920–2008) was an assistant professor of English; he left Stanford in 1959 to become a professor, later dean of faculty, at Oakland University (Michigan), and then chair of the English Department of the University of Massachusetts, Amherst. Hubert Ray Marshall (1920–2016) joined Stanford as an assistant professor of political science, in 1953, and rose through the ranks, going emeritus in 1995. He received the Gores Award for excellence in teaching in 1985. Marshall served the university and faculty, especially during the turbulent 1960s, on many key committees.

7   Hoopes-Marshall (1957) page v.

8   Ibid., page vii.

9   Sterling, "The Stanford Presidency: Part II, A Noble Purpose Shared," 32–33; Stanford News Service press release, February 9, 1956.

10   Hoopes-Marshall (1957) page vii. See also "New Program Widens General Education Course Requirements," *Stanford Today* (May 15, 1956) 1–2.

11   Stanford News Service press release, February 9, 1956. On the rise and demise of the History of Western Civilization requirement, 1935–69, see George H. Knoles, "History of Western Civilization at Stanford," *The Stanford Historian*, 6 (April 1980) 8–15, abridged in "The New/Old History Corner: 40,000 Students Took It: The History of History of Western Civilization," *Stanford Observer* (April 1980) 4–6.

12   Sterling, "The Stanford Presidency: Part II, A Noble Purpose Shared," 33. On the Overseas Campuses Program, see Chapter 9.

13   Fred Glover and Ken Cuthbertson in "A Session on Wally: Transcription of an Oral History about J. E. Wallace Sterling, Recorded for the Stanford University Archives" (1985) 58–60. Sterling believed that the low faculty morale he saw in 1949 was, at least in part, based on the sense that the administration had become distant and had grown without faculty input. See, for example, his November 17, 1948, letter to the Stanford trustees, in J. E. Wallace Sterling Presidential Papers, SC0216, box 26, SUA, excerpted in Chapter 1.

14   "A Session on Wally" (1985) 61–62.

15   Cuthbertson in "A Session on Wally" (1985) 58. According to Fred Glover, Cuthbertson originated the idea of the organizational review, given Sterling's reluctance to delegate. "Frederic O. Glover, An Oral History Interview Conducted by Harry Press, Don Carlson, and Roxanne Nilan" (1993) session two, Stanford Oral History Project, SUA.

16   Frank Medeiros, "The Sterling Years at Stanford: A Study in the Dynamics of Institutional Change," unpublished Ph.D. dissertation, Stanford University (1979) 168–69.

17   January 29, 1958, to J. L. Morrell, in SC0216 box A9. Morrell, president of the University of Minnesota, had asked for Sterling's advice about management consultants.

18   January 29, 1958, to J. L. Morrell, in SC0216 box A9.

19   Arbuckle in "A Session on Wally" (1985) 59. John J. Corson III (1905–90) was with McKinsey & Co. 1951–66, and later taught at the Wilson School of Public Affairs at Princeton.

20   Retreat was February 7–8, 1958, SC0216 box A9.

21   February 10, 1958, in SC0216 box A9.

22   April 4, 1958, in SC0216 box A9.

23   SC0216 box A9. John J. Corson, "Strengthening the Top Organization of Stanford University," McKinsey & Company, Inc. (May 28, 1958). Corson later wrote *Governance of Colleges and Universities* (New York: McGraw Hill, 1960), a study funded by the Carnegie Foundation.

24   April 4, 1958, in SC0216 box A9.

25   Corson (1958) 11, in SC0216 box A9.

26   May 29, 1958, and June 12, 1958, in SC0216 box A9.

27 Medeiros (1979) 176. Carlson in "A Session on Wally" (1985) 64.

28 Medeiros (1979) 176.

29 Sterling, "The Stanford Presidency: Part II, A Noble Purpose Shared," 66–67. "A Session on Wally" (1985) 65–66; Glover (1993) session three.

30 Trustee minutes, July 16, 1959, pp. 280–82. Cuthbertson later credited the cooperation of Dave Jacobson and Duncan McFadden in making the unique linking of finance and development work, particularly during the busy years of the PACE Campaign. (In a reorganization by President Richard Lyman in 1971, Cuthbertson was named vice president for development; business and finance was shifted elsewhere.) On these changes, see "A Session on Wally" (1985) 58–60.

31 Remarks of Robert W. Beyers at Lyle Nelson Memorial Service, 1997, reproduced in *Remembering Lyle M. Nelson* (Stanford: privately printed, 1997); Nelson in "A Session on Wally" (1985) 51.

32 *Remembering Lyle M. Nelson* (1997); *Memorial Resolution: Lyle M. Nelson (1918–1997)* Stanford University; Bob Beyers, quoted in "Knight Fellowship Program Founder Dies," *Stanford Daily*, September 19, 1997.

33 "General Studies Committee Questionnaires," *Stanford Daily*, May 19, 1961; *Stanford Daily* coverage, May 22–24, 1962; "Faculty Committee on Undergraduate Education Named," *Stanford Daily*, January 23, 1964. "Wert Named First Dean of Undergraduate Education," Stanford Daily, November 23, 1963. SES was expected to help with the overlapping jurisdiction of various university committees and offices, particularly after Robert Wert left Stanford in 1967 to become Mills College president.

34 Responses are revealing; complaints also included that there were too many athletes at such an intellectually inclined campus. "Student Poll: Frosh Express Reactions to First Stanford Year," *Stanford Daily*, May 11, 1964.

35 The Freshman Seminars linked faculty and freshmen in new ways, encouraging them to delve deeply into a subject of personal interest. "Seminars for Future Frosh Announced," *Stanford Daily*, April 16, 1965, and "New Frosh Academic Programs," *Stanford Daily*, October 29,1965. The six- to eight-person seminars, usually offered by senior faculty in 1965–66 and, later, even some deans, enrolled 260 frosh, with a waiting list of 200 its first year. "Seminar Program for Freshmen Enlarged, Extended for Two Years," *Stanford Observer*, October 1966.

36 Stanford News Service press release, October 3, 1966. On the study's organization and intent, see *The Study of Education at Stanford* (1968) I:8–17. Robert R. Hind, associate dean of undergraduate education, served as staff director.

37 Medeiros (1979) 232; Sterling, "The Stanford Presidency: Part II, A Noble Purpose Shared," 68–69.

38 Medeiros (1979) 233. *Memorial Resolution: Herbert L.*

Packer (1925–1972) Stanford University. George Packer, *Blood of the Liberals* (New York: Farrar, Straus and Giroux, 2000) 3. Re Gibbons' role, "Pitzer at Parents Day: The Overlooked Social Problems," *Stanford Observer* (November 1969) 2, and email from Jim Gibbons to Karen Bartholomew, January 2, 2021.

39 *The Study of Education at Stanford: Report to the University* (Stanford: Stanford University, 1968–69) vol. I, "The Study and Its Purposes," 9.

40 The Study of Education at Stanford (1968) I:3.

41 Sterling, "The Stanford Presidency: Part II, A Noble Purpose Shared," 69. A new Western Culture requirement, instituted in 1980, was in turn replaced by Cultures, Ideas, and Values (CIV) in 1988. In 1997, the Faculty Senate approved a new year-long Introduction to the Humanities Course, replacing CIV as a freshman requirement.

42 "Change Announced in Advising System," *Stanford Daily*, May 28, 1970; "Academic Information: Center Offers Comprehensive Services," *Stanford Daily*, November 3, 1970.

43 Sterling, "The Stanford Presidency: Part II, A Noble Purpose Shared," 67–68. Sterling recounted in his memoir attending the first two meetings, but they occurred after he left office. He likely attended one or both summer organizational meetings. See *Campus Report* 1:0 (pilot issue) (July 29, 1968), which mentions his presence. *The Study of Education at Stanford*, vol. X (February 1969) "Government of the University," 32. For information on the founding of the Faculty Senate, including Packer's early role, see Peter Stansky, et al., *The Stanford Senate of the Academic Council: Reflections on Fifty Years of Faculty Governance, 1968–2018* (Stanford: Office of the Academic Secretary, 2018).

44 Sterling, "The Stanford Presidency: Part II, A Noble Purpose Shared," 68–69. Glover later recounted that Sterling was "annoyed that he was not given credit" for initiating SES. Glover recalled "the one time I heard him speak up critically at the board" was when a trustee attributed SES to someone else. "Wally said, 'Look, by God, I started that study.'" "A Session on Wally" (1985) 45–46.

CHAPTER 15: RELIGION

1 Orrin Leslie Elliott, *Stanford University: The First Twenty-Five Years* (Stanford: Stanford University Press, 1937) 106–7.

2 Mrs. Stanford thought of Memorial Church not simply as a memorial to her husband: "To Mrs. Stanford the Church stood for high-mindedness, uprightness, unselfishness, gentleness, and for what are known as the Christian virtues," recalled pioneer faculty member John Casper Branner, "and it was as the teacher of these

virtues that she wanted to pass it and its influence on to the members of this community living and yet to live." Branner, Founders' Day Address, 1917, quoted in Elliott (1937) 139.

3   *Stanford University: The Founding Grant with Amendments, Legislation, and Court Decrees* (1987) 21–22.

4   Newton (1840–1914), "eminent, elderly and in ill health," stayed one semester, "and left in a hurricane of bad feeling." Edith Mirrielees, *Stanford: The Story of a University* (New York: G. P. Putnam's Sons, 1959) 110. He had served as rector of All Souls Church in New York City from 1869 to 1902. Newton's short stay, and mutual disappointment, is documented in the Jane Lathrop Stanford Papers, SC0033B, SUA, and Elliott (1937) 140. The imposing house Jane Stanford built for him, since remodeled and expanded, is now the student residence Hammarskjold House, on Alvarado Row. See *Historic Houses VII, South San Juan Neighborhood and Stock Farm* (Stanford Historical Society 2016) 12, 14, 16.

5   The English-born Gardner (1871–1948) had studied at a San Francisco seminary and was ordained in 1898. Gardner had preached his first sermon on campus in December 1902 and remained as chaplain while Mrs. Stanford rethought the notion of an additional "minister" for Memorial Church. He retired in 1936. Mirrielees (1959) 111; *Memorial Resolution: David Charles Gardner (1871–1948)* Stanford University; and Elliott (1937) 140–41.

6   Gardner quoted in *Memorial Resolution: David Charles Gardner.* While English Professor Edith Mirrielees, '06, called Gardner "a preacher of indifferent ability," two outspoken faculty members, historian Edgar Eugene Robinson and classics Professor Hazel Hansen, in Gardner's *Memorial Resolution*, recalled his sermons as models of helpful guidance and inspiring comment. Mirrielees also thought Gardner "a strength to the whole community, a fount of kindness and humor and practical charity . . . respected by every student who came within his orbit." Mirrielees (1959) 111.

7   Mirrielees (1959) 139, 211, and *Memorial Resolution: David Charles Gardner.*

8   Elliott (1937) 140–41. Before coming to Stanford, Trueblood held faculty and chaplain positions at Haverford College, Guilford College, and Harvard. Trueblood was a friend of fellow Quaker Herbert Hoover, and later served as an advisor to Presidents Dwight Eisenhower and Richard Nixon. On Trueblood (1900–94), see "Elton Trueblood, 94, Scholar Who Wrote Theological Works [obit]," *New York Times*, December 23, 1994, and Van A. Harvey, "Religious Studies at Stanford: An Historical Sketch," *Sandstone & Tile* 22:2–3 (Spring/Summer 1998) 3–5.

9   Minto (1908–83), born in Lilliesleaf, Roxburghshire, Scotland, retired in 1973.

10   On Faust, see Chapter 1.

11   J. E. Wallace Sterling Presidential Papers, SC0216 box A23. Paul Covey Johnston (1891–1978) was pastor of Westminster Presbyterian Church, Lincoln, Nebraska, for 17 years. In 1938, he became pastor of Third Presbyterian Church of Rochester, New York. "Paul Johnston Baccalaureate Guest Speaker," *The Oswegian* (New York), May 29, 1939.

12   May 28, 1948, in SC0216 box A23.

13   June 5, 1948, in SC0216 box A23.

14   Ibid.

15   Johnston to Eurich, June 17, 1948, and Eurich to Johnston, July 8, 1948, in SC0216 box A23.

16   December 11, 1948, in SC0216 box D2.

17   SC0216 box 23.

18   Eurich to Johnston, August 9, 1948, in SC0216 box A23.

19   Edwards to Ray Lyman Wilbur, March 2, 1949, in the Paul C. Edwards Papers, SC0170, box 2, SUA. Faust was meant to serve as acting president from January 1 to July 1, 1949, but this, too, did not work out. The trustees asked Wallace Sterling to come to Stanford in April 1949, three months earlier than planned.

20   Thomas F. Grose, letter to the editor, *Stanford Daily,* April 20, 1949.

21   SC0216 box 23.

22   Ibid.

23   June 28, 1949, in SC0216 box A23.

24   Ibid.

25   Ibid.

26   August 4, 1949, in the Paul C. Edwards Papers, SC0170, box 2.

27   July 29, 1949, in SC0216 box A23.

28   November 22, 1949, in SC0216 box A23.

29   June 20, 1950, in SC0216 box 23.

30   Transcript in SC0216 box 23.

31   Ibid.

32   *Palo Alto Times,* June 30, 1950, in SC0216 box 23.

33   July 20, 1950, in the Paul C. Edwards Papers, SC0170 box 2, folder 1.

34   Typical was the response of Hugh Moran, '05 and one of Stanford's first Rhodes Scholars, a Presbyterian minister and missionary, and influential alumnus, who wrote to the entire Board of Trustees that Johnston's dismissal "promises serious consequences for the university." July 11, 1950, in the Paul C. Edwards Papers, SC0170, box 2.

35   Transcript in SC0216 box 23.

36   July 6, 1950, in SC0216 box 23.

37   Ibid.

38   National Association of College and University Chaplains to Sterling, August 19, 1950, and Sterling response, August 29, 1950, in SC0216 box 23.

39   November 14, 1950, in SC0216 box 23.

40   November 14, 1950, in SC0216 box 23.

41   March 10, 1951, in SC0216 box 23. Johnston served the Wichita First Presbyterian Church from 1951 to 1958, when he retired, at age 67, and relocated to Southern

California. Known for his firmly held religious convictions, resonant voice, and inexhaustible energy, Johnston was said to have dominated the staff and congregation of the church. Johnston had found a good match. According to a church history, "This was a man who knew what he wanted and how to get it. From the beginning there was no doubt about who was in charge." He increased the church staff from 15 to 25 employees. *This is Who We Are: A History of First Presbyterian Church,* First Presbyterian Archives, Wichita, Kansas (1995) 79. Interestingly, Johnston does not earn any mention in either the Stanford oral history of Alvin Eurich or Sterling's memoirs, although Sterling does note the importance of Memorial Church and his interest in developing a religious studies program.

42 August 24, 1950, SC0216 box 23. Minto would serve as chaplain until 1966, when he became associate dean, as well as university chaplain, under a new dean of the chapel, B. Davie Napier.

43 National Association of College and University Chaplains to Sterling, August 19, 1950, and Sterling response, August 29, 1950, in SC0216 box 23.

44 See Harvey (1998) 3–10.

45 J. E. Wallace Sterling, "The Stanford Presidency 1949–1968: Part II, A Noble Purpose Shared," 35, in J. E. Wallace Sterling Personal Papers and Memorabilia, in SC0415 (arch 1993-061), SUA. "John Wendell Dodds: An Interview Conducted by Frederic O. Glover and Paul R. Hanna," (1983) 37–38, Stanford Oral History Project, SUA.

46 Harvey (1998) 4–5.

47 Sterling, "The Stanford Presidency: Part II, A Noble Purpose Shared," 35. Dodds (1983) 38.

48 *Memorial Resolution: Alexander Miller (1908–1960)* Stanford University.

49 Edwin (Ted) Good became emeritus in 1991. *Memorial Resolution: Edwin Good (1928–2014)* Stanford University.

50 September 29, 1953, in SC0216 box 23.

51 SC0216 box 23.

52 November 17, 1961, in SC0216 box C3.

53 Brown (1920–2001) went back to Union in 1975 but returned to California to the Pacific School of Religion in 1979. He retired in 1984. Harvey (1998) 6. "Activist Theologian Robert McAfee Brown Dead at 81," *Stanford Report,* September 7, 2001.

54 Clebsch (1923–84) received his B.A. in philosophy and history from the University of Tennessee and his bachelor of divinity from Virginia Theological Seminary, both in 1946. He continued graduate studies at VTS and Michigan State while teaching, before moving on to Union Theological Seminary. He held the position of George Edwin Burnell Professor of Religious Studies and Professor of Humanities at Stanford when he died suddenly of a heart attack in 1984. *Memorial Resolution: William Anthony Clebsch (1923–1984)* Stanford University; Robert

de Roos, "William Clebsch: 'Super Citizen of Stanford,'" *Sandstone & Tile* 19:3 (Summer 1995) 1–3.

55 *Memorial Resolution: William Anthony Clebsch (1923–1984)* Stanford University.

56 Ibid.

57 The Board of Trustees later got court approval for the change, overturning Jane Stanford's 1902 amendment to the Founding Grant. The Clubhouse also accommodated groups such as Quakers, who had for decades expressed discomfort with the opulence of Memorial Church. On the campaign, see *Stanford Daily,* 1964–66.

58 Mary Wilbur to Sterling, February 6, 1966, in SC0216 box C4. William Sloane Coffin Jr. (1924–2006), chaplain at Yale (1958–75) and later senior minister at New York City's prestigious Riverside Church (1975–87), had served in U.S. Army intelligence during World War II and the CIA during the Korean War. By the early 1960s, he had become involved in the Civil Rights Movement. An advocate of civil disobedience and nonviolence, he was considered by some to be an heir to Dr. Martin Luther King Jr. He also created the first training program for the Peace Corps. By the mid-1960s, he had become involved in the anti–Vietnam War movement. "Rev. William Sloane Coffin Dies at 81; Fought for Civil Rights," *New York Times,* April 13, 2006.

59 February 1966, in SC0216 box C4.

60 Harvey (1998) 7. Napier received his bachelor's in divinity, in 1939, and Ph.D., in 1944, from Yale Divinity School, and joined the Yale faculty in 1949. "B. Davie Napier, Dean of Stanford Chapel During 1960s, Dead at 91," *Stanford Report,* February 28, 2007.

61 September 10, 1951, in SC0216 box 54. A separate gift to Stanford for religion had been designated as the Jayne Berry Fund and was directed to the practice of religion on campus.

62 "Year of Change: 'Who Am I? How Can I Be Myself?'" *Stanford Observer* (December 1966) 7; February 16, 1968, in SC0216 box C1.

63 Sterling to Berry, February 27, 1968, in SC0216 box C1.

CHAPTER 16: ATHLETICS

1 Ray Lyman Wilbur in "Sideline Slants," *Stanford Daily,* December 15, 1943. On Stanford's wartime athletic policies, see *Annual Report of the President of Stanford University,* years 1942–48; Don Liebendorfer, *The Color of Life is Red: A History of Stanford Athletics, 1892–1972* (Stanford: Department of Athletics, 1972) 88–89; and *Stanford Daily* articles, 1942–47.

2 The University of Chicago gave up football in 1939, and later left the Big Ten Conference in all sports. On Tresider's view, see Glenn T. Seaborg, with Ray Colvig, *Roses from the Ashes: Breakup and Rebirth in Pacific Coast Intercollegiate Athletics,* Foreword by Clark Kerr (Berkeley:

Institute of Governmental Studies Press, UC Berkeley, 2000) 28–29.

3 "The University itself and the student body may be satisfied with moral victories, but the alumni will settle for nothing but the real thing." Jim Scott, "Scott's Sports Shop" [column], *Berkeley Gazette*, March 1, 1948, quoted in Seaborg (2000) 28–29.

4 "New Stanford President Takes Over Job; Sees Education as Answer to Menace of Communism," *San Jose News*, April 5, 1949. See also "Sterling Discusses Reds, Curriculum, and Athletics," *Stanford Daily*, April 6, 1949.

5 At Sterling's first press conference, reporters' two main topics of interest were football and communism. "Stanford Has a New President: Sterling Not for Red Teachers but for Study of Communism," *Palo Alto Times*, April 5, 1949.

6 "Sterling Takes Stanford Post; Assails Reds," *San Francisco Examiner,* April 6, 1949. "New Stanford Prexy Meets Press: Sterling Discusses Communist Menace," *San Jose Mercury Herald*, April 6, 1949, reported the exchange a bit differently: "Asked 'what do you like, in regard to sports?' he answered bluntly, 'Victory.' Then quickly softened this to 'a good contest.' "

7 Seaborg (2000) 29–30.

8 Ralph (Big Jim) Reynolds. See note 73.

9 Sterling to William Munro, January 3, 1950, in SC0216 box 23.

10 "The High Cost of Sports: Masters Gives Out Figures in Talk at Conference," *Stanford Alumni Review* (April 1949) 22.

11 "Happier Times for Farm Athletics," *Stanford Daily,* May 30, 1950. Sterling had taken the concept to the Board of Trustees, which approved it May 18, 1950.

12 Today's women's Division I intercollegiate teams grew from strong intramural or club teams of the 1950s and 1960s that drew public interest with national competition. Significant change, including athletic scholarships for women, came with the merger of the separate men's and women's athletics departments into the Department of Athletics, Physical Education, and Recreation, in 1975. On women's competitive sports at Stanford, see Kelli Anderson, "The Fight for Fair Play," *Stanford* [magazine], September-October 2016, and Lena Giger, "Stanford Women's Athletics, 1956–1995, *Sandstone & Tile* 43:2 (Spring-Summer, 2019) 3–17. Professor Luell Weed Guthrie, chair of the Women's Physical Education Department throughout the Sterling era, provides insight on the transition of women's competitive sports in her 1978 oral history interview with Margo Davis, SOHP, SUA.

13 "Happier Times for Farm Athletics," *Stanford Daily,* May 30, 1950.

14 On the Schwartz era, see Liebendorfer (1972) 88–96.

15 *Notre Dame Archives News & Notes*, September 21, 2011. Liebendorfer (1972) 88. Schwartz was inducted into the College Hall of Fame in 1972.

16 "Schwartz Offered 5-year Contract: SAB Aims to Do 'Best Possible for Stanford,' " *Stanford Daily,* November 6, 1950.

17 "Marchie to Head West Team," *Stanford Daily*, November 7, 1950.

18 Sterling to Northwestern University President J. Roscoe Miller, November 15, 1950, in SC0216 box 23.

19 "Marchie to Head West Team," *Stanford Daily*, November 7, 1950.

20 "The Last Play," *Stanford Daily*, November 10, 1950.

21 SC0216 box 4 folder 18.

22 "From Our Schwartzian Mailbag," *Stanford Daily*, November 13, 1950. On the Buck Club during this era, see Liebendorfer (1972) 310–12.

23 "Unchartered Alumni Assn Anti-Marchie," *Stanford Daily*, November 16, 1950. The *Daily* received only 21 petitions.

24 SC0216 box 4 folder 18. Everett S. Dean (1898–1993) had played and coached at Indiana before coming to Stanford. He was head coach of basketball for 11 years (1938–51), taking Stanford to a national basketball championship in 1942; he also coached baseball (1950–56), leading Stanford to the College World Series in 1953. He is the only college coach to be named to both the Naismith Basketball Hall of Fame and the College Baseball Hall of Fame.

25 *Football Digest* in SC0216 box 4 folder 18.

26 "Coach Marchie Ends Football Career with Brilliant Victory, Surprise Resignation Comes After West's 16–7 Triumph," *Stanford Daily*, January 3, 1951. Liebendorfer (1972) 96.

27 Pete Grothe, "MARCHIE: Students Regret Departure," *Stanford Daily*, January 4, 1951.

28 Ibid. Schwartz (1910–91) retired from coaching. He became a successful business executive in construction and real estate, and remained active in Bay Area community activities as a Palo Alto and, later, East Bay resident.

29 " 'End of Football' Rumor Squelched," *Stanford Daily*, January 4, 1951; "Unfilled Shoes," *Stanford Daily*, January 4, 1951.

30 Pete Grothe, "MARCHIE: Students Regret Departure," *Stanford Daily*, January 4, 1951; "Unfilled Shoes," *Stanford Daily*, January 4, 1951.

31 "Coffin Corner: No Pressure on SAB for Coach: Choice May Be Made by This Saturday," *Stanford Daily*, January 30, 1951.

32 *Stanford Daily* 1951: "Working Together on a New Coach," February 5; "No Pressure . . ." January 30; "Public Favors Taylor Pick," February 6; "Stanford Selects Taylor as Coach," *San Francisco Examiner,* February 4, 1951.

33 Liebendorfer (1972) 97. Taylor was drafted by the Cleveland Rams but traded to the Miami Seahawks, of the All-America Football Conference. The team lasted one year, 1946.

34 "Midweek Musings: A Bagful of Publicity Tricks," *Stanford Daily*, April 5, 1951.

35 SC0216 box 4 folder 18. Taylor (1920–94) (B.A., health education, 1943; M.A., education, 1947; Gr. '49 education) was the first individual to participate in the Rose Bowl as a player (1941), coach (1952), and athletic director (1971). On Taylor's coaching years, 1951–57, see Liebendorfer (1972) 97–112.

36 *Stanford Daily* 1957: "Card Coach to Move into Post as Assistant Athletic Director," November 22; "Win Over Cal a High Spot, But Chuck's Glad It's Over," November 25; "A New Coach? Field Is Still Wide Open," November 26.

37 Liebendorfer (1972), 306–08. Taylor was influenced, at least in part, by a Stanford Research Institute study, commissioned by the Athletics Department, regarding operation and use of Stanford Stadium. Steve Baffrey, "A Grandstand View" [column], *Stanford Daily,* October 24, 1958.

38 *Stanford Daily*, October 22, 1964, March 3, 1965; Liebendorfer (1972) 308.

39 "A New Coach? Field Is Still Wide Open," *Stanford Daily*, November 26, 1957.

40 J. E. Wallace Sterling, "The Stanford Presidency, 1949–1968: Part II, A Noble Purpose Shared," 39, in J. E. Wallace Sterling Personal Papers and Memorabilia, SC0415 (arch 1993-061), SUA. Correspondence regarding Jack Curtice is in SC0216 box 5.

41 Curtice (1907–82) had lettered in football, basketball, and baseball at Transylvania University (Lexington, Ky.). His Utah team was considered one of the best passing teams in the country. Regarding widespread enthusiasm for this appointment of "a sound teacher and tactician," see "Introducing Jack Curtice: An Interview with the New Football Coach," *Stanford Review* (February 1958); "Welcome Jack Curtice" and "Curtice Gets Five-Year Contract as New Indian Football Coach," *Stanford Daily*, January 17, 1958. (The "Indian" was Stanford's official mascot from 1930 until discontinued in 1972.)

42 Sterling quoted in "Curtice Gets Five-Year Contract as New Indian Football Coach," *Stanford Daily*, January 17, 1958; "Expected Appointment Follows Board of Trustees Approval," *Stanford Daily*, January 17, 1958; and Stanford News Service press release, January 16, 1958. On the Curtice years as coach, see Liebendorfer (1972) 113–20.

43 Liebendorfer (1972) 113.

44 See for example: "Should Stanford Throw in the Towel for Major Football?" *Stanford Daily*, October 19, 1960; "Steam and Esteem," *Stanford Daily*, October 21, 1960. Not all Stanford students equated football with Stanford spirit. See lively letters to the editor, November 18, 1958: "There are a few of us who belong to Stanford, and are fond of the school, but show this in other ways than by screaming for the lions in the arena."

45 Glover and Cuthbertson, "A Session on Wally: Transcription of an Oral History about J. E. Wallace Sterling, Recorded for the Stanford University Archives" (1985) 77–78.

46 Sterling letter, January 26, 1961, in SC0216 box 5. In "Coach Curtice Fired, Announces Masters," *Stanford Daily*, November 28, 1962, the newspaper erroneously states Curtis was fired, but notes Sterling's intervention in 1960.

47 Glover memo to Sterling, and Sterling memo, January 3, 1962, in SC0216 box 5.

48 "Ex-Card Coach Curtice Dies: 'College Football's Will Rogers,'" *San Francisco Examiner,* August 20, 1982. Liebendorfer (1972) 113.

49 SC0216 box 5. Payton Jordan (1917–2009) coached at Stanford until his retirement, in 1979. See Liebendorfer (1972) 214–24; Gary Cavalli, "Cold War, Warm Welcome," *Stanford* [magazine] (May–June 2005), subsequent Letters to the Editor: "Remembering the Coach," *Stanford* [magazine] (July–August 2005), and Payton Jordan, interview by Bob Murphy, in "Stanford Athletics Interviews Conducted by Bob Murphy" (c. 2002–03), SC1011, SUA.

50 December 18, 1962, in in SC0216 box 5.

51 "No Decision Announced on Curtice's Status Yet," *Stanford Daily*, November 27, 1962.

52 December 1962, in SC0216 box 5. Curtice went on to revive the UC Santa Barbara "Gauchos" football program (1962–69), where he also served as athletic director (1965–73).

53 January 3, 1963, and December 17, 1962, in SC0216 box 5.

54 "Coach Curtice Fired, Announces Masters," *Stanford Daily*, November 28, 1962.

55 "Stanford Signs Ralston as Head Football Coach," *Stanford Daily*, January 21, 1963.

56 Dan Hruby, *San Jose Mercury News,* November 18, 1962, in SC0216 box 5.

57 SC0216 box 5. Charles Burnham (Bud) Wilkinson (1916–94) later coached the St. Louis Cardinals (NFL) for two years. Following an unsuccessful campaign for the U.S. Senate, he served as Oklahoma's Republican Party chairman and became a special assistant to President Nixon in 1969.

58 SC0216 box 5. Wayne (Bud) Hardin (1926–2017) later coached at Temple University, from 1970 to 1982, and retired with a career record of 118–74–5. In 2013, he was inducted into the College Hall of Fame. He had played football at the College of the Pacific in Stockton under Amos Alonzo Stagg. "Wayne Hardin, Hall of Fame Football Coach at Navy, Dies at 91," *New York Times*, April 14, 2017.

59 "Stanford Signs Ralston as Head Football Coach," *Stanford Daily*, January 21, 1963.

60 "Ralston Still Not 'In' as New Card Coach," *Stanford Daily*, January 18, 1963. Bob Reynolds, a three-time

first-team All-American, had recently been elected to the College Hall of Fame (1961). He was then president of Golden West Broadcasting Corporation and president of the California Angels baseball team, and would soon become a co-owner and director of the Los Angeles Rams football team. In 1969 Governor Ronald Reagan appointed Reynolds a regent of the University of California, a post he served diligently until 1986.

61 "Stanford Signs Ralston as Head Football Coach," *Stanford Daily*, January 21, 1963.

62 There had been only two known Black football players before Warren: Ernest Houston Johnson (1871–1898), a member of the pioneer class of 1895, played at least one football season. After earning a degree in economics, Johnson enrolled in Stanford's Law Department, but he was troubled by ill health and died of tuberculosis in 1898. Jocelyn Wiener, "Regarding Ernest Johnson," *Stanford Magazine,* November/December 2004. Tom Williams, the first Black player of the modern era, played only the 1958 season. Warren, '65, who had won All-Arizona and All-American honors for South Mountain High School, turned down Harvard, Cal, and the Air Force Academy for Stanford. His collegiate football career was ended by injuries but he graduated as planned with a degree in economics and minor in math. Morrison Warren, "My American Story: How I Came to Be Stanford's First Black Recruit," Stanford Athletics (website), reprinted in *Delta Tau Delta Fraternity Rainbow* (Summer 2018) 18–23.

63 These alumni include two lawyers, a doctor, a CEO, an expert in educational policy analysis, and two professional football players: Roger Clay (B.A., sociology, 1966; J.D., UC Berkeley (Boalt), 1973); John Guillory (B.A., political science, 1967; CEO, Northbridge Group); Dave Lewis (B.A., political science, 1967, drafted by the New York Giants); Michael (Ron) Miller (B.A., political science, 1968; M.A. 1969 and Ph.D., education, 1975, school administration); Dale Rubin (B.A., psychology, 1966; J.D., UC Berkeley (Boalt), international corporate law, professor, and founder of the Stanford Black Alumni Association); Dr. Albert Wilburn (B.A., biological sciences, 1967; M.D., 1972, UCLA Medical School, prominent Central Valley physician); and Gene Washington (B.A., sociology, 1969; drafted by the San Francisco 49ers, NFL executive). Washington and Jim Plunkett joined Warren in Delta Tau Delta fraternity, helping turn a spotlight on further integration of Stanford's fraternities. See also Chapter 20.

64 William (Bill) Moultrie, at Stanford from 1969 to 1973, earned his B.A. and M.A. from Texas Southern University, a master's degree from San Francisco State, and later a degree in divinity from Howard University. He was hired as freshman football coach and served as varsity defensive backs coach for Stanford's Rose Bowl teams. He was inducted into the USA Track and Field Hall of Fame, in 2006, after an outstanding career, 1973–1999, as track and

field coach at Howard University as well as a U.S. Olympic team assistant coach and Olympic track referee. "Howard University Mourns Loss of Legendary Track Coach and Administrator," *HBCU Sports News*, July 10, 2014.

65 SC0216 box B7. Ralston (1927–2019) left Stanford to coach the Denver Broncos (NFL), 1972–76, and later was head football coach at San Jose State University, 1993–96. On his years as Stanford's coach, see Liebendorfer (1972) 121–54, and John Ralston, interview by Bob Murphy, in "Stanford Athletics Interviews Conducted by Bob Murphy" (c. 2002-03) in SC1011, SUA.

66 "Remembering John Ralston, 1927–2019," *Stanford Athletics* [website], September 16, 2019. Later coaching assistants Jim Mora and Rod Rust also became NFL coaches, while others from Ralston's coaching staff went on to collegiate head coaching positions.

67 Excellent descriptions of the complexities of the breakup of the conference and its implications can be found in Seaborg (2000) and John R. Thelin, *The Games Colleges Play: Scandal and Reform in Intercollegiate Athletics* (Baltimore: Johns Hopkins Press, 2011), chapter 5, "Faculty Control and the Irony of Reform: The Pacific Coast Conference, 1946–1959." See also "Rixford Kinney Snyder: An Interview by Frederic O. Glover and George H. Knoles, Stanford Oral History Project" (1983), SC1017, SUA; and "The West: The PCC Dies and the Big Four is Nearly Stillborn," *Sports Illustrated* (September 22, 1958).

68 Lyle Nelson, on Sterling's frustration with the PCC affair, in "A Session on Wally" (1985) 45; Thelin (2011) 128.

69 "Stanford to Join Pacific Coast Conference," *Stanford Daily*, November 29, 1916, and "Stanford Signs Up with Members of Coast Conference," *Stanford Daily*, December 4, 1916; on Stanford's first game in the conference, "Washington State Five Here Monday," *Stanford Daily*, February 1, 1917. The story behind Stanford and Cal's reunion at the 1919 Big Game is described in John Sullivan, *Cal-Stanford: The Big Game* (West Point, NY: Leisure Press, 1982). Stanford and Cal gave up American-rules football for rugby in 1906. After Cal returned to the game in 1912, Stanford-Cal football relations were tense. No official Big Game was played again until 1919.

70 Thelin (2011) 130–35. Seaborg (2000) 15, 22–23. William Brownlee Owens (1887–1973), Stanford's faculty representative, 1924–41, also served three terms as conference president and three as NCAA president. He had earned an LL.B. at Stanford in 1915, and was an expert on California's civil code and private and corporate partnerships. Owens taught from 1920 until his retirement in 1953. Charles E. Beardsley and Seth M. Hufstedler, "William Brownlee Owens," *Stanford Law Review* 4:4 (July 1952) 470–73.

71 Rube Samuelsen, *Pasadena Star-News*, April 10, 1951, clipping in SC0216 box 4. Samuelsen (1901–73) was a much-honored sportswriter. Although writing for a

smaller newspaper, he was well known for his ability to gather information from across Southern California. He authored the definitive early history of the Rose Bowl: *The Rose Bowl Game* (New York: Doubleday, 1951).

72 March 14, 1950, in SC0216 box 43.

73 See SC0216 box 28, folders 22 (1948–49), folder 23 (1951–52) and folder 24 (1950–72), and box A26, folder 10 (1955–63) for Ralph (Big Jim) Reynolds' many letters to Sterling and other administrators regarding his dominating interests in Stanford football and communist infiltration of Stanford and other campuses. All three of his children went to Stanford; his sons, Jim, '37, and Jack, '46, MBA '48, also were multi-sport athletes. The Jim Reynolds Award at Stanford is given to the most inspirational senior football player.

74 "This behavior is disheartening to the other schools who are trying sincerely to comply with the rules of the Conference." Robert Johnson to Dean Stanley Freeborn, 1948, quoted in Seaborg (2000) 29.

75 March 9, 1950, in SC0216 box 28.

76 March 29, 1950, in SC0216 box 28.

77 April 4, 1950, in SC0216 box 28.

78 SC0216 box 44.

79 *Stanford Daily*, May 17, 1954. According to the PCC code, any student permitting the use of his name or image in commercial advertising was ineligible to represent any PCC member university in any athletic contest.

80 Snyder (1983) 63. The period 1946–55 saw "both a progression of reform and regulation, and an escalating pattern of violations" of the code. Thelin (2011) 130–35.

81 Thelin (2011) 135–36; Seaborg (2000) 149–86, on the first six months of the 1956 PCC deliberations. Seaborg felt that it took "exposure in the newspapers to finally move the PCC to act against flagrant abuses," and he was convinced that top executives at UCLA and USC knew about serious violations and in some cases had known about them for years. See also Snyder (1983) 62–68.

82 Seaborg (2000) 180–83. "Pacific Coast Conference," *Sports Illustrated*, September 24, 1956.

83 "Benefits Indian Athletes Receive Are Described," *Stanford Daily*, May 26, 1956; "Looking it Over," *Stanford Daily*, October 16, 1956. "Stanford Coach Says Job Program Held Up Under Close Scrutiny," *Oakland Tribune*, July 18, 1956, and *Santa Cruz Sentinel*, July 23, 1956. *Tribune* sportswriter Ed Schoenfeld, who first investigated and exposed the undercover payoffs, later investigated 11 Palo Alto business firms employing 41 Stanford football players and found that the players were paid for their part-time work in strict accord with PCC regulations. His report was, of course, mocked by Southern California sportswriters. "LA Columnists Attack Scribe," *Oakland Tribune*, July 29, 1956.

84 Snyder (1983) 65–66; Thelin (2011) 137; Seaborg (2000) 205–14.

85 "The Pacific Coast Conference: Herman Hickman Says," *Sports Illustrated* (September 24, 1956).

86 Seaborg (2000) 30.

87 Glover, September 25, 1956, to a Los Angeles radio station, in SC0216 box 43.

88 Seaborg (2000) 222–23; "USC Players Back Arnett," *Oakland Tribune*, July 7, 1956.

89 On Taylor, "Claim Could Place USC, Cal Under PCC Rose Bowl Ban," and "The Cry-Baby Sleuths," *Stanford Daily*, May 29, 1956.

90 "Applause for Drs. Fagg and Allen," *Los Angeles Times*, July 12, 1956; Sterling to Chandler, July 16, 1956, in SC0216 box 44. Norman Chandler (1899–1973) was the son of one trustee, Harry Chandler (on the board 1923–42), brother to another (May Chandler Goodan, '14, serving 1942–62), and father to yet another (Otis Chandler, '51, a team captain in track and field, served as an alumni trustee, 1961–65). Norman's wife, Dorothy Buffam Chandler, also a Stanford alumna, was a regent of the University of California (1954–68).

91 *Stanford Review* (November 1956), and "Sterling Gives Reasons for Stand in PCC Turmoil," and "The True Purpose" (editorial), *Stanford Daily*, November 14, 1956. See also SC0216 box 44 and Stanford News Service press release, November 14, 1956. Rube Samuelsen spread Sterling's statement to a broader audience, reprinting it across two successive "Rube-Barbs" columns, *Pasadena Star News*, November 16 and 17, 1956.

92 "Pacific Coast Conference," *Sports Illustrated* (September 24, 1956).

93 "Rube-Barbs" [column], *Pasadena Star-News*, October 24, 1956.

94 "Academic Council Votes Unanimously to Support Sterling's PCC Position," *Stanford Daily*, January 14, 1957.

95 *Stanford Daily* 1957: "Student Views in Campus Opinion: Should Stanford Withdraw From the PCC if it Continues to Liberalize its Program of Aid to Athletes," January 14; "Value of Pure Athletics," January 14. Earlier, the *Daily* had editorialized: "Stanford seems to be the only school worried that the PCC is going professional," in "Isolation in the PCC," January 9.

96 "Gov. Knight Suffers Yardage Loss in Pacific Coast Football Hassle" (United Press (UP) report), in *San Bernardino Sun*, July 14, 1956, and "Between You and Me" [column], *Santa Cruz Sentinel*, August 15, 1956. Knight favored a four-member conference: Cal, UCLA, Stanford, and USC. Middleton telephoned Fred Glover to report the Hyland incident. December 19 and 28, 1956, SC216 box 44.

97 "Looking It Over," *Stanford Daily*, October 16, 1956.

98 "Sour-Grape-itis," *Stanford Daily*, May 28, 1956.

99 Seaborg (2000) 284–85; "Cal Official Favors PCC Inquiry: Subcommittee Opens Investigation of Fines Against Coast Teams," *Stanford Daily*, October 29, 1957.

100 Bonelli also was hoping to win a seat on the Los Angeles County Board of Supervisors. The Bonelli panel was a subcommittee of the Committee on Governmental Efficiency and Economy. The Bonelli hearings were covered by the United Press and widely reprinted throughout California. See *San Bernardino Sun*, December 6, 1957.

101 Sanders quoted in UP report, *San Bernardino Sun*, September 24, 1957.

102 On the UC regents' five-point program, reactions, and ensuing debate during the rest of 1957, see Seaborg (2000) 278–84, 287–312.

103 SC0216 box 44.

104 Thelin (2011) 140. On reactions around the conference, see pp. 139–42.

105 October 14, 1957, SC0216 box 44.

106 June 17, 1957, in SC0216 box 44. Chuck Taylor, tired of seeing Stanford "taking a beating" in the LA press, offered his own comments, making clear they were unofficial, "Rube-Barbs" [column], *Pasadena Star-News,* June 5, 1957.

107 "Bonelli Calls Off Probe," *Pasadena Star-News*, December 18, 1957.

108 "The West: The PCC Dies and the Big Four is Nearly Stillborn," *Sports Illustrated* (September 22, 1958).

109 "P.C.C. Break-Up Set Big Ten Against Rose Bowl," *Pasadena Star-News,* May 21, 1959; "Rube-Barbs" [column], *Pasadena Star-News*, June 7, 1959.

110 Stanford News Service press release, December 13, 1957; Sterling to Sproul, December 10, 1957, in SC0216 box 44.

111 December 23, 1957, in SC0216 box 45.

112 "Still Nine Members," *Stanford Daily*, May 27, 1957.

113 *Stanford Review* (January 1958) 11.

114 Clark Kerr, Foreword in Seaborg (2000) ix.

115 "New League," *Stanford Daily*, January 29, 1959, and "Grandstand" (column), January 30, 1959; and "Stanford Nixes Big Four and Joins National Seven," April 1, 1959, April Fools' edition. The idea of a "super league" had been floated as early as October 1956 in United Press reports throughout California. See for example, *Desert Sun,* October 24, 1956.

116 SC0216 box A5.

117 "Stanford In—Big 4 Becomes 5," *Stanford Daily,* July 23, 1959.

118 "Northwest Stays on SU Grid Slate," *Stanford Daily*, January 8, 1958; "Rube-Barbs" [column], *Pasadena Star-News*, June 7, 1959. Some Southern California newspapers continued to be suspicious, claiming Stanford was simply playing "hard to get."

119 Clark Kerr, Foreword in Seaborg (2000) ix.

120 "Stanford Joins New Conference," *San Bernardino Sun*, July 17, 1959, and "And Then There Were Five," *Desert Sun*, July 17, 1959.

121 Seaborg (2000) 287; Clark Kerr, *The Gold and The Blue: A Personal Memoir of the University of California, 1949–1967,* *Academic Triumphs,* volume 1 (Berkeley: University of California Press, 2001) 154–55. Vice Chancellor Vern Knudsen, a year from retirement, served as UCLA's chancellor until 1960 when Dr. Franklin Murphy, former dean of the University of Kansas Medical School, stepped in.

122 "Sanders' Death Ends Great Grid Career," "Coach's Death Shocks Sports and Civic Leaders," *Los Angeles Times*, August 15, 1958. Coverage was heavy in this issue and over next several days. Sanders (1905–58) is still considered second only to coach John Wooden in UCLA's pantheon of sports heros. Ben Bolch, "Red Sanders' Impact on UCLA Football Has Lasted Well Beyond His Death, 60 Years Ago Tuesday," *Los Angeles Times* (also UCLA Sports online), August 14, 2018. See also James Murray, "Red Sanders," *Sports Illustrated*, August 25, 1958, and Charles Chiccoa, "Red Sanders and a Paradise Lost [in three parts]," (c. 2002 reprinted 2018 and 2020) *Bruin Report Online* and at 247SportsCBS Sports Digital online.

123 Snyder (1983) 67. Stanford In—Big 4 Becomes 5," *Stanford Daily,* July 23, 1959.

124 The Pac-8 expanded as the Pac-10 in 1978 with the addition of Arizona and Arizona State, and became the Pac-12, in 2011, with the addition of Colorado and Utah.

125 Frank J. Taylor, "Stanford's Man with the Midas Touch," *The Saturday Evening Post* (December 3, 1960) 36ff.

126 Taylor (1960), and Stanford News Service press release, June 1959, in SC0216 box A5.

CHAPTER 17: WARM WELCOME

1 Sterling, "The Stanford Presidency: Part II, A Noble Purpose Shared," 55, in J. E. Wallace Sterling Personal Papers and Memorabilia, SC0415 (arch 1993-061), SUA.

2 "Ann Sterling, Widow of Stanford's Fifth President, Dies at 85," *Campus Report,* August 14, 1991; see also "Wally Recalls the Early Sterling Years as President, 25 Years Ago," *Campus Report*, April 24, 1974.

3 Frederick O. Glover, An Oral History Interview Conducted by Harry Press, Don Carlson, and Roxanne Nilan" (1993) session three, Stanford Oral History Project, SUA.

4 Sterling, "The Stanford Presidency: Part II, A Noble Purpose Shared," 54–55.

5 J. E. Wallace Sterling, Chancellor of Stanford University, Papers, SC0333 box 1, folder 35, Boris, Kosta 1960–78; Kosta Boris and Essie Boris, oral history interview, October 2, 1966, Herbert Hoover Oral History Program, transcript in Hoover Archives, XX028, box 3. Kosta Boris [obit], Stanford News Service, October 2, 1978; Essie (Cheerio) Boris [obit], Stanford News Service, January 11, 1995. She died December 11, 1994.

6 Quoted in Sam Childers, "Presidential Valets: Confidantes of the Wardrobe," The White House Historical Association website (available only online); Will Irwin,

"At Home with the President: His Unofficial Side Revealed," *New York Times,* April 24, 1932. Irwin served on the executive committee of Hoover's Commission for Relief of Belgium.

7   On the 1948–49 transition of Hoover House to the Sterlings, see J. E. Wallace Sterling Presidential Papers, SC0216, box 26, folders 20 and 21, SUA.

8   Essie Boris [obit] (1995).

9   Thomas P. Pike, *Memoirs of Thomas P. Pike* (San Marino, Calif., privately printed, 1979) 172–73.

10   As the Queen of England is the honorary chancellor of British universities, the heads of British universities are called vice chancellors.

11   J. E. Wallace Sterling, "The Stanford Presidency, 1949–1968: "Part III[c], Travelling *à Deux* and Otherwise," 93, 100–01, in J. E. Wallace Sterling Personal Papers and Memorabilia, SC0415 (arch 1993-061), SUA. Prince Henry, Duke of Gloucester, was the younger brother of Queen Elizabeth's father, King George VI. Princess Alice, Duchess of Gloucester, was a daughter of the 7th Duke of Buccleuch, one of Britian's wealthiest aristocrats and Scotland's richest landowner.

12   Prince William (1941–72) traveled incognito through the United States and Canada after leaving Stanford, and later joined the Foreign and Commonwealth Office after passing its rigorous exams. He died, aged 30, while piloting his airplane in a competition. He was remembered as handsome and stylish, an unusual royal who tried to "turn himself into an ordinary citizen." He was the first member of the royal family to gain university admission through open competition, and he arrived without a private security detail. His cousin, Charles, Prince of Wales, named his first son, Prince William, Duke of Cambridge, after him. A Channel 4 (England) documentary, "The Other Prince William," was released in August 2015. See also "The Other Prince William," *Daily Mail*, November 4, 2011. On Prince William, see Sterling-Pitzer Transitional Records, SC0217, box 7, "Prince William"; Sterling Chancellorship Papers SC0333, series 2, box 2, folders 51 and 53; Frederick E. Terman Papers, SC0160, series III, box 60, folder 9; and Stanford News Service, SC0122, "Alumni Prominent: William of Gloucester," SUA.

13   *Stanford Daily,* September 23, 1963.

14   Glover (1993) session three.

15   Sterling, "The Stanford Presidency: Part III[c], Travelling *à Deux* and Otherwise," 115; Glover (1993) session three.

16   Carlson in "A Session on Wally: Transcription of an Oral History about J. E. Wallace Sterling, Recorded for the Stanford University Archives" (1985) 32; Carlson and Glover in Glover (1993) session three. The campus opened in January 1966, but the dedication was in April. *Stanford Daily,* April 20, 1966.

17   Glover (1993) session four.

18   Glover (1993) session three.

19   Glover (1993) session three. Warren's address was memorable. The *Stanford Daily* reported that Warren, who was then under attack by the John Birch Society for his support of landmark civil rights legislation, told the graduating seniors that the American ideal has been to bring about unity through diversity. "All true union is the integration of diversity," and America's "pluralistic society is made up of people of diverse races, colors and religions. . . . Group pride, group capacity, the assertion of superiority, the fear of change, have always fought against it. Unity can only be brought about if it exists in the heart and mind of people and if all are accorded equal rights and opportunities."

20   In 2014, the 16.5-foot-high by 18.5-foot-wide tapestry was restored and lent to the Museum Leuven (Louvain) in Belgium, as part of a special exhibit. "Hoover Institution Tapestry Unveiled in Belgium," Hoover Institution press release, March 20, 2014.

21   Baron Robert Silvercruys of Belgium visited on March 10, 1953. Stanford Office of Information [News Service] press release March 6, 1953, in SC0216 box 11.

22   SC0216 box A36.

23   "Belgian King to Begin U.S. Tour; Will Begin Here," *Stanford Daily*, May 14, 1959; "Belgian King Baudouin Toured Campus on Friday," *Stanford Daily*, May 25, 1959.

24   Hoover to Sterling, May 1, 1959, and Sterling to Hoover, May 8, 1959, SC0216 box A36.

25   Glover (1993) session four.

26   "French Chief: de Gaulle to Visit Medical Center," *Stanford Daily*, March 30, 1960; "Crowd of 300 Shouts Welcome to de Gaulle at Medical Center," *Stanford Daily* April 29, 1960. See also Sterling Presidential Papers, SC0216 box A36.

27   Glover (1993) session four. Khrushchev visited New York, Los Angeles, San Francisco (where he toured a supermarket), San Jose, Iowa, Pittsburgh, and Washington, D.C. See also Sterling Presidential Papers, SC0216 box A36.

CHAPTER 18: CONTROVERSIES

1   "Faculty Members Endorse Stevenson: About 150 Support Columbia Petition," *Stanford Daily,* October 22, 1952. *Palo Alto Times*, October 25, 1952. *New York Times*, October 16, 1952, in J. E. Wallace Sterling Presidential Papers, SC0216 box 26, SUA.

2   October 31, 1952, in SC0216 box 26.

3   October 28, 1952, in SC0216 box 26.

4   October 22, 1952, in SC0216 box 26.

5   November 6, 1952, in SC0216 box 26.

6   October 23, 1952, and letter to the editor, in SC0216 box 26.

7   Letters in SC0216 box 26.

8   Ibid.

9   October 31, 1952, in SC0216 box 26.

10 December 11, 1952, SC0216 box 17. It is not clear if the client carried through with his threat.

11 November 5, 1952, in SC0216 box 26.

12 November 10, 1952, in SC0216 box 26.

13 November 11, 1952, in SC0216 box 26. Academic Council minutes, January 9, April 3, and June 12, 1953.

14 November 12, 1952, in SC0216 box 26.

15 For an excellent account of Arnautoff, and Stanford's handling of the case, see Robert W. Cherny, "'No Proven Communist Should Hold a Position at Stanford': Victor Mikhail Arnautoff, the House Un-American Activities Committee, and Stanford," *Sandstone & Tile* 37:3 (Fall 2013) 3–17. See also Cherny, *Victor Arnautoff and the Politics of Art* (Urbana: University of Illinois Press, 2017).

16 Cherny (2013) 4–8. Further examination of records shows that Arnautoff (1896–1979) came to Stanford in 1936 (not 1938, as published in the faculty biographical notes in the *Annual Registers*) as an acting instructor in graphic art; he became an assistant professor in 1942. Card file records, Faculty Affairs Office of the Stanford Provost's Office.

17 *Los Angeles Times*, September 18, 1955. Cherny (2013) 8.

18 September 18, 1955, in SC0216 box 9.

19 October 5, 1955, in SC0216 box 9. This letter provided the wording for similar replies.

20 Arnautoff recorded his own interpretation of his conversation with Sterling 16 years later in his memoirs. He alleged that when he asked the president if he felt awkward asking such questions, Sterling replied no, adding: "As university president I am obliged to give due regard to the views of those who finance the university," according to Arnautoff. Cherny (2013) 10.

21 Glover detailed the discussion in a typed note to Sterling, December 2, 1955, in SC0216 box 9.

22 Brown was referring to Section 842 of the War and National Defense Act, Title 50, United States Code, known as the Communist Control Act of 1954.

23 Glover to Sterling, December 2, 1955, in SC0216 box 9.

24 *San Francisco Examiner*, December 13, 1956; *Daily Palo Alto Times*, December 12, 1956.

25 Stanford News Service press release, December 1956, SC0216 box 9.

26 December 12, 1956, in SC0216 box 9.

27 On the internal debate of the Advisory Board, see Cherny (2013) 12–13.

28 "'Peace' But Behind Curtains Move Ominous Shadows," *San Francisco News,* September 27, 1957, in SC0216 box 9.

29 December 20, 1957, in SC0216 box 9.

30 SC0216 box 9.

31 On the effectiveness of labeling an individual a "Fifth Amendment Communist," and the impact of the anti-Communist investigations on colleges and universities generally, see Ellen W. Schrecker, *No Ivory Tower*: *McCarthyism and the Universities* (New York: Oxford University Press, 1986).

32 Cherny (2013) 204–06.

33 Except as noted, the source for the following section is SC0216 box A31.

34 January 23, 1957, in SC0216 box A31. Weeks was editor of the *Atlantic Month*ly, 1938–66. Three letters between Stegner and Strucinski are in the Wallace Earle Stegner Papers, M0558, box 2, folder 16, Special Collections, Stanford University Libraries.

35 Stegner to Strucinski, March 13, 1957, and Strucinski, in a 12-page typed letter to Stegner, March 24, 1957, in SC0216 box A31. Mitchell Joseph Strucinski (1922–2001) had a long history of convictions for mail fraud, check forgery, and theft of social security checks, going back to at least 1949, documented in newspapers from Wisconsin and Denver to California.

36 March 13, 1957, and April 10, 1957, in SC0216 box A31.

37 "Frederic O. Glover, An Oral History Interview Conducted by Harry Press, Don Carlson, and Roxanne Nilan" (1993) session four, Stanford Oral History Project, SUA.

38 Glover (1993) session four.

39 SC0216 box A31.

40 Robinson contacted Stanford on October 27, 1960. *San Francisco Chronicle,* November 3 and 4, 1960.

41 The FBI hunt, Strucinski's surrender, and subsequent trial were thoroughly covered in Bay Area newspapers in November and December 1960.

42 *San Mateo Times*, November 16, 1961.

43 November 21, 1960, in SC0216 box A31.

44 Stegner to Glover November 9, 1957, in SC0216 box A31.

45 "Writer with a Talent," *Time* magazine (November 28, 1960).

46 February 5, 1958, in SC0216 box 5.

47 This controversy and related faculty involvement, as well as subsequent additions to the political science faculty, is comprehensively covered in C. Stewart Gillmor, *Fred Terman at Stanford: Building a Discipline, a University and Silicon Valley* (Stanford: Stanford University Press, 2004) 405–08, 426. The provost's full dossier is preserved in Frederick E. Terman Papers, SC0160. See also Rebecca S. Lowen, *Creating the Cold War University: The Transformation of Stanford* (University of California Press, 1997) 212–22.

48 J. E. Wallace Sterling, "The Stanford Presidency, 1949–1968: Part II, A Noble Purpose Shared," 70, in J. E. Wallace Personal Papers and Memorabilia, SC0415 (arch 1993-061) SUA. Sterling discusses the situation without specifically naming Sibley.

49 SC0216 box 5.

50 March 11, 1958, in SC0216 box 5.

51 SC0216 box 5.

52 Sterling, "The Stanford Presidency: Part II, A Noble Purpose Shared," 71.

53 May 16, 1958, in SC0216 box 5.

54 *Stanford Daily*, May 10, 1958. The *San Francisco Chronicle*, May 10, 1958, reported that Sibley was a socialist and pacifist, opposed to nuclear weapons.

55 May 13, 1958, in SC0216 box 5.

56 May 14, 1958, in SC0216 box 5.

57 Ibid.

58 May 8, 1958, in SC0216 box 5. On the History Department, see Gillmor (2004) 413–19.

59 SC0216 box 5.

60 August 18 and 25, 1958, in SC0216 box 5.

61 May 27, 1958, in SC0216 box 5, folder 35.

62 Gillmor (2004) 409–11. Eulau (1915–2004) retired as William Bennett Munro Professor of Political Science, in 1986. After immigrating from Germany to the United States in 1935, he earned his degrees in political science at UC Berkeley: B.A. 1937, M.A. 1938, Ph.D. 1941. "Eulau, Pioneer in Political Behavior Research, Dead at 88," *Stanford Report,* January 28, 2004. Almond earned his degrees, including a Ph.D. in 1937, at the University of Chicago. *Memorial Resolution: Gabriel Almond (1911–2002)* Stanford University.

63 June 11, 1963, in SC0216 box A15.

64 The English-born Hilton (1911–2007) earned his bachelor's (1933) and master's (1936) degrees from Oxford University, subsequently studying at UC Berkeley (1937–39) on a Commonwealth Fund Fellowship. He joined the Stanford faculty after teaching for two years at the University of British Columbia. He was promoted to full professor in 1949. He spent two years in Spain just before the outbreak of the Spanish Civil War. "Ronald Hilton, 95, Scholar of Latin America, Dies," *New York Times*, February 24, 2007; "Ronald Hilton, Professor Emeritus of Romance languages, Dead at 95," Stanford News Service press release, February 28, 2007. See also Ronald Hilton Papers, SCM0139, SUA, and Ronald Hilton Papers, Collection 80080, Hoover Institution Archives.

65 Lyman had just taken the associate dean's part-time position at the behest of Dean Robert Sears. His perspective of this issue, one of his first tasks, is well documented in his *Stanford in Turmoil: Campus Unrest, 1966–1972* (Stanford: Stanford University Press, 2009) 52.

66 SC0216 box A15. Lyman (2009) 52.

67 SC0216 box A15.

68 Stanford News Service press releases, November 16 and 17, 1964, in SC0216 box A15.

69 Lyman (2009) 52.

70 *San Jose Mercury*, November 1, 1964, in SC0216 box A15.

71 Lyman (2009) 52.

72 Hilton to Bacchetti, December 8, 1964, and Lyman to Sterling, December 16, 1964, in SC0216 box A15.

73 Lyman to Professor Carl Spaeth, director of international studies, December 22, 1964, in SC0216 box A15.

74 Harvard historian to Lyman, December 14, 1964, and Sterling to historian, December 21, 1964, in SC0216 box A15.

75 February 4, 1965, in SC0216 box A15.

76 February 15, 1965, in SC0216 box A15.

77 March 10, 1965, in SC0216 box A15.

78 March 15, 1965, in SC0216 box A15. Hilton later claimed he suspended the *Report* after he resigned from the Hispanic American Studies Program in 1964. A year later, he founded the California Institute of International Studies (today known as the World Association of International Studies) and began editing and publishing the quarterly *World Affairs Report*. Hilton wrote several books and edited many, including the multi-volume *Who's Who in Latin America*. He became emeritus in 1976. In 1987, he was named a visiting fellow at the Hoover Institution.

79 SC0216 box A15.

CHAPTER 19: ACTIVISM 1960–1966

1 *Stanford Daily:* "Sterling Gives Frosh a View of 'The Farm,'" September 22, 1961; "Pres. Sterling Advises Frosh at Convocation," September 21, 1962; "Sterling Speech Welcomes Frosh," September 20, 1963; "Convocation Address: Sterling Welcomes Freshmen," September 25, 1964.

2 On the transformation of student governance and social regulations, see J. Michael Korff, "Student Control and University Government at Stanford: The Evolving Student-University Relationship [1891–1970]," unpublished dissertation, Stanford University (1975); Orrin Leslie Elliott, *Stanford University: The First Twenty-Five Years* (Stanford University Press, 1937) 379–450; and J. Pearce Mitchell, *Stanford University, 1916–1941* (1958) 103–08.

3 Jane Stanford, October 3, 1902, in *Stanford University: The Founding Grant with Amendments, Legislation, and Court Decrees* (Stanford University, 1987) 21–22. Leland Stanford was wary of political maneuvering often experienced by state universities, whose regents were selected by the governor and whose budgets were determined by legislators.

4 Board of Trustees' resolution, September 30, 1911, in Committee on Public Exercises, Policy Manual (June 1953), "Political Meetings," in J. E. Wallace Sterling Presidential Papers, SC0216 box 59, SUA.

5 Eisenhower was another strong candidate, winning Stanford's precinct vote just as he carried the state. "Students' GOP Preference is Consistent with Past Polls," *Stanford Daily,* November 2, 1948; "Stanford Voting," *Stanford Daily,* November 5, 1952.

6 "Political Groups Ruled Out," *Stanford Daily*, January 26, 1948. On ASSU Executive Committee support of university policy, see "Excom Ban on Political Groups Set," *Stanford Daily*, October 16, 1947. Henry A. Wallace had been Franklin Roosevelt's secretary of agriculture

when he shaped the New Deal's controversial farm relief policy, and later served as vice president (1941–44). He broke with the Democratic Party in 1946 over foreign policy, founding a new Progressive Party that advocated cooperation with the Soviet Union, strong ties with the United Nations, and arms reduction. He opposed racial and religious discrimination. The Palo Alto PCA continued to meet off-campus.

7   Committee on Academic Affairs, Board of Trustees' resolution, March 20, 1952, Board of Trustees Minutes, SC1010, SUA. See also Policy Manual. Committee on Public Exercises, "Political Meetings," in J. E. Wallace Sterling Presidential Papers, op. cit. See Chapter 18 on the controversy surrounding the 1952 election.

8   *Stanford Daily* 1958: "Demonstrators to Ask Bomb Halt Test: 'Fact Sheet,' Posters Voice Student Protest" and "Letter to the Editor [by the organizers]," April 17; "Demonstrators Protest Silently; 335 Sign Presidential Petition" and "Campus Opinion," April 18; and subsequent editorials and letters to the editor (pro and con) well into mid-May. Between 1948 and 1958, 43 nuclear tests occurred at Enewetak (official spelling was changed in 1974). Environmental restoration remains incomplete. The 1963 "Treaty Banning Nuclear Weapon Tests in the Atmosphere, in Outer Space and Under Water" discontinued testing by the U.S.S.R, U.S., and U.K., but France continued Pacific testing until the mid-1990s.

9   Herbert Dougall, chairman of the Committee on Public Exercises, to Sterling, November 8, 1949 (possibly in SC0216 box 59).

10 See extensive coverage about creation of the Political Union in the *Stanford Daily*, April through October 1953.

11 *Stanford Daily* 1960: "Kennedy to Speak at Stanford Today," February 12; "U.S. Policy on Latin America Hit by Kennedy as 'Inadequate,'" and "Unneeded Chaos," February 15; "Tickets Still Available for Nixon," April 8; and "Nixon Says U.S. Cause Needs More 'True Believers' Abroad," April 12.

12 The HUAC hearing was denounced by the State Federation of Teachers, the First Unitarian Church of San Jose, the East Bay Jewish Community Center, and the San Francisco Labor Council. The following day, the picket line grew to nearly 2,000, with another 3,500 predominantly anti-committee spectators crowded outside the building. The events were widely covered by the local and national press, and in student newspapers, including the *Stanford Daily*, May 16, 19, and 20, 1960.

13 The complete open letter to Christopher, sent to the *San Francisco Chronicle*, was printed in the *Stanford Daily*, May 19, 1960. Local coverage reinterpreted the letter and had slightly different name totals. "Stanford Group Hits Riot Cops," *San Francisco Examiner,* May 19, 1060, "Mayor Christopher Says Red Probe Riot Closed Incident," *Oakland Tribune*, May 19, 1960. See also "HUAC:

May 1960, The Events, The Aftermath," in Free Speech Movement Archives, UC Berkeley (available online).

14 Drell quoted in Lenora Ferro, with Susan Southworth, *Sidney D. Drell: Into the Heart of Matter, Passionately* (Stanford: Hoover Institution Press, 2021) 76–77.

15 September 30, 1960, in SC0216 box C4. Glover, in a different letter, noted that they had been able to identify only two students who were present at City Hall, September 27, 1960, in SC0216 box C4.

16 "Nixon Beats Kennedy by 632 Votes," *Stanford Daily*, November 9, 1960. From an undergraduate enrollment of around 5,600, some 3001 straw votes were cast by undergraduates (400 more than cast at the recent student body election). "Stanford Goes for Kennedy," *Stanford Daily*, November 9, 1960, reveals that Stanford's four precincts went for Kennedy (469 votes) over Nixon (407), but preferred the Republican incumbent for the 10th Congressional seat.

17 Rosencranz's year was heavily covered by the *Stanford Daily*, 1962–63. See also Richard W. Lyman, *Stanford in Turmoil* (Stanford University Press, 2009) 13, 15–16, and Korff (1975) 166–70, and the excellent analysis by Tom Galbraith, '66, a younger member of Rosencranz's liberal coalition, in his "An Analysis of a Stanford Student Political Party: 'The Establishment,'" unpublished anthropology paper, June 1965, SCM0453, SUA. *Daily* political editor Steve Leopold reviewed the campaign and presidency in light of subsequent ASSU presidents in "The Happy Days of Wine and Rosencranz," April 7, 1965, and "Rosencranz' Year: A GRIPping Experience," April 8, 1965.

18 "Grad Student Rosencranz Wins; Referendum Passes," May 4, 1962. Armin Rosencranz email to Karen Bartholomew, February 1, 2021.

19 Rosencranz received his A.B. (1958) from Princeton, and his J.D. (1962), M.A., (1963) and Ph.D. (1970) from Stanford. He was a law student when elected but passed the California bar exam the summer before his term began. He later became an expert on international environmental law and taught at the University of Michigan (1987–94) and Stanford (1994–2012). He also served as an alumni member on Stanford's Board of Trustees (1974–78).

20 "Armin's Address to Freshmen," *Stanford Daily,* September 24, 1962. The *Daily* editorialized that Rosencranz and two other serious speakers deserved a better platform than having to speak "while Band members fell out of trees and radios blared the account of the Tulane-Stanford game." "Orientation," *Stanford Daily*, September 24, 1962.

21 "LASSU Yields to Trustees' Decision: Armin Speaks to Legislature," *Stanford Daily,* September 28, 1962.

22 "Revolution of 'Moderates' Hailed at ASSU dinner" and "Rosencranz's Concluding Address," *Stanford Daily*, May 31, 1963. See also Galbraith (1965).

23 "Students Work with Faculty on 9 of Presidential Committees," *Stanford Daily*, November 30, 1962. Five of the Student Affairs Committee's 15 members were students. On some large committees, 7 of 20 members were students. The legislature had already lost a major student body challenge to university policy regarding the campus ban on alcohol, proposing instead to simply conform to California state law. On Sterling's recommendation, the trustees denied the legislature's right to make such a change but made an exception for married students at home at Escondido and Stanford villages as with the homes of faculty. "LASSU Yields to Trustees' Decision: Armin Speaks to Legislature," *Stanford Daily*, September 28, 1962.

24 "KPFA's License Delay Prompts Letter to FCC," *Stanford Daily*, January 23, 1963, and "Legislature, Administration Clash on Student Rights," *Stanford Daily*, January 25, 1963.

25 *Stanford Daily* 1963: "KPFA's License Delay Prompts Letter to FCC," January 23; "Legislature, Administration Clash on Student Rights," January 25; "The Winds of Freedom Blow," January 28; "An Indictment of the University for Hypocrisy," January 29; "Text of Letters from Sterling, Rosencranz," January 29; "IFC Resolution Censures LASSU," January 29; "Legislature Reaffirms Stand on Student Rights Resolve," February 1; "The KPFA Affair," February 4. Religion professor and civil rights activist Robert MacAfee Brown contributed a letter to the editor, January 28.

26 The new constitution, written largely by James Woolsey, executive assistant to Rosencranz (and future CIA director), provided for a larger and more representative legislature, and for election of a speaker of the legislature to chair its meetings, rather than the president, thus clearly distinguishing executive and legislative/judicial branches.

27 "Rosencranz's Year," *Stanford Daily*, April 8, 1965.

28 *Stanford Daily* 1964: "The Stanford Student Congress," April 8; "Sweeney Elected New Speaker to President Over Student Congress," April 25; "Student Congress Gives Rare Opportunity Here," October 2. The Student Congress apparently collapsed after Sweeney dropped out to devote himself to civil rights work in Mississippi and subsequent antiwar activism.

29 "Revolution of 'Moderates' Hailed at ASSU Dinner" and "Rosencranz's Concluding Address," *Stanford Daily*, May 31, 1963. "Legislature, Administration Clash on Student Rights," *Stanford Daily*, January 25, 1963.

30 "Rosencranz's Concluding Address," *Stanford Daily*, May 31, 1963.

31 *Stanford Daily*, 1963: "Sandperl, Weinig Will Lead Open Discussion on Shelters," April 15; "Conservative, Pacifist Debate Shelter Merits," April 16; "New Student Council Votes 70–27 to Ban SU Fallout Shelters," April 17.

32 SC0216 box C5. *Stanford Daily* 1963: "Vigil to be Kept by Peace Caucus," April 25; "Sterling's Statement," April 29; "Have All Questions Been Answered?" April 30. The Peace Caucus promoted peaceful methods of conflict resolution, particularly nonviolent alternatives to war. Its predecessor, the 1962 Forum for the Discussion of Non-Violent Alternatives to War, had been prohibited by the administration due to its allegedly partisan orientation.

33 Sterling to Lawrence Kimpton, April 25, 1963, in SC0216 box A18.

34 "Sterling's Statement," April 29, 1963, "Demonstrations Do Not Violate Fundamental Standard: LASSU" and "Shelter Controversy Leads to Student Vigil," April 26, 1963; "Official Position Given on Shelters," *Stanford Daily*, April 29, 1963.

35 "Vigil on Sterling's Home Stopped; Shelter Protest Continues," *Stanford Daily*, April 29, 1963; "Vigil on Shelters Ends, Peace Caucus Satisfied," *Stanford Daily*, May 2, 1963. Sterling felt strongly about demonstrations near his family. SC0216 box C5. See also Lyman (2009) 17–19, and Richard W. Lyman, "Stanford in Turmoil," *Sandstone & Tile* 35:1 (Winter 2011) 5–6.

36 "ST&T Panel Discusses Issue of Fallout Shelter Construction," *Stanford Daily*, May 16, 1963. See also letter to the editor by Michael Soule, May 16, 1963. Panofsky, a consultant to the Manhattan Project, advised U.S. government and military officials on detecting and designing defenses against nuclear weapons attacks. He became a noted expert on arms control and an advocate for nonproliferation of nuclear weapons.

37 June 26, 1963, in SC0216 box C5.

38 October 4, 1963, in SC0216 box C5.

39 OATQ (Once Around the Quad) announcement "Civil Rights Group," *Stanford Daily*, May 4, 1962. Glover note in SC0216 box A7. By fall 1962, a Civil Rights Caucus joined other caucuses in the Political Union and hosted Peninsula civil rights groups including the Congress of Racial Equality and the Palo Alto Fair Play Committee.

40 "New Pol Union Caucus to Discuss Civil Rights, Partisan Politics Stand," *Stanford Daily*, November 29, 1962. "Rosencranz's Concluding Address," *Stanford Daily*, May 31, 1963. The Civil Rights Caucus, beginning with 20 members, was not allowed to engage in group action but sponsored lectures, panels, and seminars on a wide array of civil rights topics, including capital punishment, restrictive real estate clauses, academic freedom, and censorship. Its principal goal was to raise student awareness.

41 "Baldwin Examines Nightmare History of Racial Problems," May 9, 1963. Breaker's Eating Club was one of several clubs where dorm students without dining facilities and off-campus students could eat and socialize.

42 "Collection at Baldwin Speech Curtailed by Student Police" and "Meeting to Protest Police Action in Birmingham," *Stanford Daily*, May 9, 1963. Baldwin's sponsors were the Civil Liberties Caucus, the Breakers Eating

Club, and the Committee on Public Exercises. Rosencranz subsequently wrote to President John F. Kennedy, describing the event and campus interest, and emphasizing that segregation was not a Black problem but a white one. He was not reprimanded this time. "Rosencranz Letter to Kennedy," *Stanford Daily*, May 13, 1963.

43 SC0216 box A7. Letters to the editor, *Stanford Daily*, November 1, 6, 7, 13, 15, 18, and 30, 1963, reveal an array of opinions about whether Stanford students should "interfere" with the racial status quo in Mississippi.

44 *Stanford Daily* 1965: "Campus Politics: Bud Wedin's Philosophy is Now Being Forgotten," February 3; "Woolsey 'Piffles' Walsh; Wedin Pilfers Presidency," April 9; "Campus Politics: Legislature May Improve But What Can It Really Do?" April 14. Wedin also played football and rugby for Stanford.

45 *Stanford Quad* (1964) 112. Galbraith (1965) offers an insightful description of the GRIP liberal coalition through 1965. Michael (Bud) Wedin (1943–) '65, dubbed the "Philosopher King" due to his philosophical analysis of the student community and its problems, received his Ph.D. in philosophy from the University of Chicago in 1971. He joined the faculty of UC Davis in 1971, becoming emeritus in 2004. He served for many years as chair of the Philosophy Department.

46 "SNCC Field Secretary Blasts 'Foggy Notions' of Crusaders," *Stanford Daily,* January 25, 1964; "Panel Advises Forethought in Civil Rights Campaign," *Stanford Daily,* January 31, 1964.

47 "Civil Rights Conference Planned," *Stanford Daily,* February 17, 1964. Fred Glover reported on November 1963 and summer 1964 Mississippi events to trustee President Richard Guggenhime, July 13, 1964, in SC0216 box A7, folder 28.

48 *Stanford Daily*, 1964: "Politics: Wedin Fails to Explain Secretariat," February 18; "Secretariat Unfinanced But In Action," February 19; "LASSU Approves Resolution Altering Open House Policy," February 28; "ASSU Adopts Partisan Position in Forming Rights Secretariat," March 3; "Secretariat Funds Frozen," May 28. The Secretariat was replaced the following year by the Mississippi Freedom Project at Stanford.

49 "Campus Politics: Secretariat Separates Presidential Candidates," *Stanford Daily*, May 4, 1964. Statements by the three ASSU presidential candidates regarding the Secretariat can be found in the *Stanford Daily*, May 4, 8, 12, 1964.

50 During 1963–64, Allard K. Lowenstein, a former assistant dean and Stern Hall director, inspired many Stanford students to become involved in civil rights activism, particularly for the Mississippi Summer project. David Harris writes about Lowenstein and Dennis Sweeney in his *Dreams Die Hard: Three Men's Journey Through the '60s* (New York: St. Martin's Press, 1982). See also William H. Chafe, *Never Stop Running: Allard Lowenstein and the Struggle to Save American Liberalism* (New York: Basic Books, 1993), Chapter 7: "Stanford and Civil Rights, 1961–63," 166–69.

51 "King Calls for Further Action Before Crowd of Over 1800," *Stanford Daily*, April 24, 1964.

52 "40 Students Going South for Summer," *Stanford Daily*, June 22, 1964. On the Stanford experience during the Mississippi Summer, see Robert W. Beyers, "Why They Went South," *Cornell Alumni News* (September 1964) 11–14; Roxanne Nilan, "Why They Went South: Stanford Newsman Bob Beyers and Mississippi Freedom Summer," *Sandstone & Tile* 38:2 (Spring-Summer 2014) 3–17; Bernard Butcher, "Freedom Summer," *Stanford* [magazine] (July-August 1996; rep. 2018) 74–81; and Bernard Butcher, "Stanford in Mississippi: A Foreign Country in Our Midst," unpublished seminar paper, Stanford University, June 1995. On the Mississippi Project, see William McCord, *Mississippi: A Long Hot Summer* (New York: W.W. Norton, 1965; University of Mississippi Press, 2016); Doug McAdam, *Freedom Summer* (New York: Oxford University Press, 1988), and "Freedom Summer: Crucible of Change" (excerpts from 50th anniversary panel discussion on campus, with an additional interview with David Harris) *Sandstone & Tile* 38:2 (Spring-Summer 2014) 18–31.

53 SC0216 box A7.

54 Ibid.

55 Nilan (2014) 7.

56 J. E. Wallace Sterling, "The Stanford Presidency 1949–1968: Part II, A Noble Purpose Shared," 80–81, in SC0415 (1993-061) SUA.

57 "Frank Morse Abducted, Beaten by Gang of Mississippi Whites," *Stanford Daily*, October 22, 1964. In March 1965, he joined Dr. King's civil rights march from Selma to Montgomery, Alabama.

58 *Stanford Daily* 1964: "The Morse Case: Student Resentment High," April 23; "Dr. Fulla Blamed for Suspension," April 27; "Morse Case: Confusion, Bad Timing Plagued Italy Hearings Pertinent Facts Overlooked on Last Day of Residence," April 28. Korff (1975) 180–85 underscores the significance of the Morse case.

59 Ibid. "Frank Morse Leads Race for Con Home King," *Stanford Daily*, April 24, 1964. Queen Trish Pad won with 3,148 votes. On the KZSU program, see "9830: The Morse Case," *Stanford Daily*, April 24, 1964, and "Discussion Continues in Morse Controversy, ACLU Waits for Dean: KZSU Analyzes Decision," *Stanford Daily*, May 4, 1964.

60 "Tact, Intelligence" (letter to the editor) Professor Morris Zelditch Jr., *Stanford Daily*, May 14, 1964.

61 The ACLU was struck by six features: the failure of the Dean's Office to apprise Morse explicitly on the grounds for his suspension; that Morse was denied an opportunity

to defend himself against the undisclosed allegations made by the Florence faculty committee; the imposition of an excessive penalty for breaking a door panel, if that was his only offense; offering no reason why Morse was treated differently from the two other students who had committed the same offense; the alleged attempt to suppress further consideration of the case and unwillingness to cooperate with the Men's Council; the need for clarifying procedures for handling disciplinary cases of students residing on foreign campuses. "Fights Florence Suspension: Stanford Student's ACLU Plea," *San Francisco Examiner*, April 17, 1964; "ACLU Asks Winbigler Opinion on Morse Case: Do Students Get Justice," *Stanford Daily*, May 1, 1964; and "ACLU Demanding Story on Student," *San Francisco Examiner*, May 1, 1964.

62 Morse graduated from Harvard Law School in 1969. In June 1967, Morse married Judith Robinson Sterling, '66, M.A. '67 (daughter of President Wallace Sterling) who also attended Stanford-in-Italy (October 1963-March 1964). *San Francisco Examiner*, June 26, 1967.

63 Nancy Steffen, "Stanford on the Edge of Greatness: Seeds of Sound and Fury Sown," *Stanford Daily,* May 27, 1964.

64 "Big McBride Victory," *Stanford Daily*, May 15, 1964; "McBride's Slow-Down Releases GRIP," April 12, 1965.

65 "The Fearful Spectator: Can it Be? Is the Daily Favorable to Sterling?" *Stanford Daily*, October 7, 1964.

66 "Four Vie for ASSU President's Post," *Stanford Daily*, May 5, 1964.

67 Stanford University Circular No. 3, May 1891; Elliott (1937) 408–09. On Jordan's approach to student discipline, see Korff (1975) 15–19, 22–28, and Elliott (1937) "Conduct and Discipline," 408–50.

68 *Annual Register 1896–97,* Stanford University, p. 25 (fundamental standard). The "Liquor Rebellion" is extensively covered by Elliott (1937) "The Problem of Liquor," 378–407, and Korff (1975) 43–55.

69 Korff (1975) 75–140. "Side-shows" in Ray Lyman Wilbur, *The Memoirs of Ray Lyman Wilbur* (Stanford: Stanford University Press, 1960) 217; Mitchell (1958) 103–08.

70 Korff (1975) 84–85. Barbara Wilcox, *World War I Army Training by San Francisco Bay: The Story of Camp Fremont* (Charleston S.C.: History Press, 2016) 64–65, 73–74.

71 Dean Winbigler was succeeded, in January 1967, by Associate Dean Joel Smith, who left two years later to become president of Denison University.

72 *Memorial Resolution: H. Donald Winbigler (1909–2000)* Stanford University. Winbigler arrived at Stanford in 1940 as an assistant professor of speech and drama, becoming full professor in 1949. He served as registrar for five years before Sterling appointed him dean of students. In 1967, he became academic secretary. After his 1974 retirement, he continued to volunteer for Stanford in many capacities, including twice serving as president of the Stanford Historical Society. See also "Don Winbig-

ler, Former Dean of Students, Dies at 91," Stanford News Service, August 11, 2000. For a recollection with amusing anecdotes and a list of the countless ways Winbigler's surname was mangled, see Fred Glover, "Speech and Drama: Don Winbigler at Stanford," *Sandstone & Tile* 16:2 (Spring 1992) 7–12.

73 "The tumult and the shouting" surrounding the Allen controversy was heavily covered by the *Stanford Daily*, February 8, 9 and 10, 1965. See also "Allen Resigns; Report Withheld," *Stanford Daily*, February 15, 1965. On the Allen Affair, see Korff (1975) 155–64, and Molly Culhane, "A More than Adequate Dose of Nonsense: Sex, Social Regulation, and Institutional Change in Stanford's Allen Controversy" and Sanford Dornbusch, "An Investigation Into Pornography and Sexual Abuse at Stanford," *Sandstone & Tile* 44:3 (Fall 2020) 10–19. Allen, formerly dean of women at Cornell, had replaced Dean Elva Fay Brown in 1961, and also was an associate professor in the School of Education.

74 *Stanford Daily* 1965: Nora Crow (Women's Council) and Darrell Halverson (Men's Council), "Text of Statement to Legislature: Report on Student Judiciary–Administration Relations," "Statement by Former Chairmen of Men's and Women's Councils," and "A Question of Values" (editorial), February 4; "Crow-Halverson Report," February 9; "Crow-Halverson: The Tumult and The Shouting," February 10. Allen released a statement on February 4 denying the allegations.

75 "Report of the Executive Committee of the Academic Council," February 12, 1965, [Lucile] Allen Controversy Papers, SC0050, SUA. Committee members were Sanford Dornbusch (sociology), Gerald Gunther (law), and Kenneth Arrow (economics); Lyman (2009) 28–29.

76 Brown's concern reported by Glover to Sterling, February 12, 1965, SC0050; Gunther, Franklin, and Manning to Sterling, February 12, 1965, SC0050.

77 "Allen Resigns; Report Withheld," *Stanford Daily*, February 15, 1965. Sterling letter quoted in Lyman (2009) 32.

78 "Judicial Resolution Gets COUP, Faculty Support: Social Regs Action Seen," *Stanford Daily,* April 12, 1965; "AWS Social Regs Report Approved: Student Affairs and Services Agrees 'With No Real Change in Substance,'" *Stanford Daily,* April 13, 1965.

79 *Stanford Daily* 1965: "Sterling Approves Social Regs: Trustees Hear Report, Regs Take Effect April 30," April 16; "Stanford Politics: A Growing Activism," September 24. The *Stanford Daily*, November 1964 to May 1965, covers the debate and the months-long study by the AWS Social Regulations Committee.

80 SC0216 box C5, folder 3.

81 SC0216 box B3.

82 *Stanford Daily* 1965: "Dean's Office Reorganized," August 6; "Major Shake-Up in Dean's Office," September 30; "H. Donald Winbigler, Dean of Students, to Stanford

Parents, April 29, 1965," News Service, SC0122, series 1, box 180, file "Sex," SUA; "Sterling Approves Social Regs: Trustees Hear Report, Regs Take Effect April 30," April 16.

83 "Mackenzie Landslide," *Stanford Daily*, May 5, 1965; "Stanford Politics: A Growing Activism," *Stanford Daily*, September 24, 1965. William (Sandy) Mackenzie (1943–2011) received his B.A. in history, 1965, and his MBA from Harvard, and followed a career in real estate. *Deseret News* (obituary), December 18, 2011. See also Joseph (Jay) Kadane Papers, 1964–1966, SC0037, SUA. Kadane, a graduate student ASSU legislator, 1964–66, served as speaker of LASSU, 1965–66. He received his Ph.D. in statistics in 1966. The GCC is covered throughout 1965–66 by the *Stanford Daily*.

84 Sterling, "The Stanford Presidency: Part II, A Noble Purpose Shared," 80–81, 86. For the experience of a student activist from New York at Stanford, see Jeanne Friedman, in Jeanne Friedman, Georgia Kelly, and Lenny Siegel, "The Roots of the Stanford Peace Movement," *Sandstone & Tile* 35:1 (Winter 2011) 16. Between 1965 and 1969, Friedman saw, and participated in, a "virtual explosion" of campus organizing and activity among students, faculty, and staff.

85 *Stanford Daily:* "Pacifists Rally In White Plaza, Urge U.S. To Exit Viet Nam Conflict," February 15, 1965; "Selma, Viet Petitions Rap LBJ," March 30, 1965; "Large Crowds Hear Pro-Con Viet Nam 'Teach-In,'" May 18, 1965; "SCPV Will Keep Protesting," July 29, 1965. Founding of SDS at Stanford cannot be pinned down, but meeting announcements were posted in the *Daily's* OATQ (Once Around the Quad), October 19, November 8 and 15, 1966. See also Friedman, et al., "The Roots of the Stanford Peace Movement" (2011).

86 SC0216 box A36. *Stanford Daily* 1966: May 6, 9, 10, 13, 18. "ROTC Students to Solicit Blood," April 11, and "Unit Takes 148 Pints in Army Blood Drive," April 13.

87 SC0216 box A36. Participation in anti-napalm protests that spring was widely covered in local newspapers. See *Stanford Daily* 1966: May 6, 9, 10, 13, 18. See also Robert M. Neer, *Napalm: An American Biography* (Cambridge: Harvard University Press, 2015) and Jennifer Tynes, "The Napalm Ladies: AKA 'The Housewife Terrorists,'" Jennifer Tynes website, 2012.

88 "Draft Test Date Nears," *Stanford Daily*, April 21, 1966. On the exam itself at this time, see Thomas J. Frusciano, "Student Deferment and the Selective Service College Qualification Test, 1954–1967" (Princeton, N.J.: Educational Testing Service, 1980, Research Paper # ETS-RM-63-1) ii, 45–50. The College Qualification Test, originally created by the Educational Testing Service in 1951 during the Korean War, consisted of 150 questions measuring basic verbal and math skills. Examples can be seen in "Samples of Questions on the Selective Service Deferment Test," *New York Times*, March 18, 1966. A

high score did not ensure deferment but could help bolster a case before one's local draft board.

89 "Rally, Night-Long Sit-in Protest Draft Test," "Irate Students 'Lobby' Demanding 'Meaningful Reply' from Sterling," and "On Protesting the Test" (editorial), *Stanford Daily*, May 20, 1966. On the events of the next few days and its aftermath, see *Stanford Daily*, May 20–26, and *Stanford Observer,* June 1966. Lyman (2009) 35–40 fills out details unknown to *Daily* reporters. Estimates of the number involved vary, and changed over the 50-hour sit-in, but an estimated 25 to at least 40 individuals took part inside.

90 "Irate Students," *Stanford Daily,* May 20, 1966; "Draft Stirs Concerned Action Across Nation," *Stanford Daily*, May 23, 1966.

91 "Protesters Quietly Leave 'Number 10,'" *Stanford Daily,* May 23, 1966. Many of the counter protesters were from the Stanford Young Republicans, a student club. Among them was future Massachusetts governor and U.S. Sen. Mitt Romney (Utah), then a freshman. (Romney transferred to BYU as a sophomore.)

92 *Stanford Daily* 1966: "On Protesting the Test," May 20. Both sides took to the "letters to the editor" section to explain themselves. See especially "Footnotes to a Sit-In," Phil O'Donnell, May 24, and "Wert Replies to the Sit-Iners," May 26.

93 Telephone calls by Robert Minge Brown and Richard Guggenhime are summarized in memos from Glover to Sterling in SC0216 box C6. See also Lyman (2009) 38–39.

94 SC0216 box C5. Michael Sweeney provides a wry analysis of the freedoms and constraints of Stanford's demonstration policy in "Demonstrations: Freedom of Expression—In Theory," *Stanford Daily*, October 11, 1965.

95 "Intransigence Forever?" *Stanford Daily*, May 24, 1966.

96 "Sterling Evaluates Trends of 'Restless Generation,'" *Stanford Daily*, April 8, 1965.

97 "Harris: Career of Commitment," *Stanford Daily*, February 23, 1967. For a contemporary review of Harris' term in office and his influence, from the student perspective, see "Harris: All-American 'Reborn' as an Anti-President," *Stanford Daily,* December 2, 1966; "Harris Resigns Presidency," "Campus Reaction," and "He Broke Fresh Ground" (editorial), *Stanford Daily,* February 23, 1967. David Victor Harris (1946–2023) was a prolific journalist and author, with a novel and 10 nonfiction books on topics as diverse as professional football, presidential elections, and the timber industry. His autobiography is included in his *Dreams Die Hard* (1982). See also "Three Who Shaped a Decade: Student Activists of a Generation Ago Look Back, Forward," *Stanford Daily*, June 1, 1994.

98 *San Jose Mercury*, May 4, 1966, and September 15, 1966. "Lessons of Mississippi: An Interview with David Harris, '67," *Sandstone & Tile* 38:2 (Spring-Summer 2014) 31. See also "Frank Morse Abducted, Beaten by Gang of Mississippi Whites," *Stanford Daily*, October 22, 1964.

Harris worked with Morse as part of a six-man Stanford contingent with the Mississippi Freedom Project that fall.

99 Harris (1982) 134–35; "Harris: All-American 'Reborn' as an Anti-President," *Stanford Daily,* December 2, 1966.

100 *Stanford Daily* (editorial), April 20, 1966.

101 "4296 Voters Register New Turnout Record" and "Harris Defeats Klein: The President-Elect—Voice of Radicalism," *Stanford Daily*, April 29, 1966.

102 *San Jose Mercury*, May 4, 1966.

103 May 21, 1966, in SC0216 box B1.

104 May 12, 1966, in SC0216 box B1.

105 "Harris: Career of Commitment" and "He Broke Fresh Ground" (editorial), *Stanford Daily*, February 23, 1967.

106 *Stanford Daily* 1966: "Bulletin," October 21; "Campus Reaction to Harris Attack Varies" and "Administration, Fraternities Condemn Harris Shavers," October 24. One of the Delts involved told the *Daily* that Harris, who did not struggle or cry out, had "really showed the Delts a lot of class. He made us feel sorry we did it," quoted in "Bulletin," October 21.

107 The details about the different investigations by the Judicial Council and the Dean's Office were not made public. "Harris: Career of Commitment," *Stanford Daily*, February 23, 1967.

108 October 30, 1966, in SC0216 box B1. Harris, too, received considerable mail from across the country as well as from alumni, ranging from crank mail and insults to letters of encouragement. "Letters Urge Harris: Cut Hair, Read Bible," *Stanford Daily*, November 23, 1966.

109 November 1, 1966, and no date available, in SC0216 box B1.

110 March 31, 1967, in SC0216 box B1.19

CHAPTER 20: ACTIVISM 1967–1968

1 "Sterling Announces Retirement, is Named Chancellor," *Stanford Observer* (April 1967).

2 Tom Galbraith, "An Analysis of a Stanford Student Political Party: 'The Establishment,'" unpublished anthropology paper, June 1965, SCM0453, SUA, 11, 13. Galbraith provides an insider's view of the political reform group that included Armin Rosencranz, Bud Wedin, Sandy Mackenzie, and their political associates, from 1962 to the election of Mackenzie in 1965.

3 "Harris Defeats Klein: President-Elect—Voice of 'Radicalism,'" *Stanford Daily,* April 29, 1966.

4 "Real Education From People, Not University, Harris Says," *Stanford Daily,* September 23, 1966; "Harris Wants Institutions to Stress Education, Not Degree," *Stanford Daily,* September 27, 1966.

5 Ibid.

6 "OFF Proposal Wins 10–1," *Stanford Daily*, November 3, 1966; "Cold Facts" (letter to editor), *Stanford Daily*, November 10, 1966.

7 "Board President Doubts Trustee Action on 'OFF,'" *Stanford Daily*, November 17, 1967; letter to Guggenhime, November 4, 1966, and Guggenhime's response in SC0216 box B2.

8 Howell's response to Guggenhime in "Board President Doubts Trustee Action on 'OFF,'" *Stanford Daily*, November 17, 1967. See also Robert Spanner, letter to editor, "Trustee Letter Irks Student," *Stanford Daily,* November 21, 1966.

9 Sterling response in "'OFF' Leader Howell Cautiously Optimistic," *Stanford Daily*, November 28, 1966.

10 December 7, 1966, in SC0216 box B2.

11 December 16, 1966, and no date available, in SC0216, box B2.

12 *Stanford Daily* 1967: January 4, 11, and 19.

13 *Stanford Daily* 1967: February 6, 14, 15, March 6, April 24, 25, May 1. "'Off' Severs University Umbilical Cord," October 11. The number 56 is reported in "Expansion of Coed Housing Approved by Trustee Board," *Stanford Observer* (April 1968) 2. "New Housing Plans Complicate Residence Draw Procedure," *Stanford Daily*, May 6, 1968.

14 "Women Off Campus," *Stanford Daily*, October 10, 1966.

15 Commission co-chair Jan Jacobi in "Housing Statement," *Stanford Daily*, November 1, 1966; Jan Jacobi, "House at Pooh Corner: In Housing Policy Students Form Prime Constituency," *Stanford Daily,* October 13, 1966. Jacobi, who later credited Harris with being a prophet, stated that after appointing the commission, Harris kept in touch but did not direct the commission. On Mackenzie's demand for a university residential philosophy statement and his criticism of current housing conditions, see "Mackenzie Lowers the Boom on Housing Dilemma," *Stanford Daily,* November 16, 1965.

16 "Advisory Committee Joins ASSU Group," *Stanford Daily,* October 11, 1966.

17 "Housing Comm Proposes Integrated Coed Dorms," *Stanford Daily*, February 13, 1967, and "Text of Housing Commission Report," *Stanford Daily,* February 15, 1967. "Integrated" in this context meant mixing freshmen with upperclassmen. The commission also recommended expansion of the role of tutors and elimination of resident assistant and sponsor positions.

18 *Stanford Daily:* Jacobi quoted in "Trustees Pass Demonstration Houses," May 19, 1967; see also "Trustees Decisions" (editorial), May 22, 1967; and "SES Report Urges More Coeducational Dorms," February 7, 1968.

19 Each student pulled a number from a large bowl; low numbers provided more freedom of choice on where to live.

20 "'Grove' Project to Offer Experiment, Coed Living," *Stanford Daily,* January 4, 1967.

21 "Letter to Sterling: Branner Lauds Coed Living," *Stanford Daily*, January 31, 1968. Branner residents, hoping to encourage more coeducational housing, presented

Sterling with a letter signed unanimously by its 174 residents, dorm sponsors, and faculty residents. It stressed that some of the freshmen intended to select single-sex housing (fraternities) the following year, but that students were united in considering the coed experience rewarding. They also pointed out that Branner was no "party dorm" and actually earned a higher GPA than Roble's women.

22 "Residence Plans: Housing Draw Set for May," *Stanford Daily*, April 12, 1968. The inclusion of Roble was the result of an administrative error, an assumption made by Roble's hall directors that was not noticed in the Dean's Office during the transition to incoming Dean of Students Peter Bulkeley. "Roble Coed Floors Approved by Error," *Stanford Daily*, October 17, 1969.

23 "Housing Report Challenges Quality of Frat Life, Traditional Hell Week," *Stanford Daily*, February 14, 1967. Not all of the subcommittee's 17 men (10 active fraternity members, 3 deactivated fraternity members, 3 freshmen, and 1 "unaffiliated" student) were involved in the drafting, or approval, of the report. Earlier in the decade, four fraternity chapters had had major conflicts with their national boards over pledging Jewish or Black students (Alpha Tau Omega, Sigma Nu, Delta Tau Delta, and Sigma Chi). In addition to *Daily* coverage, see Morrison Warren, "My American Story: How I Came to Be Stanford's First Black Recruit," Stanford Athletics (website), reprinted in *Delta Tau Delta Fraternity Rainbow* (Summer 2018) 18–23; David Kiefer, "The Catalyst: Gene Washington and the Rise of Stanford Football," Stanford Athletics (website), February 18, 2021; Mike Antonucci, "What They Stood For," *Stanford* [magazine] (March/April 2014); "On Brotherhood" (letters to the editor), *Stanford* [magazine] May/June 2014.

24 Clay Miller, '69, "This Stanford: Freshman Battle Cry 'Remember the Row'" (column), *Stanford Daily*, February 14, 1967.

25 "Commission Members Charge Bias in Report Conclusions," *Stanford Daily*, February 20, 1967; "Was the Housing Committee's Report Fair?" *Stanford Daily*, February 24, 1967.

26 *Stanford Daily* 1967: "Fraternity Rebuttal to Housing Comm Report," February 21; "Housing Report Due for Scrutiny; Frats Dissent, Deans Impressed," February 21; "IFC Symposium to Study Changes," March 10; "IFC Presidency to Quinn," April 13. On the checkered history of fraternities at Stanford and their conditions in 1985, see Charlie Gofen, "A History of Fraternities at Stanford: They're as Old as the School Itself, But the Relationship Has Been Stormy," *Stanford Daily Magazine*, January 31, 1985.

27 *Stanford Daily:* "Fraternal Discrimination," January 8, 1957; "IFC Passes Unanimous Resolution Condemning Racial Restrictions on Fraternity Membership,"

April 10, 1957; "Commendation," April 12, 1957; "Fraternity Discrimination Banned by Interfraternity Council," May 5, 1968.

28 "Harris Asks Massive Resistance to the Draft," *Stanford Daily*, January 13, 1967.

29 On the Humphrey visit from various Stanford perspectives, see *Stanford Observer* (March 1967); *Stanford Daily*, February 20, 21, 24, and 27, 1967; Lyman (2009) 57–60; Michael Novak, "Humphrey at Stanford," *Commonweal* (March 24, 1967) 7–8; Jay Neugeborn[sic], "Letter from Stanford: Humphrey and the 'Now' Generation," *New Republic* 156:11 (March 18, 1967) 32–35 (Neugeboren was a visiting lecturer in English); and News Service Collection SC0122 series 1, box 14, folder 6, "Demonstrations 1965–67, news clippings, SUA.

30 "Humphrey Welcome Mixed: HHH Stands by President's Policy," *Stanford Daily*, February 21, 1967. A protest was planned beforehand. "Students Plan Protest: Humphrey to Speak on Campus," *Stanford Daily*, February 15, 1967.

31 "Humphrey Welcome Mixed: HHH Stands by President's Policy," *Stanford Daily*, February 21, 1967.

32 March 17, 1967, in SC0216 box B1. "Chaos Reigns in Secret Service Over Humphrey Security Measures," *Stanford Daily*, February 21, 1967; "Crowd a Problem for Secret Service: Yelling Students Jam Street, Slow Humphrey's Exit," *Stanford Daily*, February 21, 1967, records the confusion and shouting, but adds that the crowd did not appear to impede Humphrey's progress.

33 "National Newspapers Deplore Student 'Attack' on Humphrey," *Stanford Daily*, February 27, 1967. Lyman quotes an eyewitness: "[Humphrey] damn well did not enjoy the taunts he could hear, but he kept up a slow, deliberate pace and if his expression varied from one of terse neutrality, it was only in the moments when someone called a friendly greeting." Lyman (2009) 58.

34 *Washington Post*, February 22, 1967, in SC0216 box B1.

35 "Humphrey Welcome Mixed: HHH Stands by President's Policy," *Stanford Daily*, February 21, 1967; Stanford News Service press release, March 6, 1967; "President Sterling: 'Deep Concern for Free Debate,'" *Stanford Observer* (March 1967). See also "Sterling, V.P. Deplore 'Welcome,'" *Stanford Daily*, March 7, 1967.

36 "When Students Heckled Mr. Humphrey," *U.S. News and World Report* (March 6, 1967) 8.

37 "$2,000 Postage: Sterling, V.P. Deplore 'Welcome,'" *Stanford Daily*, March 7, 1967.

38 "Lyman Admits Lack of Evidence for Proposed Disciplinary Action," *Stanford Daily*, March 10, 1967; "$2,000 Postage: Sterling, V.P. Deplore 'Welcome,'" *Stanford Daily*, March 7, 1967. See also opposing letters to the editor by Mary Hanson, who was involved in the march to the President's Office, and Tom Reavely, *Stanford Daily*, March 9, 1967.

39 March 15, 1967, in SC0216 box B1.

40 May 1, 1967, in SC0216 box B1.

41 March 15, 1967, in SC0216 box B1.

42 SC0216 box B1. Jay Neugenboren had been among those who marched to the President's Office on March 9. Soon after, he published his "Letter from Stanford" in the *New Republic* 156:11 (March 18, 1967) 32–35.

43 March 14, 1967, to Sterling, and response, March 30, 1967, in SC0216 box B1.

44 "Harris Resigns Presidency," *Stanford Daily,* February 23, 1967. He announced his resignation February 21 in an open letter to the student body and an interview with the *Stanford Daily,* published two days later (the *Daily* did not publish on February 22).

45 "Harris Resigns Presidency," *Stanford Daily,* February 23, 1967. Their goals were to encourage American men of draft age to refuse to cooperate with the draft, thereby overwhelming the draft boards, courts, and prisons so that the Selective Service could not continue to prosecute draft resisters. He wanted resisters to serve as moral examples themselves, knowingly facing $10,000 fines and up to five years in prison. See "The Boys Who Said NO! Draft Resistance and the Vietnam War," film directed by Judith Ehrlich, Kind Earth Productions, 2020 documentary and website.

46 "Harris Resignation Fails to Incite Strong Reaction," *Stanford Daily*, February 27, 1967.

47 Ibid.

48 *Stanford Daily* 1967: "Collins Proposes Unity of Effort," February 27; "ASSU Plans Weekend Seminars as Supplement to Packer Study," March 7; "*In Loco Parentis* Discussed," April 27.

49 "SRI Protesters Get Protests and Denials," *Stanford Daily*, April 14, 1967.

50 The Experiment charged a membership fee of $10, which was not always paid, to supplement its ASSU funding (which largely went to its catalog and publication, *Commitment*). Teachers, mostly grad students, were expected to volunteer. By winter quarter, 32 classes were offered on a wide array of subjects, from "existentialism and political commitment" and "Spanish for Revolutionaries" to sculpture and writing lyrics for rock music. Courses aimed at helping students find themselves rather than to train themselves, but some were practical efforts, such as helping with East Palo Alto's incorporation. *Stanford Daily* 1966: "'Experiment' Started; Will Offer Education Beyond the Classroom," September 28; "The Experiment," October 3; "Greenberg Parodies Stanford Awareness," October 5; "'Experiment' Starts Plans," November 17; "Experiment to Offer Additional Seminars," December 1.

51 "Dissent!" *Stanford Daily*, April 14, 1967. The four trustees were David Packard, William Hewlett, Roger Lewis, and Charles Ducommun. Campus police initially were told to take down the posters, then told to leave them. "Vietnam Posters Torn Down by Police," *Stanford Daily*, April 12, 1967.

52 *Stanford Daily* 1967: Leonard Siegel, "Who's Accusing" (letter to the editor), April 19; "The Experiment Seeks Greater Communication Among Members," April 27; "Politics in The Experiment: Asset or Albatross?" May 8. Clay L. Miller, "Has LASSU Betrayed Us to the 'Political Weirdos'?" May 1. The debate about the viability and influence of the Experiment continued in the pages of the *Daily* from mid-April through May. The Experiment and the Free University celebrated their merger with a Palo Alto park "Be-In," accompanied by the Grateful Dead. "Mary Poppins Umbrella Festival, Be-In Scheduled for Sunday," *Stanford Daily,* June 30.

53 "Peter Lyman Resigns," "News Analysis: Non-Political President," "Trend for Presidents: Harris Quit Same Position," *Stanford Daily,* November 27, 1967. Lyman (1940–2007) received his B.A. (1962) and Ph.D. (1972) from Stanford and M.A. from UC Berkeley (1963). He served on the faculty at Michigan State until his move to USC in 1987, where he became dean of university libraries in 1991. An expert in academic computing, he joined the UC Berkeley faculty in 1994 and became university librarian. He was fondly remembered as calm and serene, but willing to fight infinite battles against bureaucracies. See also Richard Lyman (2009) 200–01.

54 *Stanford Daily* 1967: "Versatile New President: Massarenti Assumes Office," "Cesare as President" (editorial), and "In Glass Houses: Goodnight Peter—Goodnight! Cesare?" all November 28. During his years at Bocconi University, Milan, he was elected four consecutive years as president of an organization representing all university students in Milan, 1960–64. After receiving his laurea (master's degree) in economics in 1964, he received a scholarship to study at Stanford, arriving with his wife in 1965. He received his M.A. in sociology in 1969. He retired from a business career and university teaching in 2015 but continues to consult in energy savings and efficiency.

55 *Stanford Daily:* "Lyman Blasts Draft," February 21, 1968. "We Will Not Fight in Vietnam," April 25, 1967; "A Declaration of Conscience," May 24, 1967.

56 *Stanford Daily*, November 2 and 3, 1967; *Stanford Observer*, November 1967. Lyman (2009) 61–63. For another perspective, see Friedman in Jeanne Friedman, Georgia Kelly, and Lenny Siegel, "The Roots of the Stanford Peace Movement," *Sandstone & Tile* 35:1 (Winter 2011) 17. Encina West Wing, site of the interviews, was vacant, pending reconstruction for the Food Research Institute. Both Sterling, in his memoirs, and Glover in Frederic O. Glover, oral history interview conducted by Harry Press, Don Carlson, and Roxanne Nilan (1993)

session three, SOHP, SUA, misidentified this crisis as involving Dow Chemical Company interviews, rather than the CIA. Dow was the target of a similar protest at the University of Wisconsin, where 3 police officers and 65 students were injured in a two-day event when police shut down the demonstration. Madison became a focal point of the national antiwar movement.

57 "Disciplinary Action Initiated Against CIA Demonstrators," *Stanford Daily*, November 10, 1967; "Students Refuse to Hear Encina CIA Protest Case," *Stanford Daily*, November 21, 1967.

58 "Legislature Ends Tie to Judiciary," *Stanford Daily*, November 22, 1967; "The Judicial Crisis," *Stanford Daily,* December 1, 1967.

59 "Committee of 15," *Stanford Quad* (1966) 85 notes that C-15 was only an advisory committee, but the quality of its membership commanded attention. The group tried, not always successfully, to avoid politics by insisting that each member act on conscience, not as a representative of a constituency. Agenda items ranged from the immediate—the closing of the Union residence—to issues relating to student advising and the nature of the Fundamental Standard. Members were selected by the Executive Committee of the Academic Council (faculty), the student legislature (students), and the president (staff).

60 "CIA Pickets Sent to Judicial Council," *Stanford Daily*, January 3, 1967.

61 "Three Who Shaped a Decade: Student Activists of a Generation Ago Look Back, Forward," *Stanford Daily*, June 1, 1994.

62 Full texts of April 4 statements by Lyman and the BSU are in Philip Taubman, "Campus Reaction: Agony and Apathy," *Stanford Daily*, April 5, 1968. See also "Martin Luther King Jr. Murdered," *Stanford Daily*, April 5, 1968.

63 *Stanford Observer* (April 1968); "Grieve Not for Dr. King, Grieve for a Nation Torn," *Stanford Daily,* April 8, 1968. On Brown's civil rights work, see Chapter 15.

64 "Campus Reaction: Agony and Apathy," *Stanford Daily*, April 5, 1968.

65 *The Study of Education at Stanford: Report to the University* (Stanford: Stanford University, 1968–69) "Minority-Group Students at Stanford—An Interim Report," April 2, 1968, in vol. IV, "Undergraduate Admissions and Financial Aid," 58–71. Statistics from pages 59–60.

66 Lyman (2009) 68–69; Robert M. Rosenzweig, oral history interview conducted by Don Carlson, Karen Bartholomew, and Roxanne Nilan (1984) 42, SOHP, SUA.

67 Lyman (2009) 70–71. Lyman provides a largely sympathetic overview, 1964–69, of the issues, events, and some of the outcomes surrounding the BSU demands, pp. 68–89.

68 Steven C. Phillips in his *Justice and Hope: Past Reflections and Future Visions of the Stanford Black Student Union*

1967–1989 (Stanford: Black Student Union, 1990) 6. During the 1960s, the number of Black students slowly increased "from invisible to the barely perceptible," Phillips notes, but points to mid-60s contributions by Gene Washington, '69 (Delta Tau Delta), and Senior Class President Ira Hall, '66, MBA '76 (Alpha Tau Omicron), a future Stanford trustee (1970–74), among others.

69 Joyce King quoted in Barbara Wilcox, "Taking the Mic: Black Students Seek Representation in Education," Stanford Graduate School of Education, 2014 (available online). See also "Negroes at Stanford: One Percent Hardly Enough," *Stanford Daily*, February 23, 1967, and "White, Middle Class Stanford: Blacks Undergo Difficult Transition," *Stanford Daily*, May 20, 1968, regarding the individual views and experiences of interviewed Black undergraduates.

70 Jean McCarter Leonard, oral history interview, Diversity Project, conducted by Katherine Toy (2011) 14–15, SOHP, SUA; Jean McCarter Leonard, oral history interview, Alumni Stories: Class of 1957 (2007) 2, SOHP, SUA; Raymond F. Bacchetti, oral history interview conducted by Susan W. Schofield (2010) 16, SOHP, SUA.

71 SES vol. IV, Admissions & Financial Aid, "Minority-Group Students at Stanford" (1968) 66–67. The report was researched and drafted by Associate Provost Robert M. Rosenzweig and John D. Black, director of counseling and testing.

72 Ray Bacchetti, who was among those who would tackle institutional racism during his long career at Stanford, viewed the argument of "We don't want them to fail here; we'd rather have them succeed someplace else," as condescension disguised as looking after their well-being. Bacchetti (2010) 20–21.

73 SES vol. IV, Admissions & Financial Aid, "Minority-Group Students at Stanford" (1968) 65–66. "Minorities Admitted to Stanford Should Have Financial Aid Priority, Says Clebsch Report," *Stanford Observer* (April 1968).

74 Interact was founded in January 1967. "Negro Group to Fill 'Leadership Vacuum,'" *Stanford Daily*, February 15, 1967. Ron Miller comments on his Stanford experience in "Negroes at Stanford: One Percent Hardly Enough," *Stanford Daily,* February 23, 1967.

75 "Plan Magazine: Black Union Formed," *Stanford Daily,* October 19, 1967. Johnie Scott, an early BSU leader, emphasized that the BSU was not a melting pot of ideas, nor an organ for "Black bourgeois intelligentsia fronts," but "is every Black face on this campus involved in some sort of meaningful social action." Johnie Scott, "Black Student Union Intends Action," *Stanford Daily*, November 15, 1967. Social anthropologist James Lowell Gibbs Jr. (1931–) (B.A. Cornell 1952 and Ph.D. Harvard 1960) joined Stanford's faculty as an associate professor in 1966 from the University of Minnesota. Gibbs, an expert on African law and society, helped found Stanford's

NOTES TO PAGES 498–502 | 627

African and Afro-American Studies Program, serving as its acting director (1968–69) until he recruited noted scholar and anthropologist St. Claire Drake as director. Gibbs later served as Stanford's first dean of undergraduate studies (1970–76) and chair of the Anthropology Department (1987–90). He was named Stanford's first Martin Luther King Jr. Centennial Professor of Anthropology in 1988, becoming emeritus in 1997. See James Lowell Gibbs Jr., oral history interview, Diversity Series, conducted by Ray Bacchetti (2011), SOHP, and James Lowell Gibbs Jr., oral history interview conducted by Joyce Kiefer (2015), SOHP, SUA.

76 On the history of the BSU and the issues behind the 1967–68 events, see Phillips (1990); Wilcox (2014); *Black70* (Stanford: Black Student Union, 1970), edited by Joyce King. The first issue of *Black on Black*, a magazine of essays, poetry, stories, and illustrations, edited by Delores Mack and Charlotte Washington, came out November 13, 1967. See also interviews in "Taking the Mic: 50 Years Later" series in Black Alumni Stories and Oral Histories, SC1473, SUA, and interviews in the "Diversity Project, 2009–13," SOHP, SC0932, SUA (particularly David Abernethy, Raymond F. Bacchetti, Mary Montle Bacon, John Bunnell, Robert M. Rosenzweig, and Willard G. Wyman Jr.).

77 "Taking the Mic: 50 Years Later: A Panel Discussion with Mary Montle Bacon, Warren C. Hayman, Frank J. Omowale Satterwhite, and Keni Washington moderated by Rosalind Conerly," April 8, 2019, in SC1473, pg. 17.

78 Louis Knowles, "The Outposts: White Paternalism Flourishes," *Stanford Daily*, October 11, 1967. In 1967–68, there were 22 Black graduate students in the School of Education, the largest representation of Stanford's graduate programs. SES vol. IV, Admissions & Financial Aid, "Minority-Group Students at Stanford" (1968) 60.

79 *Stanford Daily* 1968: Karenga, a Black nationalist and founder and chairman of the Us Cultural Center in Watts, spoke on the Black cultural revolution, February 16; "BSU Spring Talks, Panels Announced," April 8; "Damaging and Irrelevant: BSU Hits White Education," April 11.

80 "BSU Head Hits Racism Here," *Stanford Daily*, April 3, 1968.

81 Washington, in "Taking the Mic Panel Discussion" (2019) 12, 13, 16. Phil Taubman was among those escorting King and his assistant from and back to San Francisco Airport. On King's speech, see "Martin Luther King Sets 'True Equality' as Goal" and "'Sense of Direction' Needed: King Views Vietnam, Education," *Stanford Daily*, April 17, 1967.

82 Fifteen units of spring quarter academic credit had been offered. "Washington Work-Study Gets Support from 3 Departments," *Stanford Daily*, March 15, 1968. The effort was canceled April 11, 1968.

83 Bacon, in "Taking the Mic Panel Discussion" (2019) 15.

84 "Many Classes Canceled: 'Response to Racism' Today," *Stanford Daily,* April 8, 1968.

85 Ibid. Washington quoted in "University Answers Black Demands," *Stanford Daily*, April 10, 1968.

86 Washington, in "Taking the Mic Panel Discussion" (2019) 18, 19, 21.

87 Washington and Satterwhite, in "Taking the Mic Panel Discussion" (2019) 16–17. SES vol. IV, Admissions & Financial Aid, "Minority-Group Students at Stanford" (1968) 58.

88 "LASSU Confirms that TGRs Can Vote," *Stanford Daily*, February 16, 1968.

89 List of demands in "Black Student Union Presents Demands: Text of Statement Yesterday by Black Student Union," *Stanford Daily,* April 9, 1968. Lyman (2009) 73–75. See also Frank J. Omowale Satterwhite, oral history interview, Taking the Mic: 50 Years Later [series], conducted by Daniel Hartwig (2019) SOHP, SC1473, SUA.

90 "University Answers Black Demands," *Stanford Daily*, April 9, 1968. Taking the Mic Panel Discussion (2019) 17–19. Phillips (1990) 16.

91 Willard G. Wyman Jr., an oral history interview conducted by Erika Amaya (2011) 21, 23, SOHP, SUA. Keni Washington, oral history interview, Taking the Mic: 50 Years Later [series], conducted by Daniel Hartwig (2019) 17, SOHP, SC1473, SUA.

92 Wyman (2011) 19.

93 "Sterling's Statement," *Stanford Daily*, April 9, 1968. Asking the BSU to meet, it stated: "Dialogue does not take place in mass meetings. It takes place when men of good will, recognizing that none of them has truth in his exclusive possession, resolve to discuss their common problems."

94 Wyman (2011) 21, 22. As to who called for the recess, Wyman misremembered it as Packer, but it was Washington, according to Lyman (2009) 79. Wyman (2011) 18, commented, "moving policy at an academic institution is tantamount to moving a graveyard."

95 At the April 8 moratorium, Lyman announced the Human Relations Commission, to be chaired by law Professor Byron Sher. Faculty members and one student had already been selected. Additional members were added on recommendation of the BSU. "University Answers Black Demands," and "You Agree!" (editorial), *Stanford Daily*, April 9, 1968.

96 "Open Meeting: University, BSU Agree on Nine of Ten points," *Stanford Daily*, April 10, 1968. At the meeting were administrators Vice Provost Herbert Packer, Associate Provost Robert Rosenzweig, Vice President for Finance Kenneth Cuthbertson, and Associate Dean of Students Willard Wyman; professors Robert McAfee Brown, Kenneth Arrow, and Donald Kennedy (a member of the Human Relations Commission); and

BSU members Ken Washington, Charles Countee, Frank Satterwhite, and Letitia Carter. Professor James Gibbs, the BSU advisor, also attended. Lyman (2009) 78–79.

97 Attending the Thursday meeting for the BSU were Washington, Countee, Satterwhite, Warren Hayman (principal of Belle Haven Elementary School in east Menlo Park), Mary Montle, Delores Mack, and BSU advisor Jim Gibbs. Lyman, Packer, Cuthbertson, Brown, Arrow, and Rosenzweig represented the administration and faculty. "University, BSU End Conflict; Academic Council Offers Plan," *Stanford Daily*, April 12, 1968, and "Administration Answer" (editorial), *Stanford Daily*, April 12, 1968. See also Lyman (2009) 79–83.

98 On the Tresidder store incident that triggered the demand, see Lyman (2009) 80–81; Rosenzweig (1984) 46–47; and Robert M. Rosenzweig, oral history interview conducted by Ray Bacchetti (2009) 10–11, SOHP, SUA. Rosenzweig commented: "I don't blame them. I handled that really, really badly." Rosenzweig (2009) 11. Robert M. Rosenzweig (1931–) (B.A., M.A. Michigan 1951, 1952, Yale Ph.D. 1956) came to Stanford in 1962 as associate dean of the Graduate Division and lecturer in the Political Science Department. In 1967, he was appointed associate provost and director of the Center for Research in International Studies. He was later vice provost (1971–74) and vice president for public affairs (1974–83), leaving to become president of the Association of American Universities (1983–93), then president emeritus. Records on various minority affairs issues and committees are in the Robert M. Rosenzweig Papers, SC0091 (including the March 1968 East Palo Alto Day School/TMU discrimination complaint, box 2), and in SC0632, SUA.

99 Rosenzweig (1984) 45, and Rosenzweig (2009) 16, give slightly different wording.

100 Simmons, hired in May, arrived in September. A graduate of Hampton Institute (B.S. 1955) and Harvard (M.Ed. 1963), Simmons had served as deputy director of the Upward Bound program in the Office of Economic Opportunity, and as executive director of CONNTAC, a statewide program in linking Connecticut colleges and secondary schools. "Black Administrator Fills New Administrative Post," *Stanford Daily*, September 23, 1968. In 1973, he left the office, recommending integration of the needs of Black students with those of other minority groups and elimination of the separate Black Affairs Office. With more staff and faculty resources for Black students available on campus, he also recommended that its services be redeployed to the Dean of Student Affairs, the Financial Aids Office, and the Graduate Division. See the Records of the Assistant to the President for Black Affairs Office, SC0154, SUA.

101 Wyman (2011) 20, 21, 23, 36.

102 Lyman (2009) 76–77, 82–83, and 219, note 10; Bac-
chetti (2010) 12; Gibbs (2011) 10–11 notes the fortuitous momentum of SES. "Rosenzweig Relieved of Duties, Stanford Bows to BSU," *San Jose Mercury,* April 12, 1968; "Lyman Clarifies BSU Agreements," *Stanford Daily,* April 15, 1968.

103 Lyman (2009) 82–83. Trustee Committee on Academic Affairs meeting minutes April 18 and May 16, 1968, in Board of Trustees Meeting Records, SC1010. Fuller to J. R. White, April 20, 1968, quoted in Lyman (2009) 82–83.

104 Richard W. Lyman, "Richard W. Lyman Reflects on His Life and the Turbulent '60s and '70s," *Sandstone & Tile* 28:2 (Spring-Summer 2004) 8. See, for example, Wyman (2011), Bacchetti (2010), and John Bunnell, oral history interview (on admissions issues) conducted by Susan W. Schofield (2010), SOHP, SUA.

105 "Black Student Union Converts House Into Cultural Arts Center," *Stanford Daily,* April 29, 1969. Previously, the building had been used by *American Anthropologist* magazine. Black House, as it was originally known, is now the Black Community Services Center. A large deck connects the 1920s house and the 2007 separate addition, which features a large room for programs and cultural events. The cottage had been built next to his own house by University Comptroller Almon Roth as space for student renters and later for the foreman of Stanford's outside properties. Robert de Roos, '33, "Stanford Greats: Almon E. Roth: Star Athlete, Comptroller, Planner, and Trustee Also Was Lover of Roses," *Stanford Observer,* May 1988; *Annual Register,* (Stanford University) years 1928–1944 (students listed on Santa Teresa, without number, in earlier *Registers* would have been living in Roth's house or the cottage he built; there were no other student residences on Santa Teresa); "BSCS Raises Funds for Renovations: Nearly $1 Million Has Been Raised in the University-Wide Campaign," *Stanford Daily,* November 11, 2005.

106 Bacon, in Taking the Mic Panel Discussion (2019) 22, 25.

107 "Judicial Council: CIA Protest Opinion" and "Judicial Mess," *Stanford Daily,* February 29, 1968; "Judicial Council Ruling," *Stanford Daily*, April 15, 1967.

108 Lyman (2009) 62.

109 J. E. Wallace Sterling, "The Stanford Presidency 1949–1968: Part II, A Noble Purpose Shared," 86, in SC0415 (1993-061) SUA. "Judicial Mess," *Stanford Daily*, February 29, 1968.

110 *Stanford Daily* 1968: "Judicial Council Ruling," April 15; "IJB Finds Demonstrators Guilty, Asks Suspensions," May 3; and "Letters to the Editor," May 8.

111 "Sterling Rejects Demands as Students Vote Action," *Stanford Daily*, May 6, 1968.

112 Summary of law Professor William Baxter, "Faculty Urges Student Peace" (letter to the editor), *Stanford Daily*, May 6, 1968. See also letters from professors

Hubert Marshall, Kenneth Arrow, and Leonard Schiff, and from graduate student Tom Forestenzer, speaker of LASSU and a member of the Committee of 15, who was active in civil rights and antiwar protests.

113 J. E. Wallace Sterling, "University Policy on Judicial Reform," *Stanford Daily,* May 6, 1968.

114 "Sterling Rejects Demands as Students Vote Action" and editorial page, *Stanford Daily*, May 6, 1968.

115 For details about events surrounding the Old Union sit-in, see *Stanford Daily*, May 3 and May 6–9, 1968, *Stanford Observer* (May 1968), and Lyman (2009) 90–112.

116 "Protesters Holding Old Union While Lyman Rejects Demands," *Stanford Daily,* May 7, 1968. Lyman (2009) 97–100. At this time, the Committee of 15 was chaired by political science Professor Hubert Marshall.

117 Memo to Board, May 13, 1968, in SC0216 box C6.

118 Ibid. "Protesters Holding Old Union as Lyman Rejects Demands," *Stanford Daily,* May 7, 1968, and "Three Days of Protest: Students Comment on Sit-In," *Stanford Daily*, May 9, 1968, point out the relative quiet, and that police remained distant but interacted easily with the students, and that little office work got done.

119 "C-15 Judicial Overhaul," *Stanford Daily*, May 8, 1968.

120 Cassius Kirk Jr. memorandum, February 11, 1965, in SC0216 box C5.

121 Minutes of the Academic Council, May 8, 1968, in Faculty Senate Records, SC0193 (Arch 1989-214) box 3. *Stanford Observer* (May 1968) and the *Stanford Daily,* May 9, 1968. See also Lyman (2009) 102–06.

122 Minutes of the Academic Council, May 8, 1968, op. cit.

123 Donald Stokes, "The Sterling Touch: How Stanford Became a World Class University," *Stanford Observer* (November 1979).

124 Stokes (November 1979). Sterling, in his memoirs, discreetly does not name the professor but Fred Glover identifies Holman, and remembers the Holman-Sterling interchange somewhat differently, and with less sympathy for Holman, in Glover (1993) session three. Prof. Arthur D. Howard recounts the "spectacle of one member storming uninvited to the podium, shouldering President Sterling aside, grabbing the microphone . . ." in his letter to the editor, *Stanford Daily*, May 16, 1968.

125 "Sit-In Ended as Academic Council Supports Amnesty, No Suspensions," *Stanford Daily*, May 9, 1968. Sterling, "The Stanford Presidency: Part II, A Noble Purpose Shared," 88. The vote count varies by source. The May 8, 1968, minutes of the Academic Council officially recorded the vote as 284 affirmative, 241 negative, and 1 abstention. *The Stanford Observer* (June 1968) reported 284 to 241; Sterling also used those numbers in his May 18, 1968, Campus Conference speech. In its inaugural issue, however, *Campus Report*, September 18, 1968, said the tally had been 284 to 245; the *Stanford Daily* reported those same numbers May 9, 1968.

126 Stokes (November 1979). Lyman (2009) 104–05. The resolution was presented by Professor Mark Mancall and "carried by acclamation." Minutes of the Academic Council, May 8, 1968, op. cit. Wrote Arthur Howard, "The victors, having undercut the administration's position then proposed a vote of confidence in the President and his administration, a move which some of us felt was hypocritical…I wonder, had the vote gone against them, whether this group would still have proposed a vote of confidence in the administration" (letter to the editor), *Stanford Daily*, May 16, 1968.

127 Stokes (November 1979); Sterling, "The Stanford Presidency: Part II, A Noble Purpose Shared," 90.

128 Stokes (November 1979). Lyman (2009) 106–07. Lyman recalled a brief exchange with a *Stanford Daily* reporter after the Academic Council meeting. A May 10 *Daily* editorial urged him not to resign, stating: "Provost Richard W. Lyman made mistakes in dealing with the sit-in, but much of what he did not do saved this university. He did not order in the police. He tried in all sincerity and commitment to his conscience to deal with the crisis, even if others disagree with his actions and thoughts. . . . In this time of division and unrest on campus, Stanford needs Richard Lyman, and we urge him to stay."

129 Stokes (November 1979).

130 "Sit-In Ended as Academic Council Supports Amnesty, No Suspensions," *Stanford Daily*, May 9, 1968; "Sterling Grants Demands" and "The Sterling-Lyman Statement," *Stanford Daily*, May 10, 1968.

131 "Many Oppose Sit-In," *Stanford Daily,* May 8, 1968.

132 Ibid. "Hayes Wins, Cesare Censured; Students Vote to Keep ASSU," *Stanford Daily,* May 16, 1968.

133 *Stanford Daily* 1968: "Drake, Hayes Face ASSU Final Election, May 9; "Drake vs. Hayes: ASSU Race Starts Today," May 14; and "Hayes Wins, Cesare Censured; Students Vote to Keep ASSU," May 16.

134 "Statement of the Committee of Fifteen," and "C-15 Issues Final Plan for Stanford Judiciary," *Stanford Daily*, May 31, 1968; "Judicial Council Gains Faculty Jurisdiction," *Stanford Daily*, October 21, 1968. Cases involving faculty salaries or dismissal were adjudicated by the Advisory Board of the Academic Council, as before.

135 Memo to Board, March 13, 1968, in SC0216 box C6. "Another Columbia" was a potent faculty fear, recalling the Columbia campus demonstrations of April 1968 that ended with the intervention of New York City police; 132 students, 4 faculty, and 12 police officers were injured, and 700 demonstrators arrested. Protests continued during May, resulting in yet more violence, and the escalating unrest that would damage Columbia's reputation on many fronts. See also Gordon Craig's comments in his May 9, 1968, diary entry, quoted in Lyman (2009) 106.

136 "Sterling Grants Demands," *Stanford Daily*, May 10, 1968, and "Profiling a Student Radical: Weissman Explains Views," *Stanford Daily*, May 15, 1968. Herb Packer challenged the faculty to think more carefully about the implications of their vote as the campus moved from politics by debate to political brinksmanship, in his subsequent remarks, May 13, to the Stanford chapter of the Association of University Professors. He also predicted some of the key crises to come in the next few years. See *Stanford Observer* (May 1968), and "Packer Warns Faculty of 'Politics by Confrontation,'" *Sandstone & Tile* 28:2 (Spring-Summer 2004) 10–11. For an insightful view of his father's experiences at this time, see George Packer, *Blood of the Liberals* (New York, Farrar, Straus and Giroux, 2000).

137 Packer's letter quoted in Lyman (2009) 110.

138 Sterling, May 13, 1968, to a friend in Bethesda, Maryland, who wrote to him May 10, in SC0216 box C6. "Nettle, danger," is from Shakespeare's *Henry IV,* Part 1, Act 2, Scene 3.

139 May 10 and May 8, 1968, in SC0216 box C6.

140 SC0216 box C6.

141 From a commentary by an alumnus in the *Monterey Peninsula Herald*, reprinted in the May 5, 1968, *Palo Alto Times*.

142 May 10, 1968, in SC0216 box C6.

143 June 5, 1968, in SC0216 box C6. Charles Emil Ducommun (1913–91; Stanford '35 and Harvard MBA) was president, 1950–73, and chairman of the board of Ducommun Incorporated until his retirement, in 1978. He was an influential Los Angeles area civic and cultural leader, supporting major museums and classical music organizations. He was also active in Republican state and national campaigns. He served on the Stanford Board of Trustees 1961–71. The Ducommun Company, founded by his grandfather, is one of California's oldest businesses, beginning as a general store during the 1849 Gold Rush. It went on to become a successful hardware company, and later was part of the state's early aerospace industry.

144 SC0216 box C6.

145 May 9, 1968, in SC0216 box C6.

146 Wallace Sterling, "Campus Conference 18 May 1968" in Sterling Speeches files, Stanford News Service. His speech was excerpted at length in the May 1968 *Stanford Observer;* the event also is referred to in Stokes (November 1979) and in Sterling, "The Stanford Presidency: Part II, A Noble Purpose Shared," 90–91.

147 June 7, 1968, in SC0216 box C6.

148 Stanford News Service press releases, July 5 and July 10, 1968. Email from Ray Bacchetti to editor Karen Bartholomew, May 6, 2014, said that gasoline had been poured into his file cabinet drawers, in his office above Sterling's, but the files were so tightly packed that they did not burn.

149 Sterling, "The Stanford Presidency: Part II, A Noble Purpose Shared," 93–95.

150 In August 1960, Phi Gamma Delta (Fiji) house burnt to the ground. In 1961, fire destroyed the International Student Center at 539 Lasuen, and an electrical fire caused extensive damage to the Kappa Sigma fraternity house. See Theresa Johnston, "When Students Fought Fires," *Stanford* [magazine] (July/August 2002), on the transition, and the experiences of firefighters during the difficult years, 1968–72. "Some student firefighters sympathized with the antiwar movement," she noted, "whereas many of the pros were military veterans who detested the longhaired protesters. But both the amateurs and the pros knew they had to work together—particularly when the campus exploded in a string of suspicious conflagrations."

151 Speaking about this and later cases of arson on campus, Richard Lyman commented, "Every time we had a case of arson, the FBI would be in my office the next day saying, 'We're going to solve this,' and that was the last I saw of them. Arson's a tough crime. It burns its own evidence." Lyman (2004) 12.

152 Jane Morgan, "The Fire Comes Home," *Midpeninsula Observer,* July 1968, quoted in Lyman (2009) 110–11.

153 Lyman (2009) 110–11.

154 Glover (1993) session three; Beyers, "All the News," *Sandstone & Tile* 17:1 (Winter 1993) 18; recollection of Stanford firefighter Robert Bartholomew, father of editor Karen Bartholomew.

155 Hayes to Sterling, July 5, 1968, in Sterling News Releases file 1961–69, Stanford News Service.

156 Stokes (November 1979). Sterling, "The Stanford Presidency: Part II, A Noble Purpose Shared," 94. In his oral history, Glover said that two folders were found on the floor after the fire, one on SRI and a file of clippings about Professor H. Bruce Franklin. He said he had earlier told Franklin about the clips file and invited him to come see it, but Franklin never came. Glover (1993) session three.

CHAPTER 21: CHANCELLOR STERLING

1 *Stanford Daily*, April 3, 1967; see also *Palo Alto Times*, March 24, 1967; *Los Angeles Times*, March 24, 1967. The trustees had known for several years of Sterling's desire to step down, according to trustee President Richard Guggenhime.

2 Stanford News Service press release, March 24, 1967, and "Sterling Announces Retirement, Is Named Chancellor," *Stanford Observer* (April 1967).

3 Ibid.

4 "Commencement 1968," in J. E. Wallace Sterling: Speeches and Quotations file, 1965–present, Stanford News Service.

5 Ibid.

6 J. E. Wallace Sterling, "The Stanford Presidency: Part II, A Noble Purpose Shared," 95–96, in J. E. Wallace Sterling Personal Papers and Memorabilia, SC0415 (arch 1993-061), SUA. J. E. Wallace Sterling: News Clips files, 1967, 1968, Stanford News Service.

7 [Patrick McMahon], editorial, *Stanford Daily*, May 31, 1968.

8 Stanford News Service press release, June 17, 1968, regarding the Academic Council's June 14 meeting.

9 Stanford News Service press release, June 3, 1968.

10 The first recipient of the Sterling professorship was internationally known historian Gordon Craig. Richard W. Lyman also was a recipient.

11 "The Man from Stanford," *San Francisco Chronicle,* September 8, 1968.

12 Fred Glover, seeking to know the source of Pitzer's nomination, was told by John Gardner that Roger Lewis was the trustee responsible. "Frederic O. Glover, An Oral History Interview Conducted by Harry Press, Don Carlson, and Roxanne Nilan" (1993) session four, Stanford Oral History Project, SUA. It also should be noted that Stanford trustee H. Gardiner Symonds was a trustee of Rice University. Lewis, on the board from 1964 to 1982, was a Lockheed and General Dynamics executive and a former assistant secretary of the Air Force under President Eisenhower.

13 On announcing the appointment, trustee President W. Parmer Fuller III told the *Stanford Daily*, "Dr. Pitzer's academic credentials are of the highest order, and his record as president of Rice University is an enviable one. I have found him to be a man of ability, integrity, understanding, and fairness." Pitzer had just completed a $33 million fundraising drive when his new position was announced. *Stanford Daily,* September 20, 1968. Kenneth S. Pitzer (1914–97), who took office December 1, 1968, had received his B.S. from Caltech in 1935, and his Ph.D. from UC Berkeley in 1937, when he joined the Berkeley faculty. He served as dean of the College of Chemistry, 1951–60. He was appointed Rice University's third president in 1961.

14 *Stanford Daily*, July 9, 1968.

15 *Stanford Daily,* October 15, 1968.

16 See, for example, "Robert M. Rosenzweig: An Interview Conducted by Don Carlson, Karen Bartholomew, and Roxanne Nilan, Stanford Oral History Project" (1984) 32–35.

17 J. E. Wallace Sterling, "The Stanford Presidency: Part III[b], Some Extracurricular Activities," 17, in J. E. Wallace Sterling Personal Papers and Memorabilia, SC0415 (arch 1993-061), SUA. (On this page, Sterling misremembers his trustee service as 1972–76.) Glover (1993) session four.

18 Fred H. Merrill (1907–81), former president and director of Fireman's Fund Insurance Company, served on the Board of Trustees from 1964 to 1977.

19 Stanford News Service press releases, April 9, 1974, and May 2, 1977, and Fact Sheet on Campaign for Stanford, May 2, 1977. Terman Engineering Center, completed in 1977, was demolished two years after the 2010 construction of its expanded replacement, the Huang Engineering Center.

20 Pitzer's short tenure as Stanford's sixth president (December 1, 1968, to September 1, 1970) was rocked by student protests and waning trustee confidence. Exhausted and tired of spending more time as mediator than as academic administrator, he announced in June 1970, 19 months after his arrival, that he was leaving. He returned to UC Berkeley and a fruitful career as a teacher, researcher, and administrator, retiring in 1984. "Former Stanford President Renowned Chemist Ken Pitzer Dies," Stanford News Service press release, January 6, 1998, and Robert F. Curl, "Kenneth Sanborn Pitzer, 1914–1997," *National Academy of Sciences Biographical Memoir*, 2009. See also *Kenneth Sanborn Pitzer: Chemist and Administrator at UC Berkeley, Rice University, and Stanford University, and the Atomic Energy Commission 1935–1997,* an oral history conducted 1996–1998, by Sally S. Hughes and Germaine Leberge, eds. (Berkeley: Regional Oral History Office, The Bancroft Library, UC Berkeley, 1999). Pitzer died while this interview series was in progress and before he could speak at length about Stanford.

21 Sterling, "The Stanford Presidency: Part III[b] Some Extracurricular Activities," 17. Glover (1993) session four. A 1998 interview with Pitzer's wife, Jean, augmenting Pitzer's oral history (cited above), suggests that they were unaware of a number of events that had taken place at Stanford, and of efforts well underway, before their arrival. She believed strongly that her husband made excellent progress at Stanford, particularly in smoothing out faculty relations. For another perspective on President and Mrs. Pitzer as first couple of the university, Pitzer's interactions with senior administrative staff, and some major controversies during his tenure, see Glover (1993) session four.

22 Unless otherwise noted, the authors' source here and throughout this section on the Bicentennial Commission is Sterling, "The Stanford Presidency: Part III[b], Some Extracurricular Activities," 18–27, and "Sterling Head of Birthday Commission," *Stanford Daily*, September 29, 1969. Sterling kept extensive files regarding the commission. See J. E. Wallace Sterling Chancellorship Papers, SC0333, series 1, boxes 16–18, 33–34.

23 "Memories of Wally Sterling," *Los Angeles Times* (letter to editor by Godfrey Harris, Los Angeles) July 20, 1985. J. E. Wallace Sterling, "The Stanford Presidency: Part III[c], Travelling à Deux and Otherwise," 47–48. Nixon appeared April 11, 1960, to kick off a San Francisco Bay Area campaign tour. The appearance, broadcast by

KZSU, had been carefully planned by co-sponsors Pi Sigma Alpha and the Political Union, with admission by ticket only.

24 On Wilkinson, see Chapter 16.

25 Hobart (Hobe) Lewis (1910–2011) began a long career, in 1942, at *Reader's Digest,* where he was executive editor for 22 years. He became vice president of the *Digest* in 1961, taking over from *Digest* founders Lila and Dewitt Wallace when they retired, in 1965. He retired in 1976. Lewis traveled with Richard Nixon's 1960 presidential campaign as the Wallaces' deputy.

26 Melbourne L. Spector (1918–2009), a personnel management specialist who had recently retired from the State Department, had a long career in public service. He briefly served as executive director of the American Revolution Bicentennial Commission. Early in his career, Spector handled personnel matters for Marshall Plan programs that brought economic development to Europe after World War II. He was director of personnel administration for the U.S. Agency for International Development, and later executive director of the State Department's Bureau of Inter-American Affairs, operating U.S. embassies and consulates throughout the Western Hemisphere.

27 Influential Boston politician John William McCormack of Massachusetts (1891–1980), the son of a Canadian hod carrier, served in the House of Representatives from 1928 to 1971, as house majority leader three times, and as speaker of the house from 1962 to 1971. He was an early advocate for civil rights, education, and health-care legislation. A pugnacious partisan while majority leader, he was later deemed "impeccably fair and impartial" as speaker of the house. "Ex-House Speaker John McCormack Dies," *Washington Post*, November 23, 1980.

28 "Memories of Wally Sterling," *Los Angeles Times* (letter to editor by Godfrey Harris, Los Angeles) July 20, 1985.

29 David Mahoney (1923–2000) was a successful marketing executive and one of the most highly paid and highly visible corporate executives in the United States. The former president and CEO of Norton Simon Inc., and an advisor to Nixon, Carter, and Reagan, he later became an influential advocate for brain research. "David Mahoney, a Business Executive and Neuroscience Advocate, Dies at 76," *New York Times*, May 2, 2000.

30 The Order of the British Empire, the most junior and populous order of chivalry of the British and Commonwealth honors system, was founded by George V in 1917 to recognize service by non-military citizens during the Great War. Individuals who are not citizens of the United Kingdom or commonwealth countries receive an honorary award; they may use the post-nominal KBE but not the title "Sir" or "Lady."

31 Sterling, SC0333, series 1, box 3, folders 4 and 5, on his 1957 CBE and 1976 KBE. Sterling was a charter member of the Canadian-American Committee, a nongovernmental group founded in 1956 to improve through discussion and research Canadian-American relations, then at an all-time low. Sterling felt its efforts were instrumental in improving Canadian-American business and trade. An offshoot of the committee's work was creation in 1967 of the British–North American Committee along similar lines. (Sterling stepped down from both committees in 1972.) He was also a member (1962–76) of the American Advisory Board of the Ditchley Foundation, founded in Oxfordshire, England, in 1958 to promote international, but especially British-American, relations through conferences of international interest with participants drawn from the senior ranks of government, business, academia, media, and the military. Sterling's files on these efforts can be found in SC0333: Canadian-American Committee, series 1, boxes 24–25; and Ditchley Foundation, series 2, box 2.

32 J. E. Wallace Sterling, "The Stanford Presidency: Part III[a] Bits and Pieces," 17, in J. E. Wallace Sterling Personal Papers and Memorabilia, SC0415 (arch 1993-061), SUA. Hope later received the KBE, at age 95, in 1998.

33 The award now recognizes Uncommon Citizen, rather than Man (or Woman). It is not given yearly, but only when it is deemed appropriate by the president of the university, as confirmed by the Board of Governors of the Stanford Associates, to honor rare and extraordinary service. As of 2022, it has been awarded to 33 individuals.

34 "Sterling Personifies Stanford's Development as a World-Class University," *Campus Report,* March 15, 1978; Stanford News Service press release, March 10, 1978. In December 1978, Sterling was asked to present his former provost, Fred Terman, with the Uncommon Man award.

35 *Stanford Review* (November–December 1964) 5, 47. Other honorees have included John Gardner, Clark Kerr, and Fred Terman.

36 University of California alumnus James F. Crafts (1899–1980) served on Stanford's Board of Trustees from 1954 to 1968.

37 After Ann Sterling's death, in 1991, the house was sold to a private owner and the property later subdivided.

38 Sterling, "The Stanford Presidency: Part III[b], Some Extracurricular Activities," 27–32. Filoli, considered an outstanding example of early 20th-century architecture and garden design, is a California State Historic Landmark and is listed on the National Register of Historic Places.

39 Filoli.org provides a history of the estate. See also Andrew Purvis, "Filoli: Garden of a Golden Age," *Smithsonian Magazine* (May 2010); Timmy Gallagher, *Filoli* (1991); and Timmy Gallagher, *The Gardens at Filoli* (1999). On the estate as a family residence and extensive display garden, see Lurline Matson Roth, *Matson and*

Roth Family History: A Love of Ships, Horses, and Gardens, an oral history conducted 1980–81 by Suzanne B. Riess (Berkeley: Regional Oral History Office, The Bancroft Library, UC Berkeley, 1982, with extensive appendices).

40 On details of the transition, see Riess' interview with Hadley Osborn, in Roth's oral history, cited above, 136–37.

41 Arthur Hadley Osborn, an expert on rhododendrons, also was director of the American Horticultural Society and had a long association with the University of California Botanical Garden in Berkeley. Osborn promoted to garden superintendent Lucy Erickson Tolmach, who had started as a gardener in Filoli's walled garden. She was director of horticulture when she retired, after 35 years of devoted service.

42 Mary Madison, "Retirement Doesn't Stop Sterling from Dedicated Work for Stanford," *Peninsula Times Tribune*, September 17, 1980.

43 Donald Stokes, "The Sterling Touch," *Stanford Observer* (November 1979). Stokes also worked with Sterling's manuscript memoir. Although there are minor errors in the articles, Sterling reviewed them in manuscript form and was able to suggest corrections, following News Service practice on features stories.

44 "New Governor's Corner Becomes Students' Top Housing Choice," *Campus Report,* November 2, 1983.

CHAPTER 22: DEATH & REMEMBRANCES

1 Sterling to Donald Wilson, March 3, 1964; Sterling to Donald McKay, October 1, 1949, in J. E. Wallace Sterling Presidential Papers, SC0216 box 23.

2 Stanford News Service press release, October 10, 1963. Dr. Russel Lee was his personal physician. He was also attended by internists Austin Clark and William Clark.

3 October 16, 1963, SC0216 box A26.

4 Stanford News Service press release, February 13, 1964.

5 Glover in "A Session on Wally: Transcription of an Oral History about J. E. Wallace Sterling, Recorded for the Stanford University Archives" (1985) 74.

6 Carlson in "Robert M. Rosenzweig: An Interview Conducted by Don Carlson, Karen Bartholomew, and Roxanne Nilan, Stanford Oral History Project" (1984) 87–88. Editor Karen Bartholomew recalls being told more than once by Spyros Andreopoulos, director of the Medical Center News Bureau, 1963–93, that the surgery had not gone well.

7 J. E. Wallace Sterling, "The Stanford Presidency, 1949–1968: "Part III[a], Bits and Pieces," 17, in J. E. Wallace Sterling Personal Papers and Memorabilia, SC0415 (arch 1993-061), SUA.

8 J. E. Wallace Sterling, "The Stanford Presidency, 1949–1968: Part II, A Noble Purpose Shared," 53, and "Part III[c], Travelling *à Deux* and Otherwise," 116–29, esp. 122–24, in J. E. Wallace Sterling Personal Papers and Memorabilia, SC0415 (arch 1993-061), SUA.

9 "An Absent President," *Stanford Daily*, April 22, 1964.

10 Nancy Steffen, "Who is Wallace Sterling: A Profile," *Stanford Daily*, January 12, 1966 (reprinted from a 1964 *Daily* article).

11 "Sterling Announces Retirement, is Named Chancellor," *Stanford Observer* (April 1967); Stanford News Service press release, March 24, 1967.

12 Quotations from statements and eulogies can be found in similar coverage in the *Stanford Observer* (July 1985), *Campus Report,* July 3, 1985, and "J. E. Wallace Sterling, 1906–1985," *Sandstone & Tile*, 9:4 (Summer 1985). See also obituaries in the *New York Times*, July 3, 1985; "Greatness as a Memorial," *Los Angeles Times,* July 5, 1985; and "Uncommon Man," *San Jose Mercury*, July 4, 1985.

13 Working with Glover were Marlene Wine, President's Office; Professor Lyle Nelson, communication; Daryl Pearson, Office of Development; and Don Carlson, Office of Public Affairs. Eight men who had worked closely with Sterling served as ushers: Rixford Snyder, history emeritus and dean of admissions emeritus; Harold Bacon, mathematics emeritus; Donald Winbigler, speech and drama emeritus and academic secretary emeritus; George Knoles, history emeritus; Wayne Vucinich, history emeritus; Harvey Hall, registrar emeritus; Alf Brandin, former vice president for business affairs; and Douglas Walker, dean of admissions, Menlo College. Eric Hutchinson, chemistry emeritus and academic secretary emeritus, served as verger, the person who led the procession of participants to their seats in the chancel.

14 William Wallace Sterling's Remarks Recounted in "Tributes," *Sandstone & Tile* 9:4 (Summer 1985) 16–17, and "More Than 1,000 Attend Sterling Services at Stanford," Stanford News Service press release, July 9, 1985. Photos suggest that this crowd size was overestimated.

FOLLOWING >

Classic image of the Stanford Arboretum on a foggy day, 1962.

LEO HOLUB / STANFORD UNIVERSITY ARCHIVES

BIBLIOGRAPHY

PUBLISHED MATERIALS
(ARTICLES AND BOOKS)

Adamson, Paul, and Marty Arbunich. *Eichler: Modernism Rebuilding the American Dream* (Gibbs Smith, 2002) 198.

"After 30 Years, Three Presidents, Fred Glover Starts a New Life." *Campus Report,* August 3, 1977.

Allen, Peter C. *From the Foothills to the Bay* (Stanford: Stanford Historical Society/Stanford Alumni Association, 1980).

Allen, Peter C. to M. J. Lightbown (letter). *Architectural Forum*, March 6, 1954.

Allen, Wilmer C. *Stanford University School of Medicine: The First Hundred Years* (Stanford School of Medicine, 1959).

The Alway Years, 1957–1964 (Stanford University: School of Medicine, 1964).

Anderson, Kelli. "The Fight for Fair Play," *Stanford* [magazine], September/October 2016.

Andreopoulos, Spyros. "Reinventing the Stanford Medical School: A Conversation with Henry S. Kaplan," *Sandstone & Tile* 32:3 (Fall 2008) 13–21.

"Ann Sterling, Widow of Stanford's Fifth President, Dies at 85," *Campus Report,* August 14, 1991.

Antonucci, Mike. "What They Stood For," *Stanford* [magazine] (March/April 2014).

Baker, Falcon O. "City on the Campus," *The Saturday Evening Post,* December 31, 1955.

Bartholomew, Karen. "Frederic O. Glover: Exceptional Stanford Man," *Sandstone & Tile* 18:1 (Winter 1994) 1–19.

Bartholomew, Karen, and Claude Brinegar. "Leland Stanford's Grand Hotel –or– A Century of Adventure at Encina Hall," *Sandstone & Tile* 24:1 (Winter 2000) 1–35.

Bartholomew, Karen, Claude Brinegar, and Roxanne Nilan. *A Chronology of Stanford University and Its Founders, 1824–2000* (Stanford: Stanford Historical Society, 2001).

Beyers, Bob. "Ken Cuthbertson: Stanford's Financial Architect," *Sandstone & Tile* 24:2/3 (Spring-Summer 2000) 14–21.

[Beyers, Bob.] "Turbulent Waters Run Deep for Hoover, Stanford, Author Says," *Campus Report,* May 4, 1988, 1, 8–10.

Bloch, Felix. "Leonard Isaac Schiff, 1915–1971: A Biographical Memoir," *Biographical Memoirs*, vol. 54, National Academy of Sciences (1983) 300–23.

Bloch, Felix. "William Webster Hansen, 1909–1949: A Biographical Memoir," *Biographical Memoirs*, vol. 27, National Academy of Sciences (1952) 120–37.

"Bob Beyers, Longtime Stanford News Service Director, Dies at 71," *Stanford Report,* October 23, 2002.

"Bob Walker Counted 8000 Students in 15 Years Who Studied Overseas," *Stanford Historical Society Newsletter* 7:4 (Summer 1983) 2–3.

Burdick, Charles. *Ralph Lutz and the Hoover Institution* (Stanford: Hoover Institution Press, 1974).

Butcher, Bernard. "Freedom Summer," *Stanford* [magazine] (July/August 1996).

Butcher, Bernard. "The Making of Project M," *Stanford* [magazine] (May/June 1997).

"California Gold Rush," *Time,* September 22, 1961.

Campbell, Bruce. "Lack of Trust Pervades Campus," *Stanford Daily,* October 28, 1966.

Campbell, Bruce. "Trustees Fall Short of Ideal Standards," *Stanford Daily,* October 20, 1966.

Carlson, Don. "The Lighter Side of Wallace Sterling," *Sandstone & Tile* 9:4 (Summer 1985) 22. Also appeared in *Palo Alto Weekly*, September 4, 1985.

Carlson, Don. "In Memory of Wallace Sterling," *Palo Alto Weekly*, September 4, 1985.

The Case for Stanford (Stanford Pace Program, 1961).

Cavalli, Gary. "Cold War, Warm Welcome," *Stanford* [magazine] (May/June 2005), subsequent Letters to the Editor, "Remembering the Coach," (July/August 2005).

Cherny, Robert W. "'No Proven Communist Should Hold a Position at Stanford': Victor Mikhail Arnautoff, the House Un-American Activities Committee, and Stanford," *Sandstone & Tile* 37:3 (Fall 2013) 3–17.

Cherny, Robert W. *Victor Arnautoff and the Politics of Art* (Urbana, Ill.: University of Illinois Press, 2017).

Chesley, Kate. "Stanford Identifies Its Preferred

Approach for the Future of Searsville Dam and Reservoir," News Service online, May 1, 2015.

Clark, George. *Leland Stanford, War Governor of California, Railroad Builder, and Founder of Stanford University* (Stanford: Stanford University Press, 1931).

"Committee of Trustees Will Conduct Search for New Stanford President," *Stanford Alumni Review* (March 1948) 5.

Crothers, George E. *Founding of the Leland Stanford Junior University* (Stanford: Stanford University Press, 1932).

Cuban, Larry. *How Scholars Trumped Teachers: Change without Reform in University Curriculum, Teaching and Research, 1890–1990* (New York: Teachers College Press, 1999).

Culhane, Molly. "A More than Adequate Dose of Nonsense: Sex, Social Regulation, and Institutional Change in Stanford's Allen Controversy," *Sandstone & Tile* 44:3 (Fall 2020) 10–19.

Cuthbertson, Kenneth M. "Fundraising at Stanford: The First Half Century," *Sandstone & Tile* 14:4 (Fall 1990) 3–6.

Cuthbertson, Kenneth M. "Long Range Financial Planning for Institutions of Higher Education," in *Long Range Planning in Higher Education,* Owen A. Knorr, ed. (Boulder: Western Interstate Commission for Higher Education, 1965).

"Cuthbertson Energized Stanford Fundraising: A Man of Integrity and Conviction," *Stanford Daily*, May 29, 1980.

Davis, Margo, and Roxanne Nilan. *The Stanford Album: A Photographic History, 1885–1945* (Stanford: Stanford University Press, 1989).

Day, Moira, and Marilyn Potts. "Elizabeth Sterling Haynes: Initiator of Alberta Theatre," *Theatre Research in Canada* 8:1 (Spring 1987).

De Roos, Robert. "William Clebsch: 'Super Citizen of Stanford,'" *Sandstone & Tile* 19:3 (Summer 1995) 1–3.

"Deck the Halls with Ivy," *Newsweek* (February 20, 1961) 59.

Dornbusch, Sanford M. "Termanalia: Anecdotes and Reflections about Fred Terman," *Sandstone & Tile* 31:3 (Fall 2007) 2–20.

Doty, Andy. "Stanford and Palo Alto After World War II," *Sandstone & Tile* 18:2 (Spring 1994) 14.

"Dr. Sterling 'Comes Home' to Stanford and Plunges into a Rigorous Schedule of Public Appearances," *Stanford Alumni Review* (May 1949) 7–10.

Duignan, Peter. *The Hoover Institution on War, Revolution and Peace: Seventy-five Years of Its History* (Stanford: Hoover Institution Press, 1989).

Dupen, Douglas W. *The Story of Stanford's 2-Mile-Long Accelerator*, SLAC-R-62 (Stanford: Stanford Linear Accelerator Center, 1966).

Eagleson, Harvey. "William Bennett Munro: A Memoir by Harvey Eagleson," *Caltech Engineering and Science* (January 1960) 31–32, 36.

Edwards, Paul C. "Stanford Today and Tomorrow," *Stanford Alumni Review* (April 1949) 9–15.

Edwards, Paul C. *An Uncommon Man: Paul C. Edwards, His Story and Writings*, edited by Carroll Edwards Beckett (privately printed, 1991).

Elliott, Orrin Leslie. *Stanford University: The First Twenty-Five Years* (Stanford: Stanford University Press, 1937).

Endsley, Dan. "Oasis in the Asphalt," *Stanford Review* (January 1960).

Eurich, Alvin C. "Report of the President, Stanford University, 1947–1948," in *Annual Report of the President of Stanford University…Ending August 1948* (Stanford: Stanford University, 1948) 1–48.

"Fast PACE at Palo Alto," *Time*, November 9, 1962.

"Fifty Years Ago at Stanford: Recollections of the Class of 1957." *Sandstone & Tile* 32:1 (Winter 2008) 7–18.

Fraser, Jack. "Stanford's Sterling in 15th year on 'Farm,'" *San Jose News*, January 18, 1964.

"Freedom Summer: Crucible of Change" (50th anniversary panel discussion, with an additional interview with David Harris), *Sandstone & Tile* 38:2 (Spring-Summer 2014) 18–31.

Friedman, Jeanne, Georgia Kelly, and Lenny Siegel. "The Roots of the Stanford Peace Movement," *Sandstone & Tile* 35:1 (Winter 2011) 15–22.

Friend, Hallis, and Nancy Lund. "Ladera Community Association" [history], available online.

"Full Scale Electron Accelerator at Stanford to Produce Energy Exceeding a Billion Electron Volts," *Stanford Alumni Review* (October 1949) 5–6.

Fuller, William Parmer, Jr. "Address of W. P. Fuller, Jr., Delivered at the Stanford Alumni Conferences," *Annual Report of the President of Stanford University…Ending August 1948* (Stanford: Stanford University, 1948) 53–58.

Galison, Peter, Bruce Hevly, and Rebecca Lowen. "Controlling the Monster: Stanford and the Growth of Physics Research, 1935–1962," in Peter Galison and Bruce Hevly, eds., *Big Science: The Growth of Large-Scale Research* (Stanford: Stanford University Press, 1992) 46–77.

Giger, Lena. "Stanford Women's Athletics, 1956–1995," *Sandstone & Tile* 43:2 (Spring-Summer 2019) 3–17.

Gillmor, C. Stewart. *Fred Terman at Stanford: Building a Discipline, a University, and Silicon Valley* (Stanford: Stanford University Press, 2004).

Ginzton, Edward L. "An Informal History of SLAC—Part One: Early Accelerator Work at Stanford," *SLAC Beam Line*, special issue number 3 (May 1983).

Ginzton, Edward L. *Times to Remember: The Life of Edward L. Ginzton*. Edited by Anne Kinston Cottrell and Leonard Slater Cottrell (Berkeley: Blackberry Creek Press, 1995).

Glover, Frederic O. "The Overseas Studies Centers," *Stanford Observer* (February [Berlin], March [Florence], April [Vienna], May [Tours, Paris], and June [Cliveden] 1978).

Goodstein, Judith R. *Millikan's School: A History of the California Institute of Technology* (New York: Norton, 2007).

Hamrdla, G. Robert. "Four Decades of Stanford Overseas Studies," *Sandstone & Tile* 24:2–3 (Spring-Summer 2000) 8–13.

Harris, David. *Dreams Die Hard: Three Men's Journey Through the '60s* (New York: St. Martin's Press, 1982).

Harvey, Van. "Religious Studies at Stanford: An Historical Sketch," *Sandstone & Tile* 22:2–3 (Spring/Summer 1998) 3–10.

Haynes, Elizabeth. "A Granddaughter's Tribute: A Biographical Profile of Elizabeth Sterling Haynes," Edmonton Public Library (Edmonton, Alberta, 2008).

"The High Cost of Sports: Masters Gives Out Figures in Talk at Conference," *Stanford Alumni Review* (April 1949) 22.

Hoopes, Robert, and Hubert Marshall, eds. *The Undergraduate in the University: A Report to the Faculty by the Executive Committee of the Stanford Study of Undergraduate Education, 1954–1956* (Stanford: Stanford University, 1957).

Howell, Ocean. "The Merchant Crusaders: Eichler Homes and Fair Housing, 1949–1974," *Pacific Historical Review* 85:3 (August 2016) 379–407.

Jacobs, Charlotte. *Henry Kaplan and the Story of Hodgkin's Disease* (Stanford: Stanford University Press, 2010).

Jacobs, Julius. "Homeward Bound: The Sad Return of Herbert Hoover," *Sandstone & Tile* 11:2–3 (Winter-Spring 1987) 22–25.

"J. E. Wallace Sterling: Stanford's Fifth President," *Stanford Daily,* March 1, 1956.

Johns, Walter H. *A History of the University of Alberta, 1908–1969* (Edmonton: University of Alberta, 1981).

Joncas, Richard, David J. Neuman, and Paul V. Turner. *Stanford University: The Campus Guide* (New York: Princeton Architectural Press, 2004, 2nd edition) 84, 104.

Jones, Laura. "'A Little Versailles for the Sick,' Edward Durrell Stone and the Stanford Medical Center," *Sandstone & Tile* 32:3 (Fall 2008) 3–12.

Kiefer, David. "The Catalyst: Gene Washington and the Rise of Stanford Football," Stanford Athletics (website), February 18, 2021.

Kiester, Edwin, Jr. *Donald B. Tresidder: Stanford's Overlooked Treasure* (Stanford: Stanford Historical Society, 1992).

Kirk, William. *An Informal History of SLAC* (Stanford: Stanford Linear Accelerator Center, 1967–68).

Knoles, George H. "History of Western Civilization at Stanford," *The Stanford Historian*, 6 (April 1980) 8–15, abridged in "The New/Old History Corner: 40,000 Students Took It: The History of History of Western Civilization," *Stanford Observer* (April 1980).

Leslie, Stuart W. *The Cold War and American Science: The Military-Industrial-Academic Complex at MIT and Stanford* (New York: Columbia University Press, 1993).

Liebendorfer, Don E. *The Color of Life Is Red: A History of Stanford Athletics, 1892–1972* (Stanford: Stanford University Department of Athletics, 1972).

Liebert, Larry. "Year of Hope, Days of Rage: 25 Years Later," *Stanford* [magazine] (September 1995), 51–58.

Lowen, Rebecca. *Creating the Cold War University: The Transformation of Stanford* (Berkeley: University of California Press, 1997).

Lowen, Rebecca. "Exploiting a Wonderful Opportunity," *Stanford* [magazine] (July/August 1997).

Lowood, Henry. *From Steeples of Excellence to Silicon Valley: The Story of Varian Associates and Stanford Industrial Park* (Palo Alto: Varian Associates, 1988). An earlier version appeared in *Campus Report*, March 9, 1988, 11–13.

[Lyman, Richard W., and Nancy Packer.] "Richard W. Lyman Reflects on His Life and the Turbulent '60s and '70s," *Sandstone & Tile* 28:2 (Spring-Summer 2004) 3–9, 12–17.

Lyman, Richard W. "Stanford in Turmoil" and "Calling Police to Campus: May 1969," *Sandstone & Tile* 35:1 (Winter 2011) 5–14.

Lyman, Richard W. *Stanford in Turmoil: Campus Unrest, 1966–1972* (Stanford: Stanford University Press, 2009).

Lyman, Richard W. "Sterling Personifies Stanford's Development as a World Class University," *Campus Report*, March 15, 1978.

"The Man from Stanford," *San Francisco Chronicle,* September 8, 1968.

McAndrews, Rosemary. "The Birthplace of Silicon Valley: A History of Land Development at Stanford University," *Sandstone & Tile* 19:1/2 (Spring 1995) 3–11.

McCord, William. *Mississippi: A Long Hot Summer* (New York: W.W. Norton, 1965; University of Mississippi Press, 2016).

McFadden, Duncan I. "Gifts and Investment Income

Have Increased Stanford's Endowment to $37,853,000 from Original $21,298,000," *Stanford Alumni Review* (February 1949) 9–10.

Medical Care, the University, and Society: Speeches Delivered at the Dedication of the Stanford Medical Center, September 17 and 18, 1959, with a foreword by President J. E. Wallace Sterling (Stanford: Stanford University, 1959).

Medieros, Frank A. "The Sterling Years at Stanford," *Sandstone & Tile* 9:4 (Summer 1985) 3–11.

"Memories of Wally Sterling," *Los Angeles Times* (letter to editor by Godfrey Harris, Los Angeles) July 20, 1985.

Mirrielees, Edith. *Stanford: The Story of a University* (New York: G. P. Putnam's Sons, 1959).

Mirrielees, Edith, ed. *Stanford Mosaic* (Stanford: Stanford University Press, 1962).

"Miss Owen Celebrates 30 Years Work on Farm," *Stanford Daily*, April 1, 1952.

Mitchell, J. Pearce. *Stanford University, 1916–1941* (Stanford: Stanford University Press, 1958).

"Moffatt Hancock: Stanford Scholar, Gifted Photographer," *Sandstone & Tile* 19:4 (Spring 1995) 1–14.

Montella, Mary, and Roxanne Nilan. "Alta Vista: The House on the Hill" in *Historic Houses VII: South San Juan Neighborhood and Stock Farm, Stanford University* (Stanford: Stanford Historical Society 2016) 50–58.

Moulton, Robert. "Physics, Power, and Politics: Fear and Loathing on the Electron Trail," *Sandstone & Tile* 25:1 (Winter 2001) 3–13.

Naimark, Norman. "Stanford Overseas Studies: Then and Now" (Bing Overseas Studies Program, Stanford University, second revised edition 2013).

Nash, George H. *Herbert Hoover and Stanford University* (Stanford: Hoover Institution Press, 1988).

Neal, Richard B., ed. *The Stanford Two-Mile Accelerator* (New York: W. A. Benjamin, 1968).

"New Stanford President Takes Over Job; Sees Education as Answer to Menace of Communism," *San Jose News*, April 5, 1949.

"The News Behind the News: History, Headlines and Humor from the Stanford News Service," *Sandstone & Tile* 17:1 (Winter 1993) 13–20.

Nielson, Donald. *A Heritage of Innovation: SRI's First Half Century* (Menlo Park: SRI International, 2006).

[Nilan, Roxanne.] "The Incomparable Peter C. Allen," *Sandstone & Tile* 25:1 (Winter 2001) 14–26.

Nilan, Roxanne. "The Tenacious Jane Lathrop Stanford," *Sandstone & Tile* 9:2 (Winter 1985) 3–13.

Nilan, Roxanne. "Why They Went South: Stanford Newsman Bob Beyers and Mississippi Freedom Sumer," *Sandstone & Tile* 38:2 (Spring-Summer 2014) 3–17.

Nilan, Roxanne, and Karen Bartholomew. "The Palo Alto Stock Farm: Stanford's First Experimental Biological Laboratory," *Historic Houses VII: South San Juan Neighborhood and Stock Farm* (Stanford: Stanford Historical Society, 2015) 30–40.

O'Mara, Margaret Pugh. *Cities of Knowledge: Cold War Science and the Search for the Next Silicon Valley* (Princeton, NJ: Princeton University Press, 2005).

"On Brotherhood" (letters to the editor), *Stanford* [magazine] May/June 2014.

"The Other Half: Mrs. J. E. Wallace Sterling's Schedule is a Busy One," *Palo Alto Times,* February 23, 1954.

"Pacific Coast Conference," *Sports Illustrated*, September 24, 1956.

Packer, George. *Blood of the Liberals* (New York: Farrar, Straus and Giroux, 2000).

"Packer Warns Faculty on 'Politics by Confrontation,'" *Sandstone & Tile* 28:2 (Spring-Summer 2004) 10–11.

Palmer, Jim. "Sterling Dons Traveling Shoes: Farm's Genial Chief Executive Spends Ten Weeks 'On the Road' During Year," *Stanford Daily,* January 24, 1956.

Panofsky, Wolfgang K. H. "Big Physics and Small Physics at Stanford," *Sandstone & Tile* 14:3 (Summer 1990) 1–7.

Panofsky, Wolfgang K. H. "An Informal History of SLAC—Part Two: The Evolution of SLAC and Its Program," *SLAC Beam Line*, special issue number 3 (May 1983).

Panofsky, Wolfgang K. H. *Panofsky on Physics, Politics and Peace: Pief Remembers* (New York: Springer, 2007).

Panofsky, Wolfgang K. H. "SLAC and Big Science: Stanford University," in Peter Galison and Bruce Hevly, eds., *Big Science: The Growth of Large-Scale Research* (Stanford: Stanford University Press, 1992) 129–46.

Pearson, Andrew. "Beyond Sandstone and Tile: Defining Stanford's Architectural Style," *Sandstone & Tile* 14:2 (Spring 1990) 1–11, with introduction by Paul V. Turner.

Peck, Templeton. "Paul C. Edwards: From Newsman to Trustees' President," *Sandstone & Tile* 11:1 (Fall 1986) 2–11.

Petty, Claude, and Darrell Amyx. "Stanford Goes Indian," *Stanford Illustrated Review* (January 1931) 177, 195.

Phillips, Steven C. *Justice and Hope: Past Reflections and Future Visions of the Stanford Black Student Union 1967–1989* (Stanford: Black Student Union, 1990).

Pizzo, Philip. "One Hundred Years of Medicine at Stanford," *Sandstone & Tile* 33:3 (Fall 2009) 1–14.

Race and Housing: An Interview with Edward P. Eichler, President, Eichler Homes, Inc. (Center for the Study of Democratic Institutions, The Fund for the Republic, 1964).

Regnery, Dorothy F. *The History of Jasper Ridge: From Searsville Pioneers to Stanford Scientists* (Stanford: Stanford Historical Society, 1991).

Remembering Lyle M. Nelson (Stanford: privately printed, 1997).

"Remembering Wally," *Stanford Magazine* (Winter 1985) 61.

"Retirement Doesn't Stop Sterling from Dedicated Work for Stanford," *Palo Alto Times–Tribune*, September 17, 1980.

Ruffin, Herbert G., II. *Uninvited Neighbors: African Americans in Silicon Valley, 1769–1990* in Race and Culture in the American West Series #7 (Norman, OK: University of Oklahoma Press, 2014).

Rytand, David A. *Medicine and the Stanford University School of Medicine: Circa 1932, The Way It Was* (Stanford: Stanford Dept. of Medicine and Alumni Association, 1984).

Schoeck, Ellen. *I Was There: A Century of Alumni Stories About the University of Alberta* (Edmonton: University of Alberta, 2006) 204–05.

Schrecker, Ellen. *No Ivory Tower: McCarthyism and the Universities* (New York: Oxford University Press, 1986).

Seaborg, Glenn T., with Ray Colvig. *Roses from the Ashes: Breakup and Rebirth in Pacific Coast Intercollegiate Athletics*, Foreword by Clark Kerr (Berkeley: Institute of Governmental Studies Press, UC Berkeley, 2000).

"7000 Acres of Stanford's Land Studied for Future Development," *Stanford Alumni Review* (November 1950) 9–10.

"The Shrinking Stanford Lands," *Stanford Review* (May 1960) 9–13.

Siegman, Anthony E. "Edward Leonard Ginzton, 1915–1998: A Biographical Memoir," *Biographical Memoirs*, vol. 88, National Academy of Sciences (2006) 110–43.

"Stanford Has a New President: Sterling Not for Red Teachers but for Study of Communism," *Palo Alto Times*, April 5, 1949.

"Stanford Heritage is Entrusted to Dr. Sterling at Inauguration," *Stanford Alumni Review* (November 1949) 3–14.

"The Stanford Lands," *Stanford Observer* (supplement) (February 1967).

"Stanford Post for Nixon," *San Francisco Examiner*, February 23, 1961.

"The Stanford Shopping Center: Puttin' on the Ritz," the Palo Alto History Project, n.d., available online.

Stanford University Financial Report 1968 and *Financial Report 1969* (Stanford: Controllers Office, November 1968 and 1969).

Stanford University: The Founding Grant with Amendments, Legislation, and Court Decrees (Stanford: Stanford University, 1987).

"Stanford's Fifth President Dies," *Stanford Observer* (July 1985).

"Stanford's New President Feted by Friends, Associates," *Pasadena Star-News*, March 15, 1949.

Steffen, Nancy. "Who is Wallace Sterling?—A Profile," *Stanford Daily*, January 12, 1966.

Stein, Isaac. "What is Past is Prologue: The First Twenty-Five Years of the Board of Trustees," *Sandstone & Tile* 25:2 (Spring–Summer 2001) 18–23.

Sterling, J. E. Wallace. "A Lofty Purpose Shared" [inauguration speech], *Stanford Alumni Review* (November 1949) 4, 9–11.

Sterling, J. E. Wallace. "The President Speaks on Athletic Policy," *Stanford Review* (November 1956) 16–17.

Sterling, J. E. Wallace. "Stanford's National Visibility," *Stanford Review* (May 1960) 14–17.

"Sterling Announces Retirement, is Named Chancellor," *Stanford Observer* (April 1967).

"Sterling Discusses Reds, Curriculum, and Athletics," *Stanford Daily*, April 6, 1949.

"Sterling Era a Productive One," *Redwood City Tribune*, March 29, 1967.

"Sterling Gives Reasons for Stand in PCC Turmoil," *Stanford Daily*, November 14, 1956.

"Sterling Lauds Stanford Spirit," *Stanford Daily*, November 22, 1948, reprinted in *Stanford Alumni Review* (December 1948) 3.

"Sterling Likes Job, Finds Fundraising 'Inescapable' Task," *Palo Alto Times*, July 20, 1959.

"Sterling Takes Stanford Post; Assails Reds," *San Francisco Examiner*, April 6, 1949.

Stokes, Donald. "The Sterling Touch: How Stanford Became a World Class University," *Stanford Observer* (October and November 1979).

The Study of Education at Stanford: Report to the University (Stanford: Stanford University, 1968–69). 10 volumes: I The Study & Its Purposes; II Undergraduate Education; III University Residences & Campus Life; IV Undergraduate Admissions & Financial Aid; V Advising & Counseling; VI The Extra-Curriculum; VII Graduate Education; VIII Teaching, Research & the Faculty; IX Study Abroad; and X Government of the University.

Sullivan, John. *Cal-Stanford: The Big Game* (West Point, NY: Leisure Press, 1982).

"Sustained Gift Program and Gain in Tuition Have Partly Offset Drop in Investment Income," *Stanford Alumni Review* (May 1948) 11–12.

Taylor, Frank J. "Stanford's Man with the Midas

Touch," *The Saturday Evening Post*, December 3, 1960, 36ff. Unfortunately, Taylor includes some factual errors.

Thelin, John R. *The Games Colleges Play: Scandal and Reform in Intercollegiate Athletics* (Baltimore: Johns Hopkins Press, 2011).

"They Left Their Mark: Eldridge 'Ted' Spencer," *Continuity* [Preservation Action Council of San Jose] (Spring 2002) 13–14.

Torontoensis: The Yearbook of the University of Toronto, 1926 and *1927*.

"'Tough' Problems Will Stay, Outgoing President Predicts," *Stanford Daily*, January 17, 1968.

Turner, Paul V. *Mrs. Hoover's Pueblo Walls: The Primitive and the Modern in the Lou Henry Hoover House* (Stanford: Stanford University Press, 2004).

Tutorow, Norman E. *The Governor: The Life and Legacy of Leland Stanford, A California Colossus*. Two volumes. (Spokane: The Arthur H. Clark Co., 2004).

Varian, Dorothy. *The Inventor and the Pilot* (Palo Alto, CA: Pacific Books, 1983).

Villard, O. G., Jr. "Frederick Emmons Terman, 1900–1982: A Biographical Memoir," *Biographical Memoirs*, vol. 74, National Academy of Sciences (1998) 308–30.

"Wallace Sterling, Ph.D. '38, Scholar, Administrator, and Former Athlete, Takes Stanford University Helm," *Stanford Alumni Review* (December 1948) 3–10.

"Wally Recalls the Early Sterling Years as President, 25 Years Ago," *Campus Report*, April 24, 1974, 10–12.

Walsh, John. "SLAC: Stanford–AEC Accelerator is Coming Along on Schedule, but Creating Some High Tension," *Science* 143 (March 27, 1964) 1419–21.

Walsh, John. "Stanford's Search for Solutions," in *Academic Transformations: Seventeen Institutions Under Pressure*, edited by David Riesman and Verne A. Stadtman (Carnegie Commission on Higher Education, 1973).

Warren, Morrison. "My American Story: How I Came to Be Stanford's First Black Recruit," Stanford Athletics (website), reprinted in *Delta Tau Delta Fraternity Rainbow* (Summer 2018) 18–23.

Wascher, Jim. "Wallace Sterling—Giant of Two Stanford Decades," *Stanford Daily*, March 14, 1974, 7–8.

Wax, Mel. Business and Finance (column), "How University 'Wooed' Industry: Stanford Park—Weird Success," *San Francisco Chronicle*, November 16, 1958

"The West: The PCC Dies and the Big Four is Nearly Stillborn," *Sports Illustrated*, September 22, 1958.

"What It Was Like to Be an African American Freshman in 1962," *Stanford* [magazine] (September 2017).

Wilbur, Ray Lyman. *The Memoirs of Ray Lyman Wilbur, 1875–1949*, Edgar E. Robinson and Paul C. Edwards, eds. (Stanford: Stanford University Press, 1960).

Wilcox, Barbara. "Taking the Mic: Black Students Seek Representation in Education," Stanford Graduate School of Education, 2014 (available online).

Wilcox, Barbara. *World War I Army Training by San Francisco Bay: The Story of Camp Fremont* (Charleston S.C.: History Press, 2016).

Williams, James C. "Frederick E. Terman and the Rise of Silicon Valley," in *Technology in America: A History of Individuals and Ideas*, 2nd ed., ed. Carroll W. Pursell Jr. (Cambridge: MIT Press, 1990) 276–91.

Wilson, John. *Stanford University School of Medicine and the Predecessor Schools: An Historical Perspective* (Stanford Medicine's Medical History Center, 1998). Available only online.

Winslow, Ward. *Palo Alto: A Centennial History* (Palo Alto: Palo Alto Historical Association, 1993).

UNPUBLISHED MATERIALS OF NOTE

Beyers, Bob, "*Stanford Daily* Speech," November 19, 1995. Robert W. Beyers biographical file, Stanford News Service.

Chandler, Loren, and Lowell Rantz, "The Development of Stanford's School of Medicine," Committee on Future Plans, 1952–53, Stanford School of Medicine, in Stanford Medical School Committee on Future Plans, SCM092, Stanford University Archives (hereafter SUA).

Coblentz, Jean G., "Supporting Service to Stanford: Who, What, and Why are the Stanford Associates," speech to the Stanford Historical Society, February 4, 2003, transcript, Stanford Associates file, Stanford News Service.

Corson, John J. "Strengthening the Top Organization of Stanford University," McKinsey & Company, Inc. (May 28, 1958), SC0216 box A9, SUA.

Crafts, [James F.], "A Summary of the Statement made to the joint meeting of the Land Development Committee and the Special Committee appointed to review certain phases of the land development program," November 18, 1959.

Cuthbertson, Kenneth M. "Comments at Earth Day Panel Discussion on Stanford Land Use," April 22, 1970, in Kenneth Cuthbertson biographical file, Stanford News Service.

Cuthbertson, Kenneth, "Introductory Remarks for Panel at Alumni Assembly, May 25, 1968," Cuthbertson biographical file, Stanford News Service.

Cuthbertson, Kenneth M. *Long-Range Financial Planning for Institutions of Higher Education* (June 8, 1964), Cuthbertson biographical file, Stanford News Service.

Cuthbertson, Kenneth M. "Notes for a Talk by Kenneth M. Cuthbertson to the Stanford Historical Society May 27, 1990," in Cuthbertson biographical file, Stanford News Service.

Day, Moira. "Elizabeth Sterling Haynes and the Development of Alberta Theatre," unpublished dissertation, University of Toronto, 1990.

Dornbusch, Sanford. Memoir notes [2016]. In possession of author and editor.

Galbraith, Tom. "An Analysis of a Stanford Student Political Party: 'The Establishment,'" unpublished anthropology paper, June 1965, SCM0453, SUA.

Huntley, Chet. Speech delivered before the Pasadena Junior Chamber of Commerce in honor of Dr. Wallace Sterling, Pasadena, March 14, 1949, in J. E. Wallace Sterling file: miscellaneous, Stanford News Service.

Hutchison, E. Elmore. "Report on Land Use Survey of Stanford University Properties, San Mateo and Santa Clara Counties, California, June 5, 1951," in SC0486 (accession 2000-104) box 1, folder 2, and in SC0216 box 48, folder 8, SUA.

Kapp, J. [Profile of President Wallace Sterling], November 20, 1964, J. E. Wallace Sterling file: miscellaneous, Stanford News Service.

Korff, J. Michael. "Student Control and University Government at Stanford: The Evolving Student-University Relationship [1891–1970]," unpublished dissertation, Stanford University, 1975.

Linsley, Ray K., and Robert E. Lee. "The Proposed Ladera Dam: A Preliminary Economic Review," Project on Engineering-Economic Planning, Stanford University, Pub. No. 2, April 1962, SC0122 box 70, folder "Buildings & Grounds: Ladera Dam."

Medeiros, Frank A. "The Sterling Years at Stanford: A Study in the Dynamics of Institutional Change," unpublished Ph.D. dissertation, Stanford University, 1979.

Morell, George. "History of Black Mountain at Monte Bello Ridge," unpublished paper, September 1959.

Mumford, Lewis. "Memorandum on Planning" (March 6, 1947), in Donald Bertrand Tresidder Records, SC0151 box 15, folder 8, SUA.

O'Mara, Margaret Pugh. "Campus and City Plans: The Design and Influence of Stanford's Land Developments," lecture to the Stanford Historical Society,

January 22, 2004. Audio tape available in SC0683, Stanford Historical Society Program Recordings, box 1, SUA.

Phleger, Herman. "Address, Trustees and Stanford Associates Dinner honoring President and Mrs. Sterling, April 18, 1968," in SC0843, box 1, folder 1, SUA.

"Preliminary Report to President Sterling: Study on the Hoover Institution," June 1952, in SC0216, series II, box 1, SUA.

Report of the President's Advisory Committee on Land and Building Development, June 1, 1954, in SC0216 box 23, SUA.

Report of the Special Committee to Review the Land Development Program, November 17, 1959, with trustee minutes, December 17, 1959 (also in SC0216 box A33, SUA).

Rothwell, Easton. "Some Proposals Concerning the Hoover Institution, Its National Position, and Its Relation to Stanford University," Hoover Institution Records, Series T-16, Box 234C, Hoover Institution Archives.

Skidmore, Owings & Merrill. "Interim Report: Stanford Master Plan—Stanford Shopping Center, Industrial Area, Proposed Residential Development," August 15, 1953, SC0216 box 23, folder 21, SUA.

Skidmore, Owings & Merrill. "Land Use Study: Stage I," September 10, 1953, SC0486 (accession 2000-104) box 1, folder 56 [folder 56 in collection guide probably means folders 5 and 6], SUA.

Skidmore, Owings & Merrill. "Supplement 1: Economic Factors of the Master Plan," SC0486 (2000-104) box 1, folder 4, SUA.

Spencer, Eldridge T. "A Coordinated Plan for the University: Report of the Planning Department, February 1, 1947," SC0486 (accession 1999-093) box 1, folder 3, SUA.

Spencer, Eldridge T. "Master Plan Land Use, showing existing leases of proposed zoning, Stanford University, September 18, 1950" SC0486 (accession 1999-093) box 1, folder 3.

"Stanford Land Use—An Overview of Policy Determinants," Committee on Land and Buildings, January 8, 1974, pp. 77–84.

"Stanford Land Use Policies," Committee on Land and Buildings, trustee minutes, SC1010, March 12, 1974, pp. 247–49.

"Status of San Francisquito Creek Project (Ladera Dam)," February 3, 1962, and "Data Sheet: Proposed Ladera Dam Project," February 10, 1962, in SC0216 box C5, folder 6.

Sterling, J. E. Wallace. "The Stanford Presidency, 1949–1968: Part II, A Noble Purpose Shared," Part

III[a], "Bits and Pieces," Part III[b], Some Extra-curricular Activities," and "Part III[c], Travelling à *Deux* and Otherwise," J. E. Wallace Sterling Personal Papers and Memorabilia, SC0415 (arch 1993-061), SUA.

Sterling, J. E. Wallace. "Fathers and Sons: An Address by Dr. J. E. Wallace Sterling, President of Stanford University, at the Commencement Exercises of Menlo School and Menlo College, June 8, 1956," SC0216, SUA, later repeated in part for the *Edgewood Homes* supplement of the *San Francisco Examiner*, March 21, 1960.

Sterling, J. E. Wallace. "Austrian-Hungarian Diplomacy and the Austro-Hungarian Press," unpublished dissertation, Stanford University, 1938.

Sterling, J. E. Wallace. "Terman 10th Recipient of Alumni 'Uncommon Man' Award," *Campus Report*, December 13, 1978.

Sterling, J. E. Wallace. "Campus Conference" [speech], May 18, 1968, in J. E. Wallace Sterling Speeches and Quotations, 1965—present, Stanford News Service.

Sterling, J. E. Wallace. "Commencement 1968"–in J. E. Wallace Sterling Speeches and Quotations, 1965–present, Stanford News Service.

Sterling, J. E. Wallace. Stanford Today and Tomorrow program [speech], January 10, 1961, in J. E. Wallace Sterling speeches, 1961–62, Stanford News Service.

Sterling, J. E. Wallace. L.A. Conference [speech], February 1968, in J. E. Wallace Sterling Speeches and Quotations, 1965–present, Stanford News Service.

U.S. Army Corps of Engineers, South Pacific Division, San Francisco, *Notice of Survey Report for Flood Control and Allied Purposes, San Francisquito Creek, Santa Clara and San Mateo Counties*, 25 September 1961, in Lyle M. Nelson Papers, SC0989 box 1, folder 10.

Warnecke, John Carl. "Stanford's Architecture at the Crossroads," n.d. [Report to Board of Trustees, April 1949], SCM0129, SUA.

UNIVERSITY PUBLICATIONS

Stanford Academic Secretary's Office. *Stanford University Memorial Resolutions*

Stanford Alumni Association:
    Stanford Alumnus (1899–1917)
    Stanford Illustrated Review (1917–40)
    Stanford Alumni Review (1941–51)
    Stanford Review (1951–67)
    Stanford Magazine (1973–88)
    Stanford [magazine] (1989–)

Stanford Daily (titled *Daily Palo Alto*, 1892–1926)

Stanford Graduate School of Business. *Stanford Business* [magazine]

Stanford Historical Society. *Sandstone & Tile*

Stanford Linear Accelerator Center. *Beamline*

Stanford News [and Publications] Service:
    Stanford Today (1940–70) (early issues by Division of Journalism)
    Faculty-Staff Newsletter (1957–68)
    Campus Report (1968–95)
    Stanford Observer (1966–94)
    Stanford Report (1995–)

Stanford University. *Annual Register* (1891 through 1946–47) (Faculty/staff/student directory, admissions/fees, schools/departments/courses, degrees conferred)

Stanford University. *Annual Report of the President of Stanford University* (1904 through 1947–48)

Stanford University. *Directory of Students and Faculty-Staff (under various names)* (1948–)

INTERVIEWS

STANFORD ORAL HISTORY PROJECT / STANFORD UNIVERSITY ARCHIVES

"A Session on Wally: Transcription of an Oral History about J. E. Wallace Sterling, Recorded for the Stanford University Archives" (1985). Portions published as "Remembering Wally," *The Stanford Magazine* (Winter 1985) but comments were edited and some significantly changed.

Abernethy, David. Interview by Susan W. Scofield (Diversity Project, 2009).

Alway, Robert. Interview by Frederic O. Glover (1980).

Bacchetti, Raymond F. Interview by Susan W. Schofield (Diversity Project, 2010).

Bacon, Mary Montle. Interview by Ray Bacchetti (Diversity Project, 2010).

Bacon, Mary Montle. Interview by Emma Frothingham (Taking the Mic series, 2019).

Bailey, Thomas A. Interview by Frederic O. Glover (1978).

Barclay, Thomas Swain. Interview by Frederic O. Glover and Harry Press (1980).

Brandin, Alf E. Interview by Frederic O. Glover (1990).

Brandin, Alf E. Interview by Robert de Roos (1987).

Bunnell, John. Interview by Susan W. Schofield (Diversity Project, 2010).

Chandler, Loren Roscoe. Interview with Frederic O. Glover (1979).

Chase, William M. Interview by Peter Steinhart (2015).

Davis, Paul Herbert. An interview by Frederic O. Glover and Paul R. Hanna (1983).

Dodds, John Wendell. Interview by Frederic O. Glover and Paul R. Hanna (1983).

Eurich, Alvin Christian. Interview by Frederic O. Glover (1983).

Gibbs, James Lowell, Jr. Diversity Series, interview by Ray Bacchetti (2011).

Gibbs, James Lowell, Jr. Interview by Joyce Kiefer (2015).

Glover, Frederic O. Interview by Don Carlson, Roxanne Nilan, and Harry Press (1993).

Goheen, John. Interview by Judy Adams (1987).

Guthrie, Luell Weed. Interview by Margo Davis (1978).

Hayman, Warren C. Interview by Emma Frothingham (Taking the Mic series, 2019).

Jacobson, David S. Interview by Frederic O. Glover and George H. Knoles (1988).

Leonard, Jean McCarter. Interview by Katherine Toy (Diversity Project, 2011).

Leonard, Jean McCarter. Interview by Joyce Kiefer (Alumni Stories: Class of 1957 series, 2007).

Levison, Robert Mark. Interview by Frederic O. Glover (1983).

Rosenzweig, Robert. Interview by Don Carlson, Karen Bartholomew, and Roxanne Nilan (1984).

Rosenzweig, Robert. Interview by Ray Bacchetti (Diversity Project, 2010).

Satterwhite, Frank J. Omowale. Interview by Daniel Hartwig (Taking the Mic Series, 2019).

Sears, Robert. Interview by Hamilton Cravens (1988).

Snyder, Rixford Kinney. Interview by Frederic O. Glover and George H. Knoles (1983).

Washington, Keni. Interview by Daniel Hartwig (Taking the Mic series, 2019).

Whitaker, Virgil. Interview by Eleanor Bark and Harvey Hall (1983).

Wyman, Willard G., Jr. Interview by Erika Amaya (Diversity Project, 2011).

OTHER STANFORD INTERVIEWS

Jordan, Payton. Interview by Bob Murphy, in "Stanford Athletics Interviews Conducted by Bob Murphy" (c. 2002–03) in SC1011, SUA.

Kaplan, Henry. "A Conversation with Henry Kaplan," interview by Spyros Andreopoulos (1984) Stanford Medical History Center.

Murphy, Robert (Bob). An oral history by Roxanne L. Nilan, 2002, for the department of Athletics. Transcript in SC1011, SUA.

Ralston, John. Interview by Bob Murphy, in "Stanford Athletics Interviews Conducted by Bob Murphy" (c. 2002–03) in SC1011, SUA.

Spraghens, Thomas. Interview by Frederic O. Glover and Ed Kiester, February 3, 1991, in "Donald B. Tresidder: Stanford's Hidden Treasure" Research Materials, SC0438 box 1, folder 18, SUA.

"Taking the Mic: 50 Years Later: A Panel Discussion with Mary Montle Bacon, Warren C. Hayman, Frank J. Omowale Satterwhite, and Keni Washington," April 2019, moderated by Rosalind Conerly. Stanford University Archives, 2020, in SC1473, SUA.

Terman, Frederick E. "Frederick E. Terman: Oral history interview by Raymond Henle," January 1970, Herbert Hoover Presidential Library and Hoover Institution, in Hoover Institution Archives.

OTHER INTERVIEWS

Bragg, Robert. "Robert H. Bragg: African American Faculty and Senior Staff Oral History Series," interview conducted in 2002 by Nadine Wilmot, Regional Oral History Office, The Bancroft Library, University of California, Berkeley, 2005.

Charles, Caroline Moore. "The Action and Passion of Our Times," An Oral history conducted in 1974 and 1978 by Gabrielle S. Morris, Regional Oral History Office, The Bancroft Library, University of California, Berkeley, 1979.

Doyle, Morris M. "The Spirit and Morale of Private Philanthropy: Stanford University and the James Irvine Foundation," with an introduction by Kenneth M. Cuthbertson. An oral history conducted in 1989 by Gabrielle S. Morris, Regional Oral History Office, The Bancroft Library, University of California, Berkeley, 1990.

Doyle, Morris M. "An Antitrust Lawyer: Six Decades at McCutchen, Doyle, Brown & Enersen, 1932–1992. An oral history conducted in 1989 by Carole Hicke, Regional Oral History Office, The Bancroft Library, University of California, Berkeley, 1993.

Panofsky, Wolfgang. Interview of Wolfgang Panofsky by Jean Deken on 2004 May 3, Niels Bohr Library & Archives, American Institute of Physics, College Park, Maryland.

Paul, Rodman W. Interview by Caroline Bugé. Pasadena, Calif., February 5, 9, and 17, 1982. Oral History Project, California Institute of Technology Archives.

Phleger, Herman. "Herman Phleger: Sixty Years in Law, Public Service and International Affairs," with an introduction by J. E. Wallace Sterling, an interview conducted by Miriam Feingold Stein in 1977, Regional Oral History Office, The Bancroft Library, University of California, Berkeley, 1979.

Pitzer, Kenneth S. "Kenneth Sanborn Pitzer: Chemist and Administrator at UC Berkeley, Rice University, Stanford University, and the Atomic Energy Administration, 1935–1997," an oral history conducted 1996–1998, by Sally S. Hughes and Germaine Leberge, Regional Oral History Office, The Bancroft Library, University of California, Berkeley, 1999.

Sanders, Harry. "Harry Sanders: A Stanford Planner Charts the History of Campus Planning, and Church's Contribution." An oral history interview conducted by Suzanne Reiss, Regional Oral History Office, The Bancroft Library, UC Berkeley, 1978 (in Thomas D. Church, landscape architect, vol. 2).

Terman, Frederick E. "Frederick E. Terman, interviews by Arthur L. Norberg, Charles Susskind, and Roger Hahn," 1971, 1974, 1978, Bancroft Oral History Project on the History of Science and Technology; transcribed 1984 by Stanford Oral History Project, SUA.

ARCHIVAL COLLECTIONS

STANFORD UNIVERSITY ARCHIVES

Allen, Peter C. Student Demonstrations Collection, SC0157
Beyers, Robert W. Papers, SC0664
Carlson, Donald T. Papers, SC0539
Edwards, Paul C. Papers, SC0170
Ginzton, Edward L. Papers, SC0330
Glover, Frederic O. Papers, SC0234 and SC0468
Hansen, William Webster Papers, SC0004, SC0126, and SC1140
Hofstadter, Robert Papers, SC0426
Kadane, Joseph Papers, 1964–66, SC0037
Kaplan, Henry S. Papers, SC0317
Knoles, George H. Papers, SC0328
Lyman, Richard W., Provost Papers, SC0099
Nelson, Lyle Papers, SC0989
Packer, Herbert L. Papers, SC0519
Phleger, Herman Papers (presidential search committee files) SC0843
Robinson, Edgar Eugene Papers (includes History Department records), SC0029B
Rosenzweig, Robert M. Papers, SC0091
Rosenzweig, Robert M. Papers, SC0632
Schiff, Leonard I. Papers, SC0220
Sterling, J. E. Wallace, Presidential Papers, SC0216
Sterling, J. E. Wallace, Personal Papers, SC0415
Sterling, J. E. Wallace, Chancellor's Papers, SC0333
Sterling, J. E. Wallace, Speeches, SC0557
Sterling-Pitzer transitional papers, SC0217
Tresidder, Donald B., Presidential Papers, SC0151
"Donald B. Tresidder: Stanford's Overlooked Treasure" Research Materials, SC0438

Terman, Frederick E., Papers, SC0160
Varian, Russell, and Sigurd Varian Papers, SC0345
Walker, Robert Averill, Papers, SC0546
Whitaker, Douglas Merritt, Papers, SC0176

Academic Council, Faculty Senate, Minutes and Reports, SC0193
[Lucile] Allen Controversy Papers, SC0050
Alpha Tau Omega Records, SC0622
Bing Overseas Studies Program Records, SC0117
Black Affairs, Assistant to the President, Records, SC0154
Board of Trustees [Misc.] Records, SC0282
Board of Trustees Meeting Minutes and Supporting Documents, SC1010
History Department Records SC0029A
News and Publications Service Records, SC0122
Office of Development Records, SC0319
Office of General Studies Records, SC0077
Planning Office Records SC0486
Provosts Office Records (Lyman), SC0099
Public Affairs Office Records, SC0105
Stanford Associates Records, SC0833
Stanford Ranches and Lands, SC0003
Stanford Study of Undergraduate Education (SES), SC0425
Stanford University Map Collection, SC1049
University Committee on Land and Building Development Records, SC0813

STANFORD NEWS SERVICE
Faculty [and staff] biographical files
Sterling, J. E. Wallace, J. E. Biographical
Sterling, J. E. Wallace, Clippings
Sterling, J. E. Wallace, Correspondence
Sterling, J. E. Wallace, General
Sterling, J. E. Wallace, News Releases
Sterling, J. E. Wallace, Speeches and Quotations
Sterling, Mrs. Ann Shaver

HOOVER INSTITUTION ARCHIVES
Rothwell, Charles Easton, Papers, 90005
Sterling, J. E. Wallace, Papers, xx266

This May 1957 aerial view looks south down Palm Drive to the Oval and Quad, and to the foothills beyond Foothill Road (Junipero Serra Boulevard). Lagunita is full, and nearby is the recently opened Florence Moore dormitory complex. Faculty housing still closes in on the Quad's Engineering Corner, with only the new Dinkelspiel Auditorium in the area that will soon become White Plaza (Tresidder Union and the new Bookstore and Post Office would be constructed in the early 1960s). Also in the near future will be the new Medical Center (1959), in fields behind the Museum and Chemistry buildings.   STANFORD NEWS SERVICE

ROXANNE L. NILAN was Stanford's second University Archivist, 1979–90, and co-founder (with Fred Glover) and first director of the Stanford Oral History Project. She served as editor of the Stanford Historical Society's *Sandstone & Tile*, and as research historian and honorary curator at History San José. She is the author of many articles on aspects of Stanford history and co-authored *The Stanford Album: A Photographic History* (1989) and *A Chronology of Stanford University and Its Founders* (2001). Nilan received her B.A. and M.L.S. from UC Berkeley, and her master's and doctorate in American history from Stanford.

CASSIUS L. KIRK JR. received his B.A. from Stanford and graduated with honors from the UC Berkeley School of Law (then Boalt Hall). He served as staff counsel for business affairs at Stanford, 1960–78, coming to know many of the individuals featured in this book. He subsequently was business manager of Menlo College and became a successful real estate investor. Kirk, who died in 2014, was active in fundraising for both Stanford and Cal and endowed two Stanford professorships (including the Frederic O. Glover Professorship in Humanities and Social Sciences). He began researching this biography during his retirement.

KAREN E. BARTHOLOMEW, Stanford class of 1971, worked at Stanford's News and Publication Service for 25 years, including as editor of *Campus Report* and the *Stanford Observer*. Bartholomew, who is a charter member of the Stanford Historical Society, has played active roles on society committees for more than 40 years. She is a co-author of *A Chronology of Stanford University and Its Founders* and edited *Trees of Stanford and Environs* (2005), the *Historic Houses at Stanford* series, and other society publications. The Historical Society's annual service award is named in her honor.

Stanford's Wallace Sterling:
Portrait of a Presidency, 1949–1968

was produced under the auspices of
Stanford Historical Society and
Society for the Promotion of Science and Scholarship
Karen E. Bartholomew, Contributing Editor

PRODUCED BY WILSTED & TAYLOR
PUBLISHING SERVICES
Project manager Christine Taylor
Production assistant LeRoy Wilsted
Designer and compositor Nancy Koerner
Proofreader Melody Lacina
Image manager Evan Winslow Smith
Printer's devil Lillian Marie Wilsted
Type Granjon, Perpetua Titling, Myriad Pro
Paper Opus Matte
Printer and binder Friesens, Canada